Behavior Analysis and Learning

SECOND EDITION

W. David Pierce
W. Frank Epling
University of Alberta

Prentice Hall, Upper Saddle River, 07458

Library of Congress Cataloging-in-Publication Data

Pierce, W. David.
   Behavior analysis and learning / W. David Pierce & W. Frank
  Epling.—2nd ed.
     p.   cm.
   Includes bibliographical references and index.
   ISBN 0-13-080743-5
   1. Behaviorism (Psychology)   2. Learning, Psychology of.
 I. Epling, W. Frank. II. Title.
 BF199.P54 1999
 105.19′434—dc21   98–10083
                             CIP

Editor-in-Chief: *Nancy Roberts*
Acquisition Editor: *Bill Webber*
Assistant Editor: *Jennifer Hood*
Editorial Assistant: *Tamsen Adams*
Assistant Managing Editor: *Mary Rottino*
Production Liaison: *Fran Russello*
Project Manager: *Marianne Hutchinson* (Pine Tree Composition)
Prepress and Manufacturing Buyer: *Lynn Pearlman*
Cover Director: *Jayne Conte*
Director, Image Resource Center: *Lori Morris-Nantz*
Photo Research Supervisor: *Melinda Lee Reo*
Image Permission Supervisor: *Kay Dellosa*
Photo Researcher: *Beth Boyd*
Marketing Manager: *Michael Alread*

This book was set in 10/12 point Palatino medium by Pine Tree Composition and was printed and bound by RR Donnelley & Sons Company. The cover was printed by Phoenix Color Corp.

© 1999, 1995 by Prentice-Hall, Inc.
Simon & Schuster/A Viacom Company
Upper Saddle River, New Jersey 07458

Printed in the United States of America

10 9 8 7 6 5 4 3 2 1

ISBN 0-13-080743-5

Prentice-Hall International (UK) Limited, *London*
Prentice-Hall of Australia Pty. Limited, *Sydney*
Prentice-Hall Canada Inc., *Toronto*
Prentice-Hall Hispanoamericana, S.A., *Mexico*
Prentice-Hall of India Private Limited, *New Delhi*
Prentice-Hall of Japan, Inc., *Tokyo*
Simon & Schuster Asia Pte. Ltd., *Singapore*
Editora Prentice-Hall do Brasil, Ltda., *Rio de Janeiro*

Contents

CHAPTER 7
SCHEDULES OF REINFORCEMENT 147

CHAPTER 8
STIMULUS CONTROL 179

CHAPTER 9
AVERSIVE REGULATION OF BEHAVIOR 205

CHAPTER 10
CHOICE AND PREFERENCE   234

CHAPTER 11
CONDITIONED REINFORCEMENT   268

CHAPTER 12
VERBAL BEHAVIOR   293

CHAPTER 13
APPLIED BEHAVIOR ANALYSIS   327

CHAPTER 14
THREE LEVELS OF SELECTION:
BIOLOGY, BEHAVIOR, AND CULTURE   359

GLOSSARY   386

REFERENCES   404

INDEX   429

In Memoriam

It is with great sorrow that I inform you that the publication of this book will not be seen by my dear friend and colleague, Frank Epling, who died on February 1, 1998 at the age of 54 years. Frank was invited to deliver an address at the Northern California Association for Behavior Analysis in Berkeley. He went there with his wife, Judy Cameron, but was never able to present his talk. His heart stopped without warning.

Frank Epling was a complex character. Many of us will remember him as that large red-headed man who lived life to the fullest. Some people have said that Frank meant so much to them because of his satirical sense of humour. Others saw him as a person who pushed himself to excessive levels. But, excessiveness was fundamental to who Frank was. In others eyes, he was a loving, kind-mannered person who would go out of his way to help a friend, a colleague or even a stranger. Perhaps the most characterisic attribute of Frank was his ability to see issues clearly and to cut through nonsense.

Frank and I go back more than 20 years. He was my best friend and working partner. I remember how we wrote together; seated side by side, at a computer, and how Frank would say that the line I had just written was the stupidest thing he'd ever seen. After an hour of arguing, we would proceed to change that line and continue writing until our next disagreement. That's the way we got things done.

Frank was a superb instructor who had a magical ability to communicate and empathize with students even in a large lecture hall. For more than 20 years, Frank taught the basic course in Behavior Analysis to approximately 1000 students each year. He was a talented, effective, and influential teacher. In 1997, Frank was named Outstanding Teacher of the Year in Psychology at the University of Alberta.

In terms of research, Frank was the most intellectually creative scientist that I know. He had insightful ideas about research and his contribution to a theory of activity anorexia has resulted in an integrated analysis of culture, behavior, and biology. His ideas permeate the scientific community and will continue to stimulate many young students to follow in his footsteps.

Frank will be sorely missed by his students, colleagues, friends, his wife Judy, and his children Salena, Emily, Nathan, Jessica, and Anna. Personally, it will be difficult to get along without him.

W. David Pierce

Foreword

The second edition of a textbook should always be better than the first. It should profit from users' comments and from the author's extended self-critique. Furthermore, there are new findings to incorporate as the science progresses. This second edition of *Behavior Analysis and Learning* retains the many fine qualities of the first edition while adding sections and examples relating to the application of principles of behavior to everyday human issues.

Teaching the principles of behavior science cannot be overestimated as an essential educational objective. Yet many subjective, non-empirical procedures and theories of past attempts to account for and understand behavior have been of limited benefit. Although most of the critical problems in the world today are due to human behavior, at least indirectly, there does not appear to be much progress toward improvement. People perform too few of the right actions and too many destructive ones. The discovery and correct application of principles and findings of behavior science are critically needed. This second edition describes fundamental procedures and findings, and provides examples of the extension of those findings into applied environments where most other approaches have been found wanting. This textbook is one avenue toward the understanding of behavior and the application of that understanding.

The experimental analysis of behavior is an independent natural science at a level comparable to biology and physics. Behavior analysis, as represented in this book, is the scientific investigation of the interaction of organisms with the social and physical environment. The authors take the philosophical position that operant behavior is a function of its consequences. Living organisms alter their behavior as a reaction to the consequence of that action. Animals appear to be biological learning machines that, as a function of being alive, contact the environment and have their behavior literally shaped (selected) by its consequences. For example, when given a cafeteria of possible food items, animals select that which is nutritious and reject non-nutritious and toxic substances. Animals lacking such ability soon disappear. Because they learn from conditioning, animals need not possess a built-in menu of acceptable and nonacceptable food items but can adapt to nearly whatever the habitat provides.

The science of behavioral selection, proposed and brought to its current position by B. F. Skinner, has had a profound impact on all aspects of human interaction, including special and regular education, business, health care, rehabilitation, therapy, and the treatment of deviancy. This second edition systematically describes this science and how it has been brought to bear on many important human behavior issues.

In recent times, the explicit acceptance and teaching of basic experimental behavior science has sharply declined in higher education. Laboratory experiences wherein college students conduct research or perform demonstrations with living subjects (not computer simulations) has become a rare enterprise. Textbooks that describe and explain solid basic research in behavior science are relatively scarce. University and college departments infrequently offer courses to teach the experimental analysis of behavior, (which is the foundation of behavior science) using nonhuman subjects. Administrators who fail to appreciate the need for a basic behavior science education or who deny that behavior is a legitimate subject of experimental analysis, would take an entirely different position after reading Pierce and Epling's book. This book describes how the investigation of simple behaviors in simple organisms relates to such complex issues as the development of cognitive skills in children or providing therapy for depressed patients. Indeed, every effective and progressive field of endeavor has a foundation discipline to turn to when problems arise. When a pigeon is observed and its behavior systematically manipulated in an unadorned environment, many fundamental principles are exposed that apply to all living organisms. Generating hypotheses, appealing to common sense, or offering one's own original theory about the stresses on a new spacecraft rather than determining with precision from accurate calculation, is far from best-practice in aerospace engineering. Using one's own interpretation or appealing to a subjective belief system as to how best to teach reading, instead of relying on behavior science data-based educational programming is equally inappropriate. The existence of a basic science and the use of empirically determined foundations is mandatory in whatever area of discovery or application one professes.

The book in your hands contains descriptions of the best scientific foundations of behavioral research and engineering available. Without becoming encyclopedic, the second edition covers behavior analysis and conditioning in as thorough a treatment as is available for the undergraduate student. Textual transitions between principles and application, sometimes abrupt in the first edition, have been smoothed and the interrelationships between principles highlighted. The second edition is more user friendly, yet remains as scholarly and effective as the first.

Pierce and Epling have produced a text that meets the needs of the behavior science student. Books at this level should appeal not only to the sophisticated reader as a consolidated source of diverse research, but to non-behavior science and non-psychology students as well, and should help them acquire skills in the functional analysis of their own and other's behavior. Since all possible behavior problems cannot be anticipated, the student should learn the general principles of analysis and application, and the second edition of the Pierce and Epling text provides that. Just as Keller and Schoenfeld's *Principles of Psychology* (1950) was the standard for textbook presentations of behavior science and filled a critical need at that time, *Behavior Analysis and Learning* is also much needed and important today.

This book deals with what we know about learning as an adaptive process from a single and consistent point of view. The important topics are thoroughly covered. Given an objective orientation, a requirement for evidence and a basic fluency in the experimental analysis of behavior, a person may apply such to the treatment of personal, family, professional, or any other problematic behavior situation.

Behavior Analysis and Learning is written by research scientists who also teach (or are they teachers who also do research?). They know their subject because of extensive direct experience in the laboratory and from a long and close association with the appropriate literature. And they know how to present such material to students. Presenting is not teaching, but a good text helps the teacher shape appropriate repertoires in the student.

Dave Pierce and Frank Epling began their training in behavior science, behaviorism, and operant conditioning at the undergraduate level, they continued and expanded that education through graduate school. Following post-doctoral work in Great Britain, they became colleagues in different departments at the University of Alberta where they began a period of research and writing collaboration which has led to this book. The authors have conducted research, published extensively, and have taught for many years in higher education. I believe you will find this book very useful and reading it will be reinforcing.

Carl D. Cheney
River Heights, Utah

Preface

In the second edition of *Behavior Analysis and Learning*, we strive to keep the positive features of the first edition, while adding new aspects as suggested by reviewers, instructors and students. As in the first edition, the writing level is targeted to undergraduate students at university, using a lot of human examples from everyday life. At the same time, we have made a more concerted effort to tighten up technical procedures, concepts and relationships. The road between accessible and clear writing for students and scientific precision is a rough one, yet we believe that the text remains highly readable and is now more scientifically exact.

Modern behavior analysis is an exciting scientific field and we hope that we have communicated our own enthusiasm for the discipline. Principles of learning and behavior are having an impact on education, industry, medicine, animal training, clinical psychology, and environmental protection and these are only a few areas of application. There is an implicit technology available to those students who master the principles of behavior presented in this text. In many sections of the book we have attempted to draw out applications of behavior principles. Students can use these principles to change their own (and others) behavior in everyday life.

The second edition continues with the Focus On Research, Focus on Issues, and Focus on Advanced Issues sections within chapters. As in the first edition, the Advanced Issues are separate shaded sections that appear where an in-depth understanding of the material requires concentrated study. These sections are designed to stand alone and some instructors may want to omit them. Students who do not read these sections will still have a good general knowledge of behavior principles. New sections called *On the Applied Side* have been added to most chapters (except 1 and 2). Some of these sections come from material that appeared in the first edition, now reorganized under the header On the Applied Side. Other Applied Side sections present new material. These sections point students to direct applications of basic principles. For example, Chapter 7 on schedules of reinforcement has an On the Applied Side dealing with schedules of reinforcement and the regulation of cigarette smoking and abstinence. The topic is timely and provides a clear example of how schedules of reinforcement have applied importance.

The text continues to include Learning Objectives, Keywords, and a Glossary. Each chapter begins with Learning Objectives that are a set of questions intended to guide students through the material. A list of Keywords follows the end of each chapter. These are phrases and words that are key concepts in the chapter. After studying a chapter students should be able to construct sentences or paragraphs that correctly include keywords. Many of these key words are defined in the glossary that appears at the end of the book. This glossary is intended to help the reader find technical terms without searching through earlier chapters. The glossary not only provides definitions of terms, but also gives detailed accounts of how the terms are used in the discipline. Students may find the glossary a useful adjunct for study as well as definition.

We have not substantially changed or reorganized chapters that gained a high rating by reviewers. As most reviewers indicated, there is no point in changing something that is working just fine. Thus, except for corrections, minor additions, and reorganization Chapters 1, 2, 7, 8, 10, 11,12, and 14 are essentially the same as in the first edition. The chapter on imitation and rule-governed behavior is omitted from this edition based on a consideration of book length and our judgment that this material is less central to an introductory textbook.

The second edition of the text has a more thorough treatment of the principles and processes of respondent conditioning. We have divided respondent conditioning into two chapters (Chapters 3 and 4) with one chapter devoted to reflexes and simple conditioning (including second-order conditioning) and a second chapter focused on compound conditioning, complex respondent processes, and the Rescorla-Wagner model. Also, Chapter 5 on reinforcement and extinction of operant behavior, and Chapter 10 on the aversive regulation of behavior have been changed in terms of technical precision. The four basic contingencies of reinforcement are presented as based completely on procedure and effect, no longer requiring inferences about what are "positive" or "negative" stimuli. The text in these and other chapters has been altered to correspond to these changes.

Overall, there is a greater emphasis on principles of selection and the biological context of conditioning. This is evident in chapter 6 which is substantially revised. "Biological constraints" on operant conditioning are analyzed as an interplay between respondent and operant contingencies. In many situations, operant and respondent contingencies are operating at the same time, and changing over time in terms of the relative control of behavior. Our view is that behavior typically viewed as respondent is in fact operant when regulated by an operant contingency. On the other hand, behavior typically viewed as operant is in fact respondent when regulated by a respondent contingency.

There are many people who contributed to this text. Judy Cameron and Carl Cheney deserve a *special thanks* for their repeated editing for accuracy, writing style, and order of topics. Russ Powell (Grant MacEwan College, Canada), Francisco Silva (University of Redlands, CA), Barry Lowenkron (California State University, Los Angeles, CA) and Michael Ehlert (Brigham Young University, UT) served as reviewers for the second edition and many of their suggestions are reflected in the text. Of course any errors or omissions are our responsibility. Finally, our production editor, Marianne Hutchinson, made many useful suggestions and the text is, in our opinion, much improved because of her time and effort.

W. David Pierce
W. Frank Epling
Edmonton, Alberta, Canada

To B. F. Skinner

When an organism acts upon the environment in which it lives, it changes that environment in ways which often affect the organism itself. Some of these changes are what the layman calls rewards, or what are generally referred to technically as reinforcers: when they follow behavior in this way they increase the likelihood that the organism will behave in the same way again. (Ferster & Skinner, 1957, p.1)

CHAPTER 1

A Science of Behavior: Perspective, History, and Assumptions

1. Define learning and describe the difference between prescientific accounts of behavior and the modern-scientific view of behavior theory.

2. What is the experimental analysis of behavior? Give an example of such analysis based on this textbook.

3. Explain the term *behavior analysis*. What are the primary objectives of behavior analysis? How does behavior analysis differ from applied behavior analysis?

4. Summarize what is meant by respondent behavior. Write a sentence or two that includes respondent behavior, reflex, and survival value.

5. Summarize what is meant by respondent conditioning and point to the adaptive function of this process.

6. Discuss operant conditioning and give some common examples of operant behavior. Briefly compare operant and respondent conditioning.

7. Be able to write or talk about the evolution of conditioning and the implications of behavioral flexibility.

8. Discuss the meaning of the biological context of behavior. Give an example using Skinner's analysis of imprinting in young ducklings.

9. Explain what is meant by the selection of operant behavior. Compare mechanistic and selectionist models of behavior.

10. Discuss the extension of behavior analysis to human behavior and culture. Talk about the meaning of culture from a behavioral perspective and outline what selection means at the cultural level.

11. Be able to discuss the achievements and contributions of B. F. Skinner to the science of behavior. Give an example from this textbook of a popular misconception of Skinner's research and ideas.

12. Summarize the contributions of major historical figures to modern behavior analysis. Name the journals and associations that support behavior analysis. What is the split between basic and applied research?

13. Explain what is meant by the statement "The behavior of organisms is lawful."

14. Talk about how internal and private events are part of an organism's environment.

15. Summarize the behavioral viewpoint on the relationship between feelings and behavior. Be able to discuss how people can talk about their feelings and the accuracy of their reports.

16. Discuss thinking as behavior. Point to the different meanings of the verb *to think* and analyze thinking as a response tendency or as private behavior (mostly verbal).

Learning refers to the acquisition, maintenance, and change of an organism's behavior as a result of lifetime events. An important aspect of human learning concerns the influence of other people. From earliest history, people have tried to influence the behavior of other individuals. Interaction between humans is often characterized by attempts to influence behavior. Rational argument, rewards, bribes, threats, and force are used in attempts to change the behavior of people. Within society, people are required to behave in socially appropriate ways. As long as a person does what is expected, no one pays much attention. As soon as a person's conduct substantially departs from cultural norms, other people get upset and try to force conformity. Modern societies have codes of conduct and laws, and people who break them face penalties ranging from minor fines to capital punishment. Clearly, humans are concerned with regulating the behavior of others.

Theories of behavior have ranged from philosophy to natural science. When Socrates was told that new discoveries in anatomy proved that bodily movement was caused by the arrangement of muscles, bones, and joints, he replied, "That hardly explains why I am sitting here in a curved position talking to you" (Millenson, 1967, p. 3). About 2,300 years later, the philosopher Alfred North Whitehead asked the famous behaviorist B. F. Skinner a similar question. He said, "Let me see you account for my behavior as I sit here saying, 'No black scorpion is falling upon this table'" (Skinner, 1957, p. 457). Although there was no satisfactory account of behavior in the time of Socrates, a science of behavior is currently addressing such questions.

Human behavior has been attributed to a variety of causes. The causes of behavior have been located both within and outside of people. Internal causes have ranged from metaphysical entities like the soul to hypothetical structures of the nervous system. External causes of behavior have included the influence of the moon and tides, the arrangement of stars, and the whims of gods. Some of these theories of behavior remain popular today. For example, an article in the January 1991 issue of *The Economist* stated the following:

Is astrology the ultimate key to competitive advantage? That is what Divinitel, a French company specializing in celestial consulting, claims. For FFr350 ($70) a session, the firm's astrologers offer advice on anything from the timing of takeovers to exorcisms. For the busy executive, Divinitel's galaxy of services can be reached via Minitel, France's teletext system. The firm is even planning a flotation on France's over-the-counter stockmarket in March 1991.

So who is daft enough to pay for this mystical mumbo-jumbo? About 10% of French business, according to a study by HEC, a French business school. A typical client is the boss of a small or medium-sized company who wants a second, astrological opinion on job applicants. The boss of one plastics company even uses Divinitel's advice on star signs to team up salesmen. ("Twinkle, twinkle," p. 91)

The trouble with most of these accounts of behavior is that they are not scientific. That is, these theories do not hold up to testing by scientific methods. Over the last century, a scientific theory of behavior has developed. Behavior theory states that all behavior is due to a complex interaction between genetic influence and environmental experience. The theory is based on observation and experimentation, and it provides a natural-science account of the behavior of organisms, including humans. This book is concerned with such an account.

SCIENCE AND BEHAVIOR

The **experimental analysis of behavior** is a natural-science approach to understanding behavior regulation. Experimental analysis is concerned with controlling and changing the factors affecting the behavior of humans and other animals. For example, a behavioral researcher in a classroom may use a computer to arrange corrective feedback for a student's mathematical performance. The relevant condition that is manipulated or changed by the experimenter may involve presenting corrective feedback on some days and withholding it on others. In this case, the experimenter would probably observe more accurate mathematical performance on days when feedback was presented. This simple experiment illustrates one of the most basic principles of behavior—the principle of reinforcement.

The principle of reinforcement (and other behavior principles) may underlie many of the complex actions of people and animals. When a researcher identifies a basic principle that governs behavior, this is called an analysis of behavior. Thus, the experimental analysis of behavior involves specifying the basic processes and principles that regulate the behavior of organisms. Experiments are then used to test the adequacy of the analysis.

Experimental analysis occurs when a researcher notices that seagulls fly around a shoreline when people are on the beach, but not when the beach is deserted. After checking that changes in climate, temperature, time of day, and other conditions do not affect the behavior of the seagulls, the researcher offers the following analysis: People feed the birds and this reinforces flocking to the beach. When the beach is abandoned, the seagulls are no longer fed for congregating on the shoreline. This is a reasonable guess, but it can only be tested by an experiment. Pretend that the behavior analyst owns the beach and has complete control over it. The experiment involves changing the usual relationship between the presence of people and food. Simply stated, people are not allowed to feed the birds, and food is placed on the beach when people are not around. Over time, the researcher notes that there are fewer and fewer seagulls on the beach when people are present, and more and more gulls when the shoreline is deserted. The behavior analyst concludes that the presence of people regulated coming to the beach because the birds were fed, or reinforced, for this behavior. This is one example of an experimental analysis of behavior.

Behavior Analysis

Although experimental analysis is the fundamental method for a science of behavior, contemporary researchers prefer to describe their discipline as **behavior analysis.** This term implies a more general scientific approach that includes assumptions about how to study behavior, techniques to carry out the analysis, a systematic body of knowledge, and practical implications for society and culture.

Behavior analysis is a comprehensive approach to the study of the behavior of organisms. Primary objectives are the discovery of principles and laws that govern behavior, the extension of these principles over species, and the development of an applied technology. In the seagull example, the underlying principle is called discrimination. The principle of discrimination states that an organism will respond differently to two situations (e.g., presence or absence of people) if its behavior is reinforced in one setting but not in the other.

The principle of discrimination may be extended to human behavior and social reinforcement. You may discuss dating with Carmen, but not Tracey, because Carmen is interested in such conversation while Tracey is not. In a classroom, the principle of discrimination can be used to improve teaching and learning. The use of behavior principles to solve practical problems is called **applied behavior analysis** and is discussed at some length in Chapter 14.

As you can see, behavior analysis has a strong focus on environment-behavior relationships. The focus is on how organisms alter their behavior to meet the ever-changing demands of the environment. When an organism learns new ways of behaving in reaction to the changes that occur in its environment, this is called conditioning. The two basic kinds of conditioning are *respondent* and *operant*.

Two Types of Conditioning

Respondent Conditioning.   A **reflex** is behavior that is evoked by a biologically relevant stimulus. When a stimulus (S) automatically evokes a stereotypical response (R), the S $\rightarrow$ R relationship is called a reflex. This behavior had survival value in the sense that those animals that engaged in particular reflexive responses were more likely than other organisms to survive and reproduce. To illustrate, animals that startle and run when a loud noise is suddenly introduced may escape a predator, and this reflexive behavior may provide an adaptive ad-

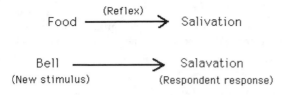

FIG. 1.1 Simple respondent conditioning. A bell rings just before feeding a dog; after several pairings of bell and food the dog begins to salivate at the sound of the bell.

vantage over organisms that don't run. Thus, reflexes are selected over species history. Of course, different species of organisms exhibit different sets of reflexes.

Respondent conditioning occurs when a neutral stimulus is paired with an unconditioned stimulus. For example, the buzz of a bee (neutral stimulus) is paired with the pain of a sting (unconditioned stimulus). After this conditioning, a buzzing bee usually causes people to avoid it. The Russian physiologist Ivan Petrovich Pavlov discovered this form of conditioning at the turn of the century. He showed that dogs salivated when food was placed in their mouths. This relation between the food stimulus and salivation is a reflex, and it occurs because of the animals' biological history. When Pavlov rang a bell just before feeding the dogs, they began to salivate at the sound of the bell. In this way, a new feature (sound of the bell) controlled the dogs' respondent behavior (salivation). As shown in Figure 1.1, a **respondent** is behavior that is elicited by the new conditioned stimulus.

Respondent conditioning is one way that organisms meet the challenges of life. A grazing animal that conditions to the sound of rustling grass by running away is less likely to become a meal than one that waits to see the predator. Almost all species on our planet, including humans, show this kind of conditioning. In terms of human behavior, many of our likes and dislikes are based on respondent conditioning. When good or bad things happen to us, we usually have an emotional reaction. These emotional responses can be conditioned to other people who are present when the positive or negative events occur (Byrne, 1971). Thus, respondent conditioning plays an important role in our social relationships—determining our friends as well as our enemies.

Operant Conditioning. Operant conditioning involves the regulation of behavior by its consequences. B. F. Skinner called this kind of behavior regulation **operant conditioning** because responses operate on the environment to produce an effect. Any behavior that operates on the environment to produce an effect is called an **operant**. During operant conditioning, an organism emits behavior that produces an effect that increases (or decreases) the frequency of the operant. In the laboratory, a hungry rat may receive food if it presses a lever. If lever pressing increases, then operant conditioning has occurred (see Figure 1.2).

Most of what we commonly call voluntary, willful, or purposive action is analyzed as operant behavior. Operant conditioning occurs when a smiling baby is picked up by its parents. If smiling increases because of parental attention, then smiling is an operant and the effect is a result of conditioning. In a more complex example, pressing a sequence of buttons while playing a video game will increase in frequency if this response pattern results in hitting a target. Other examples of operant behavior include driving a car, talking on the phone, taking notes in

$$R \xrightarrow{\text{produces}} S^r$$

Operant response
(lever press)

Environmental effect
(Food)

FIG. 1.2 Simple operant conditioning: An operant response (R) produces food (S^r) for a hungry rat.

class, walking to the corner store, reading a book, writing a term paper, and conducting an experiment.

The Evolution of Conditioning

When organisms were faced with unpredictable and changing environments, natural selection favored those individuals whose behavior could be conditioned. Organisms who condition are more flexible, in the sense that they can adjust to new requirements of the environment. Such behavioral flexibility must reflect an underlying structural change of the organism. Genes code for the anatomical and physiological characteristics of the individual. Such physical changes allow for different degrees of behavioral flexibility. Thus, differences in the structure of organisms based on genetic variation give rise to differences in the regulation of behavior. Processes of behavior regulation, like operant and respondent conditioning, lead to greater (or lesser) reproductive success. Presumably, those organisms that changed their behavior as a result of experience during their lives survived and had offspring—those that were less flexible did not. Simply stated, this means that the capacity for conditioning is inherited.

The evolution of behavioral flexibility had an important consequence. Behavior that was closely tied to survival and reproduction could be influenced by experience. Behavior related to survival and reproduction is typically regulated by specific physiological processes. However, for behaviorally flexible organisms, this control by physiology may be modified by experiences during the lifetime of the individual. The extent of such modification depends on the amount and scope of behavioral flexibility (Baum, 1983). For example, sexual behavior is closely tied to reproductive success and is regulated by distinct physiological processes. For many species, sexual behavior is rigidly controlled. In humans, however, sexual behavior is also influenced by socially mediated experiences. These experiences dictate when sexual intercourse will occur, how it is performed, and who can be a sexual partner. Powerful religious or social control can make people abstain from sex. This example illustrates that even the biologically relevant behavior of humans is partly determined by life experience.

The Biological Context of Behavior.   Although behavior analysts recognize the importance of biology and evolution, they focus on the interplay of behavior and environment. To maintain this focus, the evolutionary history and biological status of an organism are examined as part of the **context** for specific environment-behavior interactions (see Morris, 1988, 1992). This contextualist view is seen in B. F. Skinner's analysis of imprinting in a duckling:

Operant conditioning and natural selection are combined in the so-called imprinting of a newly hatched duckling. In its natural environment the young duckling moves towards its mother and follows her as she moves about. The behavior has obvious survival value. When no duck is present, the duckling behaves in much the same way with respect to other objects. Recently it has been shown that a young duckling will come to approach and follow any moving object, particularly if it is the same size as a duck—for example, a shoe box. Evidently survival is sufficiently well served even if the behavior is not under the control of the specific visual features of a duck. Merely approaching and following is enough.

Even so, that is not a correct statement of what happens. What the duckling inherits is the *capacity to be reinforced by maintaining or reducing the distance between itself and a moving objec*t [italics added]. In the natural environment, and in the laboratory in which imprinting is studied, approaching and following have these consequences, but the contingencies can be changed. A mechanical system can be constructed in which movement *toward* an object causes the object to move rapidly away, while movement *away from* the object causes it to come closer. Under these conditions, the duckling will move away from the object rather than approach or follow it. A duckling will learn to peck a spot on the wall if pecking brings the object closer. Only by knowing what and how the duckling learns during its lifetime can we be sure of what it is equipped to do at birth. (Skinner, 1974, pp. 40–41)

The duckling's biological history, in terms of capacity for reinforcement by proximity to a duck-sized object, is the context for the regulation of its behavior. Of course, the anatomy and physiology of the duck allow for this capacity. However, the way the environment is arranged determines the behavior of the individual organism. Laboratory experiments in behavior analysis identify the general principles that govern the behavior of organisms, the specific events that regulate the behavior of different species, and the arrangement of these events during the lifetime of an individual.

The Selection of Operant Behavior

Early behaviorists like John Watson used the terminology of stimulus-response (S-R) psychology. From this perspective, stimuli force responses much like meat in a dog's mouth elicits (or forces) salivation. In fact, Watson based his stimulus-response theory of behavior on Pavlov's conditioning experiments. Stimulus-response theories are mechanistic in the sense that an organism is compelled to respond when a stimulus is presented. This is similar to a physical account of the motion of billiard balls. The impact of the cue ball (stimulus) determines the motion and trajectory (response) of the target ball. Although stimulus-response conceptions are useful for analyzing reflexive behavior and other rigid response patterns, the push-pull model is not as useful when applied to voluntary actions.

The mechanistic model was rejected by B. F. Skinner, who based operant conditioning on Darwin's **principle of selection.** The basic idea is that an individual emits behavior that produces effects, consequences, or outcomes. Based on these consequences, those performances that are appropriate increase while inappropriate forms decline or become extinct. Julie Vargas is the daughter of B. F. Skinner and a professor of behavior analysis. She has commented on her father's model of causation:

> Skinner's paradigm is a *selectionist* paradigm not unlike Darwin's selectionist theory of the evolution of species. Where Darwin found an explanation for the evolution of species, Skinner looked for variables functionally related to changes in behavior over the lifetime of an individual. Both explanations assumed variation; Darwin in inherited characteristics, Skinner in individual acts. Skinner, in other words, does not concern himself with why behavior varies, only with how patterns of behavior are drawn out from the variations that already exist. In looking at the functional relationships between acts and their effects on the world, Skinner broke with the S-R, input-output transformation model. (Vargas, 1990, p. 9)

Skinner recognized that operants are selected by their consequences. He also noted that operant behavior naturally varies in form and frequency. Even something as simple as opening the door to your house is not done the same way each time. Pressure on the door knob, strength of pull, the hand that is used, and so on change from one occasion to the next. If the door sticks and becomes difficult to open, a forceful response will eventually occur. This response may succeed in opening the door and become the most likely performance for the situation. Other forms of response will occur at different frequencies depending on how often they succeed in opening the door. Thus, operants are selected by their consequences.

Similarly, it is well known that babies produce a variety of sounds called "babbling." These natural variations in babbling are important for language training. When sounds occur, parents may react to them. When the infant produces a familiar sound, parents often repeat it more precisely. Unfamiliar sounds are usually ignored. Eventually, the baby begins to talk like other people in the culture. Selection of verbal behavior by its social consequences is an important process underlying human communication.

Culture and Behavior Analysis

Although much of the research in the experimental analysis of behavior is based on laboratory animals, contemporary behavior analysts are increasingly concerned with human behavior. The behavior of people occurs in a social environment. Society and culture refer to aspects of the social environment that regulate human conduct. One of the primary tasks of behavior analysis is to show how individual behavior is acquired, maintained, and changed through interaction with others. An additional task is to account for the practices of the group, community, or society that affect an individual's behavior.

Culture is usually defined in terms of the ideas and values of a society. However, behavior analysts define culture as all the conditions, events, and stimuli arranged by other people that regulate human action (Glenn, 1988; Skinner, 1953). The principles and laws of behavior analysis provide an account of how culture regulates an individual's behavior. A person in an English-speaking culture learns to speak in accord with the verbal practices of the community. People in the community provide reinforcement for a certain way of speaking. In this manner, a person comes to talk like other members of the public and, in doing so, contributes to the perpetuation of the culture. **Cultural practices** are therefore maintained through the social conditioning of individual behavior.

Another objective is to account for the evolution of cultural practices. Behavior analysts suggest that the principle of selection (by consequences) also occurs at the cultural level. Cultural practices therefore increase (or decrease) based on consequences produced in the past. A cultural practice of making containers to hold water is an advantage to the group because it allows for the transportation and storage of water. This practice may include making and using shells, hollow leaves, or fired-clay containers. The cultural form that is selected (e.g., clay jars) is the one that proves most efficient. In other words, those containers that last the longest, hold the most, and so on are valued by the community. For this reason, people manufacture clay pots, and the manufacture of less efficient containers declines.

Behavior analysts are interested in **cultural evolution** because cultural changes alter the social conditioning of individual behavior. Analysis of cultural evolution suggests how the social environment is arranged and rearranged to support specific forms of human behavior. On a more practical level, behavior analysts suggest that the solution to many social problems requires a technology of cultural design. This possibility was addressed by B. F. Skinner in his utopian book, *Walden Two*. Although this idealistic novel was written some four decades ago, contemporary behavior analysts are conducting small-scale social experiments based on Skinner's ideas. Recently, behavioral technology has been used to manage environmental pollution, encourage energy conservation, and regulate overpopulation (Glenwick & Jason, 1980).

Focus on B. F. Skinner

B. F. Skinner (1904–1990) was the intellectual force behind behavior analysis. He was born Burrhus Frederic Skinner on March 20, 1904 in Susquehanna, Pennsylvania. When he was a boy, Skinner spent much of his time exploring the countryside with his younger brother. He had a passion for English literature and mechanical inventions. His hobbies included writing stories and designing perpetual-motion machines. He wanted to be a novelist and went to Hamilton College in Clinton, New York, where he graduated with a degree in English. After graduating from college in 1926, Skinner reported that he was not a great writer because he had nothing to say. He began reading about behaviorism, a new intellectual movement, and as a result went to Harvard in 1928 to learn more about a science of behavior. Skinner earned his master's degree in 1930 and his Ph.D. the following year.

Skinner began writing about the behavior of organisms in the 1930s when the discipline was in its infancy, and he continued to publish papers until his death in 1990. During his long career, Skinner wrote about and researched topics ranging from utopian societies, the philosophy of science, teaching machines, pigeons that controlled the direction of missiles, air cribs for infants, and techniques for improving education. Some people considered him a genius, while others were upset by his theories.

FIG. 1.3 B. F. Skinner (from the B. F. Skinner Foundation).

Skinner was always a controversial figure. He proposed a natural-science approach to human behavior. According to Skinner, the behavior of organisms, including humans, was determined. Although common sense suggests that we do things because of our feelings, thoughts, and intentions, Skinner stated that behavior resulted from genes and environment. This position bothered many people who believed that humans have some degree of self-determination. Even though he was constantly confronted with arguments against his position, Skinner maintained that the scientific facts required the rejection of feelings, thoughts, and intentions as causes of behavior. He said that these internal events were not explanations of behavior; rather these events were additional activities of people that needed to be explained.

> The practice of looking inside the organism for an explanation of behavior has tended to obscure the variables which are immediately available for a scientific analysis. These variables lie outside the organism in its immediate environment and in its environmental history. They have a physical status to which the usual techniques of science are adapted, and they make it possible to explain behavior as other subjects are explained in science. These independent variables [causes] are of many sorts and their relations to behavior are often subtle and complex, but we cannot hope to give an adequate account of behavior without analyzing them. (Skinner, 1953, p. 31)

One of Skinner's most important achievements was his theory of operant behavior. The implications of behavior theory were outlined in his book, *Science and Human Behavior*. In this book, Skinner discussed basic operant principles and their application to human behavior. Topics include self-control, thinking, the self, social behavior, government, religion, and culture. Skinner advocated the principle of positive reinforcement and argued against the use of punishment. He noted how governments and other social agencies often resort to punishment for behavior control. Although punishment works in the short run, he noted that it has many negative side-effects. Positive reinforcement, Skinner believed, is a more effective means of behavior change—people act well and are happy when behavior is maintained by positive reinforcement.

Many of the things that Skinner has said and done have been misunderstood. One popular misconception is that he raised his children in an experimental chamber—the so-called baby in a box. People claimed that Skinner used his daughter as an experimental subject to test his theories. A popular myth is that this experience drove his child crazy. His daughter, Julie, was confronted with this myth and recalls the following:

> I took a class called "Theories of Learning" taught by a nice elderly gentleman. He started with Hull and Spence, and then reached Skinner. At that time I had read little of Skinner and I could not judge the accuracy of what was being said about Skinner's theories. But when a student asked whether Skinner had any children, the professor thought Skinner had children. "Did he condition his children?" asked another student. "I heard that one of the children was crazy." "What happened to his children?" The questions came thick and fast.
>
> What was I to do? I had a friend in the class, and she looked over at me, clearly expecting action. I did not want to demolish the professor's confidence by telling who I was, but I couldn't just sit there. Finally, I raised my hand and stood up. "Dr. Skinner has two daughters and I believe they turned out relatively normal," I said, and sat down. (Vargas, 1990, pp. 8–9)

In truth, the box that Skinner designed for his children had nothing to do with an experiment. The air crib was an enclosed cot that allowed air temperature to be adjusted. In addition, the mattress cover could be easily changed when soiled. The air crib was designed so the child was warm, dry, and free to move about. Most importantly, the infant spent no more time in the air crib than other children do in ordinary beds.

Although Skinner did not experiment with his children, he was always interested in the application of conditioning principles to human problems. His many books and papers on applied behavioral technology led to the field of applied behavior analysis. Applied behavior analysis is concerned with the extension of behavior principles to socially important problems. In the first issue of the *Journal of Applied Behavior Analysis*, Baer, Wolf, and Risley (1968) outlined a program of research based on Skinner's views:

> The statement [of behavior principles] establishes the possibility of their application to problem behavior. A society willing to consider a technology of its own behavior apparently is likely to support that application when it deals with socially important behaviors, such as retardation, crime, mental illness, or education. Better applications, it is hoped, will lead to a better state of society, to whatever extent the behavior of its members can contribute to the goodness of a society. The differences between applied and basic research are not differences between that which "discovers" and that which merely "applies" what is already known. Both endeavors ask what controls the behavior under study. . . . [Basic] research is likely to look at any behavior, and at any variable which may conceivably relate to it. Applied research is constrained to look at variables which can be effective in improving the behavior under study. (p. 91)

One area of application that Skinner wrote about extensively was teaching and learning. Although Skinner recognized the importance of behavior principles for teaching people with learning disabilities, he claimed that the same technology could be used to improve our general educational system. In his book, *The Technology of Teaching*, Skinner (1968) offered a personalized system of positive reinforcement for the academic performance of students. In this system, teaching involves arranging materials, designing the classroom, programming lessons, and so on to reinforce and maintain the performance of students. Learning is defined objectively in terms of answering questions, solving problems, using grammatically correct forms of the language, and writing about the subject matter.

In the later part of his life, Skinner worked with Margaret Vaughan (1983) on positive approaches to the problems of old age. Their book, *Enjoy Old Age: A Program of Self-Management*, is written for the elderly reader and provides practical advice on how to deal with daily life. For example, the names of people are easy to forget and even more so in old age. Skinner and Vaughan suggest that you can improve your chances of recalling a name by reading a list of people you are likely to meet before going to an important occasion. If all else fails "you can always appeal to your age. You can please the friend whose name you have forgotten by saying that the names you forget are always the names you most want to remember" (p. 52).

Skinner, who held the A. E. Pierce chair, officially retired in 1974 from Harvard University. Following his retirement, Skinner continued an active program of research and writing. Each day he walked 2 miles to William James Hall, where he lectured, supervised graduate students, and conducted experiments. Eight days before his death on August 18, 1990, B. F. Skinner received the first (and only) citation for outstanding lifetime contribution to psychology from the American Psychological Association.

A BRIEF HISTORY OF BEHAVIOR ANALYSIS

Contemporary behavior analysis is based on ideas and research that became prominent at the turn of the century. The Russian scientist Ivan Petrovich Pavlov discovered the conditioned reflex, and this was a significant step toward a scientific understanding of behavior. Although Pavlov contributed greatly to behavior analysis, his main interest was in physiology.

Ivan Petrovich Pavlov (1849–1936)

Pavlov was born the son of a village priest in 1849. He attended seminary school in order to follow his father into the priesthood. However, after studying physiology he decided on a career in the biological sciences. Although his family protested, Pavlov entered the University of St. Petersburg, where he graduated in 1875 with a degree in physiology. After completing his studies in physiology, Pavlov was accepted as an advanced student of medicine. He distinguished himself and obtained a scholarship to continue his studies of physiology in Germany.

FIG. 1.4 Ivan Petrovich Pavlov (photograph by Bachrach).

In 1890, Pavlov was appointed to two prominent research positions in Russia. He was Professor of Pharmacology at the St. Petersburg Medical Academy and Director of the Physiology Department. For the next 20 years, Pavlov studied the physiology of digestion, and in 1904 he won the Nobel Prize for this work.

Ivan Pavlov worked on the salivary reflex and its role in digestion. Pavlov had dogs surgically prepared to expose the salivary glands in the dogs' mouths. The animals were brought into the laboratory and put in restraining harnesses. As shown in Figure 1.5, food was then placed in the dogs' mouths and the action of the salivary glands was observed.

The analysis of the salivary reflex was based on prevailing notions of animal behavior. At this time, many people thought that animals, with the exception of humans, were complex biological machines. The idea was that a specific stimulus evoked a particular response in much the same way that turning a key starts an engine. In other words, animals reacted to the environment in a simple cause-effect manner. Humans, on the other hand, were seen as different from other animals in that their actions were purposive. Humans were said to anticipate future events. Pavlov noticed that his dogs began to salivate at the sight of an experimenter's lab coat *before* food was placed in the animal's mouth. This suggested that the dogs anticipated food. Pavlov recognized that such a result challenged conventional wisdom.

Pavlov made an important observation in terms of the study of behavior. He reasoned that anticipatory reflexes were learned or conditioned. Further, Pavlov concluded that these conditioned reflexes were an essential part of the behavior of organisms. Although some behaviors were described as innate reflexes, other actions were based on conditioning that occurred during the animal's life. These **conditioned reflexes** were present to some degree in all animals but were most prominent in humans.

The question was how to study conditioned reflexes systematically. Pavlov's answer to this question represents a major advance in the experimental analysis

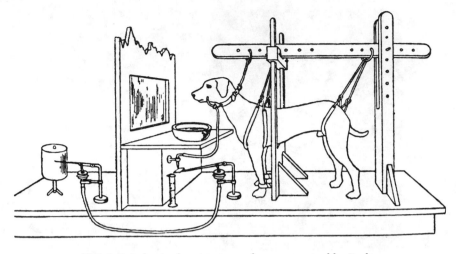

FIG. 1.5 A dog in the experimental apparatus used by Pavlov.

of behavior. If dogs reliably salivate at the sight of a lab coat, Pavlov reasoned, then any arbitrary stimulus that preceded food might also be conditioned and evoke salivation. Pavlov replaced the experimenter's lab coat with a stimulus that he could systematically manipulate and reliably control. In some experiments, a metronome (a device used to keep the beat while playing the piano) was presented to a dog just before it was fed. This procedure resulted in the dog eventually salivating to the sound of the metronome. If a particular beat preceded feeding while other rhythms did not, the dog salivated most to the sound associated with food.

Although Pavlov was a physiologist and believed in mental associations, his research was directed at observable responses and stimuli. He discovered many principles of the conditioned reflex. These principles included spontaneous recovery, discrimination, generalization, and extinction. The later part of his career involved an experimental analysis of neurosis in animals. He continued these investigations until his death in 1936.

John Broadus Watson (1878–1958)

Pavlov's research became prominent in North America, and the conditioned reflex was incorporated into a more general theory of behavior by the famous behaviorist John B. Watson. Watson acknowledged Pavlov's influence:

> I had worked the thing out [conditioning] in terms of *Habit* formation. It was only later, when I began to dig into the vague word *Habit* that I saw the enormous contribution Pavlov had made, and how easily the conditioned response could be looked upon as the unit of what we had been calling *Habit*. I certainly, from that point on, gave the master his due credit. (Watson, personal communication to Hilgard & Marquis, 1961, p. 24)

FIG. 1.6 John Watson (from the Archives of the History of American Psychology, University of Akron).

Watson went on to argue that there was no need to make up unobservable mental associations to account for human and animal behavior. He proposed that psychology should be a science based on observable behavior. Thoughts, feelings, and intentions had no place in a scientific account and researchers should direct their attention to muscle movements and neural activity. Although this was an extreme position, Watson succeeded in directing the attention of psychologists to behavior-environment relationships.

Watson was a rebellious young man who failed his last year at Furman University because he handed in a final-exam paper "backwards."[1] He graduated in 1899, when he was 21 years old. After spending a year as a public-school teacher, Watson decided to further his education and was admitted to graduate studies at the University of Chicago. There he studied philosophy with John Dewey, the famous educator. He never really appreciated Dewey's ideas and later in his life commented, "I never knew what he was talking about then, and, unfortunately for me, I still don't know" (Watson, 1936, p. 274). While a graduate student at Chicago, he also studied psychology with James Angell and biology and physiology with Henry Donaldson and Jacques Loeb. In 1903, he obtained his doctorate for research with laboratory rats. The experiments concerned learning and correlated changes in the brains of these animals.

Watson (1903) published a book called *Animal Education: An Experimental Study of the Psychical Development of the White Rat, Correlated with the Growth of Its Nervous System* that was based on his doctoral research. The book demonstrated that Watson was a capable scientist who could clearly present his ideas. Ten years later, Watson (1913) published his most influential work in *Psychological Review*, "Psychology as the Behaviorist Views It." This paper outlined Watson's views on

---

[1]This description of John Watson is partially based on a paper by James Todd and Edward Morris (1986) on "The Early Research of John B. Watson: Before the Behavioral Revolution."

behaviorism and argued that objectivity was the only way to build a science of psychology.

> I feel that *behaviorism* is the only consistent logical functionalism. In it one avoids [the problem of mind-body dualism]. These time-honored relics of philosophical speculation need trouble the student of behavior as little as they trouble the student of physics. The consideration of the mind-body problem affects neither the type of problem selected nor the formulation of the solution of that problem. I can state my position here no better than by saying that I should like to bring my students up in ignorance of such hypotheses as one finds among other branches of science. (Watson, 1913, p. 166).

In this paper, Watson also rejected as scientific data what people said about their thoughts and feelings. Further, he pointed to the unreliability of psychological inferences about another person's mind. Finally, Watson noted that the psychology of mind had little practical value for behavior control and public affairs.

Perhaps Watson's most famous experiment was the study of fear conditioning with Little Albert (Watson & Rayner, 1920). Little Albert was a normal, healthy infant who attended a day-care center. Watson and his assistant used classical-conditioning procedures to condition fear of a white rat. At first Little Albert looked at the rat and tried to touch it. The unconditioned stimulus was the sound of a hammer hitting an iron rail. This sound made Little Albert jump, cry, and fall over. After only six presentations of the noise and rat, the furry animal also produced the fear responses. The next phase of the experiment involved a series of tests to see if the child's fear reaction transferred to similar stimuli. Albert was also afraid when presented with a white rabbit, a dog, and a fur coat.

At this point, Watson and Rayner discussed a number of techniques that could be used to eliminate the child's fear. Unfortunately, Little Albert was removed from the day-care center before counter-conditioning could be carried out. In his characteristic manner, Watson later used the disappearance of Little Albert to poke fun at Freud's method of psychoanalysis. He suggested that as Albert got older, he might go to an analyst because of his strange fears. The analyst would probably convince Albert that his problem was the result of an unresolved Oedipal complex. But, Watson remarked, we would know that Albert's fears were actually caused by conditioning—so much for Freudian analysis.

Watson had many interests and he investigated and wrote about ethology, comparative animal behavior, neural function, physiology, and philosophy of science. Based on his controversial views and charisma, Watson was elected president of the American Psychological Association in 1915 when he was only 37 years old. His career came to an abrupt end in 1920 when he began having a public affair with his graduate student and collaborator Rosalie Rayner. There was also a claim that Watson carried out experiments on human sexual behavior, but these rumors have not been substantiated (Todd and Morris, 1992). Because of Watson's open love affair with Rayner his wife divorced him. This resulted in a scandal and the end of Watson's academic career. After leaving Johns Hopkins University, he became successful in industry by applying conditioning principles to advertising and public relations. Watson implemented the use of subliminal suggestion and the pairing of hidden symbols in advertising—techniques still used today.

Edward Lee Thorndike (1874–1949)

Watson's behaviorism emphasized the conditioned reflex. This analysis focuses on the events that precede action and is usually called a stimulus-response approach. Another American psychologist, Edward Lee Thorndike, was more concerned with how success and failure affect the behavior of organisms. His research emphasized the events and consequences that follow behavior. In other words, Thorndike was the first scientist to systematically study operant behavior, although he called the changes that occurred **trial-and-error learning** (Thorndike, 1898).

Edward L. Thorndike was born in 1874 in Williamsburg, Massachusetts. He was the son of a Methodist minister and had no knowledge of psychology until he attended Wesleyan University. There he read William James's (1890) book *Principles of Psychology*, which had a major impact on him. After reading the book, Thorndike was accepted as a student at Harvard, where he studied with William James. It is important to note that James's psychology focused on the mind and used the method of introspection (people's reports of feeling and thoughts). Thus, in contrast to John Watson, Thorndike was concerned with states of mind. In terms of contemporary behavior analysis, Thorndike's contribution was his systematic study of the behavior of organisms rather than his mental interpretations of animal and human behavior.

Thorndike was always intrigued with animal behavior. While at Harvard, his landlady became upset because he was raising chickens in his bedroom. By this time, James and Thorndike were good friends, and Thorndike moved his experiments to the basement of James's house when he could not get laboratory space at Harvard. He continued his research and supported himself by tutoring stu-

FIG. 1.7 Edward Thorndike (from Teachers College, Columbia University).

dents for 2 years at Harvard. Then Thorndike moved to Columbia University, where he studied with James McKeen Cattell, the famous expert on intelligence testing. Thorndike took two of his "smartest" chickens with him to Columbia, but soon switched to investigating the behavior of cats.

At Columbia University, Thorndike began his famous experiments on trial-and-error learning in cats. Animals were placed in what Thorndike called a "puzzle box" and food was placed outside the box. A cat that struggled to get out of the box would accidentally step on a treadle, pull a string, and so on. These responses resulted in opening the puzzle-box door. Thorndike found that most cats took less and less time to solve the problem after they were repeatedly returned to the box (i.e., repeated trials). From these observations Thorndike made the first formulation of the **law of effect:**

> The cat that is clawing all over the box in her impulsive struggle will probably claw the string or loop or button so as to open the door. And gradually all the other *non-successful impulses will be stamped out and the particular impulse leading to the successful act will be stamped in by the resulting pleasure* [italics added], until after many trials, the cat will, when put in the box, immediately claw the button or loop in a definite way. (Thorndike, 1911, p. 40)

Today, Thorndike's law of effect is restated as the principle of reinforcement. This principle states that all operants may be followed by consequences that increase or decrease the probability of response in the same situation. Notice that references to "stamping in" and "pleasure" are not necessary and that nothing is lost by this modern restatement of the law of effect.

Thorndike was appointed to the Teachers College, Columbia University as a professor in 1899, and he spent his entire career there. He studied and wrote about education, language, intelligence testing, comparison of animal species, the nature-nurture problem, transfer of training, sociology of the quality of life, and most importantly, animal and human learning. Thorndike published more than 500 books and journal articles. His son (Robert Ladd Thorndike, 1911–1990) became a well-known educational psychologist in his own right and in 1937 joined the same department of psychology as his father. In 1949, Edward Lee Thorndike died.

B. F. Skinner and the Rise of Behavior Analysis

Contemporary behavior analysis has been influenced by the works of Pavlov, Watson, Thorndike, and many others. Although the ideas of many scientists and philosophers have had an impact, Burrhus Fredrick Skinner (1904–1990) is largely responsible for the development of modern behavior analysis. In the "Focus on B. F. Skinner" section, we described some details of his life and some of his accomplishments. Here we will outline his contribution to contemporary behavior analysis.

Skinner was studying at Harvard during a time of intellectual change. He wanted to extend the work of Pavlov to more complicated instances of the conditioned reflex. Rudolph Magnus was a contemporary of Ivan Pavlov, and he had been working on the conditioning of physical movement. Skinner had read his book *Korperstellung* in the original German and was impressed with it. Skinner said, "I began to think of reflexes as behavior rather than with Pavlov as 'the activity of the cerebral cortex' or, with Sherrington, as 'the integrative action of the nervous system'" (Skinner, 1979, p. 46).

The idea that reflexes could be studied as behavior (rather than as a reflection of the nervous system or the mind) was fully developed in Skinner's (1938) book, *The Behavior of Organisms*. In this text, Skinner distinguishes between Pavlov's reflexive conditioning and the kind of learning reported by Thorndike. Skinner proposed that behavior was regulated by respondent and operant conditioning. These terms were carefully selected to emphasize the study of behavior for its own sake. Pavlov interpreted reflexive conditioning as the study of the central nervous system, and Skinner's respondent conditioning directed attention to environmental events and responses. Thorndike's trial-and-error learning was based on unobservable states of mind, and Skinner's operant conditioning focused on the functional relations between behavior and its consequences. Both operant and respondent conditioning required the study of observable correlations among objective events and behavior.

Skinner soon talked about a science of behavior rather than one of physiology or mental life. Once stated, the study of behavior for its own sake seems obvious, but consider that most of us say that we do something because we have made up our mind to do it or, in more scientific terms, because of a neural connection in our brain. Most people accept explanations of behavior that rely on descriptions of brain, mind, intelligence, cognitive function, neural activity, thinking, or personality. Because these factors are taken as the cause(s) of behavior, they become the focus of investigation. Skinner, however, suggested that remembering, thinking, feeling, the action of neurons, and so on are more behavior of the organism that requires explanation. He further proposed that the action of organisms could be investigated by focusing on behavior and the environmental events that precede and follow it.

Skinner's behavioral focus was partially maintained and influenced by his lifelong friend, Fred Simmons Keller. Skinner and Keller attended Harvard graduate school together, and Keller encouraged Skinner to pursue a behavioral view of psychology. By 1946, Skinner had formed a small group of behaviorists at Indiana University. At this same time, Fred Keller and his friend Nat Schoenfeld organized another group at Columbia University.

Although the number of **behavior analysts** was growing, there were no sessions on behavioral issues at the American Psychological Association annual meetings. Because of this, Skinner, Keller, Schoenfeld, and others organized their own conference at Indiana University. This was the first conference on the experimental analysis of behavior (see Figure 1.8). These new-style behaviorists rejected the extreme views of John B. Watson and offered an alternative formulation. Unlike Watson, they did not reject genetic influences on behavior; they extended the analysis of behavior to operant conditioning, and they studied behavior for its own sake.

These new behavior analysts found it difficult to get their research published in the major journals of psychology. This was because they used a small number of subjects in their experiments, did not use statistical analysis, and their graphs of response rate were not appreciated. By 1958, the group was large enough to start its own journal, and the first volume of the *Journal of the Experimental Analysis of Behavior (JEAB)* was published. As research accumulated, the practical implications of behavior principles became more and more evident, and applications to mental illness, retardation, rehabilitation, and education increased. In 1968, the *Journal of Applied Behavior Analysis (JABA)* was published for the first time.

By 1964, the number of behavior analysts had grown enough that a special division was established by the American Psychological Association. Division 25 is called The Experimental Analysis of Behavior and has several thousand members. Subsequently, the Association for Behavior Analysis (ABA) was founded in the late 1970s. This association holds an annual international conference that is at-

FIG. 1.8 Photograph taken at the first conference on the experimental analysis of behavior held in 1946 at Indiana University. From left to right in front row: Dinsmoor, Musgrave, Skinner, Keller, Schoenfeld, Lloyd. Middle row: Ellson, Daniel, Klein, Jenkins, Wyckoff, Hefferline, Wolin. Back row: Estes, Frick, Anderson, Verplanck, Beire, Hill, Craig (reprinted from *Journal of the Experimental Analysis of Behavior*, *5*, 456; copyright by the Society for the Experimental Analysis of Behavior, Inc.).

tended by behavior analysts from a variety of countries. The association publishes a journal of general issues called *The Behavior Analyst*.

A recent issue in the field of behavior analysis is the separation between applied behavior analysis and basic research. During the 1950s and 1960s, no distinction existed between applied and basic investigations. This was because applied behavior analysts were trained as basic researchers. That is, the first applications of behavior principles came from the same people who were conducting laboratory experiments. The applications of behavior principles were highly successful, and this led to a greater demand for people trained in applied behavior analysis. Soon applied researchers were no longer working in the laboratory or reading the basic journals.

This separation between basic and applied research was first described by Sam Deitz (1978), who noted the changing emphasis from science to technology among applied behavior analysts (see also Hayes, Rincover, & Solnick, 1980; Michael, 1980; Pierce & Epling, 1980). Donald Baer (1981) acknowledged the technical drift of applied behavior analysis, but suggested that this was a natural progression of the field that may have positive effects.

Today the separation issue is not resolved; however, we have written this book assuming that an acquaintance with basic research is important, even for those who are primarily concerned with behavioral applications. Students can study this text for a basic grounding in behavioral science, or for a solid foundation in human behavior and application.

SCIENCE AND BEHAVIOR: SOME ASSUMPTIONS

All scientists make assumptions about their subject matter. These assumptions are based on prevailing views in the discipline and guide scientific research. In terms of behavior analysis, researchers assume that the behavior of organisms is lawful. This means that it is possible to study the interactions between an organism and its environment in an objective manner. To carry out the analysis, it is necessary to isolate behavior-environment relationships. The scientist must identify events that reliably precede the onset of some action and the specific consequences that follow behavior. If behavior systematically changes with variation in the environmental conditions, then behavior analysts assume that they have explained the action of the organism. There are other assumptions that behavior analysts make about their science.

The Private World

Contemporary behavior analysts include internal events as part of an organism's environment. This point is often misunderstood; internal functioning like an upset stomach, full bladder, low blood sugar, and so on are part of a person's environment. Internal physical events have the same status as external stimuli such as light, noise, odor, and heat. Both external and internal events regulate behavior.

Although this is so, behavior analysts usually emphasize the external environment. This is because external events are the only stimuli available for behavior change. Many psychological studies involve giving information to a person in order to change or activate cognitive processes. The objective procedures are giving instructions and observing how the person acts. In this view, the instructions are external stimuli that regulate both verbal and nonverbal behavior. Even when a drug is given to a person and the chemical alters internal biochemistry, the direct injection of the drug is an external event that subsequently regulates behavior. To make this clear, without the drug injection neither the biochemistry nor the behavior of the person would change.

Feelings and Behavior

Most people assume that their feelings and thoughts explain why they act as they do. Contemporary behavior analysts agree that people feel and think, but they do not consider these events as causes of behavior. They note that these terms are more correctly used as verbs rather than nouns. Instead of talking about thoughts, behavior analysts point to the action word "thinking." And instead of analyzing feelings as things we possess, the behavioral scientist focuses on the action of feeling or sensing. In other words, thinking and feeling are activities of the organism that require explanation.

Feelings as Byproducts.   Because feelings occur at the same time that we act, they are often taken as causes of behavior. Although feelings and behavior are necessarily correlated, it is the environment that determines how we act, and at the same time how we feel. Feelings are real, but they are byproducts of the environmental events that regulate behavior. For this reason, a behavioral approach requires that the researcher trace feelings back to the interaction between behavior and environment.

Pretend that you are in an elevator between the 15th and 16th floors when the elevator suddenly stops, and the lights go out. You hear a sound that appears to be the snapping of elevator cables. Suddenly, the elevator lurches and then drops 2 feet. You call out, but nobody comes to your rescue. After about an hour, the elevator starts up again, and you get off on the 16th floor. Six months later, a good friend invites you to dinner. You meet downtown, and you discover that your friend has made reservations at a restaurant called The Room at the Top, which is located on the 20th floor of a skyscraper. Standing in front of the elevator, a sudden feeling of panic overwhelms you. You make a socially appropriate excuse like, "I don't feel well," and you leave. What is the reason for your behavior and the accompanying feeling?

There is no question that you feel anxious, but this feeling is not why you decide to go home. Both the anxious feeling and your decision to leave are easily traced to the negative experience in the elevator that occurred 6 months ago. It is this prior conditioning that behavior analysts emphasize. Notice that the behavioral position does not deny your feelings. These are real events. However, it is your previous interaction with the broken elevator that changed both how you feel and how you act.

Reports of Feelings.   You may still wonder why behavior analysts study overt behavior instead of feelings—given that both are changed by experience. The answer concerns the accessibility of feelings and overt behavior. Much of the behavior of organisms is directly accessible to the observer or scientist. This public behavior provides a relatively straightforward subject matter for scientific analysis. In contrast, feelings are largely inaccessible to the scientific community. Of course, the person who feels has access to this private information, but the problem is that reports of feelings are highly unreliable.

This unreliability occurs because we learn to talk about our feelings (and other internal events) as others have trained us to do. During socialization, people teach us how to describe ourselves, but when they do this they have no way of accurately knowing what is going on inside of us. Parents and teachers rely on public cues to train self-descriptions. They do this by commenting on and correcting verbal reports when behavior or events suggest a feeling. A preschooler is taught to say "I feel happy" when the parents guess that the child is happy. The parents may base their judgment on smiling, excitement, and affectionate responses from the child. Another way this training is done is that the child may be asked, "Are you happy?" in a circumstance where the parents expect the child to feel this way (e.g., on Christmas morning). When the child appears to be sad, or circumstances suggest this should be so, saying "I am happy" is not reinforced by the parents. Eventually, the child says "I am happy" in some situations and not in others.

Perhaps you have already noticed why reports of feelings are not good scientific evidence. Reports are only as good as the training of correspondence between public conditions and private events. In addition to inadequate training, there are other problems with accurate descriptions of feelings. Many of our internal functions are poorly correlated (or uncorrelated) with public conditions, and this means that we cannot be taught to describe such events accurately. Although a doctor may ask for the general location of a pain (e.g., abdomen), he or she is unlikely to ask whether the hurt is in the liver or the spleen. This report is simply inaccessible to the patient because there is no way to teach the correspondence between exact location of damage and public conditions. Generally, we are able to report in a limited way on private events, but the unreliability of such reports makes them questionable as scientific observations. Based on this realization, behavior analysts focus on the study of behavior rather than feelings.

Thinking and Behavior

Behavior analysts have also considered thinking and its role in a science of behavior. In contrast to views that claim a special inner world of thought, behavior analysts suggest that human thought is human behavior. Skinner (1974) stated that:

> The history of human thought is what people have said and done. Symbols are the products of written and spoken verbal behavior, and the concepts and relationships of which they are symbols are in the environment. Thinking has the dimensions of behavior, not a fancied inner process which finds expression in behavior. (pp. 117–118)

A number of behavioral processes, like generalization, discrimination, matching to sample, stimulus equivalence, and so on (see later chapters), give rise to behavior that, in a particular situation, may be attributed to higher mental functions. From this perspective, thinking is treated as behavior.

Thinking and Response Tendencies.

The term *think* in our culture has a variety of meanings. A person may say, "I am thinking of buying a new car" when the individual is reporting a low probability of action. Presumably, responses like "I will buy a car" or "I will definitely buy a new car" occur when the probability of action is higher. In accounting for these responses, the behavior analyst must specify the conditions that contributed to raising or lowering the probability of action (e.g., reinforcement variables) and show how the person is able to report on such tendencies to respond. Another example of people saying "I think" occurs when there is weak control of behavior by a stimulus. When shown an unfamiliar object, you may say, "I think it's a computer chip," which is contrasted with the responses "I know it's a computer chip" or "It's a computer chip." The critical factor in this episode is inadequate discrimination of the chip, as indicated by adding *think* to the sentence. In common English, when people are not sure about an object, event, or circumstance, they often add the word *think* to a descriptive sentence.

Thinking as Private Behavior.

More interesting examples of thinking are observed in a game of chess. We may ask another person, "What is the player thinking about?" A response like "She is probably thinking of moving the castle" refers to thinking that precedes the move itself. Sometimes this prior behavior is observable—the player may place a hand on the castle in anticipation of the move. At other times, behavior is covert and cannot be observed by others. An experienced chess player may think about the game and imagine the consequences of moving a particular piece.

Presumably, this behavior is overt when a person learns to play chess. For example, first the basic rules of the game are explained and a novice player is shown how the pieces move and capture. In moving the pieces from place to place, the player is asked to describe the relationships between the opposing chess pieces. This establishes the behavior of visualizing the layout of the board. As the player receives additional corrective feedback, visualizing layout becomes more skillful. The person begins to see relationships and moves that were not previously apparent. During the first few games, new players are often given instructions like "Don't move your knight there, or you'll lose it." Additionally, the player may be told "A better move would have been . . .", and a demonstration of the superior move is usually given. After some experience, the student is asked to explain why a particular move was made, and the explanation is discussed and evaluated. Eventually, the teacher stops prompting the player and encourages the person to play chess in silence. At this point, visualizing the layout of the board (e.g., white controls the center of the board) and describing the possible consequences of moves (e.g., moving the knight to this square will split the two rooks) becomes covert.

The function of thinking, as covert behavior, is to increase the effectiveness of practical action. People can act at the covert level without committing themselves publicly. An advantage is that an action can be revoked if the imagined consequences are not reinforcing. In our example, the chess player considers the possible moves and the consequences that may follow. Based on the covert evaluation, a player makes the move that appears to be best. Thus, the covert performance functions to prompt and guide overt action. Once the move is made, the player faces the objective consequences. If the move results in an advantage that could result in checkmate, then thinking about such a move in similar circumstances is strengthened. On the other hand, a bad move weakens the consideration of such moves in the future. Overall, thinking is operant behavior. Thinking that leads to effective action is likely to occur again, while thinking that prompts ineffective performance declines.

In this section, we have discussed thinking as reports on strength of response and as covert behavior. There are many other ways that the term *thinking* is used. When a person remembers, we sometimes talk about thinking in the sense of searching and recalling. Solving problems often involves private behavior that furthers a solution. In making a decision, people are said to think about the alternatives before a choice is made. The creative artist is said to think of novel ideas. In each of these instances, it is possible to analyze thinking as private behavior that is regulated by specific features of the environment. The remainder of this book discusses the behavioral processes that underlie all behavior, including thinking.

KEY WORDS

Applied behavior analysis

Behavior

Behavior analysis

Behavior analysts

Behaviorism

Conditioned reflexes

Context

Cultural evolution

Cultural practices

Culture

Experimental analysis of behavior

Law of effect

Learning

Operant

Operant conditioning

Private behavior

Reflex

Respondent

Respondent conditioning

Science of behavior

Selection

Trial-and-error learning

CHAPTER 2

The Experimental
Analysis
of Behavior

───────────────── **LEARNING OBJECTIVES** ─────────────────

1. Define the term *functional analysis*. Discuss the difference between structural and functional accounts of behavior and provide a human example based on the textbook.

2. Discuss the classification of behavior in terms of response functions. How does the concept of response class aid in a functional analysis of behavior?

3. What is the difference between the external and internal environment for a functional analysis? Discuss the classification of the environment based on stimulus functions. Give an example from the textbook of how stimulus functions may change.

   Advanced Issue

4. *Be able to talk about perception as a behavior of organisms. Discuss the traditional view of perception and contrast it with a behavior-analysis perspective.*

5. *Outline the Stroop effect and how it is understood from a traditional view of perception. How does behavior analysis account for this effect?*

6. *Talk about seeing as respondent and/or operant behavior. Describe conditioned seeing and how a person may respond to incomplete rings as if they were closed circles. What are the behavioral effects of operant seeing, as when reinforcement is arranged for seeing four-leaf clovers?*

7. Discuss the importance of stimulus class for a functional analysis.

8. Define establishing operations. Use the term *establishing operations* to show that behavior-environment relationships depend on context.

9. Be able to talk about Claude Bernard's method of experimental analysis and how it applies to his assertion that fasting rabbits are transformed into "veritable carnivorous animals."

10. Define an independent and dependent variable. What are three conditions that must be satis-

fied to show a cause-effect relationship between *X* and *Y* variables? How did Bernard eliminate rival explanations for the acidity of the rabbits' urine?

11. Discuss an A-B-A-B reversal design and some problems with reversal experiments. Show how the Goetz and Baer (1973) experiment is a modified example of this design. What is the theoretical importance of the Goetz and Baer research?

12. Define the internal validity of an experiment. Discuss the internal validity of Ayllon's (1963) experiment, referring to four possible sources of invalidity.

13. Define the external validity of an experiment. How is Ayllon's (1963) study viewed as a generalizing experiment? Discuss the correspondence between laboratory findings and the behavior of organisms in everyday life.

14. Explain the trade-off between internal and external validity.

15. What is meant by single-subject research? Discuss direct and systematic replications of single-subject experiments. What is the generality of single-subject research?

16. How does single-subject research allow for assessment of behavior change? Talk about defining the response class, measuring variability, baselines, and assessing behavior change.

17. How does variation in baseline measures affect the assessment of behavior change? Outline ways to detect behavior change when baselines are highly variable or "noisy."

18. Discuss baseline trend as a problem for the assessment of behavior change.

The experimental analysis of behavior refers to a method of analyzing behavior-environment relationships. This method is called **functional analysis**. Functional analysis involves classifying behavior according to its response functions and analyzing the environment in terms of stimulus functions. The term *function* refers to the characteristic effect produced by either a behavioral or an environmental event. Once a reliable classification has been established, the researcher uses experimental methods to show a causal relationship between the environmental event and a specified response.

FUNCTIONAL ANALYSIS OF BEHAVIOR

There are two ways to classify the behavior of organisms: structurally and functionally. In the **structural approach,** behavior is analyzed in terms of its form. For example, many developmental psychologists are interested in the intellectual growth of children. These researchers often investigate what a person does at a given stage of development. Children may show object permanence when they look for a familiar object that has just been hidden. In this case, the form of response, or what the child does (e.g., finds the hidden object), is the important aspect of behavior. The structure of behavior is emphasized because it is said to reveal the underlying stage of intellectual development. Notice that, in this example, the structural approach studies behavior to draw inferences about cognitive abilities.

In the previous chapter, we noted that behavior analysts study behavior for its own sake. To keep attention focused on behavior, structure and function are interrelated. That is, a particular form of response is traced to its characteristic effects, outcomes, or consequences. For example, a person presses a light switch with the left hand, the thumb and index finger, and a particular force. This form, or **topography,** of response occurs because it has been highly efficient, relative to other ways of turning on the light switch. Thus, the topography (structure) of a response is determined by the function of this behavior. Functionally, grasping the switch in a particular way produces light in an efficient manner.

In the more complex example of a child who finds a hidden object, a **functional analysis** suggests that this behavior also produces some specific consequence—the child gets the hidden toy. Rather than infer some intellectual stage of development, the behavior analyst suggests that a particular **history of reinforcement** is responsible for the child's capability. Presumably, a child that demonstrates object permanence has had numerous opportunities to search for and find missing objects.

A mother who breastfeeds her newborn often removes her clothing just before feeding the baby. After some experience, the baby may tug at the mother's blouse when he or she is hungry. This is one instance of the early conditioning of searching for objects. A few months later, the infant may inadvertently cover up a favorite rattle. In this situation, the child who accidentally pulls back the cover is reinforced by getting the toy. As children get older, they are directly taught to find hidden objects. This occurs when children are given presents to open at Christmas and when they hunt for Easter eggs. A functional analysis suggests that object permanence occurs because searching for objects usually results in finding them. Also, children who do not have these or similar experiences will perform poorly on a test of object permanence.

Response Functions

We have talked about behavior as if it was composed of discrete responses. In fact, it is better to consider behavior as a performance that follows a specific stimulus and/or results in a particular consequence. Although we will use the term *response* throughout this book, the term does not refer to a discrete movement like a muscle twitch or a lever press. A response is an integrated set of movements, or a performance, that is functionally related to environmental events.

Functionally, there are two basic types of behavior: respondent and operant. Respondent and operant behavior were briefly discussed in Chapter 1, but here we will emphasize the functional classification of this behavior. The term **respondent** is used to define behavior that increases or decreases because of the presentation of a stimulus (or event) that precedes the response. Such behavior is said to be **elicited,** in the sense that it reliably occurs when the stimulus is presented. The begging reflex of a young robin is respondent. It consists of opening the mouth and vigorous chirping. This behavior is elicited when a parent dangles a worm above the nestling's head. Careful testing may show that it is the position of the worm, rather than features of the parent, that reliably elicits this respondent.

There is a large class of behavior that does not depend on an eliciting stimulus. This behavior is called **emitted** and spontaneously occurs at some frequency. For example, human infants randomly emit a pattern of vocal sounds usually referred to as babbling. These sounds comprise the basic elements of all human languages. English-speaking parents attend to babbling that "sounds like" English and the baby emits more and more English sounds. When emitted behavior is strengthened or weakened by the events that follow the response, it is called **operant** behavior. Thus, operants are emitted responses that increase or decrease depending on the consequences they produce. To make clear the distinction between emitted behavior and operants, consider the action word *walking* versus the phrase *walking to the store.* Walking is emitted behavior, but it has no specified function. In contrast, walking to the store is an operant that is defined by getting food at the store. Pecking a disk is emitted behavior when there is no eliciting stimulus, but it is an operant when a bird pecks the disk for food.

Operant and respondent behavior often occur at the same time. A person who steps out of a movie theater in the middle of a bright afternoon may show both types of responses. The change from dark to bright light may elicit pupil contraction. This contraction is a reflexive response that decreases the amount of light entering the eye. At the same time, the person may shade his or her eyes with a hand or put on a pair of sunglasses. This latter behavior is operant because it is strengthened by the removal of the aversive stimulus. In another example, you find out that you have failed an important exam. The bad news may elicit a number of conditioned emotional responses like heart palpitations, changes in blood pressure, and perspiration. These physiological responses are probably felt as dread or anxiety. The person standing next to you as you read the results of the exam asks, "How did you do on the test?" You say, "Oh, not too bad" and walk down the hall. Your reply is operant behavior that avoids the embarrassment of discussing your poor performance. Although operant and respondent processes often occur at the same moment, we will often analyze them separately to clarify the factors that regulate such behavior.

Response Classes

When a person emits a relatively simple operant like putting on a coat, the performance changes from one occasion to the next. The coat may be put on using either the left or right hand; it may be grasped at the collar or held up by a sleeve. Sometimes one arm is inserted first, while in other circumstances both arms may be used. Careful observation of this everyday action will reveal an almost infinite variety of responses. The important point is that each variation of response has the common effect of staying warm by putting on a coat. To simplify the analysis, it is useful to introduce the concept of a class of responses. A **response class** refers to all the forms of the performance that have a similar function (e.g., putting on a coat to keep warm). In some cases, the responses in a class have close physical resemblance, but this is not always the case. A response class for convincing an opponent may include dramatic gestures, giving sound reasons, and paying attention to points of agreement. To get service from a restaurant server, you may call out as he or she passes, wave your hand in the air, or ask the busperson to send the server to your table.

FUNCTIONAL ANALYSIS OF THE ENVIRONMENT

In Chapter 1, we noted that behavior analysts use the term **environment** to refer to events and stimuli that change behavior. These events may be external to the organism or may arise from internal physiology. The sound of a jet aircraft passing closely overhead or an upset stomach may both be classified as aversive by their common effects on behavior. That is, both events are unpleasant and strengthen any behavior that removes them. In the case of a passing jet, people may cover their ears; a stomachache may be removed by taking antacid medication.

The location of the source of stimulation, internal versus external, is not a critical distinction for a functional analysis. There are, however, methodological problems with stomach pains that are not raised by external events like loud sounds. Internal sources of stimulation must be indirectly observed with the aid of instruments or inferred from observable behavior-environment interactions. Evidence for stomach pain may include the kinds of foods recently eaten, the health of the person when the food was ingested, and current signs of discomfort.

Stimulus Functions

All events and stimuli, whether internal or external, may acquire the capacity to affect behavior. When the occurrence of an event changes the behavior of an organism, we may say that the event has a **stimulus function.** Both respondent and operant conditioning are ways to create stimulus functions. During respondent conditioning, an arbitrary event like a tone comes to elicit a particular response, like salivation. Once the tone is effective, it is said to have a **conditioned-stimulus function** for salivation. In the absence of the conditioning history, the tone may have no specified function—it does not affect behavior.

Similarly, operant conditioning may result in establishing or changing the functions of stimuli. Any stimulus (or event) that follows a response and increases that response has a **reinforcement function** (see Chapter 1). When an organism's behavior is reinforced, those events that reliably precede responses come to have a **discriminative function.** These events are said to set the occasion for behavior and are called **discriminative stimuli.** Discriminative stimuli acquire this function because they predict reinforcement. In the laboratory, a pigeon may peck a key for food when the key is illuminated, but pecking is not reinforced when the key is dark. After some time, the illuminated key sets the occasion for the response. In everyday language, the illuminated key "tells" the bird when pecking will be reinforced. More technically, the lighted key is a discriminative stimulus since the probability of pecking is higher when the key is lit than when it is dark.

The concept of stimulus function is an important development in the analysis of behavior. Humans and other animals have evolved in such a way that they can sense those aspects of the environment that have been important for survival. Of all the stimuli that can be physically measured and sensed by an organism, at any one moment, only some affect behavior (have a stimulus function). Imagine you are sitting on a park bench with a friend on a nice sunny day. The physical stimuli include heat, wind current, sounds from traffic, birds, insects, rustling leaves, tactile pressure from sitting, and sight of kids playing ball, people walking in the park, color of flowers, grass, trees, and so on. Although all of these (and many more) stimuli are present, only some will affect your behavior—in the sense that you will turn your face into the sun, comment on the beauty of the flowers, and look in the direction of a passing fire truck. The remaining stimuli, at this moment in time, either have no function or serve as the context for those events that do.

As we are writing this book, there are many objects on the desk in front of us. We are sitting side by side; one of us is typing the text into a computer and the other is helping to compose the sentences. Functionally, the computer screen, keyboard, and conversation are regulating most of our textual or writing behavior. Other objects on the desk include computer disks, a cup with some pens in it, and several books. At this moment, the pens have no stimulus function because they are not affecting our operant or respondent behavior. It is important, however, to note that the pens may become functional in a variety of ways. If the telephone rings and the caller wants to leave a message, this circumstance will immediately make the pens functional. Another way these stimuli could be made functional is if a colleague entered the room and asked, "Do you have a pen I can borrow?"

ADVANCED ISSUE
Perceiving as Behavior

Even if you do your best to put down everything you see, will it really be *everything?* What about the singing of birds? And the freshness of the morning? And your own feeling of somehow being cleansed by it all? After all, as you paint, you perceive these things—they are inseparable from what you see. But how can you capture them in the painting so they are not lost for anyone who looks at it? Obviously they must be suggested by your composition and the color you use—since you have no other means of conveying them. (Solzhenitsyn, 1973, p. 395)

The concept of stimulus function raises some interesting issues. Most of us believe that we accurately perceive the world around us and are able to report on this with some reliability. In everyday language and in psychology, perception is an inferred, underlying process that determines behavior. In contrast, behavioral analysis suggests that perceiving is behavior that must be accounted for by environment-behavior relationships. The typical account of perception is seen in the following descriptions taken from a variety of introductory psychology textbooks:

> The view of perception that has been more or less dominant in psychology over the last 100 years holds that our experiences teach us how to draw broad inferences about the world from very limited sensory information; and that most perceptions are *constructed,* or *synthesized,* from combinations of more elementary sensations. It also maintains that these perceptual inferences are usually so accurate, highly practiced, and nearly automatic that you are almost totally unaware of making them. (Darley, Glucksberg, & Kinchla, 1991, p. 109)
>
> Perception, in its narrow usage, refers to the next stage in which an internal representation of an object is formed, and an experienced *percept* of the external stimulus is developed. The representation provides a working description of the perceiver's external environment. Information from lower-order detectors is organized and modified by higher-order brain processes to covert stimulus features and elements into patterns and forms that are recognizable. (Zimbardo, 1988, p. 185)
>
> Perception refers to the process of selecting, organizing, and interpreting sensory data into a usable mental representation of the world. (Huffman, Vernoy, Williams, & Vernoy, 1991, p. 101)
>
> Perception is the process by which we organize and make meaningful the mass of sensations we receive. Our past experience and our current state of mind influence the intricate series of steps between sensation and perception. (Martin, 1991; p. 126)

Generally, these passages reflect a view of human experience that has been popular for centuries. The basic idea is that receptors like eyes, ears, and tongue are constantly receiving sensory input that is a disorganized array of raw data. The person is said to work on the sensations by mentally organizing the input into a meaningful representation of the situation.

From a behavioral perspective, the difficulty with this view of perception is that the mental organization and representation of sensory input is not directly observable. That is, there is no objective way of getting information about such hypothetical events except by observing the behavior of the organism. Such **hypothetical constructs** are not always undesirable in science, but when used to account for behavior, these terms usually lack explanatory power because they are grounded in the very behavior that they are used to explain. This problem of explanatory power is seen in the perception account of the Stroop effect (Stroop, 1935).

In the Stroop task a person is given two lists of words for colors that are made up with different printed colors. On one list the words and colors correspond. For example, the word *red* is printed in the color red and the word *black* appears in black print. The second list contains color words that are printed with colors that are different from the meaning of the word. In this case the word *red* might be printed in yellow ink and the word *black* could appear in green print.

In a typical experiment, people are first given the list in which colors and words correspond and are told to "look at the words on the list and name the colors as fast as you can." In the second part of the experiment, they are given the noncorresponding list and asked to "look at the list and name each color while ignoring what each word says." The second task is much more difficult and takes more time. Why do you suppose it takes longer to name the colors on the list where color of print and the word do not match?

From a mental representation point of view, the explanation is as follows: ". . . the highly practiced and almost automatic perception of word meaning facilitates reading. However, this same automatically makes it difficult to ignore meaning and pay attention only to certain other aspects of the stimulus. Thus, the Stroop effect is a failure of selective perception" (Darley, Glucksberg, & Kinchla, 1991, p. 112).

From the behavioral analysis perspective, the foregoing account restates the fact that your performance is better when the words are not competing with other features of the stimulus. The meanings and attention to the words are inferences of the researcher with no independent evidence for their occurrence. For this reason, the explanation is not satisfying to the behavior analyst. The question becomes: How do environment-behavior relationships regulate performance on this task?

After people learn to read, they may be asked to say a word out loud. For example, children are often drilled with flash cards to identify words vocally, and they are given corrective feedback for performance. In behavioral terms, the sight of the word, or pattern of letters, sets the occasion for saying the word, and the corrective feedback functions as reinforcement. Thus, a child may be given a card with *red* written on it, and the correct response is saying "red." In a similar fashion, people learn to identify and label colors. Because of this conditioning, both colors and written words come to control two different response classes. When written words that refer to color are presented in a color different from the word, the two properties of the stimulus compete for the respective responses. Based on the simultaneous control by these two aspects of the blended stimulus, the time to complete the task increases. In other words, the situation is confusing, and because of this, the task takes longer to complete. Consider what you might do if you were driving and came to an intersection with a red-hexagon sign that had the word *proceed* painted on it. In contrast to the selection-perception explanation, behavior analysts point to response competition and reinforcement history as reasons for your hesitation.

There are other interesting implications of a functional analysis of perceiving. For example, you walk into a room and look around, believing that you are taking in reality. But what do you see? Seeing itself is something an organism is prepared to do based on its genetic endowment, but seeing a particular object, on a given occasion, may be analyzed as respondent or operant behavior. That is, observing an object or event is behavior that is either elicited by the event, has a high probability due to past consequences, or becomes likely due to motivating conditions (e.g., hunger, thirst, etc.).

Pretend that you have gone camping with several friends. After supper you decide to entertain your friends by telling a horror story about an axe murder that took place in the same area a few years ago. One of your companions is finishing supper, and the fried egg on her plate begins to look like a giant dead eye that is about to explode with yellow glop. As the night gets darker, another camper hears ominous sounds and begins to see figures moving in the brush. In everyday words, your friends are imagining these events. Behaviorally, the frightening story may be analyzed as a motivating condition that momentarily increases the probability of seeing things that appear to be threatening.

B. F. Skinner (1953) has described other conditions that affect seeing as a conditioned response:

Conditioned seeing explains why one tends to see the world according to one's previous history. Certain properties of the world are responded to so commonly that "laws of perception" have been drawn up to describe the behavior thus conditioned. For example, we generally see completed circles, squares, and other figures. An incomplete figure presented under deficient or ambiguous circumstances may evoke seeing a completed figure as a conditioned response. For example, a ring with a small segment missing when very briefly exposed may be seen as a completed ring. Seeing a completed ring would presumably not be inevitable in an individual whose daily life was concerned with handling incompleted rings. (pp. 267–268)

Skinner (1953) later points out that operant conditioning can also affect what is seen:

Suppose we strongly reinforce a person when he finds a four-leaf clover. The increased strength of "seeing a four-leaf clover" will be evident in many ways. The person will be more inclined to look at four-leaf clovers than before. He will look in places where he has found four-leaf clovers. Stimuli which resemble four-leaf clovers will evoke an immediate response. Under slightly ambiguous circumstances he will mistakenly reach for a three-leaf clover. If our reinforcement is effective enough, he may even see four-leaf clovers in ambiguous patterns in textiles, wallpaper, and so on. He may also "see four-leaf clovers" when there is no similar visual stimulation—for example, when his eyes are closed or when he is in a dark room. If he has acquired an adequate vocabulary for self-description, he may report this by saying that four-leaf clovers "flash into his mind" or that he "is thinking about" four-leaf clovers. (p. 271)

Epling and Cameron (1994) have reported an interesting instance of operant seeing that appeared in Euell Gibbons's book *Stalking the Wild Asparagus*. Gibbons was enthusiastic about eating wild asparagus and on a fishing trip he spotted some fine young asparagus shoots. Spying these shoots was reinforcement for seeing, looking for, and discovering other clumps of asparagus.

> . . . I was walking along the bank of an irrigation ditch, headed for a reservoir where I hoped to catch some fish. Happening to look down, I spied a clump of asparagus growing on the ditch bank, with half a dozen fat, little spears that were just the right size to be at their best. . . . Even when cutting this cluster, I saw another with several more perfect little sprouts. Alerted, I kept my eyes open and soon found another cluster and then another. . . . About this time I noticed that an old, dry, last-year's stalk stood above every clump of new asparagus tips. . . . I sat down on the ditch bank and for five minutes I did nothing but just *look* at one old dry asparagus stalk. It looked very much like the dead weeds and plants that surrounded it, and yet there were differences. The old asparagus plant stood about three feet high and had a central stem or "trunk" about a half inch in diameter which easily distinguished it from weeds with forking stems. . . . After getting the size, color and form thoroughly in my mind, I stood up and looked back along the ditch bank. Instantly, I saw a dozen old dead asparagus stalks that I had missed. I went back to where I had found the first clump and worked my way down the ditch again, and this time I re-

ally reaped a harvest. . . . That five minutes I spent [many years] ago, concentrating on one dead asparagus plant, has lead me to many pounds of this most delicious of early vegetables. The eyetraining it gave me has lasted until now. Whenever I drive, in late winter or early spring, my eye automatically picks up the dead asparagus stalks by the roadside, and I make an almost unconscious mental note of the places where the green spears will be plentiful when warm weather arrives. (pp. 28–32)

Many psychologists do not consider seeing as operant or respondent behavior. These researchers prefer to study perception as a cognitive process that guides behavior. Although the issue is not resolved here, Skinner makes it clear that analyzing seeing as behavior is one way to understand such processes. The behavior analysis of seeing (or, more generally, perceiving) also applies to other sensory dimensions such as hearing, feeling, and smelling. Notice that such an analysis accounts for perceiving without reference to mental events.

Stimulus Classes

In a preceding section, we noted that responses that produce similar effects may be many and varied. To handle this variation in form, behavior analysts use the term *response class*. Stimuli that regulate operant and respondent behavior also vary from one time to the next. When stimuli vary across physical dimension but have a common effect on behavior, they are part of the same **stimulus class**. Bijou and Baer (1978) have used the concept of stimulus class in an analysis of child development and have made the point that:

> A mother's face has a fair consistency to it, we may think, in that we know our mother's face from anyone else's face. But careful observations show that it is sometimes shiny, sometimes dusty, sometimes wet; occasionally creased into its facial lines, but sometimes smooth; the eyes range between fully open and fully closed, and assume a wide range of angles of regard; sometimes hairs fall in front of the face, sometimes not. Then let us remember that whenever we speak of a stimulus, we will almost surely mean a class of stimuli. (p. 25)

It is important to note that a stimulus class is defined entirely by the common effect of environmental events on behavior. For this reason, a stimulus class cannot be defined by the apparent similarity of the stimuli. Consider the words *boring* and *uninteresting*. In common English, we say they have the same meaning. In behavior analysis, these words have a similar effect on the person who reads or hears them; for this reason, they belong to the same stimulus class even though they have completely different physical dimensions. Other stimuli may appear physically similar but belong to different stimulus classes. For example, mushrooms and toadstools look somewhat similar, but for an experienced woods person these fungi have different functions—you pick and eat mushrooms but avoid toadstools.

Classes of Reinforcing Stimuli.   The concept of stimulus class may also be used to categorize the consequences of behavior. When behavior operates on the environment to produce effects, the effects that increase the frequency of response are a class of reinforcing stimuli. Some consequences strengthen behavior when they are presented and others strengthen it when they are removed. In this case, we can divide the general class of reinforcing stimuli into two subsets. Those events that are reinforcing when presented are **positive reinforcers,** and those that are re-inforcing when removed are **negative reinforcers.** For example, a smile and a pat on the back may increase the probability that a child will complete his or her home-work; for this reason, the smile and pat are positive reinforcers. The same child may stop dawdling and start working on a school project when a parent scolds the child for wasting time. In this case, reinforcement of working is based on the removal of scolding, and the reprimand is a negative reinforcer.

Establishing Operations

The relations between stimulus and response classes depend on the broader **con-text of behavior.** That is, environment-behavior relationships are always condi-tional—depending on other circumstances. One of the most common ways to change environment-behavior relationships is to have the person (or organism) experience a period of deprivation or satiation. For example, a pigeon will peck a key for food only if it is deprived of food for some period of time. More specifi-cally, the peck for food contingency depends on level of deprivation.

In his 1982 paper, Jack Michael (1982a) made an important distinction be-tween the discriminative and motivational functions of stimuli. In that paper, he introduced the term **establishing operation** to refer to any environmental change that had two major effects: (a) The change increased the momentary effectiveness of reinforcement supporting operant behavior, and (b) the change increased mo-mentarily the responses that had in the past produced such reinforcement. For example, the most common establishing operation is deprivation for primary re-inforcement. The procedure involves withholding reinforcement for some period of time or, in the case of food, until the organism reaches 80% of free-feeding body weight (see Chapter 5). This procedure has two effects. First, food becomes an effective reinforcer for any operant that produces it. That is, the deprivation procedure establishes the reinforcement function of food. Second, behavior that has previously resulted in getting food becomes more likely—in the wild, a bird may start to forage in places where it has previously found food. Formally, an es-tablishing operation is defined as "any change in the environment which alters the effectiveness of some object or event as reinforcement and simultaneously al-ters the momentary frequency of the behavior that has been followed by that re-inforcement" (Michael, 1982a, pp. 150–151).

Establishing operations regularly occur in everyday life. For example, televi-sion commercials are said to influence a person's attitude toward a product. One way to understand the effects of commercials is to analyze them as establishing operations. In this case, an effective commercial alters the reinforcement value of the product and increases the likelihood of purchasing the item or using it if available. For example, dairy farmers advertise the goodness of ice-cold milk.

Those who are influenced by the commercial are likely to go to the fridge and have a glass of milk. Of course, this immediate effect of the commercial depletes the amount of milk you have on hand, and eventually you buy more milk.

TACTICS OF BEHAVIORAL RESEARCH

To discover elementary relationships between functional stimuli, responses, and consequences, behavior analysts have relied on experimental methods developed in biology, medicine, and behavior analysis (Bachrach, 1962; Bernard, 1927; Bushell & Burgess, 1969; Johnston & Pennypacker, 1993; Kazdin, 1982; Sidman, 1960). In 1865, the French physician Claude Bernard outlined the central objectives for experimental analysis:

> We can reach knowledge of definite elementary conditions of phenomena only by one road, viz., by experimental analysis. Analysis dissociates all the complex phenomena successively into more and more simple phenomena, until they are reduced, if possible, to just two elementary conditions. Experimental science, in fact, considers in a phenomenon only the definite conditions necessary to produce it. (Bernard, 1927, p. 72)

In his book, *An Introduction to the Study of Experimental Medicine*, Bernard (1927) provided a classic example of experimental analysis.

> One day, rabbits from the market were brought into my laboratory. They were put on the table where they urinated, and I happened to observe that their urine was clear and acid. This fact struck me, because rabbits, which are herbivora, generally have turbid and alkaline urine; while on the other hand carnivora, as we know, have clear and acid urine. This observation of acidity in the rabbits' urine gave me an idea that these animals must be in the nutritional condition of carnivora. I assumed that they had probably not eaten for a long time, and that they had been transformed by fasting, into veritable carnivorous animals, living on their own blood. Nothing was easier than to verify this preconceived idea or hypothesis by experiment. I gave the rabbits grass to eat; and a few hours later, their urine became turbid and alkaline. I then subjected them to fasting and after twenty-four hours, or thirty-six hours at most, their urine again became clear and strongly acid; then after eating grass their urine became alkaline again, etc. I repeated this very simple experiment a great many times, and always with the same result. I then repeated it on a horse, an herbivorous animal which also has turbid and alkaline urine. I found that fasting, as in rabbits, produced prompt acidity of the urine, with such an increase in urea that it spontaneously crystallizes at times in the cooled urine. As a result of my experiments, I thus reached the general proposition which then was still unknown, to wit, that all fasting animals feed on meat, so that herbivora then have urine like that of carnivora.
> But to prove that my fasting rabbits were really carnivorous, a counter proof was required. A carnivorous rabbit had to be experimentally produced by feeding it with meat, so as to see if its urine would then be clear, as it was during fasting. So I had rabbits fed on cold boiled beef (which they eat very nicely when

they are given nothing else). My expectation was again verified, and as long as the animal diet was continued, the rabbits kept their clear and acid urine. (pp. 152–153)

Bushell and Burgess (1969) provided an outline of the basic tactics of experimental analysis used by Bernard in the rabbit experiment. The following account is loosely based on their outline. Notice that Bernard made an observation that, as a physiologist, seemed unusual and puzzling—namely, that the rabbits from the market had urine that was characteristic of carnivores. Only a trained physiologist familiar with carnivores and herbivores would notice the anomaly of the urine. Most of us would run and get a cloth to wipe it up. The point is that a researcher must have a thorough familiarity with the subject matter to find a significant problem.

Once Bernard identified the problem, he stated it in terms of a conjecture. The problem statement related type of diet to the chemistry of the urine. That is, fasting results in the animal living off its own body stores, and this produces acidity of the urine. On the other hand, when herbivores eat their usual diet of grass, their urine is alkaline. Thus, there is a clear relationship between type of diet and the nature of the animal's urine.

Experimentally, Bernard's statement suggests that we change or manipulate the type of diet and measure the chemistry of the urine. The condition that is changed by the experimenter (i.e., type of diet) is called the **independent variable** (variable X) because it is free to vary at the discretion of the researcher. Bernard changed the animal's diet and measured the effect on the urine. The measured effect in an experiment is called the **dependent variable** (variable Y), because a change in it depends on a change in the independent variable. Whether the urine was acid or alkaline (dependent variable) depended on the nature of the diet (independent variable). Figure 2.1 explains the terms used in this section.

The purpose of any experiment is to establish a cause-and-effect relationship between the independent *(X)* and dependent *(Y)* variables. To establish such a relationship, the researcher must show that changes in the independent variable are associated with changes in the dependent variable. This is called showing covariation of the X and Y variables. In addition, the experimenter must show that the

FIG. 2.1 A table of scientific terms used to discuss cause-and-effect relationships.

Independent Variable	Dependent Variable
What is changed in an experiment	What is measured in an experiment
X variable	Y variable
Commonly called a *cause*	Commonly called an *effect*
In Bernard's experiment, type of diet	In Bernard's experiment, chemistry of urine
In behavioral experiments, environmental change	In behavioral experiments, behavior of the organism

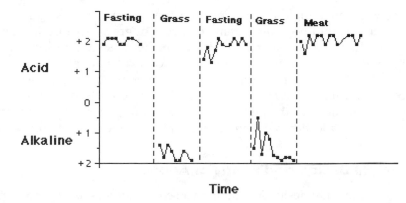

FIG. 2.2 The results of Bernard's experiment. Notice that the change in diet (independent variable) reliably changes the chemistry of the urine (dependent variable). Each time the diet is changed, the urine changes from acid to alkaline or vice versa (based on results reported by Bushell & Burgess, 1969, p. 133).

changes in the independent variable preceded changes in the dependent variable. Both of these conditions are seen in Bernard's experiment.

In Figure 2.2, you can see that changes between fasting and grass diet reliably alter the chemistry of the rabbits' urine. For this reason, changes in type of diet, the *X* variable, may be said to covary with degree of acidity of urine, the *Y* variable (see Figure 2.1 to clarify terms). Recall that Bernard changed the type of diet and then measured its effects on the urine. This procedure of manipulating the independent variable ensures that a change in *X* (type of diet) precedes the change in *Y* (chemistry of urine). At this point, Bernard has shown two of the three important conditions for causation: (1) covariation of *X* and *Y* and (2) the independent variable precedes a change in the dependent variable.

The central question in all experiments is whether the changes in the dependent variable are uniquely caused by changes in the independent variable. The problem is that many other factors may produce changes in the dependent variable, and the researcher must rule out this possibility. In the Bernard experiment, the initial change from fasting to grass diet may have been accompanied by an illness caused by contaminated grass. Suppose that the illness changed the chemistry of the animals' urine. In this case, changes from fasting to grass, or grass to fasting, will change the chemistry of the urine, but the changes are caused by the unknown illness rather than the type of diet. That is, the unknown illness confounds the effects of type of diet on the acidity of the urine. At this point, stop reading and look again at Bernard's description of his experiment and at Figure 2.2. Try to determine how Bernard eliminated this rival hypothesis.

One procedure for eliminating rival explanations is the systematic introduction and elimination of the grass diet. Notice that Bernard withholds and gives the grass diet and then repeats this sequence. Each time he introduces and removes the grass, a rapid change occurs from alkaline to acid (and vice versa). This rapid and systematic change makes it unlikely that illness accounts for the results. How can an animal recover from and contract an illness so quickly? Another procedure would be to use different batches of grass, because it is unlikely that they would all be contaminated. However, the most convincing feature of Bernard's experiment, in terms of eliminating rival explanations, is his final procedure of introducing a meat diet. The meat diet is totally consistent with Bernard's claim that the animals were living off their body stores and counteracts the rival explanation that the animals were ill. More generally, the reversal of conditions and the addition of the meat diet eliminates most other explanations.

The Reversal Design and Behavior Analysis

Bernard's experimental design is commonly used to study behavior-environment relationships. The design is called an **A-B-A-B reversal,** and is a powerful tool used to show causal relationships among stimuli, responses, and consequences. The reversal design is ideally suited to show that an organism's behavior is regulated by specific features of the environment.

The A-phase, or **baseline,** measures behavior before the researcher introduces an environmental change. During baseline, the experimenter takes repeated measures of the behavior under study, and this establishes a criterion against which any changes (caused by the independent variable) may be assessed. Following the baseline phase, an environmental condition is changed (B-phase) and behavior is repeatedly measured. If the independent variable, or environmental condition, has an effect, then the behavioral measure (dependent variable) will change (increase or decrease).

However, as we have indicated, the researcher must rule out rival explanations for the change in behavior. To do this, the baseline phase is reintroduced (A) and behavior is repeatedly measured. When the treatment is removed, behavior should return to pretreatment or baseline levels. Finally, the independent variable is changed again and the behavior is carefully measured (B). According to the logic of the design, behavior should return to a level observed in the initial B-phase of the experiment. This second application of the independent variable helps ensure that the behavioral effect is caused by the manipulated condition.

An example of the reversal design, as used in behavior analysis, is seen in an experiment conducted by Goetz and Baer (1973). The researchers were interested in the creative play of children and the role of reinforcement for such behavior. Several 4-year-old girls in a preschool were noted to lack creative skill at block building. One measure of creative behavior is the number of different forms that a child builds with blocks during a play session (form diversity). The researchers wondered if positive attention from the teacher could function as reinforcement for building new block constructions (the experimental problem).

During the baseline phase, the teacher watched the child closely but said nothing about the child's use of the blocks. After baseline measures of form diversity were taken, the teacher then socially reinforced novel block constructions. The teacher remarked with "interest, enthusiasm, and delight every time the child placed and/or rearranged blocks so as to create a form which had not appeared previously" (Goetz & Baer, 1973, p. 212). Form diversity was assessed for several sessions with this procedure in effect.

To be certain that the reinforcement procedure was responsible for the increase in diversity, Goetz and Baer altered the contingency between teacher attention and block building. During this phase, the child was reinforced for repeating a form that had previously been built. Thus, similarity of form was reinforced in this phase. Finally, reinforcement of diverse forms was reinstated. The results of this experiment are portrayed for one of the three children (Sally) in Figure 2.3.

The experimental design is a modified A-B-A-B reversal. The baseline phase (A) provides a measure of block-building diversity before any intervention by the teacher. Next, a reinforcement contingency was arranged for novel forms of construction (B). During the third phase (C) of the experiment, the contingency of reinforcement was changed to support repetitive forms. Finally, reinforcement for novel constructions was reinstated (B). The independent variable in this experiment is the contingency of reinforcement—contingent reinforcement of novelty versus contingent reinforcement of repetition. The dependent variable is the number of different forms that the child produced during each phase of the experiment. As you can see, the dependent variable reliably changes in the expected direction, with changes in the contingency of reinforcement (i.e., teacher attention).

The A-B-A-B reversal design is the most fundamental research design used in the experimental analysis of behavior. There are, however, difficulties that may make this design inappropriate for a given research question. One major problem is that behavior, once changed, may not return to baseline levels. Consider what might happen if you used a reinforcement technique to teach an illiterate adult to read. You could measure reading level, introduce your teaching technique, and after some time withdraw reinforcement for reading. It is very unlikely that the student will again become illiterate. In behavioral terms, the student's reading is maintained by other sources of reinforcement such as getting

FIG. 2.3 A reversal design in which the researchers altered the contingency between teacher attention and block building. First, a baseline measure of behavior (A) was taken for several days. During the second phase of the experiment (B), the child was reinforced (Rft) for varying a form (diversity) that had been previously built. Next, the child was reinforced for building similar block forms (C), and finally the B-phase was reinstated (from Goetz & Baer, 1973; permission granted by the Society for the Advancement of Behavior Analysis).

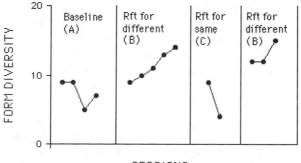

information that enables the student to behave effectively (e.g., reading a menu, traffic signs, etc.).

Another difficulty is that it is sometimes unethical to reverse the effects of a behavioral procedure. Suppose that a behavioral program to eliminate the use of crack cocaine works, but the doctors who run the program are not absolutely certain that the decline in drug use is caused by reinforcement procedures. It would be highly unethical to remove and reinsert the reinforcement therapy in order to be certain about causation. This is because removing the reinforcement procedure could lead to an increase in drug use. Nonetheless, when this and other difficulties are not encountered, the A-B-A-B reversal design is a preferable mode of analysis.

Throughout this book, we address research that uses the reversal design, modified-reversal designs (e.g., adding other control conditions), and other forms of experimental analysis. We have concentrated on the reversal design because it demonstrates the basic logic of behavioral experimentation. The task of all behavioral experiments is to establish with high certainty the cause-and-effect relationships that govern the behavior of organisms. Based on these causal relationships, behavior analysts search for general principles that organize experimental findings (e.g., principle of reinforcement).

FOCUS ON ISSUES
INTERVAL AND EXTERNAL VALIDITY IN EXPERIMENTS

A common reaction to experimental findings goes something like, "What in the world does that research have to do with anything important?" Consider an experiment in which rats are placed in a small, sound-proof chamber and are given a 45-mg food pellet after pressing a lever 50 times. The rat rapidly makes 50 responses, gets a bit of food, pauses for a few seconds, and then presses the lever another 50 times. A legitimate question might be, "Why bother doing this sort of research since all it tells us is what rats, in a highly controlled circumstance, do?" Some individuals would say that such an experiment says little about the responses of rats, never mind what people behave like. As you will see in this book, however, experiments like this build on one another and occasionally pay off in a direct sense.

More importantly for the present discussion, this research meets the minimum requirement for all experiments: The-cause-and-effect relationships that govern the behavior of the animal are identified with a reasonable amount of certainty. This is because many variables that may have accidentally produced the effect (extraneous variables) are ruled out by the control procedures of the experiment. When many extraneous variables are ruled out by an experimental design, Campbell and Stanley (1966) say that the research has high **internal validity.** That is, changes in the dependent variable may be reasonably attributed to changes in the independent variable (cause → effect).

The popular press occasionally reports scientific research that appears to have great practical value but, in fact, is difficult to interpret. Several years ago, we watched a news report on television that suggested that when parents and therapists imitated the disturbed behavior of autistic children, miraculous improvements in these children occurred. For example, a child would rock back and forth and the mother would imitate this rocking behavior. Although the observation did not make theoretical sense, we hoped it was a valid finding, because such a simple treatment offered hope to many parents and children. We contacted the researchers to discover more about their experimental methods.

The research was practically useful, easy to utilize, and appeared reasonable to many parents of autistic children; it had high external validity. **External validity** refers to the extent that an experimental finding generalizes to other behavior (not only rocking), settings, and populations (Campbell & Stanley, 1966). Unfortunately, the "experiment" was low on internal validity and could not be evaluated. There may have been many reasons for an apparent improvement in the children. The gains that the children made may have been a matter of interpretation by the researchers, or variables other than imitation could have produced the positive effect. Uncontrolled variables like extra attention from caretakers, selection of children for treatment, the particular therapist who worked with the child, etc., may have been responsible for the research outcome.

INTERNAL VALIDITY

To illustrate the distinctions between internal and external validity, consider an interesting study by Ayllon (1963). The subject was a female patient in a mental hospital who hoarded a large number of towels and collected them in her room. In desperation, the ward staff raided her room twice a week to regain the missing towels. The staff did a baseline count of the number of towels in her room and determined that she hoarded between 19 and 29 towels even though the nurses continued to remove them from her room.

The next phase involved two procedures. First, the nursing staff stopped raiding her room and taking the towels. Second, throughout the day the staff brought her towels when she was in her room. This was done without comment, and the number of towels given increased from 7 to 60 per day by the third week of the experiment. Figure 2.4 shows that the number of towels in her room increased to 625, at which time she began to remove them and the staff stopped giving towels to her. Ayllon discusses the results of the experiment as follows:

> The procedure used to reduce the amount of towel hoarding bears resemblance to satiation of a reinforcer. A reinforcer loses its effect when an excessive amount of that reinforcer is made available. Accordingly, the response maintained by that reinforcer is weakened. In this application, the towels constituted the reinforcing stimuli. When the number of towels in her room reached 625, continuing to give her towels seemed to make their collection aversive. The patient then proceeded to rid herself of the towels until she had virtually none.
>
> During the first weeks of satiation, the patient was observed patting her cheeks with a few towels, apparently enjoying them. Later, the patient was observed spending much of her time folding and stacking the approximately 600 towels in her room. A variety of remarks were made by the patient regarding receipt of towels. All verbal statements made by the patient were recorded by the nurse. The following represent typical remarks made during this experiment. First week: As the nurse entered the patient's room carrying a towel the patient would smile and say, "Oh, you found it for me, thank you." Second week: When the number of towels given to patient increased rapidly, she told the nurses, "Don't give me no

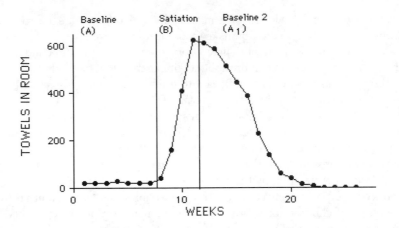

FIG. 2.4 Modification of towel hoarding by a psychotic patient. A baseline count of the number of towels in the patient's room was taken, and as you can see she hoarded between 19 and 29 towels per day. The treatment phase of the experiment involved two procedures. First, the nursing staff stopped raiding her room and taking the towels. Second, throughout the day the staff brought her towels when she was in her room. The number of towels in her room increased to 625 before she started throwing them out (based on data from Ayllon, 1963, and reprinted with permission of *Behavior Research and Therapy*).

more towels. I've got enough." Third week: "Take them towels away. . . . I can't sit here all night and fold towels." Fourth and fifth weeks: "Get these dirty towels out of here." Sixth week: After she had started taking the towels out of her room, she remarked to the nurse, "I can't drag any more of these towels, I just can't do it." (Ayllon, 1963, pp. 53–61)

The experiment was designed to stop towel hoarding by providing excessive amounts of the valued item. The researchers used the principle of satiation and applied it to the management of psychotic behavior. The experimental design was an A-B-A$_1$ where A was the initial baseline where towels were removed and a count was taken; B was the treatment phase where towels were given; and A$_1$ was a return to baseline but without the removal of towels. In terms of internal validity, the question is whether the decline in towel hoarding (dependent variable) was caused by the provision of towels (independent variable).

To the extent that there are alternative explanations for the outcome of this study, it is weak on internal validity. Any factor, other than the independent variable, that could reasonably account for the findings represents a threat to internal validity. Such threats weaken confidence in cause-and-effect conclusions. Campbell and Stanley (1966) outline a number of different threats to internal validity, some of which are applicable to operant-research designs and to Ayllon's study of towel hoarding.

History

One kind of threat to internal validity is called history. **History** refers to conditions that change at the same time as the manipulation of the independent variable. For example, the provision of towels may have cluttered the patient's room, and she discarded them to make more space. Although this appears to be a reasonable explanation for her behavior, it does not explain why she threw all the towels away. If she had kept the same 20 towels in her room, as during baseline, she would have as much space as before.

Not all history effects are so easily countered. The hospital laundry could have run out of fabric softener, or changed to a detergent with a peculiar smell, and this may have changed the texture or odor of the towels—making them aversive rather than reinforcing. This is a reasonable alternative hypothesis since it fully accounts for the patient's taking the towels out of her room and the subsequent decline to near zero hoarding. Recall that the A_1 condition, where the nurses stop giving her towels, was implemented on the basis of the patient's behavior (she started to throw towels out of her room), and this would occur if a change in the laundry happened at this time. Therefore, some sort of history effect could account for the outcome of the experiment.

Maturation

Another source of invalidity is called **maturation,** which refers to biological or psychological processes that change over time. Again, if these maturational changes occurred at the same time as the manipulation of the independent variable, they could explain the findings. Suppose that this woman had a sudden spontaneous remission of her psychosis. Presumably, this would account for why she no longer wanted to hoard towels. Although her 9 years of hospitalization argue against this possibility, the researcher should have gathered evidence about her psychiatric condition before and after the experiment.

Reactive Measurement

When a dependent variable changes just because it is being measured, the effect is called **reactive measurement.** For example, a person may lose weight because he or she is weighed daily by a researcher who is conducting an experiment on different types of diets. Daily weighing may focus attention on being overweight, and because of this the individual reduces food intake. In Ayllon's experiment, the patient could have observed the nurses counting the ever-increasing number of towels, and this was a stimulus to stop hoarding them. This explanation is unlikely since the nurses were counting during baseline, treatment, and the return-to-baseline. Also, the decline in towel hoarding after the satiation procedure is gradual rather than sudden, suggesting that feedback on the number of towels was not the critical determinant.

Instrument Decay

A fourth threat to internal validity is called instrument decay. In behavioral research, **instrument decay** refers to observers becoming better or worse at measuring the dependent variable. Such an effect can occur in reversal designs where repeated observations are made. For example, observers may be very interested and attentive when they first record the psychotic verbalizations of a mental patient. After many days of this task, the same observers may become bored and consequently miss many psychotic remarks. If the researcher was reinforcing normal speech, the apparent reduction in psychotic talk may be assigned to the reinforcement procedure rather than to the decay in measurement. In Ayllon's experiment, the before and after measures were taken by the nursing staff. Number of towels is a very concrete measure, requiring little interpretation by the staff. Also, the number of towels is steady and low in baseline, rises rapidly during satiation, and falls in the second baseline. For these reasons, instrument decay is very unlikely—only if the nursing staff was fabricating the data could such an effect occur.

Generally, in terms of internal validity, history is the most serious problem in Ayllon's study of towel hoarding. This problem could have been remedied by adding a second subject who hoarded other objects. If the satiation procedure was staggered so that the second subject received satiation at a different time than the towel-hoarding woman, then history effects would be extremely unlikely. Of course, this assumes that the procedure works or replicates for both subjects. The change in the object hoarded would rule out our laundry hypothesis, as would the staggered start of the experiment.

EXTERNAL VALIDITY

Generality of Results

External validity refers to the extent that laboratory findings generalize over time, place, dependent measures, and similar experimental manipulations. That is, do the cause-and-effect relationships found in an experiment occur at different times and places, with different organisms and diverse responses, when the original conditions are in effect?

A result is shown to have **generality** when we are able to identify the conditions that produce it. For example, the principle of reinforcement governs the behavior of organisms under specified conditions. Some of these conditions involve a genetic capacity for operant conditioning and an establishing operation that makes the response-reinforcer relationship effective. In a pigeon, the peck-for-food relationship depends on the genetic endowment of the bird and deprivation of food in the immediate past. For humans, who have an extensive capacity for operant conditioning, going to a soda machine to get a cold drink is an effective contingency on a hot afternoon. In terms of external validity and operant conditioning, the question is, to what extent do the laws and principles of operant behavior generalize over species, settings, responses, and reinforcers?

The research by Ayllon (1963) on towel hoarding may be viewed as a generalizing experiment. The principle of satiation states that any response-reinforcer relationship is weakened by repeated presentation of the reinforcer. In everyday language, the more you get something, the less valuable it becomes. How important is a free steak dinner if you just had a large meal? Ayllon used this principle of satiation to weaken the relationship between taking and accumulating towels. In this case, he assumed that stealing and hoarding towels was reinforced by the accumulation of towels in the patient's room. If this was so, then the repeated presentation of towels must reduce hoarding behavior. Since this occurred (assuming internal validity), the experiment generalizes the principle of satiation to psychiatric patients, mental hospitals, nonconsumable reinforcers, and socially significant behavior. At the time of this experiment, most mental health professionals doubted the generality of operant principles to this kind of problem. Ayllon (1963) commented that:

The ward nurses, who had undergone a three year training in psychiatric nursing, found it difficult to reconcile the procedure in this experiment with their psychiatric orientation. Most nurses subscribed to the popular psychiatric view which regards hoarding behavior as a reflection of a deep "need" for love and security. Presumably, no "real" behavioral change was possible without meeting the patient's "needs" first. Even after the patient discontinued hoarding towels in her room, some nurses predicted that the change would not last and that worse behavior would replace it. Using a time-sampling technique, the patient was under continuous observation for over a year after the termination of the satiation program. Not once during this period did the patient return to hoarding towels. Furthermore, no other behavioral problem replaced hoarding. (pp. 57–58)

Correspondence with Extra Laboratory Settings

Another index of external validity is the correspondence between laboratory findings and what organisms do under similar conditions in everyday life. For example, laboratory experiments have shown that, under certain conditions, television violence increases the aggressive behavior of children (Bandura, 1973, 1983). The basic principles involve social modeling and imitation. A child who sees violence on televised sports, movies, and cartoons may imitate such behavior if the violence is condoned by parents or other significant adults. Correspondence between laboratory findings and everyday life is suggested when naturalistic studies (e.g., surveys, observation and coding, etc.) show that the more children are exposed to violent television, the more aggressive they are at home, in school, and throughout their young lives (Eron, Huesmann, Dubow, Romanoff, & Yarmel, 1987). Although it is tempting to carry out only naturalistic research, such studies are relatively weak on internal validity and the discovery of basic principles.

In summary, there is a trade-off between internal and external validity. As internal validity increases, external validity decreases—and vice versa. When an experimenter holds all things constant and manipulates the independent variable, he or she is very certain about cause-and-effect relationships. Unfortunately, the fact that all things are held constant limits the generality of the relationship under investigation. As you will see in the next section, generality may be increased by repeating the experiment under new conditions. Ultimately, the answer to the question of generality comes from the well-known tactic of experimental replication.

SINGLE-SUBJECT RESEARCH

Behavior analysis is concerned with discovering basic principles that govern the behavior of single organisms. Each individual's behavior is studied to assess the impact of a given environmental condition. Notice that Goetz and Baer (1973) applied their reinforcement procedures to Sally and showed that her behavior reliably changed when the contingency of reinforcement was altered (she built new block constructions). The researchers applied the same procedures to two other children and found similar effects. Thus, the experimenters argued that reinforcement of diversity in block building generalized across different children. They claimed, "It seems clear that diversity of response within this delimited sphere of activity, is readily modified by simple, everyday reinforcement contingencies" (Goetz & Baer, 1973, p. 216). In other words, the researchers are suggesting that, all things being equal, any child given reinforcement for creative play will show an increase in such activity. This broader statement linking reinforcement to creative play is called an empirical generalization. Most behavior analysts assume such generality in their conclusions.

Replication of Results

Generalizing from single-subject experiments is a well-founded scientific strategy (see the preceding Focus on Issues). A single individual is exposed to all values of the independent variable, and the experiment is run on several subjects. Each subject replicates the experiment; if there are four subjects, the investigation is repeated four separate times. Thus, every additional individual in a single-subject experiment constitutes a **direct replication** of the research. Direct replication involves manipulating the independent variable in the same way for all subjects in the experiment.

Another way to increase the generality of a finding is by **systematic replication** of the experiment. Systematic replication uses procedures that are different but are logically related to the original research question (see Sidman, 1960, for a detailed discussion of direct and systematic replication). For example, in Bernard's research with the rabbits, changing the diet from fasting to grass altered the chemistry of the urine and may be considered an experiment in its own right. Feeding the animals meat may be viewed as a second experiment—systematically replicating the initial research using a grass diet. Given Bernard's hypothesis that all fasting animals become carnivores, it logically follows that meat should change the chemistry of the urine from alkaline to acid.

In a behavioral experiment, such as the creativity experiment by Goetz and Baer (1973), the researchers could have established generality by using a different task and a different kind of reinforcement (e.g., tactile contact like hugging). Here the central idea is that the **contingency of reinforcement** is the critical factor that produced the increase in creative block design. That is, the observed change in behavior does not depend on the type of activity (block building) or the nature of the reinforcer (positive attention). In fact, many behavioral experiments have shown that contingencies of reinforcement generalize across species, type of reinforcement, diverse settings, and different operants.

Generality and Single-Subject Research

A common misunderstanding about single-subject experiments is that generalizations are not possible because a few individuals do not represent the larger population. Some social scientists believe that experiments must include a large group of individuals in order to make general statements. This position is valid if the social scientist is interested in descriptions of what the average individual does. For example, single-subject research is inappropriate for questions like, "What sort of advertising campaign is most effective for getting people in Los Angeles to recycle garbage?" In this case, the independent variable might be type of advertising and the dependent variable the number of citizens in Los Angeles who recycle their waste. The central question is concerned with how many people recycle, and a group experiment is the appropriate way to approach the problem.

Behavior analysts are less interested in aggregate or group effects. Instead the analysis focuses on the behavior of the individual. These researchers are concerned with predicting, controlling, and interpreting the behavior of single organisms. The generality of the effect in a behavioral experiment is established by replication. A similar strategy is sometimes used in chemistry. The process of electrolysis can be observed in an unrepresentative sample of water from Logan, Utah. A researcher who follows the procedures for electrolysis will observe the same result in all samples of water, whether from Logan or from the Ganges. Importantly, the researcher may claim—on the basis of a single experiment—that electrolysis occurs in all water, at all times, and in all places. Of course, only replication of the experiment will increase confidence in this empirical generalization.

Assessment of Behavior Change

Single-subject experiments require a baseline period of measurement. This baseline serves as a comparison or reference for any subsequent change in behavior produced by the independent variable. To construct an appropriate baseline, it is necessary to define the response class objectively and clearly. In the animal laboratory, the response class of pressing a lever is defined by the closure of an electrical switch. There is no dispute about the state of the switch; it is either on or off. An animal may press the lever in many different ways. The left or right paw may be used as well as the hind foot, nose, mouth, and so on. The point is that no matter how the response is made, all actions that result in a switch closure define the operant class. Once the response class is defined, the number of times the response occurs can be counted and a baseline constructed.

Outside of the laboratory, response classes are usually more difficult to define. Consider that you are asked to help manage the behavior of a troublesome child in a classroom setting. The teacher complains that the child is disruptive and interferes with his teaching. On the surface, measuring the disruptive behavior of the child seems easy. Further reflection, however, suggests that it is not easy to define the operant class. What exactly does the teacher mean when he says "the child is disruptive"? After talking to the teacher and observing the child in the classroom, several "disruptive" responses may be identified: The child is often out of her seat without permission and at times when a lesson is being taught. Another behavior that occurs is talking loudly to other children during study periods. Both of these responses are more clearly defined than the label "disruptive," but objective measurement may still be difficult. Notice that each response is partially defined by prior events (permission) and the current situation (study periods). In addition, terms like *loud* and *out of seat* remain some-what subjective. How loud is loud, and is sitting on the edge of the desk out of seat? The answer is to keep refining the response definition until it is highly objective. When two observers can agree most of the time on whether a response has occurred, then a baseline can be established.

In addition to defining the response class, assessment of behavior change requires some measure of response variability. During the baseline, repeated measures are taken and the number of responses are plotted. Figure 2.5 is a graph of an idealized experiment to modify the out-of-seat behavior of the child in the foregoing classroom example. Pretend that the teacher is requested to pay attention and give tokens to the child only when she is sitting quietly in her seat. At the end of the school day, the tokens may be exchanged for small prizes. Does this procedure alter the child's behavior? The graphs in Figures 2.5(A) and 2.5(B) show two possible baselines and the results of the intervention.

FIG. 2.5 Compare your assessment of the treatment effect in graphs A and B. Notice that the range of values in the baseline of graph A is quite small when compared to graph B. The effect of an experimental manipulation can only be evaluated against a departure from baseline. Because the baseline of graph B is so variable, it is difficult to judge whether the reinforcement procedure had an effect.

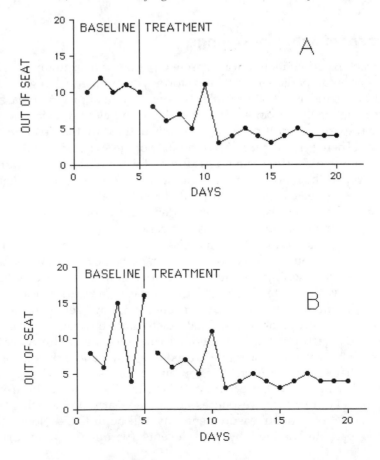

Compare your assessment of the treatment effect in Figures 2.5(A) and 2.5(B). You probably judge that the reinforcement procedure was effective in graph A but possibly not in graph B. What do you suppose led to your conclusion? Notice that the range of values in the baseline of graph A is quite small when compared to graph B. The number of times the child is out of her seat does not change much from day to day in graph A, but there is substantial variation in the baseline of graph B. The effect of the modification can only be evaluated against a departure from the baseline. Because the baseline of graph B is so variable, it is difficult to judge whether the reinforcement procedure had an effect. If you have had a course in statistics, it may occur to you that the difficulty in graph B could be solved by a statistical test. While this is possible, behavior analysts would try different tactics.

One approach is to reduce the variability of the baseline. This might involve a more precise definition of the out-of-seat response. This would reduce variation introduced by imprecise measurement of the response class. Another reasonable strategy would be to increase the power of the intervention. In this case, the attempt is to produce a larger shift in behavior, relative to the baseline. For example, the small prizes earned at the end of the school day may be changed to more valuable items. Notice that these strategies lead to refinement in measures and procedures used in the experiment. This increases the experimenter's control over the subject matter, and this is a primary objective of the experimental analysis of behavior.

Assessment of behavior change may be more difficult if there is a trend in the baseline measures. A **trend** is a systematic decline or rise in the baseline values. A drift in baseline measures can be problematic when the treatment is expected to produce a change in the same direction as the trend. Figure 2.6 is a graph of the loud-talking behavior by the child in our hypothetical experiment. Notice that the number of loud-talking episodes during baseline starts at a moderately high level and drifts downward over days. Perhaps the child's parents are getting more and more complaints from the school, and as the complaints mount they put more pressure on the child to "shut up." Regardless of why the trend is occurring, the

FIG. 2.6 A drift in baseline measures can make interpreting results difficult when the treatment is expected to produce a change in the same direction as the baseline drift.

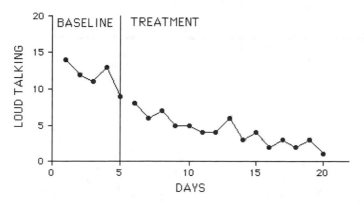

modification procedure is expected to decrease loud talking. As you can see in Figure 2.6, the trend continues throughout the experiment and the decline in talking cannot be attributed to the treatment.

A downward (or upward) drift in baseline may be acceptable if the treatment is expected to produce an opposite trend. For example, a shy child may show a declining trend in talking to other students. In this case, an intervention could involve reinforcing the initiation of conversation by the child. Because the treatment is expected to increase talking, the downward drift in baseline is acceptable. Generally, single-subject research requires a large shift in level or direction of behavior relative to baseline. This shift must be clearly observed when the independent variable is introduced and withdrawn.

KEY WORDS

A-B-A-B reversal design
Baseline
Conditioned-stimulus function
Context of behavior
Contingency of reinforcement
Dependent variable
Direct replication
Discriminative function
Discriminative stimuli
Elicited
Emitted
Environment
Establishing operation
External validity
Functional analysis

Functional analysis of behavior
Generality
History (with regard to validity in experiments)
History of reinforcement
Hypothetical constructs
Independent variable
Instrument decay (with regard to validity in experiments)
Internal validity
Maturation (with regard to validity in experiments)
Negative reinforcers
Operant
Positive reinforcers

Reactive measurement (with regard to validity in experiments)
Reinforcement
Reinforcement function
Respondent
Response classes
Response function
Single-subject research
Stimulus class
Stimulus function
Structural approach to classifying behavior
Systematic replication
Topography
Trend in baseline

CHAPTER 3

Reflexive Behavior and Respondent Conditioning

LEARNING OBJECTIVES

1. Give several examples of phylogenetic behavior and include at least one human illustration.
2. Distinguish between a fixed action pattern (FAP) and a reaction chain.
3. Outline the three primary laws of the reflex.
4. Define habituation, give an example of it, and describe its general characteristics.
5. Describe respondent conditioning, using the example of the word *lemon*.
6. Be able to define and use the terms *unconditioned stimulus* (US), *unconditioned response* (R), *reflex, conditioned stimulus* (CS), *conditioned response* (CR), and *respondent conditioning*.
7. Point to the phylogenetic origins and ontogenetic advantages of respondent conditioning.
8. Summarize the acquisition curve for the respondent conditioning of salivation to a light. What determines the asymptote of the curve?
9. Show that the US-UR relationship is not the same as the CS-CR relationship, referring to the laws of intensity magnitude and latency.
10. Define respondent extinction as a procedure and as a behavioral process.
11. What is spontaneous recovery of respondent behavior? Compare Pavlov's internal inhibition account of spontaneous recovery with the behavioral account based on context.
12. Define respondent generalization and discuss how to show generalization in an experiment.
13. Summarize what is known about generalization gradients based on respondent conditioning. How is respondent generalization an adaptive feature of the behavior of organisms?
14. Give a definition of respondent discrimination and describe a procedure to produce it. How is respondent discrimination an adaptive feature of the behavior of organisms?

15. Compare and contrast delayed, simultaneous, trace, and backward conditioning in terms of procedures and behavioral effects.

16. Cite evidence that backward conditioning can occur when the CS is biologically relevant. What does this evidence mean for a conditioning view that requires the CS to predict (or provide information about) the US?

17. Describe second-order respondent conditioning and be able to outline the experiment by Rizley and Rescorla (1972). Why is second-order conditioning important?

18. Outline the major elements of systematic desensitization and describe how a fear hierarchy is constructed.

A biological imperative, faced by all creatures, is to survive long enough to reproduce. Because of this, behavior related to survival and reproduction is often built-into the organism. That is, organisms come into the world with a range of behavior that aids survival and reproduction. Creatures that fly to avoid predators are likely born with the ability to fly. Thus, flying does not need to be taught; It results from the organism's species history. The complex array of motor movement and coordination involved in flying could be learned, but it is much more dependable when this behavior is based on genetic endowment.

For most animals, survival at birth depends on being able to breathe, take in food, and move about. When a worm is dangled over a young robin's head, this stimulus evokes opening the mouth and chirping. The behavior of the chick is innate and is released by the sight of the dangling worm. The relationship between the dangling worm (stimulus) and the open mouth (response) is a reflex. Presumably, in the evolutionary history of robins, chicks that presented a gaping mouth and chirped were fed and those that did not may have been ignored. In humans, innate or reflexive crying by an infant insures more effective care from the child's parents. Parents engage in a variety of caretaking behaviors in attempts to stop crying. Usually, parental responses such as changing a wet diaper, feeding, or burping the infant will stop the fussing.

PHYLOGENETIC BEHAVIOR

Behavior relations that are based on the genetic endowment of an organism are called **phylogenetic** and are acquired on the basis of species history. Behavior that aids survival or procreation is often (but not always) unlearned. This is because past generations of organisms that engaged in such behavior survived and reproduced. These animals passed (to the next generation) the characteristics that allowed similar behavior. Thus, species history provides the organism with a basic repertoire of responses that are evoked by environmental conditions.

Sequences of Behavior

Fixed action patterns or FAPs are sequences of behavior (a series of connected movements) that are phylogenetic in origin. All members of a particular species (often all males or all females) engage in the FAP when the appropriate releasing stimuli are presented. Fixed action patterns have been observed and documented in a wide range of animals and over a large number of behaviors related to survival and reproduction. To illustrate, Tinbergen (1951) noted that the male stickleback fish responds with a stereotyped sequence of aggressive displays and movements when other male sticklebacks intrude on its territory during mating season. The female spider *Cupiennius salei* constructs a cocoon and deposits her eggs in it by engaging in a fixed sequence of responses (Eibl-Eibesfeldt, 1975). A greylag goose presented with an egg outside its nest will automatically roll the egg into the nest by reaching over the egg (with its bill) and pulling it carefully toward the nest. If the egg is removed, the bird continues with the fixed sequence of egg-retrieval actions (Eibl-Eibelsfeldt, 1975). That is, the bird continues behaving as though the egg is present even though it has been removed. The following passage describes the fixed action pattern that the squirrel *Sciurus vulgaris L.* engages in while putting nuts away for the winter:

> The squirrel ... buries nuts in the ground each fall, employing a quite stereotyped sequence of movement. It picks a nut, climbs down to the ground, and searches for a place at the bottom of a tree trunk or a large boulder. At the base of such a conspicuous landmark it will scratch a hole by means of alternating movements of the forelimbs and place the nut in it. Then the nut is rammed into place with rapid thrusts of the snout, covered with dirt with sweeping motions and tamped down with the forepaws. (Eibl-Eibesfeldt, 1975, p. 23)

Reaction chains are similar to FAPs with one major difference, each response in a reaction chain requires an appropriate stimulus to set it off. Recall that once a fixed action pattern begins, the animal will continue the sequence even when the stimuli that set off the behavior are removed. In the previous squirrel example, if the nut is taken away from the squirrel, the animal will continue to dig a hole and bury a nonexistent nut. In contrast, a reaction chain requires the presence of a specific stimulus to evoke each link in a patterned sequence of behavior. An organism's performance produces stimuli that set off the next set of responses in the sequence; these behaviors produce the next set of stimuli and so on. Presenting stimuli that prompt responses ordinarily occurring in the middle part of the sequence will start the chain at that point rather than at the beginning. Also, unlike fixed action patterns, if the stimuli that evoke behavior are removed, the sequence is disrupted.

Reaction chains are much like consecutive sets of reflexes where the stimuli that evoke the next response in the sequence is produced by the previous reflex. The nursing reaction chain of newborn babies is diagrammed in Figure 3.1. This sequence of reflexive responses may be initiated by tactile stimulation of the infant's cheek. This stimulation elicits the unconditioned rooting response which involves turning the head towards the stimulation, opening the mouth, etc. Root-

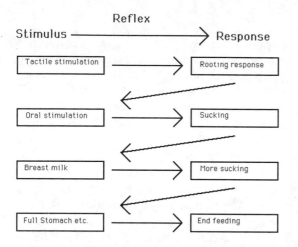

FIG. 3.1 The nursing reaction chain of newborn babies is diagrammed. This sequence of reflexive responses is initiated by tactile stimulation of the infant's cheek. Stimulation of the cheek elicits the unconditioned rooting response that involves turning the head towards the nipple, opening the mouth, etc.

ing results in mouth contact with the nipple, this oral stimulation evokes sucking. Sucking produces breast milk in the infant's mouth and this elicits further sucking. Eventually, internal stimuli arising from a full stomach, changes in blood chemistry, and so on end the sequence and the baby stops feeding.

Reflexive Behavior

The principles that describe the reflex (and its conditioning) are similar for many different kinds of reflexes. For example the laws that govern pupil contraction when a light is shined in the eye or principles describing the relationship between a sudden loud noise and a startle response also hold for the salivation produced when you eat a meal. Early work by Sherrington (1906) focused on the reflex and the relationships that he discovered, almost a century ago, generalize to a remarkable variety of reflexes. When food is placed in a dog's mouth, the animal salivates. This relationship between food in the mouth and salivation is a reflex that is based on the genetic endowment of the organism and is not learned.

All organisms are born with a set of reflexes, but the types of reflexes that occur are particular to a species. Thus, humans are born with an array of responses that are elicited by specific stimuli. As illustrated above, tactile stimulation of the human infant's cheek evokes the rooting response—turning toward the stimulation with mouth open to receive the nipple. Also, as we have noted, in young robins, the begging reflex (open mouth and chirping) serves a similar function—getting fed. Because these relationships are invariant and biologically based, we refer to the eliciting event as the **unconditioned stimulus** (US). The evoked behavior is called the **unconditioned response** (UR). The term *unconditioned* is used because the reflex does not depend on an organism's experience or conditioning during its lifetime (i.e., learning).

When an unconditioned stimulus elicits an unconditioned response (US→UR), the relationship is called a **reflex**. Reflexive behavior is automatic in the sense that a physically healthy organism will always produce the unconditioned response when presented with an unconditioned stimulus. You do not choose to salivate when you have food in your mouth; the US "food in the mouth" forces or **elicits** the UR salivation.

Laws of the Reflex. Sherrington (1906) studied many different types of reflexes, and he formulated the laws that govern reflex action. Because reflexive behavior occurs across most or all animal species from protozoa (Wawrzyncyck, 1937) to humans (Watson & Rayner, 1920) and because simple respondent conditioning builds on reflexive behavior, it is important to describe the laws of the reflex. The laws are general in that they hold for all eliciting or unconditioned stimuli (e.g., food in the mouth, a touch to a hot surface, a sharp blow just below the knee, a light shining in the eye) and the corresponding unconditioned responses (salivation, quick finger withdrawal, an outward kick of the leg, pupil contraction).

The unconditioned stimuli that elicit unconditioned responses may vary in intensity. For example, light that is shining in the eye may be bright enough to hurt or so faint that it is difficult to detect. A tap below the knee, that evokes a kick, may vary from a modest to a heavy blow, etc. The intensity of the eliciting US has direct effects on the evoked reflex. These effects are described by the three **primary laws of the reflex**.

1. **The law of the threshold** is based on the observation that at very weak intensities a stimulus will not elicit a response, but as the intensity of the eliciting stimulus increases there is a point at which the response is evoked. That is, *there is a point below which no response is elicited and above which a response always occurs.* The uncertainty region, where roughly 50% of the stimuli that are presented produce a response, is called the threshold.
2. **The law of intensity-magnitude** describes the relationship between the intensity of the eliciting stimulus and the size or magnitude of the evoked response. *As the intensity of the US increases so does the magnitude of the elicited UR.* A light tap on the patella tendon (just below the kneecap) will evoke a slight jerk of the lower leg; a stronger tap will produce a more vigorous kick of the leg (the patella reflex). Of course, there are upper limits to the magnitude of the tap. If a hammer is used to smash into the knee, the result is a broken kneecap and no movement for a long time.
3. **The law of the latency** concerns the time between the onset of the eliciting stimulus and the appearance of the reflexive response. Latency is a measure of the amount of time that passes between these two events. *As the intensity of the US increases, the latency to the appearance of the evoked UR decreases.* Thus, a strong puff of air will elicit a quick blink of the eye. A weaker puff will also elicit an eye blink, but the onset of the response will be delayed.

These three laws of the reflex are basic properties of all reflexes. They are called primary laws because taken together they define the relationship between the intensity of the eliciting stimulus (US) and the unconditioned response (UR). Reflexes, however, have other characteristics and one of these, habituation, has been shown in animals as simple as protozoa and as complex as humans.

Habituation.   One of the better documented secondary properties of the reflex is called **habituation**. Habituation occurs when an unconditioned stimulus repeatedly elicits an unconditioned response. The frequent presentation of the US produces a gradual decline in the magnitude of the unconditioned response. When the UR is repeatedly evoked it may eventually fail to occur at all. For example, Wawrzyncyck (1937) repeatedly dropped a 4-g weight onto a slide that the protozoa, *Spirostomum ambiguum* was mounted on. The weight drop initially elicited a contraction that steadily declined to near zero with repeated stimulation.

An interesting report of human habituation, in a dangerous setting, appeared in the July 1997 issue of *National Geographic*. The small island of Montserrat has been home to settlers since 1632. Unfortunately, the relatively silent volcano on the island reawakened in July 1995. Suddenly the quiet life that characterized living on Montserrat was rudely interrupted. Before the major eruption of the volcano, a large group of inhabitants refused to evacuate the island and these people suffered through several small volcanic explosions.

> . . . Gerard Dyer and his wife, Judith, [have] been staying with friends in St. John's, about as far north of the volcano as you can get. . . . People could get passes to visit the unsafe zone, which is how Gerard came to be working on the flanks of Soufriere Hills that bright morning.
>
> "If you have animals and crops, you can't just leave them" said Gerard as we walked back to his truck. "You have to come look after them and hope nothing happen." As he spoke, the volcano made a crackling sound like distant thunder— blocks of solid lava rolling down the side of the dome. Gerard didn't even look up.
>
> Montserratians have become so used to the volcano's huffing and puffing that the initial terror has gone. As one woman said, "At first when there was an ashfall, everybody run. Now when the ash falls, everybody look." (Williams, 1997, p. 66)

In this example, Gerard repeatedly has been exposed to the sound of minor volcanic explosions. At first, this sound elicited a startle/panic response, accompanied by running, but these URs habituated to near zero with repeated eruptions of the volcano. A similar process is observed when people live under a flight path; initially the sound of a jet taking off or landing is bothersome, but after some time the sound is barely noticed.

There are a number of general properties that characterize habituation (Thompson & Spencer, 1966). Some of the more important principles of habituation are: 1) The decrease in the habituated response is large at first but this decrement gets progressively smaller as habituation is continued. 2) If the unconditioned stimulus is withheld for some time, the habituated response recovers. 3) When habituation is repeatedly produced, each series of stimulus presentations generates progressively faster and faster habituation. In other words, habituation occurs more quickly on a second series of stimulus presentations than on the first, then even faster on a third set and so on.

Habituation is a behavioral process that has come about because of phylogenetic history. Those animals that habituated were more likely to survive and produce offspring. A herbivore that runs away each time the grass rustles gets less to eat than one that stands its ground. A rustling grass sound may indicate the presence of a predator, or simply the wind blowing.

ONTOGENETIC BEHAVIOR

In addition to phylogenetic history, the behavior of an organism is affected by environmental experience. Each organism has a unique **ontogenetic** history or lifetime of conditioning. This learning consists of behavior-environment interactions with events in the physical and social world. Learning builds on species or phylogenetic history to determine when, where, and what kind of behavior will occur at a given moment. For example, salivation is involved with the digestion of food. People do not learn to salivate to the taste of food; this is a phylogenetic characteristic of the species. After some experience, however, you may salivate to the sight of the golden arches of McDonald's, especially if you are hungry and like hamburgers. Salivating at the sight of McDonald's arches occurs because of respondent conditioning. It is, however, important to note that respondent conditioning (and other learning processes) evolved because of reproductive advantage. Those organisms whose behavior came under the control of arbitrary environmental events presumably survived and reproduced. Through evolution, respondent conditioning became a mode of behavioral adaptation.

Respondent Conditioning

Respondent conditioning involves the transfer of the control of behavior from one stimulus to another. In Chapter 1, we saw that the sound of a bell came to elicit salivation when the bell was associated with food. This kind of conditioning occurs in many species, including humans, and is common in everyday life. Imagine you are out for an early morning walk and pass a bakery where you smell fresh doughnuts. When this happens, your mouth begins to water and your stomach starts to growl. These conditioned responses occur because in the past, the smell has been associated (paired) with food in the mouth (doughnuts).

Figure 3.2 shows the classical conditioning of salivation described by Pavlov (1960). The upper panel indicates that an arbitrary stimulus such as a tone (CS) is presented just before food is placed in a dog's mouth (US). After several pairings of the tone with the food, the tone is presented alone. If the tone now elicits salivation (test phase), it is called a **conditioned stimulus** (CS), and salivation to the tone is the **conditioned response** (CR).[1]

---

[1]The original terms used by Pavlov were the "conditional stimulus" and "conditional response." However, we will use the word "conditioned" to refer to the CS and CR functions. This is because the term "conditional" is now used to refer to a type of discrimination training that will be presented in a later chapter.

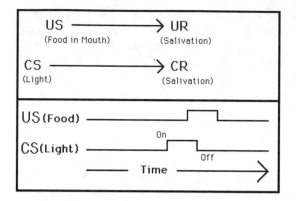

FIG. 3.2 Simple respondent conditioning. An arbitrary stimulus such as a tone (CS) is presented just before food is placed in a dog's mouth (US). After several pairings of tone and food, the tone is presented alone. If the tone now elicits salivation, it is called a conditioned stimulus (CS), and salivation to the tone is a conditioned response (CR).

Notice that a new feature of the environment (a tone) has come to regulate the behavior of the organism. Thus, classical conditioning involves the transfer of behavior control to new and often arbitrary aspects of the environment. To experience this sort of conditioning, try the following: Read the word *lemon* and consider the last time you ate a slice of lemon. Many people salivate at this CS because the word is associated with the sour taste of the fruit.

Because the CR is a response to the CS, it is often called a **respondent**. The terms *conditioned response* and *respondent* are interchangeable throughout this text. The process of presenting stimuli together in time (associating stimuli) so that a CS comes to regulate the occurrence of the conditioned response is called **respondent conditioning**. Note, however, that the association is between the CS and US (i.e., the word *lemon* and fruit in the mouth) because they have been physically presented together, not because of the cognitive association of events. This is an important point: The word association is commonly taken as an internal mental process that a person or other animal performs. In contrast, a behavior analysis points to the physical association of stimuli that occur together in time and/or place. In other words, the association is between events—it does not refer to mental associations. The word *lemon* evokes salivation because it has occurred at a time and place when the chemistry of a lemon produced salivation.

Respondent Acquisition.   In one experiment, Anrep (1920) demonstrated the conditioning of the salivary reflex to a tone stimulus. The acquisition procedure involved turning on the tone for a brief period and then placing food in a dog's mouth. Anrep measured the conditioned response as the number of drops of saliva during 30-second intervals wherein the tone occurred without food. Figure 3.3 (acquisition) shows that the amount of salivation to the tone increases rapidly during the first 25 trials and then levels off, or reaches an asymptote. In other words, with repeated pairings of the CS and US, the magnitude of the conditioned response increases. Once the conditioned reflex reaches asymptote, however, further CS-US pairings have no additional effects.

It is important to note that the asymptote for the conditioned response depends on the intensity of the unconditioned stimulus. As the intensity of the US

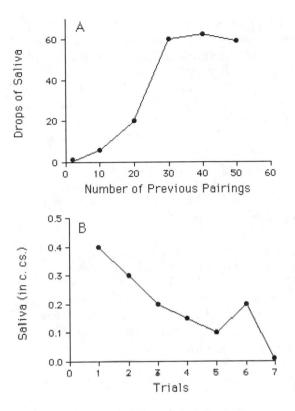

FIG. 3.3 The acquisition and extinction of salivation. The acquisition curve (A) is taken from an experiment by Anrep (1920), who paired a tone (CS) with food placed in a dog's mouth (US). The extinction curve (B) is from Pavlov (1960, p. 53), who presented the CS (sight of food) in the absence of the US (food in the mouth). Results are portrayed as a single experiment.

increases, the magnitude of the UR also increases. The magnitude of the UR limits the maximum strength of the CR. For example, the more food that a dog is given, the greater the amount of salivation. If a dog is given 2 oz of meat, there will be more salivation than if it is presented with 1 oz. A tone that is associated with 2 oz of food will evoke salivation as a CR at a higher level (at asymptote) than a tone associated with 1 oz of food. It should be obvious that these relationships are limited by an organism's physiology. If a dog is given 1 lb of steak, it will probably salivate at maximum strength and a change to 2 lb will have no effect. Similar limits are observed for reflexes such as variation in pupil size in response to light, magnitude of the knee jerk in response to a tap, and the degree of startle in response to noise.

Conditioned and Unconditioned Responses. Notice that the conditioned response of salivation appears to be identical to the unconditioned response. That is, when conditioning to the tone has occurred, turning it on will evoke salivation. This response to the tone seems the same as the salivation produced by food in the dog's mouth. In fact, early theories of learning held that the tone substituted for the food stimulus. This implies that the CS-CR relationship is the same as the US-UR relation. If the CS-CR and the US-UR relationships are the same, then both should follow similar laws and principles. The US-UR relation is governed by the laws of the reflex.

If the CS-CR and US-UR relationships are the same, then the law of intensity magnitude should hold for conditioned stimuli and responses. That is, a rise in the intensity of the CS should increase the magnitude of the CR. In addition, the CS-CR relation should follow the law of latency. An increase in the intensity of the CS should decrease the latency between the CS onset and the conditioned response. Research has shown that these, and other laws of the reflex, typically do not hold for the CS-CR relation (Millenson, 1967). Generally, a change in the intensity of the conditioned stimulus decreases the strength of the conditioned response. In Anrep's (1920) experiment, the tone occurred at a particular intensity, and after conditioning it evoked a given magnitude and latency of salivation. If Anrep had increased the sound, there would have been less salivation and it would have taken longer to occur. Thus, the CS-CR relation is specific to the original conditioning and does not follow the laws of the reflex.

Respondent Extinction.   Pavlov (1960) reported an experimental procedure that he called **extinction**. The procedure involves repeatedly presenting the CS in the absence of the US. Figure 3.3 (extinction) shows the decline in salivation when Pavlov's assistant, Dr. Babkin, repeatedly presented the CS but no longer fed the dog. As you can see, the amount of salivation declines and reaches a minimal value by the seventh trial. This minimum level of the CR is often similar to the value obtained during the first trial of acquisition and probably reflects the **respondent level** of this behavior. Respondent level refers to the strength of the target response (e.g., salivation) before any known conditioning has occurred.

A distinction should be made between extinction as a procedure and extinction as a behavioral process. The procedure of extinction involves presenting the CS without the US after conditioning has occurred. As a behavioral process, extinction refers to a decline in the strength of the conditioned response when an extinction procedure is in effect. In both instances, the term *extinction* is used correctly.

Respondent extinction for salivation occurs quickly. The decline in the strength of the CR is often rapid. This statement is true for the conditioning of salivation, but other types of conditioned responses may vary in resistance to extinction. Even with salivation, Pavlov noted that as the time between test trials increased, the CR declined more slowly. A test trial is any instance in which the CS is given in the absence of the unconditioned stimulus. Of course, repeated test trials are the same as extinction. The slower extinction of salivation with longer intervals between test trials may reflect spontaneous recovery.

Spontaneous Recovery.   **Spontaneous recovery** involves an increase in the conditioned response after respondent extinction has occurred. Recall that after repeated presentations of the CS without the US, the conditioned response declines to respondent level. Following extinction, the CS will again evoke the CR after some time passes. This effect is seen in Figure 3.4, which shows the course of extinction and spontaneous recovery from another experiment by Pavlov (1960). In this experiment, the CS was the sight of meat powder, and the US was food in

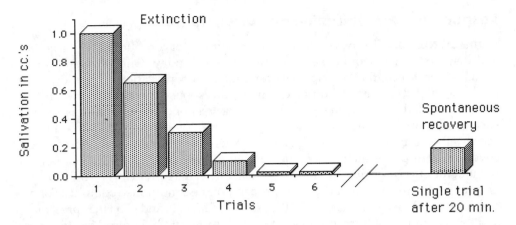

FIG. 3.4 Extinction and spontaneous recovery of salivation evoked by the sight of meat powder (Pavlov, 1960) (data replotted from Bower & Hilgard, 1981, p. 51).

the dog's mouth. As you would expect, the sight of meat powder eventually evoked a conditioned response of salivation. When extinction began, the dog responded with 1 cc of salivation at the sight of the CS. By the fifth extinction trial, the animal showed almost no salivation to the sight of food powder, but after 20 minutes of rest, the CS again evoked a conditioned response. Note, however, that the amount of salivation on the spontaneous-recovery trial is much less than the amount evoked on the first extinction trial.

Pavlov (1960) argued that spontaneous recovery shows little weakening of the CS-CR relationship during extinction. He went on to suggest that "internal inhibition" came to block the connection between stimuli and responses. Pavlov viewed conditioning phenomena as an index of brain processes, and in this regard saw behavior as a reflection of central nervous system functioning. In this sense, spontaneous recovery reflected underlying physiological processes, and one of these was an active but temporary "dampening" of associative connections between the CS and the conditioned response. Pavlov called this physiological blocking of the CS-CR relationship "internal inhibition."

In contrast to Pavlov's physiological account, a behavioral analysis of spontaneous recovery suggests that the CS-CR relation is weakened by extinction, but the context or features of the situation maintain some level of the conditioned response. During respondent conditioning, many stimuli not specified by the researcher, but present in the experimental situation, come to regulate behavior. For example, background odors, general illumination of the room, the presence of particular researchers, the passage of time, and all the events that signal the start of a conditioning series come to exert some control over the conditioned response. Each time a recovery test is made, some part of the situation that has not yet extinguished evokes the CR. This gradual decline in stimulus control through repeated extinction also accounts for progressively less recovery of the conditioned response.

Respondent Generalization and Discrimination

Generalization.   Pavlov conducted a large number of conditioning experiments and discovered many principles that remain useful today. One of his important findings concerned the principle of respondent generalization. **Generalization** occurs when an organism shows a conditioned response to values of the CS that were not trained during acquisition. For example, respondent acquisition presents a specific stimulus, such as a 60-dB tone at a known frequency (e.g., 375 Hz), and associates this stimulus with a US (e.g., food). After several pairings, the CS evokes a conditioned response such as salivation. If a 60-dB tone of 375 Hz is now presented without the US (a test trial), the animal will salivate at maximum level. To show generalization, the researcher varies some property of the conditioned stimulus. For example, a 60-dB tone of 75, 150, 225, 300, 375, 450, 525, 600, and 675 Hz is presented, and the magnitude of the conditioned response is measured. Figure 3.5 shows possible results of such an experiment. As you can see, the amount of salivation declines as the test stimulus departs from the value used in training. This graph, which plots stimulus value against magnitude of response is called a **generalization gradient.**

Interestingly, a similar generalization gradient may not occur if the intensity rather than the tonal quality of the CS is varied. That is, if decibels rather than cycles per second (hertz) are varied in the generalization test, a different result might occur. A few studies have shown that as the intensity of the CS increases, so does the magnitude of the conditioned response (Heinemann & Chase, 1970; Razran, 1949). Heinemann and Chase (1970) found that proportionally more con-

FIG. 3.5 A hypothetical generalization gradient for the salivary response. In this idealized experiment, training would occur at 375 Hz and then CSs ranging from 75 to 675 Hz would be presented.

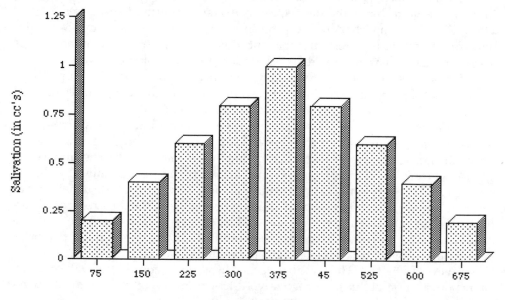

ditioned responses were evoked as the visual intensity of the CS increased. Based on this finding, Heinemann and Chase suggest that there may be consistent increases in the strength of the CR as the intensity of the CS increases, although not all research has not supported this finding (Ernst, Engberg, & Thomas, 1971). A conservative conclusion is that as the CS greatly departs from the value that was originally established, the conditioned response becomes weaker (see also Thomas & Setzer, 1972).

Generalization is an adaptive process that allows the organism to respond similarly although conditions do not remain exactly the same from trial to trial. Consider a situation in which a predator's approach (US) is associated with the sound of snapping twigs, rustling grass, and so on (CS). An organism that runs away (CR) only in the presence of these exact stimulus conditions would not last long. This is because the events that occurred during conditioning are never precisely repeated—each approach of a predator produces variations in sounds, sights, and smells. Even in the laboratory where many features of the environment are controlled, there is some variation in stimuli from one trial to the next. When a bell is paired with food, the dog may change its orientation to the bell and thereby alter the sound; room humidity and other factors may also produce slight variations in tonal quality. Because of generalization, a CS-CR relationship can be strengthened even though the stimulus conditions are never exactly the same from trial to trial. Thus, generalization was likely an adaptive process, allowing organisms to respond to the vagaries of life.

Discrimination.   Another principle that Pavlov discovered is called differentiation or discrimination. **Respondent discrimination** occurs when an organism shows a conditioned response to one stimulus but not to other similar events. A discrimination-training procedure involves positive and negative conditioning trials. For example, a positive trial occurs when a CS^+ such as a 60-dB tone is associated with an unconditioned stimulus like food. On negative trials, a 40-dB tone is presented (CS^-) but never paired with food. Because of stimulus generalization, the dog may salivate to both the 60-dB (CS^+) and 40-dB (CS^-) tones on the early trials. However, if the procedure is continued, the animal will no longer salivate to the CS^- (40-dB tone), but will show a response to the CS^+ (60-dB tone). Once such a differential response occurs, we may say that the dog discriminates between the tones.

Respondent discrimination is another adaptive process. It would be a chaotic world if an animal spent its day running away from most sounds, sights, and smells. Such an animal would not survive and reproduce because there would be no time for other essential activities, like eating, drinking, and procreating. Discrimination allows an organism to budget its time and responses in accord with the requirements of the environment. In the predator example, noises that are reliably associated with an animal that considers you a main course should become CS^+ for flight or fight. Similar noises made by the wind or harmless animals are CS^- for such behavior. Notice, however, that there is a fine line between discrimination and generalization in terms of survival.

TEMPORAL RELATIONS AND CONDITIONING

Delayed Conditioning

There are several ways of arranging the temporal relationship between the presentation of a CS and the unconditioned stimulus (US). So far we have described a procedure in which the CS is presented a few seconds before the US occurs. This procedure is called **delayed conditioning** and is shown in Figure 3.6(A). Delayed conditioning is the most effective way to condition simple autonomic reflexes like salivation. In this diagram, the CS is turned on, and 5 seconds later the US is presented. The interval between the onset of the CS and the presentation of the US (the CS-US interval) determines the effectiveness of conditioning. For autonomic responses like salivation, blood pressure, skin temperature, hormone levels, sweat secretion, and so on, a CS-US interval between 5 and 30 seconds appears to be most effective. A brief CS-US interval of about 0.5 seconds seems to be optimal for the conditioning of quick skeletal responses such as a knee jerk, eye blinks, and retraction of a limb from a hot surface.

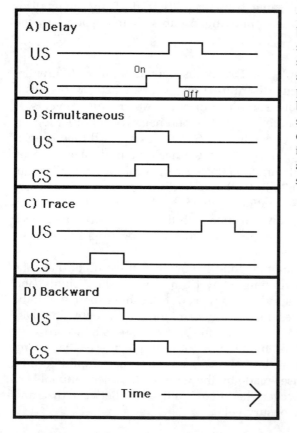

FIG. 3.6 Several temporal arrangements between CS and US commonly used for simple respondent conditioning. Time is shown in the bottom panel of the figure and moves from left to right. The other panels depict the temporal arrangement between US and CS for four basic respondent conditioning arrangements. For example, delayed conditioning is shown in panel (A), where the CS is turned on and, a few seconds later, the US is presented.

Simultaneous Conditioning

Another temporal arrangement between CS and US is called **simultaneous conditioning.** This procedure is shown in Figure 3.6(B), where the CS and US are presented at the same moment. For example, at the same time that the bell rings (CS), food is placed in the dog's mouth (US). Compared with delayed conditioning, simultaneous conditioning produces a weaker conditioned response (Smith & Gormezano, 1965; White & Schlosberg, 1952). One way to understand this weaker effect is to note that the CS does not signal the occurrence of the US in simultaneous conditioning. Based on this observation, many researchers have emphasized the predictiveness of the CS as a central feature of classical conditioning (see Rescorla, 1966). That is, the CS provides information that "tells" the organism a US will follow. Although we will address the question of predictiveness in another section, it is important to note that the occurrence of simultaneous conditioning raises problems for an informational account. In simultaneous conditioning, there can be no predictive information given by the CS and yet some conditioning occurs. This suggests that predictiveness may facilitate conditioning, but is not necessary for it (Papini & Bitterman, 1990).

Trace Conditioning

The procedure for trace conditioning is shown in Figure 3.6(C). The CS is presented for a brief period, and after some time the US occurs. For example, a light is flashed and 20 seconds later food is placed in a dog's mouth. The term **trace conditioning** comes from "memory trace" and refers to the fact that the organism must remember the presentation of the CS. Generally, as the time between the CS and US increases, the conditioned response becomes weaker (Ellison, 1964; Lucas, Deich, & Wasserman, 1981). For eyeblink conditioning (a puff of air in the eye US → an eye blink UR), the response to the CS does not occur when the CS and US are separated by as little as 2 seconds (Schneiderman, 1966). When compared to delay conditioning with the same interval between the onset of the CS followed by the US, trace conditioning is not as effective, producing a weaker conditioned response.

Backward Conditioning

As shown in Figure 3.6(D), **backward conditioning** stipulates that the US comes on before the CS. The general consensus has been that backward conditioning is unreliable, and many researchers question whether it occurs at all. It is true that backward conditioning usually does not produce a conditioned response. That is, if you place food in a dog's mouth and then ring a bell, the bell will not evoke the response of salivation. Most conditioning experiments have used arbitrary stimuli, such as lights, tones, shapes, and so on, as the conditioned stimulus. However, Keith-Lucas and Guttman (1975) found backward conditioning when they used a biologically significant CS.

These researchers reasoned that following an unsuccessful attack by a predator, the sights, sounds, and smells of the attacker would be associated with pain from the attack. Consider a situation in which a grazing animal is unaware of the approach of a leopard. The attack comes swiftly and without warning. The animal survives the onslaught, turns in the direction of the leopard, and manages to run away. In this case, the pain inflicted by the attack is a US for flight that precedes the sight of the predator (CS). For such a situation, backward conditioning would have adaptive value since the animal would learn to avoid leopards.

Keith-Lucas and Guttman (1975) designed an experiment to test this adaptive-value hypothesis. Rats were placed in an experimental chamber and fed a sugar pellet in a particular location. While eating the pellet, the rats were given a one-trial presentation of electric shock (US). After the shock, the chamber was made completely dark for 1, 5, 10, or 40 seconds. When the light in the chamber came back on, a toy hedgehog (CS) was presented to the rat. To make this experiment clear, eating sugar pellets was viewed as the laboratory equivalent of grazing, the shock represented an attack, and the appearance of the toy hedgehog substituted for the predator. Two control groups were run under identical conditions, except that one group saw the hedgehog but did not get shocked and the other group got the shock but did not see a hedgehog.

On the next day, each animal was returned to the situation and a number of responses were measured. Compared with the control groups, backward conditioning was found after a delay of 1, 5, and 10 seconds but not after 40 seconds. Relative to control animals, experimental subjects showed greater avoidance of the hedgehog, spent less time in the presence of the hedgehog, and ate less food. Presumably, the shock (US) elicited a fear-flight reaction (UR), and backward conditioning transferred this reaction to the toy hedgehog (CS). The fear induced by the hedgehog (CR) interfered with eating and produced avoidance of the toy animal. This experiment shows that with a biologically relevant CS, backward conditioning is possible. Despite this outcome, most research suggests that the backward arrangement of US then CS does not result in conditioning (but see Siegel & Domjan, 1971 and Tait & Saladin, 1986, for backward inhibitory conditioning).

SECOND-ORDER RESPONDENT CONDITIONING

Most of this chapter has been concerned with first-order conditioning. In **first-order conditioning**, an apparently neutral stimulus is paired with an unconditioned stimulus. When this occurs, the control of the response to the US is transferred to the neutral stimulus, which is now called a conditioned stimulus (CS). **Second-order conditioning** extends this transfer of control to events that have not been directly associated with the unconditioned stimulus. These events gain control over the response because of their pairing with a conditioned stimulus. Thus, second-order conditioning involves pairing a neutral stimulus with a CS, rather than pairing a neutral stimulus and US. Such higher-order conditioning is important because it extends the range of behavioral effects produced by respondent conditioning.

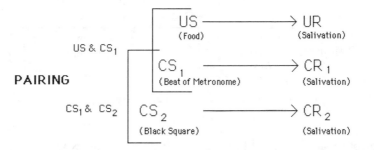

FIG. 3.7 A comparison between first- and second-order conditioning. The second-order conditioned stimulus (CS_2) comes to elicit the conditioned response (CR) even though it is never directly paired with the US.

Pavlov conducted experiments that demonstrated second-order conditioning. In these experiments, the tick of a metronome was paired with food. The sound of the metronome came to evoke salivation. Because the beat of the metronome was directly associated with the US, it is called a first-order conditioned stimulus (CS_1). Once the ticking sound reliably elicited salivation, Pavlov paired it with the sight of a black square. Following several pairings of the metronome beat with the black square, the sight of the black square (CS_2) evoked salivation. The black square is termed a second-order conditioned stimulus because it acquires control of the CR by its pairing with a first-order CS. Figure 3.7 shows a comparison between first- and second-order conditioning. An interesting point is that the second-order CS (black square) evoked the conditioned response (CR) even though it was never directly paired with food.

Since the time of Pavlov, there have been disputes about the reliability of higher-order conditioning. Even though Pavlov discovered it, he described such conditioning as fleeting—not having powerful effects. One reason that higher-order conditioning appears to produce weak effects is that each CS_1-CS_2 pairing occurs in the absence of the unconditioned stimulus. Thus, the pairing trials are also extinction trials.

The view that higher-order conditioning only produces weak effects was, however, put to rest following an experiment by Rizley and Rescorla (1972). These researchers used a conditioned suppression experiment in which a light was paired with electric shock. Rats were trained to press a lever for food, and suppression of lever pressing was used to measure the effects of conditioning.

The design of the Rizley and Rescorla (1972) experiment is shown in Figure 3.8. The paired-paired group is of most interest. Rats in this condition underwent all the procedures for second-order conditioning. For these animals, a light was paired with shock and the light was shown to suppress lever pressing for food. Next, a tone that was never associated with shock was presented just before the light came on. In this case, the tone was expected to reduce bar pressing because of its association with the light.

Two control groups were added to the experiment. The paired-unpaired group also had the light paired with shock. This group, however, received unpaired pre-

Group	Phase 1	Phase 2
PAIRED-PAIRED	LIGHT → SHOCK	TONE → LIGHT
PAIRED-UNPAIRED	LIGHT → SHOCK	TONE/LIGHT
UNPAIRED-PAIRED	LIGHT/SHOCK	TONE → LIGHT

FIG. 3.8 The design used by Rizley and Rescorla (1972) to demonstrate second-order classical conditioning.

sentations of the tone and light in the second phase of the experiment. This condition was included to ensure that the response suppression produced by the tone in the paired-paired group depended on the tone-light pairings in the second part of the experiment. A final control group was called the unpaired-paired condition. This group received unpaired presentations of the light and shocks in phase 1. For these animals, the second phase involved the same tone-light pairings as in the paired-paired condition. This insured that any observed effects of the tone were caused by second-order conditioning. That is, the effects of the light in conditioning the tone must be shown to depend on its previous association with shocks. If the light was a US rather than a CS for response suppression, then the effects of the tone would only be an example of first-order conditioning.

The effects of the tone on bar pressing for food are given as a suppression ratio. This ratio compares rate of response during the presentation of the tone with a similar period without the tone. The ratio is expressed as a proportion that varies between 0.00 and 1.00, and the lower the value the greater the response suppression. A suppression ratio of 0.50 indicates no conditioning to the tone because the rate of lever pressing for food is the same when the tone is present or absent.

Figure 3.9 is based on Rizley and Rescorla's (1972) results and presents the effects of the tone on the last two trials. The paired-unpaired group has a suppression ratio of about 0.50, indicating no conditioning of the tone. When compared to this condition, the tone dramatically disrupted bar pressing in the paired-paired group. This finding strongly supports the reality of second-order conditioning. Another result of interest is the response suppression in the unpaired-paired group. Evidently the light did have some US value, since the tone disrupted bar pressing even though the light had never been paired with shocks. This observation suggests that researchers cannot count on a stimulus being neutral before it is used in a second-order procedure. For this reason, an experimental design must control for these effects.

Second-order conditioning is important because it extends stimulus control of behavior to events that have not been directly paired with the unconditioned stimulus. Some phobic reactions (i.e., a seemingly intense and irrational fear) of people may be caused by higher-order conditioning. Consider a person who refuses to sit with friends in the backyard on a nice summer day. The sight of flowers greatly upsets her and she says that "with so many flowers there are probably bees." A possible interpretation is that the person has been stung (US) by a bee (CS_1), and she has noticed that bees hover around flowers (CS_2). The fear of flowers occurs because of the pairing of bees with flowers. Thus, phobic reactions and other emotional responses may sometimes involve higher-order respondent conditioning.

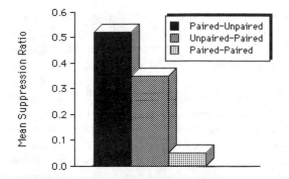

FIG. 3.9 The effects of the tone on bar pressing for food given as a suppression ratio. The ratio is expressed as a proportion that varies between 0.00 and 1.00. The lower the value of the ratio, the greater the response suppression. A suppression ratio of 0.50 indicates no conditioning to the tone.

ON THE APPLIED SIDE: TREATMENT OF FEAR

Systematic Desensitization

Systematic desensitization is a technique, based on respondent conditioning, that is used to treat phobias. Phobic reactions are intense, out-of-control fears of objects or events. Common phobias include fear of open or closed spaces, crowds, dentists, heights, taking exams, insects, snakes, and so on (see Marks, 1987; Weekes, 1976). The technique of systematic desensitization was first described by Wolpe (1958), who based the treatment on principles of respondent conditioning.

Relaxation. There are two major components to systematic desensitization—deep muscle relaxation and a fear hierarchy. The first step in the procedure is to teach the client deep muscle relaxation (Jacobson, 1938). Wolpe's idea was that relaxation was incompatible with fear responses and that the conditioned stimuli that elicited fear would eventually evoke relaxation; he called this **reciprocal inhibition**. The client is usually given a cassette audio tape with relaxation instructions on it. At home, the client plays the tape and learns to relax. Instructions for relaxation include breathing exercises and discrimination of muscle tension (see Martin & Pear, 1996, pp. 335–349). The taped instructions are given in a low, even voice and the client is taught to relax each part of the body. For example, the taped voice may say, "Make a tight fist with your left hand. Squeeze it tightly. Note how it feels. Now relax." Other instructions target different muscle groups.

The Fear Hierarchy. After the client learns to relax, a **fear hierarchy** is constructed. The first step identifies the stimulus conditions that evoke the phobic reaction. Often, this is not as straightforward as it sounds. A person may state that he or she is terribly afraid of dentists, but during an interview it may become apparent that maximum fear occurs in the dentist's waiting room rather than in the surgical chair. Once the situation of maximum fear is identified, a series of verbal stimuli are arranged that describe settings that progressively evoke less and less fear. These descriptions should be vivid in detail and include people, events, and objects that are encountered in the client's everyday life. There are usually 10 to 30 items on the anxiety hierarchy, but some behavior therapists have used over 100 items. Typically, each item is written on a separate index card and the cards are sorted so that those causing the least fear are at the top and those causing the most fear are on the bottom. Figure 3.10 shows a fear of flying hierarchy that was used in a study by Roscoe, Martin, and Pear (1980). Notice that the hierarchy is not constructed with regard to temporal order; rather it reflects the client's increasing fear of the situation.

Once the fear hierarchy has been constructed, systematic desensitization can begin. The client comes for an appointment, is seated in a comfortable chair, and is told to relax. At this point, the therapist reads the least-anxiety-provoking description and asks the client to imagine himself or herself in that circumstance. The client is also told to lift a finger if the slightest amount of anxiety is felt. If the person feels anxious, the same item is repeated until at least three repetitions occur without any anxiety. Following three or more successful repetitions, the next item on the hierarchy is presented. This continues until the last, and most fearful, item is completed.

The effectiveness of systematic desensitization was evaluated by Paul (1969a), who reviewed a number of published reports involving thousands of patients. In this review, Paul found that 80 to 90% of clients were successfully treated. On a variety of outcome measures, systematic desensitization was found to be more effective than psychotherapy, no treatment, placebo treatment, and a no-contact control group (Paul, 1966, 1968, 1969b). Other studies have also documented the effectiveness of this treatment approach (Gelder & Marks, 1966; Gelder, Marks, Wolff, & Clarke, 1967).

---

1. The plane has landed and stopped at the terminal. I get off the plane and enter the terminal, where I am met by friends.
2. A trip has been planned, and I have examined the possible methods of travel and decided "out loud" to travel by plane.
3. I have called the travel agent and told him of my plans. He gives me the times and flight numbers.
4. It is the day before the trip, and I pack my suitcase, close it, and lock it.
5. It is ten days before the trip, and I receive the tickets in the mail. I note the return address, open the envelope, and check the tickets for the correct dates, times, and flight numbers.
6. It is the day of the flight, I am leaving home. I lock the house, put the bags in the car, and make sure that I have the tickets and money.
7. I am driving to the airport for my flight. I am aware of every plane I see. As I get close to the airport, I see several planes—some taking off, some landing, and some just sitting on the ground by the terminal.
8. I am entering the terminal. I am carrying my bags and tickets.
9. I proceed to the airline desk, wait in line, and have the agent check my tickets and then weigh and check my bags.
10. I am in the lounge with many other people, some with bags also waiting for flights. I hear the announcements over the intercom and listen for my flight number to be called.
11. I hear my flight number announced, and I proceed to the security checkpoint with my hand luggage.

(continued)

12. I approach the airline desk beyond the security checkpoint, and the agent asks me to choose a seat from the "map" of the plane.
13. I walk down the ramp leading to the plane and enter the door of the plane.
14. I am now inside the plane. I look at the interior of the plane and walk down the aisle, looking for my seat number. I then move in from the aisle and sit down in my assigned seat.
15. The plane is in flight, and I decide to leave my seat and walk to the washroom at the back of the plane.
16. I notice the seat-belt signs light up, so I fasten my seat belt and I notice the sound of the motors starting.
17. Everyone is seated with their seat belts fastened, and the plane slowly moves away from the terminal.
18. I notice the seat-belt signs are again lighted, and the pilot announces that we are preparing to land.
19. I am looking out the window and suddenly the plane enters clouds and I cannot see out the window.
20. The plane has stopped at the end of the runway and is sitting, waiting for instructions to takeoff.
21. The plane is descending to the runway for a landing. I feel the speed and see the ground getting closer.
22. The plane has taken off from the airport and banks as it changes direction. I am aware of the "tilt."
23. The plane starts down the runway, and the motors get louder as the plane increases speed and suddenly lifts off.

FIG. 3.10 A fear of flying hierarchy as described by Martin and Pear (1996, p. 341, and reprinted with permission of Prentice Hall).

KEY WORDS

Backward conditioning

Conditioned response (CR)

Conditioned stimulus (CS)

Delayed conditioning

Deep muscle relaxation

Fear hierarchy

First-order conditioning

Fixed action pattern

Generalization gradient (respondent)

Habituation

Law of intensity magnitude

Law of the latency

Law of the threshold

Ontogenetic

Phylogenetic

Reaction chain

Reflex

Respondent

Respondent conditioning

Respondent discrimination

Respondent extinction

Respondent generalization

Respondent level

Second-order conditioning

Simultaneous conditioning

Spontaneous recovery (respondent)

Systematic desensitization

Trace conditioning

Unconditioned response (UR)

Unconditioned stimulus (US)

CHAPTER 4

Complexities of Respondent Conditioning

LEARNING OBJECTIVES
---

1. Define compound stimuli. How does respondent conditioning of compound stimuli extend the principles of respondent behavior to everyday settings, such as McDonald's restaurant.
2. Provide a definition and give an example of overshadowing, blocking, and sensory preconditioning.
3. What is conditioned suppression and how is it used to demonstrate the process of blocking?
4. Outline the basics of the Rescorla-Wagner model. Be able to use the terms *associative strength, maximum associative strength,* and *change in associative strength* in your discussion of the model.

Advanced Issue
5. *Be able to write the Rescorla-Wagner equation and explain the terms.*
6. *How does the Rescorla-Wagner equation account for respondent acquisition?*
7. *Provide an account of blocking using the Rescorla-Wagner equation.*
8. *Apply the Rescorla-Wagner equation to the process of respondent extinction*
9. *Explain, using a graph, how conditioned inhibition is predicted by the Rescorla-Wagner equation (or model).*
10. Show how Rescorla's (1966) experiment appears to support a correlational view of conditioning.
11. Describe how the correlational/informational view was disconfirmed. In your answer, refer to research by Estes (1969), Rescorla (1972), and Papini and Bitterman (1990).
12. Describe the counteractive effects of the CS in drug administration.

13. Summarize the research on drug tolerance and overdose.
14. Draw out the implications of context for the CS-CR relationship.

CONDITIONING AND COMPOUND STIMULI

In Chapter 3, we examined CS and US relationships in isolation, ignoring the context or background in which these events are presented. In order to investigate the effects of context in respondent behavior, researchers have arranged situations involving **compound stimuli**. In these cases, two (or more) conditioned stimuli (e.g., tone and light) are presented together and acquire the capacity to evoke a single conditioned response. Respondent conditioning to compound stimuli is a procedure that extends respondent behavior and principles to the complex situations of everyday life. For example, the odor of food at McDonald's restaurant probably becomes a CS for salivation when paired with burgers and fries (US). But other events like the presence of the order clerk, the setting of the restaurant, and the golden arches are also paired with eating. These additional features of McDonald's become conditioned stimuli that function as the context in which odor of food (CS) evokes salivation. Differences in the conditioning procedures related to compound stimuli result in the behavioral processes of sensory preconditioning, blocking, and overshadowing.

Overshadowing

Pavlov (1960) described a conditioning effect known as **overshadowing.** This effect may occur when a compound stimulus is used as the CS in a conditioning experiment. A compound stimulus consists of two or more simple stimuli presented at the same time. For example, a light and tone (CS) may be turned on at the same time and associated with an unconditioned stimulus such as food. Pavlov found that the most salient property of the compound stimulus came to regulate exclusively the conditioned response. For example, if a loud tone and a faint light were used as the compound CS, then the tone would evoke salivation while the light would not. The tone is said to overshadow conditioning to the light. This happens even though the weak light will function as a CS if it is originally presented by itself and paired with a US.

Blocking

In 1969, Kamin reported a related effect that also involved compound stimuli. This effect is known as **blocking** and describes a situation in which a CS associated with a US blocks a subsequent CS-US association. In blocking, a CS is paired with a US until the conditioned response reaches maximum strength. Following this conditioning, a second stimulus is presented at the same time as the original CS, and both are paired with the unconditioned stimulus. On test trials, the original CS evokes the CR but the second stimulus does not. For example, a tone (CS) may be associated with food (US) until the tone reliably evokes salivation. Next, the tone and a light are presented together and both are associated with food. On test trials, the tone will elicit salivation but the light will not.

In his original experiment, Kamin (1969) used a procedure called **conditioned suppression** (see Estes & Skinner, 1941). In conditioned suppression, a previously neutral stimulus (e.g., tone, light, etc.) is paired with an aversive US such as an electric shock. After several pairings, the originally neutral stimulus becomes a conditioned aversive stimulus (CS^{ave}). The CS^{ave} is said to evoke a conditioned emotional response (CER) that is commonly called anxiety or fear. Once the CS^{ave} has been conditioned, its effects may be observed by changes in an organism's operant behavior. For example, a rat may be trained to press a lever for food. After a stable rate of response is established, the CS^{ave} is introduced. When this occurs, the animal's lever pressing is disrupted, presumably because of the CER elicited by the CS^{ave}. In common English, the CS^{ave} frightens the animal and it stops pressing the bar. Conditioned suppression is a widely used procedure in respondent conditioning, and as you will see later it is important in the study of human emotions.

Using a conditioned-suppression procedure, Kamin (1969) discovered the phenomenon of blocking. Two groups of rats were used: a blocking group and a control group. In the blocking group, rats were presented with a tone (CS^{ave}) that was associated with electric shocks for 16 trials. Following this, the rats received eight trials during which the compound stimulus tone and light were followed by shock. The control group did not receive the 16 light-shock conditioning trials but did have the eight trials of tone and light paired with shock. Both groups were tested for conditioned suppression of lever pressing in the presence of the light. That is, the light was presented alone and suppression of bar pressing for food indicated the occurrence of the conditioned emotional response (CER). Kamin found that the light suppressed bar pressing in the control group but did not affect lever pressing in the blocking group. In other words, prior conditioning with the tone blocked or prevented conditioning to the light. Functionally, the light was a CS^{ave} in the control group but not in the blocking group.

Sensory Preconditioning

Sensory preconditioning is another example of stimulus control by compound events. In this case, two stimuli such as light and tone are repeatedly presented together without the occurrence of a known US (preconditioning). Later, one of these stimuli is paired with an unconditioned stimulus and the other stimulus is tested for conditioning. Even though the second stimulus was never directly associated with the US, it comes to evoke a conditioned response (Brogden, 1939; Pfautz, Donegan, & Wagner, 1978; Prewitt, 1967). For example, a rat may be repeatedly exposed to 10 seconds of light with an accompanying tone. Following this preconditioning phase, the tone is associated with an electric shock. Using a conditioned-suppression procedure, it is possible to show that the light will suppress the animal's operant behavior. Notice that the light has never been paired with the shock but comes to have a CS^{ave} function based on preconditioning with the tone. One possibility is that sensory preconditioning is a way that stimuli may acquire corresponding or equivalent functions. The light "stands for" the tone and the tone for the light.

THE RESCORLA-WAGNER MODEL OF CONDITIONING

The occurrence of overshadowing, blocking, and sensory preconditioning has led many researchers to the conclusion that cognitive processes underlie conditioning. This is because these effects (and others) seem to imply that an animal learns to expect certain events on the basis of predictive cues. That is, the sight of a predator becomes a predictive cue because the animal expects an attack. The CS is said to provide information about the occurrence of the US and redundant information, as in blocking, is not processed by the organism.

Although this is an intuitively satisfying account, cognitive processes are not necessary to describe most of the research in respondent conditioning. Bolles (1979) has commented as follows:

> Are we now in a position to conclude that conditioning is really a cognitive process, that it involves the expectancy of an ... [US], and that the expectancies reflect predictive relationships the animal perceives between cues and consequences? Some psychologists have come to this conclusion. But others have shown restraint. Indeed, it turns out to be possible to account ... [for many conditioning effects], all without recourse to any cognitive concepts. It can all be done with the clever application of [temporal pairing of stimuli] and other S-R principles. This remarkable development is the work of Wagner, and surprisingly, Rescorla himself. They have produced what is widely known as the Rescorla-Wagner model. (p. 158)

As Bolles (1979) notes, the **Rescorla-Wagner model** (Rescorla & Wagner, 1972; Wagner & Rescorla, 1972) is an S-R pairing account of respondent conditioning. That is, the Rescorla-Wagner model is a behavioral theory that does not make inferences about underlying cognitive/informational processing.

The basic idea of the Rescorla-Wagner model is that a conditioned stimulus acquires a limited amount of associative strength on any trial. We use the term **associative strength** to describe the relation between the CS and the magnitude of the conditioned response. In general, associative strength increases over conditioning trials and reaches some maximum level. It is apparent that a given CS can acquire only so much control over a conditioned response. This is the **maximum associative strength** for the CS. Thus, a tone (CS) that is paired with 1 g of food will have maximum associative strength when the amount of conditioned salivation (CR) is about the same as the unconditioned salivation (UR) elicited by the gram of food (US). That is, an unconditioned stimulus elicits a given magnitude of the unconditioned response. This magnitude sets the upper limit for the conditioned response. The CS cannot elicit a greater response than the one produced by the unconditioned stimulus.

A conditioned stimulus gains a certain amount of associative strength on any one trial. The amount of gain or increment depends on several factors. One obvious factor is the maximum associative strength that may accrue to the conditioned stimulus. As noted, this maximum is set by the magnitude of the US-UR relationship. An intense US will set a higher maximum value than a weaker one.

Another factor that affects the increment in associative strength on any trial is the **change in associative strength** or the difference between the present strength of the CS and its maximum possible value. As conditioning trials proceed, the CS gains associative strength, and this means that the difference between present and maximum strength decreases; there is less and less to gain on each trial. For example, assume a 10-trial experiment in which 1 g of meat evokes 2 cc of saliva and the meat is paired with a tone. In terms of associative strength, the most gain will occur on the first trial, there will be less gain by the fifth, and there will be almost no gain in associative strength by the 10th trial.

The change in associative strength of a conditioned stimulus (CS_1) is also affected by the strength of other conditioned stimuli (CS_2, CS_3, etc.) that evoke the conditioned response in that situation. Because there is a maximum associative strength set by the US, it follows that the associative strength of each CS will add together and reduce the difference between the present associative strength and the maximum possible value. Thus, if a tone has been frequently paired with meat, it will evoke almost maximum salivation. If a light is now introduced and presented along with the tone, it will show little control over salivation since most of the possible associative strength has accrued to the tone (blocking).

The Rescorla-Wagner model of respondent conditioning accounts for a large number of findings and has stimulated a good deal of research. The model makes counterintuitive predictions that have been confirmed in a variety of experimental settings. Since the early 1970s, scores of experiments have been conducted to test some of the implications of the model. The following Advanced Issue section provides more detail about the Rescorla-Wagner model and its predictive utility.

ADVANCED ISSUE
CONDITIONING EFFECTS AND THE RESCORLA-WAGNER EQUATION

The three limiting conditions of (a) maximum associative strength, (b) difference between the current strength and maximum, and (c) the number of additional CSs in the situation are represented by Equation 4.1 suggested by Rescorla and Wagner (1972; see also Wagner & Rescorla, 1972).

$$\Delta V_i = S_i(V_{MAX} - V_i - V_{SUM}) \qquad (4.1)$$

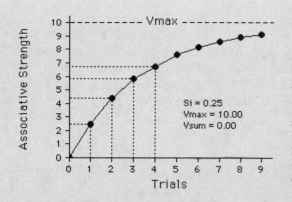

FIG. 4.1 The acquisition curve predicted by the Rescorla-Wagner equation (our Equation 4.1). Gain in associative strength, from trial to trial, declines as the CR comes closer to the asymptote. The asymptote or upper-flat portion of the curve is set in the equation by the value V_{MAX}.

The value ΔV_i stands for the amount of change in associative strength for any CS that occurs on any one trial. The symbol S_i is a constant that varies between 0.00 and 1.00, and may be interpreted as the salience (e.g., bright versus dim light) of the CS and the sensory capacities of the organism. The constant S_i is estimated after conditioning and determines how quickly the associative strength of the CS rises to maximum. The value V_{MAX} represents the maximum associative strength as measured by the magnitude of the unconditioned response (UR). The symbols V_i and V_{SUM} represent the associative strength already accrued to the CS_1 and to any other stimuli in the situation ($V_{SUM} = CS_2 + CS_3 + \ldots CS_N$).

Acquisition

Figure 4.1 shows the idealized acquisition of a conditioned response based on Equation 4.1. In this hypothetical experiment, a tone CS is repeatedly paired with an unconditioned stimulus such as food. In the figure, the S_i is set at 0.25 and the asymptote (or maximum possible strength) is 10.00 arbitrary units of the conditioned response (e.g., salivation). The value of V_{SUM} is assumed to be zero, so that all associative strength accrues to the CS. The value of ΔV_i is predicted by the equation when we substitute $S_i = 0.25$, $V_{MAX} = 10.00$, and the value of V_i is zero ($V_i = 0.00$) before conditioning begins. Based on Equation 4.1, the increase in associative strength from no conditioning to the first trial is

$$\Delta V_i = 0.25\,(10.00 - 0.00)$$
$$\Delta V_i = 2.50.$$

On each subsequent trial, the associative strength of the CS is 0.25 of the remaining distance to the asymptote. Thus for trial 2 we substitute the value 2.50 for V_i and predict an increase of 1.88:

$$\Delta V_i = 0.25\,(10.00 - 2.50)$$
$$\Delta V_i = 1.88.$$

The associative strength of the CS after the second trial is 2.50 + 1.88, or 4.38. This means that roughly one-half of the maximum associative strength of the CS has been acquired by trial 2. The ΔV_i value for trial 3 uses $V_i = 4.38$ and so on. As you can see in Figure 4.1, the equation yields a negatively accelerating curve that approaches, but never quite reaches, maximum associative strength. You can see from the horizontal and perpendicular lines that the largest increase in associative strength is on the first trial, and this change corresponds to the difference in associative strength between trial 0 and trial 1 (2.5-unit increase). The increase in ΔV_i gets smaller and smaller over trials.

Blocking Reconsidered

As Bolles (1979) noted, the Rescorla-Wagner equation accounts for many respondent conditioning effects without making assumptions about cognitive processes. One important effect that we have already discussed is blocking. Equation 4.1 provides a behavioral account of this phenomenon. Consider what will happen when V_i is almost equivalent to the value V_{MAX}, and a second conditioned stimulus (CS_2) is introduced. For example, a tone (CS_1) is paired with shock until the tone evokes close to maximum response suppression. At this point, a light (CS_2) is presented at the same time as the tone and conditioning continues. In Equation 4.1, the light is represented as V_{SUM} and the tone as V_i. After the tone acquires close to maximum strength, little is left over for the light (V_{SUM}) and the light has almost no suppressive effect on bar pressing. That is, the previous conditioning to the tone blocks conditioning to the light. Notice that it makes a big difference when the CS_2 is introduced. If CS_1 and CS_2 are paired from the start, then (all things being equal) both stimuli will gain one-half of the increase in associative strength (ΔV_i).

Extinction

Equation 4.1 can also be used to account for respondent extinction. In this case, the decline in associative strength (ΔV_i) is also determined by S_i, V_{MAX}, V_i, and V_{SUM}. As before, assume that a tone is paired with food until the tone elicits a conditioned response that is close to maximum; there are no other relevant stimuli and V_{SUM} cancels out of the equation. Since the procedure is respondent extinction, the curve must decline toward no associative strength, which means that V_{MAX} must be zero. If $S_i = 0.25$ and V_{MAX} is 0.00 then the decline in associative strength on the first extinction trial is

$$\Delta V_i = 0.25 \, (0.00 - 10.00)$$
$$\Delta V_i = -2.50$$

Thus, the value of the tone after the first extinction trial is $10.00 - 2.50$, or 7.50. Other values of the CS during extinction are determined in a similar fashion. Figure 4.2 shows that the predicted extinction curve is the exact opposite of the acquisition curve of Figure 4.1. It is important to note that the actual associative strength of the tone before extinction is never exactly equal to the V_{MAX}, but for simplicity we have assumed that it is in Figure 4.2.

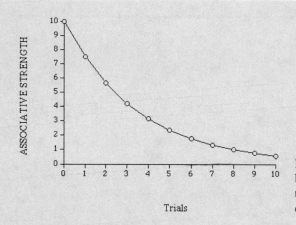

FIG. 4.2 The extinction curve predicted by the Rescorla-Wagner model. Notice that V_{MAX}, or the asymptote, is zero because extinction is in effect.

Conditioned Inhibition

The Rescorla-Wagner model can be applied to the phenomenon known as **conditioned inhibition.** When a CS^+ is repeatedly presented without the US (extinction), the conditioned stimulus is said to acquire increasing amounts of inhibition, in the sense that its presentation suppresses the response. Equation 4.1 may be expressed as $\Delta V_i = S_i (V_{MAX} - V_{SUM})$, and in this form V_i is included with the V_{SUM} term. The equation predicts that when CS^+ acquires near maximum associative strength and extinction begins, the introduction of a second stimulus makes the conditioned response decline faster. This is because the second stimulus acquires negative associative strength and further suppresses the conditioned response.

Mazur (1990) described a hypothetical experiment that illustrates and explains this effect. Consider that a light (CS) has been paired with food (US) and the light evokes a CR that is almost maximum at 100 arbitrary units of response. In terms of Equation 4.1, the maximum associative strength is 100. At this point, extinction trials are started and a tone is presented at the same time as the light. Recall that during extinction $V_{MAX} = 0.00$, associative strength drops to the preconditioning level. Based on the Rescorla-Wagner model, the tone should become a conditioned inhibitory stimulus (CS^-). This is because the model makes it clear that if V_{MAX} is less than V_{SUM}, then the associative strengths of all CSs will decline. Such a decline will be equal for the light and tone if the stimuli have the same salience (S_i). Since the tone has an initial value of zero, any decrease in associative strength must result in a negative value for this stimulus.

If salience is set at $S_i = 0.20$ for the tone and light, on the first extinction trial the decline in associative strength will be −20, since $\Delta V_i = 0.2 (0.00 - 100)$ or a decline of 20 units. On the second trial, the associative strength of the light is 80 units or $(100 - 20)$ and the tone has a value of −20 or $(0.00 - 20)$. Figure 4.3 shows the results of this experiment over 10 trials. After 10 trials, the associative strengths for the light and tone sum to approximately zero, and there can be almost no further decline in the conditioned response based on the Rescorla-Wagner model.

Trial	ΔV_i	V_{TONE}	V_{LIGHT}	V_{SUM}
1	−20.0	0.0	100.0	100.0
2	−12.0	−20.0	80.0	60.0
3	−7.2	−32.0	68.0	36.0
4	−4.3	−39.2	60.8	22.0
5	−2.6	−43.5	56.5	13.0
6	−1.6	−46.1	53.9	8.0
7	−0.9	−47.7	52.3	5.0
8	−0.6	−48.6	51.4	3.0
9	−0.5	−49.2	50.8	2.0
10		−49.6	50.4	0.0

FIG. 4.3 Table of extinction values predicted by the Rescorla-Wagner model after a light CS has been conditioned to evoke salivation. During extinction, a tone is presented along with the light.

Figure 4.4 is based on the data in Fig. 4.3 and shows three separate curves predicted by Equation 4.1. The associative strength of the light declines from an initial value of 100 units of response to an asymptote of approximately 50 units. Recall that the tone has never been paired with food, and for this reason its associative strength before the first extinction trial is zero. As extinction proceeds, the tone takes on negative values and decreases to approximately −50.00 units of response. The third curve (V_{SUM}) is obtained by summation of the associative strengths for the light and tone on each trial. This latter curve predicts the actual course of extinction based on the separate curves for light and tone. The extinction curve begins with a value of 100 units of response strength and declines to zero by the 10th trial.

Interestingly, the Rescorla-Wagner model predicts faster extinction when a CS$^+$ (light) and CS$^-$ (tone) are presented together than when a CS$^+$ is presented alone. This situation is depicted in Figure 4.5, which shows the predicted extinction curves for tone and

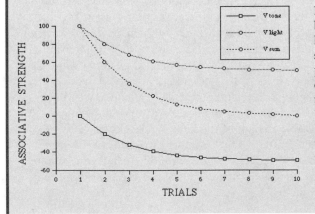

FIG. 4.4 The extinction curves predicted by the Rescorla-Wagner model after a light CS has been conditioned to evoke salivation. During extinction, a tone is presented along with the light. The curves are plotted from the values given in Figure 3.8. Notice that the V_{TONE} and V_{LIGHT} curves are summed to give the V_{SUM} curve. The V_{SUM} curve represents the expected strength of the CR as extinction proceeds.

light and for the light presented by itself. As you can see, when both light and tone are presented, the extinction curve reaches near zero associative strength by the 10th trial. When the light is presented by itself during extinction, it still has about 13 units of strength remaining after trial 10. Although more rapid extinction is predicted when both tone and light are presented concurrently, we do not know of any experiment that directly tests this possibility.

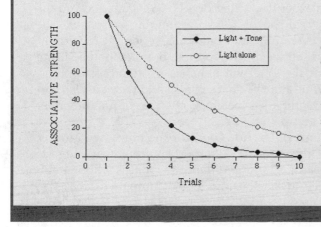

FIG. 4.5 Extinction curves predicted by the Rescorla-Wagner equation. The open circles are generated by predicting the course of simple extinction. That is, a CS is paired with a US until it evokes a CR at close to asymptote, and then the CS is placed on extinction. The closed circles show the expected curve when the CS is placed on extinction and a second stimulus (tone) is paired with it.

PAIRING, CORRELATION, AND CONDITIONING

As we have noted, the Rescorla-Wagner (Rescorla & Wagner, 1972) model is an S-R behavioral theory based on the close **temporal pairing** of stimuli. Most of the early work on respondent conditioning assumed that temporal pairing of the CS and US was necessary to establish an association. Even though the Rescorla-Wagner model is based on pairing of stimuli, Rescorla has suggested that correlation rather than temporal pairing is the critical factor in respondent conditioning. Rescorla based this conclusion on several experiments that he conducted (Rescorla, 1966, 1968, 1969). His early experiments seemed to imply that a correlation between CS and US resulted in conditioning, while mere pairing of stimuli did not. In fact, as we shall see, Rescorla-Wagner's behavioral approach was on the right track while the Rescorla correlational approach did not hold up to experimental tests.

The correlational hypothesis arose from an intriguing set of experiments in the mid-1960s. In one experiment, Rescorla (1966) placed dogs in a box that had a barrier in the center, and the dogs were trained to avoid an electric shock by jumping from one side of the box to the other. After the animal jumped to one side or the other, a shock would occur following a 30-second "safe period." The dogs could avoid all shocks by jumping back and forth about every 30 seconds. Eventually, the dogs jumped over the barrier at a steady rate. This steady rate of avoiding the shocks served as a baseline for subsequent experimental conditions.

In the next phase of the experiment, the dogs were forced to stay in one side of the box, and they were presented with tones and shocks for several sessions. For one group of dogs, a 5-second tone was always followed by shock. The tone and shock were *explicitly paired* for these animals. In a second group, the tone signaled a shock-free period of 30 seconds, but shocks were still delivered during the session. Tone and shock were *explicitly unpaired*. A third group of dogs received shocks and tones on a random basis. In this *random control group*, shocks and tones were frequently paired but there was no correlation between them.

During the final phase of this experiment, Rescorla (1966) again allowed the dogs to jump back and forth to avoid shocks. Once responding was stable, the tone was turned on for 5 seconds every now and then, in a series of probe trials. For the dogs that had the tone and shock explicitly paired, both temporal pairing and correlation views predict that the tone will enhance avoidance responses. This is because in this group, the tone and shock are paired and they are also correlated. As expected by both views, the tone increased the rate of jumping over the barrier in the explicitly paired group.

Correlation and pairing accounts differ, however, for the other two groups. When tone and shocks were explicitly unpaired, a temporal pairing view suggests that there will be no associative learning, and avoidance responses will be unaffected by the presentation of the tone. In fact, the dogs' rate of jumping decreased—suggesting that the tone had acquired associative strength because it signaled a safe period of no shocks. In casual language, the dogs did not expect to get shocked after the tone came on, and because of this they jumped the barrier less frequently.

In the random group, in which tone and shocks were often paired but the tone did not predict the occurrence of shock, a temporal pairing account suggests that the tone will gain associative strength because of its occasional pairing with the aversive stimulus. The tone should therefore increase avoidance responding when it is presented. A correlation view predicts that the tone will not gain in associative strength because there is no correlation between tone and shock—just random pairings. This was the result; the tone had no effect on rate of jumping.

Based on this and other experiments (Rescorla, 1968), Rescorla concluded that pairing theory was only one way to produce classical conditioning. He hypothesized that the CS must have informational value in the sense that it predicts the occurrence or absence of the unconditioned stimulus. He stated:

> the notion of [correlation] differs from that of pairing in that it includes not only what events are paired but also what events are not paired. As used here, [correlation] refers to the relative probability of occurrence of US in the presence of CS as contrasted with its probability in the absence of CS. The [correlation] notion suggests that, in fact, conditioning only occurs when these probabilities differ. (Rescorla, 1968, p. 1)

The central idea is that a **correlation** must exist between the CS and US. This means that when the CS occurs, the US is likely to occur or, conversely, when the CS is withheld the US is unlikely.

Rescorla's correlational hypothesis is widely accepted and has generated considerable research. Many researchers have interpreted correlation effects in cognitive terms involving information processing. The animal (or person) is said to "compute probabilities ... and the outcome of this computation determines whether a potential CS will actually be an effective CS" (Schwartz, 1989, p. 110). However, a recent review by Papini and Bitterman (1990) suggests that the correlational or informational approach is incorrect. They point out that Rescorla himself rejected the correlational hypothesis presented in his 1968 article when he proposed the Rescorla-Wagner model, which is based on a novel view of temporal pairing (Rescorla & Wagner, 1972).

FOCUS ON TEACHING
An Explanatory Note to the Student

It is important to realize that Rescorla has been on both sides of the debate between correlation and pairing accounts of classical conditioning. The Rescorla-Wagner model is a sophisticated theory of CS-US pairing and does not require cognitive interpretations involving predictiveness or information processing. Surprisingly though, Rescorla goes beyond his own behavioral theory to ask "what is learned[?] What is associated with what? . . . [A] good summary statement is that signals that are informative about the unconditioned stimulus become associated with it" (Rescorla, 1980, pp. 70–71). It appears to us that Rescorla views the Rescorla-Wagner model as a descriptive theory of conditioning, but not as an explanation.

In his late 1960s work, Rescorla conducted experiments that seemed to require a cognitive interpretation. Based on criticism by Estes (1969) and findings from his own experiments (Rescorla, 1969, 1972), Rescorla began to wonder how organisms might "bring together the effects of events separated in time in such a way as to permit all learning to depend on events occurring closely in time" (Rescorla, 1969, p. 88). According to Papini and Bitterman (1990), Wagner was also concerned with this problem and, using an idea suggested by Kamin (1969), Rescorla and Wagner invented the behavioral theory known as the Rescorla-Wagner model. This model accounted for the puzzling findings of Rescorla (1966, 1968) without reference to cognitive processes.

Rescorla, and others, continue to assert the cognitive/informational view based on the correlation approach. However, Papini and Bitterman (1990) showed that a number of experiments refute the correlation hypothesis. At present, the behavioral theory of Rescorla-Wagner, based on the close temporal pairing of stimuli, has considerable support and there is little evidence against it.

Another confusing aspect of this literature is based on terminology. The words *contiguity* and *contingency* are usually used to refer to the pairing and correlation hypotheses, respectively. These words are easily confused by students and we have not used them in the description of Rescorla's experiments. In classical conditioning, the term *contingency* refers to the percentage of conditioning trials in which the CS is followed by the US, or the percentage of trials in which the CS is not followed by the unconditioned stimulus. In other words, contingency is the same as a correlation between CS and US. *Contiguity*, on the other hand, means presenting two or more stimuli closely together in time (i.e., pairing the stimuli).

Rejection of the Information Hypothesis

In a 1969 article, Estes noted that in the Rescorla experiments, said to show the effects of correlation (Rescorla, 1966, 1968), there was a major problem. The problem concerned the effects of contextual stimuli in the random control group (see the section "Pairing, Correlation, and Conditioning" in this chapter). **Contextual stimuli** are uncontrolled sights, sounds, smells, and so on that are the background for CS-US conditioning. Estes's idea was that when conditioning occurred, the CS was accidentally paired with the shock but other stimuli were also being conditioned. Over time, the contextual stimuli would gain associative strength and eventually overshadow the effect of the CS. For this reason, Rescorla (1966, 1968) found the tone had no effect on avoidance responding. The longer the animals remained in the inescapable random-shock condition, the less effect the CS should have had on jumping the barrier. This conjecture was subsequently tested and confirmed by Rescorla (1972), who concluded that "it is not simply the [lack of correlation] between the CS and US which generates the absence of conditioning in the [random control group] but the conditioning of other [contextual] stimuli present in the situation" (Rescorla, 1972, p. 26).

The importance of this finding cannot be overstated. Originally, Rescorla had used the evidence from the random control group to argue that the CS must predict the US in order to produce conditioning. The finding that conditioning can occur with zero correlation between CS and US is damaging to an informational approach. Also, the results of Rescorla's (1972) experiment strongly suggest that pairing the CS with the US, in context, is the critical factor for conditioning. Overall, by 1972 it was apparent that a temporal paring account that included reference to background or context was correct. The Rescorla-Wagner model was offered as this account.

Since 1968, several major studies have refuted Rescorla's (1968) informational hypothesis (e.g., for aversive experiments see Ayres, Benedict, & Witcher, 1975; Benedict & Ayres, 1972; Keller, Ayres, & Mahoney, 1977; Kremer, 1971; Kremer & Kamin, 1971; Seligman, 1968; Wagner & Larew, 1985, and for positive reinforcement experiments see Durlach, 1982, 1983; Gamzu & Schwartz, 1973; Goddard & Jenkins, 1987; Rescorla, 1989). Papini and Bitterman (1990) reviewed these experiments and concluded that "the evidence suggests that CS-US [correlation] is neither necessary nor sufficient for conditioning and that the concept has long outlived any usefulness it may once have had in the analysis of conditioning" (p. 396).

Although the information hypothesis has been disconfirmed, many researchers who gathered the negative evidence (and others) still advocate a cognitive view of conditioning. In trying to explain this behavioral persistence, Papini and Bitterman (1990) stated:

> an interesting question is why the idea that conditioning depends on [correlation] should have continued to find wide acceptance in the face of so much contrary evidence. We have referred already to its [the correlation view] congruence with the cognitive and pseudoevolutionary thinking of recent decades and to the indelible influence of Rescorla's 1966 and 1968 results taken at face value and in isolation. Important, too, is a certain blurring of distinctions between the [correla-

tion] view and Rescorla-Wagner theory [the pairing view], based perhaps on common authorship and broad structural similarity, which has permitted the one to profit from the achievements of the other. The success of Rescorla-Wagner theory in accounting for Rescorla's 1966 and 1968 results has seemed somehow to validate the original interpretation of them and to create a spurious impression of compatibility.... There is no dependence of conditioning on [correlation], nor was the Rescorla-Wagner theory predicated on the assumption that there is, and many of the results that contradict the [correlation] view can be understood in terms of the Rescorla-Wagner theory, which suggested many of the experiments that produced these contradictory results in the first place. For a more complete answer to the question, we look to philosophers and historians of science, who might find much of value in entertaining it. (p. 401)

ON THE APPLIED SIDE: DRUG USE, ABUSE, AND CONDITIONING

Basic research on simple and complex (i.e., contextual effects) respondent conditioning has applied importance. Recently, the U.S. government has declared a war on the import and use of illegal drugs. One result of this is that more money is being spent on research to identify the factors that affect drug use and abuse. Several experiments have shown that conditioned stimuli can produce druglike effects in both humans and other animals, disrupting behavior and producing physiological changes. In addition, stimuli that have been paired with drugs sometimes produce internal conditioned responses that are opposite to the unconditioned effects of the drug. For example, when animals are injected with insulin, the unconditioned response is a reduction in blood sugar. The response to a stimulus that has been paired with insulin is exactly the opposite; blood sugar levels increase (Siegel, 1972, 1975).

Similar counteractive effects have been found with drugs other than insulin. For example, amphetamine reduces appetite, but a CS that has been paired with it increases food intake (Poulos, Wilkinson, & Cappell, 1981). Pentobarbital is a sedative, but the response to a conditioned stimulus associated with pentobarbital counteracts the drowsiness ordinarily associated with the drug (Hinson, Poulos, & Cappell, 1982).

Effects such as these suggest that respondent conditioning plays a major role in drug tolerance. With repeated pairings of a drug (US) and a CS, the conditioned response gains in strength and increasingly opposes the unconditioned effects of the drug. This means it will take larger and larger amounts of the drug to reach the same high. In everyday life, conditioned stimuli arise from the time of day that a drug is taken, the way it is administered (e.g., using a needle), the location such as a tavern or home, and social events like a party or dance.

Heroin Overdose and Context

A consideration of drug tolerance as a conditioned response helps to explain instances of drug overdose. Heroin addicts are known to survive a drug dose that would kill a person who did not regularly use the drug. In spite of this high level of tolerance, approximately 1% of heroin addicts die from drug overdose each year. These victims typically die from drug-induced respiratory depression. Surprisingly, many of these addicts die from a dose that is similar to the amount of heroin they usually took each day.

Siegel, Hinson, Krank, and McCully (1982) proposed that these deaths resulted from "a failure of tolerance. That is, the opiate addict, who can usually tolerate extraordinarily high doses, is not tolerant on the occasion of the overdose" (p. 436). They suggested that when a drug is administered in the usual context, the CSs that counteract the drug allow for a large dose. When the situation in which the drug is taken is changed, the CSs are not present, the opposing conditioned response does not occur, and the drug is sufficient to kill the user. Siegel and associates designed an animal experiment to test these ideas.

Male rats were injected with heroin every other day for 30 days. The amount of heroin was gradually increased to a dose level that would produce tolerance to the drug. On nonheroin days, these rats were injected with dextrose solution (i.e., sugar and water). Both heroin and dextrose injections were given in one of two distinctive contexts—the ordinary colony room that the rats lived in, or a different room with constant white noise. A control group of rats was injected only with the dextrose solution in the two situations. The researchers expected that experimental animals would develop a tolerance to the drug. This tolerance would occur if aspects of the room in which heroin was given became CSs that evoked opposing responses to the drug.

To test this assumption, Siegel and colleagues (1982) doubled the amount of heroin given to experimental animals. The same high dose of heroin was given to the control group, who had no history of tolerance. Half of the experimental animals received this larger dose in the room where the drug was usually adminis-

FIG. 4.6 Results of the experiment by Siegel, Hinson, Krank, and McCully (1982). The *same room* group of rats received the higher dose in the room where they usually were injected with heroin, and only 32% died. Twice as many animals in the *different room* condition died from the larger dose presumably because they were injected in a room where heroin had not been given. Heroin killed almost all of the animals in the control group (reprinted with permission of *Science*).

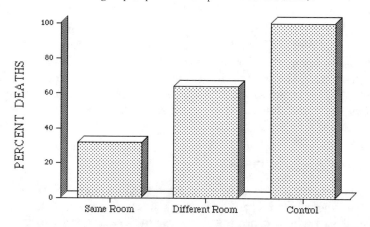

tered. The other addicted rats were injected with the higher dose in the room where they usually received a dextrose injection.

Figure 4.6 shows the results of this experiment. As you can see, the large dose of heroin killed almost all of the animals in the control group. For the two groups of animals with a history of heroin use, one group *(same room)* received the higher dose in the room where they usually were injected with heroin. Only 32% of the rats died in this condition, presumably because the CSs set off the opposing conditioned responses. This inference is supported by the mortality rate of rats in the *different room* group. These rats were injected with the double dose of heroin in a room that had never been associated with heroin administration. Twice as many animals in this condition died from the larger dose (64%) when compared to the *same room* group. As you can see, the effects of context during this kind of respondent conditioning can be a matter of life or death—tolerance to heroin (and perhaps other drugs) is relative to the situation in which the conditioning has occurred.

KEY WORDS

Associative strength

Blocking

Change in associative
  strength

Compound stimuli

Conditioned inhibition

Conditioned suppression

Contextual stimuli

Contiguity

Contingency

Correlation

Maximum associative
  strength

Overshadowing

Rescorla-Wagner model

Sensory preconditioning

Temporal pairing

CHAPTER 5

Reinforcement and Extinction of Operant Behavior

LEARNING OBJECTIVES
---

1. How do consequences regulate behavior?

2. Summarize what is meant by "operant conditioning is based on genetic endowment."

3. Discuss operant behavior, voluntary action, and the source of the term *operant*. Name and define one kind of positive consequence of operant behavior.

4. Operants are said to be emitted, while reflexes are elicited. Why?

5. What is a discriminative stimulus? Give some examples of common S^Ds and indicate when an event is operating as a discriminative stimulus. What is the relationship between an S^D and the consequences of operant behavior? Compare an S^D with a stimulus that signals extinction (S^Δ) and give an example of an S^Δ function.

6. What is a three-term contingency of reinforcement? Outline the role of the discriminative stimulus in such a contingency. Show that the S^D function depends on reinforcement of operant behavior.

7. Define the four basic contingencies and give everyday examples of each.

8. Rewards either do or do not lead to a decrease in intrinsic motivation when they are removed. What evidence supports one or the other view?

9. In terms of creativity, reinforcement seems to have several positive effects. What are these effects?

10. Discuss Thorndike's early research, his law of effect, and the modern principle of reinforcement.

11. What is wrong with so-called trial-and-error learning and measures of response latency? Why is rate of response a preferred measure of operant behavior?

12. In operant conditioning, discuss the advantage of the free operant method. How does the operant chamber structure the situation for conditioning?

13. In a demonstration of operant conditioning, what is the role of deprivation, magazine training, a well-defined response, operant level, successive approximation, and recording of behavior? Outline a model operant-conditioning experiment using a pigeon as the subject.

14. Define the procedure and processes of extinction. Discuss the extinction burst and when it occurs. Describe what happens to response topography during extinction, referring to the Antonitis (1951) experiment.

15. Summarize the research and findings of Barry Schwartz (1982a, 1982b) on reinforcement and response stereotypy. Outline Allen Neuringer's (1986) research and findings on reinforcement of response variability. What do both lines of research suggest about reinforcement, problem solving, and creativity?

16. How does extinction affect response force and emotional responses? What is discriminated extinction?

17. Discuss resistance to extinction and resistance following intermittent reinforcement. Show how discriminative stimuli play a role in resistance to extinction, using the Skinner (1950) experiment.

18. Define and discuss spontaneous recovery. Give a textbook example of human behavior that illustrates spontaneous recovery.

19 Discuss a procedural difference between forgetting and extinction. How did Skinner (1938) test this difference and what did he find?

20. What effect did the passage of time have on the behavior of pigeons used in Project Pigeon (Skinner, 1960)? Draw out the implications of this research for commonsense notions about forgetting.

21. Outline Williams's (1959) study of temper tantrums and the role of extinction in this study. What happened when the boy's aunt stayed in the room when he cried? Why?

A hungry lion returns to the waterhole where it has successfully ambushed antelope and other prey. A person who plays a slot machine and wins a large jackpot is more likely to play again than a person who does not win. Students who ask questions and are told, "That is an interesting point worth discussing" are prone to ask more questions. When a professor ignores questions or gives fuzzy answers, students eventually stop asking questions. In these cases (and many others), the consequences that follow behavior determine whether it will be repeated in the future.

Operant behavior that is followed by reinforcing consequences is selected in the sense that it increases in frequency. Behavior that is not followed by reinforcing consequences decreases in frequency. This process, called **operant conditioning,** is a major way that the behavior of organisms is changed on the basis of ontogeny or life experience. It is important, however, to recognize that operant conditioning, as a process, has evolved over species history and is based on genetic endowment. That is, operant (and respondent) conditioning as a *general be-*

havior-change process is based on phylogeny. In other words, those organisms whose behavior changed on the basis of consequences were more likely to survive and reproduce than animals that did not.

OPERANT BEHAVIOR

Operant behavior is commonly described as intentional, free, voluntary, or willful. Examples of operant behavior include conversations with others, driving a car, taking notes, reading a book, and painting a picture. From a scientific perspective, operant behavior is lawful and may be analyzed in terms of its relationship to environmental events. Formally, responses that produce a change in the environment are called **operants**. The term *operant* comes from the verb *to operate* and refers to behavior that operates on the environment to produce a consequence. The consequences of operant behavior are many and varied and occur across all sensory dimensions. When you turn on a light, dial a telephone, drive a car, or open a door, these operants result in visual clarity, conversation, reaching a destination, and entering a room. A **positive reinforcer** is defined as any consequence that increases the probability of the operant that produced it. For example, pretend that your car will not start, but when you jiggle the ignition key it fires right up. In this case, the operant—jiggling the key—is likely to be repeated the next time the car won't start.

Operants are defined by the consequences they produce. Thus, opening the door to reach the other side is the operant, not the physical movement of manipulating the door. Operants are a class of responses that may vary in **topography.** Topography refers to the physical form or characteristics of the response. Consider the number of different ways you could open a door—you may turn the handle, push it with your foot, or (if your arms are full of books) ask someone to open it for you. All of these responses vary in topography and result in reaching the other side of the door. Because these responses result in the same consequence, they are members of the same **operant class**. Thus, the term *operant* refers to a class of related responses that may vary in topography but produce a common environmental consequence (Catania, 1973).

Discriminative Stimuli

Operant behavior is said to be emitted in the sense that it often occurs without an observable stimulus preceding it. This is in contrast to reflexive responses, which are elicited by a preceding stimulus. Reflexes are tied to the physiology of an organism and, under appropriate conditions, always occur when the eliciting stimulus is presented. For example, Pavlov showed that dogs automatically salivated when food was placed in their mouths. Dogs do not learn the relationship between food and salivation; this reflex is a characteristic of the species. Stimuli may also precede operant behavior. However, these events do not force the occurrence of the response that follows them. An event that precedes an operant and alters its likelihood is said to *set the occasion for behavior* and is called a **discriminative stimulus,** or S^D.

Discriminative stimuli change the probability that an operant will be emitted. The probability of emitting an operant in the presence of an S^D may be very high, but these stimuli do not have a one-to-one relationship with the response that follows them. For example, a telephone ring increases the chances that you will emit the operant, answering the telephone, but it does not force you to do so. Similarly, a nudge under the table may set the occasion for changing the conversation or just shutting up. The events that occasion operant behavior may be private as well as public. Thus, a private event like a headache, may set the occasion for taking an aspirin.

Discriminative stimuli are defined by the operants that are occasioned by these stimuli. The probability of raising your hand in class is much greater when the instructor is present than when he or she is absent. Thus, the presence of an instructor is an S^D for asking questions in class. The teacher functions as an S^D only when his or her presence changes student behavior. The student who is having difficulty with a math problem may ask questions when the teacher enters the room. However, a student who is easily mastering the material is unlikely to do this. For this reason, the teacher functions as an S^D (for asking questions) for the first student but not the second. This discussion should make it clear that a stimulus is defined as an S^D only when it changes the probability of operant behavior. You may typically stop when you pull up to a traffic sign that reads STOP; the sign is a discriminative stimulus. If, however, you are driving a badly injured friend to the hospital, the same sign may not function as an S^D. Thus, discriminative stimuli are not defined by physical measures (e.g., color, size, tone); rather, they are defined as stimuli that precede and alter the probability of operant responses.

The consequences that follow operant behavior establish the control exerted by discriminative stimuli. When an S^D is followed by an operant that produces positive reinforcement, the operant is more likely to occur the next time the stimulus is present. For example, a student may ask a particular teaching assistant questions because in the past that teaching assistant has provided clear and concise answers. In this example, the assistant is an S^D and asking questions is the operant that increases in his or her presence. When an operant does not produce reinforcement, the stimulus that precedes the response is called an **S-delta (S^Δ)**. In the presence of an S^Δ, the probability of emitting an operant declines. For example, if a second teaching assistant answers questions in a confused and muddled fashion, the student will be less likely to ask that person questions. In this case the second teaching assistant becomes an S^Δ and the probability of asking questions declines in his or her presence.

Contingencies of Reinforcement

A **contingency of reinforcement** defines the relationship between the events that set the occasion for behavior, the operant class, and the consequences that follow this behavior. In a dark room (S^D), when you flip on a light switch (R), the light usually comes on (S^r). This behavior does not guarantee that the room will light up, the bulb may be burned out or the switch broken. It is likely that the light will come on, but it is not certain. In behavioral terms, the probability of reinforcement is high, but it is not absolute. This probability may vary between 0 and 100%. A high probability of reinforcement for turning the switch to the "on" position will establish and maintain a high likelihood of this behavior.

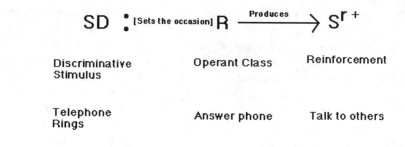

FIG. 5.1 The three-term contingency of reinforcement. A discriminitive stimulus (S^D) sets the occasion for operant behavior (R), which is followed by a consequence (S^r).

Discriminative stimuli that precede behavior have an important role in the regulation of operant responses (Skinner, 1969). Signs that read OPEN, RESUME SPEED or RESTAURANT, green traffic lights, a smile from across the room, and so on are examples of simple discriminative stimuli that may set the occasion for specific operants. These events regulate behavior because of a **history of reinforcement** in their presence. A smile from across a room may set the occasion for approaching and talking to the person who smiled. This is because, in the past, people who smiled reinforced social interaction.

Each of these events—the occasion, the operant, and the consequences of behavior—make up the contingency of reinforcement. Consider the example of this three-part contingency shown in Figure 5.1. The telephone ring is a discriminative stimulus that sets the occasion for the operant class of answering the phone. This behavior occurs because, in the past, the operant was reinforced by talking to the other party. The probability of response is very high in the presence of the ring, but it is not inevitable. Perhaps you are in the process of leaving for an important meeting, or you are in the bathtub.

Discriminative stimuli regulate behavior, but they do not stand alone. The consequences that follow behavior determine the probability of response in the presence of the discriminative stimulus. For example, most people show a high probability of answering the telephone when it rings. However, if the phone is faulty so that it rings but you cannot hear the other party when you answer it, the probability of answering the phone decreases as a function of nonreinforcement. In other words, you stop answering a phone that does not work.

Four Basic Contingencies

There are four basic contingencies of reinforcement. Events that follow behavior may be either presented or removed (environmental operation). These events can increase or decrease behavior (effect on behavior). The cells of the matrix in Figure 5.2 define the basic contingencies of reinforcement.

Positive Reinforcement. **Positive reinforcement** is one of the four basic contingencies of operant behavior. Positive reinforcement is portrayed in Figure 5.1 (cell 1), where a stimulus follows behavior and, as a result, the rate of that behav-

Effect on Behavior

Stimulus Following Behavior	Increase	Decrease
On/Presented	1 Positive Reinforcement	2 Positive Punishment
Off/Removed	3 Negative Reinforcement	4 Negative Punishment

FIG. 5.2 This figure shows the four basic contingencies of reinforcement. The stimulus following a response (consequence) can be either presented (turned on) or removed (turned off). The effect of these procedures is to increase or decrease rate of response. The cells of the matrix, in this figure, define the contingencies of reinforcement. A particular contingency of reinforcement depends whether the stimulus following behavior is presented or removed and whether behavior increases or decreases in frequency.

ior increases. For example, a child is praised for sharing a toy (operant behavior), and the child begins to share toys more regularly (increase in response strength). Positively reinforcing events usually include consequences such as food, praise, and money. *These events, however, cannot be called positive reinforcers until they have been shown to increase behavior.*

FOCUS ON RESEARCH
Reinforcement, Intrinsic Motivation, and Creativity

Over the past 25 years, many social psychologists have been critical of the practice of using rewards in business, education, and behavior modification programs. The concern is that rewards (reward and reinforcement are often used similarly in this literature) are experienced as controlling, thereby leading to a reduction in an individual's self-determination, intrinsic motivation, and creative performance (e.g., see Amabile, 1990; Deci & Ryan, 1985; Kohn, 1993; Lepper, Greene, & Nisbett, 1973). Thus, when a child who enjoys drawing is rewarded for drawing, with praise or with **tangible rewards** like points or money, the child's motivation to draw decreases. From this perspective, the child will come to draw less and enjoy it less once the reward is discontinued. Further, it is alleged that the drawings produced by the child will be less creative than those drawn by children not given the reward. In other words, the contention is that reinforcement/reward reduces people's intrinsic motivation and creativity. This view has been enormously influential and has led to a decline in the use of rewards and incentive systems in many applied settings.

In an article published in 1996 in *American Psychologist*, Dr. Robert Eisenberger, a professor of psychology at the University of Delaware, and Dr. Judy Cameron, an associate professor of educational psychology at the University of Alberta, provided an objective and comprehensive analysis of the literature concerned with the effects of reinforcement/reward on people's intrinsic motivation and creativity. Contrary to the belief of

FIG. 5.3 A). Dr. Judy Cameron.   B). Dr. Robert Eisenberger.

many psychologists, their findings indicated no inherent negative property of reward. In-stead, their research demonstrates that reward has a much more favorable effect on task interest and creativity than is generally supposed.

Rewards and Intrinsic Motivation

Those who oppose the use of rewards support their position by citing experimental stud-ies on rewards and its effects on intrinsic motivation (Schwartz, 1990). A cursory exami-nation of these experiments reveals a mixed set of findings. That is, in some studies, ex-trinsic rewards reduce performance or interest; other studies find positive effects of reward; still others show no effect. In order to make sense of these diverse findings, Judy Cameron and her colleagues (Cameron & Eisenberger, 1997; Cameron & Pierce, 1994; Eisenberger & Cameron, 1996) conducted a quantitative analysis of this literature to de-termine whether rewards really do negatively affect people's intrinsic task interest. The analysis also focused on the conditions under which rewards produce increments or decrements in task interest. Using a statistical procedure known as meta-analysis, the re-sults from over 100 experiments on rewards and intrinsic motivation were analyzed.

The findings indicated that rewards can be used effectively to enhance or maintain an individual's intrinsic interest in activities. Specifically, verbal rewards (praise, positive feedback) were found to increase people's performance and interest on tasks. In terms of tangible rewards, the results from the meta-analysis point to the importance of reward contingency as a major determinant of intrinsic motivation. When tangible rewards were offered to people for solving problems, completing a task, or for attaining a specific level of performance, intrinsic task interest was enhanced. The only situation in which tangible rewards were found to slightly decrease intrinsic motivation involved offering a reward to individuals regardless of task completion or performance quality.

Eisenberger and Cameron (1996) concluded that intrinsic task interest and performance can be enhanced when individuals receive verbal praise, positive feedback, or when tangible rewards are offered for task completion or for attaining or exceeding a performance standard. The view that rewards undermine people's intrinsic motivation is an overgeneralization. Eisenberger and Cameron pointed out that these findings run contrary to the popular argument that rewards have generalized negative effects on people's intrinsic motivation.

Rewards and Creativity

The generalization that rewards lessen creativity has also been commonly accepted as a fact. The most widely studied form of creativity is divergent thinking, involving varied novel responses to a problem or a question that has multiple possible solutions. Many researchers have reported that offering an individual a reward results in reduced divergent thinking (e.g., Amabile, 1990; Condry, 1977; Deci & Ryan, 1985). Robert Eisenberger has suggested that failures to find increased creativity, resulting from reward, may have occurred because the reward was not actually contingent on creative performance. Because people are rewarded more for conventional performance in their everyday lives, they may fall back on conventional performance when a reward is offered with no indication that creativity is preferred. Given this interpretation, Eisenberger and his associates hypothesized that promising reward for creative performance should increase creativity. In one experiment, Eisenberger, Armeli, and Pretz (1998) reported that children who were told explicitly that drawing novel pictures would produce a monetary reward drew more unusual pictures than children who were promised a reward for undefined drawing performance or for children who were told to draw novel pictures without any mention of reward.

Eisenberger and his colleagues also investigated the generalized effects of reward for a high degree of creativity. Eisenberger (1992) assumed that individuals learn which dimensions of performance (e.g., speed, accuracy, or novelty) are rewarded, and generalize rewarded performance in those dimensions to new activities. In his theory of *learned industriousness,* Eisenberger predicts that rewarding high divergent thinking on one task should increase creativity in an entirely different task. In a test of this contention, Eisenberger and Armeli (1997) asked children to state unusual uses of everyday objects (e.g., paper bag, chair) for which they received no reward, a small monetary reward, or a large monetary reward. When next asked to draw pictures, without the promise of reward, the children who had previously received a large monetary reward (for giving unusual uses of objects) drew the most creative pictures.

Taken together, Eisenberger and Cameron's research and their 1996 *American Psychologist* review article, suggests that (a) the explicit promise of reward for creative performance increases creativity; (b) reward for creative performance produces a generalized increase in novel performance that affects new tasks; (c) in general, rewards increase intrinsic interest and task enjoyment; and (d) the view that rewards undermine people's intrinsic motivation is an overgeneralization based on a restricted set of conditions. In summary, Eisenberger and Cameron point out that rewards can have strong positive effects on creativity and intrinsic motivation.

Negative Reinforcement.   When a response results in the removal of an event, and this procedure increases the rate of that response, the contingency is called **negative reinforcement**. This contingency is shown in cell 3 of the matrix in Figure 5.2. Negative reinforcement is commonly misunderstood as punishment. However, the matrix makes it clear that negative reinforcement involves completely different procedures and effects than positive or negative punishment.

Negative reinforcement plays a major role in the regulation of everyday human behavior. For example, you put on sunglasses because in the past this behavior removed the glare of the sun. You open your umbrella when it is raining because doing so has prevented you from getting wet. You leave the room when someone is rude or critical because this behavior has ended other similar conversations. Consider that you live in a place with a very sensitive smoke detector. Each time you are cooking, the smoke detector goes off. You might remove the sound by tripping the breaker or fuse that controls the alarm. In fact, you will probably learn to do this each time before cooking. As a final example, a mother may pick up and rock her crying baby because, in the past, comforting the child has stopped the crying. In each of these instances, an operant is strengthened by removing an aversive event.

Positive Punishment.   Cell 2 of the matrix in Figure 5.2 depicts a situation in which responses produce an event and rate of behavior decreases. This contingency is called **positive punishment**. For example, spanking a child who runs onto a busy road is positive punishment if the child now stops or turns before reaching the road. In everyday life, people often talk about punishment (and reinforcement) without reference to behavior. For example, a mother scolds her child for playing with matches. The child continues to play with matches, and the parents may comment that "punishment doesn't work with Nathan." In behavior analysis, positive punishment is defined functionally (i.e., by its effects). When behavior is not changed by apparently aversive events, punishment has not occurred. In other words, the parents are arranging an ineffective contingency. The parents could identify an aversive event that reliably decreases behavior; however, this strategy may backfire. For example, as you will see in Chapter 9, punishment may produce serious emotional and aggressive behavior. Because of this, punishment should be used only as a last resort for the modification of severe behavior problems.

Negative Punishment.   Punishment can also be arranged by removing stimuli contingent on behavior (cell 4 in Figure 5.2). This contingency is called **negative punishment**. In this case, the removal of an event or stimulus decreases operant behavior. Two children are watching a favorite television program and begin to fight with one another. The parent says, "that's enough fighting" and turns off the television. You tell a sexist joke and people stop talking to you. At school, a student who is passing notes is required to leave the room for a short period of time. In these examples, watching television, talking to others, and participating in classroom activities are assumed to be reinforcing events. When removal of these events contingent on fighting, telling sexist jokes, and passing notes decreases such behavior, negative punishment has occurred.

As you have seen, there are four basic contingencies of reinforcement. In each case, a stimulus is presented or removed contingent on operant behavior. The contingency is defined as punishment or reinforcement (either positive or negative) by its effects on behavior. One hundred dollars will probably strengthen operants that produce it (e.g., betting 25 cents and pulling the handle on a slot machine). Once a stimulus has been shown to increase the rate of operant behavior it may be called a **positive reinforcer.** The stimulus $100 may be defined as reinforcement *after its effects are demonstrated.* That is, a positive reinforcer or reinforcing stimulus is one that increases the rate of operant that it follows.

This definition of reinforcement is circular. One hundred dollars is defined as a positive reinforcer because it increases the frequency of betting 25 cents and pulling the handle on the slot machine. At the same time, betting and pulling the handle on the slot machine is said to increase because it is reinforced with a hundred dollars. In order to avoid this circularity of definition, Meehl (1950) introduced the concept of **trans-situationality.** Simply stated, once a stimulus is identified as a reinforcing (or punishing) stimulus in one situation, it will also be a reinforcer (or punisher) in other situations. That is, a consequence that has been shown to increase (or decrease) the frequency of behavior may, with only a very few exceptions (see Chapter 6), be used to strengthen (or weaken) other operants in other settings.

Another way that circularity is circumvented has to do with a consideration of what is called the **Premack principle.** David Premack (1959) proposed that reinforcement involved a contingency between two sets of behaviors, operant behavior and reinforcing behavior (behavior^{operant} → behavior^{Sr+}), rather than between an operant response (behavior) and a stimulus (R → S^{r+}). That is, it is more accurate to describe reinforcing events as actions of the organism rather than as discrete stimuli. Thus, reinforcement involves eating rather than food; drinking rather than water; reading rather than a book, and so on.

Premack's principle has obvious applied implications (see Chapter 14), and it provides a way to define reinforcement in a non-circular fashion. Behavior is measured in a situation where all relevant behavior can occur without restriction. For example, a child is observed in a situation where doing homework, watching television, playing with toys, recreational reading, etc. may all freely occur. Once baseline measures of behavior have been taken, the **Premack principle** predicts that any higher frequency (or duration) behavior may serve as reinforcement for any lower frequency behavior. If television watching is longer in duration than doing homework, watching television may be made contingent on completing homework assignments. This contingency will increase the number of completed homework assignments.

Operant Conditioning

Operant conditioning refers to an increase or decrease in operant behavior as a function of a contingency of reinforcement. In a simple demonstration of operant conditioning, an experimenter may alter the consequences that follow operant behavior. The effects of environmental consequences on behavior were first described in 1911 by the American psychologist E. L. Thorndike, who reported results from a series of animal experiments that eventually formed the basis of operant conditioning. Cats, dogs, and chicks were placed in situations in which they could obtain food by performing complex sequences of behavior. For example, hungry cats were confined to an apparatus that Thorndike called a puzzle box, shown in Figure 5.4. Food was placed outside the box, and if the cat managed to pull out a bolt, step on a lever, or emit some other behavior, the door would open and the animal could eat the food.

After some time in the box, the cat would accidentally pull the bolt or step on the lever and the door would open. Thorndike measured the time from closing the trap door until the cat managed to get it open. This measure, called a **latency,** tended to decrease with repeated exposures to the box. In other words, the cats took less and less time to escape from the apparatus as they were given more trials. According to Thorndike, the puzzle-box experiment demonstrated learning by trial and error. That is, the cats repeatedly tried to get out of the box and made fewer and fewer errors. Thorndike made similar observations with dogs and chicks and, on the basis of these observations, formulated the **law of effect.** A modern paraphrase of this law is the principle of reinforcement: Operants that

FIG. 5.4 Thorndike's puzzle box for cats. Food was placed outside the box, and if the cat managed to pull out a bolt, step on a lever, and so on, the door would open and the animal could get out of the box and eat the food. When the cats were given repeated trials in the box, they became faster and faster at getting out (from Rachlin 1976, p. 228, based on E. L. Thorndike, 1911).

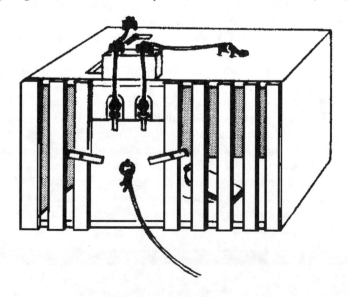

produce positive reinforcers increase in frequency. Skinner (1988) has commented on Thorndike's analysis of trial-and-error learning:

> Thorndike thought he solved *his* problem by saying that the successful cat used trial-and-error learning. The expression is unfortunate. "Try" [from *trial*] implies that a response has already been affected by relevant consequences. A cat is "trying to escape" if it engages in behavior which either has been selected in the evolution of the species because it has brought escape from comparable situations or has been reinforced by escape from aversive stimulation during the life of the cat. The term "error" does not describe behavior, it passes judgment on it. The curves for trial-and-error learning plotted by Thorndike and many others do not represent any useful property of behavior—certainly not a single process called problem solving. The changes which contribute to such a curve include the adaptation and extinction of emotional responses, the conditioning of reinforcers, and the extinction of unrelated responses. Any contribution made by an increase in the probability of the reinforced response is hopelessly obscured. (p. 219)

In other words, Skinner suggests that simply measuring the time (or latency) taken to complete a task misses changes that occur across several operant classes. Responses that resulted in escape and food were selected while other behavior decreased in frequency. Eventually those operants that produced reinforcement came to predominate the cat's behavior. For this reason, the cat got out of the box in progressively less time as trials were repeated. Thus, latency was an indirect measure of a change in the animal's operant behavior. Today, rate of response (frequency of response divided by time) is considered a better measure of operant behavior. Operant rate provides a direct measure of the selection of behavior by its consequences.

Procedures in Operant Conditioning

Rate of Response as a Measure of Response Strength.   Rate of response refers to the number of operant responses that occur in some defined unit of time. For example, if you ask 5 questions during a 2-hour class, your rate is 2.5 questions per hour. An animal that presses a lever 1,000 times in a 1-hour session generates a rate of 1,000 bar presses per hour (or 16.7 responses per minute). The importance of rate of response as a measure of operant behavior was recognized by Skinner (1938). Skinner suggested that rate of response should be the basic datum (or measure) for operant analysis. This is because rate of response is an index of the probability that an operant will occur in the future. In other words, a response that occurs at high rate in one situation has a high probability of being emitted in a similar situation in the future. This increased probability of response is observed as a change in operant rate. Of course, probability of response may decrease and in this case is seen as a decline in rate.

The Free Operant Method.   In the **free operant method,** an animal may repeatedly respond over an extensive period of time. The organism is free to emit many responses or none at all. That is, responses can be made without interference from the experimenter. For example, a laboratory rat may press a lever for food pellets. Lever pressing is under the control of the animal, which may press the bar rapidly, slowly, or quit pressing. Importantly, this method allows the researcher to observe changes in rate of response. This is important because rate of response is used as a measure of response probability. Rate of response must be free to vary if it is used to index the future probability of operant behavior.

The analysis of operant rate and probability of response is not easily accomplished when an organism is given a series of trials (as in the Thorndike experiments). This is because the animal's rate of behavior is largely controlled by the experimenter. For example, a rat that runs down a T-maze for food reward is picked up at the goal box and returned to the starting point. The number of trials (and response opportunities) is set by the experimenter. For this reason, changes in rate of response cannot be directly observed and measured. The free operant method is clearly demonstrated by the procedures involved in operant conditioning.

The Operant Chamber.   To study operant conditioning in a laboratory, a device called an **operant chamber** is used. Of course, operant conditioning is also investigated outside laboratories. Nonetheless, many principles of behavior have been discovered by investigating the behavior of animals in operant chambers. Figure 5.5 shows an operant chamber designed to accommodate a laboratory rat. The chamber is a small enclosed box that contains a lever with a light above it, and a food magazine or cup connected to an external feeder. The feeder delivers a small food pellet (typically, 45 mg) when electronically activated. In this situation, the food pellet serves as reinforcement for lever pressing. The operant cham-

FIG. 5.5 An operant chamber for a rat. The chamber is a small box that has a lever that the animal can press. There is a light above the lever that can be turned on or off. A food magazine or cup is connected to an electronically activated feeder. The feeder delivers a small, 45-mg food pellet to the cup. In this situation, the food pellet serves as reinforcement for lever pressing (photograph by permission of Gerbrands Corporation, Arlington, MA).

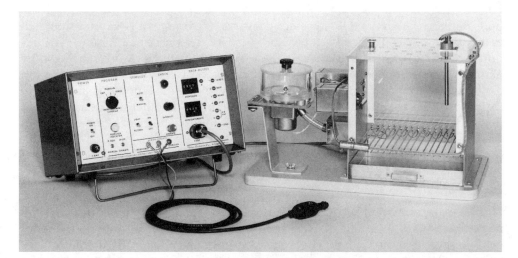

ber structures the situation so that the desired behavior will occur and incompatible behavior is reduced. Thus, lever pressing is highly likely, while behavior like exploring the chamber is minimized.

Deprivation.   Because the delivery of food is used as reinforcement, an animal must be motivated to obtain food. An objective and quantifiable measure of motivation for food is percentage of free-feeding body weight. Prior to a typical experiment, an animal is brought from a commercial (or research) colony into a laboratory, placed in a cage, given free access to food, and weighed on a daily basis. The average weight is calculated, and this value is used as a baseline. Next, the daily food ration is reduced until the animal reaches 85% of its free-feeding weight. The procedure of restricting access to food (the potentially reinforcing stimulus) is called a **deprivation operation.** At this point, the experimenter assumes, but does not know if, food is a reinforcing stimulus. This is because food delivery must increase the frequency of an operant before it can be defined as a reinforcer.

The weight-loss or deprivation criterion is less severe than it first appears. Laboratory animals typically have food freely available 24 hours per day while animals in the wild must forage for their food. The result is that lab animals tend to be heavier than their free-ranging counterparts. Alan Poling and his colleagues (Poling, Nickel, & Alling, 1990) nicely demonstrated this point by showing that captured free-range pigeons gained an average 17% body weight when housed under laboratory conditions. Notice that weight gain, for these birds, is roughly equal to the weight loss typically imposed on laboratory animals.

Magazine Training.   After deprivation for food is established, **magazine training** starts. For example, a rat is placed in an operant chamber and a microcomputer periodically turns on the feeder. When the feeder is turned on, it makes a click and a small 45-mg food pellet falls into the food magazine. Because the click and the appearance of food are associated in time, you would, after training, observe a typical rat staying close to the food magazine; also, the animal would move quickly toward the magazine when the feeder operated and the click occurred. Because the click of the feeder reliably precedes the appearance of food, it becomes a **conditioned positive reinforcer** (see Chapter 11 for a more complete discussion of conditioned reinforcement).

The Response Class.   Staying close to the food cup and moving toward it are operants that have been selected by their reinforcing consequences. In other words, these responses have been reliably followed by food presentation, and as a result they have increased in frequency. However, hovering around a food cup or moving toward it are operants that are difficult to measure objectively. In contrast, a lever press may be easily defined as a switch closure that makes an electrical connection. Any behavior emitted by the rat that results in a switch closure defines the operant class. A lever press with the left or right paw produces an identical electrical connection. Another advantage of lever pressing as an operant is that it may be emitted at high or low rates of response. This is an advantage because the primary focus of operant research is on the conditions that affect rate of response.

Operant Level.   After magazine training, the food-deprived rat is again placed in the operant chamber. The researcher may first want to measure the rate of lever pressing before these responses produce food pellets. Rats emit many exploratory and manipulative responses and as a result may press the lever at some low frequency, even when this behavior is not reinforced with food. This baseline rate of response is called the **operant level.** Next, the environment is arranged so that each lever press results in the click of the feeder and the delivery of a food pellet. When each response produces food, the schedule of reinforcement is called **continuous reinforcement (CRF).** The food pellets are contingent on lever pressing. This contingency between the operant behavior and food reinforcement increases the frequency of lever pressing above operant level.

The Method of Successive Approximation.   In the preceding example, we took advantage of a rat's behavioral **repertoire.** The animal's repertoire refers to the behavior it is capable of naturally emitting on the basis of species and environmental history. Suppose you want to train some response that the animal does not emit. For example, you may want the rat to activate the switch by an upward thrust of its nose. A baseline period of observation shows that the animal fails to emit this response (in other words, the operant level is zero). In this case, the **method of successive approximation** or **shaping** may be used to establish the response. This method involves reinforcing closer and closer approximations to the final performance (i.e., nosing the lever).

   At first, the rat is reinforced for standing in the vicinity of the lever. It is important to note that the most immediate consequence is the sound of the pellet feeder, and this conditioned reinforcer may be used to shape the desired response. Once the animal is reliably facing the lever, a movement of the head toward the bar is reinforced with a click of the feeder and presentation of food. Next, closer and closer approximations of lifting the lever with the nose are reinforced. Each step of the procedure involves reinforcing closer approximations and nonreinforcement of more distant responses. Eventually, the rat emits a response that activates the electrical switch. Many novel forms of behavior may be shaped by the method of successive approximation.

Recording Operant Behavior

A commonly used laboratory instrument that records the frequency of operant behavior in time is called a **cumulative recorder.** Figure 5.6 illustrates this device; each time a lever press occurs, the pen steps up one increment. When reinforcement occurs, this same pen makes a downward deflection. Once the pen reaches the top of the paper, it resets to the bottom and starts to step up again. Since the paper is drawn across the roller at a constant speed, the cumulative recorder depicts a real-time measure of the rate of operant behavior. The faster the lever presses, the steeper the slope or rise of the cumulative record.

   A cumulative record of key pecking by a pigeon is shown in Figure 5.7. In this illustration, a bird responded 50 times in order to produce one food delivery. Notice that periods of responding are followed by reinforcement (indicated by the

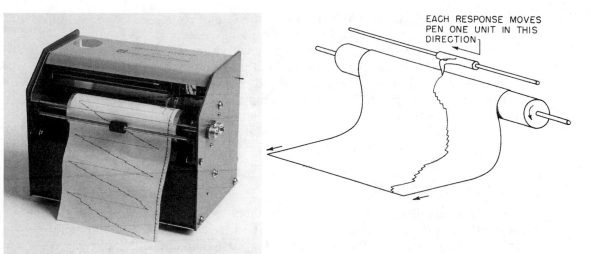

FIG. 5.6 A laboratory instrument used to record operant responses, called a cumulative recorder. The recorder gives a real-time measure of the rate of operant behavior. The faster the lever presses, the steeper the slope or rise of the cumulative record. This occurs because paper is drawn across the roller at a constant speed and the pen steps up a defined distance for each response (photograph by permission of Gerbrands Corporation, Arlington, MA).

FIG. 5.7 A cumulative record of key pecking by a pigeon. In this illustration, a bird responded 50 times to produce one food delivery. Notice that 50 pecks are followed by reinforcement and that this is indicated by a downward deflection of the pen. Following reinforcement, the rate of response is zero, as indicated by the plateaus or flat portions of the record.

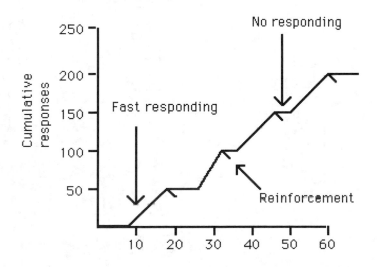

deflection of the pen). After reinforcement, the rate of response is zero, as indicated by the plateaus or flat portions of the cumulative record.

In a modern operant laboratory, the cumulative recorder is used to provide the experimenter with an immediate report of the animal's behavior. Many basic principles of behavior have been discovered by examining cumulative records (Ferster & Skinner, 1957). Today, microcomputers allow researchers to collect and record measures of behavior that are later submitted to complex numerical analyses. In this book, we present examples of cumulative records and numerical analyses that have been important to the experimental analysis of behavior.

A Model Experiment

In the previous discussion of operant behavior, some basic principles were illustrated using the laboratory rat. It is important to realize that these same principles can be extended to a variety of species (later chapters will focus more on human behavior). In the following demonstration of operant conditioning, pigeons are used as the experimental subjects. Pigeons are placed in an operant chamber and required to peck a small plastic disk or **key** that is illuminated by a white light. A peck at the key activates a micro-switch and makes an electrical connection that controls a food hopper. Presentation of food functions as reinforcement for pecking. A food hopper filled with grain swings forward and re-

FIG. 5.8 An operant chamber for birds. The chamber contains a small plastic disk illuminated by a light. A peck at the disk activates a micro-switch and makes an electrical connection. When reinforcement is scheduled to occur, the food hopper swings forward and remains available for a few seconds. The bird can eat grain from the hopper by sticking its head through the opening in the chamber wall. In principle, the chamber is similar to the one used to study the operant behavior of rats (from Ferster & Skinner, 1957).

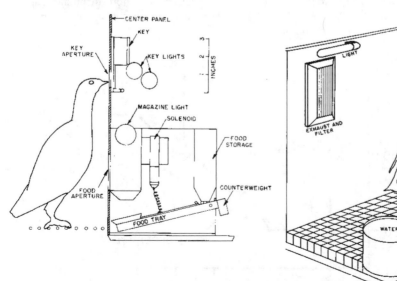

mains available for a few seconds. The bird can eat the grain by sticking its head through an opening. Figure 5.8 shows an operant chamber designed for birds. Note that the chamber is very similar to the one used to study the operant behavior of rats.

Before an experiment, the bird is taken from its home colony and is placed alone in a cage. Each pigeon is given free access to food and water. The bird is weighed each day for about a week and its baseline weight is calculated. Next, the daily food ration is reduced until the bird reaches approximately 80% of free-feeding or **ad libitum weight**. After the deprivation procedure, the pigeon is placed in the operant chamber for magazine training.

When the bird is put in the chamber for the first time, it may show a variety of emotional responses including wing flapping and defecating. This is because the chamber presents a number of novel stimuli that are initially aversive. For example, the operation of the feeder makes a loud sound that may startle the bird. Eventually, these emotional responses are extinguished by repeated exposure to the apparatus. As the emotional responses dissipate, the bird explores the environment and begins to eat from the food magazine. Since the sound of the hopper is paired with food, the sound becomes a conditioned positive reinforcer. At this point, the bird is said to be magazine trained.

The purpose of this demonstration is to train the pigeon to peck the key for food reinforcement. To show that the behavior occurs because of the contingency between pecking and food, an operant level or baseline of pecking the key must be measured. This is accomplished by placing the bird in the operant chamber and recording pecks on the key before a peck-food contingency is established. In other words, pecking the key does not produce food during this phase of the experiment. The operant level serves as a baseline or control period for assessing a change in behavior.

A bird's operant level of key pecking is typically very low, and it is convenient to train these responses by the method of successive approximation. Shaping key pecking in a pigeon involves reinforcing closer and closer approximations to the final performance. As each approximation occurs, it is reinforced with the presentation of the food hopper. Earlier approximations are no longer reinforced and reduce in frequency. This process of **differential reinforcement** eventually results in the pigeon pecking the key with sufficient force to operate the micro-switch.

The key peck that operates the micro-switch to produce food is the first definable response. The switch closure and electrical connection define the operant class of pecking for food. At this point, a microcomputer is programmed so that each key peck results in the presentation of food for a few seconds. Because each response produces reinforcement, the schedule is called continuous reinforcement, or CRF.

Figure 5.9 shows the acquisition of key pecking on continuous reinforcement. Notice that the rate of response is low when the pigeon is initially placed in the chamber. This period is called the warm-up and probably occurs because of the abrupt change from home cage to the operant chamber. After the brief warm-up period, the rate of response is high and stable.

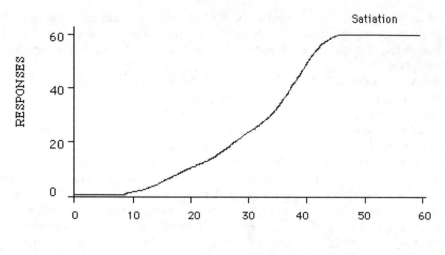

FIG. 5.9 Typical acquisition of key pecking on CRF or continuous reinforcement. Because every response is reinforced, downward deflections indicating reinforcement are omitted. Rate of response is low when the animal is initially placed in the chamber. After this brief period, rate of response is high and stable. Finally, rate of response declines and then levels off. This latter effect is caused by satiation.

Finally, the record shows that rate of response declines and the plateau indicates that the bird stops pecking the key. This latter effect is called **satiation,** and it occurs because the bird has eaten enough food. More technically, rate of response declines because repeated presentations of the reinforcer weaken its effectiveness. A satiation operation decreases the effectiveness of reinforcement. This

FIG. 5.10 Performance on CRF and extinction. Responses are maintained when they are reinforced. However, when responding is no longer reinforced, rate of response declines and eventually stops.

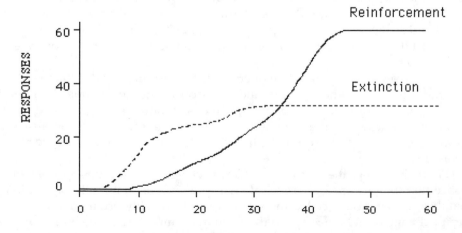

effect is opposite to deprivation, in which the effectiveness of a reinforcer is increased by withholding it.

To be sure that an increase in rate of response is caused by the contingency of reinforcement, it is necessary to withdraw that contingency. In other words, if food is no longer presented, the pigeon should no longer peck the key. If the peck-food contingency caused key pecking, then withdrawal of the contingency will result in a decline in key pecking toward the operant level.

Figure 5.10 presents cumulative records for periods in which pecking produces, or does not produce, food. The initial peck-food contingency produces a steady rate of response. When pecking no longer produces food, the rate of response declines and eventually key pecking stops. Thus, key pecking clearly is caused by the contingency of reinforcement.

EXTINCTION

The procedure of withholding reinforcement for a previously reinforced response is called **extinction.** To produce extinction, you could disconnect the food hopper after the bird had been reinforced for key pecking. It is important to note that the procedure of extinction is a contingency of reinforcement. The contingency is defined as zero probability of reinforcement for the operant response. Extinction is also a behavioral process and, in this case, refers to a decline in rate of response caused by withdrawal of reinforcement. For example, you may raise your hand to ask a question and find that a certain professor ignores you. Asking questions may decline because the professor no longer reinforces this behavior.

Behavioral Effects of Extinction

Extinction produces several behavioral effects in addition to a decline in rate of response. In the section that follows, we consider the range of effects generated by the cessation of reinforcement.

Extinction Burst.   When extinction is started, operant behavior tends to increase in frequency. A pigeon will initially increase the rate of key pecking, and you may raise your hand more often than you did in the past. You may explain your increased hand raising by telling a friend, "The instructor doesn't see me; I have an important point to make" and so on. If the bird could talk it might also "explain" why it was pecking at an increased rate. The point is that an initial increase in rate of response, or **extinction burst,** occurs when reinforcement is first withdrawn.

Response Topography.   In addition to extinction bursts, operants become increasingly variable in form or topography as extinction proceeds. You may wave your hand about in an attempt to catch the professor's eye; the bird may strike the key in different locations and with different amounts of force. A classic experiment by Antonitis (1951) demonstrated this effect. Rats were taught to poke their noses through a 50-cm-long slot for food reinforcement. When this occurred, a photocell was triggered and a photograph of the animal was taken. The position of the rat and the angle of its body were recorded at the moment of reinforcement. After the rat reliably poked its nose through the slot, it was placed on extinction. Following this, reinforcement was reinstated, then extinguished, and in a final phase the operant was again reinforced.

Antonitis reported that reinforcement produced a stereotyped pattern of response. The rat repeatedly poked its nose through the slot at approximately the same location, and the position of its body was held at a particular angle. When extinction occurred, the nose poking and position of the body varied. During extinction, the animal poked its nose over the entire length of the slot. Reinforcing the operant after extinction produced even more stereotyped behavior than the original conditioning.

Pear (1985) found a similar effect with pigeons. When birds were reinforced for pecking a key after an average of only 15 seconds, they stayed close to the key and emitted routine patterns of head and body movements. When these animals were reinforced on a similar schedule, but one that required an average wait of 5 minutes, they strayed further from the key. Both of these patterns developed during extinction, but as extinction continued their behavior became much more variable.

The effect of reinforcement on response stereotypy is a controversial issue in the field of behavior analysis. On the one hand, Dr. Barry Schwartz of Swarthmore College has interpreted this effect as a negative outcome of reinforcement procedures. Schwartz (1980, 1982a, 1982b) showed that reinforcement produces stereotyped responses in pigeons and college students. In the human experiment, this effect prevented students from discovering solutions to novel problems. More technically, response stereotypy resulted in students behaving less effectively under new contingencies of reinforcement. On the other hand, Dr. Allen Neuringer of Reed College reports that reinforcement may be used to train variable response patterns in pigeons and college students. The human research by Neuringer (1986) showed that students generated random sequences of behavior when given reinforcing feedback for randomness. An implication is that reinforcement contingencies may sometimes produce novel and creative behavior patterns.

FOCUS ON RESEARCH
Reinforcement, Problem Solving, and Creativity

Dr. Barry Schwartz, at the time of this writing, a professor of psychology at Swarthmore College in Pennsylvania, stated that he "decided to study the Skinnerian program and come to know it well, so that I would be able to criticize it" (1981, p. 12). As an undergraduate, Schwartz read Skinner's book *Science and Human Behavior* and was appalled that behaviorists used principles derived from laboratory research with animals to account for human behavior. According to Schwartz, human action is misrepresented by behaviorists who insist on a scientific account of behavior. Schwartz finds it hard to believe that our commonsense understanding of human nature is wrong. In the everyday account of

FIG. 5.11 Dr. Barry Schwartz (photograph by John Brodsky).

human action, people refer to desires, intentions, and expectations. From this position, people are said to be free and responsible for their actions. If the commonsense account is correct, then the behavioral interpretation of human behavior must be inaccurate. Furthermore, Schwartz argues that principles of reinforcement may actually interfere with human intellectual capacities.

Schwartz (1982a) carried out a series of experiments with pigeons to show that reinforcement produced response stereotypy. In these experiments, reinforcement produced a set pattern of responding that occurred over and over. Once he established this result in pigeons, Schwartz (1982b) used similar procedures with college students to demonstrate the negative effects of reinforcement for human problem solving.

College students were given points on a counter when they completed a complex sequence of responses. The responses were left and right key presses that moved a light on a checkerboard-like matrix of 25 illuminated squares. Figure 5.12 shows the matrix, with

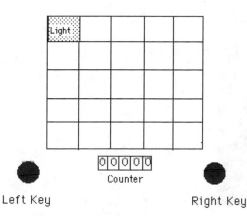

FIG. 5.12 The matrix task used by Schwartz (1982b). A right press moved the light one square to the right; a left button press moved the light down one square.

the light in the top left square. The task required that the subject press the keys to move the light from the top left corner to the bottom right square. A press on the right key moved the light one square to the right. When the left-hand key was pressed, the light moved one square down. Schwartz required exactly four left (L) and four right (R) presses in any order (e.g., LRLRLRLR, LLLLRRRR, etc.). There were 70 different orders of left and right key presses that would move the light to the bottom right corner. When the light reached the bottom right corner, a point registered on the counter. The points were later exchanged for money. If the subject pressed any key a fifth time (e.g., RRRRR), all matrix lights were turned off and the trial ended without reinforcement.

In a series of experiments, Schwartz found that students developed a stereotyped pattern of responding. That is, they repeated the same sequence over and over. For example, two students produced the same left and right sequences (LLLLRRRR) over and over again. Another subject repeatedly produced the sequence LRLRLRLR to satisfy the contingency. The point is that as soon as a student hit on a correct sequence, he or she repeated it and rarely tried another pattern. Schwartz also asked the students to discover the rule that would result in moving the light to the bottom-right corner. The actual rule was any four presses on the left key and any four on the right. However, students who produced a stereotyped pattern of response had difficulty describing this simple rule. They often described the rule in terms of their stereotyped response pattern. For example, although any four left and right responses resulted in reinforcement, a student might claim that the particular sequence of LLRRLLRR was the necessary pattern. When Schwartz compared such students with others who had not worked on the task, he found that the inexperienced students were better at discovering the actual underlying rule.

In other experiments (Schwartz, 1982b), subjects were explicitly reinforced for varying their response pattern. When this was done, the students developed higher-order stereotypes. When students were reinforced for changing their pattern of button presses from trial to trial, they developed a stereotyped set of sequences that occurred in a regular

FIG. 5.13 Dr. Allen Neuringer (photograph by Vera Jagendorf, Portland, OR).

order. For example, a subject might respond with LLLLRRRR, then LRLRLRLR, followed by RRRRLLLL. Patterns like this were repeated over and over by the students. From these experiments, Schwartz (1982b) concluded that reinforcement interfered with problem solving, because it produced stereotyped response patterns.

Dr. Allen Neuringer, at the time of this writing, is a professor of psychology at Reed College in Portland, Oregon. He received his Ph.D. in 1967 from Harvard University, where he was trained as a behavior analyst. Since that time, he has published extensively in the experimental analysis of behavior. Several years ago, Neuringer became interested in variability, randomness, and behavior. He said that this interest developed from a game that involved predicting his own behavior. The game consisted of predicting the movement of his index finger. If he could move his finger up or down in a random fashion, then by definition the behavior was unpredictable. This game prompted Neuringer to investigate the question of randomness and human behavior.

A review of the literature suggested that humans could not behave in a random manner. At the same time, Neuringer read Schwartz's research on problem solving and disagreed with the conclusion. Schwartz claimed that reinforcement necessarily produced response stereotypy. Neuringer suggested that the contingencies of the Schwartz experiments produced response stereotypy and that this was not an inevitable outcome of reinforcement. The requirement to emit exactly four left and four right responses was arbitrary and may have resulted in response stereotypy.

In their 1985 experiments, Neuringer and his honors student, Suzanne Page (Page & Neuringer, 1985), used the light matrix task to investigate variability of response pattern in pigeons. The birds pecked left and right keys to move the light and were reinforced with food. The researchers designed a contingency that was identical to the one used by Schwartz (1982a, 1982b). They compared this to a condition in which response variability was not constrained by exactly four pecks on each key. In this condition, the birds could emit any sequence of eight left or right responses to obtain reinforcement. This difference in procedure is important because it increases the number of correct sequences from 70 to 256. The Neuringer procedure increased the rate of reinforcement for response variability and eliminated time out (negative punishment) for emitting novel sequences. To make this clear, in the Schwartz experiments the fifth left or right response resulted in the lights going out and the end of the trial. In other words, students and pigeons received time out from reinforcement (negative punishment) for varying their response patterns. Time out from reinforcement does not occur when any sequence of eight left and right responses is emitted. Thus, the procedures used by Schwartz punished trying out new patterns. This occurred because a mistake (a fifth left or right response) turned the trial off and reinforcement was not available. Additionally, the requirement of exactly four left and right presses limited the number of possible sequences to 70.

Page and Neuringer (1985) investigated contingencies of reinforcement that could generate behavioral variability. Pigeons had to peck left and right keys eight times in any order to produce food reinforcement. In their third experiment, the researchers required pigeons to vary their pattern of response on the current trial from the ones produced on the previous trials. In different phases of the experiment, the sequence had to differ from the last 5, 10, 15, 25, or 50 response patterns. For example, at lag 5 there were five preceding sequences (e.g., RRRRRRRR, LLLLLLLL, LLLLRRRR, LLRRRRRR, RRRLLLLL) and the next sequence had to be different from these five (e.g., RLLLLLLL). Results showed that the pigeons were able to generate highly variable response patterns when the contingencies required this behavior. Generally, sequence variation increased with the lag requirement. At lag 25, approximately 85% of the emitted response patterns differed from all others for a session. Another experiment showed that behavioral variability or stereotypy is an acquired response. Pigeons learned to respond with a variable pattern in the presence of one color and respond with a stereotyped sequence when another color was presented. Apparently, the degree of response variability is a conditionable property of operant behavior. In other words, when variation in response is reinforced, it increases in frequency.

A subsequent study by Neuringer (1986) extended the findings on response variability to humans. In two experiments, Neuringer demonstrated that college students could learn to generate random sequences of two numbers on the keyboard of a computer. Subjects were required to press the 1 and 2 keys as randomly as possible. Initially, the students were not able to generate random sequences. However, when they were given feedback from statistical estimates of chance, the students learned to emit sequences that were indistinguishable from computer-generated random numbers. Neuringer concluded that "randomlike behaviors are learned and controlled by environmental feedback, as are other highly skilled activities" (p. 72).

In summary, Dr. Barry Schwartz argues that reinforcement produces behavioral inflexibility and rigidity. Such inflexibility interferes with finding solutions to complex problems that require innovation and creativity. He argues that in educational settings, the use of reinforcement procedures may be counterproductive because the natural problem-solving capabilities of humans are overridden by reinforcement contingencies. In contrast, the work of Dr. Allen Neuringer suggests that response stereotypy is not an inevitable outcome of reinforcement. Neuringer's research shows us that the effects of reinforcement depend on the contingencies. If the contingencies of reinforcement support stereotyped behavior, then this will occur. On the other hand, contingencies may generate novel sequences of behavior if these patterns result in reinforcement (see also Machado, 1989; 1992; 1997).

One way to view this issue is to consider that solutions to some problems require flexibility and solutions to others require rigidity. For example, in writing a poem, behavioral variability is reinforced. This makes the poem different and may contribute to its artistic merit. On the other hand, solving a long division problem must be done in a rigid and repetitive manner. Behavioral flexibility in long division is not reinforced.

Force of Response.   Reinforcement may be made contingent on the force of response. Notterman (1959) measured the force that rats used to press a lever during periods of reinforcement and extinction. During reinforcement sessions, animals came to press the lever with a force that varied within a relatively narrow range. When extinction occurred, the force of lever pressing became more variable. Interestingly, some responses were more forceful than any emitted during reinforcement or during operant level. This increase in response force may be due to emotional behavior generated by extinction procedures.

For example, imagine that you have pushed a button for an elevator but the elevator does not arrive, and you have an important appointment on the 28th floor. At first you increase the frequency of pressing the elevator button; you also change the way you hit the button. You probably feel angry and frustrated and you may smash the button. These responses and accompanying feelings occur because of the change from reinforcement to extinction.

Emotional Responses.   Consider what happens when someone puts money in a vending machine and is not reinforced with an item (e.g., a beverage). The person who is placed on extinction may hit the machine, curse, and engage in other emotional behavior. Several U.S. soldiers were once killed by soda machines. Young soldiers at the peak of physical fitness are capable of emitting forceful operants. When some of the soldiers put money in soda machines that failed to operate, extinction-induced emotional behavior became so powerful that the men pulled over the 2-ton machines. Thus, their deaths were an indirect outcome of emotional behavior produced by extinction.

A variety of emotional responses occur under conditions of extinction. Birds flap their wings, rats bite the response lever, and humans may swear and kick at a vending machine. One important kind of emotional behavior that occurs during extinction is aggression. Azrin, Hutchinson, and Hake (1966) trained pigeons to peck a key for food. After training, a second immobilized pigeon was placed in the operant chamber. The "target" bird was restrained and placed on an apparatus that caused a switch to close whenever the bird was attacked. Attacks to the target reliably occurred when the contingencies of reinforcement were changed from CRF to extinction. Many of the attacks were vicious and unrelenting, lasting up to 10 minutes.

Discriminated Extinction.   Suppose that a pigeon was reinforced for pecking a key in the presence of a green light. However, when a red light came on, pecking was not reinforced. During the course of training, the animal would emit emotional responses, extinction bursts, and so on when the red light was turned on. Following training, the bird would not emit this behavior and it would simply stop responding when the light changed from green to red. The red light became a discriminative stimulus (S^Δ) that signaled a period of extinction. This effect is called **discriminated extinction** and is commonly observed in human behavior. A sign on a vending machine that reads OUT OF ORDER is an S^Δ that signals extinction for putting money in the machine.

The respondent procedures for conditioned inhibition and rapid extinction (see Chapter 3) seem close to the operant procedure of discriminated extinction. Comparing the procedures, we assume that the conditioned response to the light is similar to the emission of an operant on a given occasion. Discriminative extinction involves signaling extinction periods with an extroceptive stimulus, such as a change in key color from green to red. This change from green to red in the operant procedure is like adding the tone during respondent extinction. When the key is green, a pigeon is trained to peck it for food. Every once in a while the key color changes to red, and reinforcement for pecking no longer occurs. During these extinction periods, rate of response should decline. This decline would occur more rapidly when extinction is signaled by a change in color than when the key color remains the same. Finally, since the red key is consistently associated with extinction, it acquires a discriminative function (S$^{\Delta}$), suppressing responding when it is presented.

Resistance to Extinction

As extinction proceeds, emotional behavior subsides and rate of response declines. When extinction has been in effect long enough, behavior may return to operant level. In practice, however, a return to operant level is rarely accomplished. This is because many extinction sessions are usually required before operant level is attained. Extinction is typically assessed by measuring the total number of responses, or rate of response, after some amount of time. For example, a bird may be reinforced on CRF for 10 consecutive daily sessions; following this, extinction is initiated. The pigeon's responses are recorded over three extinction sessions. The number of responses emitted by the bird or the rate of response during the last session may be used to index **resistance to extinction.** Operants are rapidly extinguished after a few reinforced responses, but when operants are reinforced many times, resistance to extinction increases. Several experiments (Hearst, 1961; Perin, 1942) have shown that resistance to extinction reaches a maximum after 50 to 80 reinforced responses.

Intermittent Reinforcement.   Resistance to extinction is substantially increased when an **intermittent schedule of reinforcement** has been used to maintain behavior. On an intermittent schedule, only some responses are reinforced. For example, instead of reinforcing each response (CRF), the experimenter may program reinforcement after 100 key pecks have been emitted. In this situation, the bird must emit 100 pecks before food is presented. This intermittent schedule will generate many more responses during extinction than continuous reinforcement. When people are described as persistent or tenacious, their behavior may reflect the effects of intermittent reinforcement.

Resistance to extinction following intermittent reinforcement increases because it takes the organism longer to contact the change in the contingencies. For example, a rat that has been reinforced for every 100 responses must emit 100 responses before contacting the change from reinforcement to extinction. In contrast, an animal that is reinforced for each response contacts the extinction contingency immediately. Since each response is a nonreinforced occurrence, the animal repeatedly encounters the change to extinction. If an animal on CRF emits 50 responses during extinction, it has contacted the extinction contingency 50 times. A rat on intermittent reinforcement may have to emit 5,000 responses to have equal experience with the contingencies.

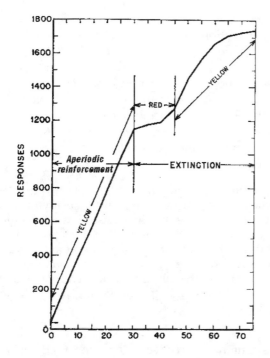

FIG. 5.14 Responding during extinction as a function of discrimination. Responding in the presence of the yellow triangle is high during the first 30 minutes of intermittent reinforcement. When the red triangle and extinction are introduced, rate of response declines. Extinction is continued and the yellow triangle is reinstated. When the yellow triangle is presented, rate of response recovers and then declines toward extinction (from Skinner, 1950).

Discriminative Stimuli and Extinction.

Intermittent reinforcement is not the only factor that determines the return to operant level during extinction. Resistance to extinction is also affected by discriminative stimuli that are conditioned during sessions of reinforcement. Skinner (1950) showed that "maximal responding during extinction is obtained only when the conditions under which the response was reinforced are precisely reproduced" (p. 204).

Pigeons were trained to peck a yellow triangle on an intermittent schedule of food reinforcement. After training, a red triangle was substituted for the yellow one and extinction was started. During 15 minutes of extinction in the presence of the red triangle, rate of response substantially declined. At this point, the red triangle was replaced by the yellow one but extinction was continued. The effect of introducing the yellow triangle was that rapid responding began immediately, and the usual extinction curve followed. This effect is portrayed in Figure 5.14, in which responding in the presence of the yellow triangle is at a high rate during the first 30 minutes of intermittent reinforcement. When the red triangle and extinction were introduced, rate of response declined. Finally, extinction was continued and the yellow triangle was reinstated. Notice that rate of response immediately recovers and then declines toward extinction.

Spontaneous Recovery.

An interesting phenomenon that occurs during extinction is called **spontaneous recovery**. After a session of extinction, rate of response may be close to operant level. At this point, the animal is taken out of the operant chamber and returned to a holding cage. The next day, the organism is again placed in the operant chamber and extinction is continued. Surprisingly, the animal begins to respond above operant level, and this defines spontaneous recovery. Over repeated sessions of extinction, the amount of recovery decreases. If many sessions of extinction are provided, rate of response will no longer recover.

Spontaneous recovery is really not spontaneous. Stimuli that have accompanied reinforced responding are usually presented at the beginning of extinction sessions. Skinner (1950) has noted that handling procedures and the stimulation arising from being placed in an operant chamber set the occasion for responding at the beginning of each extinction session. Skinner (1950) states:

> No matter how carefully an animal is handled, the stimulation coincident with the beginning of an experiment must be extensive and unlike anything occurring in the latter part of an experimental period. Responses have been reinforced in the presence of, or shortly following, this stimulation. In extinction it is present for only a few moments. When the organism is again placed in the experimental situation the stimulation is restored; further responses are emitted as in the case of the yellow triangle [see aforementioned experiment]. The only way to achieve full extinction in the presence of the stimulation of starting an experiment is to start the experiment repeatedly. (pp. 199–200)

Human behavior also shows spontaneous recovery. Imagine that you are stranded in a secluded mountain cabin during a week-long snowstorm. The telephone rings, you answer, but all you get is the dial tone. You shout at the dial tone and bang the disconnect button repeatedly. Next, you try to contact the telephone company and discover that you are not able to dial out. Over the course of the first day the phone rings many times, you answer, but it does not work. By the end of the day, you may not be inclined to answer the telephone; you just let it keep on ringing. The next morning you are having breakfast and the phone rings. What do you do? The best guess is that you will again answer the phone. You may say to yourself, "Perhaps they have fixed the line." On this second day of extinction, you answer the phone but give up more quickly. On day 3, the phone rings at 10:00 A.M. and even though you doubt that it will work, you answer it "just to check it out." By day 4, you have had it with the "damn phone and the stupid telephone company" and extinction is complete.

Extinction and Forgetting

During extinction, operant behavior decreases over time. People often talk about the weakening of behavior as loss of memory or forgetting. An important question concerns the procedural differences between forgetting and extinction. Extinction is a procedure in which a previously reinforced response no longer produces reinforcement. The opportunity to emit the operant remains available during extinction. Thus, the pigeon may still peck the illuminated key, or the rat may continue to press the response lever. In contrast, forgetting is said to occur after the mere passage of time. An organism who has learned a response is tested for retention after some amount of time has passed. In this case, there is no apparent opportunity to emit the behavior.

Skinner (1938) designed an experiment to assess the behavioral loss that occurs after the passage of time. In this experiment, four rats were trained to press a lever, and each animal received 100 reinforced responses. After 45 days of rest, each animal was placed in the operant chamber and responding was extinguished. The number of responses emitted during extinction was compared with the performance of four other rats selected from an earlier experiment. These animals were similar in age, training, and number of reinforced responses to the experimental subjects. The comparison animals had received extinction 1 day after reinforced bar pressing.

Figure 5.15 shows the results of Skinner's experiment. Results are presented as the cumulative-average number of responses emitted by each group of animals. The group that received extinction 1 day after response strengthening emitted an average of 86 responses in 1 hour. The group that was extinguished after 45 days made an average of 69 responses in 1 hour. Notice that both groups of animals show a similar number of responses during the first few minutes of extinction. In other words, animals in both groups immediately began to press the lever when placed in the operant chamber. This shows that the rats who had received extinction after 45 days had not forgotten what to do to get food (Skinner, 1938).

Following the first few minutes of extinction, there is a difference in the cumulative-average number of responses for the two groups. Resistance to extinction is apparently reduced by the passage of time. Rats that were required to wait 45 days before extinction generated fewer responses per hour than those given extinction 1 day after reinforcement. Although the curves rise at different rates, animals in both groups appear to stop responding after approximately 90 nonreinforced lever presses. Overall, the results suggest that the passage of time affects resistance to extinction, but a well-established performance is not forgotten.

In a later experiment on forgetting, Skinner (1950) trained 20 pigeons to strike a key with a complex pattern. The pigeons had been used for a World War II naval research project involving missile guidance systems (Project Pigeon, see Skinner, 1960). Skinner had taught the birds to peck at a complex visual image. A particular feature of the New Jersey coastline was projected onto a translucent key. The pigeons were required to strike the specified target in order to obtain food on an intermittent schedule of reinforcement. Reinforcement was contingent on a high and steady rate of pecking at the specified visual feature.

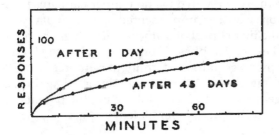

FIG. 5.15 Average extinction curves of four rats, 1 day after training and 45 days after training (from Skinner, 1938).

In a personal conversation (1989), Skinner indicated that he kept some of the birds from Project Pigeon when funding was discontinued. The birds were housed in a coop in his garden. Skinner said that over a period of 6 years, he tested the birds for retention. The birds were food deprived and placed in the original apparatus after 6 months, 1 year, 2 years, 4 years, and 6 years.

Unfortunately, Skinner said that most of the data were unavailable. However, he was impressed that the birds responded immediately to the target image at a high and steady rate. All subjects produced extensive extinction curves even after several years had passed since the initial training. One remarkable observation was that "the extinction curves became smaller" with greater passage of time. Again, passage of time does not seem to affect forgetting, since the birds immediately pecked the target. However, as with the rats, resistance to extinction declined as a function of the retention interval.

ON THE APPLIED SIDE

Extinction as a Modification Procedure for Temper Tantrums

Williams (1959) has shown how extinction effects play an important role in the modification of human behavior. In this study, a 20-month-old child was making life miserable for his parents by having temper tantrums when put to bed. If the parents stayed up with the child, he did not scream and cry and eventually went to sleep. A well-known source of reinforcement for children is parental attention, and Williams reasoned that this was probably maintaining the bedtime behavior. That is, when the parents left the bedroom, the child began screaming and crying. These tantrums were reinforced by the return of the parents to the bedroom. The parental behavior stopped the tantrum and for this reason it continued. The parents were spending a good part of each evening in the child's room waiting for him to go to sleep. At this point, the parents were advised to implement extinction by leaving the room and closing the door after the child was put to bed. Figure 5.16 demonstrates the rapid decline in duration of crying when this was done (first extinction).

When extinction was first attempted, the child screamed and cried for 45 minutes. However, on the next night he did not cry at all. On the third night, the child emitted tantrums for 10 minutes. By the end of 10 days, the boy was smiling at his parents when they left the room. Unfortunately, the boy was put to bed by his aunt, who reinforced crying by staying in the room with him and temper tantrums reoccurred. A second extinction procedure was then implemented. Duration of crying was longer for the second than for the first period of extinction. The higher probability of response during the second extinction phase is presumably caused by the intermittent reinforcement of tantrums. Recall that intermittent reinforcement increases resistance to extinction. Fortunately, the boy was not reinforced again and tantrums eventually declined to a zero rate. At a 2-year follow-up, the parents reported that bedtime tantrums had been completely eliminated.

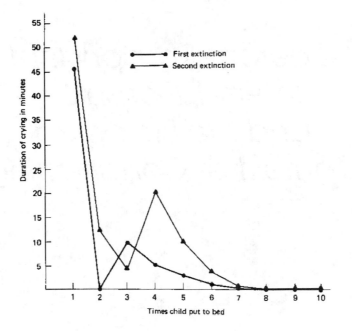

FIG 5.16 First and second extinction procedures for a child's temper tantrums (from Williams, 1959).

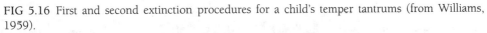

KEY WORDS

Ad libitum weight

Conditioned positive
  reinforcer

Contingency of
  reinforcement

Continuous
  reinforcement (CRF)

Cumulative recorder

Deprivation operation

Differential
  reinforcement

Discriminated extinction

Discriminative stimulus
  (S^D)

Elicited

Emitted

Extinction

Extinction burst

Free operant method

History of reinforcement

Intermittent schedule of
  reinforcement

Intrinsic motivation

Latency

Law of effect

Magazine training

Negative punishment

Negative reinforcement

Operant chamber

Operant class

Operant level

Premack principle

Positive punishment

Positive reinforcement

Positive reinforcer

Rate of response

Repertoire

Resistance to extinction

S-delta (S^Δ)

Satiation

Selection by
  consequences

Shaping

Spontaneous recovery

Successive
  approximation

Topography

Trans-situationality

CHAPTER 6

Operant-Respondent Interrelationships and the Biological Context of Conditioning

1. State what is meant by the dual function of a stimulus. Give an example of such a stimulus.

2. Discuss a pigeon's key pecking as an operant and as a respondent.

3. Outline the Brelands' effect of instinctive drift. How does this effect fit within a respondent conditioning view?

4. What is sign tracking and how does it apparently challenge the operant, three-term contingency model (S^D: R → S^r)? Describe the Jenkins, Barrera, Ireland, and Woodside (1978) experiment and its findings. How do respondent relations help to explain these findings?

5. Compare shaping by successive approximation with the autoshaping procedure of Brown and Jenkins (1968). Describe the research on autoshaping and the basic findings.

6. How could accidental reinforcement account for autoshaping? Show how Williams and Williams (1969) used omission training to test a reinforcement account of autoshaping. Be able to give a respondent analysis of this experiment.

Advanced Issue

7. *Describe the Schwartz and Williams (1972a,1972b) experiments and the relevance of these studies for the autoshaping controversy. What other evidence suggests that autoshaping involves both operant and respondent processes?*

8. What do sign tracking, autoshaping, and instinctive drift have in common? How can the dispute between operant and respondent accounts of biologically relevant behavior be resolved?

9. Summarize the experiments on reinforcement of reflexive behavior. Show how Miller and DiCara (1967) solved the problem of operant behavior mediating reinforcement of a reflex. State and discuss the findings.

10. What does Morris (1992) mean by context? How does the biological context establish and change operant (or respondent) relations (SD: R → S^r)?

11. Be able to describe how organisms acquire food aversions based on biologically relevant visual and taste cues. Use respondent conditioning and the concept of preparedness in your answer.

12. Describe the Garcia and Koelling (1966) experiment on taste aversion and its major findings. What is unusual about their results and how can we explain them? After a dinner date at which you became ill, why would you probably give up pasta alfredo rather than your date?

13. What three distinct types of behavior occur between food reinforcement on interval- or time-based schedules? Define the term *polydipsia* and explain how it occurs.

14. Describe the adjunctive behavior that occurs for different reinforcers and species.

15. What are the major conditions that regulate adjunctive behavior? How is the schedule of reinforcement related to the amount of adjunctive behavior? What about deprivation and adjunctive behavior?

16. Discuss adjunctive responses as displacement behavior. Point to the adaptive value of such behavior.

17. How are eating and exercise motivationally interrelated? What is the relationship between food deprivation and the reinforcement value of running? How does running affect the reinforcement value of eating? What is the evolutionary analysis of these relations and activity anorexia?

So far, we have considered operant and respondent behavior as separate domains. Respondent behavior is evoked by the events that precede it, and operants are strengthened (or weakened) by stimuli that follow them. Pretend that you are teaching a dog to sit and you are using food reinforcement. You might start by saying "sit," and then push the animal into a sitting position and follow this posture with food. After training, you present the dog with the discriminative stimulus "sit," and it quickly sits. This sequence nicely fits the operant paradigm—the S^D "sit" sets the occasion for the response of sitting, and food reinforcement strengthens this behavior.

In most circumstances, however, both operant and respondent conditioning occur. If you look closely at what the dog does, it should be apparent that the "sit" command also evokes respondent behavior. Specifically, the dog salivates just after you say "sit." This occurs because the "sit" command reliably preceded the presentation of food, and it becomes a conditioned stimulus that evokes respondent salivation. For these reasons, the stimulus "sit" is said to have a dual function: It is an S^D in the sense that it sets the occasion for operant responses, and it is a CS because it evokes respondent behavior.

Similar effects are seen when a warning stimulus (i.e., a tone) is turned on that signals imminent shock if a rat does not press a lever. The signal is a discriminative stimulus that increases the probability of bar pressing, but it is also a CS that evokes changes in heart rate, hormone levels, and so on (all of which can be called fear). Consider that you are out for a before-breakfast walk and you pass a doughnut and coffee shop. The aroma from the shop may be a CS that evokes salivation and an S^D that sets the occasion for entering the store and ordering a doughnut. These examples should make it clear that in many settings respondent and operant conditioning are intertwined.

ANALYSIS OF OPERANT/RESPONDENT CONTINGENCIES

In some circumstances, the distinction between operant and respondent behavior becomes even more difficult. Experimental procedures (contingencies) can be arranged in which responses typically considered reflexive increase when followed by reinforcement. Other research has shown that behavior usually thought to be operant may be evoked by the stimuli that precede it. Many students (and more than a few psychologists) incorrectly label operant or respondent behavior in terms of its form or topography. That is, pecking a key is automatically called an operant and salivation, no matter how it comes about, is labeled a reflex. Recall, though, that operants and respondents are defined by the experimental procedures that produce them, not by their topography. When a pigeon pecks a key for food, pecking is an operant. If another bird reliably strikes a key when it is lit up, and does this because the light has been paired with food, the peck is a respondent.

When biologically relevant stimuli, like food, are contingent on an organism's behavior, species-characteristic behavior is occasionally evoked. One class of species-characteristic responses that are occasionally evoked (when operant behavior is expected) is reflexive behavior. This intrusion of reflexive behavior occurs because *respondent procedures are sometimes embedded in operant contingencies of reinforcement*. These respondent procedures evoke species-characteristic responses that may interfere with the regulation of behavior by operant contingencies.

At one time, this intrusion of respondent conditioning in operant situations was used to question the generality of operant principles and laws. The claim was that the biology of an organism overrode operant principles (Hinde & Stevenson-Hinde, 1973; Stevenson-Hinde, 1983; Schwartz & Lacey, 1982) and behavior drifted towards its biological roots.

Operant (and respondent) conditioning is, however, part of the biology of an organism. Conditioning arose on the basis of species history; organisms that changed their behavior as a result of life experience had an advantage over animals that did not change their behavior. Behavioral flexibility allowed for rapid adaptation to an altered environment. As a result, organisms that conditioned (or learned) were more likely to survive and produce offspring.

Respondent Contingencies Predominate over Operant Regulation of Behavior

The Breland and Breland Demonstration.   Marion and Keller Breland worked with B. F. Skinner and established a successful animal training business. They conditioned a variety of animals for circus acts, arcade displays, and movies. In an important paper (Breland & Breland, 1961), they documented occasional instances in which species-specific behavior interfered with operant responses. For example, when training a raccoon to deposit coins in a box, they noted:

> the response concerned the manipulation of money by the raccoon (who has "hands" rather similar to those of primates). The contingency for reinforcement was picking up the coins and depositing them in a 5-inch metal box.
>
> Raccoons condition readily, have good appetites, and this one was quite tame and an eager subject. We anticipated no trouble. Conditioning him to pick up the first coin was simple. We started out by reinforcing him for picking up a single coin. Then the metal container was introduced, with the requirement that he drop the coin into the container. Here we ran into the first bit of difficulty: he seemed to have a great deal of trouble letting go of the coin. He would rub it up against the inside of the container, pull it back out, and clutch it firmly for several seconds. However, he would finally turn it loose and receive his food reinforcement. Then the final contingency: we put him on a ratio of 2, requiring that he pick up both coins and put them in the container.
>
> Now the raccoon really had problems (and so did we). Not only could he not let go of the coins, but he spent seconds, even minutes rubbing them together (in a most miserly fashion), and dipping them into the container. He carried on the behavior to such an extent that the practical demonstration we had in mind—a display featuring a raccoon putting money in a piggy bank—simply was not feasible. The rubbing behavior became worse and worse as time went on, in spite of non-reinforcement. (Breland & Breland, 1961, p. 682)

Breland and Breland documented similar instances of what they called instinctive drift in other species. **Instinctive drift** refers to species-characteristic behavior patterns that became progressively more invasive during training. The term instinctive drift is problematic because the concept suggests a conflict between nature (biology) and nurture (environment). Behavior is said to drift toward its biological roots. There is, however, no need to talk about behavior "drifting" toward some end. Behavior is appropriate to the operating contingencies. Recall that respondent procedures may be embedded in an operant contingency and this seems to be the case for the Brelands' raccoon.

In the raccoon example, the coins were presented just before the animal was reinforced with food. For raccoons, food elicits rubbing and manipulating food items. Since the coins preceded food delivery, they became CSs that elicited the respondent behavior of rubbing and manipulating (coins). This interpretation is supported by the observation that the behavior increased as training progressed. As more and more reinforced trials occurred, there were necessarily more pairings of coins and food. Each pairing increased the strength of the $CS_{(coin)} \rightarrow CR_{(rubbing)}$ relationship, and the behavior became more and more prominent.

Sign Tracking. Suppose that you have trained a dog to sit quietly on a mat, and you have reinforced the animal's behavior with food. Once this conditioning

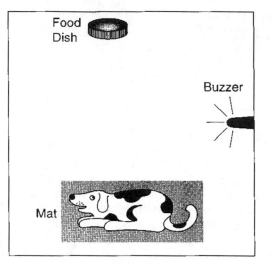

FIG. 6.1 Diagram of apparatus used in sign tracking.

is accomplished (the dog sits quietly on the mat), you start a second training phase. During this phase, you turn on a buzzer that is on the dog's right side. A few seconds after the sound of the buzzer, a feeder delivers food to a dish that is placed 6 feet in front of the dog. Figure 6.1 is a diagram of this sort of arrangement.

When the buzzer goes off, the dog is free to engage in any behavior it is able to emit. From the perspective of operant conditioning, it is clear what should happen. When the buzzer goes off, the dog should stand up, walk over to the dish, and eat. This is because the sound of the buzzer is an S^D that sets the occasion for the operant going to the dish, and this response is reinforced by food. In other words, the three-part contingency, SD: R → S^r, specifies this outcome and there is little reason to expect any other result. A careful examination of this contingency, however, suggests that the sign could be either an S^D (operant) that sets the occasion for approaching and eating the reinforcer (food); or a CS+ (respondent) that is paired with the US (food). In this latter case, the CS would be expected to elicit food-related conditioned responses.

Jenkins, Barrera, Ireland, and Woodside (1978) conducted an experiment very much like the one described here. Dogs were required to sit on a mat and a light/tone stimulus compound was presented either on the left or right side of the animal. When the stimulus was presented on one side, it signaled food, and on the other side it signaled extinction. As expected, when the extinction stimulus came on, the dogs did not approach the food tray and for the most part ignored the signal. However, when the food signal was presented, the animals approached the signal and made, what was judged by the researchers to be, "food-soliciting responses" to the stimulus. Some of the dogs physically contacted the signal source, and others seemed to beg at the stimulus by barking and prancing. This behavior is called **sign tracking** because it refers to approaching a sign (or stimulus) that signals a biologically relevant event (in this case, food).

The behavior of the dogs does not make sense in terms of operant contingencies of reinforcement. As stated earlier, the animals should simply trot over to the food and eat it. Instead the dogs' behavior appears to be elicited by the signal that precedes food delivery. Importantly, the ordering of stimulus → behavior resembles the CS → CR arrangement that characterizes classical conditioning. Of course, S^D: R follows the same time line, but in this case, the response should be a direct approach to the food, not to the signal. Additionally, behavior in the presence of the stimulus appears to be food directed. When the tone/light comes on, the dog approaches it, barks, begs, prances, licks the signal source, and so on. Thus, the temporal arrangement of stimulus followed by response, and the form or topography of the animal's behavior, suggests respondent conditioning. Apparently, in this situation the unconditioned stimulus features of the food are stronger (in the sense of regulating behavior) than the operant-reinforcement properties of the food. Because of this, the light/tone gains strength as a CS with each pairing of light/tone and food.

Autoshaping.   Shaping is the usual way that a pigeon is taught to strike a response key. In a laboratory experiment, closer and closer approximations to the final performance (key peck) are reinforced by a researcher. Once the bird makes the first complete peck at the key, electronic programming equipment activates a food hopper and the response is reinforced. The contingency between behavior and reinforcement, both during shaping and after the operant is established, is clearly operant (R → S^r). The method of successive approximation requires considerable patience and a fair amount of skill on the part of the experimenter.

Brown and Jenkins (1968) reported a way to teach pigeons automatically to peck a response key. In one experiment, they first taught birds to approach and eat grain whenever a food hopper was presented. After the birds were magazine trained, they turned on a key light 8 seconds before the grain was delivered. Next, the key light went out and the grain hopper was presented. After 10 to 20 pairings of key light followed by food, the birds started to orient and move toward the lighted disk. Eventually all 36 pigeons in the experiment began to strike the key, even though pecking did not produce food. Figure 6.2 shows the arrangement between key light and food presentation. Notice that the light onset precedes the presentation of food and appears to elicit the key peck.

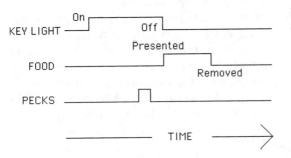

FIG. 6.2 Autoshaping procedures based on Brown and Jenkins (1968).

The researchers reported this effect as **autoshaping,** an automatic way to teach pigeons to key peck. Brown and Jenkins offered several explanations for their results. In their view, the most likely explanation had to do with species characteristics of pigeons. They noted that pigeons have a tendency to peck at things they look at. The bird notices the onset of the light, orients toward it, and "the species-specific look-peck coupling eventually yields a peck to the [key]" (Brown & Jenkins, 1968, p. 7). In their experiment, after the bird made the response, food was presented, and this could have accidentally reinforced the peck.

Another possibility was that key pecking resulted from respondent conditioning. The researchers suggested that the lighted key could have become a CS that evoked key pecks. This could occur because pigeons make unconditioned pecks (UR) when grain (US) is given to them. In their experiment, the key light preceded grain presentation and may have elicited a conditioned peck (CR) to the lighted key (CS). Brown and Jenkins comment on this explanation and suggest that although it is possible, it "seem[s] unlikely because the peck appears to grow out of and depend upon the development of other motor responses in the vicinity of the key that do not themselves resemble a peck at grain" (1968, p. 7). In other words, the birds began to turn toward the key, stand close to it, make thrusting movements with their heads, and so on, all of which led to the eventual key peck. It does not seem likely that these are reflexive responses.

In addition, reflexive behavior like salivation, eye blinks, startle, knee jerks, pupil dilation, and others do not depend on the development of some other behavior. When you touch a hot stove, you rapidly and automatically pull your hand away. This response simply occurs when a hot object is contacted. A stove does not evoke approach to it, orientation toward it, movement of the hand and arm, and other responses. All of these other responses seem to be operant because similar behavior is regulated by the consequences that it has produced in the past.

Autoshaping extends to other species and other types of reinforcement and responses. Chicks have been shown to make autoshaped responses when heat was the reinforcer (Wasserman, 1973). When food delivery is signaled for rats by lighting a lever or by inserting it into the operant chamber, the animals lick and chew on the bar (Peterson, Ackil, Frommer, & Hearst, 1972; Stiers & Silberberg, 1974). These animals also direct social behavior toward another stimulus rat that signals the delivery of food (Timberlake & Grant, 1975). Rachlin (1969) showed autoshaped key pecking in pigeons using electric shock as negative reinforcement. The major question that these and other experiments raise is: What is the nature of the behavior that is observed in autoshaping and sign-tracking experiments?

In general, research has shown that autoshaped behavior is respondent, but when the contingency is changed so that pecks are followed by food, the peck becomes operant. Pigeons reflexively peck (UR) at the sight of grain (US). Because the key light reliably precedes grain presentation, it acquires a conditioned stimulus function that evokes the CR of pecking the key. However, when pecking is followed by grain, it comes under the control of contingencies of reinforcement and it is an operant. To make this clear, autoshaping produces respondent behavior that can then be reinforced. Once behavior is reinforced, it is regulated by consequences that follow it and it is operant.

ADVANCED ISSUE
The Nature of Autoshaped Responses

Negative Automaintenance.   When scientists are confronted with new and challenging data, they are typically loathe to accept the findings. This is because researchers have invested time, money, and effort in experiments that may depend on a particular view of the world. Consider a person who has made a career of investigating the operant behavior of pigeons, with key pecks as the major dependent variable. The suggestion that key pecking is respondent, rather than operant behavior, would not be well received by such a scientist. If key pecks are reflexive, then conclusions about operant behavior based on these responses are questionable. One possibility is to explain the data within the context of operant conditioning.

In fact, Brown and Jenkins (1968) suggested just this sort of explanation for their results. Recall that these experimenters pointed to the species-specific tendency of pigeons to peck at stimuli they look at. When the light is illuminated, the bird looks and pecks. Some of these responses are followed by food, and pecks increase in frequency. Other investigators noted that when birds are magazine trained, they stand in the general area of the feeder, and the response key is typically at head height, just above the food tray. Anyone who has watched a pigeon knows that they constantly bob their heads. Since they are close to the key and are making pecking (or bobbing) motions, it is possible that a strike at the key is unintentionally followed by food delivery. From this perspective, key pecks are superstitious in the sense that they are accidentally reinforced. The superstitious explanation has an advantage because it does not require postulating a look-peck connection and it is entirely consistent with operant conditioning.

Although these explanations of pecking as an operant are plausible, the possibility remains that the autoshaped peck is respondent behavior. An ingenious experiment by Williams and Williams (1969) was designed to answer this question. In their experiment, pigeons were placed in an operant chamber and key illumination was repeatedly followed by food. This is, of course, the same procedure that Brown and Jenkins (1968) used to show autoshaping. The twist in the Williams and Williams procedure was that if the bird pecked the key, food was not presented. This is called omission training because if the pigeon pecks the key, it is not reinforced.

The logic of this procedure is that if pecking is respondent, then it is elicited by the key light and the pigeon will reflexively strike the disk. If, on the other hand, pecking is operant, then striking the key prevents reinforcement and responses should not be maintained. Thus, the clear prediction is that, with the **omission procedure** in place, if the bird pecks the key it is respondent behavior. Using this procedure, Williams and Williams (1969) found that pigeons frequently pecked the key even though responses prevented reinforcement. This finding suggests that, for pigeons, the sight of grain is an unconditioned stimulus that elicits an unconditioned response peck at the food. When a key light stimulus precedes grain presentation, it becomes a CS that evokes a peck at the key (CR). Figure 6.3 shows this arrangement between stimulus events and responses.

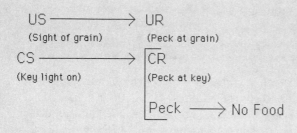

FIG. 6.3 Omission training procedures based on Williams and Williams (1969).

In discussing their results, Williams and Williams state that "the stimulus-reinforcer pairing overrode opposing effects of . . . reinforcement indicate[ing] that the effect was a powerful one, and demonstrate[ing] that a high level of responding does not imply the operation of . . . [operant] reinforcement" (1969, p. 520). The puzzling aspect of this finding is that in most cases pecks to a key are regulated by reinforcement and are clearly operant. Many experiments have shown that key pecks increase or decrease in frequency depending on the consequences that follow behavior.

The Nature of the Autoshaped Response.
Because of this apparent contradiction, several experiments were designed to investigate the nature of autoshaped pecking. Schwartz and Williams (1972a) preceded grain reinforcement for pigeons by turning on a red or white light on two separate keys. The birds responded by pecking the illuminated disk (i.e., they were autoshaped). On some trials, the birds were presented with both the red and white keys. A peck on the red key prevented reinforcement, as in the omission procedure used by Williams and Williams (1969). However, pecks to the white key did not prevent reinforcement.

On these choice trials, the pigeons showed a definite preference for the white key that did not stop the delivery of grain. In other words, the birds more frequently pecked the key that was followed by the presentation of grain. Because this is a description of behavior regulated by an operant contingency (peck → food), autoshaped key pecks cannot be exclusively respondent. In concluding their paper, Schwartz and Williams wrote:

> a simple application of respondent principles cannot account for the phenomenon as originally described . . . and it cannot account for the rate and preference results of the present study. An indication of the way operant factors can modulate the performance of automaintained behavior has been given. . . . The analysis suggests that while automaintained behavior departs in important ways from the familiar patterns seen with arbitrary responses, the concepts and procedures developed from the operant framework are, nevertheless, influential in the automaintenance situation. (Schwartz & Williams, 1972a, p. 356)

Schwartz and Williams (1972b) went on to investigate the nature of key pecking by pigeons in several other experiments. The researchers precisely measured the contact duration of each peck that birds made to a response key. When the omission procedure was in effect, pigeons produced short duration pecks. If the birds were autoshaped but key pecks did not prevent the delivery of grain, peck durations were long. These same long-duration pecks occurred when the pigeons responded for food on a schedule of reinforcement. Generally, it appears that there are two types of key pecks: short-duration pecks evoked by the presentation of grain, and long-duration pecks that occur when the bird's behavior is brought under operant control.

Other evidence also suggests that both operant and respondent conditioning are involved in autoshaping. It is likely that the first autoshaped peck is a respondent that is evoked by light-food pairings. However, once pecking produces food, it comes under operant control. Even when the omission procedure is in effect, a similar process probably occurs. During omission training, a response to the key turns off the key light and food is not delivered. If the bird does not peck the key, the light is eventually turned off and food is presented. Because on these trials turning the light off is associated with reinforcement, a dark key becomes a conditioned reinforcer. Thus, the bird pecks the key and is reinforced when the light goes off. Hursh, Navarick, and Fantino (1974) provided evidence for this view. They showed that birds quit responding during omission training if the key light did not immediately go out when a response was made.

Contingencies of Sign Tracking, Autoshaping and Instinctive Drift.   In discussing their 1968 experiments on autoshaping, Brown and Jenkins report that:

> experiments in progress show that location of the key near the food tray is not a critical feature [of autoshaping], although it no doubt hastens the process. Several birds have acquired the peck to a key located on the wall opposite the tray opening or on a side wall. (p. 7)

This description of autoshaped pecking by pigeons sounds similar to sign tracking by dogs. Both autoshaping and sign tracking involve species-characteristic behavior that is evoked by food presentation. Instinctive drift also appears to be reflexive behavior that is elicited by food. Birds peck at grain and make similar responses to the key light. Dogs make food-soliciting responses to the signal that precedes food reinforcement. Raccoons rub and manipulate food items and make similar responses to coins that precede food delivery. It is likely that autoshaping, sign tracking, and instinctive drift represent the same (or very similar) processes (for a discussion, see Hearst & Jenkins, 1974).

One proposed possibility is that all of these phenomena (instinctive drift, sign tracking, and autoshaping) are instances of **stimulus substitution.** That is, when a CS (e.g., light) is paired with a US (e.g., food) the conditioned stimulus is said to substitute for the unconditioned stimulus. This means that responses evoked by the CS (rubbing, barking and prancing, pecking) are similar to the ones evoked by the US. While this is a parsimonious account, there is evidence that it is wrong.

Recall from Chapter 3 that the laws of the reflex (US → UR) do not hold for the CS → CR relationship, suggesting there is no substitution of the CS for the US. Also, in many experiments, the behavior evoked by the US is opposite in direction to the responses elicited by the conditioned stimulus (see Chapter 4 on Drug Use, Abuse, and Conditioning). Additionally, there are experiments conducted within the autoshaping paradigm that directly refute the stimulus substitution hypothesis.

In an experiment by Wasserman (1973), chicks were placed in a very cool enclosure. In this situation, a key light was occasionally turned on and this was closely followed by the activation of a heat lamp. All the chicks began to peck the key light in an unusual way. The birds moved toward the key light and rubbed their beaks back and forth on it; behavior described as snuggling. These responses resemble the behavior that newborn chicks direct toward their mothers, when soliciting warmth. Chicks peck at their mothers' feathers and rub their beaks from side to side, behavior that results in snuggling up to their mother.

At first glance, the "snuggling to the key light" seems to illustrate an instance of stimulus substitution. The chick behaves to the key light as it does toward its mother. The difficulty is that the chicks in Wasserman's (1973) experiment responded completely differently to the heat lamp than to the key light. In response to heat from the lamp, a chick extended its wings and stood motionless, behavior that it might direct toward intense sunlight. In this experiment, it is clear that the CS does not substitute for the US because these stimuli evoke completely different responses (also see Timberlake and Grant, 1975).

An alternative to stimulus substitution has been proposed by Timberlake (1983; 1993) who suggested that each US (food, water, sexual stimuli, warmth, and so on) controls a distinct set of species-specific responses or a **behavior system.** That is, for each species there is a behavior system related to procurement of food, another related to obtaining water, still another for securing warmth, and so on. For example, the presentation of food to a raccoon evokes the behavior system that consists of procurement and ingestion of food. One of these behaviors, rubbing and manipulating the item, is evoked. Other behaviors like bringing the food item to the mouth, salivation, and chewing and swallowing of the food are not elicited. Timberlake goes on to propose that the particular responses evoked by the CS depend, in part, on the physical properties of the stimulus. Presumably, in the Wasserman experiment, properties of the key light (a visual stimulus raised above the floor) were more related to snuggling than to standing still and extending wings.

At the present time, it is not possible to predict which response in a behavior system will be evoked by a given CS. That is, a researcher can predict that the CS will elicit one or more of the responses controlled by the US, but cannot specify which responses will occur. One possibility is that the salience of the US affects which responses are elicited by the CS. For example, as the intensity of the heat source increases (approximating a hot summer day) the chicks response to the CS key light may change from snuggling to behavior appropriate to standing in the sun (open wings and motionless).

Operant Contingencies Predominate over Respondent Regulation of Behavior

As you have seen, there are circumstances in which both operant and respondent conditioning occur. Moreover, responses that on the basis of topography are typically operant are occasionally regulated by respondent processes (and as such are respondents). There are also occasions in which behavior that, in form or topography, appears to be reflexive is regulated by the consequences that follow it.

Reinforcing Reflexive Behavior.   In the 1960s, a number of researchers attempted to show that involuntary reflexive or autonomic responses could be operantly conditioned (Kimmel & Kimmel, 1963; Miller & Carmona, 1967; Shearn, 1962). Miller and Carmona (1967) deprived dogs of water and monitored their respondent level of salivation. The dogs were separated into two groups. One group was reinforced with water for increasing salivation and the other group was reinforced for a decrease. Both groups of animals showed the expected change in amount of salivation. That is, the dogs that were reinforced for increasing saliva flow showed an increase, and the dogs reinforced for less saliva flow showed a decrease.

At first glance, this result seems to demonstrate the operant conditioning of salivation. However, Miller and Carmona (1967) noticed an associated change in the dogs' behavior that could have produced the alteration in salivation. Dogs that increased saliva flow appeared to be alert, and those that decreased it were described as drowsy. For this reason, the results are suspect—salivary conditioning may have been mediated by a change in the dogs' operant behavior. Perhaps drowsiness was operant behavior that resulted in decreased salivation, and being alert increased the reflex. In other words, the change in salivation could have been part of a larger, more general behavior pattern that was reinforced. Similar problems occurred with other experiments. For example, Shearn (1962) showed operant conditioning of heart rate, but this dependent variable can be affected by a change in pattern of breathing.

The Miller Experiments.   It is difficult to rule out operant conditioning of other behavior as a mediator of reinforced reflexes. However, Miller and DiCara (1967) conducted a classic experiment in which this explanation was not possible. The researchers reasoned that operant behavior could not mediate conditioning if the subject had its skeletal muscles immobilized. To immobilize their subjects, which were white rats, they used the drug curare. This drug paralyzes the skeletal musculature and interrupts breathing.

There are a number of technical problems associated with experiments like this. Because breathing is affected by curare, the rats had to be given artificial respiration. Careful monitoring of the animals' physiological or autonomic responses was necessary to show any conditioning effects. When curarized, the rats could not swallow food or water, and this made it difficult to reinforce the animals' behavior. Miller and DiCara solved this last problem by using electrical stimulation of the rats' pleasure center, which is located in the brain, as reinforcement for visceral reflexes.

Before starting the experiment, the rats had electrodes permanently implanted in their hypothalamus. This was done in a way that allowed the experimenters to connect and disconnect the animals from the equipment that pulsed the pleasure center. To make certain that the stimulation was reinforcing, the rats were trained to press a bar in order to turn on a brief microvolt pulse. This procedure demonstrated that the pulse was, in fact, reinforcing since the animals pressed a lever for the stimulation.

At this point, Miller and DiCara curarized the rats and reinforced half of them with electrical stimulation for decreasing their heart rate. The other animals were reinforced for an increase in heart rate. Figure 6.4 shows the results of this experiment. Both groups start out with heart rates in the range of 400 to 425 beats per minute. After 90 minutes of contingent reinforcement, the groups are widely divergent. The group that was reinforced for slow heart rate is at about 310 beats per minute, and the fast rate group is at approximately 500 beats per minute.

Miller and Banuazizi (1968) extended this finding. They inserted a pressure-sensitive balloon into the large intestine of rats, which allowed them to monitor intestinal contractions. At the same time, the researchers measured the animals' heart rate. As in the previous experiment, the rats were curarized and reinforced with electrical brain stimulation. In different conditions, reinforcement was made contingent on increased or decreased intestinal contractions. Also, the rats were reinforced on some occasions for a decrease in heart rate, and at other times for an increase.

The researchers showed that reinforcing intestinal contractions or relaxation changed them in the appropriate direction. The animals also showed an increase or decrease in heart rate when this response was made contingent on brain stimulation. Finally, Miller and Banuazizi (1968) demonstrated that a change in intestinal contractions did not affect heart rate and, conversely, changes in heart rate did not affect contractions.

Thus, contingent reinforcement modified behavior, usually considered to be reflexive, under conditions in which skeletal responses could not affect the outcome. Also, the effects were specific to the response that was reinforced, showing that brain stimulation was not generating general physiological changes that produced the outcomes of the experiment. It seems that responses, which are usually elicited, can be conditioned using an operant contingency of reinforcement. Greene and Sutor (1971) extended this conclusion to humans, showing that a galvanic skin response, or GSR, could be regulated by negative reinforcement (for a review of operant autonomic conditioning, see DiCara, 1970; Jonas, 1973; Kimmel, 1974; Miller, 1969).

Although this conclusion is probably justified, the operant conditioning of autonomic responses like blood pressure, heart rate, and intestinal contraction

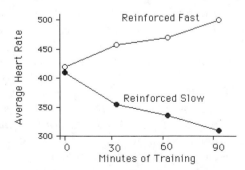

FIG. 6.4 Effects of curare immobilization of skeletal muscles on conditioning of heart rate in Miller and DiCara (1967) experiment.

has run into difficulties. Miller has even had problems replicating the results of his own experiments (Miller & Dworkin, 1974). The weight of the evidence does suggest that reflexive responses are, at least in some circumstances, affected by the consequences that follow them. However, this behavior is also subject to control by contiguity or pairing of stimuli. It is relatively easy to change heart rate by pairing a light (CS) with electric shock and then using the light to change heart rate. It should be evident that controlling heart rate with an operant contingency is no easy task. Thus, autonomic behavior may not be exclusively tied to respondent conditioning, but respondent conditioning is particularly effective with these responses.

FOCUS ON TEACHING
Operants and Respondents

Clearly, the fundamental distinction between operant and respondent conditioning is operational. The distinction is operational because conditioning is defined by the operations that produce it. Operant conditioning involves a contingency between behavior and its following consequences. Respondent conditioning entails the pairing of stimuli.

Autonomic responses are usually respondents and are best modified by respondent conditioning. If, however, they are changed by the consequences that follow them, they are operants. Similarly, skeletal responses are usually operant and they are most readily changed by contingencies of reinforcement, but when they are modified by the pairing of stimuli they are respondents.

THE BIOLOGICAL CONTEXT OF CONDITIONING

As we stated in Chapter 1, the evolutionary history, ontogenetic history, and current physiological status of an organism is the context for conditioning. Edward Morris (1992) has described the way we use the term *context*:

> Context is a funny word. As a non-technical term, it can be vague and imprecise. As a technical term, it can be vague and imprecise—and has been throughout the history of psychology. In what follows, I mean to use it technically and precisely.... First, the historical context—phylogenetic and ontogenetic, biological and behavioral—establishes the current structure and function of biology (anatomy and physiology) and behavior (form and function). Second, the form or structure of the current context, organismic or environmental, affects (or enables) what behavior can physically or formally occur. Third, the current context affects (actualizes) the functional relationships among stimuli and response (i.e., their "meaning" for one another). (p. 14)

Reinforcing events, responses, and stimuli may vary from species to species. A hungry dog can be reinforced with meat for jumping a hurdle, and a pigeon will fly to a particular location to get grain. These are obvious species differences, but there are more subtle effects of the biological context. The rate of acquisition and level of behavior once established may be influenced by an organism's physiology, as determined by species history. Moreover, within a species, reinforcers, stimuli, and responses can be specific to particular situations.

Behavior that is observed with any one set of responses, stimuli, and reinforcers may change when different sets are used. In addition, different species may show different environment-behavior relationships when the same set of responses and events is investigated. However, within a particular set of events, the principles of behavior hold. Also, principles of behavior like extinction, discrimination, spontaneous recovery, and so on generalize across species. The behaviors of school children working at math problems for teacher attention and of pigeons pecking keys for food are regulated by contingencies of reinforcement.

As early as 1938, Skinner recognized that a comprehensive understanding of the behavior of organisms required the study of more than "arbitrary" stimuli, responses, and reinforcers (Skinner, 1938, pp. 10–11). However, by using simple stimuli, easy-to-execute responses, and precise reinforcers, Skinner hoped to identify general principles of conditioning. By and large, this same strategy is used today in the modern operant laboratory.

The biological context suggests that the needed element is a specification of how behavior principles apply given the organism and the environmental situation. Also, it is worth noting that in many instances, principles of behavior generalize across responses, reinforcers, stimuli, and organisms. With regard to this generalization, human conduct is probably more sensitive to environmental influence than the behavior of any other species. In this sense, humans may be the organisms best described by general principles of behavior.

Taste Aversion Learning

In an experiment by Wilcoxon, Dragoin, and Kral (1971), quail and rats were given blue salty water. After the animals drank the water, they were made sick. Following this, the animals were given a choice between water that was not colored but tasted salty, and plain water that was colored blue. The rats avoided the salty-flavored water, and the quail would not drink the colored solution. This finding is not difficult to understand—when feeding or drinking, birds rely on visual cues; and rats are sensitive to taste and smell. In the natural habitat, drinking liquids that produce illness should be avoided, and this has obvious survival value. Because quail typically select food on the basis of what it looks like, they avoided the colored water. Rats, on the other hand, associated the taste of the water with sickness.

In this experiment, the taste or color of the water was a CS that was paired with the US illness. Both species came to avoid one or the other of these stimulus elements based on biological history. In other words, the biology of the organism dictated which cue became a CS, but the conditioning of the aversion, or CS-US

Type of water

		Bright-Noisy	Flavored
Type of aversive stimulus	Shock	Bright-Noisy drinking followed by shock	Flavored drinking followed by shock
	Poison	Bright-Noisy drinking followed by poison	Flavored drinking followed by poison

FIG. 6.5 Conditions used to show taste aversion conditioning by rats in an experiment by Garcia and Koelling (1966). Relation of cue to consequence in avoidance learning (from *Psychonomic Science*, 4, 123–124, reprinted by permission of Psychonomic Society, Inc.).

pairing, was the same for both species. Of course, a bird that relied on taste for food selection would be expected to associate taste and illness. This phenomenon has been called **preparedness**—quail are more biologically prepared to associate sights with illness, and rats quickly make a flavor-illness association. Other experiments have shown that within a species the set of stimuli, responses, and reinforcers may be affected by the biology of the organism.

Garcia and his colleagues conducted several important experiments that were concerned with the conditions that produce taste aversion in rats.[1] Garcia and Koelling (1966) had thirsty rats drink tasty (saccharin-flavored) water or unflavored water that was accompanied by flashing lights and gurgling noises (bright-noisy water). After the rats drank the water, one half of each group was immediately given an electric shock for drinking. The other animals were poisoned and made ill by injecting them with lithium chloride or by irradiating them with X-rays. Lithium chloride and high levels of X-rays poison the rats and produce nausea roughly 20 minutes after administration. Figure 6.5 shows the four conditions of the experiment.

After avoidance training, the rats were allowed to drink and their water intake was measured. The major results of this experiment are shown in Figure 6.6. Baseline measures of drinking were compared to fluid intake after shock or poison were paired with a visual or flavor stimulus (CS). Both shock and illness induced by X-ray exposure suppressed drinking. Those rats that received shock for drinking the bright-noisy water and the ones that were poisoned after ingesting the flavored water substantially reduced their fluid intake. Water intake in the other two groups was virtually unaffected. The animals that were poisoned and made sick after drinking the bright-noisy water and those that were shocked for ingesting the flavored water did not show a conditioned aversion.

[1]It is worth noting that the rat is an ideal subject in these experiments for generalizing to humans. Like humans the rat is omnivorous—it eats both meats and vegetables. Rats live wherever humans do and are said to consume twenty percent of the worlds human food supply.

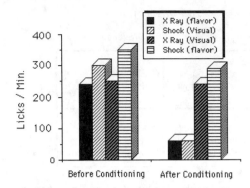

FIG. 6.6 Major results of the taste-aversion experiment by Garcia and Koelling (1966). Relation of cue to consequence in avoidance learning (from *Psychonomic Science, 4,* 123-124, reprinted by permission of Psychonomic Society, Inc.).

These results are unusual for several reasons. During respondent conditioning, the CS and US typically overlap or are separated by a few seconds. In the Garcia and Koelling (1966) experiment, the taste CS was followed much later by the US, poison. Also, it is often assumed that the choice of CS and US are irrelevant for respondent conditioning. However, taste and poison produced aversion, but taste and shock did not condition. Finally, for other kinds of classical conditioning many CS-US pairings are required, but aversion to taste conditioned after a single pairing of flavor-poison.

These results can be understood by considering the biology of the rat. The animals are omnivorous and as such eat a wide range of meat and vegetable foods. Rats eat 10 to 16 small meals each day and frequently ingest novel food items. The animals are sensitive to smell and taste but have relatively poor sight. When contaminated, spoiled, rotten, or poisonous food is eaten, it typically has a distinctive smell and taste. For this reason, taste and smell but not visual cues are associated with illness. Conditioning after a long time period between CS and US occurs because there is usually a delay between ingestion of a toxic item and nausea. It would be unusual for a rat to eat and have this quickly followed by an aversive stimulus (flavor-shock); hence there is little conditioning. The survival value of one-trial conditioning, or quickly avoiding food items that produce illness, is obvious—eat that food again and it may kill you.

Taste aversion learning has been replicated and extended in many different experiments (see Barker, Best, & Domjan, 1977; Rozin & Kalat, 1971). Revusky and Garcia (1970) showed that the interval between a flavor CS and a poison US could be as much as 12 hours. Other findings suggest that a new taste is more easily conditioned than one that an animal has had experience with (Revusky & Bedarf, 1967). Novelty in setting (as well as taste) has been shown to increase avoidance of food when poison is the unconditioned stimulus. For example, Mitchell, Kirschbaum, and Perry (1975) fed rats in the same container at a particular location for 25 days. Following this, the researchers changed the food cup and made the animals ill. After this experience, the rats avoided eating from the new container.

Taste aversion learning also occurs in humans (Logue, 1979, 1985, 1988a). Dr. Alexandra Logue of the State University of New York, Stony Brook, has concluded:

conditioned food aversion learning in humans appears very similar to that in other species. As in other species, aversions can be acquired with long CS-US delays, the aversion most often forms to the taste of food, the CS usually precedes the US, aversions frequently generalized to foods that taste qualitatively similar, and aversions are more likely to be formed to less preferred, less familiar foods. Aversions are frequently strong. They can be acquired even though the subject is convinced that the food did not cause the subject's illness. (1985, p. 327)

Pretend that on a special occasion you spend an evening at your favorite restaurant. Stimuli at the restaurant include your date, waiters, waitresses, candles on the table, china, posters on the wall, and so on. You order several courses, most of them familiar, and "just to try it out" you have pasta alfredo for the first time. What you do not know is that a flu virus has invaded your body and is percolating away while you eat. Early in the morning, you wake up with a clammy feeling, rumbling stomach, and a hot acid taste in the back of your throat. You spew alfredo sauce, wine, and several other ugly bits and pieces on the bathroom mirror.

The most salient stimulus at the restaurant was probably your date. Alas, is the relationship finished? Will you get sick at the sight of your lost love? Is this what the experimental analysis of behavior has to do with romance novels? Of course, the answer to these questions is no. It is very likely that you will develop a strong aversion to pasta alfredo. Interestingly, you may be aware that your illness was caused by the flu, not the new food. You may even understand taste aversion learning but, as one of the authors of this book can testify to, it makes no difference. The novel-taste CS, because of its single pairing (delayed by several hours) with nausea, will likely be avoided in the future.

Adjunctive Behavior

On time-based or interval schedules, organisms may emit behavior patterns that are not required by the contingency of reinforcement (Staddon & Simmelhag, 1971). If you received $5 for pressing a lever once every 10 minutes, you might start to pace, twiddle your thumbs, have a sip of soda, or scratch your head between payoffs on a regular basis. Staddon (1977) has noted that during the time between food reinforcers, animals engage in three distinct types of behavior. Immediately after food reinforcement, **interim behavior** like drinking water may occur; next an organism may engage in **facultative behavior** that is independent of the schedule of reinforcement (e.g., rats may groom themselves); finally, as the time for reinforcement gets close, animals engage in food-related activities called **terminal behavior**, such as orienting toward the lever or food cup. The first of these categories, interim or **adjunctive behavior**,[2] is of most interest for the present discussion, because it is behavior that is not required by the schedule but is induced by reinforcement.

---

[2]Induced behavior that immediately follows reinforcement has been called interim by Staddon (1997), and adjunctive by Falk (1961; 1964; 1969). The terms are interchangeable in this book.

When a hungry animal is placed on a schedule of reinforcement, it may, if allowed to drink, ingest an excessive amount of water. Falk (1961, 1964, 1969) has suggested that this **polydipsia,** or excessive drinking, is adjunctive behavior induced by the time-based delivery of food. A rat that is working for food on an intermittent schedule may drink as much as half its body weight during a single session (Falk, 1961). This drinking occurs even though the animal is not water deprived. The rat may turn toward the lever, press for food, obtain and eat the food pellet, drink excessively, groom itself, and then repeat the sequence. Pressing the lever is required for reinforcement, and grooming may occur in the absence of food delivery, but polydipsia appears to be induced by the schedule.

In general, adjunctive behavior refers to any excessive and persistent behavior pattern that occurs as a side-effect of reinforcement delivery. The schedule may require a response for reinforcement, or it may simply be time based, as when food pellets are given every 30 seconds no matter what the animal is doing. Additionally, the schedule may deliver reinforcement on a fixed time basis (e.g., every 60 seconds) or it may be constructed so that the time between reinforcers varies (e.g., 20 seconds, then 75, 85, 60 seconds, and so on).

Schedules of food reinforcement have been shown to generate such adjunctive behavior as attack against other animals (Flory, 1969; Hutchinson, Azrin, & Hunt, 1968), licking at an airstream (Mendelson & Chillag, 1970), drinking water (Falk, 1961), and chewing on wood blocks (Villareal, 1967). Adjunctive behavior has been observed in pigeons, monkeys, rats, and humans; reinforcers have included water, food, shock avoidance, access to a running wheel, money, and for male pigeons the sight of a female (see Falk, 1971, 1977; Staddon, 1977, for reviews). Thus, adjunctive behavior occurs in different species, is generated by a variety of reinforcement procedures, and extends to a number of induced responses.

A variety of conditions affect adjunctive behavior, but the schedule of reinforcement delivery and the deprivation status of the organism appear to be the most important. As the time between reinforcement deliveries increases from 2 to 180 seconds, adjunctive behavior increases. After 180 seconds, adjunctive behavior drops off and reaches low levels at 300 seconds. For example, a rat may receive a food pellet every 10 seconds and drink a bit more than a normal amount of water between pellet deliveries. When the schedule is changed to 100 seconds, drinking increases; polydipsia goes up again if the schedule is stretched 180 seconds. As the time between pellets is further increased to 200, 250, and then 300 seconds, water consumption goes down. This increase, peak, and then drop in schedule-induced behavior is illustrated in Figure 6.7 and is called a bitonic function. The function has been observed in species other than the rat, and occurs for other adjunctive behavior (see Keehn & Jozsvai, 1989, for contrary evidence).

In addition to the reinforcement schedule, adjunctive behavior becomes more and more excessive as the level of deprivation increases. A rat that is at 80% of its normal body weight and is given food pellets every 20 seconds will drink more water than an animal that is at 90% weight and on the same schedule. Experiments have shown that food-schedule-induced drinking (Falk, 1969), airstream licking (Chillag & Mendelson, 1971), and attack (Dove, 1976) go up as an animal's

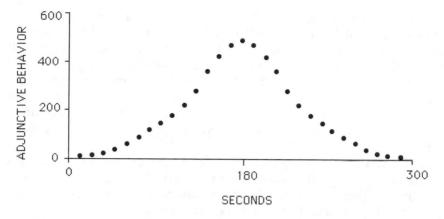

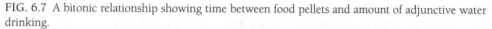

FIG. 6.7 A bitonic relationship showing time between food pellets and amount of adjunctive water drinking.

body weight goes down. Thus, a variety of induced activities escalate when deprivation for food is increased and when food is the scheduled reinforcer.

Falk (1977) has noted that "on the surface" adjunctive behavior does not seem to make sense:

> [Adjunctive activities] are excessive and persistent. A behavioral phenomenon which encompasses many kinds of activities and is widespread over species and high in predictability ordinarily can be presumed to be a basic mechanism contributing to adaptation and survival. The puzzle of adjunctive behavior is that, while fulfilling the above criteria its adaptive significance has escaped analysis. Indeed, adjunctive activities have appeared not only curiously exaggerated and persistent, but also energetically quite costly. (p. 326)

Falk (1977) goes on to argue that, in fact, induced behavior does make biological sense.

The argument made by Falk is complex and beyond the scope of this book. Simply stated, adjunctive behavior may be related to what ethologists call displacement behavior. **Displacement behavior** is seen in the natural environment and is "characterized as irrelevant, incongruous, or out of context. . . . For example, two skylarks in combat might suddenly cease fighting and peck at the ground with feeding movements" (Falk, 1971, p. 584). The activity of the animal does not make sense given the situation, and the displaced responses do not appear to follow from immediately preceding behavior. Like adjunctive behavior, displacement activities arise when consummatory (i.e., eating, drinking, etc.) activities are interrupted or prevented. In the laboratory, a hungry animal is interrupted from eating when small bits of food are intermittently delivered.

Adjunctive and displacement activities occur at high strength when biologically relevant behavior (i.e., eating or mating) is blocked. Recall that male pigeons engage in adjunctive behavior when reinforced with the sight (but not access to) female members of the species. These activities may increase the chance that other possibilities in the environment are contacted. A bird that pecks at tree bark when prevented from eating may find a new food source. Armstrong (1950) has suggested that "a species which is able to modify its behavior to suit changed circumstances by means of displacements, rather than by the evolution of ad hoc modifications starting from scratch will have an advantage over other species" (Falk, 1971, p. 587). Falk, however, goes on to make the point that evolution has probably eliminated many animals that engage in nonfunctional displacement activities.

Adjunctive behavior is another example of activity that is best analyzed by considering the biological context. Responses that do not seem to make sense may ultimately prove adaptive. The conditions that generate and maintain adjunctive and displacement behavior are similar. Both types of responses may reflect a common evolutionary origin, and this suggests that principles of adjunctive behavior will be improved by analyzing the biological context.

ON THE APPLIED SIDE

The Interrelations between Eating and Physical Activity

In 1967, Dr. Carl Cheney (who was then at Eastern Washington State University) ran across a paper (Routtenberg & Kuznesof, 1967) that reported self-starvation in laboratory rats. Cheney thought this was an unusual effect since most animals are reluctant to kill themselves for any reason. Because of this, he decided to replicate the experiment, and he recruited W. Frank Epling, an undergraduate student at the time, to help run the research. The experiment was relatively simple. Cheney and Epling (1968) placed a few rats in running wheels and fed them for 1 hour each day. The researchers recorded daily number of wheel turns, weight of the rat, and amount of food eaten. Surprisingly, the rats ran more and more, ate less and less, lost weight, and if allowed to continue in the experiment died of starvation. Importantly, the rats were not required to run and they had plenty to eat, but they stopped eating and ran as much as 10 miles a day.

Twelve years later, Dr. W. Frank Epling (who was then an assistant professor of psychology at the University of Alberta) began to do collaborative research with Dr. W. David Pierce. Pierce, a professor of sociology at the same university, wondered if anorexic patients were hyperactive, like the animals in the self-starvation experiments. If they were, it might be possible to develop an animal model of anorexia. Clinical reports indicated that, indeed, many anorexic patients were excessively active. For this reason, Epling and Pierce began to investigate the relationship between wheel running and food intake (Epling & Pierce, 1988; Epling, Pierce, & Stefan, 1983; Pierce & Epling, 1991). The basic finding is that physical activity decreases food intake and that decreased food intake increases activity. We call this feedback loop **activity anorexia** and argue that a similar cycle occurs in anorexic patients (see Epling & Pierce, 1992).

This analysis of eating and exercise suggests that these activities are interrelated. Depriving an animal of food should increase the reinforcing value of exercise. Rats that are required to press a lever in order to run on a wheel should work harder for wheel access when they are deprived of food. Additionally, engaging in exercise should reduce the reinforcing value of food. Rats that are required to press a lever for food pellets should not work as hard for food following a day of exercise. The authors designed two experiments to test these ideas (Pierce, Epling, & Boer, 1986).

Reinforcement Value of Exercise

We asked whether food deprivation increased the reinforcing effectiveness of wheel running. If animals worked harder for an opportunity to exercise when deprived of food, this would show that running had increased in its capacity to support behavior. That is, depriving an animal of food should increase the reinforcing value of running. This is an interesting implication because increased reinforcement effectiveness is usually achieved by withholding the reinforcing event. Thus, to increase the reinforcement value of water, a researcher typically withholds access to water, but (again) in this case food is withheld in order to increase the reinforcing value of wheel access.

We used nine young rats of both sexes to test the reinforcing effectiveness of wheel running as food deprivation changed. The animals were trained to press a lever to obtain 60 seconds of wheel running. When the rat pressed the lever, a brake was removed and the running wheel was free to turn. After 60 seconds, the brake was again activated and the animal had to press the lever to obtain more wheel movement for running. The apparatus that we constructed for this experiment is shown in Figure 6.8.

Once lever pressing for wheel running was stable, each animal was tested when it was food deprived (75% of normal weight) and when it was at free-feeding weight. Recall that the animals were expected to work harder for exercise

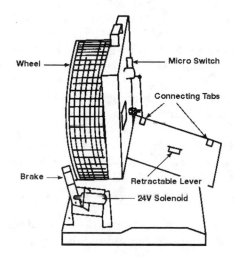

FIG. 6.8 Wheel-running apparatus used in Pierce, Epling, and Boer (1986) experiment on the reinforcing effectiveness of physical activity as a function of food deprivation (copyright 1986 by the Society for the Experimental Analysis of Behavior, Inc.).

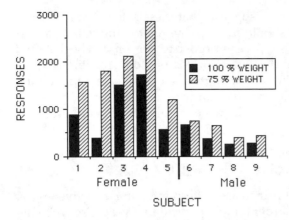

FIG. 6.9 Number of bar presses for 60 seconds of wheel running as a function of food deprivation (from Pierce, Epling, and Boer 1986, copyright 1986 by the Society for the Experimental Analysis of Behavior, Inc.).

when they were food deprived. To measure the reinforcing effectiveness of wheel running, the animals were required to press the lever more and more for each opportunity to run. Specifically, the rats were required to press five times to obtain 60 seconds of wheel running, then 10, 15, 20, 25, and so on. The point at which they gave up pressing for wheel running was used as an index of the reinforcing effectiveness of exercise.

The results of this experiment are shown in Figure 6.9. All animals lever pressed for wheel running more when food deprived than when at normal weight. In other words, animals worked harder for exercise when they were hungry. Further evidence indicated that the reinforcing effectiveness went up and down when an animal's weight was made to increase and decrease. For example, one rat pressed the bar 1,567 times when food deprived, 881 times at normal weight, and 1,882 times when again food deprived. This indicated that the effect was reversible and was tied to the level of food deprivation.

Reinforcement Value of Food

In a second experiment, we investigated the effects of exercise on the reinforcing effectiveness of food. Four male rats were trained to press a lever for food pellets. When lever pressing occurred reliably, we tested the effects of exercise on each animal's willingness to work for food. In this case, we expected that a day of exercise would decrease the reinforcement effectiveness of food on the next day.

Test days were arranged to measure the reinforcing effects of food. One day before each test, animals were placed in their wheels without food. On some of the days before a test, the wheel was free to turn and on other days it was not. Three of the four rats ran moderately in their activity wheels on exercise days. One lazy rat did not run when given the opportunity. This animal was subsequently forced to exercise on a motor-driven wheel. All animals were well rested (3 to 4 hours of rest) before each food test. This ensured that any effects were not caused by fatigue.

Reinforcement effectiveness of food was assessed by counting the number of lever presses for food as food became more and more difficult to obtain. For ex-

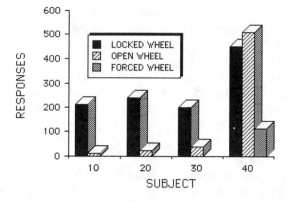

FIG. 6.10 Number of bar presses for food when rats were allowed to run on a wheel as compared with no physical activity (from Pierce, Epling, and Boer, 1986, copyright 1986 by the Society for the Experimental Analysis of Behavior, Inc.).

ample, an animal had to press 5 times for the first food pellet, 10 for the next, then 15, 20, 25, and so on. As in the first experiment, the giving-up point was used to measure reinforcement effectiveness. Presumably, the more effective or valuable the reinforcer (i.e., food) the harder the animal would work for it.

Figure 6.10 shows that when test days were preceded by a day of exercise, the reinforcing effectiveness of food decreased sharply. Animals pressed the lever more than 200 times when they were not allowed to run but no more than 38 times when running preceded test sessions. Food no longer supported lever presses following a day of moderate wheel running, even though a lengthy rest period preceded the test. Although wheel running was moderate, it represented a large change in physical activity since the animals were previously sedentary.

Prior to each test, the animals spent an entire day without food. Because of this, the reinforcing effectiveness of food should have increased. Exercise, however, seemed to override the effects of food deprivation since responding for food went down rather than up. Other evidence from these experiments suggested that the effects of exercise were similar to feeding the animal. This finding is important for understanding activity anorexia, since exercise appears to substitute for eating.

The rat that was forced to run also showed a sharp decline in lever pressing for food (see Figure 6.9). Exercise was again moderate but substantial relative to the animal's sedentary history. Because the reinforcement effectiveness of food decreased with forced exercise, we concluded that both forced and voluntary physical activity produce a decline in the value of food reinforcement. This finding suggests that people who increase their physical activity because of occupational requirements (e.g., ballet dancers) may value food less.

The Biological Context of Eating and Activity

In our view, the motivational interrelations between eating and physical activity have a basis in natural selection. Natural selection favored those animals that increased locomotor activity in times of food scarcity. During a famine, organisms can either stay and conserve energy or become mobile and travel to another location. The particular strategy adopted by a species depends on natural selection. If travel led to reinstatement of food supply and remaining resulted in starvation, then those animals that traveled gained reproductive advantage.

A major problem for an evolutionary analysis of activity anorexia is accounting for the decreased appetite of animals who travel to a new food patch. The fact that increasing energy expenditure is accompanied by decreasing caloric intake seems to violate common sense. From a homeostatic (i.e., energy balance) perspective, food intake and energy expenditure should be positively related. In fact, this is the case if an animal has the time to adjust to a new level of activity and food supply is not greatly reduced.

When depletion of food is severe, however, travel should not stop when food is infrequently contacted. This is because stopping to eat may be negatively balanced against reaching a more abundant food patch. Frequent contact with food would signal a replenished food supply, and this should reduce the tendency to travel. Recall that a decline in the reinforcing value of food means that animals will not work hard for nourishment. When food is scarce, considerable effort may be required to obtain it. For this reason, animals ignore food and continue to travel. However, as food becomes more plentiful and the effort to acquire it decreases, the organism begins to eat. Food consumption lowers the reinforcement value of physical activity and travel stops. On this basis, animals that expend large amounts of energy on migration become anorexic.

KEY WORDS

Activity anorexia

Adjunctive behavior

Autoshaping

Biological context of
behavior

Displacement behavior

Facultative behavior

Instinctive drift

Interim behavior

Negative
automaintenance

Omission training

Polydipsia

Preparedness

Schedule-induced
behavior

Sign tracking

Taste aversion learning

Terminal behavior

CHAPTER 7

Schedules of Reinforcement

LEARNING OBJECTIVES

1. Define a schedule of reinforcement. Compare humans and other organisms on similar schedules of reinforcement.

2. Discuss the behavior-analysis approach to science. In your answer, refer to the use of highly controlled settings, discouragement of speculation about the organism, study of behavior for its own sake, biological status as context, search for principles of behavior, accumulation of research, and integration of research by behavioral theory.

3. According to Reynolds (1966b), why is the study of schedules of reinforcement central to understanding behavior regulation? Why are the early studies of schedule performance still important?

4. Describe how orderly patterns of response develop on schedules of reinforcement. Use the terms *contingency of reinforcement* and *steady-state performance* in your answer.

5. What happens when a hungry rat presses a lever for food and obtains a pellet for every 10 responses?

6. Be able to discuss schedules of reinforcement in everyday life. How does a bird's foraging relate to schedules of reinforcement? Refer to the Cheney, Bonem, and Bonem (1985) experiment in your answer.

7. What role does intermittent reinforcement play in the regulation of human interaction?

8. Based on Azrin (1959), how does punishment affect behavior maintained on a fixed-ratio schedule of reinforcement?

9. Why did Azrin's findings (Azrin, 1959; Azrin & Holz, 1961) on schedule effects and punishment lack generality? Refer to behavior reinforced after a fixed amount of time in your answer.

10. What does Mechner notation describe? Write the notation for nine event symbols. Do the same for time and number symbols. What does R → S^r mean? What about R$_a$ → R$_b$? Write in Mechner notation (1) A and B occur at the same time, and B produces C; (2) A and B occur at the same time, A produces C, and B prevents C; (3) A and B occur at the same time, and B repeatedly produces C.

11. Define CRF and discuss resistance to extinction on this schedule. Compare CRF with intermittent reinforcement in terms of resistance to extinction. Refer to experiments by Hearst (1961) and Williams (1959) in your answer.

12. Discuss response stereotypy on CRF using a classic study by Antonitis (1951).

13. What does the research with pigeons tell us about response variability and rate of reinforcement? Give an interpretation of the findings based on this textbook. How would you produce a performance that is variable in form and resistant to extinction?

14. Define ratio and interval schedules. Name the four basic schedules of reinforcement. Write the Mechner notation for a FR25 schedule of reinforcement. Describe the characteristic effects of fixed ratio (FR) schedules, using run of responses and postreinforcement pause (PRP) in your answer.

15. Discuss FR schedules and building a sun deck. Analyze piece-rate work in factories as schedule performance. Why do management and workers often disagree about piece-rate contingencies?

16. What is a variable ratio (VR) schedule of reinforcement? Write the Mechner notation for a VR10 schedule. Compare FR and VR schedules in terms of behavioral effects. Give examples of VR schedules in everyday life.

17. Define a fixed interval (FI) schedule. Give the Mechner notation for FI 90 seconds. Describe the characteristic effects of FI schedules. Outline a hypothetical experiment with humans responding for money on an FI schedule. What pattern of behavior is likely to occur at steady state? What happens to FI performance if mediating behavior times out the interval?

Advanced Issue

18. *Distinguish between molar and molecular accounts of schedule performance.*

19. *Provide an IRT analysis of differences in rate of response on interval versus ratio schedules of reinforcement.*

20. Discuss transition states and performance during transition from one schedule to another. Relate transition of schedule to important human behavior.

21. Outline the experiment by Roll, Higgins, and Badger (1996) concerned with abstinence from cigarette smoking and schedule of reinforcement. What schedule of reinforcement for abstinence was most effective? Why was this schedule the most effective?

The stimuli that precede operants and the consequences that follow them may be arranged in many different ways. A **schedule of reinforcement** describes this arrangement. In other words, a schedule of reinforcement is a prescription that states how and when discriminative stimuli and behavioral consequences will be presented (Morse, 1966). In the laboratory, sounding a buzzer in an operant chamber may be a signal (S^D) that sets the occasion for each lever press (operant) to produce food (consequence). A similar schedule operates when a dark room sets the occasion for a person to turn on a lamp, which, of course, is followed by light in the room.

At first glance, a rat pressing a lever for food and a person turning on a light seem to have little in common. Humans are very complex organisms: They build cities, write books, go to college, go to war, conduct experiments, and do many other things that rats cannot do. In addition, pressing a bar for food appears to be very different from switching on a light. Nonetheless, performance on schedules of reinforcement has been found to be remarkably similar for different organisms, many types of behavior, and a variety of reinforcers. When the schedule of reinforcement is the same, a child solving math problems for teacher approval may generate behavior that is comparable to a bird pecking a key for water.

THE IMPORTANCE OF SCHEDULES OF REINFORCEMENT

Schedules of reinforcement have been investigated over the last 5 decades. They were first described by B. F. Skinner in the 1930s and were a major discovery. Today, few studies focus directly on simple schedules of reinforcement. However, the lawful relations that have emerged from the analysis remain an important part of the science of behavior.

FOCUS ON ISSUES
Science and Behavior Analysis

The experimental analysis of behavior is a progressive enterprise. Research findings are accumulated and integrated to provide a general account of the behavior of organisms. Often, simple animals in highly controlled settings are studied. The strategy is to build a comprehensive theory of behavior that rests on direct observation and experimentation.

The field emphasizes a descriptive approach and discourages speculations that go beyond the data. Such speculations include reference to the organism's memory, thought processes, expectations, and undocumented accounts based on presumed physiological states. For example, a behavioral account of schedules of reinforcement provides a description of how behavior is altered by contingencies of reinforcement. One such account is based on evidence that a particular schedule sets up differential reinforcement of the time between responses (interresponse times, or IRT; see later in this chapter). This sort of analysis provides an understanding of an organism's performance in terms of specific environment-behavior relationships.

Behavior analysts study the behavior of organisms, including people, for its own sake. Behavior is not studied in order to make inferences about mental states or physiological processes. Although most behaviorists emphasize the importance of biology and physiological processes, they focus on the interplay of behavior and environment.

To maintain this focus, the evolutionary history and biological status of an organism are examined as part of the context for specific environment-behavior interactions. For example, some people seem more driven by sexual stimuli than others. Natural selection may have resulted in a distribution of susceptibility to sexual reinforcement (of course, cultural conditioning will also contribute). People who are strongly affected by sexual consequences may develop a broad repertoire of behavior that leads to sexual gratification. When given a choice between sexual and nonsexual reinforcement, the person will often select the sexual alternative. In extreme cases, behavior regulated by sexual stimuli may be so exaggerated that the person is called a criminal and is subjected to legal sanctions. A man who makes obscene phone calls is strongly reinforced by a woman's reaction to his words. The woman's reaction is a conditioned reinforcer for his call. Although he has learned the relationship between obscene talk and her reaction, his biological history plays a role in the effectiveness of the reinforcement contingency.

Accumulating information about environment-behavior relations has, in recent years, led to the formulation of several principles of behavior. For example, animals and people are much more persistent on a task when they have been reinforced on a schedule that only pays off occasionally. This persistence is especially pronounced during extinction and is called the **partial reinforcement effect**. Other principles of behavior (e.g., discrimination and conditioned reinforcement) have been identified through the experimental analysis of schedule effects.

As more and more information becomes available, the goal of a comprehensive behavior theory comes closer. Chapter 10 presents the work on concurrent schedules of reinforcement. This research has been prominent over the past 20 years and today is used to formulate theories and models of behavioral choice and preference. These theories draw on earlier work and become more sophisticated as data accumulate.

Contemporary behavior analysis continues to build on previous research. The extension of behavior principles to more complex processes and to human behavior is of primary importance. The analysis remains focused on the environmental conditions that regulate the behavior of organisms. Schedules of reinforcement concern the arrangement of environmental events that support behavior. The analysis of schedule effects is currently viewed within a biological context. In this analysis, biological factors play several roles. One way biology affects behavior is through specific physiological events that function as reinforcement and discriminative stimuli (see Chapter 1). Biological variables may also constrain or enhance environment-behavior relationships, as we have noted. As behavior analysis and the other biological sciences progress, an understanding of biological factors becomes increasingly important for a comprehensive theory of behavior.

The knowledge that has accumulated about the effects of schedules is central to understanding behavior regulation. G. S. Reynolds (1966b) underscored this point and wrote that

schedules of reinforcement have regular, orderly, and profound effects on the organism's rate of responding. The importance of schedules of reinforcement can-

not be overestimated. No description, account, or explanation of any operant behavior of any organism is complete unless the schedule of reinforcement is specified. Schedules are the mainsprings of behavioral control, and thus the study of
schedules is central to the study of behavior.... Behavior that has been attributed
to the supposed drives, needs, expectations, ruminations, or insights of the organism can often be related much more exactly to regularities produced by
schedules of reinforcement. (p. 60)

Modern technology has made it possible to analyze performance on schedules of reinforcement in increasing detail. Nonetheless, early experiments on
schedules remain important. The experimental analysis of behavior is a progressive science in which observations and experiments build on one another. In this
chapter, we will present early and later research on schedules of reinforcement.
The analysis of schedule performance will range from a global consideration of
cumulative records to a detailed consideration of the time between responses.

Schedules and Patterns of Response

Patterns of response develop on schedules of reinforcement (Ferster & Skinner,
1957). These patterns come about after an animal has experience with the **contingency of reinforcement** defined by a particular schedule. Subjects are exposed to
a schedule of reinforcement and, following an acquisition period, behavior typically settles into a consistent or **steady-state performance.** It may take many experimental sessions before a particular pattern emerges, but once it does, the or-
derliness of behavior is remarkable.

The first description of schedule performance was provided by B. F. Skinner
(1938) in his book, *The Behavior of Organisms.* In the preface to the seventh printing
of that book, Skinner writes that "the cumulative records ... purporting to show
orderly changes in the behavior of individual organisms, occasioned some surprise and possibly, in some quarters suspicion" (p. xii). Any suspicion was put to
rest when Skinner's observations were replicated in many other experiments (see
Morse, 1966, for a review of early work on schedules of reinforcement).

The steady-state behavior generated when a fixed number of responses is reinforced illustrates one of these patterns. For example, a hungry rat might be required to press a lever 10 times to get a food pellet. Following reinforcement, the
animal has to make another 10 responses to produce the next bit of food, then 10
more responses, and so on.

When organisms are reinforced for a fixed number of responses, a pause-
and-run pattern of behavior develops. Responses required by the schedule are
made rapidly and result in reinforcement. Following each reinforcement, there is
a pause in responding, then another quick burst of responses (see the section on
fixed ratio later in this chapter for more detail). This pattern repeats over and
over and occurs even when the size of the schedule is changed. A pause-and-run
pattern has been found for horses (Myers & Mesker, 1960), chickens (Lane, 1961),
a vulture (Witoslawski, Anderson, & Hanson, 1963), and children (Orlando &
Bijou, 1960).

Schedules and Natural Contingencies

In the everyday environment, behavior is often reinforced on an **intermittent** basis. That is, operants are reinforced occasionally rather than each time they are emitted. Every time a child cries, he or she is not reinforced with attention. Each time a predator hunts, it is not successful. When you dial the number for airport information, you get through sometimes, but often the exchange is busy. Buses do not immediately arrive when you go to a bus stop. In concluding his review of schedule research, Dr. Michael Zeiler (1977) states:

> it is impossible to study behavior either in or outside the laboratory without en-
> countering a schedule of reinforcement: whenever behavior is maintained by a
> reinforcing stimulus, some schedule is in effect and is exerting its characteristic
> influences. Only when there is a clear understanding of how schedules operate
> will it be possible to understand the effects of reinforcing stimuli on behavior.
> (p. 229)

Consider a bird foraging for food. The bird turns over sticks or leaves and once in a while finds a seed or insect. These bits of food occur every now and then, and the distribution of reinforcement is the schedule that maintains the animal's foraging behavior. If you were watching this bird hunt for food, you would probably see the animal's head bobbing up and down. You might also see the bird pause and look around, change direction, and so on. This sort of activity is often attributed to the animal's instinctive behavior patterns. Although biology certainly plays some role in this episode, so does the schedule of food reinforcement.

Dr. Carl Cheney and his colleagues created a laboratory analog of foraging that allowed pigeons to choose between two food patches (Cheney et al., 1985). The density of food was based on two schedules of reinforcement that increased or decreased with the amount of foraging. They found that the greater the cost of hunting in a patch, the more the effort to change patches, and the higher the gains in the alternative patch, all contributed to the likelihood that an animal would change patches. This research is an interesting laboratory model of animal foraging in the wild that uses schedules of reinforcement to simulate natural contingencies.

Intermittent reinforcement plays an important role in the regulation of human social interaction. In this case, the behavior of one person affects what another individual does. For example, John asks his friend George, who is looking out the window, if the pizza delivery person has arrived yet. The operant is John's question, "Is the pizza here?" Reinforcement for the question is the reply from George. Importantly, George's reply is not certain and depends on many factors. George may not hear the question; he may be preoccupied with other things; he may have just had an argument with John and refuse to talk. No matter what the reason, John's question may not be reinforced on this occasion. Of course, most of the time George answers when asked a question. This means that John's verbal behavior is on an intermittent schedule of social reinforcement. Thus, one reason schedules are important is that they approximate some of the complex contingencies that operate in the everyday environment.

Ongoing Behavior and Schedule Effects

Zeiler's (1977) point that schedules of reinforcement typically affect operant behavior is well taken. Experimenters risk misinterpreting results when they ignore possible schedule effects. This is because schedules of reinforcement may interact with a variety of other independent variables and produce characteristic effects. For example, Azrin (1959) found that when every response on a fixed-ratio schedule of reinforcement (reinforcement occurs after a fixed number of responses) was punished, the pause after reinforcement increased. However, once the animal emitted the first response, operant rate was unaffected. In other words, the pause increased but otherwise behavior on the schedule remained the same. A possible conclusion is that punishment reduces the tendency to begin responding; however, once started, behavior is not suppressed by contingent aversive stimulation.

This conclusion is not correct because further experiments have shown that punishment has other effects when behavior is maintained on a different schedule of reinforcement (Azrin, 1958; Azrin & Holz, 1961). When behavior is reinforced after a fixed amount of time (rather than responses), an entirely different result occurs. On this kind of schedule, when each operant is punished, the pattern of behavior remains the same and rate of response declines. It should be obvious that conclusions concerning the effects of punishment on pattern and rate of response cannot be made without considering the schedule of reinforcement maintaining behavior.

In summary, schedules of reinforcement are important for an analysis of behavior regulation. The interplay of punishment and schedule performance is one example of how behavior regulated by schedules of reinforcement may interact with other independent variables. Schedules produce reliable patterns of response, and these patterns are consistent for different reinforcers, organisms, and for a variety of different operants. In our everyday environment, schedules of reinforcement are so common that we take such effects for granted. We wait for a taxi to arrive, line up at a bank to negotiate a transaction, solve 10 math problems for homework, and so on. All of these behavior-environment interactions illustrate schedules of reinforcement in our everyday lives. Social or behavioral scientists who ignore schedules of reinforcement do so at considerable risk.

FOCUS ON TEACHING
A System of Notation

This notation system is based on Mechner's (1959) description of reinforcement contingencies. We have simplified the notation and relabeled some of the symbols. The system of notation only describes independent variables. That is, **Mechner notation** describes what the experimenter does, not the behavior of subjects. In other words, Mechner notation represents the way that schedules of reinforcement are arranged. Cumulative records or other data describe what a subject does (i.e., the dependent variable) on those schedules.

Event	Symbols
S	Stimulus or event
S^r	Reinforcer
S^{r+}	Positive reinforcer
S^{r-}	Negative reinforcer (aversive stimulus)
S^D	Discriminative stimulus (event signaling reinforcement)
S$^\Delta$	S-delta (a discriminative stimulus that signals extinction)
S^{ave}	Conditioned aversive stimulus (an event that has signaled punishment)
R	Response (operant class)
R$_a$	Response of type a (i.e., a response on lever a)

Time and Number Symbols

F	Fixed
V	Variable
T	Time
N	Number

Relationships.   The horizontal arrow connecting two events (i.e., A → B) indicates that one event follows another. When the arrow leads to a consequence, as in R → S^r, the arrow is read as *produces*. In this case, a response (R) produces a consequence (S^r). If the arrow leads to a response, as in R$_a$ → R$_b$, it is read as *produces a condition where*. In other words, response R$_a$ "sets up" or allows response R$_b$ to produce an effect. For example, a press on lever *a* creates a situation where a press on lever *b* results in food.

Brackets.   All conditions listed vertically inside a bracket go into effect simultaneously. For example, A and B are conditions that occur at the same time, and the occurrence of B leads to event C.

When a vertical arrow cuts across a horizontal arrow, it means that the diagrammed event is prevented. In the following example, A and B occur at the same time. Event A leads to condition C, but event B blocks the A → C relationship. In other words, A leads to C but not if A and B occur together.

When events repeat, this may be shown by a horizontal arrow that starts at the end of a sequence and goes back to the beginning.

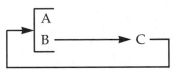

In the presence of A, the event B produces C; and after C occurs, the sequence repeats.

SCHEDULES OF POSITIVE REINFORCEMENT

Continuous Reinforcement

Continuous reinforcement, or **CRF**, is the simplest schedule of reinforcement. On this schedule, every operant required by the contingency is reinforced. For example, every time a hungry pigeon pecks a key, food is presented. When every operant is followed by a reinforcer, responses are emitted relatively fast. The organism continues to respond until it is satiated. In plain words, when the bird is hungry (food deprived), it rapidly pecks the key for food until it is full (satiated). If the animal is again deprived of the reinforcer and exposed to CRF, this pattern of responding followed by satiation occurs again. Figure 7.1 is a typical cumulative record of performance on continuous reinforcement.

CRF and Resistance to Extinction. Continuous reinforcement generates little **resistance to extinction**. Resistance to extinction is a measure of persistence when reinforcement is discontinued. This perseverance can be measured in several ways. The most obvious way to measure resistance to extinction is to count the number of responses and measure the length of time until **operant level** is

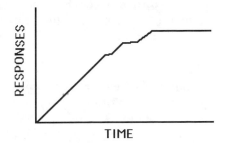

FIG 7.1 Performance on a continuous reinforcement schedule. Hatch marks indicating reinforcement are omitted since each response is reinforced. The flat portion of the record occurs when the animal stops making the response because of satiation.

reached. Operant level refers to the rate of a response before behavior is reinforced. For example, a laboratory rat could be placed in an operant chamber with no explicit contingency of reinforcement in effect. The number of times the animal pressed the response bar during a 2-hour exploration of the chamber is a measure of operant level. Measuring the time taken and number of responses made until operant level is attained is the best gauge of resistance to extinction.

Although continuing extinction until operant level is obtained provides the best measure of behavioral persistence, this method requires considerable time and effort. For this reason, measures that take less time are usually used. Resistance to extinction may be estimated by counting the number of responses emitted over a fixed number of sessions. For example, after exposure to CRF, reinforcement could be discontinued and the number of responses made in three daily 1-hour sessions counted. Another index of resistance to extinction is based on how fast rate of response declines during nonreinforced sessions. The point at which no response occurs for 5 minutes may be used to index extinction. The number of responses and time taken to that point are used as an estimate of behavioral persistence. These measures and others may be used to index resistance to extinction. The important criterion is that the method must be quantitatively related to extinction responding.

When compared to intermittent schedules, continuous reinforcement produces less resistance to extinction. This is called the partial or **intermittent reinforcement effect.** That is, when reinforcement is presented occasionally rather than for every response (as on CRF), behavior becomes more persistent during extinction. Hearst (1961) investigated the resistance to extinction produced by CRF and intermittent schedules. In this experiment, birds were trained on CRF and two intermittent schedules that provided reinforcement for pecking a key. The number of extinction responses that the animals made during three daily sessions of nonreinforcement were then counted. Basically, Hearst found that the birds made many more extinction responses after training on an intermittent schedule than after exposure to continuous reinforcement.

The intermittent reinforcement effect has been documented in humans. Williams (1959) reports that bedtime temper tantrums in a young child increased following one unintentional presentation of social reinforcement by the child's aunt (see the section in Chapter 5, "Extinction as a Modification Procedure for Temper Tantrums"). When the aunt reinforced the child's tantrum, a continuous reinforcement schedule was changed to an intermittent one. Thus, what is typically called persistence, perseverance, or endurance may actually be the effects of intermittent reinforcement. Persons who have difficulty sticking with a task may reflect a history of continuous reinforcement. Conversely, individuals who are described as stubborn or as having a great deal of persistence may show the effects of intermittent schedules.

Response Stereotypy on CRF.   On continuous reinforcement schedules, the form or topography of response becomes stereotyped or highly regular. In a classic study, Antonitis (1951) found that on CRF, operants were repeated with very little change in topography. In this study, rats were required to poke their noses anywhere along a 50-cm horizontal slot in order to get a food pellet (see Figure 7.2). Although not required by the contingency, the animals frequently responded at the same position on the slot. When the rats were placed on extinction, responses became more variable. These findings are not limited to laboratory rats and may reflect a principle of behavior.

Further research with pigeons suggests that response variability may be inversely related to the rate of reinforcement. In other words, as more and more responses are reinforced, less and less variation occurs in the members of the operant class. Herrnstein (1961a) reinforced pigeons for pecking on an intermittent schedule. The birds pecked at a horizontal strip and were occasionally reinforced with food. When some responses were reinforced, most of the birds pecked at the center of the strip — although they were not required to do so. During extinction, the animals made fewer responses to the center and more to other positions on the strip. Eckerman and Lanson (1969) replicated this finding in a subsequent study with pigeons. They varied the rate of reinforcement by comparing response variability under CRF, intermittent reinforcement, and extinction. Responses were stereotyped on CRF and became more variable when the birds were on extinction or on an intermittent schedule.

One interpretation of these findings is that organisms become more variable in their responding as reinforcement becomes less frequent. When a schedule of reinforcement is changed from CRF to intermittent reinforcement, the rate of reinforcement declines and response variability increases. A further change in rate of reinforcement occurs when extinction is started. In this case, operants are no longer reinforced and response variation is maximum. The general principle appears to be, "When things do not work, try new ways of behaving." In solving a problem, people usually employ a solution that has worked in the past. When the solution does not work, people try novel approaches to the problem. Pretend that you are a camper who is trying to start a fire. Most of the time, you gather leaves

FIG. 7.2 The apparatus used by Antonitis (1951). Rats could poke their noses anywhere along the 50-cm horizontal slot to obtain reinforcement.

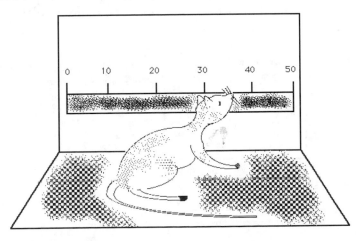

and sticks, place them in a heap, strike a match, and start the fire. This time the fire does not start. What do you do? If you are like most of us, you try different ways to get the fire going. You may change the kindling, add newspaper, use lighter fluid, build a shelter, and so on. Clearly, your behavior becomes more variable when reinforcement is withheld.

In summary, CRF is the simplest schedule of positive reinforcement. On this schedule, every response produces a reinforcer. Continuous reinforcement produces little resistance to extinction. This schedule also generates stereotyped response topography. Both resistance to extinction and variation in form of response increase on intermittent schedules.

RATIO AND INTERVAL SCHEDULES OF REINFORCEMENT

On intermittent schedules of reinforcement, some rather than all responses are reinforced. **Ratio schedules** are response based; that is, these schedules are set to deliver reinforcement following a number of responses. **Interval schedules** pay off when one response is made after some amount of time has passed. Interval and ratio schedules may be fixed or variable. Fixed schedules set up reinforcement after a fixed number of responses, or a constant amount of time, has passed. On variable schedules, response and time requirements may vary from one reinforcer to the next. Thus, there are four basic schedules: fixed ratio, variable ratio, fixed interval, and variable interval. In this section, we define these four basic schedules of reinforcement (shown in Figure 7.3) and describe the typical effects they produce. Following this discussion, some of the reasons for these effects are analyzed.

Ratio Schedules

Fixed Ratio.   A **fixed ratio,** or **FR,** schedule is programmed to deliver reinforcement after a fixed number of responses is made. Continuous reinforcement is FR 1; that is, after each response a reinforcer is delivered. Figure 7.4 presents a fixed-ratio schedule diagrammed in Mechner notation. In the presence of a discrimina-

REINFORCEMENT
CONTINGENT ON

		RESPONSES	TIME**
RESPONSE/TIME REQUIREMENT	FIXED	FIXED-RATIO (FR)	FIXED-INTERVAL (FI)
	VARIABLE	VARIABLE-RATIO (VR)	VARIABLE-INTERVAL (VI)

**The first response after a given amount of time

FIG. 7.3 A table of the four basic schedules of positive reinforcement (from Ferster, Culbertson, & Boren, 1975).

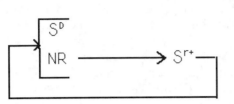

FIG. 7.4 A fixed-ratio schedule of positive reinforcement diagrammed in Mechner notation. In the presence of an S^D, a fixed number of responses results in reinforcement (S^{r+}). As indicated by the returning arrow, the sequence repeats such that another fixed number of responses will again produce reinforcement, and so on.

tive stimulus (S^D), a fixed number *(N)* of responses produces a reinforcer (S^{r+}). In a simple animal experiment, the S^D is sensory stimulation arising from the operant chamber, the response is a lever press, and food functions as reinforcement. On fixed-ratio 25 (FR 25), 25 lever presses must be made before food is presented. After reinforcement, the returning arrow indicates that another 25 responses will again produce the reinforcer.

The symbol *N* is used to indicate that fixed-ratio schedules can assume any value. Of course, it is unlikely that very high values (say, FR 100,000,000) would ever be completed. Nonetheless, this should remind you that Mechner notation describes independent variables, not what the organism does. Indeed, FR 100,000,000 could be easily programmed, but this schedule is essentially an extinction contingency since that animal will never complete the response requirement for reinforcement.

In 1957, Ferster and Skinner published a catalog of schedule contingencies and the characteristic effects of schedules of reinforcement. Their observations remain valid: FR schedules produce a rapid **run of responses,** followed by reinforcement, and then a pause in responding (Ferster & Skinner, 1957; Weissman & Crossman, 1966). A cumulative record of behavior on fixed ratio is presented in Figure 7.5. The record looks somewhat like a set of stairs (except at very small FR values, as shown by Crossman, Trapp, Bonem, & Bonem, 1985). There is a steep period of responding (the run), followed by reinforcement, and finally a flat portion. The flat part of the cumulative record is called the **postreinforcement pause, or PRP.**

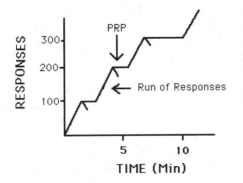

FIG. 7.5 A cumulative record of well-developed performance on FR 100. The typical pause-and-run pattern is presented. Reinforcement is indicated by the hatch marks. This is an idealized record that is typical of performance on many fixed-ratio schedules.

The pause in responding after the reinforcer is delivered does not occur, because the organism is consuming the reinforcer. Conditioned reinforcers like money, praise, and successful completion of a task also produce a pause when they are scheduled on fixed ratio. Consider what you might do if you had five sets of 10 math problems to complete for a homework assignment. A good bet is that you would solve 10 problems, then take a break before starting on the next set. When constructing a sun deck, one of the authors bundled nails into lots of 50 each. This had an effect on the "nailing behavior" of friends who were helping build the deck. The pattern that developed was to put in 50 nails, then stop, drink some beer, look over what was accomplished, have a chat, and finally start nailing again. In other words, a pause-and-run pattern typical of FR was generated by this simple scheduling of the nails.

In a factory, piece rates of payment are examples of fixed-ratio schedules. A worker may receive a dollar for sewing 20 pieces of elastic waistband. When the ratio of responses to reinforcement is large, FR schedules produce long pauses following reinforcement. This means that the overall productivity of the workers may be low and plant managers may complain about slacking off by the employees. The problem, however, is the schedule of reinforcement that relates a fixed number of responses to payment.

Piece work has been a contentious issue between management and workers. The fixed ratio may be gradually increased so that the company's labor cost remains the same while the number of units produced spirals upward (an increase in profit). A similar effect may be obtained in the laboratory when an animal is given the same amount of food for more and more lever presses. If carefully engineered, gradual increases in the ratio requirement may support an enormous amount of behavior for a single delivery of reinforcement. One of the roles of labor unions is the negotiation of the schedules of payment to the advantage of the workers. For instance, a union may negotiate the size of the fixed ratio, the amount of payment (magnitude of reinforcement), and alternative schedules that are based on both time and productivity.

Variable Ratio. Variable-ratio, or **VR,** schedules are similar to FRs except that the number of responses required for reinforcement changes after each reinforcer is presented. The average number of responses is used to define the schedule. A subject may press a lever for reinforcement 5 times, then 15, 7, 3, and 20. Adding these response requirements for a total of 50 and then dividing by the number of separate response runs (5) yields the schedule value, VR 10. The symbol *V* in Figure 7.6 indicates that the number of responses required for any one reinforcer is variable. Other than this change, the contingency is identical to fixed ratio (see Figure 7.4).

In general, ratio schedules produce a high rate of response. When VR and fixed-ratio schedules are compared, responding is typically faster on variable ratio. One reason for this is that pausing after reinforcement (PRP) is reduced or eliminated when the ratio contingency is changed from fixed to variable. This provides further evidence that the PRP does not occur because the animal is consuming the reinforcer (i.e., eating food). A rat or pigeon responding for food on VR does not

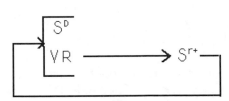

FIG. 7.6 A variable-ratio schedule of positive reinforcement. The symbol *V* indicates that the number of responses required for reinforcement is varied from one sequence to the next. The schedule is indexed by the average number of responses required for reinforcement. That is, a VR 10 requires an average of 10 responses before reinforcement is presented.

pause as many times, or for as long after reinforcement. When VR schedules are not excessive, postreinforcement pauses may occur (Kintsch, 1965; Webbe, DeWeese, & Malagodi, 1978). However, these pauses are typically smaller than those generated by fixed-ratio schedules (Mazur, 1983). Figure 7.7 portrays a typical pattern of response on a variable-ratio schedule of positive reinforcement.

In everyday life, variability is routine; for this reason, variable-ratio schedules are more common than FR schedules. You may have to hit a nail three times to drive it in, and the next may take six swings of the hammer. It may, on the average, take 70 casts of a fly rod to catch a trout, but any one strike is unpredictable. In baseball, the batting average refers to the player's schedule of reinforcement. A batter with a .300 average gets 3 hits for 10 times at bat. The schedule depends on a complex interplay among conditions set by the pitcher and the skill of the batter.

Many contingencies set by games of chance are similar to variable-ratio schedules. Gambling is often called addictive, but from a behavioral perspective it may be understood as persistent high-rate behavior generated by ratio contingencies of reinforcement. A bird may rapidly make thousands of responses for a few brief presentations of grain. When reinforcement is withdrawn, the animal will continue to respond at a high rate for a long period of time. As with fixed-ratio schedules, the average-ratio size may be increased to very large values. It is possible to set the average ratio so high that an animal will spend all of its time working for a small amount of food. The animal will show a net energy loss when effort expended exceeds caloric intake. A similar self-defeating response is seen in the behavior of gambling. Gambling involves the operant behavior of placing a

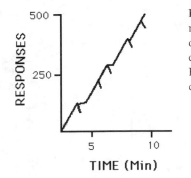

FIG. 7.7 A cumulative graph of typical responding on a variable-ratio schedule of reinforcement. Reinforcement is indicated by the hatch marks. Notice that PRPs are reduced or eliminated when compared with fixed-ratio performance.

bet that is reinforced with money after a variable number of bets. A person may feed money into a slot machine even though the overall payoff does not cover the cost of gambling. The seemingly irrational behavior of the gambler (spending more than winning) is generated by an unfavorable variable-ratio schedule.

Interval Schedules

Fixed Interval.   On **fixed-interval (FI)** schedules, an operant is reinforced after a fixed amount of time has passed. For example, on a fixed-interval 90-second schedule, one bar press after 90 seconds results in reinforcement. Following reinforcement, another 90-second period goes into effect, and after this time has passed, another response will produce reinforcement. It is important to note that responses made before the time period has elapsed have no effect. Notice that in Figure 7.8, one response (R) produces reinforcement (S^{r+}) after the fixed time period (FT) has passed.

When organisms are exposed to interval contingencies, they typically produce many more responses than the schedule requires. Fixed-interval schedules produce a characteristic pattern of responding. There is a pause after reinforcement (PRP), then a few probe responses, followed by more and more rapid responding as the interval times out. This pattern of response is called **scalloping.** Figure 7.9 is an idealized cumulative record of FI performance.

Pretend that you have volunteered to be in an operant experiment. You are brought into a small room, and on one wall there is a lever with a cup under it. Other than those objects, the room is empty. You are not allowed to keep your watch while in the room, and you are told, "Do anything you want." After some time, you press the lever to see what it does. Ten dollars falls into the cup. A good bet is that you will press the lever again. You are not told this, but the schedule is FI 5 minutes. You have 1 hour per day to work on the schedule. If you collect all 12 (60 min ÷ 5 min = 12) of the scheduled reinforcers, you can make $120 a day.

Assume you have been in this experiment for 3 months. Immediately after collecting a $5 reinforcer, there is no chance that a response will pay off (discriminated extinction). However, as you are standing around, or doing anything else, the interval is timing out. You check out the contingency by making a probe response. The next response occurs more quickly because even more time has gone by. As the interval continues to time out, the probability of reinforcement increases and your responses are made faster and faster. This pattern of responding

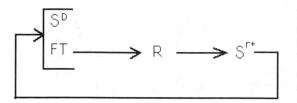

FIG. 7.8 A fixed-interval schedule. In the presence of an S^D, one response is reinforced after a fixed amount of time. Following reinforcement, the returning arrow states that the sequence starts again. This means that the fixed-time interval starts over and, after it has elapsed, one response will again be reinforced.

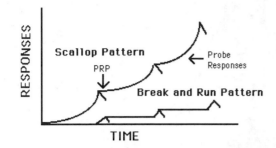

FIG. 7.9 Fixed-interval schedules usually produce a pattern that is called scalloping. There is a PRP following reinforcement, then a gradual increase in rate of response to the moment of reinforcement. Less common is the break-and-run pattern. Break-and-run occasionally develops after organisms have considerable experience on FI schedules. There is a long pause (break) after reinforcement, followed by a rapid burst (run) of responses.

is described by the scallop given in Figure 7.9 and is typical of fixed-interval schedules (Dews, 1969; Ferster & Skinner, 1957).

Following considerable experience with FI 5 minutes, you may get very good at judging the time period. In this case, you would wait out the interval and then emit a burst of responses. Perhaps you decide to pace back and forth during the session, and you find out that after 250 steps the interval has almost elapsed. This kind of mediating behavior may develop after experience with FI schedules. Other animals behave in a similar way and occasionally produce a **break-and-run** pattern of responding (Ferster & Skinner, 1957).

FOCUS ON RESEARCH
The Generality of Schedule Effects

Many behavior analysts assume that basic research with animals will yield general principles that extend to many different species, including humans. This assumption applies to the research on schedules of reinforcement. In this context, experimenters who describe patterns of behavior on a given schedule believe that similar regularities will develop for any species that has evolved the capacity for operant conditioning. The **assumption of generality** implies that the effects of contingencies of reinforcement extend over species, reinforcement, and behavior. For example, a fixed-interval schedule is expected to produce the scalloping pattern for a pigeon pecking a key for food, as well as for a child solving mathematics problems for teacher approval.

This assumption is clearly stated in a variety of passages from books in behavior analysis. In their popular text, Whaley and Malott (1971) comment that "past research has shown that nearly all of the results of animal experimentation are just as true of humans as they are of animals" (Whaley & Malott, 1971, p. 8). A similar view was expressed by Morse (1966) in the early handbook of operant behavior. He wrote that "any member of most species will give a similar performance on the same schedules" (Morse, 1966, p. 59). Finally, B. F. Skinner (1969) supported the assumption of generality when he suggested that "the fact is that methods first developed for the study of lower organisms, as well as the concepts and principles arising from that study have been successfully applied

FIG. 7.10 Fergus Lowe.

to human behavior, both in basic analysis and in many technological applications" (1969, p. 101).

Dr. Fergus Lowe is a professor of psychology at the University College of North Wales who has questioned the generality of schedule effects. He states that "the question which provides the main focus of my research is one which should be central to all behavior analysis, namely, how do the principles of behavior derived from animal experiments apply to human behavior?" (personal communication, March 20, 1989). Lowe has devoted much of his research to an analysis of performance on fixed-interval schedules of reinforcement. He has investigated the operant behavior of rats, pigeons, chimpanzees, human adults, and children of differing ages and language ability.

Lowe (1979) has conducted numerous studies of fixed-interval performance with humans, who press a button to obtain points that are later exchanged for money. Figure 7.11 shows typical performances on fixed-interval schedules by a rat and two human subjects. Building on research by Harold Weiner (1969), Lowe argues that animals show the characteristic scalloping pattern, and humans do not. Humans often produce one of two patterns—an inefficient high, steady rate of response, or an efficient low-rate, break-and-

FIG. 7.11 Typical animal performance on FI and the high- and low-rate performance usually seen with adult humans (data reprinted from Lowe, 1979, p. 162).

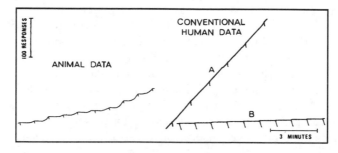

run performance. Experiments by Lowe and his colleagues have focused on the conditions that produce the high- or low-rate patterns in humans.

The basic idea is that schedule performance in humans reflects the influence of language (see Chapter 12 on verbal behavior). In conditioning experiments, people figure out a rule and behave according to the rule rather than the experimentally arranged contingencies. Lowe, Beasty, and Bentall (1983) commented that:

> verbal behavior can, and does, serve a discriminative function that alters the effects of other variables such as scheduled reinforcement. Unlike animals, most humans are capable of describing to themselves, whether accurately or inaccurately, environmental events and the ways in which those events impinge upon them; such descriptions may greatly affect the rest of their behavior. (p. 162)

In most cases, people who follow self-generated rules satisfy the requirements of the schedule, obtain reinforcement, and continue to follow the rule. For example, one person may think, "I should press the button fast" while another believes that "I should count to 50 and then press the button." Only when the contingencies are arranged so that self-generated rules conflict with programmed reinforcement do people abandon the rule and behave in accord with the contingencies (Baron & Galizio, 1983).

Although conditions may be arranged to override the effects of rules, most adult human behavior is rule governed (see Skinner, 1969). The implication is that humans who have not developed language skills will show characteristic effects of schedules. Lowe et al. (1983) designed an experiment to show typical FI performance by children less than a year old. The infants sat in a high chair and were able to touch a round metal cylinder. When the cylinder was touched, one infant (John) received a small bit of food (pieces of fruit, bread, or candy) on fixed-interval schedules of reinforcement. A second infant, Ann, was given 4 seconds of music played from a variety of music boxes on the same schedules. Both infants produced a response pattern similar to the rat's performance in Figure 7.11. Thus, infants who are not verbally skilled behave in accord with the FI contingencies and are substantially different from adult humans.

Based on this finding and other research, Lowe argues that "these studies have shown 1) that the operant behavior of verbally-able humans differs very markedly from that of non-verbal organisms (i.e., animals and human infants) and 2) that verbal behavior plays a major role in bringing about these differences" (personal communication, 1992). These conclusions have encouraged Dr. Lowe to increasingly concentrate his investigations on the interactions between verbal and nonverbal behavior, particularly in early childhood when verbal control of behavior is first established.

Although the effects of verbal behavior and self-instruction may account for human performance on FI schedules, there are alternative possibilities. Dr. Michael Perone and his colleagues, Drs. Mark Galizio and Alan Baron, in an article concerning the relevance of animal-based principles for human behavior, noted:

> when comparisons are made between the performances of humans and animals, discrepancies . . . are not difficult to find and, in themselves, provided little basis for satisfaction. The challenge for the student of human operant conditioning is to identify the similarities in the variables underlying the discrepant performances and ultimately to bring them under experimental control. (Perone, Galizio, & Baron, 1988, p. 80)

There is no doubt that humans become more verbal as they grow up. However, there are many other changes that occur in the movement from infancy to adulthood. An important consideration is the greater experience that adults have with ratio-type contingencies of reinforcement. Infants rely on the caregiving of other people. This means that most of the infant's reinforcement is delivered on the basis of time and behavior. A baby is fed when the mother has time to do so, although fussing may decrease the interval. As children get older, they begin to crawl and walk and reinforcement is delivered more and more on the basis of their behavior. When this happens, many of the contingencies of reinforcement change from interval to ratio schedules. This experience with ratio schedules of reinforcement may account for the differences between adult human and animal performance on fixed-interval schedules.

Recent research by Wanchisen, Tatham, and Mooney (1989) has shown that rats perform like adult humans on FI schedules after a history of ratio reinforcement. The animals were exposed to variable-ratio reinforcement and then were given 120 sessions on a fixed-interval 30-second schedule (FI 30 seconds). Two patterns of response developed on the FI schedule—a high-rate pattern and a low-rate pattern with some break-and-run performance. These patterns of performance are remarkably similar to the schedule performance of adult humans (see Figure 7.11). One implication is that human performance on schedules may be explained by a special history of reinforcement rather than self-generated rules. At this time, it is reasonable to conclude that both reinforcement history and verbal ability contribute to fixed-interval performance of humans.

Variable Interval.   On a **variable-interval,** or **VI,** schedule responses are reinforced after a variable amount of time has passed (see Figure 7.12). For example, on a VI 30 second schedule, the time to each reinforcement changes but the average time is 30 seconds. The symbol *V* indicates that the time requirement varies from one reinforcer to the next. The average amount of time required for reinforcement is used to index the schedule.

Interval contingencies are common in the ordinary world of people and other animals. People line up, sit in traffic jams, wait for elevators, time a boiling egg, and are put on hold. In everyday life, variable time periods occur more frequently than fixed ones. Waiting in line to get to a bank teller may take 5 minutes one day and half an hour the next time you go to the bank. A wolf pack may run down prey following a long or short hunt. A baby may cry for 5 seconds, 2 minutes, or a quarter of an hour before a parent picks up the child. A cat waits vary-

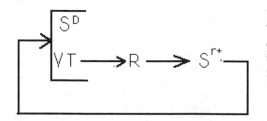

FIG. 7.12 A variable-interval schedule. The symbol *V* stands for variable and indicates that the schedule is indexed by the average time requirement for reinforcement.

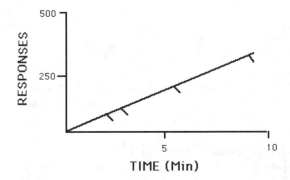

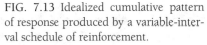

FIG. 7.13 Idealized cumulative pattern of response produced by a variable-interval schedule of reinforcement.

ing amounts of time in ambush before a bird becomes a meal. Waiting for a bus is rarely on a fixed schedule, despite the efforts of transportation officials.

Figure 7.13 portrays the pattern of response generated on a VI schedule. On this schedule, rate of response is moderate and steady. The pause after reinforcement that occurs on FI usually does not appear in the variable-interval record. Because rate of response is moderate, VI performance is often used as a baseline for evaluating other independent variables. Rate of response on VI schedules may increase or decrease as a result of experimental manipulations. For example, tranquilizing drugs such as chlorpromazine decrease rate of response on variable-interval schedules (Waller, 1961), while stimulants increase VI performance (Segal, 1962). Murray Sidman (1960) has commented on the usefulness of VI performance as a baseline.

> An ideal baseline would be one in which there is as little interference as possible from other variables. There should be a minimal number of factors tending to oppose any shift in behavior that might result from experimental manipulation. A variable-interval schedule, if skillfully programmed, comes close to meeting this requirement. (p. 320)

In summary, VI contingencies are common in everyday life. These schedules generate a moderate steady rate of response. Because of this pattern, variable-interval performance is frequently used as a baseline.

ADVANCED ISSUE
Analysis of Schedule Performance

Each of the basic schedules of reinforcement (FR, FI, VR, VI) generates a unique pattern of responding. Ratio schedules produce a higher rate of response than interval schedules. A reliable pause after reinforcement (PRP) occurs on fixed-ratio and fixed-interval schedules but not on variable-ratio or variable-interval schedules.

Rate of Response on Schedules

The issue about what produces rapid responding on ratio schedules and moderate rates on interval schedules has not been resolved. The two major views concern molecular versus molar conceptions of schedule control. **Molecular approaches** focus on small moment-to-moment relationships between behavior and its consequences. **Molar** accounts are concerned with large-scale factors that may occur over the length of an entire session.

Molecular Account of Rate of Response.

The time between any two responses, or what is called the **interresponse time (IRT)**, may be treated as an operant. Consider Figure 7.14, in which 30-second segments of performance on VR and VI schedules are presented. Responses are portrayed by the vertical marks, and the occurrence of reinforcement is given with the familiar symbol S^{r+}. As you can see, IRTs are much longer on VI than on variable ratio. On the VR segment, 23 responses occur in 30 seconds, which gives an average time between responses of 1.3 seconds. The VI schedule generates longer IRTs, with a mean of 2.3 seconds.

Generally, ratio schedules produce shorter IRTs and consequently higher rates of response than interval schedules. Skinner (1938) suggested that this came about because ratio and interval schedules reinforce short or long interresponse times, respectively. To understand this, consider the definition of an operant class. It is a class of behavior that may increase or decrease in frequency as a consequence of contingencies of reinforcement. In other words, if it could be shown that the time between responses changes as a function of selective reinforcement then the IRT is by definition an operant in its own right. To demonstrate that the IRT is an operant, it is necessary to identify an IRT of specific length (e.g., 2 seconds between any two responses) and then reinforce that interresponse time and show that it increases in frequency.

Computers and other electronic equipment have been used to measure the IRTs generated on various schedules of reinforcement. A response is made and the computer starts timing until the next response is emitted. Typically, these interresponse times are slotted into time bins. For example, all IRTs between zero and 2 seconds are counted, then those that fall in the 2- to 4-second range, next the number of 4- to 6-second IRTs, and so on. This method results in a distribution of interresponse times. Several experiments have shown that the distribution of IRTs may in fact be changed by selectively reinforcing interresponse times of a particular duration (for a review, see Morse, 1966). Figure 7.15

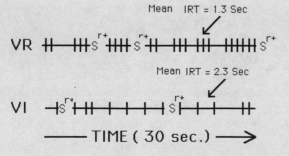

FIG. 7.14 Idealized distributions of response on VR and VI schedules of reinforcement. Responses are represented by the vertical marks, and S^{r+} stands for reinforcement.

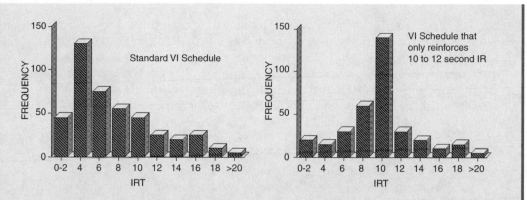

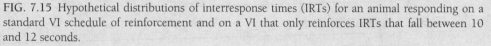

FIG. 7.15 Hypothetical distributions of interresponse times (IRTs) for an animal responding on a standard VI schedule of reinforcement and on a VI that only reinforces IRTs that fall between 10 and 12 seconds.

shows the results of a hypothetical experiment in which IRTs of different duration are reinforced on a VI schedule. On the standard VI, most of the IRTs are 2 to 4 seconds long. When an additional contingency is added to the VI schedule that requires IRTs of 10 to 12 seconds, the IRTs increase in this category. Also, a new distribution of IRTs is generated.

Anger (1956) conducted a complex experiment demonstrating that IRTs are a conditionable property of behavior. In this experiment, the interresponse time was considered to be a stimulus that set the occasion for the next response (i.e., an S^D). Reynolds (1966a), in fact, showed that the IRT could affect performance that followed it. In other words, interresponse times can function as discriminative stimuli. The difficulty with this conception is that stimulus properties are inferred from performance. Zeiler (1977) has pointed out:

> if the IRT is treated as a differentiated response unit [an operant], unobservable stimuli need not be postulated as controlling observable performance. Given the one-to-one correspondence between response and inferred stimulus properties, however, the two treatments appear to be equivalent. (p. 223)

For these reasons, we treat the IRT as an operant rather than as a discriminative stimulus. As an operant, the IRT is considered to be a conditionable property of the response that ends the time interval between any two responses. For example, a rat may press a lever R_1, R_2, R_3, R_4, and R_5 times. The time between lever presses R_1 and R_2 is the interresponse time associated with R_2. In a similar fashion, the IRT for R_5 is the elapsed time between R_4 and R_5, and so on.

As part of Anger's (1956) experiment, animals were placed on a VI-300 second schedule of reinforcement. On this schedule, the response that resulted in reinforcement had to occur 40 seconds or more after the previous response. If the animal made many fast responses with IRTs of less than 40 seconds, the schedule requirements would not be met. In other words, IRTs of more than 40 seconds were the operant that was reinforced. Anger found that this procedure shifted the distribution of IRTs toward 40 seconds. Thus, the IRT that is reinforced is more likely to be emitted than other interresponse times. Additional experiments have demonstrated a similar effect (Dews, 1963; Ferster & Skinner, 1957; Kelleher, Fry, & Cook, 1959; Platt, 1979; Shimp, 1969), and Morse (1966) provides a formal analysis supporting the conclusion that IRTs are a conditionable property of operant behavior. Lattal and his colleagues at West Virginia University have extended these findings. Their research on delay of reinforcement suggests that basic behavioral units, like IRTs, are conditioned even when the contingencies of reinforcement do not directly require it (Arbuckle & Lattal, 1988; Lattal, 1984; Lattal & Ziegler, 1982).

Ratio schedules generate rapid sequences of responses with short interresponse times (Gott & Weiss, 1972; Weiss & Gott, 1972). On a ratio schedule, consider what the probability of obtaining reinforcement is following a burst of very fast responses (short IRTs) or a series of responses with long IRTs. Recall that ratio schedules are based on the number of responses that are emitted. Bursts of responses with short IRTs count down the ratio requirement and are more probably reinforced than sets of slow responses. Responses that occur slowly do not excessively affect the schedule requirements and are less likely to be reinforced. Thus, ratio schedules, because of the way they are constructed, differentially reinforce short IRTs. According to the molecular IRT view of schedule control, this is why rate of response is high on these schedules.

When compared to ratio schedules, interval contingencies generate longer IRTs and consequently a lower rate of response. Interval schedules pay off after some amount of time has passed and a response is made. As IRTs become longer, more and more of the time requirement on the schedule elapses. This means that the probability of reinforcement for a response increases with longer IRTs. In other words, longer IRTs are differentially reinforced on interval schedules (Morse, 1966). In keeping with the molecular view, interval contingencies differentially reinforce long IRTs, and rate of response is moderate on these schedules.

Molar Accounts of Rate Differences.   There are several problems with the IRT account of rate differences on ratio and interval schedules. A logical objection is that showing that the reinforcement of IRTs can change behavior does not mean that this is what is happening on other schedules. In other words, demonstrating that IRTs can be selectively reinforced does not prove that this occurs on interval or ratio schedules. Also, there is evidence that when long IRTs are reinforced, organisms continue to emit short bursts of rapid responses. Animals typically produce these bursts even on schedules that never reinforce a fast series of responses (i.e., differential reinforcement of low rate). For these reasons, molar hypotheses about the rate of response difference have been advanced.

Molar explanations of rate differences are concerned with the global relationship between responses and reinforcement. In general terms, the correlation between responses and reinforcement produces the difference in rate on interval and ratio schedules. Generally, if a high rate of response is associated with a higher frequency of reinforcement, then subjects will respond rapidly. When increased rate of response does not affect rate of reinforcement, organisms do not respond faster.

Consider a VR-100 schedule of reinforcement. On this schedule, a subject could respond 50 times per minute and in a 1-hour session obtain 30 reinforcers. On the other hand, if the rate of response was 300 per minute (not outside the range of pigeons or humans), the number of reinforcers earned would increase to 180 an hour. According to supporters of the molar view, this correlation between increasing rate of response and increased frequency of reinforcement is responsible for rapid responding on ratio schedules.

A different correlation between rate of response and frequency of reinforcement is set up on interval schedules. Recall that interval schedules program a reinforcer after time has passed and one response is made. Suppose you are responding on a VI 3-minute schedule for $5 reinforcers. You have 1 hour a day to work on the schedule. If you respond at a reasonable rate, say 30 lever presses per minute, you will get most or all of the 20 scheduled reinforcers. Now pretend that you increase your rate of response to 300 a minute. The only consequence is a sore wrist, and rate of reinforcement stays at 20 per hour. In other words, after some moderate value, it does not pay to increase rate of response on interval schedules.

PostreInforcement Pause on Fixed Schedules

Fixed-ratio and fixed-interval schedules generate a pause that follows reinforcement. Accounts of pausing on fixed schedules also may be classified as molecular or molar. Molecular accounts of pausing are concerned with the moment-to-moment relationships that immediately precede reinforcement. Such accounts are concerned with the relationship between the number of bar presses that produce reinforcement and the subsequent postreinforcement pause. In contrast, molar accounts of pausing focus on the overall rate of reinforcement for a session and the average pause length.

Generally, it is well established that the postreinforcement pause is a function of the **interreinforcement interval (IRI).** As the time between reinforcements becomes longer, the PRP increases. On fixed-interval schedules, in which the time between reinforcement is controlled by the experimenter, the postreinforcement pause is approximately one-half the interreinforcement interval. For example, on a FI 300-second schedule (in which the time between reinforcements is 300 seconds), the average PRP will be 150 seconds. On fixed ratio, the evidence suggests similar control by the IRI (Powell, 1968)—as the ratio requirement increases, the PRP becomes longer.

There is, however, a difficulty with analyzing the postreinforcement pause on FR schedules. On ratio schedules, the time between reinforcements is partly determined by what the animal does. That is, the animal's rate of pressing the lever affects the time between reinforcements. Another problem with ratio schedules, for an analysis of pausing, is that rate of response goes up as the size of the ratio is increased (Boren, 1961). Unless rate of response exactly coincides with changes in the size of the ratio, adjustments in ratio size alter the interreinforcement interval. For example, on FR 10 a rate of five responses per minute produces an IRI of 2 minutes. This same rate of response produces an IRI of 4 minutes on a FR 20 schedule. Thus, changes in postreinforcement pause as ratio size is increased may be caused by the ratio size, the interreinforcement interval, or both.

A Molar Interpretation of Pausing.   We have noted that the average PRP is one-half of the interreinforcement interval. Another finding is that the postreinforcement pauses are normally distributed (bell curve) over the time between reinforcements. In

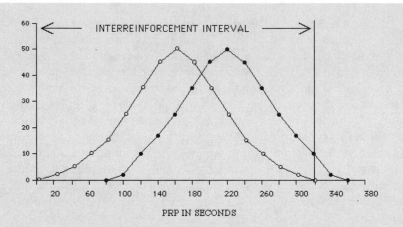

FIG. 7.16 Two possible distributions of PRPs on a fixed-interval 320-second schedule. The distribution given by the open circles has a mean of 160 seconds and does not exceed the interreinforcement interval set on the FI schedule. The bell curve for the distribution with the dark circles has an average value at 225 seconds, and many pauses are longer than the IRI.

other words, on a FI 320-second schedule, pauses will range from zero to 320 seconds with an average pause around 160 seconds. As shown in Figure 7.16, these results can be accounted for by considering what would happen if the bell curve moved upward so that the mean pause was 225 seconds. In this case, many of the pauses would exceed the FI interval and the animal would get fewer reinforcements for the session. An animal that was sensitive to overall rate of reinforcement (maximization) should come to emit pauses that are on average one-half the FI interval, assuming a normal distribution. Thus, maximization of reinforcement provides a molar account of the postreinforcement pause.

Molecular Interpretations of Pausing.   There are two molecular accounts of pausing on fixed schedules that have some amount of research support. One account is based on the observation that animals often emit other behavior during the postreinforcement pause (Staddon & Simmelhag, 1971). For example, rats may engage in grooming, sniffing, scratching, and stretching after the presentation of a food pellet. Because this behavior reliably follows reinforcement, it is said to be induced by the schedule. Schedule-induced behaviors (see Chapter 6) may be viewed as operants that automatically produce reinforcement. For example, stretching may relieve muscle tension and scratching may eliminate an itch. One interpretation is that pausing occurs because the animal is maximizing local rates of reinforcement. That is, the rat gets food for bar pressing as well as the automatic reinforcement from the induced activities (see Shull, 1979). The average pause should therefore reflect the allocation of time to induced behavior and to the operant that produces scheduled reinforcement (e.g., food). At present, experiments have not ruled out or clearly demonstrated the induced-behavior interpretation of pausing.

A second molecular account of pausing is based on the run of responses or amount of work that precedes reinforcement (Shull, 1979, pp. 217–218). This "work-time" interpretation holds that the previously experienced run of responses regulates the length of the postreinforcement pause. Work time affects the PRP by altering the value of the next scheduled reinforcement. In other words, the more effort or time expended for the previous reinforcer, the lower the value of the next reinforcer and the longer it takes for the animal to initiate responding (i.e., pause length). Interestingly, Skinner made a similar interpretation in 1938 when he stated that pausing on fixed-ratio schedules occurred because "the preceding run which occurs under reinforcement at a fixed ratio places the [reflex] reserve in a state of strain which acts with the temporal discrimination of reinforcement to produce a pause of some length" (p. 298). Skinner's use of the strained reserve seems equivalent to the more current emphasis on work time. Overall, this view suggests that the harder one works for reinforcement, the less valuable the next reinforcement and therefore the longer it takes to start working again.

Neither the induced behavior nor the work-time accounts of pausing are sufficient to handle all that is known about patterning on schedules of reinforcement. A schedule of reinforcement is a procedure for combining a large number of different conditions that regulate behavior. Some of the controlling factors arise from the animal's behavior, and others are set by the experimenter. This means that it is exceedingly difficult to unravel the exact processes that produce characteristic schedule performance. Nonetheless, the current interpretations of pausing point to some of the more relevant factors that play a role in the regulation of behavior on fixed schedules.

The Dynamics of Schedule Performance.

There are reasons for detailed research on the postreinforcement pause and interresponse time. The hope is to analyze schedule effects in terms of a few basic processes. This area of research, called **behavioral dynamics**, is an important endeavor because the environment of people and other animals can be arranged in an infinite number of ways. If performance on schedules can be reduced to a small number of fundamental principles, then reasonable interpretations may be made about any particular arrangement of the environment. Also, it should be possible to predict behavior more precisely from knowledge of the operating contingencies and the axioms that govern reinforcement schedules.

Behavioral dynamics is at the leading edge of behavior analysis and, like most scientific research, it requires a high level of mathematical sophistication. Both linear and nonlinear calculus are used to model the behavioral impact of schedules of reinforcement. A recent issue of the *Journal of the Experimental Analysis of Behavior* was devoted to this important subject and included topics like chaos theory and performance on fixed-interval schedules, dynamics of behavioral structure, behavioral momentum, resistance to behavior change, and feedback functions for variable-interval schedules (see Baum, 1992; Galbicka, 1992; Gibbon & Church, 1992; Harper & McLean, 1992; Hoyert, 1992; Killeen, 1992; Marr, 1992; McDowell, Bass, & Kessel, 1992; Nevin, 1992; Palya, 1992; Rachlin, 1992; Shimp, 1992; Zeiler, 1992). In this same issue, Dr. Peter Killeen, a professor at Arizona State University, builds on his previous work and suggests that "behavior may be treated as basic physics" with responses viewed as movement through behavioral space (Killeen, 1974, 1975, 1985, 1992). Although these issues are beyond the scope of this book, the student of behavior analysis should be aware that the physics of schedule performance is an advanced area of the science of behavior.

SCHEDULE PERFORMANCE IN TRANSITION

We have described typical performances generated by different schedules of reinforcement. The patterns of response on these schedules take a long time to develop. Once behavior has stabilized, showing little change from day to day, the organism's behavior is said to have reached a steady state. As we have pointed out, the pause and run pattern that develops on FR schedules is a steady-state performance and is only observed after an animal has considerable exposure to the contingencies. Similarly, the steady-state performance generated on other intermittent schedules takes time to evolve. When an organism is initially placed on a schedule of reinforcement, behavior patterns are not consistent or regular. This early performance on a schedule is called a **transition state.**

Consider how you might get an animal to press a lever 100 times for each small presentation of food (FR 100). First, you shape the animal to press the bar on continuous reinforcement (see Chapter 4). After steady-state performance is established on CRF, you are faced with the problem of how to program the steps from CRF to FR 100. Notice that there is a large shift in the rate of reinforcement for bar pressing. If you simply move from CRF to the large-ratio value, the animal will show **ratio strain** in the sense that it produces longer and longer pauses after reinforcement. This occurs because the time between successive reinforcements regulates the postreinforcement pause. The pause gets longer as the inter-reinforcement interval increases. Because the PRP makes up part of the interval between reinforcements and is controlled by it, the animal eventually stops responding. Thus, there is a negative-feedback loop between increasing PRP length and the time between reinforcements.

Large increases in schedule values may also produce extinction. For this reason, a slow progression to higher schedule values is typically programmed. Even when a small change in the fixed ratio is made, an animal is momentarily exposed to a period of extinction. Recall that during the early phase of extinction, behavior becomes more variable and a burst of responses is likely to occur. This eruption of responses may be used to support the transition to a higher-ratio requirement. In other words, when continuous reinforcement (FR 1) is changed to FR 5, the animal makes several rapid responses and the fifth response is reinforced. Following several reinforced sequences of five responses, the ratio requirement may be raised again. The transition to the next FR requirement also produces an extinction burst and enables the animal to contact the next scheduled value.

Extinction bursts and increased behavioral variability allow for adaptation to changing environmental contingencies. When an organism changes its behavior on the basis of life experience, this is called **ontogenetic selection.** In this ontogenetic form of adaptation, the form and frequency of behavior increase when reinforcement is withheld. These behavioral changes during extinction allow for the selection of behavior by new contingencies of reinforcement. Thus, a wild rat that has been exploiting a compost heap may find that the home owner has covered it. In this case, the rat emits various operants that may eventually uncover the food. The animal may dig under the cover, gnaw a hole in the sheathing, or search for some other means of entry. A similar effect occurs when food in the compost heap is depleted and the animal emits behavior that results in getting to a new food patch. In the laboratory, this behavior is measured as an increase in the form and frequency of bar pressing as the schedules of reinforcement change.

Transitions from one reinforcement schedule to another play an important role in human development. Developmental psychologists have described periods of life in which major changes in behavior typically occur. One of the most important life stages in Western society is the transition from childhood to adolescence. Although this phase involves many biological and behavioral processes, one of the most basic changes involves schedules of reinforcement.

When a youngster reaches puberty, parents, teachers, peers, and others require more behavior and more skillful performance than they did during childhood. A young child's reinforcement schedules are usually simple, regular, and immediate. In childhood, food is given when the child says "Mom, I'm hungry" after playing a game of tag, or is scheduled at regular times throughout the day. On the other hand, a teenager is told to fix his or her own food and clean up the mess. Notice that the schedule requirement for getting food has significantly increased. The teenager may search through the refrigerator, open packages and tins, sometimes cook, get out plates, eat the food, and clean up. Of course, any part of this sequence may or may not occur depending on the disciplinary practices of the parents. Although most adolescents adapt to this transition state, others may show signs of ratio strain and extinction. Poor eating habits by teenagers may reflect the change from regular to intermittent reinforcement.

Many other behavioral changes may occur during the transition from childhood to adolescence. Ferster, Culbertson, and Boren (1975) have noted the transition to intermittent reinforcement that occurs in adolescence.

> With adolescence, the picture may change quite drastically and sometimes even suddenly. Now money becomes a reinforcer on a fixed-ratio schedule instead of continuous reinforcement as before. The adolescent may have to take a job demanding a substantial amount of work for the money which heretofore he received as a free allowance. Furthermore, he now needs more money than when he was younger in order to interact with people he deals with. A car or a motorcycle takes the place of the bicycle. Even the price of services such as movies and buses is higher. Money, particularly for boys, frequently becomes a necessary condition for dealing with the opposite sex. The amount of work required in school increases. Instead of simple arithmetic problems, the adolescent may now have to write a long term paper, cover more subjects, or puzzle through a difficult algebra problem which will require much trial and error. (pp. 416–417)

There are other periods of life in which our culture demands large shifts in schedules of reinforcement. A current problem involves a rapidly aging population and the difficulties generated by forced retirement. In terms of schedules, retirement is a large and rapid change in the contingencies of reinforcement. Retired people face significant alterations in social, monetary, and work-related consequences. For example, a person who has enjoyed his or her academic career as a professor is no longer reinforced for research and teaching by the university community. Social consequences for these activities may have included approval by colleagues, academic advancement, interest of students, and intellectual discussions. Upon retirement, these social reinforcers are reduced in frequency or completely eliminated. It is not surprising, therefore, that retirement is an unhappy time of life for many people. Although retirement is commonly viewed as a problem of old age, a behavior analysis points to the abrupt change in rates of reinforcement.

Transitions in the schedules of reinforcement also occur with major life events. Significant life events that produce shifts in schedules of reinforcement include going to school, making a living, getting married, having children, divorcing, and experiencing the death of a loved one. The authors are both familiar with the shift in contingencies of reinforcement that happens following a divorce. A person's sexual behavior may have to adjust to new requirements. This adjustment involves finding new partners and meeting the contingencies set by these individuals. Some people who go through a divorce may not be able to meet the new contingencies of reinforcement. Feelings of loneliness and depression often accompany marital breakdown. These feelings may be generated by ratio strain and extinction that result from a change in the contingencies of reinforcement. In contrast, there are people who readily adapt to this life crisis. Presumably, behavioral variability and an initial flurry of responding produced by extinction allow such persons to contact the new schedules of sexual reinforcement.

ON THE APPLIED SIDE

Schedules of Reinforcement of Abstinence from Cigarette Smoking

The use of drugs is operant behavior maintained in part by the reinforcing effects of the drug. One implication of this analysis is that reinforcement of an incompatible response (i.e., abstinence) can reduce the probability of taking drugs. The effectiveness of an abstinence contingency depends on the magnitude and schedule of reinforcement for nondrug use (e.g., Higgins, Bickel, & Hughes, 1994).

In a recent investigation of cigarette smoking, Roll, Higgins and Badger (1996) assessed the effectiveness of three different schedules of reinforcement for promoting and sustaining drug abstinence. These researchers conducted an experimental analysis of cigarette smoking because a) cigarettes can function as reinforcers, b) smoking can be reduced by reinforcement of alternative responses, and c) it is relatively more convenient to study cigarette smoking than illicit drugs. Furthermore, cigarette smokers usually relapse within several days following abstinence. This suggests that reinforcement factors regulating abstinence exert their effects shortly after the person stops smoking and it is possible to study these factors in a short-duration experiment.

Sixty adults, who smoked between 10 and 50 cigarettes a day, took part in the experiment. The smokers were not currently trying to give up cigarettes. Participants were randomly assigned to one of three groups: progressive reinforcement, fixed rate of reinforcement, and a control group. They were told to begin abstaining from cigarettes on Friday evening so that they could pass a carbon monoxide (CO) test for abstinence on Monday morning. Each person in the study went at least two days without smoking before reinforcement for abstinence began. On Monday through Friday, participants agreed to take three daily CO tests. These tests could detect prior smoking.

Twenty participants were randomly assigned to the progressive reinforcement group. The progressive schedule involved increasing the magnitude of reinforcement for remaining drug free. Participants earned $3.00 for passing the first carbon monoxide test for abstinence. Each subsequent consecutive CO sample that indicated abstinence increased the amount of money participants received by $0.50. The third consecutive CO test passed earned a bonus of $10.00. That is, passing the first CO test yielded $3.00, passing the second $3.50, the third $14.00 ($4.00 and bonus of $10.00), the fourth $4.50, and so on. In addition, a substantial response cost was added for failing a CO test. If the person failed the test, the payment for that test was withheld and the value of payment for the next test was reset to three dollars. Three consecutive CO tests indicating abstinence following a reset returned the payment schedule to the value at which the reset occurred (p. 497), supporting efforts to achieve abstinence.

Participants in the fixed reinforcement group (N = 20) were paid $9.80 for passing each CO test. There were no bonus points for consecutive abstinences and no resets. The total amount of money available for the progressive and fixed groups was the same. Smokers in both the progressive and fixed groups were informed in advance of the schedule of payment and the criterion for reinforcement. The schedule of payment for the control group was the same as the average payment obtained by the first 10 participants assigned to the progressive condition. For these people, the payment was given no matter what their carbon monoxide levels were. The control group was, however, asked to try and cut their cigarette consumption, reduce CO levels, and maintain abstinence.

Participants in the progressive and fixed reinforcement groups passed more than 80% of the abstinence tests while the control group only passed about 40% of the tests. The effects of the schedule of reinforcement are shown in Figure 7.17a. the figure indicates the percentage of participants who passed three consecutive tests for abstinence and then resumed smoking over the five days of the experiment. Only 22% of those on the progressive schedule resumed smoking compared with 60% and 82% in the fixed and control groups. Thus, the progressive schedule of reinforcement was superior at preventing the resumption of smoking (after a period of abstinence).

Figure 7.17b shows the percentage of smokers who gave up cigarettes throughout the experiment. Again, a strong effect of schedule of reinforcement is apparent. Fifty percent of those on progressive reinforcement schedule remained abstinent for the five days of the experiment. This compares with 30% and 5% of the fixed and control participants.

Overall, these results indicate that a progressive reinforcement schedule, combined with an escalating response cost, is an effective short-term intervention for abstinence from smoking. Further research is necessary to see whether a pro-

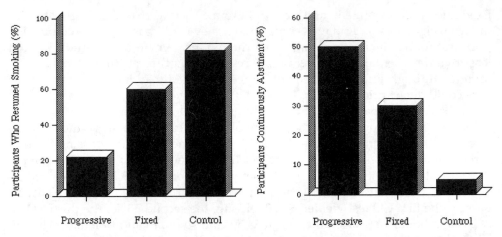

FIG. 7.17 Percentage of participants in each group who obtained three consecutive abstinences, but then resumed smoking (7.17a). Percentage of smokers in each group who were abstinent on all trials during the entire experiment (7.17b).

gressive schedule maintains abstinence after the schedule is withdrawn. Long term follow-up studies of progressive and other schedules are necessary to assess the lasting effects of reinforcement schedules on abstinence. What is clear, at this point, is that schedules of reinforcement may be an important component of stop-smoking programs.

KEY WORDS

Assumption of generality

Behavioral dynamics

Break and run

Contingency of
   reinforcement

Continuous
   reinforcement (CRF)

Fixed interval (FI)

Fixed ratio (FR)

Intermittent
   reinforcement

Intermittent
   reinforcement effect

Interreinforcement
   interval (IRI)

Interresponse time (IRT)

Interval schedules

Mechner notation

Molar accounts of
   schedule performance

Molecular accounts of
   schedule performance

Ontogenetic selection

Operant level

Partial reinforcement
   effect

Postreinforcement pause
   (PRP)

Ratio schedules

Ratio strain

Resistance to extinction

Run of responses

Scalloping

Schedule of
   reinforcement

Steady-state performance

Transition state

Variable interval (VI)

Variable ratio (VR)

CHAPTER 8

Stimulus Control

1. Define a controlling stimulus. Discuss two kinds of controlling stimuli and provide examples of these in everyday life.

2. In behavioral terms, what is discrimination? Describe the contingency of differential reinforcement. Discuss the effects of this procedure in an idealized experiment with pigeons pecking red and green keys.

3. What is meant by stimulus control? Give an example in the laboratory and in everyday settings.

4. Define a multiple schedule of reinforcement and write the Mechner notation for a multiple VI, extinction (MULT VI, EXT) schedule. How can the mere alternation of the red and green components in a multiple schedule confound the results? What is the likely result of a bird responding on a multiple VI 2-minute extinction (MULT VI 2-minute, EXT) schedule?

5. Discuss the discrimination index and write a simple equation for it. How does the index vary and what are the meanings of different values?

6. Discuss a study by Pierrel, Sherman, Blue, and Hegge (1970) on differences in sound intensity, using the discrimination index. What do the results of this experiment mean?

7. Summarize the problem faced by the student with a "bird-brained" pigeon. How did the student solve the problem using Mechner notation? In your answer, refer to adventitious reinforcement on multiple schedules, superstitious behavior, and a differential reinforcement of other behavior (DRO) contingency. Draw out the implications for teaching and learning.

8. Define behavioral contrast and how it occurs on a MULT VI, EXT schedule. Name two kinds of contrast and define them. Give a relative rate of reinforcement analysis of behavioral contrast. What other conditions affect contrast? How could contrast have adaptive value?

9. In terms of the Focus On the research of Ben Williams, which component of an A→B→C sequence of schedules is the target? In relation to the target schedule, which schedule produces weak and fleeting contrast effects? Which schedule produces strong and durable contrast effects? Describe the transitory contrast effect elicited by the preceding schedule. Describe the more robust effect of anticipatory contrast. Where do we stand today in terms of behavioral contrast?

10. What is stimulus generalization? Give several common examples. Discuss generalization gradients using a classic experiment by Guttman and Kalish (1956). Define a peak shift. Recount an experiment by Hanson (1959) on the peak-shift phenomenon.

11. Define absolute and relative stimulus control. How is peak shift an instance of relative stimulus control? Compare successive and simultaneous discrimination.

12. Use an experiment by Gonzalez, Gentry, and Bitterman (1954) to illustrate simultaneous discrimination. What were the results? Give an example of simultaneous discrimination on the television program *Sesame Street.*

13. How does extinction interfere with establishing a discrimination? What is errorless discrimination? Discuss the Terrace (1963) experiment on errorless discrimination. Compare the effects of early progressive training with standard successive discrimination.

14. What are some additional effects of errorless-discrimination procedures? Discuss the importance of errorless training in educational settings.

15. Describe two basic procedures that underlie errorless training. What is fading? Give a practical example of fading used by Sherman (1965). How is fading important in everyday life?

16. What is identity matching? Describe delayed matching to sample in a pigeon experiment. How is this procedure used to investigate behavior said to reflect cognition and memory? Provide a behavior analysis of symbolic delayed matching to sample (DMTS) in terms of sources stimulus control regulating reference and working remembering.

17. Summarize the Herrnstein and Loveland (1964) research on concept formation by pigeons. What were the results? How general is concept formation? Draw out the implications of this research area.

18. Outline conditional discrimination using a pigeon and matching to sample procedure. How does conditional discrimination help explain complex human behavior?

19. How did Verhave (1966) teach pigeons to be quality control inspectors? What did Verhave do to keep performance accurate on the inspection line when the match between the sample and the comparison capsules was unknown? What contingencies does management face that prevents the adoption of pigeons as quality control inspectors?

In the everyday world, human behavior is changed by signs, symbols, gestures, and spoken words. Behavior is also regulated by sounds, smells, sights, and other sensory stimuli that do not depend on social conditioning. When social or nonsocial events precede operant behavior and affect its occurrence, they are called controlling stimuli. A **controlling stimulus (S)** is said to alter the probability of an operant, in the sense that the response is more (or less) likely to occur when the stimulus is present.[1]

One kind of controlling stimulus that we discussed in Chapter 5 is the S^D or **discriminative stimulus.** An S^D is a controlling stimulus that sets the occasion for reinforcement of an operant. In a pigeon experiment, a red light may reliably signal the presentation of food for pecking a key. After some experience, the bird will immediately strike the key when it is illuminated with the red light. Thus, the discriminative stimulus sets the occasion for a high probability of response.

The discriminative stimuli that regulate human behavior may be as simple as in the pigeon experiment or far more complex. A green traffic light and the word *walk* sets the occasion for pedestrians to cross a street. In a library, the call numbers posted above the stacks and on the books are discriminative stimuli for stopping, turning corners, and so on that result in finding a book. On the football field, a quarterback who is about to pass the ball must decide whether to pick the left or right receiver. Throwing the ball to a receiver is based on the degree of coverage (number and proximity of defensive players). In this example, the degree of coverage is a complex S^D that controls the direction, speed, and elevation of the quarterback's pass.

Another kind of controlling stimulus is called an S^Δ **(S-delta)** or an **extinction stimulus.** An S^Δ is a stimulus that sets the occasion for nonreinforcement or extinction of an operant. A rat may press a lever on a VI schedule of food reinforcement. Every now and then, a tone comes on and a period of extinction is in effect. After some time, the rat will stop pressing the bar as soon as the tone is presented. Thus, the tone is defined as an S^Δ because lever pressing has a low probability of occurrence in its presence.

Extinction stimuli that regulate human behavior also range from simple to complex. When your car is almost out of gas, a service-station sign that says CLOSED is an S^Δ for turning into that station. A tennis opponent who usually wins the match may become an extinction stimulus for playing the game. In this case, you may play tennis with others, but not with the person who always wins. Sometimes breakdown of communication between a married couple may be caused by stimuli that signal extinction for conversation. A wife may try to talk to her husband about a variety of issues, and he pretends to read the newspaper. The husband's behavior is an S^Δ for conversation if the wife reliably stops talking when he picks up the paper.

---

[1]In this chapter, we have invented a classification scheme for stimuli that precede and set the occasion for reinforcement, extinction, or punishment of operant behavior. We introduce the generic term controlling stimulus (S) to stand for all events that exert stimulus control over operant behavior. There are three kinds of controlling stimuli: S^D, S^Δ, and S^{ave}. Notice that in each case the controlling stimulus is modified to reflect its function based on the contingencies of reinforcement that have established it (i.e., reinforcement, extinction, or punishment). See Chapter 9 for a discussion of the S^{ave} function of controlling stimuli.

DIFFERENTIAL REINFORCEMENT AND DISCRIMINATION

When an organism makes a response in one situation but not in another, we say that the animal shows a discrimination between the situations. The simplest way to train a **differential response** or **discrimination** is to reinforce an operant in one situation and withhold reinforcement in the other.

Figure 8.1 shows the development of a differential response to a single key that is alternately illuminated red and green for 5 minutes. The graph shows the cumulative number of responses over a 90-minute session. Pecks to the red light by a pigeon are intermittently reinforced with food. Responses emitted in the presence of the green light are extinguished.

As you can see in this idealized experiment, the pigeon begins by emitting about the same number of responses to the red and green stimuli. After about 20 minutes, the cumulative response curves start to separate. This indicates that the bird is pecking in the presence of red more than the green. At about 60 minutes, the pigeon seldom responds when the key is green, and this is shown by the leveling off of the curve for this stimulus. Notice, however, that the cumulative curve for pecking the red key continues to rise. Because the bird pecks in the presence of red, but does not respond when the key is green, we may say that the pigeon discriminates between these two stimuli. At this point, it is possible to label the red and green stimuli in terms of their functions. The red light is called a discriminative stimulus, or S^D, and the green color is an S^Δ, or extinction stimulus.

Suppose that the bird is returned to its home cage after 90 minutes of such differential reinforcement. On the next day, the pigeon is again placed in the operant chamber and the key is illuminated with the red light. During this test session, reinforcement is not given for pecking in the presence of either red or green. Because of its previous training, a high probability exists that the bird will strike the red key. Over a 60-second period, the bird may emit many responses when the S^D is present. After 60 seconds, the key light is changed from red to green. When the green light comes on, the probability of response declines and the bird makes few pecks to the green key. By continuing to alternate between red and green, the researcher can show the stimulus control exerted by the respective stimuli.

Stimulus control refers to a change in behavior that occurs when either an S^D or S^Δ is presented. When an S^D is presented, the probability of response increases;

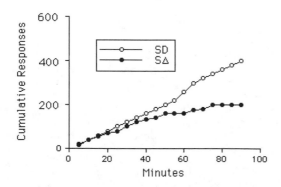

FIG. 8.1 Development of a differential response in the presence of red and green stimuli. Cumulative number of responses over a 90-minute session in which responses in the presence of red are reinforced and responses in the presence of green are on extinction.

when an S^Δ is presented, the probability of response decreases. The stimuli that commonly control human behavior occur across all sensory dimensions. Stopping when you hear a police siren, coming to dinner when you smell food, expressing gratitude following a pat on the back, elaborating an answer because the student looks puzzled, and adding salt to your soup because it tastes bland are instances of stimulus control in human behavior.

STIMULUS CONTROL AND MULTIPLE SCHEDULES

Behavior analysts often use multiple schedules of reinforcement to study stimulus control in the laboratory. On a **multiple schedule,** two or more simple schedules are presented one after the other and each schedule is accompanied by a distinctive stimulus. The idealized experiment that we have just discussed is one example of a multiple schedule. Pecking was reinforced when a red light appeared on the key, and a schedule of extinction was in effect when the green light was on. The schedules and the associated stimuli alternated back and forth every 5 minutes. As indicated, these procedures result in a differential response to the colors.

In an actual experiment, presenting the component schedules for a fixed amount of time or on an FI schedule (e.g., 5 minutes) would confound the results. Without a test procedure, the researcher may not be sure that the bird discriminates on the basis of color rather than time. That is, time itself may have become a discriminative stimulus. For this reason, variable interval schedules are often used for discrimination training.

Figure 8.2 is one example of a multiple variable-interval extinction schedule of reinforcement (MULT VI, EXT). The Mechner notation shows that in the presence of the red S^D, the first response after an average of 2 minutes produces reinforcement. Following reinforcement, the key light changes from red to the green S^Δ, and pecking the key no longer results in reinforcement. After an average of 2 minutes of extinction, the green light goes out and the red stimulus appears again. Pecking the key is now reinforced on the VI 2-minute schedule and the components continue to alternate in this fashion.

A likely result of this multiple schedule is shown in Figure 8.3. The graph portrays the total number of responses during the red and green components for 1-hour daily sessions. Notice that the bird begins by pecking equally in the presence of the red and green stimuli. Over sessions, the number of pecks to the green extinction stimulus, or S^Δ, declines. By the last session, almost all responses occur in the presence of the red S^D and almost none when the green light is on. At this

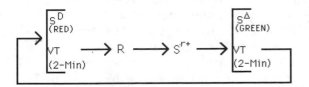

FIG. 8.2 Mechner notation for a MULT VI 2-minute, EXT 1-minute schedule of reinforcement.

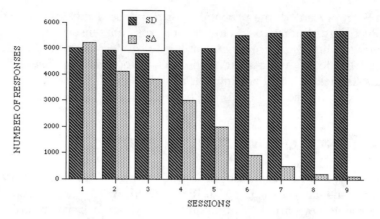

FIG. 8.3 Idealized results for a MULT VI 2-minute, EXT 1-minute schedule of reinforcement. Relative to the red VI component, pecking declines over sessions to almost zero responses per minute in the green extinction phase.

point, pecking the key can be controlled easily by presenting the red or green stimulus. When red is presented the bird will peck the key at a high rate, and if the color changes to green the pigeon will immediately stop.

One way to measure the stimulus control exerted by the S^D and S^Δ at any moment is to use a **discrimination index (I_D).** This index compares the rate of response in the S^D component to the sum of the rates in both S^D and S^Δ phases (Dinsmoor, 1951):

$$I_D = (S^D \text{ rate})/(S^D \text{ rate} + S^\Delta \text{ rate}).$$

Prior to discrimination training, the measure varies between 0.00 and 1.00. Using the I_D measure, when the rates of response are the same in the S^D and S^Δ components, the value of I_D is 0.50, indicating no discrimination. When all responses occur during the S^D phase, the S^Δ rate is zero and I_D equals 1.00 in value. Thus, a discrimination index of 1.00 indicates a perfect discrimination and maximum stimulus control of behavior. Intermediate values of the index signify more or less control by the discriminative stimulus.

A study by Pierrel et al. (1970) illustrates the use of the discrimination index. The experiment concerned the effects of sound intensity on acquisition of a discrimination. The researchers were interested in sound-intensity relationships (measured in decibels) between the S^D and S^Δ. The basic idea was that the more noticeable the difference in sound, the better the discrimination. For example, some people have doorbells for the front and back entrances to their houses. If the chimes are very close in sound intensity, a ring will be confusing and you may go to the wrong door. One way to correct this problem is to change the intensity of sound for one of the chimes (of course, another is to replace one chime with a buzzer).

In one of many experimental conditions, 16 rats were trained to respond on a MULT VI 2-minute, EXT schedule. The animals were separated into four equal groups, and for each group the auditory S^D for the VI component was varied while the S^Δ for the extinction phase was held constant. For each group, the S^Δ

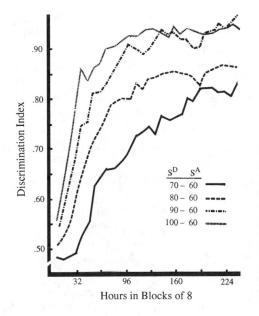

FIG. 8.4 Discrimination index (I_D) curves for different values of S^D and S^Δ. Each curve is a plot of the average I_D values based on a group of four animals, repeatedly exposed to 8-hour sessions of discrimination training (based on Figure 1B from Pierrel, Sherman, Blue, & Hegge 1970; copyright 1970 by the Society for the Experimental Analysis of Behavior, Inc.). The labels for the *x*- and *y*- axes have been simplified to promote clarity.

was a 60-dB tone but the S^D was different, a choice of 70, 80, 90, or 100 dB. Thus, the difference in decibels, or sound intensity, between the S^D and S^Δ increased over groups (70–60, 80–60, 90–60, and 100 versus 60 dB). The rats lived in operant chambers for 15 days. Two 8-hour sessions of the multiple schedule were presented each day, with a 4-hour break between sessions.

Figure 8.4 shows the average acquisition curves for each experimental group. A mean discrimination index based on the four animals in each group was computed for each 8-hour session. As you can see, all groups begin with an I_D value of approximately 0.50, or no difference in responding between the S^D and S^Δ components. As discrimination training continues, a differential response develops and the I_D value rises toward 1.00, or perfect discrimination. The accuracy of the discrimination, as indicated by the maximum value of I_D, is determined by the difference in sound intensity between S^D and S^Δ. In general, more rapid acquisition and a more accurate discrimination occurs when the difference between S^D and S^Δ is increased.

FOCUS ON TEACHING
Discrimination and the "Bird-Brained" Pigeon

Pretend that you are doing a class assignment that involves training a pigeon to discriminate between red and green components of a multiple schedule. The assignment counts for 30% of the course grade, and you must show the final performance of the bird to your instructor. All students are given a pigeon, an operant chamber, and a microcomputer that allows you to control key color and the delivery of food from a hopper. Sessions are scheduled for 1 hour a day over a 2-week period that ends with the professor's evaluation of your project. The pigeon has been food deprived, magazine trained, and taught to peck at a white-illuminated key on a VI 60-second schedule.

You and the other students follow the Mechner notation for a MULT VI 60-second EXT 60-second schedule in which you signal the VI component with a red-key light and a minute of extinction by turning the key green. To create the VI schedule and the variable 60 seconds of extinction, you use operant-conditioning software to program your computer. The software program is set up to record the number of key pecks in both components of the multiple schedule. Your program starts a session with the key illuminated red, and the first response after an average of 60 seconds is reinforced with food (VI 60 seconds). After food is presented, the key color changes to green and extinction is in effect for an average of 60 seconds.

Day after day, your bird pecks at a similar rate in both the red and green components. You become more and more concerned since other students have trained their birds to peck when the key is red and stop when it is green. By the 11th session, you are in a panic because everyone else is finished, but your bird has not made much progress. You complain to your instructor that you were given a dumb or color-blind bird, and it is not fair to get a low mark because you tried your best. Your professor is a strict behavior analyst who replies, "The fault is with the program, not with the pigeon; go study your computer program in terms of Mechner notation." You spend the night pondering the program, and just like Kohler's apes (Kohler, 1927) you "have an insight." Pecking in the extinction component has been reinforced with the presentation of the red-key light.

You realize that the red color is always associated with food reinforcement, and this suggests that the stimulus has more than one function. It is obviously an S^D that sets the occasion for reinforced pecking. In addition, the stimulus is a conditioned reinforcer because of its association with food. Presumably, during the extinction component the bird sometimes pecked the green key, and on the basis of the computer program, the color changed to red. This change in color accidentally or adventitiously reinforced pecking in the extinction component. From the bird's point of view, pecking the key during extinction turns on the red light that allows food reinforcement. In fact, the pigeon's behavior is **superstitious** because pecking in the green component does not affect the presentation of the red color.

Figure 8.5 shows how to solve the adventitious reinforcement problem in Mechner notation. The first part of the diagram presents the notation for a simple MULT VI

FIG. 8.5 Mechner diagram of how to solve the adventitious reinforcement problem on a multiple schedule of reinforcement.

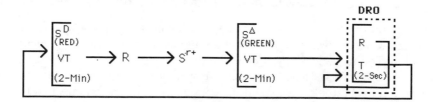

60-second EXT 60-second schedule. Enclosed within the dotted lines is an additional contingency. This contingency prevents the onset of the red stimulus if responding is occurring at the moment that the extinction phase ends. That is, if the extinction period ends with the bird pecking the key, the onset of the red stimulus is delayed. The added contingency is called **differential reinforcement of other behavior,** or **DRO.** Notice that when extinction ends, the DRO contingency requires an additional 2-second period before the red stimulus is presented. During this time, each response or peck resets the 2-second interval. If the bird does anything other than strike the key, the red stimulus will occur.

With this insight, you rush to the laboratory and add DRO to your computer program. At the first opportunity, you place your dumb or color-blind pigeon in the operant chamber and pray. As you watch the bird's performance on the cumulative recorder, the rate of response during the S^D and S^{Δ} components begins to separate. After two more sessions, the discrimination index (I_D) is almost 0.90, indicating good discrimination between reinforcement and extinction phases. The instructor is impressed with your analytical skills, and you get the highest mark possible for the assignment (A+).

This analysis has implications for teaching and learning. When most people learn from instruction but a few do not, educators, psychologists, and parents often blame the poor student, confused client, or stubborn child. They see the failure to learn as a deficiency of the person rather than a problem of contingencies of reinforcement. The ones that fail to learn are said to be learning disabled, low in intelligence, dim-witted, and so on. Of course, some people and animals may have neurological and/or sensory impairment (e.g., color blindness, deafness, organic brain damage) that contributes to their poor performance. Nonetheless, defective contingencies of reinforcement also may contribute to, or exclusively produce, problems of discrimination and learning. In the case of the apparently dumb pigeon, the fault was caused entirely by adventitious reinforcement of responding during extinction. A small change in the contingencies of reinforcement (adding DRO) made a "bird-brained" pigeon smart.

Behavioral Contrast

Consider an experiment by Guttman (1977) in which rats were exposed to a two-component multiple schedule with a variable-interval 30-second schedule in both components (MULT VI 30 seconds VI 30 seconds). One component was signaled by sound (white noise) and the other by a light. The sound and light alternated every 3 minutes, and the rats made about the same number of responses in both components. Next, in the presence of the sound stimulus the contingencies were changed from VI to extinction (MULT VI EXT). As you might expect, rate of response declined in the extinction component. Surprisingly, rate of response increased on the VI component signaled by the light. The increase occurred even though the reinforcement contingencies for the VI component remained the same. Thus, changing the contingencies of reinforcement on one schedule affected reinforced behavior on another schedule.

This effect is called **behavioral contrast** (Reynolds, 1961a, 1961b, 1963). Contrast refers to a negative association between the response rates in the two components of a multiple schedule—as one goes up, the other goes down. There are two forms of contrast, positive and negative. **Positive contrast** occurs when rate of response in an unchanged setting increases with a decline in behavior in another situation. **Negative contrast** occurs when rate of response declines in an unaltered situation with increases in behavior in another setting.

There are many different accounts of why behavioral contrast occurs. These include the addition of autoshaped key pecks to responding in the unchanged component, fatigue or rest attributed to the amount of responding on the changed schedule, and compensating for response rate changes on the altered component (see de Villiers, 1977; McSweeney, Ettinger, & Norman, 1981; Schwartz & Gamzu, 1977, for a discussion). Although there is some dispute, one account suggests that behavioral contrast results from changes in relative rates of reinforcement. On a multiple VI schedule, relative rate of reinforcement for the unchanged component increases when the number of reinforcers goes down on the other schedule. Of course, relative rate of reinforcement for the unchanged component goes down when the number of reinforcers is increased on the other schedule.

For example, if an animal obtains 30 reinforcers each hour on the unchanged component and gets another 30 on the other schedule, then 50% of the reinforcement occurs on both components. If the schedule is changed to MULT VI EXT, then 100% of the reinforcements occur on the unaltered component. As the relative rate of reinforcement goes up on the unchanged component, so does the rate of response. Similarly, response rate on the unaltered schedule will go down if relative rate of reinforcement declines, because of an increase in reinforcement on the changed component. Relative rates of reinforcement provide an account of performance on multiple schedules that is consistent with a behavioral analysis of choice and preference (see Chapter 10).

Although relative rates of reinforcement are important for an analysis of behavioral contrast, there is evidence that other conditions may also contribute to such effects. Research has shown that contrast may only occur in some species and may depend on the type of response required for reinforcement, although the data are inconsistent and sometimes contradictory (e.g., Beninger & Kendall, 1975; Hemmes, 1973; Pear & Wilkie, 1971; Westbrook, 1973).

Recently, McSweeney and her colleagues (Ettinger & McSweeney, 1981; McSweeney, Melville, & Higa, 1988) have examined how different kinds of responses and different types of reinforcement (e.g., food, water, alcohol, etc.) affect behavioral contrast. Her recent research on food and alcohol reinforcement suggests that the nature of the reinforcers on a multiple schedule may limit the impact of relative rates of reinforcement.

Changes in relative rates of reinforcement produced positive contrast (i.e., rate of response went up on the unchanged schedule) when food reinforcement was continued in one component and extinction for alcohol was introduced in the other. However, behavioral contrast did not occur when alcohol reinforcement was continued and responding for food was placed on extinction. One possibility is that alcohol is an economic substitute for food (as rice is for potatoes), but food is not a substitute for alcohol. Relative rates of reinforcement may produce contrast only when reinforcers are substitutable, based on reinforcement history or biology.

After hundreds of studies of behavioral contrast, it is clear that contrast effects may occur in pigeons, rats, and even humans. In addition, contrast has been shown with various schedules of reinforcement (both ratio and interval), different kinds of responses (e.g., lever pressing, key pecking, and treadle pressing), and different types of reinforcement (e.g., food, water, and alcohol) in the component schedules. This suggests that contrast is an important behavioral process that may have adaptive value. A bird that forages successively in two patches would be expected to increase searching for food in one patch if the other began to deplete (i.e., positive contrast). Similarly, negative contrast may occur when food in one of the patches becomes more abundant than in the other. In this case, the bird would decrease foraging in the less plentiful location.

A problem with the research on behavioral contrast is that some of the findings are puzzling. Many experiments result in contrast but others with apparently similar procedures do not, and it is not clear how this happens. Generally, there are many theories of behavioral contrast, but none of the accounts handle all the data.

FOCUS ON RESEARCH
Searching for the Determinants of Contrast

Behavioral contrast is a topic that has interested many behavior analysts. Although contrast is not difficult to describe as a behavioral process, its analysis has been a puzzle for several decades. One of the more prominent researchers in this area is Dr. Ben Williams, at the time of this writing a professor of psychology at the University of California, San Diego. After obtaining a Ph.D. at Harvard University, Dr. Williams pursued a career in basic research. His interests include concurrent schedules of reinforcement, delay of reinforcement, conditioned reinforcement, and stimulus control of operant and respondent behavior. He has been actively involved in an analysis of behavioral contrast for more than 20 years (see Williams, 1974).

As one of his programs of research on behavioral contrast, Williams investigated the sequencing of schedules and stimuli. That is, Williams (1976, 1979, 1981, 1990, 1992) began to investigate how contrast depends on the contingencies that preceded or followed a target schedule. For example, in the schedule sequence A → B → C, the target schedule is component B and response rates for this schedule may be influenced by the contingencies set by A or C.

Generally, Williams (1981) found that the schedule preceding the target component produced weak, variable, and transitory contrast effects. This transitory effect is shown in Figure 8.7 (panel A) where the rate of response is high following reinforcement and drops-off to pre-contrast levels. The schedule that followed the target component gener-

FIG. 8.6 Dr. Ben Williams.

ated strong contrast effects that increased as training progressed (Fig. 8.7, panel B). Williams called this strong contrast effect **anticipatory contrast** to distinguish it from the weak elicited responding evoked by the preceding schedule.

Today, the causes of behavioral contrast still are not completely understood. What is clear from this research is that performance on a schedule of reinforcement is affected by the contingencies that precede and follow the current schedule. As in other areas of behavior analysis, performance on a schedule is a function of the operating contingencies and the context.

FIG. 8.7 Two patterns of behavioral contrast. The drop-off pattern presented in panel A is often elicited by contingencies that precede the target schedule. The linear pattern presented in panel B is called anticipatory contrast and is a function of the contingencies that follow the target schedule.

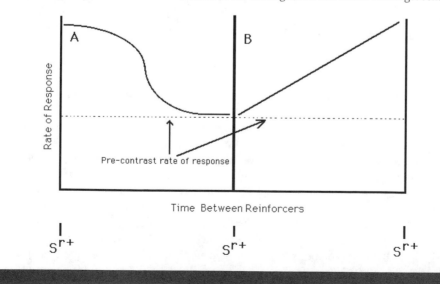

GENERALIZATION

An organism that responds in one situation but not in another is said to discriminate between the settings. An organism that behaves similarly in different situations is said to **generalize** across circumstances. Generalization is a common observation in everyday life. A child may call all adult males "daddy," label all small furry animals as dogs, and drink anything that looks like juice (one reason for child-proof caps on dangerous liquids). Some students call all university teachers "profs" even though professors are only the senior academics. Most of us have seen an old friend at a distance only to find out that the person was not who we expected. A rude person is one who tells vulgar jokes no matter who is listening. In these and many more examples, it appears that common properties of the different stimuli set the occasion for operant behavior.

The problem is that an observer cannot be sure of the stimulus properties that regulate a common response. That is, it is difficult to specify the geometry of dad's face, the physical characteristics that differentiate dogs from other animals, the common aspects of different audiences for the joke teller, and so on. In the operant laboratory, however, it is possible to specify the exact physical dimensions of stimuli in terms of wavelength, amplitude, size, mass, and other physical properties. On the basis of experiments that use well-defined stimuli, it is possible to account for everyday examples of generalization and discrimination.

Stimulus Generalization

Formally, stimulus generalization occurs when an operant that has been reinforced in the presence of a specific discriminative stimulus also is emitted in the presence of other stimuli. The process is called stimulus generalization because the operant is emitted to new stimuli that presumably share common properties with the discriminative stimulus. Generalization and discrimination refer to differences in the precision of stimulus control. Discrimination refers to the precise control of an operant by a stimulus, and generalization involves less precise regulation of operant behavior.

Generalization Gradients. A classic study of generalization was conducted by Guttman and Kalish (1956). Pigeons were trained to peck a key on a VI 1-minute schedule of reinforcement. The key was illuminated with a green light of 550 nanometers (nm), which refers to a wavelength of light that is approximately in the middle of the color spectrum.[2] Once rate of key pecking for food had stabilized in the presence of the green light, the researchers tested for stimulus generalization. To do this, the pigeons were exposed to 10 additional values of wavelength (variations in color) and the original green light. All 11 colors were presented in a random order and each wavelength was shown for 30 seconds.

---

[2]The visible color spectrum is seen when white light is projected through a prism. The spectrum ranges from violet (400 nm) on one end to red (700 nm) on the other.

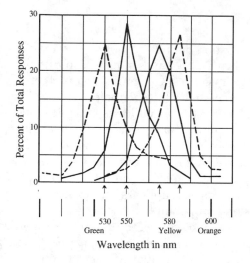

FIG. 8.8 Stimulus generalization gradients of wavelength obtained from four groups of pigeons trained at different wavelengths (from Guttman & Kalish, 1956).

During these test trials, pecking the key was not reinforced (extinction). After the 11 wavelengths were presented (one block of trials), a new random series of the same colors was initiated. A total of 12 blocks of trials were given to the birds. Of course, as the test for generalization continued, key pecking decreased because of extinction, but the decline was equal over the range of stimuli because different wavelengths were presented randomly.

As shown in Figure 8.8, generalization gradients resulted from the experiment. A **generalization gradient** shows the relationship between probability of response and stimulus value. In the experiment by Guttman and Kalish (1956), probability of response is measured as the number of responses emitted by the pigeons and stimulus value is wavelength of light. As you can see, a symmetrical curve with a peak at 550 nm (yellow-green training stimulus) describes stimulus generalization for pigeons trained at this wavelength. The more the new stimulus differed from the wavelength used in training, the fewer the number of responses. Importantly, these results were typical of the curves for individual birds. In addition, similar generalization gradients were found for three other groups of pigeons using 530, 580, and 600 nm as the training stimuli. Generally, probability of response is highest for a stimulus that has signaled reinforcement (S^D), less for stimuli that are similar but not identical to the S^D, and low for stimuli that substantially depart from the discriminative stimulus.

Peak Shift.   Multiple schedules may also be used to study generalization gradients. Hanson (1959) reported an experiment with pigeons that was similar to the Guttman and Kalish (1956) study we just discussed. The procedural difference was that four groups of birds were exposed randomly to periods of VI reinforcement and extinction. For the experimental groups, the S^{Δ} period was either 555, 560, 570, or 590 nm and the S^D phase was always 550 nm. A control group only received training on the VI schedule, with 550 nm of light on the response key.

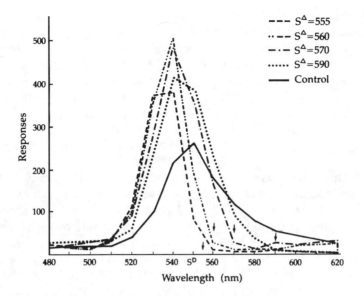

FIG. 8.9 Peak shift of a generalization gradient shown by Hanson (1959).

Notice that the S^D for all groups was a key light of 550 nm, replicating one of the stimulus values used by Guttman and Kalish.

Figure 8.9 shows the major results of Hanson's (1959) experiment. The control group that received only VI training produced a generalization gradient that replicates the findings of Guttman and Kalish. The peak of the distribution is at 550 nm and is symmetrical around this value. In contrast, the experimental groups uniformly showed a shift in the peak of the distribution from 550 nm to 540 nm, moving away from the stimulus value of the S^Δ, which was always greater than 550 nm. For this reason, **peak shift** refers to the change in the peak of a generalization gradient away from the stimulus that signals extinction. Also, the number of responses made at the peak of each distribution is greater for the experimental groups when compared to the control subjects. This latter finding reflects positive behavioral contrast, which occurs on multiple schedules with S^D and S^Δ components (see the foregoing section, "Behavioral Contrast").

Absolute and Relative Stimulus Control. Peak shift is an unusual effect from the point of view of absolute control by a stimulus. **Absolute stimulus control** means that the probability of response is highest in the presence of the stimulus value used in training. In fact, this occurs when reinforcement is the only procedure used to establish stimulus control. This is clearly seen in the results of the Guttman and Kalish (1956) study and in the control group of Hanson's (1959) experiment. In both studies, the peak of the generalization gradient is at the exact (or absolute) value of the stimulus presented during training (550 nm). However, when both S^D and S^Δ procedures are scheduled, the peak of the distribution shifts away from the absolute value of the training stimulus.

The shift in the peak of the generalization gradient may reflect relative, rather than absolute, stimulus control. **Relative stimulus control** means that an organism responds to differences among the values of two or more stimuli. For example, a pigeon may be trained to peck the "larger" of two triangles projected on a response key, rather than respond to the absolute size of the discriminative stimulus. Similarly, the birds in the peak-shift experiments may have come under the control of the relative value of the wavelengths. That is, the S^D was "greener" than the yellow-green S^As used in discrimination training. Because of this, the birds pecked most at stimuli that were relatively "greener," shifting the peak to 540 nm.

There are other ways of showing relational control by stimuli. To study generalization gradients and peak shift, the researcher usually arranges the presentation of S^D and S^A so that one follows the other. This is called **successive discrimination.** An alternative procedure is labeled **simultaneous discrimination**—the S^D and S^A are presented at the same time and the organism responds to one or the other. For example, a pigeon may be presented with two keys, both illuminated with white lights, but one light is brighter than the other. The bird may be reinforced for pecking the "dimmer" of the two keys. Pecks to the other key are placed on extinction. After training, the pigeon will mostly peck the darker of the two keys. To test that the bird's performance is caused by the difference between the two stimuli, it is necessary to present new values of luminosity and observe whether the pigeon pecks the dimmer of two keys.

Gonzalez et al. (1954) provide an example of complex simultaneous discrimination and relational stimulus control in the chimpanzee. The animals were presented with nine squares that were rank ordered in size from 1 (the smallest) to 9 (the largest). Discrimination training involved the simultaneous presentation of 1st-, 5th-, and 9th-ranked squares, and reinforcement was arranged for selecting the intermediate square (5th ranked). To rule out position of the square as an S^D, the researchers varied the position of the three squares from trial to trial.

After this training, the animals were allowed to choose from several new sets of three squares. A chimpanzee might be presented with a choice among squares that ranked 1, 3, and 5. If the animal selected square 3, it showed relational control by the intermediate stimulus. Similarly, choosing square 7 from the set 5, 7, and 9 shows the same kind of stimulus control. In contrast, the chimpanzee could have selected square 5, which would indicate absolute control by the stimulus. In fact, the animals typically chose the middle-sized square in most of the new sets. This finding indicates that relational properties of stimuli often control the operant behavior of organisms, especially if the S^D and S^A are presented at the same time.

Simultaneous discrimination tasks are often used in education. The television program *Sesame Street* teaches youngsters the relations of "same" and "different" by presenting several objects or pictures at the same time. The jingle "one of these thing is just like the others" sets the occasion for the child to identify one of several items. After the child makes a covert response, something like "it's the blue ball," the matching item is shown. In this case, getting the correct answer is reinforcement for the discriminative response.

ERRORLESS DISCRIMINATION AND FADING

When the S^D and S^Δ are alternately presented as in successive discrimination, the organism initially makes many errors. That is, the animal or person continues to respond in the presence of the S^Δ on the basis of generalization. As extinction and reinforcement progress, a differential response occurs to the S^D and S^Δ. A pigeon is taught to peck a green key for food. Once this behavior is well established, the color on the key is changed to blue and pecking is not reinforced. The blue and green colors are alternately presented and the corresponding schedules of extinction or reinforcement are in effect. During the early sessions, the onset of extinction will generate emotional behavior that interferes with ongoing operant behavior.

Extinction is an aversive procedure. Pigeons flap their wings in an aggressive manner and will work for an opportunity to attack another bird during the presentation of the S^Δ on a multiple schedule. Birds will peck a different key if pecking turns off the extinction stimulus, implying that the stimulus is aversive. There are other problems with successive discrimination procedures. Because emotional behavior is generated, discriminative responding takes a long time to develop. In addition, spontaneous recovery of S^Δ responding from session to session interferes with the acquisition of a discrimination. Finally, even after extensive training, birds and other organisms continue to make errors by responding in the presence of the signal for extinction.

Errorless Discrimination

These problems can be eliminated with a discrimination procedure described by Terrace (1963). The method is called **errorless discrimination** because the trainer or teacher does not allow the organism to make mistakes by responding to the extinction stimulus. In his 1963 experiment, Terrace used early progressive training to reduce errors of discrimination. This training began when pigeons were conditioned to peck a red key for food reinforcement. The birds were started on continuous reinforcement and moved gradually to a variable-interval 1-minute schedule. Early in this training, the key light was turned off for 5 seconds and extinction was in effect. Thus, a dark key was the S^Δ in this early phase. It is important to note that pigeons usually do not peck at a dark key, and Terrace made use of this fact.

As discrimination training continued, the dark key was gradually illuminated with a green light. The light became progressively brighter and remained on for longer and longer intervals, until it stayed on the same amount of time as the red key light. At this point, the duration of the S^D (red) was increased to 3 minutes and the S^Δ (green) was gradually increased from 5 seconds to 3 minutes.

Now the birds were responding on a MULT VI 1-minute EXT 3-minute schedule. On this schedule, the red key was presented for 3 minutes and the pigeons pecked for food on a VI 1-minute schedule for this period. After 3 minutes in the reinforcement component, the key color was changed from red to green and extinction was in effect for 3 minutes. With these new contingencies in effect, the pigeons had sufficient time in the S^{Δ} component to make numerous errors, but they did not respond in the presence of the red light.

When this early progressive training was compared with standard successive discrimination procedures, there were far less mistakes with the errorless technique. Figure 8.10 shows that the three pigeons trained with errorless discrimination procedures made about 25 pecks each to the extinction stimulus (errors). Another three birds had the S^{Δ} introduced later in the experiment, at full intensity and for 3 minutes (standard method); these pigeons made between 2,000 and 5,000 pecks to the S^{Δ}. Compared with the errorless group, most of the pecks to the S^{Δ} in the standard condition occurred during the first three sessions. Overall, errorless discrimination procedures result in faster acquisition of a discrimination and substantially less incorrect responding.

Errorless training has other important effects. In a 1972 report, Terrace suggested that his procedures reduced the aversiveness of the S^{Δ} when compared with traditional discrimination methods. Because of this, Terrace claimed that errorless training eliminated the peak-shift effect and positive behavioral contrast. Animals are also less likely to show emotional behavior such as attack or aggressive wing flapping (see Rilling, 1977, for an alternative view). For these reasons, errorless discrimination procedures may be useful in educational settings. Students will enjoy learning, learn as rapidly as possible, and make few mistakes.

Once a discrimination is established with errorless training, it may be difficult to reverse the roles of the S^D and S^{Δ}. Marsh and Johnson (1968) trained two groups of birds to discriminate between red (S^D) and green (S^{Δ}) stimuli. One group received errorless training and the other got the standard discrimination procedure. After performance stabilized, the S^D and S^{Δ} were reversed so that the green stimulus now signaled reinforcement and the red indicated extinction. The birds trained by the errorless method continued responding in terms of their initial training—they would not respond to the S^{Δ} (the new S^D from the point of view of the researcher) even when explicitly reinforced for such behavior. Birds

FIG. 8.10 Results of errorless discrimination procedure used by Terrace (redrawn from Fig. 1 of Terrace, 1963; copyright 1963 by the Society for the Experimental Analysis of Behavior, Inc.).

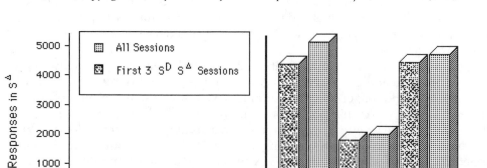
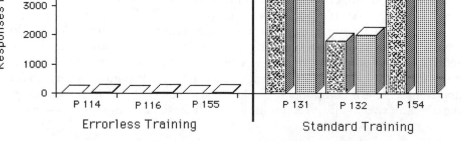

given standard discrimination training were not as persistent since they quickly discriminated the change in contingencies.

These findings suggest that errorless procedures may be most useful in education when there is little chance of a change in the contingencies of reinforcement. For example, students may be best taught multiplication tables, standard word spellings, rules for extracting a square root, and other types of rote learning with the errorless method. In problem-solving situations where there are many alternative solutions or where the contingencies of reinforcement change, the standard method of trial-and-error learning may produce more flexibility in responding.

Fading

Errorless discrimination involves two basic procedures: early introduction of the S^Δ and gradual transfer of stimulus control. It is the latter procedure, called fading, that has received the most attention by clinicians and educators. **Fading** involves transfering stimulus control from one value of a stimulus to another. This is done by gradually changing a controlling stimulus from an initial value to some designated criterion. When Terrace (1963) gradually changed the dark key toward the green color, this was fading.

A practical example of fading is given by Sherman (1965), who used the procedure to get a mute psychotic to say his first words. The patient was described by Sherman as:

> a 63-year-old man, diagnosed, in 1916, as dementia praecox, hebephrenic type. He had been in the hospital continuously for 47 years, with a history of mutism for 45 of those years. At the time of this study he was not receiving any medication or participating in psychotherapy. Periodically, when seen on the ward, ... [he] could be observed walking around mumbling softly to himself. However, all of this mumbling appeared to be nonsensical vocal behavior. In his 45-year history of mutism [he] had not exhibited any recorded instance of appropriate verbal behavior. (1965, p. 157)

After many sessions of reinforcement and imitation training, Sherman succeeded in getting the patient to say "food"—his first distinct utterance in 45 years. At this point, Sherman used fading to bring this response under appropriate stimulus control—responding "food" to the question, "What is this?" The training was as follows:

> To obtain the word "food" from the subject when the experimenter asked "What is this?" a fading procedure was used. With the fading procedure, the experimenter continued to hold up a bite of food each time and to deliver instructions to the subject. The behavior of the subject—that is saying "food"—was maintained with reinforcement while the instructions to the subject were gradually changed in the following steps: (a) "Say food"; (b) "Say foo_"; (c) "Say f___"; (d) "What is this? Say f___"; (e) "What is this? Say ____"; (f) "What is this?" (Sherman, 1965, p. 158)

This example shows that the patient initially replied "food" after the experimenter said "say food." The original verbal stimulus for the response "food" was gradually faded and replaced with a new stimulus of "What is this?"

In everyday life, fading is an important aspect of complex human behavior that often goes unrecognized because of its gradual nature. Children learn to identify many objects in the world by the step-by-step transfer of stimulus control. A parent may present a glass of milk to a 2-year-old and state, "Say milk." Eventually, the child says "milk" when a glass of milk is given. Once the response "milk" is established, stimulus control may be gradually transferred from "say milk" to questions such as "What is this?" by fading. In another example, a parent may initially stay at a day-care center in order to make the child comfortable in the new setting. Once the child starts to participate in activities, the parent sneaks out and stimulus control for a variety of behavior is transferred to the new situation and the teacher. A similar process occurs in adults. When you meet a stranger who is an acquaintance of an old friend, conversation proceeds normally as long as the old friend is present, but becomes awkward if the friend leaves. Over time, the old friend can spend less and less time with you and the new person because stimulus control of conversation is passed to the new acquaintance.

COMPLEX STIMULUS CONTROL

To this point, we have discussed the control of behavior by relatively simple configurations of stimuli, as when a red color signals reinforcement and green does not. There are other procedures that allow for the investigation of performance regulated by more complex stimulus arrays.

Matching to Sample

One procedure that is often used to investigate identity discriminations is **matching to sample.** In a simple identity procedure, a pigeon may be presented with three keys, as in Figure 8.11. Panel A shows a triangle projected onto the center key. The triangle is the sample stimulus in the sense that it is an instance of a larger set of geometric forms. To ensure that the bird attends to the sample, it is required to peck the sample key. When this happens, two side keys are illuminated with a triangle on one and a square on the other, called the comparison stimuli. If the bird pecks the comparison stimulus that corresponds to the sample, this behavior is reinforced and leads to the presentation of a new sample. Panel B shows a nonreinforced sequence in which pecks to the noncorresponding stimulus result in extinction and the next trial. Over a number of trials, the comparison stimuli appear on the left or right keys with equal probability. After some training, pigeons will accurately match to sample even with new (never reinforced) samples and comparison stimuli (Blough, 1959, 1982). The evidence suggests that pigeons' behavior can be regulated by the identity or similarity among stimuli.

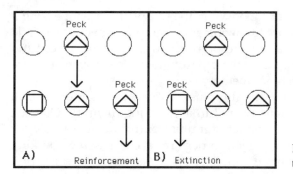

FIG. 8.11 Procedures used to train identity matching by a pigeon.

Delayed Matching to Sample. A twist on the standard matching to sample task is called **delayed matching to sample (DMTS).** This procedure was first described by Blough (1959) and involves delay between the offset of the sample stimulus and the onset of the two comparison stimuli. For example, a pigeon is presented with a center key that is illuminated with a red light. The red sample turns off and 10 seconds later red and green comparison stimuli are presented on the side keys. A response to the stimulus that matches the sample is reinforced and responses to the other stimulus are not. The basic finding is that the percentage of correct responses decreases as the delay increases (Blough, 1959; Grant, 1975).

Delayed matching to sample has been used to investigate behavior that is said to reflect cognition and memory. For example, the time between the offset of the sample stimulus and the onset of the comparison stimuli is usually called the retention interval. The idea is that during this interval the organism is covertly doing something that helps to retain the information about the sample. Thus, Grant (1981) found that pigeons would forget the sample if they were given a sign (a vertical line on the key) that indicated that the comparison stimuli would not appear on that trial. In terms of remembering the sample, Grant reported that the pigeons performed poorly if the forget cue was presented soon after the sample went off (see also Maki & Hegvik, 1980; Stonebraker, Rilling, & Kendrick, 1981). Performance was not as disrupted if the signal was given later in the interval. One interpretation is that the cue to forget interferes with covert rehearsal of the sample stimulus (Grant, 1981; Stonebraker & Rilling, 1981).

The cognitive metaphor of memory processes (coding, storage, retrieval, rehearsal, etc.) is popular in our culture, but it is less acceptable to behavior analysts because the account is based on inferred mental processes. Behavior analysts argue that a scientific analysis of the behavioral processes called remembering must refer to contingencies of reinforcement and basic behavior principles. For example, cognitive researchers use the concepts of reference (long-term) and working (short-term) memory to account for performance on delayed matching to sample tasks. Behavioral researchers discuss the pigeon's performance in terms of **sources of stimulus control** (personal communication, Serdikoff, 1997) For example, in a symbolic DMTS task, the researcher sets the reinforcement contingencies so that when a red sample has been presented the pigeon is required to peck a circle for food. When the sample is green, pecking a square is reinforced. Pecks to a square following a red sample or pecks to a circle following a green sample are "incorrect" responses and are not reinforced (no food). These stable features of the task—the environmental contingencies—are what cognitive researchers call reference memory.

In contrast, behavior that is under the stimulus control of features of the task that change from trial to trial is often referred to as working memory. On each trial, pecking the comparison keys is under stimulus control of the sample for that trial, and so on. In order for the pigeon to perform accurately (i.e., pecking the designated comparison based on the sample), *both the stable (reinforcement contingencies) and fluctuating (sample on that trial) sources of stimulus control* must be considered. Reference remembering is shown when the pigeon demonstrates a history of pecking the comparison keys in accord with reinforcement contingencies (RED : PECK CIRCLE →FOOD; GREEN : PECK SQUARE→FOOD). Working remembering is shown when the pigeon pecks the appropriate comparison given the sample on that trial (RED : PECK CIRCLE). Adding a delay on a given trial weakens the stimulus control by the sample overworking remembering. On the other hand, manipulating the rate of reinforcement for matching to sample presumably affects reference remembering. One possibility is that an experimental analysis of remembering based on complex stimulus control will eventually replace the cognitive account using inferred memory structures and processes.

FOCUS ON RESEARCH
Concept Formation by Pigeons

Principles of stimulus control are involved in many instances of concept formation and abstract reasoning. People usually assume that conceptual thinking is a defining feature of humans that separates them from other animals. Although this kind of behavior is common in humans, it occurs in a more limited way in other organisms. Herrnstein and Loveland (1964) designed an experiment to teach pigeons to identify humans from other objects.

Consider what it means to know that this is a human being and other objects are not. Humans come in a variety of sizes, shapes, colors, postures, and so on. Characteristics of the stimulus "human" are abstract and involve multiple stimulus dimensions rather than a single property such as wavelength of light. For example, human faces differ in terms of presence or absence of hair, geometric form, and several other factors. Defining characteristics of faces include bilateral symmetry, two eyes, a nose, a mouth, and many additional features common to all people.

Although a precise physical description of humans is elusive, Herrnstein and Loveland (1964) asked whether pigeons could respond to the presence or absence of human beings in photographs. If a bird can do this, then its behavior is controlled by the abstract property of humanness. There is no concrete set of attributes that visually equals a human being, but there are relations among such attributes that define the stimulus class. The bird's task is to respond correctly to instances of the stimulus class and by doing so demonstrate concept formation. Herrnstein and Loveland (1964) described the experiment as follows:

It is well known that animals can use one or a few distinguishing features to discriminate stimuli such as simple visual arrays differing in size, shape, or color. In the experiment described here, however, pigeons were trained to detect human beings in photographs, a class of visual stimuli so diverse that it precludes simple characterization.

[After pigeons were trained to peck at a hinged switch in the presence of a translucent plate] . . . the plate was illuminated throughout each session with projections of 35-m color slides from a projector that housed 81 slides. . . . Over 1200 unselected slides obtained from private and commercial sources were available. Before each session, the projector was loaded with 80 or 81 different photographs of natural settings, including countryside, cities, expanses of water, lawn, meadow, and so on. For any one session, approximately half the photographs contained at least one human being; the remainder contained no human beings—in the experimenter's best judgment. In no other systematic way did the slides appear to differ. Many slides contained human beings partly obscured by intervening objects: trees, automobiles, window frames, and so on. The people were distributed throughout the pictures: in the center or to one side or the other, near the top or the bottom, close up or distant. Some slides contained a single person; others contained groups of various sizes. The people themselves varied in appearance: they were clothed, semi-nude, or nude; adults or children; men or women; sitting, standing or lying; black, white, or yellow. Lighting and coloration varied: some slides were dark, others light; some had either reddish or bluish tints, and so on.

. . . Pictures containing people . . . meant an opportunity to feed . . . and pictures without people meant no such opportunity. . . . Each day the slides themselves and also the random sequence of positive (SD) slides (that is, containing a person) and negative (SΔ) slides (without people), were changed for each pigeon. Many slides were used again in later sessions, but never in the order with other slides in which they had appeared earlier. The pigeons had no opportunity, therefore, to learn groups of particular slides or sequences of positives and negatives in general. (pp. 549–550)

The results showed that the pigeons could discriminate between slides with people and ones without them. Within 10 sessions of this training, every bird was responding at a higher rate to slides with humans in them. Over several months, the performance of the birds steadily improved. After extensive training, the birds were given 80 (or 81) slides that they had never seen before. Pigeons pecked at a high rate to new slides with people and at lower rates to slides without them. Generally, this experiment shows that pigeons can differentially respond to the abstract stimulus class of human being.

Additional experiments on concept formation have been conducted with other stimulus classes and different organisms. Pigeons have discriminated trees (Herrnstein, 1979), geometric forms (Towe, 1954), letters of the alphabet (Blough, 1982), fish (Herrnstein & de Villiers, 1980), one person from another (Herrnstein, Loveland, & Cable, 1976), and aerial photographs of human-made objects (Lubow, 1974). Concept formation has also been reported for monkeys (Schrier & Brady, 1987), an African gray parrot (Pepperberg, 1981), and mynah birds (Turney, 1982).

Overall, this research suggests that animals differntially respond to abstract properties of stimulus classes. These stimulus classes are commonly called categories when humans make similar discriminations. When people describe different categories, they are said to understand the concept. People can easily identify a computer disk and an automobile as human-made objects. When a similar performance is shown by other animals, we are reluctant to attribute the discriminative behavior to the creature's understanding of the concept.

Rather than attribute understanding to complex performances by humans or animals, it is possible to provide an account based on evolution and the current demands of the environment. Natural selection shapes sensory capacities of organisms that allow for discrimination along abstract dimensions. Birds obtain food, navigate, care for young, find mates, and so on largely on the basis of visual stimuli. Many of these activities require subtle adjustments to a complex and changing visual world. It is not surprising, therefore, that these creatures are readily able to discriminate abstract properties of visual objects, especially when reinforcement contingencies favor such a discrimination.

Conditional Discrimination.   In everyday life, stimuli that regulate behavior (S^D and S^Δ) often depend on the context. Consider a matching-to-sample experiment in which a bird has been trained to match to triangles and squares based on the sample stimulus. To turn this experiment into a conditional-discrimination task, a red or green light illuminates the sample stimulus. The bird is required to match to the sample when the background light is green and to choose the noncorresponding stimulus when the light is red. That is, when a green triangle is the sample, the bird must peck the comparison triangle, but when a red triangle is presented, pecks to the circle are reinforced. Of course, if a green circle is the sample, pecks to the circle are reinforced, and when the sample turns red, pecking the triangle is the correct response. Conditional matching to sample involves simultaneous discrimination of three elements in a display. The animal must respond to geometric form depending on the background color of the sample. It also must respond to the correspondence or noncorrespondence of the comparison stimuli.

Conditional discrimination is a common aspect of human behavior. A person who is hurrying to an appointment on the 15th floor of an office building will ordinarily enter the first available elevator. This same person may wait for the next lift if the elevator is full. Thus, getting on the elevator (operant) when the doors open (S^D) is conditional on the number of people in the car. In another example, you will say "eight" when shown 3 + 5 and "fifteen" if the relation is 3 × 5. Your response to the 3 and 5 is conditional on the + and × symbols. In the chapter on verbal behavior (Chapter 12), we will see that conditional discrimination is also important for the emergence of symbolic behavior. When people say that the spoken word *cat*, the written word *CAT*, and a picture of a cat are the same, their behavior is a result of such complex discrimination training.

ON THE APPLIED SIDE

The Pigeon as a Quality Control Inspector

In industrial settings, workers often are hired as quality control inspectors. Quality control usually is a monotonous job of checking samples of a product to identify any defects. The most important skills or attributes needed for such jobs are good visual acuity and color vision. Based on these visual requirements, Thom Verhave (1966) suggested to the management of a drug company that the laboratory pigeon (*Columba livia domestica*) would be a cheap and efficient quality control inspector. Although skeptical, the director of research for the company gave Verhave the go ahead to train pigeons as inspectors.

The procedures were similar to a matching to sample (identity matching) task. Pigeons were trained to inspect a line of drug capsules, accepting those that met a fixed standard and rejecting defective ones. In this procedure (Figure 8.12), a bird compared a drug capsule with a standard sample (a perfect one) and pecked Key 1 if it matched or pecked Key 2 if there was a defect (a skag).

The standard capsule was fixed in position behind an inspection window. A line of capsules passed by the same window one at a time; some were perfect and others were defective. In order to initiate an inspection, the pigeon pecked at the inspection window activating a beam of light that illuminated the sample and the comparison capsules. During training, all capsules on the inspection line were pre-coded by an electrical switch as either perfect or skags. If a capsule on the line was pre-coded as perfect, then the pigeon's response to Key 1 (matching response) resulted in food, turned off the beam of light behind the inspection window and moved a new capsule into place. If a capsule was pre-coded as a skag, then a response to Key 2 (non-matching response) turned off the illumination, moved a new capsule into the inspection window, and resulted in presentation of the food hopper. All other responses were false alarms or misses that were not reinforced and resulted in a 30-second blackout. With these contingencies in effect, the birds were about 99% accurate in identifying perfect capsules and skags.

FIG. 8.12. Drawing depicts Verhave's (1966) discrimination procedures as described in the text. Pigeons were trained to inspect a line of drug capsules, accepting those that met a fixed standard and rejecting defective ones. The illustration is taken from Ferster, Culbertson & Boren (1975, p.558) and republished with the permission of Prentice Hall Inc.

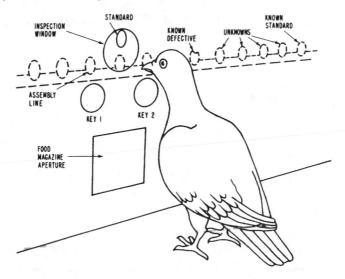

One practical problem that Verhave faced concerned the persistence of a pigeon's performance on a real-life inspection line. In everyday life, there is no experimenter to designate perfect capsules, skags, misses, and false alarms. Without this monitoring, differential reinforcement for "hits versus misses" cannot be maintained and a bird's performance will deteriorate over time to chance levels. A solution was to introduce capsules "known to be perfect or defective" occasionally onto the inspection line. Reinforcement or punishment were only in effect for "known" instances of matching (or non-matching) to sample. With this procedure, sufficient differential reinforcement occurred to maintain stimulus control by the sample and comparison capsules.

In addition to Verhave (1966), there have been other attempts to use pigeons for navigation of missiles (Skinner, 1960) or to run assembly lines (Cumming, 1966). Most of these projects began with the company's management (or military officers) being skeptical and amused by the claim that pigeons could perform such feats. Once it became clear that behavioral researchers could establish and maintain precise performance in pigeons, upper-level management no longer found this research humorous or acceptable and immediately stopped all funding.

Analysis of the reinforcement contingencies related to upper management's rejection of pigeons in industry is informative. For example, although pigeons can be effective quality control inspectors, customers might complain about the lack of sanitary conditions. This could result in sales losses that would offset the benefits of having pigeons as low-cost employees. Other contingencies for managers may involve the complaints of union workers. Even though the quality control task is boring and monotonous, union workers could complain about the loss of jobs and use strikes to back up their demands. Again, the benefits of pigeons as inspectors is offset by human labor disputes. Overall, while pigeons are excellent, low-cost employees, the social and economic contingencies of the human marketplace insure that pigeons' pecking will not prevail.

KEY WORDS

Absolute stimulus
control

Anticipatory contrast

Behavioral contrast

Conditional
discrimination

Controlling stimulus (S)

Delayed matching to
sample

Differential
reinforcement of other
behavior (DRO)

Differential response

Discrimination

Discrimination index
(I_D)

Discriminative stimulus
(S^D)

Errorless discrimination

Extinction stimulus (S^Δ)

Generalization gradient

Matching to sample

Multiple schedule

Negative contrast

Peak shift

Positive contrast

Relative stimulus control

Simultaneous
discrimination

Sources of stimulus
control

Stimulus control

Stimulus generalization

Successive
discrimination

Superstitious behavior

CHAPTER 9

Aversive Regulation
of Behavior

1. Define and give an example of primary and conditioned aversive stimuli. According to Azrin and Holz (1966), why is punishment a fact of life?

2. What is meant by aversive regulation of behavior? Discuss positive punishment and extend the analysis to a child who is spanked for hitting a friend.

3. Outline the procedure of negative punishment. Give an example of negative punishment involving a child who is watching television. Distinguish between negative punishment and extinction.

4. Does punishment teach new behavior? Why is it important to study punishment and aversive control of behavior? What are the advantages of laboratory experiments on punishment?

5. Outline the effects of gradual and sudden punishment. Give an example of graduated punishment involving a messy kid playing with Mike's new disk player.

6. How does the intensity of positive punishment relate to response suppression? Why have Skinner and others argued that punishment only produces temporary suppression of behavior?

7. Discuss immediacy of positive punishment and how reflexive behavior may disrupt operant responding. What is the most effective schedule of positive punishment? Why?

8. Outline the issues about use of aversive procedures in behavior therapy. What are two possible side-effects in the use of positive punishment? Discuss Solomon's recommendation to solve disputes about punishment. Why hasn't it worked?

9. How effective is punishment at different levels of food deprivation? Discuss the practical implications of the motivation-punishment relationship by pointing to the modification of self-destructive behavior (Lovaas & Simmons, 1969).

10. Outline how response alternatives make punishment more effective. Give an everyday example of response alternatives and punishment.

11. Distinguish between escape and avoidance. Define negative reinforcement. Why is the distinction between escape and avoidance somewhat artificial? Use shock-shock interval and response-shock interval in your answer.

12. Give some examples of escape conditioning. Know the Mechner notation for an escape contingency. Why are escape responses more easily acquired than avoidance behavior? Discuss escape conditioning and the compatibility of reflexive and operant behavior.

13. Define avoidance and give some common examples. Outline discriminative avoidance and the Mechner notation for this contingency. Discuss the rate of acquisition for discriminative avoidance.

14. Comment on nondiscriminative avoidance as compared with discriminative avoidance. Discuss the experiment and findings of Murray Sidman (1953).

15. Analyze the S-S and R-S intervals and the effectiveness of an avoidance contingency. Discuss the relationship between shock frequency and avoidance, referring to the molar and molecular views.

16. What happens when a period of avoidance precedes or follows a session of food reinforcement (Hakenberg & Hineline, 1987)?

17. Be able to outline Skinner's argument against aversive techniques.

18. Discuss behavioral persistence as a side-effect of punishment, referring to operant-respondent interactions. How could you place avoidance behavior on extinction? Provide an example of behavioral persistence in the Nazi concentration camps.

19. What is learned helplessness? How is this behavior acquired in animals (Seligman & Maier, 1967)? Does learned helplessness occur in people? Give an example. Explain how learned helplessness is a side-effect of punishment.

20. Analyze the relationship between learned helplessness and depression, referring to relevant studies.

21. Describe respondent (pain-elicited) aggression as a side-effect of positive punishment, indicating the appropriate studies. As the frequency and intensity of shocks increase, what happens to aggression?

22. What happens to aggression if rats can escape or avoid the shocks? How does the amount of space affect pain-elicited aggression?

23. Describe the effects of random shocks on aggression of other species. Does the same kind of aversive stimulus lead to aggression in all animals? What about humans?

24. What is operant aggression? Give an example. Within the aggressive episode, how is aggressive behavior maintained by negative reinforcement?

25. Discuss the problems of investigating human aggression in the laboratory.

26. Provide a behavior analysis of how aggression breeds aggression, referring to Skinner's account of the sailors' game during the 18th century.

27. What have controlled experiments with humans shown about how aggression breeds aggression?

28. Discuss the side-effect of punishment known as social disruption. Why does this side-effect occur?

29. Based on Sidman's (1989) analysis of coercion, why do children drop out of school? Can anything be done to turn dropping out into "tuning in"?

Aversive stimuli are those events that organisms avoid or escape from. Stings, attacks, foul odors, bright light, and very loud noises, are examples of aversive events that organisms are phylogenetically prepared to evade. Escaping or avoiding these **primary aversive stimuli** had survival value, presumably because those animals that emitted this behavior survived and reproduced. In other words, organisms do not learn that these stimuli are aversive; they are biologically prepared to avoid or escape such events.

Other stimuli become aversive because they are associated with primary aversive events during an animal's lifetime. For people, **conditioned aversive stimuli** include threats, public criticism, a failing grade, a frown, and verbal disapproval. A 1-week-old infant is not affected by a reprimand such as, "Don't do that!" However, by the time the child is 2 years old, the command may stop the toddler from tearing pages out of your favorite book. Animals also learn to respond to conditioned stimuli as aversive events. People commonly shout "No!" when pets misbehave, and this auditory stimulus eventually reduces the probability of the response it follows (e.g., chewing on your new chair). A wolf may snap at a yellow-jacket wasp, but following a sting or two the animal will avoid yellow-and-black striped insects.

There are good reasons for not using aversive contingencies in the regulation of behavior, and these reasons will be discussed later in this chapter. Nonetheless, a large amount of human (and animal) behavior is regulated by contingent aversive stimuli, and for this reason the analysis is necessary. Azrin and Holz (1966) have recognized this:

> We have seen that several methods other than punishment are available for eliminating behavior. For whatever the reasons, we may wish to use methods other than punishment. To what extent is this objective practicable? At the institutional level, it would seem to be quite possible to eliminate the use of physical punishment. Conceivably, administrative regulations could be altered such that public punishment in the form of flogging, spankings, or other physical abuse would be excluded. At the level of individual behavior, it seems somewhat more difficult but still not impossible to eliminate the use of physical punishment. One type of punishment, however, seems to be virtually impossible to eliminate, and that is the punishing contingencies that are arranged by the physical world. Whenever we interact with the physical world, there are many punishing contingencies awaiting us. A good example of this would be any behavior that moves us through space such as walking, running, or reaching. It is only necessary to shut one's eyes while running to realize the extent to which punishing contingencies surround our movement. The degree to which these punishing contingencies are actually applied can be seen in the initial efforts of the young child in learning to walk and to run. So powerful are these potential punishing contingencies that they exist even when we sleep. The response of rolling off a bed is punished immediately and severely by collision with the floor below. Elimination of punishing contingencies by the physical world would appear to require elimination of all behavior that involves interaction with physical world. (p. 438)

This passage makes it clear that, at least in the physical world, punishment (and other forms of aversive regulation) are a fact of life.

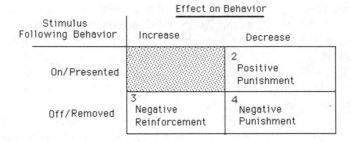

FIG. 9.1 Aversive contingencies of reinforcement and punishment (adapted from Figure 5.2 in Chapter 5). When a stimulus or event follows operant behavior, then the behavior increases or decreases in frequency. It is this relationship between behavior and consequence that defines the contingency.

CONTINGENCIES OF PUNISHMENT

When a behavioral consequence results in a decrease in rate of response the contingency is called punishment. Figure 9.1 makes it clear that it is the relationship between the consequence and its effects on behavior that defines the aversive contingency. At this point, we discuss contingencies of punishment; negative reinforcement is addressed later in this chapter.

Positive Punishment

Positive punishment occurs when a stimulus is presented following an operant and the operant decreases in rate of response. The contingency, positive punishment, is shown in cell 2 of Figure 9.1. When a parent spanks a child for running into the street and the child stops doing it, this is positive punishment. Of course, spanking is a punishing consequence *only if it decreases the probability of running into the street.* This is an important point because in usual language people talk about punishment without considering its effects on behavior. For example, you may shout and argue with another person when he or she expresses a particular political position. Your shouting is positive punishment only if the other individual stops (or decreases) talking about politics. In fact, the person may increase his or her rate of political conversation (as often happens in arguments). In this case, you have by definition reinforced rather than punished the person for arguing with you. Thus, positive punishment is defined as a decline in operant behavior because of the presentation of a stimulus that follows it.

Negative Punishment

Negative punishment is portrayed in cell 4 of Figure 9.1. When a stimulus is taken away contingent on a response and this removal results in a decrease in rate of behavior, the contingency is called **negative punishment.** In other words, if the organism responds, the stimulus is taken away and behavior decreases. A

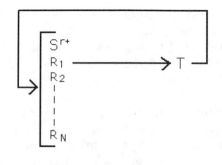

FIG. 9.2 Negative punishment occurs when operant responses R_2 through R_N do not affect ongoing reinforcement (S^{r+}). If the response R_1 is emitted, however, reinforcement is removed for some period of time (T). After that time period has passed, reinforcement is reinstated.

hungry bird is given continuous access to food, but if it pecks the key, food is removed. A child is watching TV, but if the child swears, the television is turned off. In these cases, reinforcement that is in the situation (i.e., food is available, the TV is turned on) is removed contingent on behavior.

Negative punishment is often confused with extinction. *Extinction occurs when a previously reinforced response no longer produces reinforcement.* In this case, a response has produced reinforcement; extinction for that response is in effect when the response → reinforcer contingency is discontinued. A pigeon may peck a key for food, but when extinction is programmed, pecking no longer produces the food reinforcer. Similarly, a child may be allowed to watch a favorite television show after completing homework assignments. When the TV is broken the contingency is no longer in effect and doing homework is on extinction.

In Figure 9.2, ongoing reinforcement could be eating a meal with the family, and responses $R_2 \ldots R_N$ may involve talking to a sister, passing food around the table, turning on a compact disk player, and so on. Licking your plate is represented by R_1 and results in father telling you to leave the table for a period of time (negative punishment). Forcing you to leave your supper reduces your tendency to engage in this nasty habit when you next have a meal with your family.

How to Make Punishment Most Effective

It is important to note that punishment does not teach or condition new behavior. Contingencies of punishment eliminate or, more often, temporarily suppress the rate of operant behavior. In this section, we describe some of the conditions that increase the effectiveness of contingencies of punishment.

Experimental investigations of punishment are important. In the everyday world of people (and other animals), many consequences of behavior are aversive. Parents scold and spank children, people fall off bicycles, individuals are forced to pay fines, and school kids are made to stand in a corner. All modern cultures use legal sanctions to control their citizens, and these sanctions are generally aversive. Experiments on punishment have shown how to make punishment most effective. Other research has suggested strong reasons for avoiding the use of punishment whenever possible.

The study of punishment is complicated by the fact that punished responses are typically maintained on some schedule of reinforcement. In other words, a schedule of punishment is superimposed on a baseline schedule of positive reinforcement. This means that we are really investigating the effects of punishment on behavior maintained by a schedule of reinforcement, and results may reflect both of these variables. Nonetheless, there are reasonably clear findings that suggest how to make punishment most effective.

Abrupt Introduction of Punishment.   Azrin, Holtz, and Hake (1963) found that birds would continue to respond even when intense levels of electric shock (130 volts) were delivered for key pecks. This effect occurred when the aversive stimulus was introduced at 60 volts or less and gradually increased. On the other hand, animals that suddenly received moderate-intensity shocks, at 80 volts, completely quit responding (see also Azrin, 1959; Miller, 1960). Importantly, the key-pecking behavior of the birds given sudden shock was irreversibly suppressed—they never pecked the key again.

Consider the following scenario: Mike has bought a new stereo system and his friend, Joe, and Joe's 2-year-old daughter drop in for a visit. The child is eating a glob of peanut butter and makes a beeline for the new equipment. Nervously, Mike looks at his friend, who says, "Emily, don't touch—that's Mike's new disk player." The child continues to fondle the knobs on Mike's $900 music system and Joe says, "Please leave that alone!" Emily is still smearing peanut butter on Mike's investment, so Joe glowers at his child and loudly says, "I said *stop* that!" Emily does not stop and is now threatened with, "*If you don't stop, Dad will give you a spanking!*" Emily still plays with the stereo. In desperation, Joe gives Emily a light tap on the bottom, which she ignores. In this circumstance, aversive stimuli are introduced at low intensity and gradually increased. Laboratory research suggests that this is a formula for creating a masochist. Of course, the best solution for the stereo problem would be to wipe the child's hands off, or place the equipment out of reach.

Intensity of Punishment.   The preceding discussion should make it clear that if punishment is going to be used, it should be introduced at a moderate intensity on the first occasion. Generally, the higher the intensity of the aversive stimulus, the greater the response suppression. Low-intensity positive punishment may leave behavior relatively unaffected, while severe values of the aversive stimulus may permanently change behavior (Appel & Peterson, 1965; Azrin, 1960). Several experiments have shown that intense punishment can completely eliminate responding (Appel, 1961; Storms, Boroczi, & Broen, 1962). One interesting implication is that once complete suppression of responding occurs, behavior is unlikely to recover for some time when the aversive stimulus is withdrawn. This is because the organism stops responding and the absence of punishment is not contacted.

If organisms do respond after punishment is withdrawn, behavior eventually recovers to prepunishment levels. For this reason, Skinner (1953) and others have suggested that punishment only produces a temporary suppression of behavior:

> Recently, the suspicion has ... arisen that punishment does not in fact do what it is supposed to do. An immediate effect in reducing a tendency to behave

is clear enough, but this may be misleading. The reduction in strength may not be permanent. (p. 183)

This passage reflects Skinner's lifelong objection to the use of aversive stimuli for behavior regulation.

Nonetheless, research shows that high-intensity positive punishment can permanently eliminate responding. This elimination of responses does not seem to be affected by time away from the experimental situation (Azrin, 1959, 1960). For example, Masserman (1946) placed cats in a situation in which they had been punished 20 months earlier. The animals did not emit the punished response, even though the aversive stimulus was discontinued. Thus, high-intensity punishment can reduce rate of response to absolute zero, and this appears to be an enduring effect.

Immediacy of Punishment.
Punishment is most effective at reducing responses when it closely follows behavior (Azrin, 1956; Cohen, 1968). This effect can be missed easily because aversive stimuli generate emotional behavior that may disrupt operant responses. In other words, when first introduced, positive punishment elicits reflexive behavior that prevents the occurrence of many operants. Watch a child (or adult) who has just been chastised severely. You will probably see the person sit quietly, possibly cry, look away from others, and so on. In common language, we may say that the child is pouting but, in fact, what is happening is that reflexive emotional behavior is disrupting all operant responses. If the child was punished immediately for making rude noises, those noises and many other operants would decrease in frequency. However, in the long run, making noises would be relatively unaffected if punishment did not closely follow that response.

Estes (1944) punished some rats immediately after they made a response, while another group received delayed punishment. Both groups of animals showed a similar reduction in bar pressing. This finding was replicated 11 years later by Hunt and Brady (1955) and suggests that positive punishment reduces operant responses because it elicits competing respondent behavior. Later research by Azrin (1956) found that after the first hour of exposure to positive punishment, immediate versus delayed punishment makes a large difference. Responses that were punished after a time delay recovered substantially, but when the aversive stimulus was immediately delivered, responses were often completely eliminated. Thus, it appears that the introduction of punishment generates reflexive responses that may at first disrupt operant behavior. However, the contingency is eventually contacted and, in the long run, makes a large difference. To make punishment most effective, it should be delivered immediately after the response.

Schedule of Punishment.
In general, positive punishment is most effective when it is delivered for each response (Zimmerman & Ferster, 1963). Azrin, Holz, and Hake (1963) trained pigeons to peck a key on a VI 3-minute schedule of food reinforcement. Once responding was stable, they shocked the bird when it

pecked the key. Shocks were presented after 100, 200, 300, 500, or 1,000 key pecks. Rate of response substantially declined even when punishment was delivered after 1,000 responses. As rate of punishment increased, the number of responses per hour declined. In other words, as more and more responses were punished, operant rate decreased. Continuous punishment (FR 1) produced the greatest response suppression. This effect is similar to increasing the intensity of the aversive stimulus—to maximize suppression of responses, deliver the aversive stimulus as frequently as possible and increase its intensity.

FOCUS ON ISSUES
Use of Aversives in Treatment

There are behaviorally deficient and psychotic people who, for a variety of reasons, engage in self-destructive behavior. This behavior may escalate to the point at which the person is hitting, scratching, biting, or gouging himself or herself most of the day. In some cases, self-destructive acts are so frequent and intense that the person is hospitalized. Occasionally physical injury is irreversible, as when a child bangs his or her head on a wall until brain damage occurs. Although positive-reinforcement programs have been used to alleviate severe behavior problems, these contingencies are not always successful. Because of this, behavior therapists have resorted to punishment as a way of reducing self-destructive behavior.

The use of positive punishment as a treatment technique has been controversial (Feldman, 1990). Opponents of punishment argue that such procedures are morally wrong and they advocate a total ban on its use (e.g., Guess, Helmstetter, Turnbull, & Knowlton, 1986; Sobsey, 1990). These researchers also suggest that punishment is not necessary because many positive methods are available to treat severe behavior problems. They further propose that positive techniques are as effective as punishment for eliminating self-destructive responses. On the other side of the issue are therapists and parents of self-abusive children who advocate the individual's right to effective treatment (e.g., Matson & Taras, 1989; Van Houten et al., 1988). The proponents of effective treatment claim that a combination of positive reinforcement and punishment is the best way to manage severely self-injurious behavior.

One reason given for not using punishment in applied settings is that aversive techniques may generate emotional distress and aggression (LaVigna & Donnellan, 1986; Meyer & Evans, 1989). Opponents of positive punishment often support this view by pointing to research with animals concerning electric shock and pain-elicited aggression (see the section "Side-Effects of Aversive Procedures" later in this chapter). Essentially, when animals are given noncontingent electric shock, they attack other animals or inanimate objects. A broader, but similar, position has been advanced by Murray Sidman (1989) in his book, *Coercion and Its Fallout*. Sidman argues that violence within and between nations is the product of punitive contingencies. In a treatment setting, these effects imply that aversive therapy may produce as many problems as it alleviates.

Solomon (1969) recognized that there must be certain conditions that lead to the side-effects of punishment—under specified conditions punishment may have devastating effects, under other conditions punishment may not. Solomon (1969) stated:

> when punishments are asserted to be ineffective controllers of [operant] behavior, they are in contrast, often asserted to be devastating controllers of emotional reactions, leading to neurotic and psychotic symptoms, and to general pessimism, depressiveness, constriction of thinking, horrible psychosomatic diseases, and even death! This is somewhat of a paradox, I think. The convincing part of such generalizations is only their face validity. There are experiments, many of them carefully done, in which these neurotic outcomes were clearly observed. . . . The side effects are frightening, indeed, and should *not* be ignored! But there *must be* some rules, some principles, governing the appearance of such side effects, for they *do not* appear in all experiments involving the use of strong punishment or the elicitation of terror. (p. 89)

Solomon clearly believes that an in-depth scientific analysis of punishment will solve the value question of whether or not to use punishment in a given situation. Although we agree with Solomon's hopes, current research on punishment is not sufficient to answer value questions. That is, research evidence suggests that complex interactions may occur between the reinforcement schedule maintaining behavior and punishment (Epling & Pierce, 1990; Linscheid & Meinhold, 1990). Most of these interactions, however, have not been sufficiently studied and replicated to draw any firm conclusions.

One reason for the lack of modern research is that many people think that it is not right to expose animals to aversive procedures. On the basis of animal ethics, investigations of punishment have almost been eliminated at the basic level. Until our society finds it more important to understand punishment, questions about the use of aversives cannot be informed by scientific analysis.

Motivation for the Response.   Punishment is most effective when the motivation to respond is reduced (Dinsmoor, 1952). Azrin, Holz, and Hake (1963) trained pigeons to peck a key on a VI 3-minute schedule of food reinforcement. After responding was stable, they introduced an intense 160-volt shock for every 100th response. Birds were exposed to the schedule of reinforcement plus punishment at several levels of food deprivation. Increased deprivation for food should increase the pigeon's motivation to respond. The animals were punished for responding at 60, 65, 70, 75, and 85% of free-feeding body weight. At 85% weight, punishment virtually stopped the birds' responding. However, at 60% weight the pigeons maintained a high, stable rate of response. As shown in Figure 9.3, rate of response was ordered by level of deprivation—the less the deprivation for food, the more effective punishment was.

Thus, behavior that is punished may be completely suppressed when the motivation to respond is low. Interestingly, there is evidence that once complete suppression has occurred, the behavior does not recover even when motivation is in-

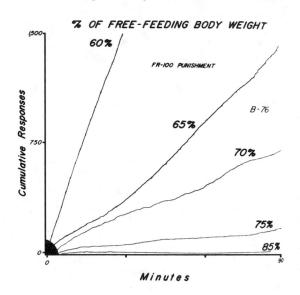

FIG. 9.3 Level of food deprivation and punished responding maintained by a VI food reinforcement schedule (reprinted from Azrin, Holz, & Hake, 1963; copyright 1963 by the Society for the Experimental Analysis of Behavior, Inc.).

creased (Masserman, 1946; Storms et al., 1962). For example, a rat may be punished when it responds for food and its behavior completely eliminated. Next, the level of food deprivation is increased but responding remains at zero rate.

These findings may have practical implications. Punishment is sometimes used to reduce the frequency of human behavior (see the preceding Focus on Issues). As we have said, there are side effects of aversive regulation that suggest that these techniques should be used with caution. Nonetheless, there are circumstances in which punishment may be a reasonable option for changing behavior. When people behave in ways that hurt themselves or others, punishment can be used to quickly suppress these operants. In the preceding discussion, we described children who severely hurt themselves by banging their heads, hitting themselves, chewing on their flesh, and so on. In some of these cases, positive punishment can be used to rapidly reduce self-injurious behavior.

Some self-abusive behavior may be maintained by unintentional contingent attention from caretakers. Lovaas and Simmons (1969) treated three severely self-destructive children who were placed on extinction (adult attention was withdrawn) for hitting themselves. During extinction, one child (John) hit himself 9,000 times before stopping. The other child who was treated with extinction demonstrated similar behavior, emitting many self-injurious acts before extinction was complete. Lovaas and Simmons (1969) commented that:

> this procedure of withdrawing or making potential reinforcers unavailable has an undesirable attribute, in that it is not immediately effective and temporarily exposes the child to the danger of severe damage from his own self-destruction, which is particularly intense during the early stages of the extinction run. In some cases of severe self-destruction, it is ill-advised to place the child on extinction. Marilyn, . . . for example, could have inflicted serious self-injury or possibly even killed herself during an extinction run. (p. 155)

In contrast, when positive punishment was made contingent on this behavior, all three children hit themselves a few times and then quit. In cases like these, punishment seems warranted, but the animal research suggests a humane modification of the basic procedure.

The children treated by Lovaas and Simmons were apparently engaging in self-injurious behavior because of contingent social attention from adult caretakers. The motivation for attention might be reduced by having adults provide lots of noncontingent attention to a child before using a punishment procedure. This would be easy to implement: simply have staff hold, cuddle, and talk to the child for a few days before punishment is used to stop self-abusive responses. Once this is done, a mild aversive stimulus may eliminate the responses. Interestingly, the basic research also suggests that when motivation increases, responding will not recover.

Response Alternatives.   A straightforward way to make punishment more effective is to give a person or animal another way to obtain the same reinforcers that support target responses. This is another way that moderate levels of punishment can be used effectively to suppress behavior. It is essential to identify the consequences that are maintaining the behavior that is to be punished. After this is accomplished, motivation may be reduced, or the organism can be given another response opportunity to get the same reinforcer. Herman and Azrin (1964) had people lever press on a VI schedule of reinforcement. These individuals were punished with an annoying buzzing sound for each response, and this procedure slightly reduced their rate of response. When people were given another response opportunity that did not produce the buzzer, they quickly changed to that alternative and punished responses were eliminated (see also Azrin & Holz, 1966, p. 405).

Pretend that there is a convenience store in the middle of the block directly behind your house. You often walk to the store, but if you turn left to go around the block you pass a chained pit bulldog that lunges and growls at you. On the other hand, if you turn right you do not pass the dog. It's obvious that most of us will choose the nonpunished route to the store. If, however, turning right leads to a path that does not get you to the store, you may continue walking past the dog. In reality, of course, you could walk on the other side of the street or drive to the store—these are also nonpunished alternative responses.

CONTINGENCIES OF NEGATIVE REINFORCEMENT

When an organism emits an alternative nonpunished response, this may be viewed as escape or avoidance. If the response is made in the presence of the aversive stimulus, it is an **escape** response. The pit bulldog growls at you, and you cross to the other side of the street. When the operant prevents the aversive stimulus, it is an **avoidance** response. You turn right, to go around the block, and do not walk by the dog. In both cases, the removal or prevention of an aversive event strengthens operant behavior. A contingency of negative reinforcement is presented in cell 3 of

Figure 9.1. **Negative reinforcement** occurs when an operant results in the removal (or prevention) of a stimulus and the operant increases in rate.

In everyday life, the distinction between negative and positive reinforcement is occasionally uncertain (Michael, 1975). For example, do you open a window on a hot day to get a cool breeze or to escape the heat? Putting on glasses clarifies vision but also removes a blurry view of the world. Hineline (1984) has made a similar point:

> The addition of one event is the removal of another, and vice versa: Adding heat is removing cold; adding food is decreasing deprivation; adding a smile removes a frown. However, there is a fundamental asymmetry, for if a stimulus or situation is to be reducible or removable by some response, that response must occur in its presence. In contrast, positively reinforced responses necessarily occur in the absence of the stimuli upon which reinforcement is based. (pp. 496–497)

This difference between positive and negative reinforcement is reasonably easy to arrange in an operant laboratory, and experimental investigations of negative reinforcement are relatively clear cut. When a response results in the removal or postponement of a stimulus and rate of response increases, **negative reinforcement** has occurred (see also Catania, 1973).

The distinction between escape and avoidance is somewhat artificial. Consider an experiment on escape, in which an animal makes a response that turns off a continuous electric shock. Hineline (1977) has suggested that in experiments like this:

> electric shock continuously delivered may not be continuously received. For example, if it is grid shock the animal may produce intermittency by jumping up and down. Nevertheless the escape procedure is treated as a clear case of negative reinforcement by removal of shock. The experimenter may even arrange an escape procedure by explicitly presenting intermittent pulses of shock several times per second, rather than presenting it continuously. But if shock is presented several times per second, why not just twice per second, or once per second, or even less frequently? At some point we tend to stop labeling it continuous shock, and call it a stream of shocks. Responses are reinforced by interruption of (escape from) a stream of shocks. But as the pulses of shocks are spaced out still further, to one every five, ten, or twenty seconds, we tend to characterize suspension of this situation not as removal of shock . . . but as reduction in shock frequency [avoidance]. (p. 369)

To make this clear, when an animal presses a lever to turn off a stream of shocks that are occurring every 0.2 seconds, we call this escape. If, however, the same animal makes a response that interrupts shocks that are scheduled every 20 seconds, then shocks are postponed and the procedure is usually called avoidance.

The only difference between escape and avoidance, presented in Figure 9.4, is the time between shocks, or the **shock-shock interval.** In both procedures, time away from shock produced by responses, or the **response-shock interval,** is 10 seconds. Thus, escape and avoidance may represent endpoints on a continuum of negative reinforcement. For this reason, escape and avoidance may be analyzed as behavior regulated by the same processes.

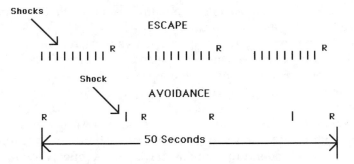

FIG. 9.4 In the escape contingency, shocks (indicated by the vertical line) are scheduled once every second and a response (R) delays the aversive stimulus for 10 seconds. The amount of time that a response delays shock onset is called the response-shock interval. During avoidance, shocks occur once every 10 seconds and a response produces a 10-second delay. Notice that the only difference in the two procedures is the time between shock deliveries, called the shock-shock interval.

In this chapter, we make the traditional distinction between escape and avoidance. In avoidance, an organism evades an aversive event; in escape, it removes the stimulus (or itself) from the aversive situation. A person may escape a boring party by leaving it, or the party may be avoided by never going to it.

Escape

In escape conditioning, an operant response changes the situation from one in which an aversive stimulus is present to one in which it is absent for some period of time. A pigeon could be exposed to continuous loud white noise, and when the bird pecks a key the noise is turned off. If pecking the key increases, then this defines the procedure as negative reinforcement. A person hangs up the telephone to cut off an obscene caller. Children may run home after school because a bully picked on them. A dog will readily jump across a barrier (leave the situation) to escape electric shock. Figure 9.5 is a diagram of a shuttle-box apparatus that is used to train escape responses in dogs. The figure also shows the notation for an

FIG. 9.5 (A) An escape contingency: In the presence of an aversive event (S^{r-}), an operant (R) produces a period of time (T) in which the aversive stimulus is absent. The increase in the operant is the process of negative reinforcement. (B) A shuttle box that may be used to condition escape responses in dogs. The animal is placed in the left compartment at the start of a trial. Electric shock is turned on, and the dog can escape the aversive stimulus by jumping the hurdle and going to the safe area, on the right side of the box.

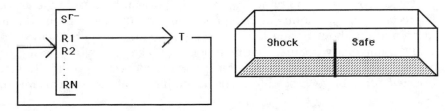

escape contingency. Notice that there are many responses that may be emitted, but only R_1 removes the aversive stimulus.

In general, organisms acquire escape responses more readily than avoidance responses. This is easy to understand: Escape and avoidance behavior is strengthened by the removal or prevention of the aversive stimulus. In escape (but not avoidance), there is an immediate change from the presence of the aversive stimulus to its absence.

Another factor that affects how quickly an escape response is acquired is its compatibility with behavior elicited by an aversive stimulus. Evolution has ensured that organisms respond to many aversive events reflexively. In the everyday world, animals may only get one chance to save their lives in the presence of an aversive stimulus. Running like crazy makes good sense (in many cases) when a predator appears. Those animals that "ponder over" the situation are likely to contribute calories to the predator, but not genes to the next generation. For this reason, species-specific stereotyped responses often are elicited by aversive stimuli. For example, rats will typically run, freeze, or fight when they are shocked.

Conditioning lever pressing as an escape response is often difficult. When rats are presented with intense electric shock, they typically freeze. Depressing and then releasing a lever is not compatible with this species-typical response to shock. If the animal is simply required to press the lever and hold it down, the escape response is more readily acquired because holding the lever down is compatible with freezing. In other words, aversive events frequently elicit reflexive behavior that interferes with the acquisition of operants that are supported by negative reinforcement.

As stated earlier, holding a lever down is an escape response that is usually not difficult to condition. In general, ease of conditioning with negative reinforcement increases when the operant is similar to reflexive behavior elicited by the aversive stimulus. A rat can be readily trained to run on a wheel to escape an electric shock, but conditioning the animal to stand up is much more difficult (Bolles, 1970). This occurs because running is a species-typical response to electric shock but standing is not. Although respondent and operant conditioning interact in escape training, once behavior is established it comes under the control of the operant contingency. For example, if rats are trained to run on a wheel (or hold down a bar) to escape shock, they will stop running (or bar holding) if this response does not terminate the aversive stimulus.

Avoidance

When an operant prevents the occurrence of an aversive stimulus, the contingency is called avoidance. You typically walk the shortest distance to the university, but recently an acquaintance has joined you, at the halfway mark, and blabbed on and on about boring topics. Now you walk a longer distance than needed to the university because that path does not take you by the boring person's house. During their annual migration, young wildebeests stop to drink at a river infested with large crocodiles. The crocodiles wait each year for this

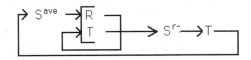

FIG. 9.6 Discriminated avoidance occurs when a warning stimulus (S^{ave}) leads to a condition in which, after some time (*T*), an aversive event (S^{r-}) is presented. If a response (R) is made, the aversive stimulus is delayed and further responses continue to prevent the onset of the aversive event. Once the aversive stimulus is presented, some amount of time passes and the warning stimulus again comes on.

gourmet lunch and "pig out" on rare wildebeest. Survivors of the crocodile picnic choose a different watering spot the next year.

Discriminated Avoidance. Avoidance may involve responding when a warning signal precedes an aversive stimulus. Because the organism only responds when the warning signal occurs, the procedure is called **discriminated avoidance.** A parent may say to a child, "Nathan, keep the noise down or else you will have to go to bed." An antelope may smell a lion and change the direction it is traveling. In these cases, the child is told what not to do and the antelope detects what direction to avoid. Pretend that you are all set to go to a party but are told that Dr. Hannibal Sloat will be attending. Dr. Sloat is an unusually obnoxious professor, and you have just flunked his human sexuality class. In this case, the warning that he will be at the bash may result in you avoiding the party. Figure 9.6 is a diagram of discriminated avoidance in an experimental situation. In the presence of a warning stimulus (S^{ave}), a response postpones for some time, *T*, the onset of an aversive stimulus (S^{r-}). If the response does not occur, the aversive stimulus is presented and after some time the warning stimulus comes on again.

In the operant laboratory, discriminated avoidance is typically acquired only after many hours of training. Rats will quickly learn to lever press for food, but take a surprisingly long time to acquire lever pressing in order to avoid electric shock (Solomon & Brush, 1956). Pigeons are also slow at acquiring avoidance behavior when they are required to peck a key to avoid an aversive event. A major reason for this is that in the discriminated avoidance procedure, the warning stimulus is also a CS that elicits respondent behavior (like freezing) that interferes with operant behavior (Meyer, Cho, & Wesemann, 1960). As stated earlier, other responses like running and jumping are elicited by shock and are acquired much more readily than bar pressing. For example, Macphail (1968) found that pigeons required 120 trials to learn to avoid shock by running down a straight alley. Rats require only two or three trials to learn to jump onto a platform (Baum, 1965, 1969). Thus, to produce rapid acquisition of avoidance responses, choose behavior that is elicited by the aversive stimulus.

Nondiscriminated Avoidance. In the laboratory, a rat may press a lever to avoid the delivery of an electric shock. Shocks are scheduled every 60 seconds, and each lever press prevents the shock and starts another 1-minute cycle. The shocks

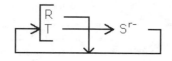

FIG. 9.7 A Mechner diagram of nondiscriminated avoidance. A response (R) produces some time (T) in which aversive stimuli (S^r-) are not presented.

are simply programmed to occur on the basis of time, and there is no warning that they are about to be presented. When there are no warning stimuli present, the contingency is called **nondiscriminated avoidance.** There are people who compulsively wash their hands to get rid of unseen germs. In this case, hand washing is the operant and the supposed absence of germs negatively reinforces the behavior. As you will see in later chapters, negative reinforcement appears to underlie many so-called abnormal behavior patterns. Figure 9.7 illustrates simple nondiscriminated avoidance in which the aversive event is presented without a warning signal.

This book was written on a computer, and we soon learned (or more accurately contacted the contingency) that an unexpected power failure could result in many hours of lost work. To prevent this aversive event, we regularly emitted the avoidance behavior of hitting the save key. This response saved the text to a disk and was maintained because it prevented computer crashes from costing us a day's work.

Nondiscriminated avoidance was first investigated by Murray Sidman (1953). Periodic shocks were given to a rat unless the animal emitted an operant response. The time between shocks was (and still is) called the shock-shock (S-S) interval. When a response occurred, it delayed the onset of shock for some specified period of time called the response-shock (R-S) interval (see Figure 9.4). Avoidance responding is more quickly acquired when the R-S interval is longer than the S-S interval (Leaf, 1965; Sidman, 1962). In other words, when the operant delays the aversive stimulus for a period that exceeds the time between scheduled shocks, conditioning is enhanced.

FOCUS ON RESEARCH
An Analysis of Avoidance Behavior

Pretend that you live in a world in which evil professors have absolute authority over students. One day you walk into class and your professor says, "Class, from today until the end of term you are subjects in a shocking experiment." You notice the straps attached to your desk and the two large electrodes embedded in your chair. Although you protest vigorously, the teaching assistant straps you to the chair and says, "Press the button on your desk, if you want to." You look at the button and wish you had taken another course. A powerful (but your professor says harmless) electric shock is delivered every 20 seconds (S-S = 20 seconds). In desperation, you press your button and notice that the frequency of shock delivery declines (you get fewer shocks). Each press of the button delays shock for 30 seconds (R-S = 30 seconds), and after some experience you regularly press your button and avoid most or all of the shocks. Consider, however, what would happen if the S-S interval remained at 20 seconds but the R-S interval changed to 5 seconds. Pressing the button would increase the frequency of shocks unless you maintained a high rate of response. This occurs because a response brings the next shock closer than not responding does (5 seconds versus 20 seconds). Animal research suggests that under these conditions avoidance responding is poorly maintained.

Shock Frequency and Avoidance Behavior

In the preceding example, avoidance behavior is weak because reducing the frequency of aversive stimulation appears to be a major factor maintaining responses (Sidman, 1962). In a classic experiment, Herrnstein and Hineline (1966) exposed 18 rats to a random sequence of electric shocks. The animals could press a lever to reduce the frequency of shocks, but some responses were still followed by the aversive stimulus. That is, bar pressing reduced the number of shocks per second but did not completely eliminate them. Seventeen of the 18 rats in this experiment showed avoidance responding—they reliably pressed the lever.

This finding has generated a debate over the critical factors that regulate avoidance behavior. Essentially, the issue concerns molar versus molecular control of behavior in avoidance. From a molecular perspective, the moment-to-moment time between shocks and the time from response to shock represent the essential variables regulating avoidance responding (Dinsmoor, 1977). Nonetheless, the bulk of the evidence suggests that the molar variable, overall reduction in shock frequency, can produce and maintain operant avoidance (Gardner & Lewis, 1976; Hineline, 1970; Lewis, Gardner, & Hutton, 1976; Mellitz, Hineline, Whitehouse, & Laurence, 1983).

Consider what happens when another person persistently nags at you to stop watching television and start working on your term paper. You may tell your friend, "Leave me alone, I'll get to it after the movie is over." This will likely reduce the frequency of nagging but not eliminate it. In fact, your reply sometimes may be followed by, "I can't understand how you can just sit there glued to the idiot box, when you have so much to do." Assuming that the nagging is aversive, how can your vocal operant ("leave me alone . . . ") be maintained? The answer, of course, is that it has reduced the overall number of nagging episodes while you are engrossed in *Return of the Killer Tomatoes*.

Although reduction in shock frequency can establish and maintain avoidance behavior, Hineline (personal communication, May, 1989) has stated that "rather than trying to establish either the molar or molecular view as correct, the point [is] to discover what determines the scale of process. That is, under what circumstances is behavior sensitive to its more remote consequences, as contrasted with its more immediate ones?" Dr. Philip Hineline is a professor of psychology at Temple University in Philadelphia. He has been interested in negative reinforcement and the regulation of operant behavior over short- and long-time scales. In his recent work with Dr. Timothy Hackenberg, he has drawn these two interests together.

Long-Term Effects of Negative Reinforcement

Hakenberg and Hineline (1987) used a conditioned-suppression paradigm (see Chapter 3) to show the interrelations between avoidance and behavior maintained by positive reinforcement. Recall that conditioned suppression is a procedure in which a conditioned aversive stimulus (a tone that has signaled shock) is presented when an animal is responding for food reinforcement. The tone usually suppresses the operant behavior regulated by food. The interesting twist that Hackenberg and Hineline (1987) introduced was to show that a similar effect could be obtained when a period of avoidance either preceded or followed entire sessions of food reinforcement.

In their experiment, eight rats were trained to press a lever for food on a fixed-interval 3-minute schedule (FI 3 minutes). After response rates were stable on the FI schedule, animals were exposed to 100 minutes of unsignaled shock avoidance. During this period, shocks occurred every 5 seconds (shock-shock interval = 5 seconds) unless the rat pressed a lever that postponed the shocks for 20 seconds (response-shock interval = 20 seconds). These avoidance periods were presented to four rats just before the food reinforcement sessions. The other four animals were given the avoidance period immediately after they responded for food. The question was whether the avoidance periods would suppress responding during food reinforcement sessions.

Results indicated that operant responding for positive reinforcement was disrupted when avoidance periods either preceded or followed the food sessions. This suppression occurred even though the rats responded at a level that was high enough to obtain most of the available food. This means that the avoidance periods had an effect on responding that was independent of any interference with the schedule of positive reinforcement. When avoidance periods came after food reinforcement sessions, there was more disruption of food-related operants than when avoidance periods preceded fixed-interval responding. In addition, when avoidance was discontinued, operant responses for food took longer to recover if the avoidance periods came after positive-reinforcement sessions.

In everyday language, it seems that the rats were worried about their appointment with doom (since they had experienced previous appointments). This is not unlike a student who has difficulty studying because he or she is scheduled to have a wisdom tooth extracted a few hours later. People, and apparently rats, respond to long-term aversive consequences in their environment. This disruption of responding is severe when long-term negative consequences are impending. Immediately delivered aversive events can also suppress operant behavior but, all things being equal, do not appear to affect responses as strongly as long-term aversive consequences. By implication, a child who receives reprimands from a teacher for talking out of turn will show little disruption of play and school work. In contrast, a student who is regularly harassed by a bully after school is over may show general disruption of school activities throughout the day.

SIDE-EFFECTS OF AVERSIVE PROCEDURES

There are obvious ethical reasons for not using aversive contingencies to change behavior. In addition to ethical concerns, there are serious side-effects that often arise when contingencies of punishment and negative reinforcement are employed. Skinner (1953, 1971) has consistently argued against the use of aversive techniques:

> The commonness technique of control in modern life is punishment. The pattern is familiar: if a man does not behave as you wish, knock him down; if a child misbehaves, spank him; if the people of a country misbehave, bomb them. Legal

and police systems are based on such punishments as fines, flogging, incarceration, and hard labor. Religious control is exerted through penances, threats of excommunication, and consignment to hell-fire. Education has not wholly abandoned the birch rod. In everyday personal contact we control through censure, snubbing, disapproval, or banishment. In short, the degree to which we use punishment as a technique of control seems to be limited only by the degree to which we can gain the necessary power. All of this is done with the intention of reducing tendencies to behave in certain ways. Reinforcement builds up these tendencies; punishment is designed to tear them down.

The technique has often been analyzed, and many familiar questions continue to be asked. Must punishment be closely contingent upon the behavior punished? Must the individual know what he is being punished for? What forms of punishment are most effective and under what circumstances? This concern may be due to the realization that the technique has unfortunate by-products. In the long run, punishment, unlike reinforcement, works to the disadvantage of both the punished organism and the punishing agency. The aversive stimuli which are needed generate emotions, including predispositions to escape or retaliate, and disabling anxieties. For thousands of years men have asked whether the method could not be improved or whether some alternative practice would not be better. (1953, pp. 182–183)

Behavioral Persistence

As noted, punishment may, under some circumstances, produce a rapid decline in behavior. Consider that when positive punishment is used, it is almost always in a circumstance in which one person is attempting to reduce the aversive behavior of another. A teacher punishes a child who talks loudly out of turn in class; a wife shouts at her husband for making sexist comments at a party; and a boss threatens to fire an employee who is insubordinate. In each of these examples the teacher, wife, and boss are negatively reinforced by a reduction in talking out of turn, sexist jokes, and insubordinate comments. For this reason, individuals who effectively use punishment are more likely to use aversive regulation on future occasions. This is an important point: The "successful" use of punishment leads to further use of the technique, which produces the other side-effects of aversive behavior regulation.

Operant-Respondent Interactions and Persistence.   Consider a person who has received a painful wasp sting. The sight and buzz of the insect precede the sting and (for some people) become powerful conditioned stimuli that elicit anxiety. The CS- that is established will likely generalize to similar sights and sounds (i.e., the sight of other flying insects, the buzz of a harmless fly). The CS- also has a dual function: In terms of Pavlovian conditioning, it elicits anxiety; in an operant sense, it functions as a conditioned aversive stimulus (S^{ave}) and will strengthen behavior that removes it (negative reinforcement). To extinguish the effects of the CS-, it must be presented in the absence of the unconditioned stimulus (respondent extinction). Under ordinary circumstances the CS- would rapidly extinguish since buzzing sounds and flying insects (CS-) are rarely accompanied by pain (US). However, people who are afraid of wasps and bees avoid places in which they may be found and leave locations in which they encounter buzzing sounds and flying insects. Thus, avoidance behavior, maintained by operant conditioning, prevents respondent extinction.

One way to place avoidance behavior on extinction is to expose the organism to aversive stimulation while preventing effective escape responses.[1] A rat may be trained to press a lever to turn off electric shock, but during extinction bar presses have no effect. Extinction occurs most rapidly when it is clearly signaled—a buzzer could be turned on during extinction and turned off when responses prevented shock. However, in many everyday settings, escape and avoidance responses are resistant to extinction. This persistence occurs when the difference between the acquisition and extinction setting is low (extinction is not clearly signaled). When the difference between the extinction setting and conditions under which the contingency is in effect is slight, extinction is not discriminated and avoidance responding continues. In everyday life, a particular dentist's office smells and looks similar to one in which pain was experienced; flying insects and buzzing sounds were accompanied by a sting; and so on.

A moving account of behavioral persistence was given by the famous psychiatrist Bruno Bettelheim, who survived the Nazi concentration camps:

> Often an SS man would for a while enforce some nonsensical rule, originating in a whim of the moment. Usually it was quickly forgotten, but there were always some old prisoners who continued to observe it and tried to enforce it on others long after the SS had lost interest. Once, for example, an SS man was inspecting the prisoners' apparel and found that some of their shoes were dirty on the inside. He ordered all prisoners to wash their shoes inside and out with soap and water. Treated this way, the heavy shoes became hard as stone. The order was never repeated, and many prisoners did not even try to carry it out the first time, since the SS, as was often the case, gave the order, stood around for a few minutes and then left. Until he was gone, every prisoner busied himself with carrying out the order, after which they promptly quit. Nevertheless there were some old prisoners who not only continued to wash the insides of their shoes every day but cursed all who failed to do so as being negligent and dirty. These prisoners believed firmly that all rules set down by the SS were desirable standards of behavior, at least in the camp. (in Scott, 1971, p. 206)

The prisoners were, of course, washing their shoes to escape the aversive consequences that the SS would administer if the prisoners did not obey the order. Some of the men became very persistent and continued washing their shoes even when the SS did not require them to do so. Generally, it was the older prisoners, who had more experience with the aversive contingencies of the SS, that were likely to persist in washing their shoes. For these men, the concentration camp experience generated escape *and* avoidance behavior. The older prisoners in the concentration camp also accepted the rules of the SS and preached these standards to their fellow inmates. These responses are more complex than simple avoidance and may be analyzed as rule-governed behavior (Skinner, 1969; see also chapter 12).

---

[1]Another way to place avoidance behavior on extinction is to stop the delivery of aversive stimuli.

Learned Helplessness

A similar persistence effect occurs when animals are exposed to unavoidable aversive stimulation and then are given an opportunity to escape. In the phenomenon called **learned helplessness,** an animal is first exposed to inescapable and severe aversive stimulation. Eventually the animal gives up and stops attempting to avoid or escape the situation. Next, an escape response (which under ordinary circumstances would be acquired easily) is made available, but the animal does not make the response. In an early experiment, Seligman and Maier (1967) exposed dogs to intense, inescapable electric shock. Following this, they attempted to teach the animals to avoid signaled shocks by jumping across a shuttle-box barrier (see Figure 9.5). The dogs failed to avoid the shocks, and even after the shocks came on (for 50 seconds) they would not escape by crossing the barrier to safety. The researchers suggested that the dogs had learned to give up and become helpless when presented with aversive stimulation. Of course, dogs that are not first exposed to inescapable shock learn quickly to escape and avoid shocks in a shuttle box.

Learned helplessness has been found in a large number of experiments and has been documented in other animals (Baker, 1976; Glazer & Weiss, 1976a, 1976b; Maier, 1970; Maier, Albin, & Testa, 1973; Maier & Seligman, 1976; Maier, Seligman, & Solomon, 1969; Overmier & Seligman, 1967; Seligman & Maier, 1967). For example, Jackson, Alexander, and Maier (1980) found that rats in a maze had difficulty learning to escape electric shocks after exposure to inescapable aversive stimuli.

Similar results have been reported for humans. Hiroto and Seligman (1975) exposed college students to a series of inescapable loud noises. Following this procedure, the students had to solve a number of anagram problems. Students who were exposed to inescapable noise had more difficulty solving problems than students who did not get the loud noise. Most control subjects solved all the anagrams and reached solutions faster and faster. In contrast, students exposed to inescapable noise failed many problems and made slow improvements in performance.

The practical implication of these findings seems obvious. When people are exposed to inescapable punishment, they may learn to give up and become helpless. A parent who punishes a child on the basis of his or her mood rather than for the child's misbehavior may create a socially withdrawn individual. The child has learned "No matter what I do, I get a spanking." A husband that frequently "blows up" for no apparent reason might produce a similar set of responses in his partner.

Helplessness and Depression.   Seligman (1975) argued that the research on learned helplessness provides a model for clinical depression. Thousands of people each year are diagnosed as depressive. These individuals show insomnia, report feeling tired, often say that life is not worth living, have difficulty performing routine tasks, and may be suicidal. Clinical depression is severe, long lasting, and is not easily traced to a recent environmental experience.

Seligman (1975) has suggested that the behavior of helpless dogs may be relevant to the origin and treatment of clinical depression. Depression may arise when a person has a history of inescapable abuse. This could occur when a parent, spouse, or caretaker unreasonably and severely mistreats a child, partner, or elderly person. In later writings, Seligman and his co-workers have pointed out that, although animal experiments may shed light on human depression, there are differences (Abramson, Seligman, & Teasdale, 1978; Peterson & Seligman, 1984). For the most part, Seligman points to differences that occur because of human verbal behavior. For example, a person may attribute depression to either internal or external causes.

In terms of treatment, research on learned helplessness has practical importance. When helpless dogs are forced to make a response that escapes the electric shocks, they eventually begin to make the escape response on their own (i.e., a dog that fails to jump the barrier is forcibly guided across it). Based on this finding, Seligman has suggested that depressed individuals should be placed in situations in which they cannot fail. In this manner, the person may eventually learn to emit appropriate responses in the presence of aversive events.

Other studies have suggested that learned helplessness can be prevented by what Seligman called immunization. In these experiments, animals are first placed in a situation where they may escape an electric shock (by turning a wheel or making some other response). Next, the animal is exposed to the learned helplessness procedure by presenting inescapable shocks. Finally, the subjects in these experiments are placed in a situation where a new response (e.g., jumping over a barrier) allows the organism to escape from shock. The finding is that the initial conditioning of escape from shock prevents the onset of learned helplessness (Maier & Seligman, 1976; Williams & Lierle, 1986).

Aggression

Respondent Aggression.　　When two organisms are placed in the same setting and painful stimuli are delivered, the organisms may attack one another (Ulrich, Wolff, & Azrin, 1964). The fighting generated by this circumstance is called **respondent** or **pain-elicited aggression** because it follows the presentation of aversive events. Attack occurs even though neither individual is responsible for the delivery of the painful stimuli. Ulrich and Azrin (1962) placed two rats in an operant chamber and noted that the animals showed no signs of aggression. However, when the rats were shocked, they turned and attacked each other. Elicited aggression has been documented in several species including humans (Azrin, Hutchinson, & Hake, 1963; Hutchinson, 1977), and it has been found with painful stimuli other than electric shock (Azrin, Hake, & Hutchinson, 1965). Most people recognize that they are more prone to aggression when exposed to painful stimuli. When feeling good you may never shout at your boyfriend, but you may do so if you have a severe toothache. It is probably good advice to stay clear of your boss when he or she has a headache, and so on.

Pain-elicited aggression was first described by O'Kelly and Steckle (1939). In these early experiments, rats were placed in a small enclosure and electric shock occurred periodically, no matter what the animals did. When the rats were shocked, they began to fight. This response to noncontingent electric shock was systematically investigated 23 years later by Ulrich and Azrin (1962). These investigators began by testing whether or not two rats would fight when simply placed in a small operant chamber. They noted that the animals did not usually attack one another when placed in a confined space. However, when random shocks were given, the animals would immediately stand up and vigorously strike and bite one another (see Figure 9.8).

Shocks were delivered at increasing frequencies, and the number of attacks increased as more and more shocks were presented. In addition, Ulrich and Azrin (1962) found that the probability of attack for any single shock increased as the number of shocks went up. When the animals got one shock every 10 minutes, attack followed approximately 50% of the shocks. When the animals received 38 shocks a minute, fighting followed 85% of the shocks.

Further experiments conducted by Ulrich and Azrin (1962) examined the effects of shock intensity on aggressive behavior. As shock intensity increased in milliamperes (mA), from 0.5 to 2.0 mA, the number of aggressive episodes went up. When shock intensity exceeded 2.0 mA, fighting decreased because the high-intensity shocks elicited running, jumping, and so on—responses that were incompatible with fighting.

An important question is whether such fighting occurs when animals are able to escape or avoid the electric shock. The floor of the operant chamber was made of metal rods, and some of these were electrically charged positive and others were charged with negative voltage. Animals could evade the shocks by standing on two positive or two negative rods. The rats readily learned this response, and

FIG. 9.8 Two rats in the attack position induced by electric shock (reprinted from Ulrich & Azrin, 1962; copyright 1962 by the Society for the Experimental Analysis of Behavior, Inc.).

since they did not get shocked, they did not fight. That is, allowing the animals to escape the shocks effectively eliminated the aggression.

Ulrich and Azrin (1962) varied the size of the operant chamber in another experiment. When there was little floor space (0.25 square feet), almost all shocks resulted in fighting. As floor space increased to 2.25 square feet, the chances of attack for any one shock decreased. It seems that the size of the chamber regulated pain-elicited fighting through the changing proximity of the opponents. In other words, the closer the animals were to each other, the greater the chances of attack attributable to shock.

To determine whether these findings occurred in other species, the researchers placed different animals in the shock box. Hamsters also fought when shocked, and these attacks occurred at shock intensities that did not elicit aggression in rats. One possibility is that hamsters have less padding or more pain receptors on their feet, making them more susceptible to low levels of shock. In contrast, mature guinea pigs would not fight when shocked. This passive response even occurred when a guinea pig was placed in the shock box with a rat. The rat attacked the guinea pig when it was shocked, but the guinea pig "reacted only by withdrawing from the rat's biting attacks following the shock delivery" (Ulrich & Azrin, 1962, p. 517). These findings suggest that there are species differences in the tendency to fight when exposed to painful stimulation.

There are other limitations on pain-elicited aggression. Ulrich and Azrin (1962) found that rats fought when exposed to intense heat or shock, but not to intense noise or cold temperature. Apparently there are specific forms of painful stimulation that elicit attack in a given species. Presumably, the type and intensity of painful stimulation that triggers attack is not the same for different kinds of animals.

Painful stimulation also produces attack-like responses in humans and monkeys (Azrin et al., 1966; Azrin, Hutchinson, & Sallery, 1964; Hutchinson, 1977). In one experiment, squirrel monkeys were strapped into a small test chamber and electric shock was delivered to the animals' tails (Azrin et al., 1964). As with rats, attack was elicited by electric shocks. The animals attacked other monkeys, rats, mice, and inanimate objects such as a stuffed doll, round ball, and a rubber hose that they could bite. As shock intensity increased, so did the probability and duration of the attacks—a result that parallels the findings with rats.

In a review of the side-effects of aversive control, Hutchinson (1977) described bite reactions by humans to aversive stimulation. Subjects were paid volunteers who were given noncontingent loud noise at regular intervals. Because the noise was delivered on a predictable basis, the subjects came to discriminate the onset of the aversive stimulus. Unobtrusive measures indicated that humans would show aggressive responses (or more precisely bite on a rubber hose) following the presentation of loud noise. This response by humans parallels the elicited fighting found in monkeys and other animals. However, Hutchinson suggests that the human results should be interpreted with caution. The subjects were told that they would receive aversive stimulation, but the intensity would be tolerable. Also, he noted that subjects were paid to stay in the experiment, and most people would leave such a situation in everyday life.

Operant Aggression. When one person punishes another, the punished individual may retaliate. This is not difficult to understand; one way to escape aversive stimulation is to eliminate or neutralize the person who is delivering it (Azrin & Holz, 1966). This strategy is called **operant aggression,** and it is shaped and maintained by negative reinforcement (i.e., removal of the aversive event). When two people have a fist fight, the winner of the combat is reinforced by the absence of punches from the other person. Unfortunately, this analysis suggests that physical aggression will increase in frequency for those individuals who successfully use counter aggression to stop the delivery of aversive stimuli. Consider a situation in which a husband and wife argue and the husband loses his temper and strikes his spouse. Because men are typically larger and stronger than women, this probably ends the argument and the husband is negatively reinforced (by withdrawal of the wife's arguing) for physical abuse. Although this does not completely explain spouse abuse, it does suggest that negative reinforcement plays a large role in many cases.

Investigating Human Aggression. Although human aggression is easily recognized, it is difficult to study in the laboratory. This is because aggression is a dangerous form of human behavior. For this reason, researchers have developed procedures that protect the victim from harm. In the laboratory situation, subjects are led to believe that they have an opportunity to hurt another person when in reality they do not (e.g., Baron, Russell, & Arms, 1985; Gustafson, 1989; Zillmann, 1988). In a typical experiment, subjects are told that they can deliver an aversive stimulus (e.g., loud noise, electric shock, etc.) to another person by pressing a button on a response panel. The other person is, in fact, an accomplice or confederate of the researcher and acts the role of victim but does not receive the aversive stimulus.

There has been a debate about the reality or external validity of these procedures. However, evidence suggests that these methods constitute a reasonable analog of human aggression in everyday life. Participants in aggression experiments are convinced that their actions harmed the confederate (Berkowitz & Donnerstein, 1982). When the accomplice provokes (e.g., with insults) the subjects, they deliver greater amounts of painful stimulation than when they are not provoked (Baron & Richardson, 1993). Finally, people who are known to be violent usually select and deliver stronger levels of aversive stimulation than those without such a history (Gully & Dengerink, 1983; Wolfe & Baron, 1971).

Aggression Breeds Aggression. Operant and respondent principles suggest that the presentation of an aversive stimulus may evoke or set the occasion for aggressive behavior. Provocation by others is a common form of aversive stimulation that occurs in a variety of social settings. Consider a situation in which you have worked extremely hard on a term paper and you feel it is the best paper you have ever written. Your professor calls you to his office and says, "Your paper is rubbish. It lacks clarity, scholarship, organization, and is riddled with grammatical mistakes. Only an idiot could write and submit such trash!" You probably protest the unfair treatment, but to no avail. You storm out of the office mumbling a few choice words, and once down the hall you kick the elevator door.

Later in the term you are asked to fill out a teaching evaluation and, in retaliation, you score the professor as one of the worst teachers you have known. In this example, the professor's insulting remarks generated aggressive responses that ranged from kicking doors to counter-attack by negative evaluation. Generally, aggression breeds aggression (Patterson, 1976).

Skinner (1953) described how aggression breeds aggression in his account of a game played by sailors during the 18th century.

> Sailors would amuse themselves by tying several boys or younger men in a ring to a mast by their left hands, their right hands remaining free. Each boy was given a stick or whip and told to strike the boy in front of him whenever he felt himself being struck by the boy behind. The game was begun by striking one boy lightly. This boy then struck the boy ahead of him, who in turn struck the boy next ahead, and so on. Even though it was clearly in the interest of the group that all blows be gentle, the inevitable result was a furious lashing. The unstable elements in this interlocking system are easy to identify. We cannot assume that each boy gave precisely the kind of blow he received because this is not an easy comparison to make. It is probable that he underestimated the strength of the blows he gave. The slightest tendency to give a little harder than he received would produce the ultimate effect. Moreover, repeated blows probably generate an emotional disposition in which one naturally strikes harder. A comparable instability is seen when two individuals engage in a casual conversation which leads to a vituperative quarrel. The aggressive effect of a remark is likely to be underestimated by the man who makes it, and repeated effects generate further aggression. The principle is particularly dangerous when the conversation consists of an exchange of notes between governments. (p. 309)

Skinner's analysis is confirmed by controlled experiments showing that both physical and verbal provocation produces aggression. In terms of physical provocation, experiments show that people respond to attacks with escalating counter-attacks (Borden, Bowen, & Taylor, 1971; O'Leary & Dengerink, 1973; Taylor & Pisano, 1971). In these experiments, subjects tried to beat their opponents on a reaction time game in which the loser received an electric shock. In fact, there were no actual opponents, but subjects received shocks that were programmed by the researchers. In this game, subjects were made to lose on a number of trials and the shocks from the fictitious opponent increased in magnitude. Faced with increasing physical provocation, subjects retaliated by escalating the intensity of the shocks they gave when the "opponent" lost.

Verbal insults also evoke and set the occasion for strong counterattacks. Wilson and Rogers (1975) suggest that verbal provocation can lead to physical retaliation, and they have noted incidents that began with verbal taunts escalating into violent fist fights. In a laboratory study of verbal insults, Geen (1968) found that subjects who were exposed to unprovoked, nasty comments from a confederate would retaliate with physical aggression. The subjects in this study were allowed to deliver shocks to the insulting confederate (in fact, no shocks were actually given). Compared with personal frustration (a confederate prevents them from competing an assigned task) and task frustration (the task did not have a solution), verbal insults produced the highest level of aggression toward the confederate. Generally, aggression (both verbal and physical) breeds aggression, and aggressive episodes escalate toward greater levels of violence.

Social Disruption

When punishment is used to decrease behavior, the attempt is usually made to stop a particular response. The hope is that other nonpunished behavior is unaffected. Two factors work against this: The person who delivers punishment and the setting in which punishment occurs can both become conditioned aversive stimuli (S^{ave}). Because of this, individuals will attempt to escape from or avoid the punishing person or setting. Azrin and Holz (1966) have called this negative side-effect of punishment **social disruption:**

> It is in the area of social disruption that punishment does appear to be capable of producing behavioral changes that are far-reaching in terms of producing an incapacity for an effective life.... For example, a teacher may punish a child for talking in class, in which case it is desired that the unauthorized vocalization of the child be eliminated but his other behaviors remain intact. We have seen previously, however, that one side-effect of the punishment process was that it reinforced tendencies on the part of the individual to escape from the punishment situation itself. In terms of the example we are using, this means that punishment of the vocalization would not only be expected to decrease the vocalization, but also increase the likelihood of the child leaving the classroom situation. Behavior such as tardiness, truancy, and dropping out of school would be strengthened. The end result would be termination of the social relationship, which would make any further social control of the individual's behavior impossible. This side effect of punishment appears to be one of the most undesirable aspects of having punishment delivered by one individual against another individual since the socialization process must necessarily depend upon continued interaction with other individuals. (pp. 439–440)

It is also worth recalling the general suppressive effects of aversive stimuli. A teacher who frequently uses aversive techniques becomes a conditioned punishing stimulus. Once this occurs, the mere presence of the teacher can disrupt all ongoing operant behavior. This means that positive behavior falls to low levels in the presence of the teacher. Of course, these effects are not restricted to schools and can occur in families, places of employment, and even recreational settings.

ON THE APPLIED SIDE

Coercion and Its Fallout

Murray Sidman is a prominent researcher in behavior analysis. He is known for his work on nondiscriminated avoidance and other aspects of negative reinforcement and punishment (see the section on nondiscriminated avoidance in this chapter). Dr. Sidman has published over 100 scientific articles and is the author of the book *Tactics of Scientific Research,* a definitive account of single-subject

FIG. 9.9 Murry Sidman

research and methodology (Sidman, 1960). In a more recent book, *Coercion and Its Fallout,* Sidman (1989) provides a behavior analysis of coercion and its frequent use in North American society. An interesting part of this book concerns escape and "dropping out" of the family, community, and society.

One kind of escape contingency is dropping out—a major social problem of our time. People drop out of education, family, personal and community responsibility, citizenship, society, and even life. Sidman (1989, p. 93) points out that the *common element in all of these forms of conduct is negative reinforcement.* Once involved in an aversive system, people can get out by removing themselves from the coercive situation and this strengthens the behavior of dropping out. Sidman notes that society is the loser when individuals cease to participate; dropping out is nonproductive since drop-outs no longer contribute to their own or society's welfare.

An unfortunate, but common, example is the school drop-out. Day after day, students are sent to schools where coercion is a predominant way of teaching. That is, often the teacher's job is to "get students to learn" by punishing them when they fail. The pupil who is slow to answer or who errs on obvious questions is subjected to ridicule. Written work is filled with negative comments and low grades are observed by classmates as papers are returned from front to rear. Report cards emphasize failing grades in red ink; poor students are seated at the back of the room as examples of what happens to failures. Students who cannot deal with the normal workload are required to do extra work at school and home, making those who fail social outcasts who are deprived of play and other activities. Children who fail eventually conclude that learning and pleasure are not compatible—the more learning the less the pleasure.

As the aversive control escalates, escape is inevitable and students show increasingly severe forms of dropping out. Tardiness, feigned illness, "playing hooky," and never showing up for school are common responses to the escalation of coercion in schools. Sidman summarizes the problem as follows:

The current discipline and dropout crises are the inevitable outcome of a history of educational coercion. One may long for the days when pupils feared their teachers, spoke to them with respect, accepted extra work as punishment, submitted to being kept after school, and even resigned themselves to being beaten. But through the years, all these forms of coercive control were sowing the seeds of the system's destruction. Wherever and whenever coercion is practiced, the end result is loss of support of the system on the part of those who suffered from it. In every coercive environment, the coerced eventually find ways to turn upon the coercers. An adversarial relationship had developed between pupils and teachers, and the former victims, now parents, no longer support the system against their children. (Sidman, 1989, p. 95)

As Sidman goes on to note, not all teachers (or school systems) use coercion or negative reinforcement as a way to induce students to learn. Some teachers and educators are familiar with and use positive reinforcement effectively. A teacher who does use positive reinforcement looks to reward small steps of success rather than punishing instances of failure. Schools who adopt positive reinforcement methods are likely to promote the enjoyment of learning as well as high academic performance. Positive reinforcement turns dropping out into "tuning in."

KEY WORDS

Avoidance	Negative punishment	Primary aversive stimuli
Coercion	Negative reinforcement	Punishing stimulus
Conditioned aversive stimuli	Nondiscriminated avoidance	Punishment
Discriminated avoidance	Operant aggression	Respondent aggression
Escape	Pain-elicited aggression	Response-shock interval
Learned helplessness	Positive punishment	Shock-shock interval
		Social disruption

CHAPTER 10

Choice and Preference

1. In a behavioral view, what is meant by choice and preference? Give a common example.

2. Compare a single-operant analysis with an analysis based on alternative sources of reinforcement.

3. Describe the two-key procedure in terms of a pigeon experiment. Why have concurrent schedules of reinforcement received so much attention?

4. What are concurrent-ratio schedules and what is the steady-state effect of such contingencies? What about concurrent fixed-interval schedules? Describe the advantage of concurrent VI VI schedules.

5. Summarize the analytical problems of rapid switching or changing over between concurrent schedules. Why does switching occur? How does a changeover delay (COD) help solve the problem?

6. State four laboratory procedures used to study choice. What is a Findley procedure and how does it compare with the two-key method? When would you use a Findley procedure?

7. State the relationship known as the matching law. Describe Herrnstein's (1961b) experiment and what he found.

8. Know how to calculate the proportional rate of response and proportional rate of reinforcement. Write the matching equation in terms of proportions and know what each term means. Create a graph showing the matching relationship.

9. Cite evidence about the generality of the matching law. Give an example of matching in human communication.

10. How can departures from matching occur? What is time matching and when is it applicable? Write a matching equation for time spent on alternatives and know what the terms mean.

11. Be able to write a matching equation for more than two alternatives.

Advanced Issue

12. *In a concurrent VI VI experiment in which matching is expected, how can sources of error arise?*

13. *Transform the proportional matching equation to a ratio matching expression. Write the power law for matching of ratios.*

14. *Define the a and k values of the generalized matching equation. Be able to discuss bias and sensitivity.*

15. *Write the algebraic equation for a straight line. Know the concepts of slope and intercept. Write the generalized matching (power law) equation in log-linear form. What is the slope and intercept of the log-linear equation?*

16. *Be able to read a table of results that shows ratio matching. Understand how the logarithms of the ratios are obtained. Know that the logarithm of a number is simply a transformation of scale.*

17. *State what the slope and intercept values must be for ideal matching. Know how to plot the log ratios of reinforcement and response on xy-coordinates. Explain where the line intercepts the y-coordinate and the rate at which the line rises (i.e., slope).*

18. *What is undermatching (refer to slope)? Be able to tell the difference between ideal matching and undermatching by plots on xy-coordinates. Do the same for bias (refer to intercept).*

19. *Know how to set the values of log ratio reinforcement for a matching experiment. Explain how the log-ratio of response is obtained. How do we show the relationship between relative rate of reinforcement and relative rate of response?*

20. *Discuss the plot of pigeon 22 by White and Davison (1973). How are statistical estimates of slope (sensitivity) and intercept (bias) obtained?*

21. *What were the bias and sensitivity estimates for pigeon 22 and what do the values mean? Read a plot on xy-coordinates of the results. How does a measure of explained variance relate to prediction accuracy?*

22. Draw out the implications of the matching law in terms of child compliance and parental rates of reinforcement.

23. Why do Myerson and Hale (1984) recommend the use of VI schedules in behavior modification?

24. Be able to show how the proportional-matching equation may be used to obtain an expression of absolute response rate (quantitative law of effect). Write the Herrnstein's absolute rate equation and know what each term means.

25. According to the quantitative law of effect, how do background sources of reinforcement (Re) modify the impact of a schedule of reinforcement? Give an example based on dialing for dollars. Read a graph of the dialing-for-dollars experiment and interpret the two hyperbolic curves in terms of Re.

26. Read Herrnstein's graph of the data from six birds (Catania & Reynolds, 1968) using the quantitative law of effect. How generalizable is the absolute rate equation?

27. Distinguish between melioration and maximization of reinforcement. What is the steady state outcome of melioration? Describe Baum's (1974b) experiment on a flock of free-ranging wild pigeons. Did his results support melioration or maximization?

28. Discuss McDowell's (1981, 1988; Carr & McDowell, 1980) use of the quantitative law of effect in behavior modification. Read a graph of self-injurious behavior, relating reprimands per

hour to the number of scratches each hour. What is the theoretical importance of this relationship?

29. According to the quantitative law of effect, why does differential reinforcement of other behavior (DRO) work? Give an example of McDowell's use of DRO in the modification of aggressive behavior. Explain how Herrnstein's equation predicted the treatment outcome.

Over the course of a day, an individual makes many decisions that range from ones of great importance to ones of small consequence. A person is said to make a decision when buying a new car, when choosing to spend an evening with one friend rather than another, or when deciding what to eat for supper. Animals also make a variety of decisions; they may choose mates with particular characteristics, select one type of food over another, or decide to leave a territory.

From a behavioral view, the analysis of **choice** is concerned with the distribution of operant behavior among alternative sources of reinforcement. When several choices are available, one alternative may be chosen more frequently than others. When this occurs, it is called **preference** for an alternative source of reinforcement. For example, a person may choose between two food markets (a large supermarket and the corner store) on the basis of price, location, and variety. Each time the individual goes to one store rather than the other, he or she is said to choose. Eventually, the person may shop more frequently at the supermarket than the local grocery, and when this occurs the person is showing preference for the supermarket alternative.

Many people describe choosing to do something, or a preference for one activity over another, as a subjective experience. For example, you may simply like one person better than others, and based on this you feel good about spending a day with that person. From a behavioral perspective, your likes and feelings are real but they do not provide an objective scientific account of what you decide to do. To provide that account, it is necessary to identify the conditions that affected your attraction to (or preference for) the individual.

EXPERIMENTAL ANALYSIS OF CHOICE AND PREFERENCE

For behavior analysts, the study of choice is based on principles of operant behavior. In previous chapters, operant behavior was analyzed in situations in which one response class was reinforced on a single schedule of reinforcement. For example, a child is reinforced with contingent attention from a teacher for correctly completing a page of arithmetic problems. The teacher provides one source of reinforcement (attention) when the child emits the target operant (math solutions). The single-operant analysis is important for the discovery of basic principles and applications. However, this same situation may be analyzed as a choice among alternatives. The child may choose to do math problems or emit other behavior (e.g., look out the window or talk to another child). This analysis of choice extends the operant paradigm or model to more complex environments in which several response and reinforcement alternatives are available.

In the natural environment, there are many alternatives that schedule reinforcement for operant behavior. A child may distribute time and behavior among parents, peer group, and sport activities. Each alternative may require specific behavior and provide reinforcement at a particular rate and magnitude. To understand, predict, or change the child's behavior, all of these response-consequence relationships must be taken into account. Thus, the operant analysis of choice and preference begins to contact the complexity of everyday life and offers new principles for application.

The Choice Paradigm

The Two-Key Procedure. In the laboratory, choice and preference are investigated by arranging **concurrent schedules of reinforcement.** Figure 10.1 shows a concurrent operant setting. In the laboratory, two or more simple schedules (i.e., FR, VR, FI, or VI) are simultaneously available on different response keys (Ferster & Skinner, 1957). Each key is associated with a separate schedule of reinforcement, and the organism is free to distribute behavior between the alternative schedules. The distribution of time and behavior among alternatives is the behavioral measure of choice and preference. For example, a food-deprived bird may be exposed to a situation in which the left response key is programmed to deliver 20 presentations of the food hopper each hour, while the right key delivers 60 re-

FIG. 10.1 A two-key operant chamber for birds. Schedules of food reinforcement are arranged simultaneously on each key.

inforcers an hour. To obtain reinforcement from either key, the pigeon must respond according to the schedule on that key. If the bird responds exclusively to the right key (and never to the left) and meets the schedule requirement, then 60 reinforcers will be delivered each hour. Because the bird could have responded to either side, we may say that it prefers to spend its time on the right alternative.

Concurrent schedules of reinforcement have received considerable research attention because they may be used as an analytical tool for understanding choice and preference. This selection of an experimental paradigm or model is based on the reasonable assumption that contingencies of reinforcement contribute substantially to choice behavior. Simply stated, all other factors being equal, the more reinforcement provided by an alternative, the more time and energy spent on that alternative. For example, in choosing between spending an evening with two friends, the one who has in the past provided the most social reinforcement will probably be the one selected. Reinforcement may be social approval, affection, interesting conversation, or other aspects of the friend's behavior. The experience of deciding to spend the evening with one rather than the other may be something like, "I just feel like spending the evening with John." Of course, in everyday life choosing is seldom as uncomplicated as this, and a more common decision might have been to spend the evening with both friends. However, to understand how reinforcement processes are working, it is necessary to control the other factors so that the independent effects of reinforcement on choice may be observed.

Concurrent Ratio Schedules.   Figure 10.2 shows a two-key concurrent-operant setting for humans. Consider that you are asked to participate in an experiment in which you may earn up to $50 an hour. As an experimental participant, you are taken to a room that has two response keys separated by a distance of 8 feet. Halfway between the two keys is a small opening just big enough to place your hand in. The room is empty, except for the unusual-looking apparatus. You are told to do anything you want. What do you do? You probably walk about and inspect your surroundings and, feeling somewhat foolish, eventually press one of the response keys. Immediately following this action, $1 is dispensed by a coin machine and is held on a plate inside the small opening. The dollar remains available for about 5 seconds, and then the plate falls away and the dollar disappears. Assuming that you have retrieved the dollar, will you press one of the keys again? In reality, this depends on several factors: perhaps you are wealthy and the dollar is irrelevant; perhaps you decide to "get the best of the experimenter" and show that you are not a rat; maybe you do not want to appear greedy, and so on. However, assume for the moment that you are a typical poor student and you press the key again. After some time pressing both keys and counting the number of key presses, you discover a rule. The left key pays a dollar for each 100 responses, while the right side pays a dollar for 250 responses. Does it make sense to spend your effort on the right key when you can make money faster on the other alternative? Of course it does not, and you decide to spend all of your work on the key that pays the most. This same result has been found with other organisms. When two ratio schedules are programmed as concurrent schedules, then the alternative that produces more rapid reinforcement is chosen exclusively (Herrnstein & Loveland, 1975).

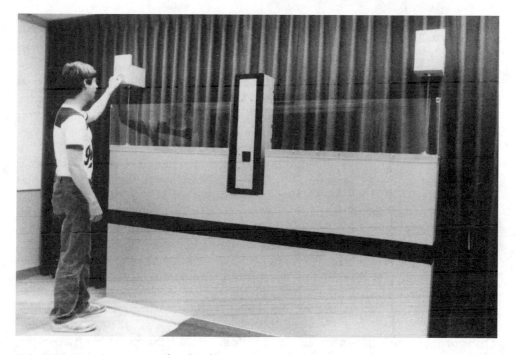

FIG. 10.2 A two-key operant chamber for humans. Pressing the keys results in money from a coin dispenser (middle), depending on the schedules of reinforcement.

Because ratio schedules result in exclusive responding to the alternative with the highest rate of payoff, these schedules are seldom used to study choice. We have discovered something about choice: Ratio schedules produce exclusive preference (in contrast, see McDonald, 1988 on how to program concurrent ratio schedules to produce response distributions similar to those that occur on interval schedules). Although this result is interesting, it suggests that other schedules should be used to investigate choice and preference. This is because once exclusive responding occurs, it is not possible to study how responses are distributed between the alternatives.

Concurrent Interval Schedules. Consider, however, what you might do if interval schedules were programmed on the two keys. Remember that on an interval schedule a single response must occur after a defined amount of time. If you spend all of your time pressing the same key, you will miss reinforcement that is programmed on the other alternative. For example, if the left key is scheduled to pay a dollar every 2 minutes and the right key every 6 minutes, then a reasonable tactic is to spend most of your time responding on the left key but every once in a while check out the other alternative. This behavior will result in obtaining most of the money set up by both schedules. In fact, when exposed to concurrent interval schedules, most animals distribute their time and behavior between the two alternatives in such a manner (de Villiers, 1977). Thus, the first prerequisite of the choice paradigm is that interval schedules must be used to study the distribution of behavior.

Interval schedules are said to be independent of one another when they are presented concurrently. This is because responding on one alternative does not affect the rate of reinforcement programmed for the other. For example, a fixed-interval 6-minute schedule (FI 6 minutes) is programmed to deliver reinforcement every 6 minutes. Of course, a response must be made after the fixed interval has elapsed. Pretend that you are faced with a situation in which the left key pays a dollar every 2 minutes (FI 2 minutes). The right key delivers a dollar when you make a response after 6 minutes. You have 1 hour a day in the experiment. If you just respond to the FI 2-minute schedule, you would earn approximately $30. On the other hand, you could increase the number of reinforcers an hour by occasionally pressing the FI 6-minute key. This occurs because the left key pays a total of $30 each hour and the right key pays an additional $10. After many hours of choosing between the alternatives, you may develop a stable pattern of responding. This steady state performance is predictable. You should respond for approximately 6 minutes on the FI 2-minute alternative and obtain three reinforcers (i.e., $3). After the third reinforcer, you may feel like switching to the FI 6-minute key, on which a reinforcer is immediately available. You obtain the money on this key and immediately return to the richer schedule (left key). This steady-state pattern of responding may be repeated over and over with little variation.

Concurrent Variable-Interval Schedules.

Recall that there are two major types of interval schedules. On variable-interval schedules (VI), the time between each programmed reinforcer changes and the average time to reinforcement defines the specific schedule (e.g., VI 60 second). Because the organism is unable to discriminate the time to reinforcement on VI schedules, the regular switching pattern that characterizes concurrent FI FI performance does not occur. This is an advantage for the analysis of choice because the organism must respond on both alternatives since switching does not result always in reinforcement. Thus, operant behavior maintained by concurrent VI VI schedules is sensitive to the rate of reinforcement on each alternative. For this reason, VI schedules are typically used to study choice.

Alternation and the Changeover Response.

At this point, the choice paradigm is almost complete. Again, however, consider what you would do in the following situation. The two keys are separated and you cannot press both at the same time. The left key now pays a dollar on a VI 2-minute schedule, and responses to the right alternative are reinforced on VI 6 minutes. The left key pays $30 each hour, and the right one delivers $10 if you respond. Assuming you obtain all programmed reinforcers on both schedules, you may earn $40 for each experimental session. What can you do to earn the most per hour? If you stay on the VI 2-minute side, you end up missing the 10 reinforcers on the other alternative. However, if you frequently change over from key to key, most of the reinforcers on both schedules will be obtained. This is in fact what most animals do when faced with these contingencies (de Villiers, 1977).

Simple alternation between response alternatives prevents an analysis of choice because the distribution of behavior remains the same (approximately 50/50) no matter what the programmed rates of reinforcement. Frequent switching between alternatives may occur because of the correlation between rate of switching and overall rate of reinforcement (dollars per session). In other words, as the rate of switching increases, so does the hourly payoff. Another way of looking at this alternation is that organisms are accidentally reinforced for the **changeover response.** This alternation is called concurrent superstition (Catania, 1966) and occurs because as time is spent on an alternative, the other schedule is timing out. As the organism spends more time on the left key, the probability of a reinforcer being set up on the right key increases. This means that a changeover to the right alternative will be reinforced even though the contingencies do not require the changeover response. Thus, switching to the other response key is an operant that is inadvertently strengthened.

The Changeover Delay. The control procedure used to stop rapid switching between alternatives is called a **changeover delay,** or **COD** (Shull & Pliskoff, 1967). The COD contingency stipulates that responses do not have an effect immediately following a change from one schedule to another. After switching to a new alternative, a brief time is required before a response is reinforced (e.g., 3-second delay). For example, if an organism has just changed to an alternative that is ready to deliver reinforcement, there is a 3-second delay before a response is effective. As soon as the 3-second delay has elapsed, a response is reinforced. Of course, if the schedule has not timed out, the COD is irrelevant because reinforcement is not yet available. The COD contingency operates in both directions whenever a change is made from one alternative to another. The COD prevents frequent switching between alternatives. To obtain reinforcement, an organism must spend a minimal amount of time on an alternative before switching to another schedule. For example, with a 3-second COD, changing over every 2 seconds will never result in reinforcement. The COD is therefore an important and necessary feature of the operant-choice procedure for the investigator.

Experimental Procedures to Study Choice. The basic paradigm for investigating choice and preference is now complete. In summary, a researcher interested in behavioral choice should

1. arrange two or more concurrently available schedules of reinforcement
2. program interval schedules on each alternative
3. use variable rather than fixed interval schedules
4. require a COD in order to stop frequent alternation between or among the schedules

The Findley Procedure. An interesting variation on the basic choice procedure was described by Findley (1958). The procedure involves a single response key that changes color. Each color is a stimulus that signals a particular schedule of reinforcement. The color and the associated schedule may be changed

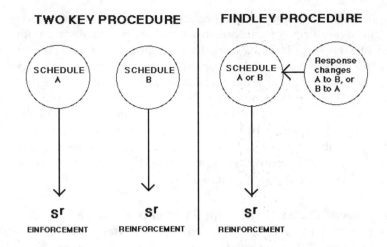

FIG. 10.3 Comparison of two-key and Findley procedures. Notice that the Findley method highlights the changeover response.

when a response is made to a second key. This key is called the changeover key. For example, a pigeon may respond on a VI 30-second schedule that is signaled by red illumination of the response key. When the bird pecks a second changeover key, the color on the response key changes from red to blue. In the presence of the blue light, the pigeon may respond on a VI 90-second schedule of reinforcement. Another response on the changeover key reinstates the red light and the VI 30-second schedule. The advantage of the Findley procedure is that the response of changing from one alternative to another is explicitly defined and measured. Figure 10.3 compares the two-key and Findley procedures, showing that the Findley method allows for the measurement and control of the changeover response.

Current evidence suggests that the same principles of choice account for behavior in both the two-key and changeover procedures. For this reason, researchers have not made a theoretical distinction between them. However, such a distinction may be important for the analysis of human behavior. Sunahara and Pierce (1982) have suggested that the two-key procedure may provide a model for social interaction. For example, in a group discussion a person may distribute talk and attention to several group members. These members may be viewed as alternative sources of social reinforcement for the person. On the other hand, the changeover-key procedure may model role taking, in which an individual responds differentially to another person. In this case, the individual may change over between the reinforcement schedules provided by the other person as a friend or as a boss. For example, while at work the changeover may be made by saying, "Could I discuss a personal problem with you?" In other words, a person who is both your friend and supervisor at work may sometimes deliver social reinforcers as a friend and at other times as a boss. Your social role may change when differential reinforcement (from supervisor or friend) is provided by the other individual.

FIG. 10.4 Richard Herrnstein.

THE MATCHING LAW

In 1961, Richard Herrnstein published an influential paper that described the distribution of behavior on concurrent schedules of positive reinforcement. He found that pigeons matched relative rates of behavior to relative rates of reinforcement. For example, when 90% of the total reinforcement was provided by schedule A (and 10% by schedule B), approximately 90% of the bird's key pecks were on this schedule. This relationship is known as the **matching law.** To understand this law, we turn to Herrnstein's (1961b) experiment.

Proportional Matching

Herrnstein's Experiment.   In this study, Herrnstein investigated the behavior of pigeons on a two-key concurrent schedule. Concurrent VI VI schedules of food reinforcement were programmed with a 1.5-second COD. The birds were exposed to different pairs of concurrent variable-interval schedules for several days. Each pair of concurrent schedules was maintained until response rates stabilized. That is, behavior on each schedule did not significantly change from session to session. After several days of stable responding, a new pair of schedule values was presented. Overall rate of reinforcement was held constant at 40 per hour for all pairs of schedules. Thus, if the schedule on the left key was programmed to deliver 20 reinforcers an hour (VI 3 minute), then the right key also provided 20 reinforcers. If the left key supplied 10 reinforcers, then the right key supplied 30 reinforcers. The schedule values that Herrnstein used are presented in Figure 10.5.

The data in Figure 10.5 show the schedules operating on the two keys, A and B. As previously stated, the total number of scheduled reinforcers is held constant for each pair of VI schedules. This is indicated in the third column, in which the sum of the reinforcements per hour (Rft/h) is equal to 40 for each set

Key	Schedule	Rft/h	Rsp/h	Relative reinforcement	Relative responses
A	VI 3 min	20.00	2000	0.50	0.50
B	VI 3 min	20.00	2000	0.50	0.50
A	VI 9 min	6.7	250	0.17	0.10
B	VI 1.8 min	33.30	3000	0.83	0.90
A	VI 1.5 min	40.00	4800	1.00	1.00
B	Extinction	0.00	0000	0.00	0.00
A	VI 4.5 min	13.30	1750	0.33	0.31
B	VI 2.25 min	26.70	3900	0.66	0.69

FIG. 10.5 A table of schedule values and data extrapolated from Figure 1 of Herrnstein (1961b). Reinforcement per hour (Rft/h), responses per hour (Rsp/h), relative reinforcement (proportions), and relative responses (proportions) are shown (copyright 1961 by the Society for the Experimental Analysis of Behavior, Inc.).

of schedules. Because the overall rate of reinforcement remains constant, changes in the distribution of behavior cannot be attributed to this factor. Note that when key A is programmed to deliver 20 reinforcers an hour, so is key B. When this occurs, the responses per hour (Rsp/h) are the same on each key. However, the responses per hour (or absolute rate) are not the critical measure of preference. Recall that choice and preference are measured as the distribution of time or behavior between alternatives. To express the idea of distribution, it is important to direct attention to relative measures. Because of this, Herrnstein focused on the relative rates of response. In Figure 10.5, the relative rate of response is expressed as a proportion. That is, the rate of response on key A is the numerator and the sum of the rates on both keys is the denominator. The proportional rate of response on key A is shown in the final column, labeled "Relative Responses."

Calculation of Proportions.   To calculate the proportional rate of responses to key A for the pair of schedules VI 4.5 minutes VI 2.25 minutes the following simple formula is used:

$$B_a/(B_a + B_b).$$

The value B_a is behavior measured as the rate of response on key A, or 1,750 pecks per hour. Rate of response on key B is 3,900 pecks per hour and is represented by the B_b term. Thus, the proportional rate of response on key A is

$$1,750/(1,750 + 3,900) = 0.31.$$

In a similar fashion, the proportion of reinforcement on key A may be calculated as

$$R_a/(R_a + R_b).$$

The R_a term refers to the scheduled rate of reinforcement on key A, or 13.3 reinforcers per hour. Rate of reinforcement on key B is designated by the symbol R_b and is 26.7 reinforcers each hour. The proportional rate of reinforcement on key A is calculated as

$$13.3/(13.3 + 26.7) = 0.33.$$

These calculations show that the relative rate of response (0.31) is very close to the relative rate of reinforcement (0.33). If you compare these values for the other pairs of schedules, you will see that the proportional rate of response approximates the proportional rate of reinforcement.

Importance of Relative Rates.   Herrnstein showed that the major dependent variable in choice experiments was **relative rate of response.** He also found that **relative rate of reinforcement** was the primary independent variable. Thus, in an operant-choice experiment, the researcher manipulates the relative rates of reinforcement on each key and observes the relative rate of response to the respective alternatives.

Figure 10.5 shows that Herrnstein manipulated the independent variable, relative rate of reinforcement on key A, over a range of values. Because there are several values of the independent variable and a corresponding set of values for the dependent variable, it is possible to plot the relationship. Figure 10.6 shows the relationship between proportional rate of reinforcement, $R_a/(R_a + R_b)$, and proportional rate of response, $B_a/(B_a + B_b)$ for pigeon 231 based on the values in Figure 10.5.

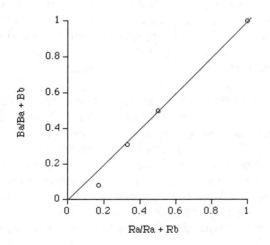

FIG. 10.6 Matching between proportional rate of response and proportional rate of reinforcement for bird 231. Figure is based on results from Herrnstein (1961b) and the data reported in Figure 10.5 (copyright 1961 by the Society for the Experimental Analysis of Behavior, Inc.).

The Matching Equation. As relative rate of reinforcement increases, so does the relative rate of response. Further, for each increase in relative reinforcement there is about the same increase in relative rate of response. This equality of relative rates of reinforcement and relative rates of response is expressed as proportions in equation 10.1.

$$B_a/(B_a + B_b) = R_a/(R_a + R_b) \qquad (10.1)$$

Notice that we have simply taken the $B_a/(B_a + B_b)$ and the $R_a/(R_a + R_b)$ expressions which give the proportion of responses and reinforcers on key A and mathematically stated that they are equal. In verbal form, we are stating that relative rate of response matches (or equals) relative rate of reinforcement. This statement, whether expressed verbally or mathematically, is known as the matching law.

In Figure 10.6, **matching** is shown as the solid black line. Notice that this line results when the proportional rate of reinforcement exactly matches the proportional rate of response. The matching law is an ideal representation of choice behavior. The actual data from pigeon 231 approximates the matching relationship. Herrnstein (1961b) also reported the results of two other pigeons that were well described by the matching law.

Extension of the Matching Law

The Generality of Matching. This equality of rates of response and reinforcement is called a law of behavior because it describes how a variety of organisms choose among alternatives (de Villiers, 1977). Animals such as pigeons (Davison & Ferguson, 1978), wagtails (Houston, 1986), cows (Matthews & Temple, 1979), and rats (Poling, 1978) have demonstrated matching in choice situations. Interestingly, this same law applies to humans in a number of different settings (Bradshaw & Szabadi, 1988; Pierce & Epling, 1983). Reinforcers have ranged from food (Herrnstein, 1961b) to points that are subsequently exchanged for money (Bradshaw, Ruddle, & Szabadi, 1981). Behavior has been as diverse as lever pressing by rats (Norman & McSweeney, 1978) and conversation in humans (Conger & Killeen, 1974). Environments in which matching has been observed have included T-mazes, operant chambers, and open spaces with free-ranging flocks of birds (Baum, 1974a). Thus, the matching law describes the distribution of behavior across species, type of response, reinforcers, and settings.

Matching and Human Communication. An interesting test of the matching law was reported by Conger and Killeen (1974). These researchers assessed human performance in a group discussion situation. A group was composed of three experimenters and one subject. The subject was not aware that the other group members were confederates in the experiment and was asked to discuss attitudes toward drug abuse. One of the confederates prompted the subject to talk. The other two confederates were assigned the role of an audience. Each listener reinforced the subject's talk with brief positive words or phrases when a hidden cue light came on. The cue lights were scheduled so that the listeners gave different rates of reinforcement to the speaker. When the results for several subjects were combined, relative time spent talking to the listener matched relative rate of agreement from the listener. These results suggest that the matching law operates in everyday social interaction.

Departures from Matching. Of course, in the complex world of people and other animals matching does not always occur. This is because in complex environments, contingencies of positive and negative reinforcement may interact, reinforcers differ in value, and histories of reinforcement are not controlled. In addition, discrimination of alternative sources of reinforcement may be weak or absent. For example, pretend you are talking to two people after class at the local bar and grill. You have a crush on one of these two and the other you do not really care for. Both of these people attend to your conversation with equal rates of social approval, eye contact, and commentary. You can see that even though the rates of reinforcement are the same, you will probably spend more time talking to the person you like best. Because this is a common occurrence in the nonlaboratory world, you might ask, "What is the use of matching and how can it be a law of behavior?"

The principle of matching is called a law because it describes the regularity underlying choice. Many scientific laws work in a similar fashion. Anyone who has an elementary understanding of physics can tell you that objects of equal mass fall to the earth at the same rate. Observation, however, tells you that a pound of feathers and pound of rocks do not fall at the same velocity. We can only see the lawful relations between mass and rate of descent when other conditions are controlled. In a vacuum, a pound of feathers and a pound of rocks fall at equal rates and the law of gravity is observed. Similarly, with appropriate laboratory control, relative rate of response matches relative rate of reinforcement.

Matching Time on an Alternative. Behavioral choice can also be measured as time spent on an alternative (Baum & Rachlin, 1969; Brownstein & Pliskoff, 1968). Time spent is a useful measure of behavior when the response is continuous, as in talking to another person. In the laboratory, rather than measure the number of responses, the time spent on an alternative may be used to describe the distribution of behavior. The matching law can also be expressed in terms of relative time spent on an alternative. Equation 10.2 is similar to equation 10.1 but states the matching relationship in terms of time.

$$T_a/(T_a + T_b) = R_a/(R_a + R_b) \tag{10.2}$$

In this equation, the time spent on alternative A is represented by T_a and the time spent on alternative B is T_b. Again, R_a and R_b represent the respective rates of reinforcement for these alternatives. The equation states that relative time spent on an alternative equals relative rate of reinforcement from that alternative. This extension of the matching law to continuous responses such as standing in one place or looking at objects is important. Most behavior outside of the laboratory does not occur as discrete responses. In this case, Equation 10.2 may be used to describe choice and preference.

Matching on More Than Two Alternatives.   Equations 10.1 and 10.2 state that relative behavior matches relative rate of reinforcement. A consideration of either equation makes it evident that to change behavior, the rate of reinforcement for the target response may be changed; alternatively, the rate of reinforcement for other concurrent operants may be altered. Both of these procedures change the relative rate of reinforcement for the specified behavior. Equation 10.3 represents relative rate of response as a function of several alternative sources of reinforcement.

$$B_a/(B_a + B_b + \ldots B_n) = R_a/(R_a + R_b + \ldots R_n) \qquad (10.3)$$

In the laboratory, most experiments are conducted with only two concurrent schedules of reinforcement. However, the matching law also describes the situation in which an organism may choose among several sources of reinforcement (Pliskoff & Brown, 1976). In Equation 10.3, behavior allocated to alternative A (B_a) is expressed relative to the sum of all behavior directed to the known alternatives ($B_a + B_b + \ldots B_n$). Reinforcement provided by alternative A (R_a) is stated relative to all known sources of reinforcement ($R_a + R_b + \ldots R_n$). Again, notice that an equality of proportions (matching) is stated.

ADVANCED ISSUE
Quantification of Behavioral Choice and the Generalized Matching Law

The proportion equations (Equations 10.1, 10.2, and 10.3) describe the distribution of behavior when alternatives differ only in rate of reinforcement. However, in complex environments other factors also contribute to choice and preference.

Sources of Error in Matching Experiments.   Suppose a pigeon has been trained to peck a yellow key for food on a single VI schedule. This experience establishes the yellow key as a discriminative stimulus that controls pecking. In a subsequent experiment, the animal is presented with concurrent VI VI schedules of reinforcement. The left key is illuminated with a blue light and the right with a yellow one. Both of the variable-interval schedules are programmed to deliver 30 reinforcers each hour. Although the programmed rates of reinforcement are the same, the bird is likely to distribute more of its behavior to the yellow key. In this case, stimulus control exerted by yellow is an additional variable that affects choice.

In this example, the yellow key is a known source of experimental error that came from the bird's history of reinforcement. However, many unknown variables also affect choice in a concurrent-operant setting. These factors arise from the biology and environmental history of the organism. For example, sources of error may include different amounts of effort for the responses, qualitative differences in reinforcement such as food versus water, a history of punishment, a tendency to respond to the right alternative rather than the left, and sensory capacities.

Matching of Ratios.   To include these and other conditions within the matching law, it is useful to express the law in terms of ratios rather than proportions. A simple algebraic transformation of Equation 10.1 gives the matching law in terms of ratios:

A. Proportion equation: $B_a/(B_a + B_b) = R_a/(R_a + R_b)$
B. Cross-multiplying: $B_a/(R_a + R_b) = R_a/(B_a + B_b)$
C. Then: $(B_a * R_a) + (B_a * R_b) = (R_a * B_a) + (R_a * B_b)$
D. Canceling: $B_a * R_b = R_a * B_b$
E. Ratio equation: $B_a/B_b = R_a/R_b$

In the ratio equation, B_a and B_b represent rate of response or time spent on the A and B alternatives. The terms R_a and R_b express the rates of reinforcement. When relative rate of response matches relative rate of reinforcement, the ratio equation is simply a restatement of the proportional form of the matching law.

The Power Law.   A generalized form of the ratio equation may, however, be used to handle the situation in which unknown factors influence the distribution of behavior. These factors produce systematic departures from ideal matching but may be represented as two constants (parameters) in the generalized matching equation, as suggested by Baum (1974b):

$$B_a/B_b = k(R_a/R_b)^a \qquad (10.4)$$

In this form, the matching equation is represented as a **power law** in which the coefficient k and the exponent a are values that represent two sources of error for a given experiment. When these parameters are equal to 1, Equation 10.4 is the simple ratio form of the matching law.

Bias.   Baum suggested that variation in the value of k from 1 reflects preference caused by some factor that has not been identified. For example, consider a pigeon placed in a chamber in which two response keys are available. One of the keys has a small dark speck that is not known to the experimenter. Recall that pigeons have excellent visual acuity and a tendency to peck at stimuli that approximate a piece of grain. Given a choice between the two keys, there will be a systematic response **bias** for the key with the spot on it. The presence of such bias is indicated by a value of k different than 1. Generally, bias is some unknown asymmetry between the alternatives that affects preference over and above the relative rates of reinforcement.

Sensitivity.   When the exponent a takes on a value other than 1, another source of error is present. A value of a greater than 1 indicates that changes in the response ratio (B_a/B_b) are larger than changes in the ratio of reinforcement (R_a/R_b). Baum (1974b) called this outcome **overmatching** because relative behavior increased faster than predicted from relative rate of reinforcement. Although overmatching has been observed, it is not the most common result in behavioral-choice experiments. The typical outcome is that the exponent a takes on a value less than 1 (Baum, 1979; Davison & McCarthy, 1988; Myers & Myers, 1977; Wearden & Burgess, 1982). This result is described as **undermatching.** Undermatching refers to a situation in which changes in the response ratio are less than changes in the reinforcement ratio.

One interpretation of undermatching is that changes in relative rates of reinforcement are not well discriminated by the organism (Baum, 1974b). Sensitivity to the operating schedules is adequate when the value of a is close to 1. An organism may not detect subtle changes in the schedules, and its distribution of behavior lags behind the current distribution of reinforcement. This slower change in the distribution of behavior is reflected by a value of a less than 1. For example, if a pigeon is exposed to concurrent VI VI schedules without a COD procedure, then the likely outcome is that the bird will rapidly and repeatedly switch between alternatives. This rapid alternation usually results in the pigeon being less sensitive to changes in the reinforcement ratio, and undermatching is the outcome. However, a COD may be used to prevent the superstitious switching and increase sensitivity to the rates of reinforcement on the alternatives. The COD is therefore a procedure that reduces undermatching, and this is reflected by values of a that are close to 1.

Although problems of discrimination or sensitivity may account for deviations of a from 1, some researchers believe that undermatching is so common that it should be regarded as an accurate description of choice and preference (Davison, 1981). If this position is correct, then matching is not the lawful process underlying choice. Most behavior analysts have not adopted this position and view matching as a fundamental process. Nonetheless, the origin of undermatching is currently a focus of debate and is not resolved at this time (Allen, 1981; Baum, 1979; Prelec, 1984; Wearden, 1983).

Estimating Bias and Sensitivity

Dr. William Baum (1974b) formulated the **generalized matching law,** as shown in Equation 10.4. In the same article, he suggested that Equation 10.4 could be represented as a straight line when expressed in logarithmic form. In this form, it is relatively easy to por-

FIG. 10.7 William Baum.

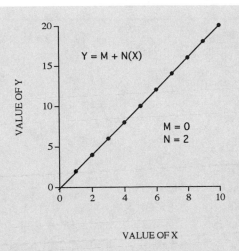

FIG. 10.8 A plot of the algebraic equation for a straight line. Slope is set at 2.0, and intercept is zero.

tray and interpret deviations from matching (i.e., bias and sensitivity) on a line graph. Baum suggested that in linear form, the value of the slope of the line measured sensitivity to the reinforcement schedules, while the intercept reflected the amount of bias.

Algebra for a Straight Line.   The algebraic equation for a straight line is

$$Y = m + n(X)$$

In this equation, n is the slope and m is the intercept. The value of X (horizontal axis) is varied, and this changes the value of Y (vertical axis). Assume that X takes on values of 1 through 10, $m = 0$, and $n = 2$. When X is 1, the simple algebraic equation is $Y = 0 + 2$ (1) or $Y = 2$. The equation can be solved for the other nine values of X and the (X,Y) pairs plotted on a graph. Figure 10.8 is a plot of the (X,Y) pairs over the range of the X values. The rate at which the line rises, or the slope of the line, is equal to the value of n and has a value of 2 in this example. The intercept m is zero in this case and is the point at which the line crosses the Y-coordinate.

A Log-Linear Matching Equation.   To write the matching law as a straight line, Baum suggested that Equation 10.4 be expressed in the logarithmic form of Equation 10.5.

$$\log(B_a/B_b) = \log(k) + a * \log(R_a/R_b) \tag{10.5}$$

Notice that in this form, $\log(B_a/B_b)$ is the same as the Y value in the algebraic equation for a straight line. Similarly, $\log(R_a/R_b)$ is the same as the X term. The value a is the same as n and is the slope of the line. Finally, $\log(k)$ is the intercept, as is the m term in the algebraic equation.

The Case of Matching.   Figure 10.9 shows the application of Equation 10.5 to idealized experimental data. The first and second columns give the number of reinforcers an

Rft/hr A	Rft/hr B	(R_a/R_b)	X - Value $\log (R_a/R_b)$	Slope (a)	Intercept (log k)	Y - Value $\log (B_a/B_b)$
			MATCHING			
5	5	1	0.00	1.00	0.00	0.00
30	5	6	0.78	1.00	0.00	0.78
100	5	20	1.30	1.00	0.00	1.30
600	5	120	2.08	1.00	0.00	2.08
			UNDERMATCHING			
5	5	1	0.00	0.50	0.00	0.00
30	5	6	0.78	0.50	0.00	0.39
100	5	20	1.30	0.50	0.00	0.65
600	5	120	2.08	0.50	0.00	0.14
			BIAS			
5	5	1	0.00	1.00	1.50	1.50
30	5	6	0.78	1.00	1.50	2.28
100	5	20	1.30	1.00	1.50	2.80
600	5	120	2.08	1.00	1.50	3.58

FIG. 10.9 Application of log-linear matching equation (equation 10.5) to idealized experimental data. Shown are reinforcements per hour (Rft/h) for alternatives A and B, the ratio of the reinforcement rates (R_a/R_b), and the log ratio of the reinforcement rates (X-values). The log ratios of the response rates (Y-values) were obtained by setting the slope and intercept to values that produce matching, undermatching, or bias.

hour delivered on the A and B alternatives. Notice that the rate of reinforcement on alternative B is held constant at 5 per hour, while the rate of reinforcement for alternative A is varied from 5 to 600 reinforcers. The relative rate of reinforcement is shown in column 3, expressed as a ratio (i.e., R_a/R_b). For example, the first ratio for the data labeled "matching" is 5/5 = 1, and the other ratios may be obtained in a similar manner.

The fourth column is the logarithm of the ratio values. Logarithms are obtained from a calculator and are defined as the exponent of base 10 that yields the original number. For example, 2.0 is the logarithm of 100 since 10 raised to the second power is 100. Similarly, in Figure 10.9 the logarithm of the ratio 120 is 2.08 because 10 to the 2.08 power is equal to the original 120 value.

Notice that logarithms are simply a transformation of scale of the original numbers. Such a transformation is suggested because logarithms of ratios plot as a straight line on X-Y coordinates, while the original ratios may not be linear. Actual experiments involve both positive and negative logarithms since ratios may be less than 1. For simplicity, the constructed examples in Figure 10.9 only use values that yield positive logarithms.

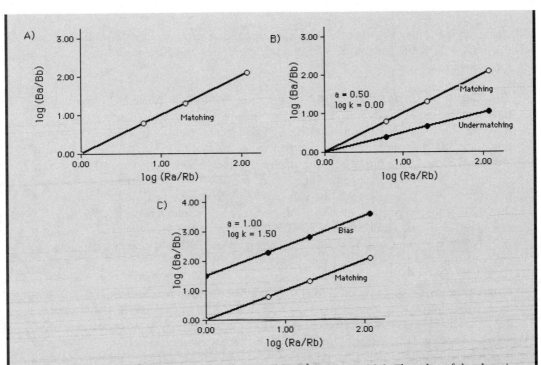

FIG. 10.10 (A) An *X-Y* plot of the data for "Matching" from Figure 10.9. The value of the slope is set at 1 ($a = 1.00$), and the intercept is set at zero (log $k = 0.00$). The matching line means that a unit increase in relative rate of reinforcement [log(R_a/R_b)] produces a unit increase in relative rate of response [log(B_a/B_b)]. (B) An *X-Y* plot of the data for "Undermatching" from Figure 10.9. The value of the slope is set at less than 1 ($a = 0.50$), and the intercept is set at zero (log $k = 0.00$). Undermatching with a slope of 0.50 means that a unit increase in relative rate of reinforcement [log(R_a/R_b)] produces a half-unit increase in relative rate of response [log(B_a/B_b)]. (C) An *X-Y* plot of the data for "Bias" from Figure 10.9. The value of the slope is set at 1 ($a = 1.00$), and the intercept is more than zero (log $k = 1.50$). A bias of this amount means that the new *X-Y* plot is deflected 1.5 units from the matching line.

Columns 5 and 6 provide values for the slope and intercept for the log-ratio equation. When relative rate of response is assumed to match (or equal) relative rate of reinforcement, the slope (a) assumes a value of 1.00 and the value of the intercept (log k) is zero. With slope and intercept so defined, the values of Y or [log(B_a/B_b)] may be obtained from the values of X or [log(R_a/R_b)], by solving equation 10.5. For example, the first Y value of 0.00 for the final column is obtained by substituting the appropriate values into the log-ratio equation, log(B_a/B_b) = 0.00 + 1.00 * (0.00). The second value of Y is 0.78, or log(B_a/B_b) = 0.00 + 1.00 * (0.78), and so on.

Figure 10.10(A) plots the "matching" data. The values of X or [log(R_a/R_b)] were set for this idealized experiment, and Y or [log (B_a/B_b)] values were obtained by solving equation 10.5 when $a = 1.00$ and log $k = 0.00$. Notice that the plot is a straight line that rises at 45 degrees. The rate of rise in the line is equal to the value of the slope (i.e., $a = 1.00$). This value means that a unit change in X (i.e., from zero to 1.00) results in an equivalent change in the value of Y. With the intercept (log k) set at zero, the line passes through the origin ($X = 0$, $Y = 0$). The result is a matching line in which log ratio of responses equals log ratio of reinforcement.

The Case of Undermatching.   The data of Figure 10.9 labeled "undermatching" represent the same idealized experiment. The value of the intercept remains the same (log $k = 0.00$); however, the slope now takes on a value less than 1 ($a = 0.50$). Based on Equation 10.5, this change in slope results in new values of Y or [log(B_a/B_b)]. Figure 10.10(B) is a graph of the line resulting from the change in slope. When compared with the matching line ($a = 1.00$), the new line rises at a slower rate ($a = 0.50$). This situation is known as undermatching and implies that the subject gives less relative behavior to alternative A [log(B_a/B_b)] than expected on the basis of relative rate of reinforcement [log(R_a/R_b)]. For example, if log-ratio reinforcement changes from zero to 1.00, the log ratio of behavior will change only from zero to 0.50. This suggests poor discrimination by the subject of the operating schedules of reinforcement (i.e., sensitivity).

The Case of Bias.   It is also possible to have a systematic bias for one of the alternatives. For example, a right-handed person may prefer to press a key on the right side more than a left-hand key. This tendency to respond to the right side may occur even though both keys schedule equal rates of reinforcement. Recall that response bias refers to any systematic preference for one alternative that is not explained by the relative rates of reinforcement. In terms of the idealized experiment, the data labeled "bias" in Figure 10.9 show that the slope of the line is 1.00 (matching), but the intercept (log k) now assumes a value of 1.50 rather than zero. A plot of the X or [log(R_a/R_b)] and Y or [log(B_a/B_b)] values in Figure 10.10(C) reveals a line that is systematically deflected 1.5 units from the matching line.

Experiments and Log-Linear Estimates

Setting the Values of the Independent Variable.   In actual experiments on choice and preference, the values of the slope and intercept are not known until the experiment is conducted. The experimenter sets the values of the independent variable, log(R_a/R_b), by programming different schedules of reinforcement on the alternatives. For example, one alternative may be VI 30 seconds and the other VI 60 seconds. The VI 30-second schedule is set to pay off at 120 reinforcers per hour, and the VI 60-second schedule is set to pay off at 60 reinforcers each hour. The relative rate of reinforcement is expressed as the ratio 120/60 = 2.00. To describe the results in terms of Equation 10.5, the reinforcement ratio, 2.00, is transformed to a logarithm, using a calculator with logarithmic functions. Experiments are designed to span a reasonable range of log-ratio reinforcement values. The minimum number of log-ratio reinforcement values is 3, but most experiments program more than three values of the independent variable.

Each experimental subject is exposed to different pairs of concurrent schedules of reinforcement. The subject is maintained on these schedules until rates of response are stable, according to preset criteria. At this point, relative rates of response are calculated (B_a/B_b) and transformed to logarithms. For example, a subject on concurrent VI 30-second VI 60-

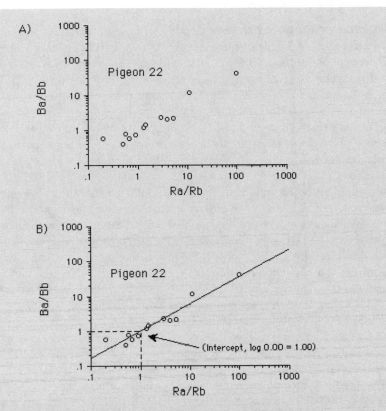

FIG. 10.11 (A) Reinforcement and response ratios for pigeon 22 plotted on logarithmic coordinates, based on Table 1 from White and Davison (1973; copyright 1973 by the Society for the Experimental Analysis of Behavior, Inc.). (B) The line of best fit for the data of pigeon 22, also from White & Davison (1973; copyright 1973 by the Society for the Experimental Analysis of Behavior, Inc.).

second schedule may generate 1,000 responses per hour on the VI 30-second alternative and 500 on the VI 60-second schedule. Thus, the ratio is 1,000/500 = 2.00, or 2 to 1. The response ratio, 2.00, is transformed to a logarithm. For each value of $\log(R_a/R_b)$, the observed value the dependent variable $\log(B_a/B_b)$ is plotted on X, Y coordinates.

To illustrate the application of Equation 10.5, consider an experiment conducted in 1973 by White and Davison. In this experiment, several pigeons were exposed to 12 sets of concurrent schedules. Each pair of schedules programmed a different reinforcement ratio. The pigeons were maintained on the schedules until key pecking was stable from day to day. The data for pigeon 22 are plotted in Figure 10.11(A) on logarithmic coordinates. Plotting the reinforcement and response ratios on logarithmic coordinates is the same as plotting the log ratios on ordinary graph paper. Notice that actual results are not as orderly as the data of the idealized experiment. This is because errors in measurement, inconsistencies of procedure, and random events operate to affect response ratios in actual experiments. The results appear to move upward to the right in a linear manner, but it is not possible to draw a simple line through the plot.

Estimates of Slope and Intercept. To find the line that best fits the results, a statistical technique (i.e., least squares regression) is used to estimate values for the slope and intercept of Equation 10.5. The idea is to select slope and intercept values that minimize the errors in prediction. For a given value of the reinforcement ratio (x-axis), an error is the difference between the response-ratio value on the line (called the predicted value) and the actual or observed response ratio.

The mathematics that underlie this statistical technique are complicated and beyond the scope of this book. However, most personal computers have programs that will do the calculations for you. In this case, a Macintosh™ computer solved this problem with a program called Cricket Graph™ in a matter of seconds. The estimate of slope was $a = 0.77$, indicating that pigeon 22 undermatched to the reinforcement ratios. The estimate of the intercept was zero (log k = zero), indicating that there was no response bias. With these estimates of slope and intercept, Equation 10.5 may be used to draw the best-fitting line.

In Figure 10.11(B), the line of best-fit has been drawn. You can obtain the line of best-fit by substituting values for $\log(R_a/R_b)$ and finding the predicted $\log(B_a/B_b)$ values. You only need to find two points on the X, Y coordinates to draw the line. Notice that the data and best-fit line are plotted on a graph with logarithmic coordinates. Because there was no bias (log k = 0.00), the line must pass through the point $X = 1, Y = 1$ when Ra/Rb and Ba/Bb values are plotted on logarithmic paper.

As a final point, you may be interested in how well the matching equation fit the results of pigeon 22. One measure of accuracy is called explained variance. This measure varies between zero and 1.00 in value. When the explained variance is zero, it is not possible to predict the response ratios from the reinforcement ratios. When the explained variance is 1.00, there is perfect prediction from the reinforcement ratios to the response ratios. In this instance, the explained variance is 0.92, indicating 92% accuracy. The log-linear matching equation is a good description of the pigeon's behavior on concurrent schedules of reinforcement.

IMPLICATIONS OF THE MATCHING LAW

The matching law has practical implications. A few researchers have shown that the matching equations are useful in applied settings (Epling & Pierce, 1983; McDowell, 1981, 1982, 1988; Myerson & Hale, 1984). For example, a common problem with children is that they do not obey their parents (Patterson, 1976). In some cases, this problem becomes severe and parents complain that their children are out of control. When this happens, the parents may seek professional help.

Matching and Child Compliance

A traditional applied behavior analysis of this problem involves objectively identifying the target responses, finding effective reinforcers, and then establishing contingencies between behavior and consequences. However, the matching equations suggest that other sources of reinforcement should be taken into account.

$$\frac{\text{Child's Compliance to Mother}}{(\text{Compliance to Mother}) + (\text{Compliance to Others})} = \frac{\text{Reinforcement from Mother}}{(S^{r+} \text{ Mother}) + (S^{r+} \text{ Others})}$$

For example, according to the proportion equation, to change the child's rate of compliance to the mother, the applied analyst should consider the father and siblings as additional sources of reinforcement. Rate of compliance with the requests of one parent may be low because this behavior is concurrently reinforced at a high rate by other family members. For example, if maternal reinforcement (e.g., praise, approval, and attention) is given at a lower rate than the father's, then modification of the rate of maternal attention for compliant behavior will increase obedience only if the father's rate of reinforcement remains the same. Frequently, however, parents compete for their children's behavior, and a shift away from the father can easily lead to an increase in rate of social reinforcement from him. An increase in the father's attention and approval could further decrease the frequency of child compliance toward the mother, even though she has increased her rate of reinforcement. This analysis reflects the typical two-key concurrent paradigm. The child responds to, and switches among, alternative schedules of reinforcement set up by parents and siblings.

Matching, Modification, and Reinforcement Schedules

The matching law has implications for the kind of reinforcement schedules that should be used for behavior modification. Myerson and Hale (1984) discussed the applied setting in terms of concurrent schedules of reinforcement. People emit a variety of responses, many of which are maintained by concurrently available sources of reinforcement. Some of these responses may be socially appropriate, while others are considered undesirable. In a classroom, appropriate behavior for students includes working on assignments, following instructions, and attending to the teacher. In contrast, yelling and screaming, talking out of turn, and throwing paper airplanes are usually viewed as undesirable. All of these activities, appropriate or inappropriate, are presumably maintained by teacher attention, peer approval, sensory stimulation, and other sources of reinforcement. However, the schedules of reinforcement maintaining behavior in complex settings like a classroom are usually not known. When the objective is to increase a specific operant and the competing schedules are unknown, Myerson and Hale (1984) recommend the use of VI schedules to reinforce target behavior.

To simplify the analysis, we will treat all on-task operants as part of the more general class of appropriate behavior and off-task operants as inappropriate behavior. Assume that the reinforcement for inappropriate behavior is delivered on a ratio schedule. To increase desired behavior by a student, ratio contingencies may be arranged by the teacher. This means that the situation is analyzed as a concurrent ratio schedule. Recall that on concurrent ratio schedules, exclusive preference develops for the alternative with the higher rate of reinforcement (Herrnstein & Loveland, 1975). Ratio schedules are in effect when a teacher implements a grading system based on the number of correct solutions for assignments. The teacher's intervention will increase the students' on-task behavior only if the rate of reinforcement by the teacher is higher than the ratio schedule controlling inappropriate behavior. Basically, an intervention is either completely successful or a total failure when ratio schedules are used to modify behavior. In contrast, interval schedules of reinforcement will always redirect behavior to the desired alternative, although such a schedule may not completely eliminate inappropriate responding.

When behavior is maintained by interval contingencies, interval schedules remain the most desirable method for behavior change. Myerson and Hale (1984) used the matching equations to show that behavior-change techniques based on interval schedules are more effective than ratio interventions. They stated that "if the behavior analyst offers a VI schedule of reinforcement for competing responses two times as rich as the VI schedule for inappropriate behavior, the result will be the same as would be obtained with a VR schedule three times as rich as the schedule for inappropriate behavior" (pp. 373–374). Generally, behavior change will be more predictable and successful if interval schedules are used to reinforce appropriate behavior.

THE QUANTITATIVE LAW OF EFFECT

The matching law suggests that operant behavior is determined by rate of reinforcement for one alternative relative to all other known sources of reinforcement. Even in situations in which a contingency exists between a single response and a reinforcement schedule, organisms may have several reinforced alternatives that are unknown to the researcher. Also, many of the activities that produce reinforcement are beyond experimental control. A rat that is lever pressing for food may gain additional reinforcement from exploring the operant chamber, scratching itself, and so on. In a similar fashion, rather than work for teacher attention a pupil may look out the window, talk to a friend, or even daydream. Thus, even in a single-operant setting, multiple sources of reinforcement are operating. R. J. Herrnstein (1970, 1974) argued this point and suggested that all operant behavior must be understood as behavior emitted in the context of other alternative sources of reinforcement.

An Equation for Absolute Rates

Based on these ideas, Herrnstein proposed an equation for the single operant that is now called the **quantitative law of effect.** The equation relates absolute (rather than relative) response and reinforcement rates, using alternative sources of reinforcement as the context. Because the equation is expressed in absolute rates, it is usually considered a more fundamental expression of matching theory. Herrnstein's equation may be derived from a restatement of the proportional matching law.

$$B_a/(B_a + B_e) = R_a/(R_a + R_e)$$

The difference between this equation and the proportional equation (Equation 10.1) is that B_e refers to all behavior directed to **extraneous sources of reinforcement,** and R_e represents these sources. For example, lever pressing is the specified operant (B_a) that produces food at some rate of reinforcement (R_a). Notice that pressing the lever is expressed relative to the other activity of the organism (B_e). This activity is reinforced by events that are not under experimental control (R_e). A rat may obtain reinforcement from grooming even though this is not prescribed by the experimental procedures. Many other activities result in extraneous sources of reinforcement.

To solve the equation for the absolute rate of response (B_a), it is important to recognize that $B_a + B_e$ is equal to the total behavioral output for a given situation. Because B_a represents lever pressing and B_e represents all other activity, the sum must equal all the behavior of the animal in the experimental setting. It is convenient to express this sum as the value k or the total behavioral output. The quantity k may now be substituted into the preceding equation.

$$B_a/k = R_a/(R_a + R_e)$$

When each side of the equation is multiplied by k, the absolute response rate (B_a) is expressed as:

$$B_a = k\,(R_a)/(R_a + R_e) \tag{10.6}$$

This kind of equation produces a hyperbolic line that rises to asymptote on X, Y coordinates. Herrnstein's equation therefore states that the absolute rate of response (B_a) is a hyperbolic function of the scheduled rate of reinforcement (R_a) and all extraneous sources of reinforcement (R_e). The constant k or the total behavioral output sets the upper limit on the hyperbolic curve (McDowell, 1986).

Background Sources of Reinforcement

The constant R_e represents background sources of reinforcement and modifies the impact of the scheduled rate of reinforcement. In Equation 10.6, extraneous reinforcement (R_e) is added to the programmed rate of reinforcement (R_a), and R_a is divided by this sum. As the value of R_e increases, the impact of R_a must decline. This means that, for a given schedule of reinforcement, the absolute rate of response (B_a) will be low when R_e is large, and high when R_e is small.

Pretend that you volunteer to participate in an experiment that involves dialing for dollars. Your task is to dial phone numbers that result either in an answer or a busy signal. When a call is completed, a message says, "Congratulations, you have just won a dollar" and simultaneously a coin machine dispenses money to you. The experiment is controlled by a computer that schedules the rate of reinforcement for dialing. Reinforcement consists of the message and the dollar. Experimental sessions are held after classes for 1 hour, 5 days a week, for 6 months. During this period, the scheduled payoff for dialing the phone is varied to produce different rates of reinforcement. Sometimes the rate of reinforcement is high (e.g., $120 per hour) and during other sessions it is low (e.g., $2 per

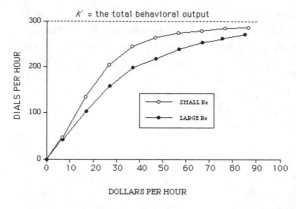

FIG. 10.12 Two idealized plots of Equation 10.6, Herrnstein's hyperbola. Both curves approach the asymptote k, which represents the total behavioral output for the experiment. The value of R_e, or extraneous reinforcement, is large for one curve and is small for the other.

hour). A given rate of reinforcement is maintained until dialing occurs at a stable rate.

Figure 10.12 shows the possible results of this experiment in terms of Equation 10.6. Number of phone calls per hour is plotted against number of dollars earned each hour. Herrnstein's hyperbolic equation suggests that your rate of dialing will increase rapidly as rate of reinforcement goes up. As rate of reinforcement becomes larger and larger, the increase in rate of response becomes less and less, and the curve flattens out.

Two hyperbolic curves are presented in Figure 10.12. Both curves rise toward (but never meet) the line k, which represents all your activity in the experimental setting. These curves depict the effects of high versus low values of R_e or extraneous reinforcement. Comparison of the curves indicates that your rate of dialing may be high or low for the same rate of reinforcement (R_a). The impact of scheduled rate of reinforcement on response rate is modified by the value of R_e in the situation.

In a rich environment, R_e is large and monetary payments produce a relatively low response rate. When the environment is lean, R_e has a small value and the dollars produce a higher rate of dialing. For example, if you are dialing in a laboratory cubicle (small R_e), your rate of calls should be higher than if you are dialing in a spacious, well-decorated room with a picturesque view of the countryside (large R_e). Add a television set to the room and your dialing will be even lower. Thus, your behavior in the dialing-for-dollars experiment varies in accord with the scheduled payoffs and the background or context, as represented by the R_e value.

Experimental Evidence and Herrnstein's Equation

The quantitative law of effect (Equation 10.6) has been analyzed in laboratory experiments. In an early investigation, Catania and Reynolds (1968) conducted an exhaustive study of six pigeons that pecked a key for food on different variable-interval (VI) schedules. Rate of reinforcement ranged from 8 to 300 food presentations each hour. Herrnstein (1970), in his classic article on the law of effect, replotted the data from the Catania and Reynolds experiment on X, Y coordinates.

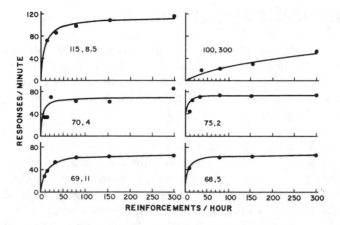

FIG. 10.13 Rate of response as a function of rate of food reinforcement for six pigeons on single VI schedules. The k and R_e values and percentage variance accounted for by the curve fit are shown (reprinted from Figure 8 of Herrnstein, 1970, which in turn is based on data from Catania & Reynolds, 1968; copyright 1970 by the Society for the Experimental Analysis of Behavior, Inc.).

Figure 10.13 shows the plots for the six birds, with reinforcements per hour on the X-axis and responses per minute on the Y-axis.

Herrnstein used a statistical procedure to fit Equation 10.6 to the data of each pigeon. Figure 10.13 presents the curves that best fit these results. Notice that all of the birds produce rates of response that are described as a hyperbolic function of rate of reinforcement. Some of the curves fit the data almost perfectly (e.g., P281) while others are less satisfactory (e.g., P129). Overall, Herrnstein's quantitative law of effect is well supported.

The quantitative law of effect, as represented by equation 10.6, has been extended to magnitude of food reinforcement, brain stimulation, quality of reinforcement, delay of positive reinforcement, rate of negative reinforcement, magnitude or intensity of negative reinforcement, and delay of negative reinforcement (see de Villiers, 1977, for a thorough review). In a summary of the evidence prior to 1980, Peter de Villiers (1977) stated:

> The remarkable generality of Herrnstein's equation is apparent from this survey. The behavior of rats, pigeons, monkeys and ... people is equally well accounted for, whether the behavior is lever pressing, key pecking, running speed, or response latency in a variety of experimental settings. The reinforcers can be as different as food, sugar water, escape from shock or loud noise or cold water, electrical stimulation of a variety of brain loci, or turning a comedy record back on. Out of 53 tests of Equation [10.6] on group data the least-squares fit of the equation accounts for over 90% of the variance in 42 cases and for over 80% in another six cases. Out of 45 tests on individual data, the equation accounts for over 90% of the variance in 32 cases and for over 80% in another seven cases. The literature appears to contain no evidence for a substantially different equation than Equation [10.6]. ... This equation therefore provides a powerful but simple framework for the quantification of the relation between response strength and both positive and negative reinforcement. (p. 262)

OPTIMAL FORAGING, MATCHING AND MELIORATON

One of the fundamental problems of evolutionary biology and behavioral ecology concerns the concept of "optimal foraging" of animals (Krebs and Davies, 1978). Foraging involves prey selection where prey can be either animal or vegetable. Thus, a cow taking an occasional mouthful of grass throughout a field, or a redshank wading in the mud and probing with its beak for an occasional worm are examples of foraging behavior. Because the function of foraging is food, foraging can be viewed as operant behavior regulated by food reinforcement. The natural contingencies of foraging present animals with alternative sources of food called patches. Food patches provide items at various rates and in this sense are similar to concurrent schedules of reinforcement arranged in the laboratory.

Optimal foraging is said to occur when animals obtain the highest overall rate of reinforcement from their foraging. That is, over time organisms are expected to select between patches so as to optimize (obtain the most possible of) their food resources. In this view, animals are like organic computers comparing their behavioral distributions with overall outcomes and stabilizing on a response distribution that **maximizes overall rate of reinforcement.**

In contrast to the optimal foraging hypothesis, Herrnstein (1982) proposed a process of **melioration** (doing the best at the moment). Organisms, he argued, are sensitive to fluctuations in the momentary rates of reinforcement rather than to long-term changes in overall rates of reinforcement. That is, an organism remains on one schedule until the local rates of reinforcement decline relative to that offered by a second schedule. Herrnstein showed that the steady state outcome of the process of melioration is the matching law where relative rate of response matches relative rate of reinforcement. Thus, in a foraging situation involving two patches, Herrnstein's melioration analysis predicts matching of the distributions of behavior and reinforcement. Optimal foraging theory, on the other hand, predicts maximization of overall rate of reinforcement.

It is not possible to examine all the evidence for melioration, matching, and maximizing in this chapter, but Herrnstein (1982) has argued convincingly that melioration and matching are the basic processes of choice. That is, when melioration and matching are tested in choice situations that distinguish matching from maximizing, matching theory has usually predicted the actual distributions of the behavior.

One example of the application of matching theory to natural foraging is reported by Baum (1974a) for a flock of free-ranging wild pigeons. The subjects were 20 pigeons that lived in a wooden frame house in Cambridge, Massachusetts. An opening allowed them to freely enter and leave the attic of the house. An operant apparatus with a platform was placed in the living space opposite to the opening to the outside. The front panel of the apparatus contained three translucent response keys and, when available, an opening allowed access to a hopper of mixed grain. Pigeons were autoshaped to peck to the center key, and following this training a perch replaced the platform so that only one pigeon at a time could operate the keys to obtain food. Pigeons were now shaped to peck the illuminated center key on a VI 30-s schedule of food reinforcement. When a stable performance was observed, the center key was no longer illuminated or operative, and the two side keys became active. Responses to the illuminated side keys were reinforced on two concurrent VI/VI schedules. Relative rates of reinforcement on the two keys were varied and the relative rate of response was measured.

Although only one bird at a time could respond on the concurrent schedules of reinforcement, Baum (1974b) treated the aggregate pecks of the group as the dependent measure. When the group of 20 pigeons chose between the two side keys, each of which occasionally produced food, the ratio of pecks to these keys approximately equaled the ratio of grain presentations obtained from them. That is, the aggregate behavior of the flock of 20 pigeons was in accord with the generalized matching equation (see this chapter). This research suggests that the matching law applies to the behavior of wild pigeons in natural environments. Generally, principles of choice based on laboratory experiments can predict the foraging behavior of animals in ecologically valid settings.

ON THE APPLIED SIDE

Application of the Quantitative Law of Effect

Dr. Jack McDowell was the first researcher to use the quantitative law of effect (Equation 10.6) to describe human behavior in a natural setting. Many people are interested in his work on applications of matching theory to the treatment of clinical problems. However, McDowell states, "I really think of myself as a basic researcher" (personal communication, March 3, 1989). As a college student, he started out as a physics major and gained a strong background in natural science. He recalls that "I regarded psychology as a discipline with interesting problems but terrible methods. Indeed, I thought it was absurd to consider psychology a science. Then I took a course in what we now call behavior analysis. I was sur-

FIG.10.14 Dr. Jack McDowell.

prised to find a specialty in psychology that looked like what I had always thought of as science. So I changed my major to psychology and later entered a behavioral graduate program" (personal communication, March 3, 1989). In 1972, at Yale University, McDowell worked on the philosophical foundations of behavior modification. By 1978, he had completed a clinical internship at the State University of New York, Stony Brook, and a year later he received his Ph.D. in clinical psychology. McDowell's doctoral dissertation focused on the mathematical description of behavior, and he has maintained this emphasis throughout his career. At the time of this writing, he is a professor of clinical psychology and psychobiology at Emory University in Atlanta, Georgia; he also maintains a private practice in behavior therapy.

Mathematics and Behavior Modification.   McDowell's expertise in mathematics and behavior modification spurred him to apply Herrnstein's equation to a clinically relevant problem. Carr and McDowell (1980) had been involved in the treatment of a 10-year-old boy who repeatedly and severely scratched himself. Before treatment the boy had a large number of open sores on his scalp, face, back, arms, and legs. In addition, the boy's body was covered with scabs, scars, and skin discoloration, where new wounds could be produced. In their 1980 paper, Carr and McDowell demonstrated that the boy's scratching was operant behavior. Careful observation showed that the scratching occurred predominantly when he and other family members were in the living room watching television. This suggested that the self-injurious behavior was under stimulus control. In other words, the family and setting made scratching more likely to occur.

Next, Carr and McDowell looked for potential reinforcing consequences maintaining the boy's self-injurious behavior. The researchers suspected that the consequences were social because scratching appeared to be under the stimulus control of family members. In any family interaction there are many social exchanges, and the task was to identify those consequences that reliably followed the boy's scratching. Observation showed that family members reliably reprimanded the boy when he engaged in self-injury. Reprimands are seemingly negative events, but the literature makes it clear that both approval and disapproval may serve as reinforcement.

Although social reinforcement by reprimands was a good guess, it was still necessary to show that these consequences in fact functioned as reinforcement. The first step was to take baseline measures of the rate of scratching and the rate of reprimands. Following this, the family members were required to ignore the boy's behavior. That is, the presumed reinforcer was withdrawn (i.e., extinction) and the researchers continued to monitor the rate of scratching. Next, the potential reinforcer was reinstated by having the family members again reprimand the boy for his misconduct. Relative to baseline, the scratching decreased when reprimands were withdrawn and increased when they were reinstated. This test identified the reprimands as positive reinforcement for scratching. Once the reinforcement for scratching was identified, behavior modification was used to eliminate the self-injurious behavior.

In a subsequent report, McDowell (1981) analyzed the boy's baseline data in terms of the quantitative law of effect. He plotted the reprimands per hour on the *x*-axis and scratches per hour on the *y*-axis. McDowell then fit Equation 10.6 to the points on the graph. Figure 10.15 shows the plot and the curve of best fit. Equation 10.6 provides an excellent description of the boy's behavior. You will notice that most of the points are on, or very close to, the hyperbolic curve. McDowell has pointed to the significance of this demonstration. He states:

> as shown in the figure [10.15] the single-alternative hyperbola accounted for nearly all the variance in the data. This is especially noteworthy because the behavior occurred in an uncontrolled environment where other factors that might have influenced the behavior had ample opportunity to do so. It may be worth emphasizing that the rates of reprimanding ... occurred naturally; that is, they were not experimentally arranged.... Thus, the data ... demonstrate the relevance of matching theory to the natural ecology of human behavior. (McDowell, 1988, pp. 103–104)

Why DRO Works.   The quantitative law of effect provides an explanation for the success of many well-known behavior-modification procedures. Differential reinforcement of other behavior (DRO) is often used to reduce problem behavior. The technique involves reinforcing any behavior other than the inappropriate response. For example, a person who always complains about his or her health when doctors cannot find a problem is called a hypochondriac. This behavior is likely maintained by the serious attention provided by others. Pretend that you have such a friend and you value the person's company, but you are sick of hearing about his health problems. One solution is suggested by the DRO procedure. The idea is to provide your friend with the same amount of attention, but only when he is talking about something other than health problems. Being human, you do your best to implement the procedure but every now and then you cannot help attending to his outlandish complaints.

The principle of intermittent reinforcement suggests that your friend's complaints will be maintained and be more resistant to extinction. According to the

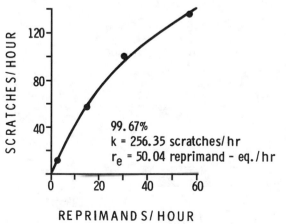

FIG. 10.15 Rate of social reinforcement and self-injurious scratching of a young boy. The data were fitted by Herrnstein's single-operant equation (Equation 10.6). Values of k and R_e and percentage variance accounted for by the curve fit are shown (these results are from McDowell, 1981; copyright 1981 by the American Psychological Association; reprinted by permission).

99.67%
k = 256.35 scratches/hr
r_e = 50.04 reprimand - eq./hr

quantitative law of effect, however, this intervention will reduce health complaints because it changes the environmental context of reinforcement. In terms of equation 10.6 the value of R_a, rate of reinforcement for complaints (B_a), is reduced and the value of R_e is increased because you provide reinforcement for other behavior.

McDowell used a DRO procedure that was based on a consideration of Equation 10.6 to treat a difficult behavior problem. The case history was as follows:

> The client was a mildly retarded 22-year-old male who had been dismissed from a sheltered workshop for threatening a staff member with a pair of scissors. The client exhibited other types of oppositional behavior as well, including noncompliance, argumentativeness, and temper tantrums, the last of which frequently escalated in intensity and sometimes culminated in assault. In addition to an incident at the workshop, the young man had a history of assaulting his mother, sometimes with a lighted cigarette. Assessment information indicated that the client's oppositional behavior at home was supported by social reinforcement from his parents. Traditional treatment procedures could not be applied in this case. Extinction was contraindicated because assault during the extinction run was an unacceptable risk. Similarly, punishment of the behavior was ruled out because no one was willing to enforce a time-out contingency with this assaultive client. The treatment procedure decided upon was based on Equation [10.6]. Token reinforcement was arranged for behaviors unrelated to the oppositional behavior. The client earned points, which could be exchanged for money at the end of each week, for personal-maintenance behaviors like shaving, job tasks like helping with dinner, and educational tasks like reading. According to Equation [10.6] this intervention increases the total amount of reinforcement in the environment and so should decrease the frequency of the oppositional behavior $[B_a]$, even though the contingencies directly affecting the oppositional behavior do not change. The outcome of the treatment procedure is shown in Figure [10.16]. Before treatment the client exhibited almost daily episodes of escalating oppositional behavior. Token reinforcement of unrelated behavior reduced the frequency of the oppositional behavior by about 80%. During the ninety weeks of treatment a response cost (point deduction) contingency was added but, as

FIG. 10.16 The results of a treatment procedure for the aggressive behavior of a mildly retarded man (data are from McDowell, 1988, and are reprinted with permission of *The Behavior Analyst* and the Society for the Advancement of Behavior Analysis).

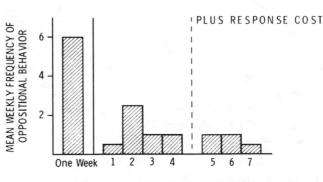

shown in the figure, this failed to reduce the behavior much further. At the end of treatment the mother reported that the young man's oppositional behavior had decreased in intensity as well as in frequency. (McDowell, 1988, p. 105)

The research by McDowell demonstrates the progression from laboratory experiments with animals, to basic research with humans, and then to the treatment of human behavior. The final step is to use this knowledge in practically important ways. McDowell has shown the application of matching theory to the modification of clinically relevant behavior. Other researchers are working on more global social problems like economics (Herrnstein, 1990; Hursh, 1980; Lea, Tarpy, & Webley, 1987). Generally, the research on choice and preference illustrates the close tie between behavior principles and application.

KEY WORDS

Bias

Changeover delay (COD)

Changeover response

Choice

Concurrent schedules of reinforcement

Extraneous sources of reinforcement (R_e)

Findley procedure

Generalized matching law

Log-linear matching equation

Matching law

Maximization

Melioration

Overmatching

Power law for matching

Preference

Quantitative law of effect

Relative rate of reinforcement

Relative rate of response

Two-key procedure

Undermatching

CHAPTER 11

Conditioned Reinforcement

LEARNING OBJECTIVES

1. What is conditioned reinforcement? Give some common examples. Distinguish between primary and conditioned reinforcers.

2. Describe Skinner's (1938) procedure for rats that resulted in conditioned reinforcement. Summarize the new-response method and the problem with this technique for analyzing conditioned reinforcement.

3. Define a chain schedule of reinforcement. Write the Mechner notation for a chain VI FR FI schedule of reinforcement.

4. Discuss multiple functions of stimuli on chain schedules. Compare the performance of pigeons on tandem and chain fixed-interval schedules, referring to an experiment by Gollub (1958). What accounts for these performance differences?

5. Distinguish between homogeneous and heterogeneous chains. Give an everyday example of a heterogeneous chain. Why do the conditioned reinforcers remain effective in such a chain? How much detail should be given when describing human performance on a chain schedule?

6. What is backward chaining? When is backward chaining most useful in training human behavior? Describe backward chaining in the performance of making a bed. How can backward chaining be applied to playing golf? Why is backward chaining effective in training complex and skillful athletic performance?

7. Describe the relationship between frequency of primary reinforcement and strength of conditioned reinforcement. How do variability of primary reinforcement, establishing operations, and delay to primary reinforcement affect conditioned reinforcement?

8. Be able to describe the established-response method and how it differs from the new-response technique.

9. Outline the S-S account of conditioned reinforcement. What is the alternative operant account? Currently, is there a definitive test? Why or why not?

10. State the information hypothesis of conditioned reinforcement. Summarize Egger and Miller's (1962) experiment and how it relates to this hypothesis.

11. What does the information hypothesis imply about good and bad news? Describe Wyckoff's (1969) experimental procedures and results. What finding suggested that Wyckoff's (1969) pigeons may only respond for good news?

12. How did Dinsmoor, Brown, and Lawrence (1972) clarify the conditioned-reinforcement effectiveness of good and bad news?

13. State how the conditioned-reinforcement value of good news (but not bad) is shown with aversive procedures. Give a common example of the good and bad news effect. Be able to state the general principle underlying the good and bad news effect.

14. State Fantino's (1969a) delay-reduction hypothesis. What procedures do contemporary researchers use to evaluate conditioned reinforcement and delay reduction?

15. In Mechner notation, write two separate chain schedules (VI 20 seconds VI 10 seconds; VI 20 seconds VI 60 seconds). Now write a concurrent-chains schedule using the same basic schedules.

16. How is the concurrent-chains procedure used to study delay reduction? What are the two functions of stimuli correlated with the onset of the terminal-link schedule? What is the measure of relative effectiveness of the conditioned reinforcers?

17. Be able to talk about a businessperson calling Delta and American Airlines as an example of delay reduction and conditioned reinforcement.

Advanced Issue

18. *In the Delta and American example, how is the average time in the initial link (time-to-hold message) calculated?*

19. *Calculate the average time in the terminal links in terms of the example.*

20. *Now obtain the average total time to terminal reinforcement. Obtain the delay reduction at Delta and the same at American. Write the relative delay reduction for Delta and relate this to the distribution of dialing the respective airlines.*

21. *Write a general equation for delay reduction and know what each term means. Show how Fantino (1969a) varied the initial-link schedules to test the delay-reduction hypothesis. What does proportional matching predict for Fantino's experiment?*

22. Define generalized conditioned reinforcement. How is a generalized reinforcer relatively independent of the momentary condition of an organism?

23. Discuss generalized reinforcement and social contingencies involving attention, approval, and affection.

24. Analyze an aggressive episode in terms of submissiveness of the victim (generalized reinforcement) and cessation of threats and physical injury by the attacker. How do these contingencies extend to other cases of abuse in our society? What can be done?

25. Discuss token reinforcement with chimpanzees. How does token reinforcement relate to human behavior and money? What is the applied advantage of money and tokens?

26. What is a token economy? Describe some uses of token systems. Outline the modification program used by Schaefer and Martin (1966) and the major findings. How can the behavioral gains of a token economy be maintained in everyday life?

Human behavior is often regulated by consequences that depend on a history of conditioning. Praise, criticism, good grades, and money are consequences that may strengthen or weaken behavior. These events acquire a conditioned-reinforcement function because of the different experiences that people have had throughout their lives. Some people value what others say about their actions—others are indifferent. Lee Iacocca markets and sells cars because of monetary reinforcement, status, and power, but Mother Teresa took care of the poor for other reasons. In these examples, the effectiveness of a behavioral consequence depends on a personal history of conditioning.

Conditioned reinforcement occurs when behavior is strengthened by events that have an effect because of a conditioning history. The critical aspect of this history involves a correspondence between the arbitrary event and a reinforcer. Once the arbitrary event increases the frequency of an operant, it is called a **conditioned reinforcer.** For example, the sound of the pellet feeder becomes a conditioned reinforcer for a rat that presses a lever because it is associated with food. The immediate effect of lever pressing is the sound of the feeder, not the food. Food is a biological or **primary reinforcer** that accompanies the sound of the feeder. One way to demonstrate the reinforcing effectiveness of the sound is to arrange a contingency between some other operant (e.g., pressing a spot on the wall) and only the sound. If operant rate increases, the process is conditioned reinforcement and the sound is a conditioned reinforcer.

In his book, *The Behavior of Organisms*, Skinner (1938) described a procedure that resulted in conditioned reinforcement. Rats were exposed to a clicking sound and were given food. Later the animals were not fed, but the click was used to train lever pressing. Lever pressing increased although it only produced the clicking sound. Because the click was no longer accompanied by food, each occurrence of the sound was also an extinction trial. For this reason, the sound declined in reinforcing effectiveness and lever pressing for clicks decreased at the same time.

This **new-response method** for studying conditioned reinforcement results in weak effects. Because of extinction, the conditioned reinforcer quickly loses its effectiveness and is only capable of maintaining a few responses (see Kelleher & Gollub, 1962; Miller, 1951; Myers, 1958; Wike, 1966). Animals, however, typically engage in long and complex sequences of behavior that are often far removed from primary reinforcement. This is particularly true for humans. People get up in the morning, take buses to work, carry out their jobs, talk to other workers, and so on. These operants occur day after day and are maintained by conditioned reinforcement. Thus, conditioned reinforcement is a durable process, but the new-response method does not reveal how this occurs. Because of this, behavioral re-searchers have turned to procedures that clarify the long-lasting effects of condi-tioned reinforcement.

CHAIN SCHEDULES AND CONDITIONED REINFORCEMENT

One way to investigate conditioned reinforcement is to construct sequences of be-havior in the laboratory. A **chain schedule of reinforcement** involves two or more simple schedules (CRF, FI, VI, FR, or VR), each of which is presented se-quentially and is signaled by an arbitrary stimulus. Only the final or terminal link of the chain results in primary reinforcement. Figure 11.1 shows the Mechner no-tation for a three-component chain schedule of reinforcement. The schedule is a chain VI FR FI, and each link (or component) of the chain is signaled by a red, blue, or green light. For example, in the presence of the red light, a pigeon must emit a key peck after an average of 1 minute has elapsed (VI 60 seconds). When the peck occurs, the light changes from red to blue and the bird must peck the key 50 times (FR 50) to produce the green light. In the presence of the green light, a single peck after 2 minutes (FI 120 seconds) produces food and the light changes back to red (i.e., the chain starts over).

When the pigeon pecks in the red component, the only consequence is that the light changes to blue. Once the blue condition is in effect, 50 responses turns on the green light. If the bird pecks for the blue and green lights, the change in color is reinforcement. Recall that any stimulus that strengthens behavior is by definition a reinforcing stimulus. Thus, these lights have multiple functions: They are S^Ds that set the occasion for pecking the key in each link and conditioned re-inforcement, $S^{r(cond)}$, for behavior that produces them. The notation in Figure 11.1 indicates that the red light is only a discriminative stimulus. You might suspect that it is a conditioned reinforcer, and it may have this function. However, the chain procedure as outlined does not require a separate response to produce the red light (the last response in the chain produces food and afterward the red light

FIG. 11.1 Mechner notation for a three-component chain schedule of reinforcement, VI 60 seconds FR 50 FI 120 seconds. Notice that the red light only has a discriminative stimulus function, while the blue and green lights have multiple functions, including S^D and $S^{r(cond)}$.

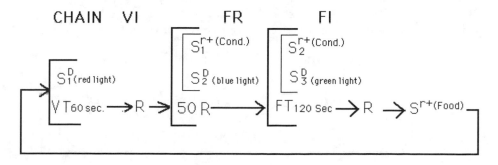

automatically comes on), and for this reason a conditioned reinforcing function is not demonstrated.

Multiple-Stimulus Functions

Consider a sequence of two schedules, FR 50 FI 120 seconds, in which the components are not signaled. Formally, this is called a **tandem schedule.** A tandem is a schedule of reinforcement in which primary reinforcement is programmed after completing two or more schedules, presented sequentially without discriminative stimuli. In other words, a tandem schedule as shown in Figure 11.2 is the same as an unsignaled chain.

Gollub (1958) compared the behavior of pigeons on similar tandem and chain schedules of reinforcement. On a tandem FI 60 seconds FI 60 seconds, performance resembled the pattern observed on a simple FI 120-second schedule. The birds produced the typical scallop pattern observed on fixed-interval schedules—pausing after the presentation of food, and accelerating in response rate to the moment of reinforcement. When the tandem schedule was changed to a chain FI 60 seconds FI 60 seconds by adding distinctive stimuli to the links, the effect of conditioned reinforcement was apparent. After some experience on the chain schedule, the birds responded faster in the initial link than they had on the tandem. In effect, the birds produced two FI scallops rather than one during the 120 seconds. This change in behavior may be attributed to the discriminative stimulus in the final link that also reinforced responses in the first component. In other words, the discriminative stimulus signaling the terminal link is also a conditioned reinforcer for responses in the first component of the chain (see also Ferster & Skinner, 1957).

Homogeneous and Heterogeneous Chains

Operant chains are classified as **homogeneous** when the topography or form of response is similar in each component. For example, in the chain schedule discussed earlier, the bird pecks the same key in each link. Because a similar response occurs in each component, this is a homogeneous chain. In contrast, a **heterogeneous** chain requires different responses for each link. Dog trainers make use of heterogeneous chains when they teach complex behavioral sequences to their animals. In going for a walk, a seeing-eye dog stops at intersections, moves forward when the traffic is clear, pauses at a curb, avoids potholes, and finds the

FIG. 11.2   A tandem schedule of reinforcement is the same as an unsignaled chain.

TANDEM   FR   FI

$$\rightarrow 50\,R \longrightarrow FT_{120\,Sec} \rightarrow R \rightarrow S^{r+(Food)}$$

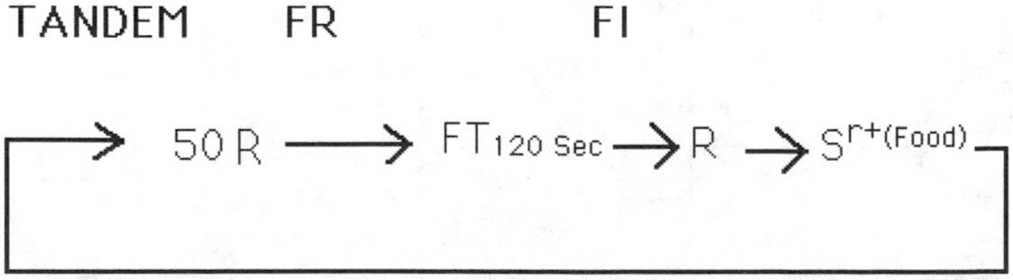

way home. Each of these different responses are occasioned by specific stimuli and result in conditioned reinforcement. Although heterogeneous chains are common in everyday life and are created easily in the laboratory, they are usually too complex for experimental analysis. For this reason, conditioned reinforcement is typically investigated with homogeneous chains.

Chain schedules show how sequences of behavior are maintained by conditioned reinforcement in everyday life. Acquired reinforcers in chains remain effective because the terminal link continues to schedule primary reinforcement. Viewed as a heterogeneous chain schedule, going to a restaurant may involve the following links: A person calls and makes a reservation, gets dressed for the occasion, drives to the restaurant, parks the car, enters and is seated, orders dinner, and eats the meal. In this example, the S^Ds are the completion of the response requirements for each link. That is, being dressed for dinner (S^D) sets the occasion for going to the car and driving to the restaurant. Conditioned reinforcement involves the opportunity to engage in the next activity—bringing you closer to primary reinforcement.

Of course, each of these components may be subdivided into finer and finer links in the chained performance. For example, dressing for dinner is comprised of many different responses with identifiable discriminative stimuli (e.g., putting on shoes sets the occasion for tying laces). Even tying shoelaces may be separated into finer and finer links of a heterogeneous chain. The degree of detail in describing a chain performance depends on the analytical problem. An analysis of going out for dinner does not require details about how a person ties his or her shoes. On the other hand, a behavior analyst teaching a retarded child to dress may focus on fine details of the chained performance.

FOCUS ON ISSUES
Backward Chaining

Imagine that you have just been hired as a behavioral technician at a group home for retarded children. One of your first assignments is to use the principle of conditioned reinforcement to teach a child to make his bed. The child is profoundly retarded and cannot easily follow instructions or examples. He does have good motor coordination and is reinforced by potato chips. You and the child are in one of the bedrooms with sheets, blankets, and pillowcases stacked on the bed. You have decided to use potato chips as a reinforcer for bed making.

Many people would start at the beginning of the sequence by unfolding a sheet, shaking it out, and placing it over the mattress. This tactic works for students (or children) who are easily able to follow instructions. However, this is not the case for this child and the initial links of the chain are far removed from primary reinforcement. Also, there are no conditioned reinforcers established along the way for completing the components.

The alternative way of teaching is to use a technique called **backward chaining**. The idea is to begin training at the end of the sequence. That is, you first teach the behavior in the final link of the chain. The child is reinforced with chips when he places the top of the bedspread over the pillow. Once this behavior is well established, the bedspread is pulled down further. Primary reinforcement now occurs when the child pulls covers up to the pillow and then finishes making the bed. In this manner, responses that are more and more remote from the final performance are maintained by conditioned reinforcement (engaging in the next sequence). Of course, you eventually pair chips with social approval (i.e., "Your bed looks great!") and maintain the behavior without direct primary reinforcement.

In everyday life, backward chaining has been used to train athletic skills. O'Brien and Simek (1983) taught golf using principles of backward chaining. In their article they state:

> the teaching of sports has been largely unaffected by the advances in learning other oper-
> ants. Golf, for example, is still routinely taught by handing the novice a driver and in-
> structing him verbally how to get his body, arms and head to combine to hit a 250 yard
> drive. The usual result of such instruction is a series of swings that end in wiffs, tops and
> divots. This is followed by more verbal explanations, some highly complex modeling, and
> loosely administered feedback. Endless repetitions of this chain then follow.
>
> A behavioral analysis of golf would suggest that the reinforcer for this exercise is
> putting the ball in the hole. The trip from tee to green represents a complex response
> chain in which the swing of the club up over the head and back to hit the ball is short-
> ened as one gets closer to the hole. The final shot may be a putt of six inches or less lead-
> ing to the reinforcement of seeing the ball disappear into the ground. This putt requires a
> backswing of only a few inches but involves the same basic stroke as the long back-
> swinged shot from the tee. Since the short putt seems to be the simplest response and the
> one closest to reinforcement, it would seem appropriate to teach the golf chain by starting
> with the putt and working back to the drive. (pp. 175–176)

O'Brien and Simek designed two experiments to compare the acquisition of golf by backward chaining against traditional teaching methods.

In one of their experiments, 12 college students were randomly assigned to eight lessons of backward chaining or traditional methods of learning golf. Students in both groups received standard instruction from an amateur golfer who had experience teaching the sport. In the backward-chaining condition, students were first taught to make 6-inch putts until they were able to sink the ball four times in a row. Over a series of 10 steps, the putting distance was increased to 30 feet, and the students consistently had to come within 2 feet of the hole. Next, approach shots using clubs appropriate to the distance from the hole were trained to a stipulated criterion. On the last step, a 200-yard shot from the tee had to come within 90 feet of the hole one-third of the time.

After eight lessons, students in both groups played 18 holes of golf on a course that was rated by The Professional Golfers Association as par 70 or moderately difficult. The average score for the backward-chaining group was 98 strokes, and the traditional group scored 116 swings. Four out of six golfers in the backward-chaining condition broke 100 strokes, but only one of the traditionally taught students was able to do this.

The superiority of the backward-chaining method in athletics or other areas of learning results from the principle of conditioned reinforcement. Behavior that is closest to primary reinforcement is taught first. By doing this, the instructor ensures that operants in the sequence are maintained by effective consequences. With this method, each step in the chain may be added as the previous link is mastered.

DETERMINANTS OF CONDITIONED REINFORCEMENT

Operant chains show how complex sequences of behavior can be maintained by events that have acquired a reinforcement function based on the past experience of an organism. The task for experimental analysis is to identify the critical conditions that contribute to the strength of conditioned reinforcement. It is also important to specify the factors that determine the reinforcing effectiveness of conditioned stimuli.

Strength of Conditioned Reinforcement

Frequency of Primary Reinforcement. The effectiveness of a conditioned reinforcer depends on the frequency of primary reinforcement correlated with it. Autor (1960) found that preference for a conditioned reinforcer increased with the frequency of primary reinforcement in its presence. The power or effectiveness of a conditioned reinforcer increases with more and more presentations of primary reinforcement, but eventually levels off. As the frequency of primary reinforcement goes up, the strength of a conditioned reinforcer reaches a maximum value. This relationship is strikingly similar to the increase in associative strength of a CS as described by the Rescorla-Wagner model of classical conditioning (see Chapter 3).

Variability of Primary Reinforcement. Variability of primary reinforcement also affects the strength of a conditioned reinforcer. Fantino (1967) showed that birds preferred a conditioned reinforcer that was correlated with an alternating schedule (FR 1 half of the time and FR 99 for the other 50% of the trials) to one that was associated with a fixed schedule with the same rate of payoff (FR 50). Thus, variability of primary reinforcement increases the value of a conditioned reinforcer (see also Davison, 1969, 1972; Fantino, 1965; Herrnstein, 1964a). Variable schedules increase the effectiveness of conditioned reinforcement because these schedules occasionally program short intervals to reinforcement. Compared with fixed schedules, these short intervals enhance responding and the value of stimuli correlated with them (Herrnstein, 1964b).

Establishing Operations. The effectiveness of a conditioned reinforcer is enhanced by events that establish primary reinforcement. A bird will respond for a light correlated with food more when it is hungry than when it is well fed. People attend to signs for washrooms, restaurants, and hospitals when their bladders are full, they have not eaten for some time, or they are sick. Generally, conditioned reinforcement depends on stimuli that establish primary reinforcement (Michael, 1982a).

Delay to Primary Reinforcement. On a chain schedule, the longer the delay between a discriminative stimulus and primary reinforcement the less effective it is as a conditioned reinforcer. Gollub (1958) compared the performance of pigeons on three different schedules—FI 5 minutes, chain FI 1 FI 1 FI 1 FI 1 FI 1 minute, and tandem FI 1 FI 1 FI 1 FI 1 FI 1 minute. On the simple FI 5-minute schedule a blue key light was on throughout the interval. On the chain, a different key color was associated with each of the five links. The components of the tandem schedule were not signaled by separate colored lights, but a blue key light was on throughout the links. Birds responded to the tandem as they did to the simple FI—producing the typical FI scallop. On the extended chain schedule, responding was disrupted in the early components, and some of the birds stopped responding after prolonged exposure to the schedule (see also Fantino, 1969b). Disruption of responding occurs because the S^Ds in the early links (farthest from primary reinforcement) signal a long time to reinforcement and are weak conditioned reinforcers. A similar effect occurs when people give up when faced with a long and complex task. Students who drop out of school may do so because the signs of progress are weak conditioned reinforcers—far removed from a diploma or degree.

Establishing Conditioned Reinforcement

Many experiments have used an extinction procedure to investigate conditioned reinforcement. In most of these experiments, a conspicuous stimulus is presented just before the delivery of food. The new-response method involves pairing a distinctive stimulus such as a click with primary reinforcement. After several pairings, the stimulus is presented without primary reinforcement and is used to shape a new response. Another extinction technique is called the **established-response method.** An operant that produces primary reinforcement is accompanied by a distinctive stimulus, just prior to reinforcement. When responding is well established, extinction is implemented but half of the subjects continue to get the stimulus that accompanied primary reinforcement. The other subjects undergo extinction without the distinctive stimulus. Generally, subjects with the stimulus present respond more than the subjects who do not get the stimulus associated with primary reinforcement. This result is interpreted as evidence for the effects of conditioned reinforcement.

Pairing, Discrimination, and Conditioned Reinforcement.   Both extinction methods for analyzing conditioned reinforcement involve the presentation of a stimulus that was closely followed by primary reinforcement. This procedure is similar to CS-US pairings used in respondent conditioning. One interpretation, therefore, is that conditioned reinforcement is based on classical conditioning. This interpretation is called the stimulus-stimulus or **S-S account of conditioned reinforcement.** That is, all CSs are also conditioned reinforcers.

Although this is a straightforward account, the experimental procedures allow for an alternative analysis. In both the new-response and established-response methods, the stimulus (e.g., a click) sets the occasion for behavior that produces primary reinforcement. For example, the click of a feeder (S^D) sets the occasion for approaching the food tray (operant) and eating food (S^{r+}). Thus, the **discriminative-stimulus account** is that an S^D is a conditioned reinforcer only and does not function as a CS associated with food.

There have been many experiments that have attempted to distinguish between the S^D and S-S accounts of conditioned reinforcement (see Gollub, 1977;

Hendry, 1969, for reviews). For example, Schoenfeld, Antonitis, and Bersh (1950) presented a light for 1 second as an animal ate food. This procedure paired food and light, but the light could not be a discriminative stimulus since it did not precede the food delivery. Following this training, the animals were placed on extinction and there was no effect of conditioned reinforcement.

Given this finding, it seems reasonable to conclude that a stimulus must be discriminative in order to become a conditioned reinforcer. Unfortunately, current research shows that simultaneous pairing of CS and US results in weak conditioning (see Chapter 3). For this and other reasons, it has not been possible to have a definitive test of the S^D and S-S accounts of conditioned reinforcement.

On a practical level, distinguishing between these accounts of conditioned reinforcement makes little difference. In most situations, procedures that establish a stimulus as an S^D also result in that stimulus becoming a conditioned reinforcer. Similarly, when a stimulus is conditioned as a CS it almost always has an operant reinforcement function. In both cases, contemporary research (Fantino, 1977) suggests that the critical factor is the temporal delay between the onset of the stimulus and the later presentation of primary reinforcement.

Information and Conditioned Reinforcement. Stimuli that provide information about primary reinforcement may become effective conditioned reinforcers. Egger and Miller (1962) used the extinction method to test for conditioned reinforcement. They conditioned rats by pairing two different stimuli (S_1 and S_2) with food. Figure 11.3 describes the procedures and major results. In their experiment (panel A), S_1 came on and S_2 was presented a half-second later. Both

FIG. 11.3 Procedures and major results of an experiment by Egger and Miller (1962) using the extinction method to test for conditioned reinforcement (reprinted with permission of the *Journal of Experimental Psychology*).

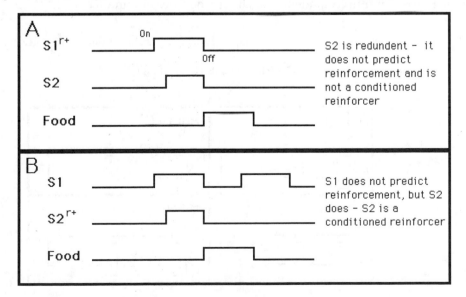

stimuli were turned off when the animals were given food. Both S_1 and S_2 were paired with food, but only S_1 became an effective conditioned reinforcer. In another condition (panel B), S_1 and S_2 were presented as before, but S_1 was occasionally presented alone. Food was never given when S_1 occurred by itself. Under these conditions, S_2 became a conditioned reinforcer.

To understand this experiment, consider the informativeness of S_2 in each situation. When S_1 and S_2 are equally correlated with food, but S2 always follows S_1, then S_2 is redundant—providing no additional information about the occurrence of food. Because it is redundant, S_2 gains little conditioned reinforcement value. In the second situation, S_1 only predicts food in the presence of S_2 and for this reason S_2 is informative and becomes a conditioned reinforcer. These results, along with later experiments (e.g., Egger & Miller, 1963), suggest that a stimulus will become a conditioned reinforcer if it provides information about the occurrence of primary reinforcement.

Good News and Bad News.   The informativeness of a stimulus should not depend on whether it is correlated with positive or negative events, because bad news is just as informative as good news. Wyckoff (1952, 1969) designed an observing-response procedure to evaluate the strength of a conditioned reinforcer that predicted good or bad news. In this procedure, periods of reinforcement and extinction alternate throughout a session, but the contingencies are not signaled by S^Ds or S^Δs. The contingency is called a **mixed schedule of reinforcement.** A mixed schedule is the same as a multiple schedule, but without discriminative stimuli. Once the animal is responding on the mixed schedule, an observing response is added to the contingencies. The observing response is a topographically different operant that functions to produce an S^D or S^Δ depending on whether reinforcement or extinction is in effect. In other words, an observing response changes the mixed to a multiple schedule. Figure 11.4 shows the relationships among mixed, multiple, tandem, and chain schedules of reinforcement.

FIG. 11.4 The relationships among mixed, multiple, tandem, and chain schedules of reinforcement.

PRIMARY REINFORCEMENT

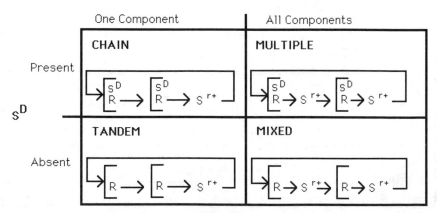

Wyckoff (1969) showed that pigeons would stand on a pedal in order to observe red and green colors associated with FI 30-second reinforcement or EXT 30 seconds. Before the birds had an observing response available, they pecked equally in the reinforcement and extinction phases—showing failure to discriminate the schedules. When the observing response was added, the pigeons showed a high rate of pecking in the reinforcement phase and very low rates during extinction. Because the observing response was maintained, the results suggest that stimuli correlated with either reinforcement or extinction (good or bad news) became conditioned reinforcers.

Although Wyckoff's data are consistent with an information view of conditioned reinforcement, it is noteworthy that his pigeons only spent about 50% of the time making the observing response. One possibility is that the birds were observing the stimulus correlated with reinforcement (red color) but not the stimulus that signaled extinction (green color). In other words, the birds may have only responded for good news.

In fact, a subsequent experiment by Dinsmoor et al. (1972) supported the good-news interpretation of conditioned reinforcement. Pigeons were trained to peck a key on a VI 30-second schedule of food reinforcement that alternated with unpredictable periods of extinction. The birds could peck another key in order to turn on a green light correlated with reinforcement and a red light correlated with extinction. That is, if reinforcement was in effect, an observing response turned on the green light, and if extinction was occurring, the response turned on the red light.

Observing responses were maintained when they produced information about both reinforcement and extinction. In the next part of the experiment, observing responses only produced the green light signaling reinforcement, or the red light associated with extinction. In this case, observing responses produced either good or bad news, but not both. When observing responses resulted in the green light correlated with reinforcement, the birds pecked at a high rate. In contrast, the pigeons would not peck a key that only produced a stimulus (red) signaling extinction. Thus, good news functions as conditioned reinforcement, but bad news does not.

The good-news conclusion is also supported by research using aversive, rather than positive, consequences. Badia, Harsh, Coker, and Abbott (1976) exposed rats to electric shocks. The shocks were delivered on several variable-time schedules, independent of the rats' behavior. During training, a light was always on and a tone occurred just before each shock. In Experiment 2 of their study, the researchers allowed the animals to press a lever that turned on the light for 1 minute. During this time, if shocks were scheduled, they were signaled by a tone. In one condition, the light was never accompanied by tone and shocks. That is, when the light was on the animal was completely safe from shocks. Other conditions presented more and more tones and shocks when the animal turned on the light. In these conditions, the light predicted less and less safety, and responding for the light decreased. In other words, the animals responded for a stimulus correlated with a shock-free period, but not for information about shock given by the tone signals (see also DeFran, 1972; Dinsmoor, Flint, Smith, & Viemeister, 1969). Once again, conditioned reinforcement is based on good news but not on bad news.

There are human examples of the good- and bad-news effect. Students who usually do well on mathematics exams quickly look up their marks on posted lists, while those who have done poorly wait for their grades to come in the mail. Seeing a grade is a conditioned reinforcer for students who are skilled at mathematics, but not for those who find the subject difficult. People who have taken care of their teeth find it easy to make a dental appointment, but those with inadequate dental health postpone the visit. Visiting the dentist is a safe period for patients with good teeth, but it signals "pulling and drilling" for those with poor dental hygiene. Unfortunately, the worse things get in such situations, the less likely people are to do anything about them—until it is too late.

Overall, research has shown that stimuli correlated with positive or negative reinforcement maintain an observing response (Dinsmoor et al., 1972; Fantino, 1977), and stimuli that are correlated with extinction or punishment do not (Blanchard, 1975; Jenkins & Boakes, 1973; Katz, 1976). For this reason, the mere informativeness of a stimulus is not the basis of conditioned reinforcement.

DELAY REDUCTION AND CONDITIONED REINFORCEMENT

Fantino and Logan (1979) have reviewed the observing response studies and point out that:

> only the more positively valued of two stimuli should maintain observing, since the less positive stimulus is correlated with an increase, not a reduction, in time to positive reinforcement (or a reduction, not an increase, in time to an aversive event).... Conditioned reinforcers are those stimuli correlated with a reduction in time to reinforcement (or an increase in time to an aversive event). (p. 207)

This statement is based on Edmund Fantino's (1969a) **delay-reduction hypothesis.** Stimuli closer in time to positive reinforcement, or further in time from an aversive event, are more effective conditioned reinforcers. Stimuli that signal no reduction in time to reinforcement (S^Δ) or no safety from an aversive event (S^{ave}) do not function as conditioned reinforcement. Generally, the value of a conditioned reinforcer is due to its delay reduction—how close it is to reinforcement or how far it is from punishment.

Modern views of conditioned reinforcement are largely based on the concept of delay reduction (Fantino, 1969a; Squires & Fantino, 1971). The idea is to compare the relative value of two (or more) stimuli that are correlated with different amounts of time to reinforcement. To do this, a complex-choice procedure involving concurrent-chains schedules is used. On these schedules, an organism may choose between alternatives that signal different amounts of time to reinforcement.

Concurrent-Chains Schedules of Reinforcement

In Chapter 10, we discussed the analysis of choice based on concurrent schedules of reinforcement. We have also noted the importance of chains schedules for the study of conditioned reinforcement. These schedules allow a researcher to change the temporal location of a stimulus in relation to primary reinforcement. For example, the terminal-link discriminative stimulus (S^D2) on a chain VI 20 seconds VI 10 seconds is six times closer to primary reinforcement than it is on a chain VI 20 seconds VI 60 seconds. This relation is shown in Figure 11.5. In terms of time, the terminal-link S^D that is closest to primary reinforcement should be a stronger conditioned reinforcer than one associated with a longer delay. Thus, the terminal-link S^D accompanying the VI 10-second schedule ought to be a more effective conditioned reinforcer than a discriminative stimulus correlated with VI 60 seconds.

To assess the effects of delay, organisms must be able to choose between stimuli associated with different reductions in time to primary reinforcement. For example, using a two-key choice procedure, a chain VI 20 seconds VI 10 seconds may be programmed on the left key and a chain VI 20 seconds VI 60 seconds on the right key.

This two-key **concurrent-chains** procedure is diagrammed in Figure 11.6. Consider the situation in which responses to the left key are eventually reinforced with food. To start, both left and right keys are illuminated with white lights. A bird makes left- and right-key pecks and after the left VI 20-second schedule times out, the first peck to the left key has two effects. The light on the right key goes out and the VI 20-second schedule on that key stops timing. That is, the key becomes dark and inoperative. At the same time, the left key changes from white to a diamond pattern. In the presence of this pattern, pecking the left key is reinforced with food on a VI 10-second schedule. After primary reinforcement, both left and right keys are again illuminated white and the bird chooses between the two alternatives.

A similar sequence occurs when the right key times out and the bird pecks this key. The left key becomes dark and inoperative and the right key changes from white to a dotted pattern. In the presence of this pattern, pecking the right key is re-

FIG. 11.5 Comparison of chain VI 20 seconds VI 10 seconds with chain VI 20 seconds VI 60 seconds. Notice that the S^D closer to primary reinforcement should be a more effective conditioned reinforcer.

CHAIN VI 20 sec VI 10 sec

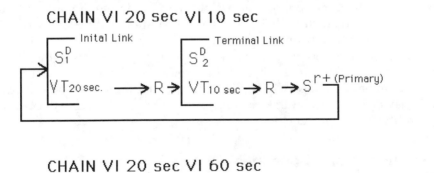

CHAIN VI 20 sec VI 60 sec

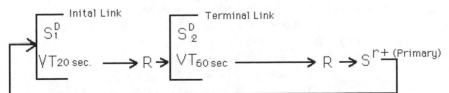

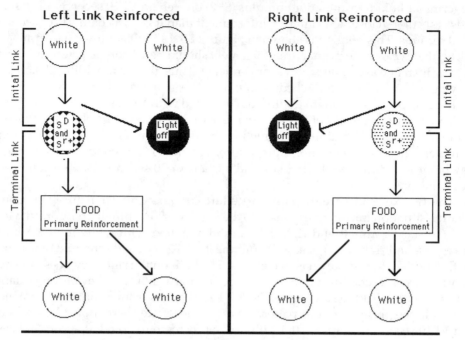

FIG. 11.6 A two-key concurrent-chains schedule of reinforcement. Chain VI 20 seconds VI 10 seconds is programmed on the left key, and a chain VI 20 seconds VI 60 seconds on the right.

inforced with food on a VI 60-second schedule. Following reinforcement, the discriminative stimuli in the initial links of the two chains (left and right white keys) are in effect and the bird again chooses to enter one of the terminal links (left or right).

The patterned stimuli on the left and right keys have two functions. These stimuli are S^Ds that set the occasion for pecking for food in the terminal links of the two chain schedules. In addition, the patterned stimuli function as conditioned reinforcement for pecking one or the other white keys in the initial links, or choice phase of the experiment. That is, reinforcement for pecking in the choice phase is the onset of the stimuli (S^D and S^r) associated with primary reinforcement in the terminal links. Because the bird is free to distribute pecks, the distribution of behavior in the initial links is a measure of the relative effectiveness of the two conditioned reinforcers.

Delay Reduction and Concurrent Chains

Humans often respond on concurrent-chains schedules of reinforcement. A businessperson who frequently flies from Kansas City to Denver may call either Delta or American Airlines to book a ticket. Many people are trying to book flights, and the telephone lines to both companies are always busy. To contact an agent, the businessperson calls one airline and then the other. Eventually, one of the calls is successful, but both companies have recorded messages that state, "All lines are busy at the moment; please hold until an agent is available." After waiting for some time, an agent answers and the ticket is booked.

In this example, calling the two airlines is the choice phase. The length of time to complete a call and get the hold message (initial-link schedules) is determined by the number of telephone lines at each airline and the number of people phoning the companies. The recorded message is conditioned reinforcement for dialing that company. The amount of time waiting on hold to book a flight (terminal-link schedule) is a function of the number of available agents. Waiting in the terminal link is reinforced by booking the flight. The sequence is repeated the next time the businessperson has a meeting in Denver.

To predict how much more (or less) reinforcing it is to be placed on hold at Delta relative to American Airlines, it is useful to consider a situation in which the initial- and terminal-link schedules are known for each company. Say that, on average, the telephone lines of both companies are busy for 120 seconds before a call is successful. In other words, the initial links for Delta and American are similar to concurrent VI 120-second schedules. The terminal-link schedules are different for the two airlines. It takes an average of 30 seconds to talk to a Delta agent after being placed on hold. That is, the terminal link for Delta is similar to a VI 30-second schedule. After being placed on hold at American, it takes an average of 90 seconds to reach an agent, so that the terminal link for American is similar to a VI 90-second schedule. Thus, the sequence for booking a ticket at Delta is chain VI 120 seconds VI 30 seconds, and it is chain VI 120 seconds VI 90 seconds at American.

In this situation, Fantino's delay-reduction hypothesis predicts that the businessperson will prefer Delta more than American. This is because more of the total time to reinforcement has elapsed when the person is placed on hold at Delta when compared to American. The conditioned reinforcement in this situation is getting the message, "All lines are busy at the moment; please hold until an agent is available." After the message occurs, it is faster to book a ticket at Delta compared with American. There has been relatively more reduction in delay to reinforcement when the Delta message occurs.

ADVANCED ISSUE
Quantitative Analysis of Conditioned Reinforcement

Consider how long it takes to get placed on hold at the two airlines. The average time to be placed on hold at both airlines is 120 seconds. If the person is dialing back and forth between Delta and American, the average time to get through is 120 seconds divided by the two choices, or 60 seconds (i.e., 120/2 = 60). This is because the initial-link schedules are simultaneously available and are both timing out.

Next, consider how long it takes to contact an agent once placed on hold at one or the other airlines. In this case, the person is stuck on hold at one airline and can no longer dial the other company. The average time in the terminal links of the two chains is 30 seconds for Delta plus 90 seconds for American divided by the two links, or 60 seconds [i.e., $(30 + 90)/2 = 60$]. That is, over many bookings the person has sometimes waited 90 seconds for an American agent and at other times 30 seconds for a Delta agent. On average, the length of time spent waiting on hold is 60 seconds.

Based on the average times in the initial and terminal links (60 seconds + 60 seconds), the overall average total time, T, to book a flight is 120 seconds or 2 minutes. Given that it takes an average of $T = 120$ seconds to book a flight, how much will the businessperson prefer booking at Delta relative to American Airlines? Recall that it takes an average of 30 seconds to contact an agent at Delta and 90 seconds at American, after being placed on hold. This terminal-link time is represented as $t_{2\,DELTA} = 30$ seconds, and $t_{2\,AMERICAN} = 90$ seconds.

Of the average total time, 90 seconds has elapsed when the person is placed on hold at Delta ($T - t_{2\,DELTA} = 120 - 30 = 90$ seconds). That is, the reduction in delay to reinforcement (booking a flight) is 90 seconds at Delta. The delay reduction at American is 30 seconds ($T - t_{2\,AMERICAN} = 120 - 90 = 30$ seconds).

The greater the delay reduction at Delta relative to American, the more the conditioned reinforcement value of Delta compared with American. This relation may be expressed as follows:

$$\frac{R_{DELTA}}{R_{DELTA} + R_{AMERICAN}} = \frac{T - t_{2DELTA}}{(T - t_{2DELTA}) + (T - t_{2AMERICAN})}$$

$$= \frac{120 - 30}{(120 - 30) + (120 - 90)}$$

$$= \frac{90}{90 + 30}$$

$$= 0.75$$

The R values represent responses or, in this example, the number of calls to Delta (R_{DELTA}) and American ($R_{AMERICAN}$), respectively. The relative number of calls made to Delta is equal to the relative reduction in time to book a flight (reinforcement). This time is calculated as the proportion of delay reduction at Delta to the total delay reduction. According to the calculation, 0.75 or 75% of the businessperson's calls will be directed to Delta Airlines.

Experimental Test of Delay Reduction

Edmund Fantino (at the time of this writing, a professor of psychology at the University of California, San Diego) first proposed and tested the delay-reduction analysis of conditioned reinforcement. He was trained in operant conditioning at Harvard University, where he worked in B. F. Skinner's laboratory and graduated with a Ph.D. in 1964. After a brief stay at Yale University, he joined the faculty at San Diego and continued his research on the experimental analysis of choice. Fantino recounts his discovery of the delay-reduction hypothesis in the following passage:

> One of my first experiments at [San Diego], on choice behavior, was producing strange but consistent results in each of four pigeons. I was losing sleep over these results until one morning I awoke with the following hypothesis: Choice responses don't match rates of reinforcement of the outcomes but instead match the relative reduction in delay to reinforcement associated with these outcomes. This delay-reduction hypothesis then served to guide scores of experiments assessing its generality and limitations in areas such as choice, conditioned reinforcement, elicited responding, self-control, observing and experimental analogs of foraging decisions. (personal communication, Feb., 1992).

Fantino (1969a) proposed a general equation for preference on a concurrent-chains schedule that was based on delay reduction. Equation 11.1 is a generalized statement of the formula used to calculate preference for Delta and American.

$$\frac{R_L}{R_L + R_R} = \frac{T - t_2}{(T - t_{2L}) + (T - t_{2R})} \tag{11.1}$$

In this equation, R_L and R_R represent the rate of response on the left and right initial links of a concurrent-chains schedule of reinforcement. The symbol T is the average time to reinforcement (see the airlines example for calculation). The time required in the left and right terminal links is represented by t_{2L} and t_{2R} in the equation. The equation states that relative rate of response is a function of relative reduction in time to primary reinforcement.

The delay-reduction equation emphasizes conditioned reinforcement as a major determinant of choice. This is because the onset of the terminal-link S^D for each chain is correlated with a reduction in time to primary reinforcement. This reduction is $T - t_{2L}$ for the left alternative and is $T - t_{2R}$ for the right. Recall that the greater the reduction in time to primary

FIG. 11.7 Edmund Fantino.

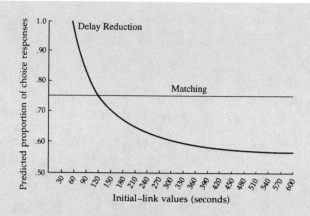

FIG. 11.8 Proportion of responses predicted by the delay-reduction equation for the shorter (VI 30 seconds) terminal link as time is added equally to the initial links of the concurrent-chains schedule (reprinted from Figure 1 of Fantino, 1969b; copyright 1969 by the Society for the Experimental Analysis of Behavior, Inc.).

reinforcement signaled by a stimulus, the greater the conditioned-reinforcement value of that stimulus. The delay-reduction equation is a mathematical expression of this idea.

Fantino (1969a) designed an experiment to test the delay-reduction equation. The subjects were six pigeons who responded for food on concurrent-chains schedules of reinforcement. In this experiment, the terminal links were always set at t_{2L} = 30 seconds and t_{2R} = 90 seconds. Notice that for the left alternative the relative rate of primary reinforcement is 0.75 and according to the matching law the birds should spend 75% of their time on the left key. The situation becomes more complex when initial-link schedules are varied. Fantino's experiment involved adding initial links to the VI 30-second and VI 90-second schedules. That is, he investigated concurrent-chains schedules with 30- and 90-second terminal links. The schedules in the initial links were always the same for both alternatives, but the values of these schedules were varied over the course of the experiment. For example, in one condition the initial links were VI 30 seconds on the left and VI 30 seconds on the right. In another condition, the initial-link schedules were both VI 600 seconds. Other initial-link values between these two extremes were also investigated. The important question is what happens to the pigeons' preference for the shorter (VI 30 seconds) terminal link as time is increased in the first link of the chains.

Figure 11.8 shows the proportion of responses predicted by Equation 11.1 for the shorter (VI 30 seconds) terminal link as time is added equally to the initial links of the concurrent-chains schedule. When the schedules were chain VI 30 seconds VI 30 seconds on the left and chain VI 30 seconds VI 90 seconds on the right, the birds responded almost exclusively to the left alternative. When the chains were VI 120 seconds VI 30 seconds on the left and VI 120 seconds VI 90 seconds on the right, the pigeons showed response distributions close to matching (0.75 responses on the left). Finally, when time in the initial links was greatly increased to VI 600 seconds, the birds showed no preference for either alternative. As you can see in Figure 11.8, these results are in accord with the declining preference predicted by the delay-reduction equation.

GENERALIZED CONDITIONED REINFORCEMENT

Formally, a **generalized conditioned reinforcer** is any event or stimulus that is associated with, or exchangeable for, many sources of primary reinforcement. Generalized reinforcement does not depend on deprivation or satiation for any specific reinforcer. Skinner (1953) describes its effects in the following passage:

> A conditioned reinforcer is generalized when it is paired with more than one primary reinforcer. The generalized reinforcer is useful because the momentary condition of the organism is not likely to be important. The operant strength generated by a single reinforcement is observed only under an appropriate condition of deprivation—when we reinforce with food, we gain control over the hungry man. But if a conditioned reinforcer has been paired with reinforcers appropriate to many conditions, at least one appropriate state of deprivation is more likely to prevail upon a later occasion. A response is therefore more likely to occur. When we reinforce with money, for example, our subsequent control is relatively independent of momentary deprivations. (p. 77)

Generalized Social Reinforcement

A major source of generalized reinforcement is mediated by the behavior of other people. Social consequences such as praise, attention, status, and affection are powerful reinforcers for most people. Approval, attention, affection, and praise function as **generalized social reinforcement** for human behavior (see Kazdin & Klock, 1973; Kirby & Shields, 1972; Ruggles & LeBlanc, 1982). In a classroom, a child's misbehavior may be followed regularly by attention, as when the teacher says, "What are you doing out of your seat?" The teacher may complain that the student is an unmanageable child. But the problem may concern the social reinforcement contingency between the student's misbehavior and the teacher attention.

Misbehavior usually captures the teacher's attention because it is highly intense (even aggressive) activity. Attention is reinforcing to most children because it necessarily precedes other types of reinforcement from people. When attention is contingent on misbehavior, then misbehavior increases. The solution to the problem is not to change the child, but to alter the contingency of reinforcement. One possibility is to ignore misbehavior (extinction) and attend to the child at any time other than when he or she is misbehaving (differential reinforcement of other behavior, or DRO).

The importance of generalized social reinforcement involving approval and affection is recognized in the following passage from Skinner (1953):

> Another person is likely to reinforce only that part of one's behavior of which he approves, and any sign of his *approval* therefore becomes reinforcing in its own right. Behavior which evokes a smile or the verbal response "That's right" or "Good" or any other commendation is strengthened. We use this generalized reinforcer to establish and shape the behavior of others, particularly in education. For example, we teach both children and adults to speak correctly by saying "That's right" when appropriate behavior is emitted.

A still stronger generalized reinforcer is *affection*. It may be especially connected with sexual contact as a primary reinforcer but when anyone who shows affection supplies other kinds of reinforcement as well, the effect is generalized.

It is difficult to define, observe, and measure attention, approval, and affection. They are not things but aspects of the behavior of others. Their subtle physical dimensions present difficulties not only for the scientist who must study them but also for the individual who is reinforced by them. If we do not easily see that someone is paying attention or that he approves or is affectionate, our behavior will not be consistently reinforced. It may therefore be weak, may tend to occur at the wrong time, and so on. We do not "know what to do to get attention or affection or when to do it." The child struggling for attention, the lover for a sign of affection, and the artist for professional approval show the persevering behavior which . . . results from only intermittent reinforcement. (pp. 78–79)

Skinner goes on to discuss the submissiveness of others as generalized reinforcement (see also Patterson, 1982). In an aggressive episode, two people use threats and possibly physical attack to control each other's behavior. Eventually, one of the combatants gives up, and this submissive behavior serves as reinforcement for the aggressive behavior of the other person. Giving up the argument often results in cessation of the attack by the aggressor, and this is reinforcement for the submissive behavior displayed by the other. Unfortunately, the contingencies of aggression and submission arrange for an indefinite escalation of conflict, which may inadvertently result in serious harm that is legally judged as assault or murder.

The contingencies of aggression may account for many instances of abuse involving children, spouses, the elderly, and individuals incarcerated in prisons and mental hospitals. To the extent that these people are dependent on the benevolence of their parents, spouses, or caretakers, they must give in to the demands of their keepers. Consider a woman who is unemployed, has few friends, and is married to a man who physically assaults her. When her husband becomes aggressive, she has little recourse other than submission. If she calls the police or tells a neighbor, she risks losing her home and income, and she may have learned that her husband will only become more angry. For these reasons, the husband's aggressive behavior is shaped to more extreme levels.

Occasionally, victims develop an emotional attachment to the people who mistreat them. This kind of affectionate behavior may be shaped as part of the aggressive episode. The contingencies could involve negative reinforcement, as when the aggressor's attack is reduced or removed by signs of affection from the victim. After some exposure to these contingencies, victims may even claim to love their abusers.

There are several steps that may be taken to reduce the incidence of victim abuse in our society. One solution involves the issue of control and countercontrol. To prevent abusive control, the victim must be able to arrange consequences that deter the actions of the aggressor. This countercontrol by victims is established when society provides agencies or individuals who monitor abusers and take action on behalf of the victims. Countercontrol may also involve passing laws to protect the rights of persons who are in highly dependent situations. Another possibility is to teach alternative behavior in terms of negotiation and conflict resolution. Finally, a society that supports aggression for entertainment in sports, television, and movies should not be surprised at having high levels of violence in daily life.

Tokens, Money, and Generalized Reinforcement

Other conditioned reinforcers are economic in the sense of being exchangeable for goods and services. Awards, prizes, and scholarships support an enormous range of human activity. Perhaps the most important source of economic reinforcement is money. One way to understand the reinforcing effects of money is to view it as a type of token (coins or bills) exchangeable at a later time for a variety of goods and services.

Token reinforcement has been demonstrated in chimpanzees (Figure 11.9; see also Cowles, 1937). Chimpanzees were trained to exchange poker chips for raisins. After tokens and fruit were paired, the animals learned to select one of several patterns to get poker chips that were later exchanged for raisins. The animals collected several tokens and went to another room, where they inserted the chips in a vending machine for raisins. Because the discriminative operant (pattern selection) was maintained, the chips were by definition conditioned reinforcers.

Another study (Wolfe, 1936) also showed that chimpanzees would tolerate a delay between getting a token and exchanging it for food. The animals earned white chips, which could be inserted into a vending machine that immediately

FIG. 11.9 Token reinforcement and chimpanzee behavior (with permission from Yerkes Regional Primate Research Center of Emory University.)

delivered grapes. Inserting the chip into the machine was shaped by successive approximation. The experimenter placed a token partway in the vending slot, and any push by the chimpanzee caused the chip to drop—resulting in a grape. This procedure continued until the animals started retrieving the chips and inserting them in the slot. Following this training, the animals were taught to pull a lever to get chips. At this point, access to the vending machine was delayed but the chimpanzees continued to work for tokens. Some animals even began saving their tokens much like people save money. When delays occurred after the chimpanzees had inserted the tokens into the vending machine, the reinforcing effectiveness of the tokens declined. This suggests that the token bridged the interval between earning and spending.

For people, money also functions to bridge long delays between earning and spending. A major difference between the chimpanzees' tokens and money is that money is exchangeable for many different reinforcers. For this reason, money is a generalized conditioned reinforcer. Most behavioral experiments involving humans have used money as reinforcement. Money is relatively independent of momentary deprivation, is easily quantified, and is exchangeable for numerous goods and services outside of the laboratory.

Schedules of monetary reinforcement have been used to assess matching (see Chapter 10) and delay reduction with humans. Belke, Pierce, and Powell (1989) created a human-operant chamber, and people were required to pick up tokens from a dispenser and exchange them for 25¢ a piece. At first, a single token was exchanged for 25¢, then two tokens for 50¢, and then four tokens for $1. By extending the delay between earning and exchanging tokens, subjects learned to collect up to 40 tokens before trading them for $10.

In this experiment, there were no instructions and pressing left or right keys was shaped by monetary reinforcement. Various reinforcement schedules were then programmed to test matching, maximizing, and delay-reduction accounts of human choice and preference. Human performance on monetary schedules of reinforcement was better described by matching and maximizing models than by the delay-reduction equation. Relative rate of monetary reinforcement was the most important determinant of behavior in this situation.

The applied advantage of money and tokens is that they are tangible objects that are observed easily, and their exchange value can be specified precisely. For this reason, a large amount of research has been conducted on experimental communities in which economic reinforcement is scheduled for effective patterns of behavior.

ON THE APPLIED SIDE

The Token Economy

One of the most important applications of behavior analysis is based on using tokens as generalized conditioned reinforcement. Tokens are arbitrary items like poker chips, tickets, coins, checkmarks in a daily log, and stars or happy-face symbols given to students. To establish these objects as reinforcement, the applied researcher has a person exchange tokens for a variety of backup reinforcers.

A child may exchange five stars for a period of free play, a selection of toys, access to drawing materials, or an opportunity to use a LEGO™ set.

A **token economy** is a set of contingencies or a system based on token reinforcement. That is, the contingencies specify when, and under what conditions, particular forms of behavior are reinforced with tokens. It is an economy in the sense that the tokens may be exchanged for goods and services much like money is in our economy. This exchange of tokens for a variety of backup reinforcers ensures that the tokens become conditioned reinforcers.

Systems of token reinforcement have been used to improve the behavior of psychiatric patients (Ayllon & Azrin, 1968), juvenile delinquents (Fixsen, Phillips, Phillips, & Wolf, 1976), pupils in remedial classrooms (Breyer & Allen, 1975), and medical patients who must follow a plan of treatment (Dapcich-Miura & Hovell, 1979). Token economies also have been designed for alcoholics, drug addicts, prisoners, nursing-home residents, and retarded persons (see Kazdin, 1977, for a review).

One of the first token systems was designed for psychiatric patients who lived in a large mental hospital. Schaefer and Martin (1966) attempted to modify the behavior of 40 female patients who were diagnosed as long-term schizophrenics. A general characteristic of these women was that they seemed disinterested in the activities and happenings on the ward. Additionally, many of the women showed little interest in personal hygiene (i.e., they showed a low probability for washing, grooming, brushing teeth, and so on). In general, Schaefer and Martin referred to this class of behavior as apathetic and designed a token system to increase social and physical involvement by these patients.

The women were randomly assigned to a treatment or control group. Women in the control group received tokens no matter what they did (i.e., noncontingent reinforcement). Patients in the contingent reinforcement group obtained tokens that could be traded for a variety of privileges and luxuries. Tokens were earned for specific classes of behavior. These response classes were personal hygiene, job performance, and social interaction. For example, a patient earned tokens when she spoke pleasantly to others during group therapy. A social response like "Good morning, how are you?" resulted in a ward attendant giving her a token and praising her effort. Other responses that were reinforced included personal hygiene like attractive use of cosmetics, showering, and generally maintaining a well-groomed appearance. Finally, tokens were earned for specified jobs such as wiping tables and vacuuming carpets and furniture.

Notice that the reinforcement system encouraged behavior that was incompatible with the label "apathetic." A person who is socially responsive, well groomed, and who carries out daily jobs is usually described as being involved with life. To implement the program, general response classes such as personal hygiene had to be specified and instances of each class, such as brushing teeth or combing hair, had to be defined. Once the behavior was well defined, ward staff were trained to identify positive instances and deliver tokens for appropriate responses.

Over a 3-month period of the study, the ward staff counted instances of involved and apathetic behavior. Responses in each class of behavior—hygiene, social interaction, and work—increased for women in the contingent-token system, but not for patients who were simply given the tokens. Responses that were successful in the token economy apparently were also effective outside the hospital.

Only 14% of the patients who were discharged from the token system returned to the hospital, and this compared favorably with an average return rate of 28%.

Although Schaefer and Martin (1966) successfully maintained behavioral gains after patients were discharged, not all token systems are equally effective (see Kazdin, 1983, for a review). Programs that teach social and life skills have lower return rates than those that do not. This presumably occurs because patients taught these skills can take better care of themselves and interact more appropriately with others. Of course, these operants are valued by members of the social community who reinforce and thereby maintain this behavior.

Token economies that gradually introduce the patient to the world outside the hospital also maintain behavior better than those programs with abrupt transitions from hospital to home. A patient on a token-economy ward may successively earn day passes, overnight stays, weekend release, discharge to a group home, and eventually a return to normal living. This gradual transition to everyday life has two major effects. Contrived reinforcement on the token system is slowly reduced or faded and, at the same time, natural consequences outside of the hospital are contacted. Second, the positive responses of patients are shifted from the relatively dense schedules of reinforcement provided by the token system to the more intermittent reinforcement of the ordinary environment.

Because of increasing budget constraints for many mental hospitals in the United States, there has been an alarming increase in the rapid discharge of psychiatric patients. Many of these individuals have been relegated to the ranks of the poor and homeless. According to our analysis of the token economy, this kind of policy is shortsighted. Programs that teach a range of useful skills and that allow for successful entry into work and community settings are more humane and economically productive in the long run. Generally, programs of behavior management and change offer alternative solutions for many social problems (Glenwick & Jason, 1980).

KEY WORDS

Backward chaining

Chain schedule of reinforcement

Concurrent-chains schedule

Conditioned reinforcement

Conditioned reinforcer

Delay-reduction hypothesis

Discriminative-stimulus account of conditioned reinforcement

Established-response method of conditioned reinforcement

Generalized conditioned reinforcer

Generalized social reinforcement

Heterogeneous chains schedule

Homogeneous chains schedule

Information account of conditioned reinforcement

Mixed schedule of reinforcement

New-response method for conditioned reinforcement

Primary reinforcer

S-S account of conditioned reinforcement

Tandem schedule

Token economy

CHAPTER 12

Verbal Behavior

LEARNING OBJECTIVES

1. How do behavior analysts use the term *verbal behavior*? What are some of the meanings of the term *language*? Why do Lee (1981a) and Catania (1984) argue against the use of the term *language* in behavior analysis? According to Skinner (1957), what is the study of verbal behavior?

2. Discuss the verbal interaction of speaker and listener, using a waiter and customer as an example. How does verbal behavior operate indirectly on the environment?

3. Describe the range of verbal behavior as outlined in this textbook.

4. Distinguish between speaking and listening in terms of function. What is the term used to describe the behavior of the listener?

5. Why does verbal behavior require special attention? What is the verbal community, and how does grammatical form depend on this community?

6. What is the name of Skinner's book on verbal behavior? Why is Skinner's analysis of verbal behavior better viewed as a set of testable hypotheses?

7. Provide a functional definition of a mand. Be able to diagram and describe a simple interaction sequence (cafeteria and ketchup) of a mand relation. What are the controlling variables of a mand relation? Give examples of manding in everyday life.

8. Give a functional definition of a tact. Be able to diagram and describe a simple verbal episode (teacher-student interaction) involving a tact relation. What are the controlling variables of a tact relation? Compare mand and tact relations. Give everyday examples of tacts that are difficult to distinguish from mands (or vice versa).

9. Be able to describe a conditional discrimination experiment with pigeons, involving red and green circles and similarly colored triangles.

10. Extend the conditional discrimination experiment to a child's behavior of naming the number and type of coins. Why is it inappropriate to call the conditional-discrimination performance of a pigeon verbal behavior?

11. Describe the Jack and Jill experiment concerning communication by pigeons. Be able to distinguish the contingencies regulating the behavior of speaker and listener.

12. Outline the Lubinski and MacCorquodale (1984) experiment on communication and generalized reinforcement. What is the value of experiments on communication by pigeons?

13. Give a behavior analysis of reporting on private events. Describe Lubinski and Thompson's (1987) experiment on the reporting of private stimulation by pigeons. What did additional experiments show? Why is this research important?

14. Give some common examples of symbolic behavior. Analyze the Jack and Jill experiment in terms of symbolic behavior and equivalence relations.

15. Define three basic equivalence relations. How are these relations examined in the laboratory (refer to identity and symbolic matching procedures)? Describe how identity matching is used to train reflexivity of color or form by pigeons.

16. Outline how symbolic matching is used to train and test for symmetry. Refer to the training of a color-to-form discrimination and the reversal test for emergent relations.

17. Building on the symmetry relation, how can transitivity be established? What tests are necessary to show transitivity?

18. What is the evidence that nonhuman subjects can pass tests for reflexivity, symmetry, and transitivity? What happens when retarded children who pass a test for reflexivity are reinforced for symbolic matching involving symmetry and transitivity?

19. Know what is meant by the functional independence of verbal response classes. How do researchers train mand relations? What is a blocked-response conditioned establishing operation, or CEO, and how did Hall and Sundberg (1987) use it?

20. Discuss other forms of mand training as used with chimpanzees. Compare the teaching of mands by pointing and speaking.

21. How is tacting trained? What procedural cautions must be used to insure tacting rather than manding? Outline Savage-Rumbaugh's (1984) training of tacts by chimpanzees. How did Michael, Whitley, and Hesse (1983) train pigeons to tact based on changes in response topography?

22. Describe behavioral experiments on tact training with language-delayed humans. How does this research relate to the question of functional independence of verbal response classes? Cite further evidence of tact training in humans involving positions and quantity of objects.

23. Define an intraverbal response. Give some common examples of intraverbals. How does intraverbal behavior relate to free association? Show that a serial learning of nonsense syllables tests for intraverbal relations.

24. Define an echoic response. Give an example of echoic (imitation) behavior using the game "pat a cake." Compare echoic behavior with the mere duplication of sound by some organisms. When is echoic behavior most prevalent in human speech?

25. What is a textual response? Give an example of textual behavior.

26. Outline Moerk's (1990) research on three-term contingencies and natural speech. Be able to state Moerk's observational categories. In terms of three-term sequences (e.g., mother-child-mother), what did Moerk's results show?

27. What is Moerk's evidence that the mother's behavior, saying "right" or repeating Eve's words, provided reinforcement for the child's utterances?

28. How do maternal expansions relate to the process of successive approximation? Describe how maternal expansion is important for acquisition of syntax. What is the overall importance of Moerk's research for behavior analysis?

Humans are social animals. Most of the daily life of people takes place in the company of others. An important aspect of human social behavior involves regulating others' actions by speaking, writing, signing, and gesturing. Behavior analysts use the term *verbal behavior* to refer to this kind of human activity. In this chapter, verbal behavior is analyzed according to the same principles of behavior that have been used throughout this book. The analysis explores the role of contingencies of reinforcement in the regulation of verbal behavior.

LANGUAGE AND VERBAL BEHAVIOR

People usually use the term *language* when they talk about speaking and other forms of communication. Although some researchers argue that language is behavior (Baer & Guess, 1971), others use the term to refer to a set of linguistic habits (Hockett, 1958, 1968), while still others point to the underlying mental rules that are presumed to organize spoken and written words (e.g., Chomsky, 1959). Finally, some view language as a cultural phenomenon that does not depend on individual behavior and mental rules (Sanders, 1974). As you can see, there is little agreement on the definition of language. The most important implication of this confusion is that language may not be a useful concept for a natural-science approach to speech (and other forms of verbal behavior).

In terms of behavior analysis, Lee (1981a) notes that language tends to obscure environment-behavior relationships. Language usually directs research attention to unobservable mental representations and processes, rather than to the objective conditions that influence the behavior of a speaker. Catania (1984) also has noted that the "language of reference" implicitly proceeds from words to objects in the world. The possibility that environmental contingencies regulate our speech is usually not considered. Catania (1984) states:

> We must therefore consider the possibility that the everyday vocabulary of language has prejudiced the ways in which we can analyze verbal behavior. Particular words are uttered or written in particular circumstances. We do not ordinarily say that we utter nouns in the presence of relevant objects, or that sentences are occasioned by relevant events. Instead we say that the words refer to objects, or that sentences are about events. There are good reasons for this usage in everyday vocabulary ... [but] the usage may be misleading when applied to the analysis of the behavior of speakers and listeners or readers and writers. (p. 221)

To rectify these problems, Skinner (1957) introduced the term *verbal behavior*. The term helps to redirect attention to the operating contingencies. In contrast with the term *language*, **verbal behavior** deals with the performance of a speaker and the environmental conditions that establish and maintain such performance.

VERBAL BEHAVIOR: SOME BASIC DISTINCTIONS

Verbal behavior refers to the vocal, written, and gestural performances of a speaker, writer, or communicator. This behavior operates on the listener, reader, or observer, who arranges for reinforcement of the verbal performance. A woman who is hungry may ask a waiter for "the tossed green salad with the egg sandwich." The speaker's behavior affects the listener, who in turn supplies reinforcement (i.e., placing the meal on the table). A similar effect is produced if the woman writes her order on a piece of paper. In this case, the written words function like the spoken ones; the waiter reads the order and brings the meal. Verbal behavior therefore expands the ways that humans can produce effects on the world.

Verbal behavior allows us to affect the environment indirectly. This contrasts with nonverbal behavior, which often results in direct and automatic consequences. When you walk toward an object, you come closer to it. If you lift a glass, there is a direct and automatic change in its position. Verbal behavior, on the other hand, only works through its effects on other people. To change the position of a lamp, the speaker says, "Lift the blue lamp at the back of the room" to a listener who is inclined to respond. Notice that reinforcement of the verbal response is not automatic, since many conditions may affect what the listener does. The listener may not hear you, may be distracted, or may not understand (i.e., picks up the red lamp rather than the blue one). Generally, the contingencies that regulate verbal behavior are complex, subtle, and highly flexible.

The Range of Verbal Behavior

Although verbal behavior is usually equated with speaking, vocal responses are only one of its forms. In addition to talking, a person emits gestures and body movements that indirectly operate on the environment through their effects on others. In most cultures, a frown sets the occasion for others to remove some aversive event, while a smile may signal the observer to behave in ways that produce positive reinforcement. In fact, frowns and smiles have such consistent and pervasive effects on others that some researchers have considered these gestures as universal symbols (Ekman, Friesen, & Ellsworth, 1972).

Another kind of verbal behavior involves manual signing rather than speech sounds. In American Sign Language (ASL), the speaker produces arm and hand movements that are functionally similar to speech sounds. In this case, regulation of the listener's behavior is along a visual dimension. Deaf speakers may also acquire complex finger movements known as "finger spelling" that function like

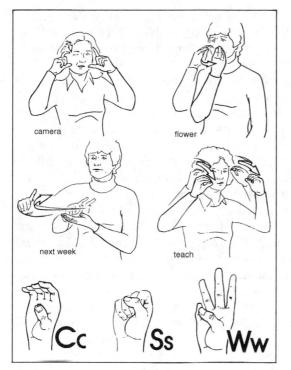

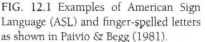

FIG. 12.1 Examples of American Sign Language (ASL) and finger-spelled letters as shown in Paivio & Begg (1981).

letters in the English alphabet. Figure 12.1 illustrates some of the basic manual movements of ASL and digital positions for finger spelling.

In the behavioral view, writing is verbal behavior that functions to regulate the behavior of a reader. Although written words and sentences have little formal similarity to spoken ones, the two modes of communication have equivalent functions. Recall that behavior analysts classify responses in terms of their functions, and for this reason both writing and speaking are commonly categorized as verbal operants.

Speaking, Listening, and the Verbal Community

The behavior of the speaker (or writer) is functionally different from the behavior of the listener (or reader). That is, the conditions that regulate speaking are distinct from those that affect listening. In the field of psycholinguistics, the distinction between speaking and listening is often blurred by talking about language encoding and decoding. Since both are treated as aspects of language (i.e., the transmission of meaning), there is little attempt to analyze the separate functions of such behavior. In fact, Skinner (1969) used the term **rule-governed behavior** to describe the behavior of the listener and *verbal behavior* to specify the performance of the speaker.

Rule-governed behavior refers to the effects of instructions, advice, maxims, and laws on the listener's behavior. In this view, rules are seen as complex discriminative stimuli, and the principles that govern stimulus control also regulate the behavior of the listener. While many behavior analysts have accepted this perspective, others have suggested that rule-governed behavior involves additional processes (see Parrott, 1987, for a discussion of these issues).

Regardless of one's view about the behavior of the listener, verbal behavior requires special attention because the consequences of verbal behavior are mediated by the actions of others. The way a person speaks is shaped by the consequences supplied by the listener. A busy mother may not respond to the polite response of "milk, please" by her child. However, a change in form to *"Give me milk!"* may induce compliance. Inadvertently, the mother is teaching her child to give commands in a loud voice. Subtle contingencies of reinforcement shape the style, dialect, tonal quality, and other properties of speaking.

The contingencies that regulate verbal behavior arise from the practices of people in the community. These practices are part of the culture of the group and they have evolved over time (Skinner, 1953). The practices of the **verbal community** therefore refer to the customary ways that people reinforce the behavior of a speaker. In an English-speaking community, the speaker who substitutes "also" for "in addition" or "besides" is likely to be reinforced, especially if repetition is bothersome to the listener. When linguists analyze the grammar of a language, they state rules that describe the reinforcing practices of the verbal community. For example, the grammatical rule *"i before e except after c"* describes a requirement for reinforcement set by the community; the written word *received* is reinforced while *recieved* is not. Thus, verbal behavior is established and maintained by the reinforcing practices of the community or culture.

OPERANT FUNCTIONS OF VERBAL BEHAVIOR

In his book *Verbal Behavior*, Skinner (1957) presented a preliminary analysis of this kind of human activity. Although some linguists have treated Skinner's work as a behavioral theory of language, it is more likely that the book represents a set of testable hypotheses about verbal behavior (MacCorquodale, 1970). Skinner described verbal behavior in terms of the principles found in the operant laboratory. Such an analysis must ultimately be judged in terms of its adequacy. That is, it must deal with the facts of the speaker's behavior in natural settings and the experimental evidence that supports or refutes such an account. In this section, the basic verbal classes are outlined using Skinner's (1957) distinctions as well as clarifications made by others (e.g., Michael, 1982b; Oah & Dickinson, 1989).

Mands and Tacts

Verbal behavior may be separated into two broad classes, mands and tacts, based on the regulating conditions. When you say "Give me the book," "Don't do that," "Stop," and so on, your words are regulated by motivational conditions—deprivation for the book, or another person doing something unpleasant. In behavior analysis, these verbal responses are called mands. The **mand** is a class of verbal

SPEAKER

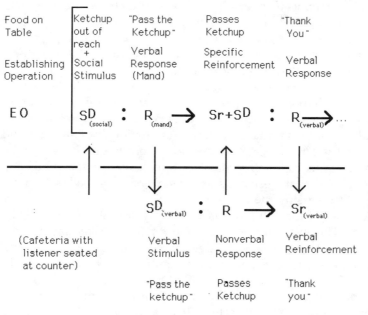

FIG. 12.2 Analysis of the mand relation between speaker and listener based on Skinner (1957). EO = establishing operation; S^D = discriminative stimulus; R = operant; S^r = reinforcement. See text for a description of the verbal contingencies.

operants whose form is regulated by specific establishing operations (e.g., deprivation, aversive stimulation, etc.). The word *mand* comes from the common English word *command*, but commands are only a small part of this operant class.

Figure 12.2 is a formal analysis of the mand relation. A verbal episode involves the social interaction of speaker and listener. The line through the middle of the diagram separates the speaker's events and actions from those of the listener. Each person completes a behavioral sequence or chain, and social interaction involves the intermingling of these chains.

In this example, we assume that two people are seated at a counter in a cafeteria. Dinner is placed in front of the speaker, but the ketchup is out of reach and situated near the listener. In this context, the presence of food on the table is an **establishing operation (EO)** for behavior that has produced ketchup in the past. The establishing operation also makes getting ketchup a reinforcing event in this situation.

In addition to the EO, the speaker's response ("pass the ketchup") in Figure 12.2 is regulated by the presence of ketchup near the listener or audience. The effect of the audience is shown as an arrow passing from the listener's side of the interaction to the speaker's side. If there were no other people in the restaurant, it is likely that the speaker would get out of his or her seat and get the ketchup. The presence of a listener increases the probability that the speaker will say "pass the ketchup" rather than get it himself or herself. This means that the audience functions as a discriminative stimulus (S^D) in this social episode. Together, the out-of-reach ketchup and the audience set the occasion for $(:)$ a verbal response (R_{mand}) by the speaker.

The speaker's verbal response of "pass the ketchup" affects the listener as a stimulus. The words are a verbal stimulus (S^D_{verbal}) that sets the occasion for the listener to pass the ketchup ($R_{nonverbal}$). In this episode, the listener's response of passing the ketchup is reinforcement for the speaker's verbal response (S^r). Since the speaker's verbal response produces specific reinforcement from the listener, the verbal response is formally a mand. As previously stated, a mand is a verbal response that is set up by an establishing operation (out-of-reach ketchup) and maintained by specific reinforcement (getting ketchup) delivered by a listener.

In this situation, the listener's response of passing the ketchup has dual functions ($S^r + S^D$). Passing the ketchup not only functions as reinforcement for the mand, but it also functions as a discriminative stimulus for the next response by the speaker. This event sets the occasion for the speaker saying "thank you," a verbal response that serves as social reinforcement for the listener's behavior. The "thank you" response also serves as the ending point for this social episode, releasing the listener from obligations with respect to the speaker.

Everyday examples of manding include asking someone for a glass of water when thirsty, or requesting directions from a stranger when lost. Notice that specific reinforcement is made effective for the mand by some motivating condition. A glass of water reinforces asking for it when you are deprived of water, and directions are reinforcement for requesting them when you are lost. The establishing operations have two effects: Such events increase the probability of an appropriate mand (i.e., asking for water, or requesting directions) and make a specific consequence momentarily effective (e.g., water, directions, etc.). Common forms of mands include speaking or writing orders, asking questions, requesting objects or things, giving flattering comments to others, and promoting commercial products (i.e., "buy this detergent").

There is another major class of verbal operants. The **tact** is defined as a class of verbal operants whose form is regulated by specific nonverbal discriminative stimuli. The word *tact* comes from the more familiar term *contact*. Tacts are verbal responses that make contact with the environment. Figure 12.3 is a formal analysis of the tact relation. As with the mand, the verbal episode begins with a speaker and listener. In this example, the speaker is a student and the listener is a teacher. The social interaction begins in a classroom with the teacher showing pictures of objects to a young student.

A picture of a red ball is displayed (S^{cond}), and the teacher says, "What color is the ball?" The teacher's question (R_{verbal}) supplies a verbal stimulus to the student. In this situation, the student's answer depends on both the nonverbal stimulus ($S^D_{red\ ball}$) and the teacher's question (S^D_{verbal}). Notice that the student will give a different answer if the question is, "What shape is the ball?"

The student's answer of "the ball is red" is formally a tact because it is regulated by a nonverbal stimulus (redness of ball). In this example, the student's tact produces a verbal stimulus (S^D_{verbal}) for the teacher that may or may not correspond to the specified physical property of the ball (SD_{red}). If the student's answer corresponds to the requested property, the teacher's question is reinforced (S^r).

In terms of analysis, the teacher's question, "What color is the ball?" is a mand. This verbal response is reinforced by correspondence between the student's tact and the actual color of the object. When correspondence occurs, this condition sets the occasion for the teacher saying, "Yes, that's right" and turning to the next picture (noncorrespondence may lead to repeating the question, perhaps in a different way). The teacher's verbal response supplies generalized reinforcement for the student's tact and functions to maintain the verbal response class. Finally, because the presentation of the next picture allows for the continuation of the lesson, this event is reinforcement for the teacher's behavior.

It is useful to compare the tact and mand relations. As we have seen in the teacher-student example, the form or topography of a tact depends on an appropriate nonverbal stimulus. The redness of the ball regulated the student's verbal response. In contrast, the mand depends on an establishing operation (EO) such as deprivation. Generalized reinforcement serves to strengthen and maintain the response class of tacts, but it does not determine the kind of response that occurs.

FIG. 12.3 Analysis of the tact relation between speaker and listener, based on Skinner (1957). S COND = conditional stimulus; SD = discriminative stimulus; R = operant; S^r = reinforcement. See text for a description of the verbal contingencies.

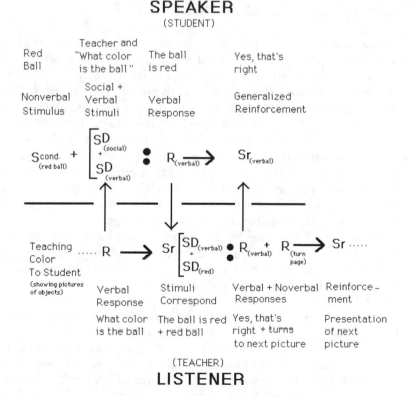

SPEAKER
(STUDENT)

(TEACHER)
LISTENER

As previously stated, the form of the tact depends on the nonverbal discriminative stimulus that precedes it. In terms of the mand, specific reinforcement is the major variable regulating the form of response.

Everyday examples of tacts include describing a scene, identifying objects, providing information about things or issues, and reporting on your own behavior and that of others. Occasionally, it is difficult to distinguish between mands and tacts. A person who says "I believe you have the sports page" may be tacting the nonverbal stimulus (the sports page), or manding specific reinforcement (getting the sports page). The issue is often resolved by the listener saying "Yes, I do" and returning to read the paper. If the original response was a mand, the listener's reply will not function as reinforcement. In this case, the speaker is likely to clarify the disguised mand by stating, "May I please have the sports page!"

Many advertisements and television commercials are disguised mands, in the sense that the verbal responses of an announcer seem to describe the benefits of the product (tacts), but are in fact requests to buy it (mands). Given these contingencies, listeners learn how to reveal the disguised mands of a speaker, and speakers learn to conceal their obvious mands of a listener. Persuasion and attitude change may be analyzed therefore in terms of mands, tacts, and the interaction of speakers and listeners (see Bem, 1965).

COMPLEX BEHAVIOR IN THE LABORATORY

Faced with the complexity of verbal behavior, many people find it hard to believe that basic behavior principles, such as stimulus control and schedules of reinforcement, can eventually account for this kind of human activity (see Chomsky, 1957). It is therefore useful to begin the analysis with a consideration of complex behavior in the laboratory. Although there are many distinctions between human verbal behavior and the behavior generated in pigeons, the laboratory analog is useful in identifying some of the contingencies that result in complex behavior.

Consider a **conditional-discrimination** experiment described by Catania (1980), in which a pigeon is placed in an operant chamber with left and right keys. Stimuli can be projected on the keys, and a light is situated in one corner of the response panel, allowing general illumination of the chamber (i.e., a houselight). The stimuli consist of red and green circles and similarly colored triangles. Centered below the keys is a feeder that provides reinforcement depending on the prevailing conditions. When the houselight is on, pecks to the keys are reinforced according to color (on = peck by color). If the houselight is off, pecks produce food on the basis of form (off = peck by form).

Figure 12.4 portrays the contingencies based on whether the houselight is on or off. During a session when the houselight is on, pecks to the left key are reinforced if the key colors are red (red = peck left key). Pecks to the right key produce food if the two keys are green (green = peck right key). Notice that the form of the stimuli (triangles or circles) has no function when the houselight is illuminated. In contrast, when the houselight is off, key pecks are reinforced depending on form, and color no longer has a stimulus function. If circles are presented,

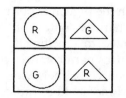

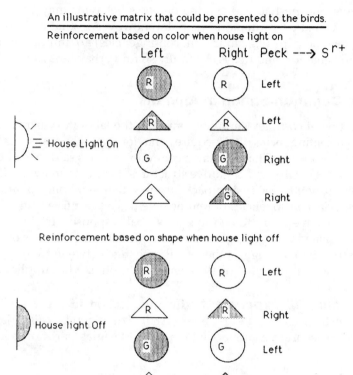

An illustrative matrix that could be presented to the birds.

FIG. 12.4 A conditional discrimination experiment as described in the text (the hypothetical experiment is based on Catania, 1984, and reprinted with the permission of *Behaviorism*).

pecks to the left key are reinforced (circles = peck left key). When triangles are projected, pecks to the right key produce food (triangles = peck right key).

Assuming that the bird's pecking is regulated by the appropriate stimuli, we may say that the performance demonstrates a conditional discrimination. Pecking the keys depends on color or form conditional on the illumination of the houselight. These conditional relations among stimuli and responses are also observed in verbal behavior. A child may provide the answer of "five" when presented with a picture of five dimes and the question, "How many coins?" When asked "What kind of coins are these?" the child will respond "dimes." This kind of verbal performance involves contingencies similar to the ones that produce conditional discrimination in the laboratory.

This does not mean that the pigeon's performance should be called verbal. The laboratory procedure shows that nonverbal processes (conditional discrimination) may play a role in verbal behavior. In the pigeon experiments, the bird responded to color and form only within the narrow context of the operant chamber. Verbal behavior in humans is not limited to specific situations or circumstances. You may also have noted that the bird's performance was maintained by food, and this is seldom the case with human verbal behavior. Additionally, no audience responded to the performance and mediated reinforcement. In each of these respects, and perhaps others, the pigeon's behavior may be distinguished from human verbal performance. The point, however, is that conditional stimulus-control relationships (e.g., four term contingencies) are important in an analysis of human behavior, and this is especially so for verbal behavior.

Symbolic Communication in Animals

One implication of complex stimulus control in the laboratory is that animals exposed to such contingencies often acquire behavior that in humans is said to reflect higher mental processes. That is, human communication is said to be caused by our expanded brain capacity and cognitive structures. Behavior analysts offer an alternative to the mental capacity approach, arguing that symbolic communication is caused by special contingencies of reinforcement. To test this assumption, nonhuman organisms have been trained to emit verbal responses. In this research, one subject is designated the speaker and the other the listener. The roles of speaker and listener are used here to suggest the verbal exchange between two organisms, one who asks for and uses information (listener) and the other who supplies it (speaker).

The Jack and Jill Experiment. Communication in pigeons was first reported by Epstein, Lanza, and Skinner (1980). The pigeons, called Jack and Jill, were placed in separate chambers with a clear Plexiglas partition between them

FIG. 12.5 The chambers and key arrangement for the Jack and Jill experiment as described by Epstein, Lanza, and Skinner (1980). R = red; Y = yellow; G = green. See text for a description of the contingencies.

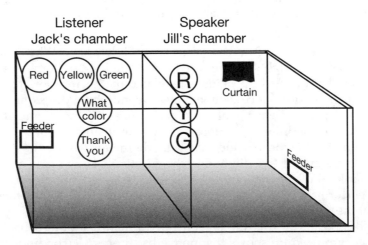

(see Figure 12.5). In the original procedure, Jack was the listener and Jill was the speaker (see Epstein & Skinner, 1981, for implications of training both birds as speaker and listener). The interaction began when Jack pecked a key with the words *What color?* on it. When this happened, one of three colors—red, green, or yellow—was illuminated in Jill's chamber. Importantly, the color of the light was hidden by a curtain and could not be seen by Jack.

The speaker, Jill, thrust her head behind the curtain and looked at the color. Following this, she pecked one of three symbol keys, labeled R, G, and Y (e.g., R = red), that matched the color behind the curtain. When Jack looked into Jill's chamber and saw which symbol she had pecked, he pecked a *Thank you* key that operated Jill's feeder. Following this, Jack pecked one of three colored keys in his chamber that corresponded to the symbol (R, G, or Y) selected by Jill. If Jack matched the color to the symbol, this response operated his feeder for a few seconds. After 5 days of this interaction, the pigeons were accurate on more than 90% of the trials.

Formally, the experiment involved training pigeons in the use of mands and tacts. The role of listener required the training of the mand, *What color?* The mand, in this case a question, is a verbal operant reinforced when the speaker supplies the answer, reporting a color by pecking one of the three symbol keys. This "report" by the speaker allows the listener to peck the corresponding color on his panel. Because pecking the correct color is part of a sequence that leads to food, hiding the color from the listener may be viewed as a conditioned establishing operation (blocked-response procedure) in this experiment.

The speaker's sequence is initiated when the listener pecks *What color?* In the presence of this verbal stimulus, the speaker must look at the color behind the curtain and report on the color. Pecking the correct symbol key is formally tact. The verbal response qualifies as a tact because it is controlled by a nonverbal aspect of the environment (the hidden color) and results in nonspecific reinforcement (i.e., the food supplied when the listener pecks *Thank you*). A nonspecific reinforcer is one that does not specify the form of a subsequent tact. The speaker pecks Y, G, or R (form of response) and is reinforced with grain. The presentation of grain at the end of the listener-speaker interaction does not control which color symbol the speaker pecks on the next trial.

Communication and Generalized Reinforcement.

In human communication, tacts emitted by a speaker almost never result in food reinforcement. It is therefore important to know whether pigeons will continue to tact when this behavior is supported by generalized conditioned reinforcement. An experiment by Lubinski and MacCorquodale (1984) was designed to answer such questions.

These researchers established a generalized conditioned reinforcer for the speaker by associating a flashing light with the presentation of both food and water. On some days the pigeon was food deprived, and on other days it was deprived of water. Occasionally, the bird was deprived of both food and water. When food deprived, the pigeon could peck a key that operated a feeder. When the bird was thirsty, it could peck a different key to produce water. Importantly, responses for food or water were only effective when a light was flashing in the chamber. The flashing light became a generalized reinforcer because it was associated with more than one source of primary reinforcement (food and water).

The interaction of the pigeons was similar to the performances of Jack and Jill (Epstein et al., 1980). This occurred even though the keys, procedures, and chambers were different (see Figure 12.6). As in the Jack and Jill experiment, one bird (the listener) started the interaction by pecking the *What color?* key. This response produced a letter (R, Y, or W) on the other bird's (the speaker) sample disk. The speaker then pecked one of three colored keys—red, yellow, or white—that corresponded to the letter on the sample disk. Notice that in this experiment by Lubinski and MacCorquodale (1984), the speaker is presented with a letter and reports by pecking the appropriate color; in the Jack and Jill experiment, the bird sees a color and reports by pecking a letter.

When the speaker pecked a colored key, the listener had to peck a *Thank you* key that activated a flashing light in the speaker's chamber. When the light started flashing, the speaker could produce reinforcement by pecking the food or water keys. The *Thank you* response also turned on a sample disk in the listener's chamber. The disk was illuminated with the color that corresponded to the one pecked by the speaker. Finally, the listener was reinforced with food if it pecked one of the three letter keys that matched the color presented on its sample disk. Overall, the birds were highly successful at mastering this kind of symbolic communication.

As the experiment progressed, the researchers tested whether the speaker would continue to emit tact responses (i.e., pecking the color key corresponding to a sample letter) when satiated on primary reinforcement. On some days the pigeon was satiated on both food and water, so that the only consequence of tacting was the flashing light (generalized conditioned reinforcement). Under these con-

FIG. 12.6 The chambers and key arrangements for speaker and listener in the experiment on generalized reinforcement and tacting as described by Lubinski and MacCorquodale (1984). R = red; Y = yellow; G = green. See text for a description of the contingencies.

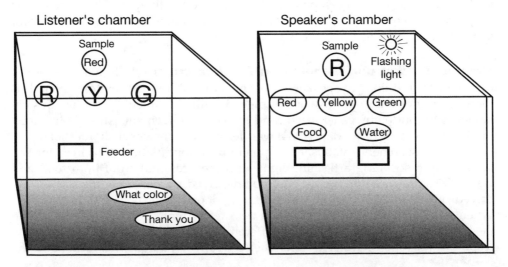

ditions, accurate tacting was maintained but the frequency of tact responses decreased substantially. Apparently, some level of deprivation is required on at least one reinforcement dimension to maintain the effectiveness of generalized reinforcement and a high probability of tact responses.

Research on nonhuman communication plays an important role in behavior analysis. In such experiments, the researcher must guess about the kind of experiences that allow for "language-like" verbal interactions. To do this, the behavior analyst must consider the principles of behavior and how they might apply to such a complex problem. Notice that communication depends on one organism manding (*What color?*) and the other tacting (e.g., pecking R for red). The behavior of the speaker supplies reinforcement (i.e., the color) for the listener's mand ("What color is it?"). The subsequent response by the listener, Thank *you*, provides generalized reinforcement for the speaker's tact. These sources of reinforcement maintain the interlocking behavioral sequences that compose a social interaction.

Although human communication involves far more than the manding and tacting of symbols and colors, these nonhuman experiments point to the basic elements that underlie symbolic communication. This research also shows that social interaction may arise from the simultaneous interplay of relatively simple principles of behavior—in this case, shaping, fading, chaining, and discrimination procedures.

FOCUS ON RESEARCH
Reports of Private Events by Pigeons

One of the actions that is said to separate humans from other animals is the ability to report on internal states and feelings. Behaviorists have maintained that humans do not have special capabilities that give them knowledge of themselves. Rather, behavior analysts suggest that self-description is something a person learns by interacting with others who ask questions about the person (e.g., "How do you feel?"). It is only because of special verbal contingencies that a person acquires a repertoire of self-description (Bem, 1965; Skinner, 1957).

As we have seen in earlier chapters, behavior analysts treat the internal and external happenings of an organism as physical events. The only difference between the external environment and the one inside of us is that internal events are private. This privacy means that internal events are less accessible to others and, as a result, it is more difficult for the verbal community to teach a person to describe internal events accurately.

When a verbal response is controlled by a nonverbal discriminative stimulus, this response is functionally defined as a tact. A person who has learned to describe the up-and-down flight of a butterfly may say "I have butterflies in my stomach" when upset or nervous. This response is analyzed as an extended or generalized tact—the person describes an upset stomach the same as a person describing the motion of a butterfly. This suggests that self-description is, in part, based on the verbal relations involved in tacting.

To set up a report on a private event (tact), it is necessary to have a public event that is well correlated with this private happening. For example, a bump on the head and crying usually accompany painful private stimulation. A child who bumps her head and cries may occasion the response "Oh, you're hurt" by the parent. In this situation, the child is asked where it hurts and how she feels. The youngster is reinforced when she accurately reports "I hurt my head" and "it hurts a lot." Although parents use public events (bumps and crying) to train self-description, the public cues are usually well correlated with private stimulation (physical damage). Because of this correspondence, private stimulation eventually comes to regulate self-descriptive responses (e.g., "I am hurt") even in the absence of public signs like crying.

The verbal relations that are presumed to set up a self-descriptive repertoire may be arranged in a laboratory. A pigeon is a useful organism to test these ideas because pigeons are not usually able to describe themselves. Lubinski and Thompson (1987) therefore used pigeons that were trained to discriminate among the private stimulation produced by different drugs and report how they felt in each condition. This is another example of communication in nonhuman organisms, but the experiment involves reporting on internal drug effects rather than external events like colors.

Two pigeons were placed in separate chambers, as shown in Figure 12.7. One bird was the "mander" and the other was the "tacter." The first step was to develop a generalized reinforcer for the tacter. That is, pecking a key for food or a key for water was reinforced only when a blue light was flashing (see Lubinski & MacCorquodale, 1984). After this training, the tacter bird was given a drug that was either a depressant, a stimulant, or a saline solution (salt water). Private stimulation consisted of introceptive effects produced by the different kinds of chemicals.

FIG. 12.7 The chambers and key arrangements for speaker and listener in the experiment on pigeons' reports of internal states as described by Lubinski and Thompson (1987; copyright 1987 by the Society for the Experimental Analysis of Behavior, Inc.).

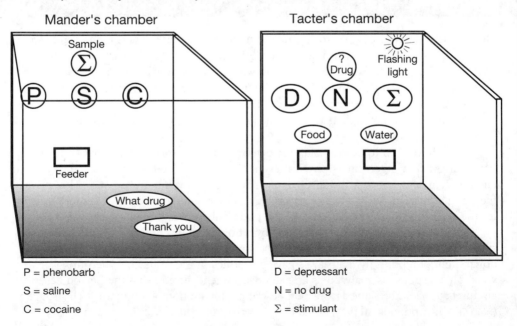

Mander's chamber

Tacter's chamber

P = phenobarb   D = depressant
S = saline   N = no drug
C = cocaine   Σ = stimulant

The interaction began with the mander (listener) pecking a *How do you feel?* key in its chamber. This response illuminated three keys in the tacter's (speaker's) chamber. Each key had a symbol, D for depressant, N for no drug, and Σ for stimulant. The tacter pecked a symbol key that corresponded to the drug it had received. When this occurred, a sample disk illuminated in the mander's chamber with the chosen symbol, and a *Thank you* key was illuminated. Pecks to this key by the manding bird activated a flashing blue light in the tacter's chamber. The tacting bird could then receive food or water by pecking the corresponding keys.

The interaction ended with the mander pecking one of three comparison keys that matched the sample (D, N, Σ) reported by the other bird. The mander's three keys had the letters S for saline, C for cocaine, and P for pentobarb. If the symbol N (no drug) was the sample, pecking the S key for saline resulted in food reinforcement. Reinforcement also occurred if the mander pecked its P key for pentobarb when D (depressant) was the sample, or pecked the C key for cocaine when Σ (stimulant) was the stimulus. Notice that this experiment is similar to the experiments in which pigeons reported on a hidden color or letter. The interesting twist on the procedure is that the bird reports an internal and private drug state ("boy oh boy, do I feel good!" = C).

Although these complex sequences took a long time to train, eventually the tacter's "reports" and the mander's "comprehensions" were highly accurate—exceeding 90% reliability. At this point, Lubinski and Thompson (1987) conducted additional experiments on the communication of internal events, in order to extend the findings to human behavior. In a test for generalization, the researchers substituted the drug Dexedrine (*d*-amphetamine) for cocaine and Librium (chlordiazpoxide) for pentobarbital. Although the Dexedrine and Librium differ chemically and pharmacologically from cocaine and pentobarbital, both share pharmacological properties with these agents. The generalization tests showed that accurate reporting of drug effects occurred even when the same bird was given a different depressant and stimulant. This finding suggested that the tacting response (i.e., pecking the symbol key that corresponded to the drug effect) had generalized to a class of drugs with common chemical effects. Most importantly, the experiments showed that accurate tacting of the drug effects could be maintained by generalized conditioned reinforcement. In this case, the tacting bird was satiated on food and water, and the only result of the report was the blue flashing light. Even though the number of tacts declined, the pigeon was still highly reliable at reporting on the internal effects of the drugs.

The research on private events by Lubinski and Thompson (1987) is an important step in the analysis of verbal behavior and self-description. The contingencies arranged by the researchers resulted in a complex sequence of behavior between two pigeons. When birds are exposed to verbal contingencies that are presumed to operate in human behavior, they begin to act something like humans—reporting on how they feel to one another.

Self-reference in humans is also trained through the socialization practices of the community (Bem, 1965). People in different parts of the world (e.g., India) are able to contact and describe internal events that are usually unavailable to North Americans. These people receive religious and educational training that make them more "aware" of themselves. Although mystical explanations have been given for such abilities, contingencies of reinforcement provide a scientific account of this kind of human behavior.

SYMBOLIC BEHAVIOR AND STIMULUS EQUIVALENCE

For most Americans, the flag is a significant symbol. When we see the flag, we may think of the United States, mother, and apple pie. This suggests that symbolic behavior involves the training of **stimulus equivalence.** The presentation of one class of stimuli (e.g., flags) occasions responses made to other stimulus classes (e.g., countries). This seems to be what we mean when we say that the flag stands for, represents, or signifies our country. Equivalence relations such as these are an important aspect of verbal behavior. For example, in teaching a child to read, spoken words (name of animals) are trained to visual stimuli (pictures of animals) and then to written symbols (written words for animals). Eventually, the written word is then said to stand for the actual object, in the same sense that a flag stands for a country. In this section, we will examine the behavior analysis of equivalent relations as an account of such symbolic activity.

Recall that symbolic communication in pigeons is based on a procedure known as matching to sample. In the Jack and Jill experiment by Epstein et al. (1980), the listener, Jill, looked behind a curtain at a color projected on a plate (red, green, or yellow) and then pecked and illuminated one of three symbol keys with black on white letters (R, G, or Y). Although this performance seems to involve symbolic behavior, this is not the only possibility. Jill may simply have learned a stimulus-response chain, or a conditional (if red, peck R) relation.

If the stimuli were functioning as symbols for Jill, then each letter would stand for a color, and each color would stand for its corresponding letter. The stimuli would be equivalent—the colors would substitute for letters, and vice versa. In the communication experiments, Jill was taught to match a set of colors to a set of letters. This may be called an A to B relation (A = B). Given a member of Set A (e.g., red), the pigeon is reinforced for pecking the corresponding member of Set B (e.g., R). If the A class of stimuli is equivalent to the B class, it follows that Jill should be able to do the reverse, without any further training. That is, if Jill is presented with a member of Set B (e.g., Y), she should peck the corresponding stimulus in Set B (yellow). In this case, a B to A relation (B = A) would have emerged from the initial A to B training. Unfortunately, Epstein et. al. (1980) did not test for this emergent performance, and we cannot be sure that Jill's communication involved stimulus-equivalence relations.

Basic Equivalence Relations

When stimulus class A is shown to be interchangeable with stimulus class B (if A = B then B = A), we may say that the organism shows **symmetry** between the stimulus classes. Symmetry is only one form of equivalence relation. A more elementary form of equivalence is called **reflexivity.** In this case, an A to A relation (A = A) is established so that given the color red on a sample key, the organism responds to the comparison key with the identical color (red). A child who is given a picture of a cat and then finds a similar picture in a set of photographs is showing reflexivity.

Reflexivity and symmetry are basic logical relations of mathematics. A child who is presented with the number 1 shows reflexivity when she points to 1 in an array of numbers {2,3,1,4,5}. The same child shows symmetry if, when given the number 2, she selects the set {X,X} rather than {X} or {X,X,X}, and when given {X,X} she selects 2 from the array {3,2,1,5,4}.

There is one other equivalence relation in mathematics. This is the relation of **transitivity.** If the written numbers *one, two, three* are equivalent to the arithmetic numbers 1, 2, and 3, and these arithmetic numbers are equivalent to sets {X}, {X,X}, and {X,X,X}; it logically follows that *one, two,* and *three* are equivalent to sets {X}, {X,X}, and {X,X,X}. That is, if A = B and B = C, then A = C (transitivity).

Experimental Analysis of Equivalence Relations

Although equivalences are logically required by mathematics, it is another thing to show that the behavior of organisms is governed by such relations. In terms of behavior, three stimulus classes (A, B, and C) are called equivalent when an organism has passed tests for reflexivity, symmetry, and transitivity.

A complete experiment for stimulus equivalence consists of both identity and symbolic matching procedures. In **identity matching,** the researcher presents a sample stimulus (e.g., red) and two options (e.g., red and green). The organism is reinforced for choosing the red option that corresponds to the sample (i.e., matching to sample). **Symbolic matching** involves presenting one class of stimuli as the sample (e.g., geometrical forms) and another set of stimuli (e.g., different colors) as the options. Reinforcement depends on an arbitrary relation (e.g., triangle = red). After the reinforced relations are trained, tests are made for each kind of equivalence relation. The question is whether reflexivity, symmetry, and transitivity spontaneously emerge without further training. To make this clear, identity and symbolic matching are training procedures that allow for stimulus equivalence, but the procedures do not guarantee the emergence of it. We will describe such an experiment in a step-by-step manner.

Figure 12.8 presents the identity-matching procedures used to show reflexivity for color or form by a pigeon. The bird is presented with three keys that may be illuminated as shown in the two displays. For each display, two sets alternate on the three keys. A set includes a sample key and two option keys. For the sake of clarity, in our example the option that matches the sample is always shown on the left of the displays, and the nonmatching stimulus is on the right. In real experiments, of course, the position of the matching stimulus varies from trial to trial. A peck on the sample key illuminates the option keys (left and right), and pecks to the matching stimulus produce food and the next sample. Pecks to the nonmatching stimulus are not reinforced and lead to the next trial (i.e., the next sample stimulus).

Reflexivity.   Reflexivity for color may be shown using this identity-matching procedure. In the Display A (color match) of Figure 12.8, the sample key is illuminated red. When the pigeon pecks this key the red and green options are presented. Pecks to the red matching key are reinforced with food, while pecks to

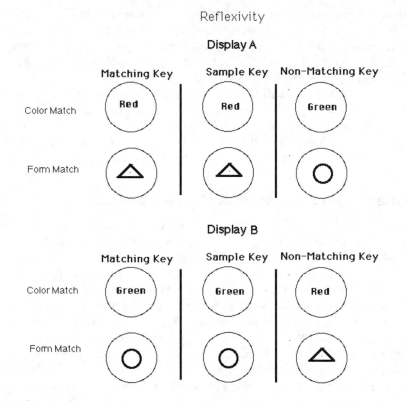

FIG. 12.8 The stimulus-equivalence procedures that could be used to establish reflexivity in pigeons as described by Catania (1984). See text for a description of the contingencies.

green are not. The next trial may present Display B (color match). Now the sample is illuminated green. If the bird pecks the green key, it receives food, but pecks to the red key are extinguished. Based on this training, the bird learns to identify colors.

Similar procedures may be used to train reflexivity based on form. In Figure 12.8 Display A (form match), the form display is based on triangles and circles. When Display A is in effect, the sample key is illuminated with a triangle. Pecks to the sample produce the two options—triangle and circle. Pecks to the key that matches the sample stimulus are reinforced, while pecks to the nonmatching form are placed on extinction. A new trial may result in Display B (form match). In this case, the sample is a circle. When the bird pecks, the sample two options (circle and triangle) are presented. Pecks to the key with a circle produce food, but pecks to the triangle are extinguished. Using these procedures, the pigeon learns to identify forms.[1]

[1]In this case, identity matching simply occurs when the bird matches to sample. A test for emergent reflexivity could involve testing for generalization of identity matching. For example, a bird could be trained to match color to a sample stimulus and then be tested with forms as sample and comparison stimuli.

Symmetry

Display A

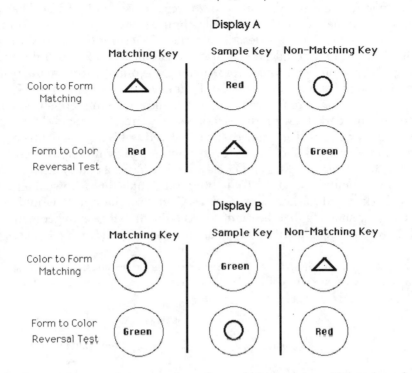

FIG. 12.9 The stimulus-equivalence procedures that could be used to establish and test for symmetry in pigeons as described by Catania (1984). See text for a description of the contingencies.

Symmetry. Figure 12.9 shows the procedures used to train symbolic matching and the tests for symmetry. These procedures are implemented only after a bird has shown identity matching. At this point, the bird is trained to discriminate form on the basis of color (i.e., a color-to-form discrimination) and tested for reversal (form to color).

This procedure is shown by the color-to-form display of Figure 12.9 (Display A). Pecks to the red sample illuminate the options—triangle or circle. In the presence of the red sample, pecks to the triangle are reinforced while pecks to the circle are not. When set 2 is presented, as shown in the form-to-color display (Display B), the sample is illuminated green and pecks to the circle are reinforced.

Once the matching of color to form (or form to color) is well established, a reversal test is conducted without any further reinforcement. In test 1, the bird is presented with a triangle and the question is whether it pecks red. Because red = triangle was trained, the bird shows symmetry if it pecks red when presented with a triangle. Similarly, because green = circle on the basis of training, symmetry is shown if the bird pecks green when the circle is presented. In everyday English, the bird responds as if red stands for triangle, and as if green means circle. The percentage of "correct" responses is the usual measure of symbolic performance on this task.

Transitivity. Figure 12.10 illustrates the procedures that may be used to train and test a pigeon for transitivity. These procedures are used only if a bird has passed the tests for symmetry. Rows 1 and 5 of the figure present the color-to-form procedures for symmetry that were described earlier. To test for transitivity, the pigeon is trained to produce an additional discrimination. Rows 2 and 6 illustrate this training. The pigeon is reinforced for matching a geometric form to intensity of illumination on the option keys—dark or light key. For example, in row 2, pecking the lighter option key is reinforced when a triangle is the sample; also, row 6 shows that pecking the darker key produces food when a circle is the sample.

Notice that the bird is trained such that red = triangle and green = circle (rows 1 and 5) and has shown the reverse on tests of symmetry. Given this performance, if triangle = lighter and circle = darker (rows 2 and 6), then the following relations should emerge: red = lighter and lighter = red (rows 3 and 4), also green = darker, and darker = green (rows 7 and 8). These tests would establish transitivity by showing that the set of colors is equal to the set of geometric forms, which in turn are equivalent to the set of light intensities (A = B = C). This perfor-

FIG. 12.10 The stimulus-equivalence procedures that could be used to establish and test for transitivity in pigeons as described by Catania (1984). See text for a description of the contingencies.

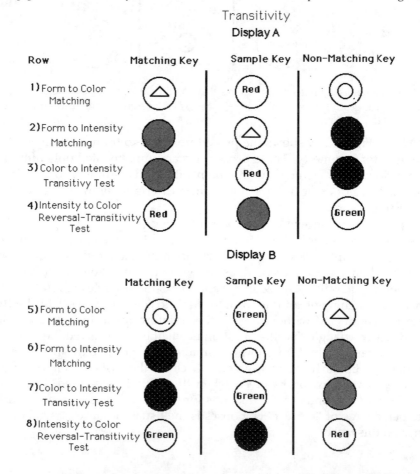

mance is similar to a person who responds to the written word *dog* in the same way as to a picture of a dog or the spoken word "dog." The stimuli are said to be equivalent because they regulate the same operant.

Although stimulus-equivalence training has been given to both human and nonhuman subjects, only two nonhuman studies have claimed that animals can pass tests for reflexivity, symmetry, and transitivity (McIntire, Cleary, & Thompson, 1987; Vaughn, 1988). These studies are controversial since some researchers assert that the animals did not demonstrate emergent or novel relations—all the relations were directly trained (e.g., Hayes, 1989a; Saunders, 1989). This is an important point because, in humans, equivalence relations are easily trained and demonstrated, even in people who are behaviorally retarded.

Researchers have used developmentally delayed people who could pass a reflexivity test (identity matching) but, before training, failed to show symmetry or transitivity (Sidman & Cresson, 1973; Sidman, Cresson, & Wilson-Morris, 1974; see also Lazar, 1977). These subjects were given training in symbolic matching. They were presented with one of 20 spoken names and asked to select the corresponding picture from a comparison set (A = B training). Next, the subjects were trained to select printed words from a set when given one of the 20 names (A = C training). After both training procedures, subjects displayed four emergent relations without further training—two symmetry and two transitivity relations. Subjects showed B to A and C to A reversals—given a picture they emitted the corresponding name, and given a printed word they said it. In addition, subjects showed two transitivity relations. When given a picture (e.g., car, boy, dog, etc.), subjects selected the corresponding printed word (B = C), and when given the printed word, they selected the corresponding picture (C = B).

During training the subjects were presented with three stimulus classes that contained 20 elements in each class (spoken words, pictures, and written words). Forty instances of symbolic matching were reinforced (spoken words = pictures, and spoken words = written words). Tests revealed that 80 new instances of correspondence emerged indirectly from training (B = A; C = A; B = C; and C = B).

As you can see, the reinforcement of symbolic matching resulted in a preliminary form of reading by these individuals. The limits on this training have not been established, but it seems obvious that equivalence relations make up a large part of human education (mathematics, science, reading, etc.). These equivalence classes are not the same as discriminative stimuli because S^Ds cannot be exchanged for the responses they occasion. Clearly, equivalence relations define symbolic performance and are an important part of the experimental analysis of verbal behavior (see, Sidman, 1994 for an overview of stimulus equivalence research).

RESEARCH ON VERBAL BEHAVIOR

Training of Verbal Operants: Mands and Tacts

According to Skinner (1957), the basic classes of verbal behavior are functionally independent in the sense that the relations involved in mands are distinct from those that define tacts. This functional independence means that it is possible to teach mands and tacts as separate response classes. It also implies that there is no basic ordering of the verbal repertoire; that is, it is not necessary to train mands in order to train tacts, or vice versa. In this section, research on basic verbal relations will be outlined and assessed in terms of functional independence of the response classes.

Training Mand Relations.   Recall that the mand relation is defined by an establishing operation (EO). An establishing event regulates the topography or form of the verbal response and sets up a specific consequence as reinforcement. To train mand relations, the most direct procedure is to manipulate an EO and reinforce the verbal response with the specified consequence. In the laboratory, establishing operations usually involve a history of deprivation for some event that functions as primary reinforcement (e.g., food).

Most human behavior, however, is regulated by conditioned reinforcement. To investigate the manding of conditioned reinforcement, Michael (1988) suggested the use of a conditioned establishing operation (CEO). The procedure is called the blocked-response CEO, in which a response that usually occurs is blocked because of the temporary absence of a specific condition, stimulus, or event. You may leave your seminar notes at home as you rush to the university. Because you cannot complete the behavioral sequence of giving a seminar presentation, obtaining the notes would function as reinforcement for making a telephone call to get them. The notes would not have a reinforcement function during a casual lunch with an old friend, because they are not necessary to this behavioral sequence. Whenever an event or stimulus is required to complete a behavior chain, withholding the event will establish it as reinforcement for operant behavior.

Hall and Sundberg (1987) used the blocked-response CEO to train manding by deaf subjects. The first step was to teach a sequence or chain of responses. For example, a subject was taught to open a can of fruit with a can opener, to pour the contents into a bowl, and eat it with a spoon. When the sequence was trained, the subject was given the items to complete the chain, except that one was missing. In this situation, a previously trained verbal response that specified the missing item was reinforced by the teacher supplying the object. Since subjects came to emit such verbal responses, it appears that CEO and specific reinforcement are regulating conditions for such behavior (see also Carroll & Hesse, 1987; Yamamoto & Mochizuki, 1988).

There are other studies of mand training that did not manipulate an establishing operation (Hung, 1980; Rogers-Warren & Warren, 1980; Savage-Rumbaugh, 1984; Simic & Bucher, 1980; Sundberg, 1985). In these studies, humans and animals were required to produce a response that specified a particular object (food items or toys). The objects were shown to the subject to evoke an appropriate mand response. When the verbal response occurred, the object was given and this functioned as reinforcement.

For example, in the study by Savage-Rumbaugh (1984), chimpanzees were shown a number of food items. If the animal pointed to the corresponding symbol on a communication panel, the item was given as reinforcement. Chimpanzees readily acquired this kind of behavior. However, there is some question as to the regulating conditions. The food items may have functioned as discriminative stimuli that set the occasion for selecting the corresponding symbol key, in which case the chimpanzee was emitting tacts rather than mands. Because the sources of control were complex, the behavior is best described as an impure mand (i.e., it is attributable to the control exerted by the food items as discriminative stimuli and specific reinforcement).

In chimpanzee studies, pointing to a food symbol is taken as a mand since it results in getting the item. Pointing is a type of mand in which the response topography remains constant but the response is directed at different stimuli. This contrasts with human speech, in which the topography varies with the establishing operation and specific reinforcement (i.e., "give food" versus "give water"). Mands that vary in topography facilitate discrimination by a listener and may therefore produce more rapid and precise compliance to a request. Although pointing to what you want is formally a mand, saying what you want is much more effective—especially if the listener is in another room, or the object is out of sight.

Training Tact Relations.   To train tact responses, a speaker must come to emit a verbal operant whose form depends on a nonverbal discriminative stimulus. A second requirement is that the operant class be acquired and maintained by nonspecific reinforcement. Reinforcement is nonspecific if the reinforcer for one response exerts no stimulus control over the form of the next response. In animal studies, a response may qualify as a tact even if it is reinforced with food, as long as food reinforcement does not set the occasion for a subsequent verbal response or the selection of the next symbol. For example, a chimpanzee may be offered an apple, and when it selects the symbol key for apple it is given a piece of banana. The presentation of the banana cannot set the occasion for pressing the symbol for apple on the next trial.

In humans, the consequences of tacts are conditioned generalized reinforcers (e.g., praise, attention, approval, etc.), but this is not a defining feature of the tact relation. Recall that tacts are verbal responses controlled by a nonverbal discriminative stimulus; reinforcement maintains the response class but does not specify what response will occur. It is the discriminative stimulus that regulates the tact. Thus, studies using either nonspecific or generalized reinforcement may qualify as tact-training experiments.

Tact relations have been investigated with chimpanzees. Savage-Rumbaugh (1984) used pointing to symbol keys as the verbal response. When the experimenter displayed an item of food, a response to the corresponding symbol resulted in praise and the delivery of a food item. Importantly, the item of food always differed from the one on display. In this situation, the presentation of an item of food was a nonverbal S^D that set the occasion for a response to the appropriate symbol key (tact). Since reinforcement was nonspecific, the consequences of behavior could not regulate pointing to a particular symbol. Because the chimpanzee points to the apple symbol and is reinforced with a banana, we can be sure that the verbal response is a tact rather than a mand. Chimpanzees' symbol pointing came under the control of the displayed food items and therefore qualified as tacting. In this experiment, the form of the tact was the same (i.e., pointing), but its location changed. In contrast, tacts in human speech involve changes in form depending on the nonverbal stimulus (i.e., "that's a chair" or "there's a table").

Michael et al. (1983) attempted to train tacts based on changes in response topography. Pigeons received nonspecific reinforcement (food) that depended on a bird emitting a particular form of response in the presence of a nonverbal discriminative stimulus. For example, a thrust of the head was reinforced when a red ball was presented, and turning in a circle produced reinforcement when a blue ball was the discriminative stimulus. Functionally, this is equivalent to a child who says, "That's a red coat" and "This is a brown coat" and is reinforced by acceptance of the description by the listener. Tacting in the pigeons was successfully established even though the contingencies required correspondence between the nonverbal stimulus and the form of the bird's response. A question that is left unanswered by this research is whether pigeons (or chimps) can show generalization of a tact relation. That is, without further training, would the respective responses for blue and red occur when the objects were triangles or squares rather than balls?

There are behavioral experiments with language-delayed humans that trained tact responses as part of a more general program of language acquisition (Carroll & Hesse, 1987; Guess, 1969; Guess & Baer, 1973; Guess, Sailor, Rutherford, & Baer, 1968; Lamarre & Holland, 1985; Lee, 1981a). Carroll and Hesse (1987) investigated the effects of alternating between mand and tact training. During mand training, a response to an object produced the item. When tacts were trained, the experimenter presented the objects as discriminative stimuli and provided praise as reinforcement for correct responses. Results indicated that subjects responded appropriately to the verbal contingencies, and that mand training facilitated the acquisition of tacts. That is, mands such as "give cup" increased the acquisition of tacts like "that's a cup." This latter finding is interesting because it suggests that under some conditions, mands and tacts are not independent classes of behavior. Apparently, these verbal operants may interrelate when parts of the response forms are shared (i.e., both involve the word cup).

Experiments by LaMarre and Holland (1985) and Lee (1981b) also concerned the acquisition of tacting by language-delayed humans. In these experiments, one object was placed on the left and another on the right. The tact response was saying "on the right" or "on the left" depending on the position of the object. For example, the experimenter would prompt "Where is the dog?" The subject who answered "on the right" when the dog was on the right of a flower was reinforced with social praise. This type of training successfully established verbal responses that contacted the position of an object. In another version of tact training, Guess (1969), Guess and Baer (1973), and Guess et al. (1968) trained verbal responses that contacted the quantity of an object. Subjects with language deficits were taught to emit the singular form of a noun when a single object was shown, and to emit the plural form if two identical items were presented.

In these experiments, correct responses produced food, rather than praise. Thus, the subject was presented with a single cup and saying "cup" rather than "cups" was reinforced with food. Food may be defined as nonspecific reinforcement in such studies since it does not exert any stimulus control over the next verbal response "cup." In humans, both generalized reinforcement (e.g., praise) and nonspecific reinforcement (e.g., food in the preceding example) may be used to establish tacts to various features of the nonverbal environment (e.g., position of objects, quantity, etc.).

ADDITIONAL VERBAL RELATIONS: INTRAVERBALS, ECHOICS, AND TEXTUALS

Intraverbals

Other verbal responses also depend on discriminative stimuli. The **intraverbal** is a class of verbal operants regulated by verbal discriminative stimuli. Verbal stimuli arise from verbal behavior; a previous verbal response by a speaker may be a stimulus for a subsequent verbal operant by the same speaker. When a verbal response exactly replicates the verbal stimulus, we may say there is correspondence between them. Intraverbals, however, have no point-to-point correspondence between the verbal stimulus and the response. When there is exact correspondence between a verbal stimulus and response, the behavior is echoic rather than intraverbal.

In everyday language, thematically related words (or sentences) are examples of intraverbals. For example, the verbal response "fish" to the spoken words "rod and reel" is an intraverbal; saying "water" to the written word "lake" is also intraverbal behavior. On the other hand, the person who says "water" to the spoken sound "water" is not showing intraverbal regulation; in this case, there is exact correspondence between the response and the stimulus, and the response is echoic.

The technique of free association (Galton, 1879) seems to depend on intraverbal regulation. Free association has been used in psychoanalysis. The psychiatrist begins by saying neutral words like "soap," "cup," and "book," and the client is asked to say the first word that comes to mind. As the session continues, the therapist introduces words that may have thematic and emotional relevance in terms of the client's problem. For example, the words *dominant*, *overbearing*, and *punitive* may evoke the common response "father"—suggesting a special history of aversive conditioning.

An individual who says sexual words to noncorresponding verbal stimuli also shows a particularly strong history of reinforcement. This is because the immediate consequences of free associations are not obvious and the verbal stimulus may set the occasion for a variety of different responses. Skinner (1957) analyzed free association as intraverbal behavior in the following passage:

> One verbal response supplies the stimulus for another in a long series. The net effect is revealed in the classical word-association experiment. Here the subject is simply asked to respond verbally to a verbal stimulus, or to report out loud any responses he may "think of"—that is, find himself making silently.... Such an experiment, repeated on many subjects or on one subject many times, produces a fair sample of the responses under the control of a standard stimulus in a given verbal community....

> Many different responses are brought under the control of a given stimulus word, and many different stimulus words are placed in control of a single response. For example, educational reinforcement sets up many different intraverbal operants involving the cardinal numbers. *Four* is part of the occasion for *five* in learning to count, for *six* in learning to count by twos, for *one* in learning the value of *pi,* and so on. On the other hand, many different verbal stimuli come to control the response *four,* e.g., *one, two, three* ... or *two times two makes.*... Many different connections between verbal responses and verbal stimuli are established when different passages are memorized and different "facts" acquired. The word-association experiment shows the results. (pp. 73–74)

As you can see, intraverbal relations are an important part of human behavior. This class of verbal behavior has been studied in the laboratory for many years, and it was called "verbal learning" (e.g., Ebbinghaus, 1885). From the behavioral perspective, verbal learning experiments using nonsense syllables are studies of intraverbal behavior. The use of nonsense syllables enables researchers to control for previous experience and allows for the regulation of verbal responses by arbitrary combinations of stimuli.

A nonsense syllable is usually a three-letter sequence of consonant-vowel-consonant. For example, subjects are instructed to say "BEF" in the presence of the stimulus BEF, "JAH" in the presence of JAH, "PUC" for PUC, and so on. In serial learning, a list of nonsense words is presented and the subject has to remember the list. For instance, in learning the list BEF-JAH-PUC, saying "BEF" must come to occasion the response "JAH," which in turn regulates the spoken word "PUC."

Notice that this problem concerns the acquisition of intraverbal behavior. The occurrence of the verbal stimulus BEF regulates the verbal response JAH, which is acoustically different from the verbal stimulus (the verbal stimulus and verbal response do not correspond). Similarly, the occurrence of the verbal stimulus JAH sets the occasion for PUC—the noncorresponding verbal response.

Echoics

When there is point-to-point correspondence between the stimulus and response, verbal behavior may be classified as either echoic or textual, depending on the criterion of formal similarity. Formal similarity requires that the verbal stimulus and the product of the response be in the same mode (auditory, visual, etc.) and have exact physical resemblance (e.g., same sound pattern). An **echoic** is a class of verbal operants regulated by a verbal stimulus in which there is correspondence and formal similarity between the stimulus and response. Saying "this is a dog" to the spoken stimulus "this is a dog" is an example of an echoic response in human speech. Echoic behavior may also be seen in writing or typing a copy of a text.

Echoic operants occurs at an early age in an infant's acquisition of speech. The term *imitation* is often used to describe this form of operant behavior. The child who repeats "pat a cake, pat a cake, baker's man" to the same words uttered by a parent is showing echoic operant behavior. In this situation, behavior that closely replicates the verbal stimulus is reinforced by the parent.

Although this kind of verbal behavior is often taken for granted, echoic relations are actually quite complex. A verbal stimulus consists of a complex pattern of sounds. The verbal response involves coordinated movements of the larynx, tongue, and lips that result in a sound pattern acoustically similar to the verbal stimulus. Reinforcement (by the listener's acceptance of the verbal response) only occurs when the speaker's performance results in an acoustical pattern that matches the original verbal stimulus.

It is important to note that echoic behavior is not simply the duplication of sounds. As a verbal operant, echoic performance is regulated by specific reinforcement contingencies arranged by others. Echoic contingencies in humans involve reinforcing correspondence of speech units rather than the mere reproduction of sounds. These units begin as phonemes (i.e., smallest sound units to which listeners react), expand to words, and eventually may include full phrases and sentences (Catania, 1984). In contrast, parrots and other birds duplicate the sounds they hear (see Pepperberg, 1981) but their behavior is not verbal in Skinner's sense. This is because the parrot's speech does not depend on reinforcement mediated by a listener. Parrots will reproduce repetitious sounds or noises even when these responses produce no change in the behavior of the listener. For this reason, an infant's imitation of speech is classified as an echoic, but a parrot's "speech" is not.

Echoic contingencies are most prevalent during language acquisition. This means that an infant's vocalizations will have more echoic components than the speech of an adult. It also implies that adult speech will become more echoic when a person is learning to speak a second language. Thus, a Spanish teacher may demonstrate word pronunciation to a student who initially makes many errors. The teacher gives many examples, and the student is reinforced for correct pronunciation. After some practice and correction, the student's pronunciation is close to that of the teacher's. Only when the speech units correspond is the student said to show competence in pronunciation of Spanish.

Textuals

Verbal behavior is textual when there is no formal similarity between the stimulus and response. A **textual** is defined as a class of verbal operants regulated by verbal stimuli where there is correspondence between the stimulus and response, but no formal similarity. The most common example of textual behavior is reading out loud. The child looks at the text "See Dick, see Jane" and emits the spoken words "See . . . Dick, . . . see . . . Jane." In adult reading, the behavior is also textual but the "out loud" aspect is no longer emitted—the person reads silently so that the response is now a private event. Textual behavior is also observed when a secretary takes dictation from his or her boss. In this case, hearing the spoken words "Dear Mr. Smith . . ." by the boss sets the occasion for writing these words by the secretary. Again, correspondence between the stimulus and response occurs but there is no formal similarity.

ON THE APPLIED SIDE

Three-Term Contingencies and Natural Speech

At the most basic level, behavior analysts suggest that the acquisition of verbal behavior is governed by contingencies of reinforcement. We have already discussed some of the elementary contingencies that contribute to human speaking and writing. When different responses by a speaker produce specific reinforcements, the speaker learns a repertoire of mands. The speaker usually learns a generalized response such as "Give me [something]"—where the thing specified depends on the motivational conditions. If the contingencies are changed, the speaker may acquire a repertoire of tact responses. In this case, a nonverbal S^D is presented and the speaker must emit a response with respect to a discriminative stimulus. Correspondence between the verbal response and the stimulus conditions results in generalized (or nonspecific) reinforcement arranged by a listener. The tact contingency seems to contribute to humans' ability to identify features of the environment and describe the world in which they live.

An important question is whether humans arrange similar verbal contingencies in their everyday interactions. Evidence of operant contingencies in casual speech is important for a comprehensive account of verbal behavior. When observational research shows natural dependencies between speaker and listener, we can be more confident that our understanding of speaking (and writing) is not an artifact of laboratory procedures. Also, evidence of verbal contingencies without explicit control by an experimenter suggests that laboratory findings may eventually have general applicability. For both of these reasons, Moerk's (1990) analysis of contingency patterns in mother-child verbal episodes is an important contribution to the behavior analysis of speech.

One interesting aspect of this study is that Ernst Moerk is not a behaviorist, although he has always been interested in language training and learning. His research program goes back almost 20 years and builds on Roger Brown's (1958; Brown & Bellugi, 1964; Brown & Fraser, 1963) empirical approach to first language acquisition. In his recent article in the *Journal of the Experimental Analysis of Behavior*, Moerk (1990) states:

> from the beginning ... [my] program borrowed eclectically from the behavioral, observational learning, system theoretical, and functional/ecological tradition, while retaining cognitive and linguistic perspectives where they seemed most useful. *With more detailed focus on interactional data, it appeared increasingly necessary to adopt learning theoretical concepts and principles in order to explain the training and learning of language skills* [italics added].... [The] stream of verbal behavior (as it unfolds in the interactions between mother/adult and child), the contingencies between successive utterances, and the functional relationships were central to the analyses. (p. 294)

Although Moerk has numerous publications on language training and learning (e.g., Moerk, 1972, 1976a, 1976b; 1977a, 1977b, 1980, 1983a, 1983b, 1985a, 1985b, 1986, 1989, 1990), his recent discovery of three-term contingency patterns in the acquisition of human speech (Moerk, 1990) is of specific interest. The data are based on a reanalysis of the verbal interactions between a child named Eve and her mother. The original observations were collected by Roger Brown (1973) as part of a larger study of mother-child interaction. Eve and her mother were observed in their home during everyday activities. When the study began, Eve was 18 months old and she was 28 months old at the end of the research. Brown collected numerous samples of verbal interaction between Eve and her mother over this 10-month period. Moerk selected all odd-numbered samples and analyzed 2 hours of transcribed audio recoding for each of these samples.

Transcripts were coded by Moerk and two trained research assistants. Observational categories included verbal behavior emitted by both mother and child (Eve). For example, sentence expansion involved the mother adding syntactic elements to her child's utterance (Eve says "see boy" and her mother says "You see the boy"), while sentence reduction occurred when Eve omitted elements that were originally present in her mother's speech (mother says "give the toy to mommy" and Eve says "give toy mum"). Figure 12.11 shows the entire range of speech categories used by Moerk. The research focuses on the arrangement of these verbal utterances in mother-child-mother interactions, and child-mother-child episodes.

As shown in Figure 12.12, many different verbal sequences end with maternal reinforcement. Reinforcement was defined as feedback from the mother that confirmed that Eve's utterance was linguistically acceptable. A contingency that often occurred was the mother saying a new word that was repeated by Eve (vocabulary preservation) and followed by her mother saying "yeah," "right," "yes," and so on (reinforcement). Another three-term pattern involved the mother repeating what she had just said (self-repetition), Eve emitting an approximation to this utterance (reduction), and her mother ending the sequence with words of acceptance (reinforcement).

There are 31 verbal sequences in Figure 12.12. Each one of these contingent relations between mother and child occurred far more often than would be expected by chance. Moerk (1990) suggested that

> the general dynamics, as well as the specific training/learning principles, are apparent in [this table]. Many linguistic skills are first modeled by the mother; they are more or less directly imitated by the child and rewarded by a maternal "yes" or a closely equivalent reinforcing response. In accordance with the age and early stages of Eve's language acquisition, vocabulary training is still predominant, but many grammatical exercises are also encountered, with a strong emphasis on basic syntactic training. (p. 298)

Notice that Moerk assumed that maternal acceptance functioned as reinforcement for Eve's utterances. To show that the mother's acceptance had this function, it is necessary to show an increase in the child's response class. Moerk analyzed child-mother-child sequences to gather evidence on the reinforcement function of maternal acceptance. In this case, the child emitted a response that was followed by the mother saying "yes" (or equivalent) and the subsequent response of the child was assessed against chance levels. Moerk (1990, p. 299) found that "in nine of the 11 three-term patterns, Eve repeats part or all of her rewarded utterance, which can be vocabulary items or the antecedent sentence. For syntax learning, buildups are

The Categories of Maternal Teaching Techniques and Filial Learning Strategies

Labels	Definitions
Expansion /[a] reduction	Minor syntactic elements (i.e., functors) are added/deleted while retaining other elements.
Chaining	Combines item from partner with own newly produced or repeated items.
Self-repetition	Repeats own statement almost identically.
Buildup	Adds constituents to preceding utterance; can be combined with deletions of other elements.
Breakdown	Eliminates words or constituents from preceding utterance making the subsequent one shorter.
Morpheme perseveration	Specific morphemes or morpheme categories are repeated.
Substitution	Most elements and the structure are retained, one or a few items are substituted.
Frame variation	The content is fully or partially repeated, the syntactic structure is changed. Excludes transformation.
Transformation	Syntactic structural changes that result in changes in the elocutionary force.
Vocabulary perseveration	New or rare vocabulary items are repeated.
Provides a label	Provides a noun label without any additional major content elements.
Mapping	Two or more observable nonlinguistic elements are encoded linguistically.
Asks for label	Asks for a noun label.
Requests repetition	Requests partner to repeat preceding utterance.
Item specification	Singles out one specific element of a preceding utterance that needs repetition or specification.
Reinforcement	Feedback confirming that the preceding utterance was linguistically acceptable.
Other	No recognized strategy or technique or those for which no category exists in the present system.
Uncodable	Includes simple exclamations, *yes* or *no* responses referring to the truth value of utterances, and gaps in the transcripts.

[a] A slash indicates that the specific code had a different meaning for the mother and the child. The meaning for the mother is stated before the slash and that for the child after it. The child's conversation partner was mostly her mother, but rarely the father or one of the observers joined in with a few remarks that were also coded. Sections with only the observers or the father as communication partner were excluded from the analysis because the goal was to analyze mother–child interactions.

FIG. 12.11 Response labels and definitions for the study of three-term contingencies in mother-child verbal interactions (from Moerk, 1990; copyright 1990 by the Society for the Experimental Analysis of Behavior, Inc.).

Mother	Child	Mother	Observed Frequency	Expected Frequency[a]
Vocabulary perseveration (.05)[b]	Vocabulary perseveration (.043)	Reinforcement (.029)	30	3.2
Self-repetition (.01)	Reduction (.024)	Reinforcement (.029)	20	0.4
Frame variation (.047)	Reduction (.024)	Reinforcement (.029)	19	1.7
Frame variation (.047)	Vocabulary perseveration (.043)	Reinforcement (.029)	13	3.0
Substitution (.046)	Reduction (.024)	Reinforcement (.029)	12	1.7
Substitution (.046)	Vocabulary perseveration (0.43)	Reinforcement (.029)	12	3.0
Mapping (.027)	Reduction (.024)	Reinforcement (.029)	12	1.0
Substitution (.046)	Provides a label (.014)	Reinforcement (.029)	11	1.0
Morpheme perseveration (.056)	Mapping (.03)	Reinforcement (.029)	10	2.5
Asks for label (.006)	Provides a label (.014)	Reinforcement (.029)	10	0.1
Morpheme perseveration (.056)	Vocabulary perseveration (.043)	Reinforcement (.029)	10	3.6
Breakdown (.02)	Vocabulary perseveration (.043)	Reinforcement (.029)	9	1.3
Breakdown (.02)	Reduction (.024)	Reinforcement (.029)	9	0.7
Expansion (.038)	Mapping (.03)	Reinforcement (.029)	8	1.7
Frame variation (.047)	Mapping (.03)	Reinforcement (.029)	8	2.1
Substitution (.046)	Mapping (.03)	Reinforcement (.029)	8	2.1
Expansion (.038)	Reduction (.024)	Reinforcement (.029)	7	1.4
Asks for label (.006)	Vocabulary perseveration (.043)	Reinforcement (.029)	7	0.4
Item specification (.02)	Mapping (.03)	Reinforcement (.029)	7	0.9
Transformation (.037)	Reduction (.024)	Reinforcement (.029)	7	1.3
Expansion (.038)	Provides a label (.014)	Reinforcement (.029)	6	0.8
Vocabulary perseveration (.05)	Self-repetition (.016)	Reinforcement (.029)	6	1.2
Frame variation (.047)	Chaining (.006)	Reinforcement (.029)	6	0.4
Buildup (.018)	Vocabulary perseveration (.043)	Reinforcement (.029)	6	1.1
Transformation (.037)	Vocabulary perseveration (.043)	Reinforcement (.029)	6	2.4
Expansion (.038)	Vocabulary perseveration (.043)	Reinforcement (.029)	6	2.5
Self-repetition (.01)	Self-repetition (.016)	Reinforcement (.029)	5	0.2
Self-repetition (.01)	Vocabulary perseveration (.043)	Reinforcement (.029)	5	0.6
Frame variation (.047)	Provides a label (.014)	Reinforcement (.029)	5	1.0
Uncodable (.029)	Vocabulary perseveration (.04)	Reinforcement (.029)	5	1.7
Vocabulary perseveration (.05)	Mapping (.03)	Reinforcement (.029)	5	2.3

[a] Expected frequencies = $(p / j)(p / k)(p / l)(N / 3)$.

[b] The numbers in parentheses are the simple or unconditional probabilities of occurrence of each specific category.

FIG. 12.12 Three-term contingency patterns for mother-child-mother sequences ending with maternal reinforcement. Expected frequency is the number of sequences of a specific type expected by chance. Observed frequency is the actual number of these sequences based on the interactional data (from Moerk, 1990; copyright 1990 by the Society for the Experimental Analysis of Behavior, Inc.).

of special interest, because they indicate that the child produced a more complex sentence in adding to a previous utterance." Although the data support a reinforcement interpretation, continuous time analysis is needed to capture the full implications of maternal acceptance as reinforcement for a child's speech.

We have focused on the contingencies among maternal speech samples, child's utterances, and maternal acceptance. Moerk also described other three-term sequences that characterized mother-child interactions. These sequences had the common feature of ending with maternal expansion. Expansion involved the mother repeating Eve's preceding utterance and adding items that were omitted by the child. For example, in one common sequence the mother might introduce the word *cup* (vocabulary preservation), Eve responds "kuh" (vocabulary preservation), and her mother repeats "cup" (expansion). From a behavioral perspective, expansion appears to involve two separate functions: The repetition of Eve's utterance functions as reinforcement for her approximation, and the insertion of omitted elements exerts stimulus control over Eve's next attempt at the word.

Moerk also noted the importance of verbal sequences ending in maternal expansion for the child's acquisition of syntax or grammar. He states:

> From the perspective of language learning, which has focused largely on the controversy of syntax acquisition, the frequent occurrences of *mapping* in the second position of this three-term contingency pattern are of considerable importance. Mapping refers to the child's encoding of environmental relations and events in syntactic [grammatical] form—a complex tact in Skinner's terminology [e.g., "cup on table"]. The mother approves and improves this filial construction by repeating and expanding it in Step 3 of the contingency pattern [e.g., "the cup is on the table"]. (Moerk, 1990, p. 300)

Overall, Moerk's (1990) research on the three-term contingency and human speech is an important contribution to behavioral science. In terms of behavior analysis, this research suggests that contingencies of reinforcement are fundamental to the acquisition of speaking. In addition, this research suggests that natural contingencies are arranged by the verbal community (e.g., parents, teacher, etc.) that govern when, where, and how a person speaks. Although Moerk's research is not based on functional classes of responses, it seems apparent that his response categories are compatible with Skinner's system of mands, tacts, intraverbals, and so on.

Finally, it is necessary to note that contemporary behavior analysts accept a broader view of contingency than used in Moerk's research. The procedures of conditional discrimination imply a four-term contingency, and five-term relations are not uncommon in human behavior—for example, establishing stimulus (ES), conditional stimulus (S^{cond}), discriminative stimulus (S^D), response (R), and reinforcement (S^r). Given this expanded view of contingency, it is not hard to believe that almost all verbal behavior is regulated to some extent by contingencies of reinforcement. Evidence for this assumption will, however, require much more research at both the experimental and observational levels.

KEY WORDS

Conditional discrimination	Identity matching	Symbolic matching
Echoic	Intraverbal	Symmetry
Establishing operation (EO)	Mand	Tact
Establishing stimulus (ES)	Reflexivity	Textual
	Rule-governed behavior	Transitivity
	Stimulus equivalence	Verbal behavior
		Verbal community

CHAPTER 13

Applied Behavior Analysis

LEARNING OBJECTIVES

1. What is one rationale for application of behavior principles? Give examples of behavioral applications.

2. Know the term *applied behavior analysis* and distinguish it from the experimental analysis of behavior.

3. Discuss the concentration on research as a characteristic of applied behavior analysis. Show that human behavior is the central focus of applied behavior analysis. What does this mean for treatment of human problems?

4. How did Dr. Epling help Tammi, the girl who talked of suicide? State how conditioning principles are used in the analysis of Tammi's neurosis.

5. Explain how staff at an institution could inadvertently condition a child to bang her head repeatedly. How could this behavior be eliminated by conditioning principles?

6. Give examples of biological factors that produce behavior change. Can conditioning principles help in these cases?

7. Explain what is meant by the direct treatment of behavior problems. What is a behavioral contract? State the principles of behavioral contracting.

8. In terms of therapy, what do applied behavior analysts focus on? Is there a role for "talk therapy" in applied behavior analysis?

9. How do applied behavior analysts attempt to ensure lasting change or modification of behavior? In terms of generality of behavior change, what are the roles of stimulus generalization, response generalization, and behavior maintenance?

10. Outline and analyze Don Baer's example of hypertension and how to program for lasting behavior change. Explain what is meant by behavior trapping. How can it be used to modify hypertension?

11. Explain what Jim Holland (1978) means when he says, "It takes changed contingencies to change behavior." Discuss changing behavior by changing the social environment.

12. State some of the practical and ethical difficulties with a reversal design. Name three types of multiple baseline designs. In terms of design, discuss the multiple baseline across stimulus conditions used by Hall, Cristler, Cranston, and Tucker (1970) to modify tardiness.

13. Outline the multiple baseline across subjects design. How did Hall and associates (1970) use this design to improve academic performance?

14. What is a multiple baseline across behavior design? Explain how Hall and associates (1970) used this design to modify three target responses of a 10-year-old girl. Are there other designs not detailed in this textbook? Name one.

15. Discuss problems of definition and measurement of behavior in applied settings. According to Kazdin (1989), what are three criteria for adequate response definition? Even with adequate response definition, how can a modification procedure be unfair and inappropriate?

16. Distinguish among the various methods of recording behavior. How do applied behavior analysts ensure reliability of observation?

17. Be able to talk about the evolving relationship between applied and basic behavior analysis. What does Deitz (1978) mean when he says that "the field is shifting from *applied* behavior analysis to *applying* behavior analysis"? According to Baer (1981), why is the separation of applied and basic research good news? Do this textbook's authors agree with Baer's perspective?

18. What is the Premack principle? Describe the Premack (1962) experiment and draw out the implications of the results. How did Homme, deBaca, Devine, Steinhorst, and Rickert (1963) use the Premack principle for behavior modification?

19. Define self-control from a behavioral perspective. Distinguish between the controlling and controlled responses.

20. Give several examples of self-management discussed by Skinner (1953).

21. Discuss self-control as a problem of immediate and long-term consequences. What is commitment and how does it work to increase self-control?

22. How did Belles and Bradlyn (1987) use self-control techniques to modify the smoking of a 65-year-old man? Did the modification work?

23. What is a personalized system of instruction (PSI)? How does this kind of instruction (PSI) differ from the traditional lecture-based instruction? In your answer consider what the role of lectures are in the two kinds of college teaching.

24. Describe the major characteristics that distinguish autistic children from other children. Discuss the Lovaas method of autism treatment and how these methods are incorporated by Morrow and Terzich at Applied Behavior Consultants (ABC). How successful has ABC been at the treatment of autism?

25. What is activity-based anorexia and how is it different from anorexia nervosa? Outline the evidence that physical activity is central to the onset of human anorexia.

26. Describe the process of activity anorexia in animals and its motivational basis. How does activity anorexia develop in humans and how can it be treated and prevented?

27. Discuss the program of MammaCare for prevention of breast cancer. What is the prevalence of breast cancer? How important is early detection?
28. Outline the behavioral procedures (components) used in the MammaCare program. How effective is the program and how has it been extended to new applications?

The experimental analysis of behavior is a science that easily lends itself to application. This is because the focus of the discipline is on those environmental events that directly alter the behavior of organisms. Almost half a century ago (e.g., Dollard & Miller, 1950; Skinner, 1953), behavior analysts suggested that since operant and respondent principles regulate behavior in the laboratory, they likely affect human behavior in the everyday world. Thus, principles of behavior can be used to change socially significant human conduct.

Principles of behavior change have been used to improve the performance of university students (Keller, 1968), increase academic skills (Sulzer-Azaroff, 1986), teach developmentally delayed children self-care (O'Brien & Azrin, 1972), reduce phobic reactions (Bandura, Blanchard, & Ritter, 1969), get people to wear seat belts (Sowers-Hoag, Thyer, & Bailey, 1987), prevent industrial accidents (Sulzer-Azaroff & De Santamaria, 1980), and help individuals stop cocaine abuse (Budney, Higgins, Delaney, Kent, & Bickel, 1991). Behavioral interventions have had an impact on clinical psychology, medicine, counseling, job effectiveness, sports training, and environmental protection. Applied experiments have ranged from investigating the behavior of psychotic individuals to analyzing (and altering) contingencies of entire institutions (see Kazdin, 1989).

CHARACTERISTICS OF APPLIED BEHAVIOR ANALYSIS

Behavioral principles, research designs, observational techniques, methods of analysis, and so on transfer readily to an applied science. When this is done to improve performance or solve social problems, the technology is called **applied behavior analysis** (Baer et al., 1968). Thus, applied behavior analysis is a field of study that focuses on the application of the principles, methods, and procedures of the science of behavior. Because applied behavior analysis is a wide field of study, it cannot be characterized by a single definition. Nonetheless, several features in combination distinguish applied behavior analysis as a unique discipline.

Concentration on Research

Behavior therapists and applied researchers are committed to a scientific analysis of human behavior. What a person does and the events that govern behavior are objectively identified. In this regard, operant and respondent conditioning are assumed to regulate much human action. However, verbal behavior, generalized imitation, equivalence relationships, and physiology complicate human behavior.

Applied behavior analysis involves two major areas of research. The application of operant and respondent principles to improve human behavior has concerned many behavior analysts. A good deal of literature has documented the success of this enterprise (see the *Journal of Applied Behavior Analysis* for many examples). Many experiments have shown how basic conditioning principles can be used in a variety of complex settings. Problems that are unique to the applied context have been addressed, and treatment packages that are designed for the modification of behavior have been described and evaluated (see Martin & Pear, 1996).

Another set of studies have not focused directly on behavior change, but are a part of applied behavior analysis. Such investigations are involved with an analysis of everyday human behavior and have long-range implications for improving the human condition. For example, studies that investigate environmental factors that produce cooperation, competition, successful teaching, and coercive family dynamics may identify basic principles of complex human interaction (Epling & Pierce, 1986). Researchers in this area of applied behavior analysis are attempting to specify the contingencies that produce social problems.

Behavior Is the Primary Focus

Applied behavior analysts focus on the behavior of people. Behavior is not considered to be an expression of inner causes like personality, cognition, and attitude. Marital difficulties, children who are out of control, littering, phobic reactions, poor performance on exams, excessive energy use, and negative self-descriptions are analyzed as problems of behavior. Interventions for these and other problems are directed at changing environmental events to improve behavior.

Of course, people think, feel, and believe a variety of things associated with what they do. Individuals experiencing difficulty in life may have unusual thoughts and feelings. A depressed person may feel worthless and think that nobody likes him or her. The same person does not spend much time visiting friends, going to social events, or engaging in the usual activities of life. A behavioral intervention for this problem would likely focus on increasing the person's activity, especially social interaction. The individual may be asked to set goals for completing various tasks, and reinforcement is arranged when they are accomplished. When people become more socially involved, physically active, and complete daily tasks, they do not describe themselves as depressed. In this and many more cases, a change in behavior produces a change in feelings and cognition.

A Case Study.   In other cases, what a person says about his or her feelings and thoughts may be treated as verbal operants that require change. Tammi was an 8-year-old girl who was diagnosed as neurotic by a physician who saw her in his general practice. She was referred to one of this textbook's authors, Dr. Epling, for evaluation and treatment.

When she was 6 years old, Tammi had witnessed a gruesome farm accident in which her brother was killed. The girl frequently talked about killing herself and joining her brother in heaven. She had also cut herself with a kitchen knife on two occasions. Her parents were asked to record the circumstances that preceded and followed these episodes and the number of times they occurred.

Tammi had cut herself on two occasions since her brother's death, but had not done so during the past year. Talking about suicide had, however, increased, and she did this about three times a week. This talk usually took place at the evening meal when both parents were present. She did not talk about dying to her older siblings or to other people. Quite naturally, these episodes upset her mother and father and they routinely attempted to "calm her down and reason with her" when they occurred.

This information suggested stimulus control and (unintentional) reinforcement by parental attention. After the mother and father were taught a few simple principles of extinction, they withdrew social reinforcement when talk about suicide occurred. The parents were instructed to avoid eye contact, make no comment, and if possible turn away from Tammi when she talked about killing herself. They were also told that extinction would likely produce an initial increase in the form and frequency of the behavior. In other words, Tammi would temporarily get worse, but a rapid improvement could be expected to follow. At the end of 5 weeks and at a 6-month follow-up, talk of killing herself went to zero and cutting herself did not occur again.

The Importance of Conditioning

This discussion should make it clear that problem behavior may, in many cases, be understood in the same fashion as any other behavior. Principles of conditioning are neutral with respect to the form and frequency of behavior. Maladaptive, annoying, or dangerous responses may be inadvertently produced by environmental contingencies.

Consider an institutional setting in which three staff nurses are in charge of 20 disabled children. The nurses are busy and as long as the children behave, they are left alone. This natural response to a strenuous work schedule may, for some children, result in deprivation for adult attention. When one of the children accidentally hits his or her head and is hurt, a staff member rushes over and comforts the child. It is possible that head hitting will increase in frequency because it has been reinforced by contingent attention (e.g., Lovaas & Simmons, 1969). Of course, when people are injured they cannot be ignored. One way to deal with the problem would be to provide social reinforcement for appropriate play, academic activities, ward chores, self-hygiene, and so on. This tactic is called **differential reinforcement of other behavior,** or **DRO** (e.g., Burgio & Tice, 1985; Lowitz & Suib, 1978). In the preceding example, the procedure would strengthen responses that are incompatible with self-injury and reduce deprivation for adult attention.

Although much human behavior is a function of contingencies of reinforcement, biological factors also produce behavior change. A person who has experienced a stroke, a child with fetal alcohol syndrome, an individual in the later stages of syphilis, and an adult suffering from Huntington's chorea may emit responses that are a function of brain damage, toxic agents, disease, and genetics. Even when this is the case, principles of conditioning can often be used to improve behavior (see Epling & Pierce, 1990, pp. 452–453).

Direct Treatment of Problem Behavior

Applied behavior analysts usually focus directly on the environmental events that generate and maintain behavior. Typically, target behavior and the events that precede and follow those responses are counted for several days. During this baseline, treatment is withheld so that a later change in behavior can be evaluated. This assessment also provides information about stimulus control (events that precede the behavior) and contingencies of reinforcement (events that follow behavior) that maintain responses.

Following a baseline period of assessment, a behavioral plan of action may be negotiated between the behavior therapist, the client, and concerned others. This plan usually includes a statement of target responses, consequences that follow different actions, and long-term goals. In many cases, a detailed **behavioral contract** is drawn up that objectively specifies what is expected of the client and the consequences that follow behavior (Bristol, 1976; De Risi & Butz, 1975; Hall & Hall, 1982; Stuart, 1971; Upper, Lochman, & Aveni, 1977). Figure 13.1 outlines the major principles of behavioral contracts. At a minimum, the behavior analyst should clearly identify the problem behavior; and the contract should specify in a

FIG. 13.1 Steps in writing a behavioral contract (based on Hall & Hall, 1982).

A Guide to Behavioral Contracting

1. Specify the target behavior.
2. Describe the behavior in a way that an observer may count or time.
3. Collect baseline data on the frequency of response or time spent responding.
4. Identify consequences that may be used to increase desired behavior (positive and negative reinforcers).
5. Find people who will monitor the behavior and provide the consequences.
6. Write the contract in clear statements of behavior and consequences (e.g., "if you do x, then you receive y").
7. Collect data on frequency of response or time spent responding and compare with baseline level.
8. Modify the contract if the desired behavior does not increase (e.g., try different consequences).
9. Gradually, remove arbitrary consequences and replace with natural reinforcers—rewrite the contract and monitor the behavior.
10. Plan for generalization—implement the contract in a variety of settings.

straightforward manner the reinforcement for meeting behavioral objectives, the people who provide reinforcement, and the contingencies of reinforcement.

Applied behavior analysts do not typically focus on what has been called the therapeutic process. This is because they do not place much faith in talking about problems to relieve stress or develop insight. They prefer to arrange contingencies of reinforcement to alter behavior problems. Although this is the case, Dr. Steven Hays at the University of Nevada–Reno is a behavior analyst who has recognized the importance of rule-governed behavior in a therapeutic setting. From his perspective, talking is a form of social influence that may be used to change the client's actions. That is, instructions and other verbal stimuli may directly alter the probability of behavior (see Hayes, 1987; Zettle & Hayes, 1982). Today, most applied behavior analysts prefer contingency management, but others are investigating the practical importance of instructions, rules, and therapeutic advice (see Hayes, 1989b).

Programming for Generality

In terms of direct treatment of problem behavior, applied behavior analysts have been concerned with the generality of behavior change (Baer, 1982; Stokes & Baer, 1977). That is, researchers attempt to ensure that their interventions produce lasting changes in behavior that occur in all relevant settings. As noted in Chapter 7, when organisms are reinforced in the presence of a particular stimulus, they typically produce a gradient of generalization that falls on both sides of the discriminative stimulus. Rather than rely on the organism to generalize automatically in an appropriate manner, the applied behavior analyst attempts to program for generality.

Generality of behavior change involves three distinct processes: stimulus generalization, response generalization, and behavior maintenance (Martin & Pear, 1996). Behavior change has generality if the target response(s) occurs in a variety of situations, spreads to other related responses, and persists over time. **Stimulus generalization** occurs when the person responds similarly to different situations (e.g., a person greets one friend as she does another). **Response generalization** occurs when a target response is strengthened and other similar responses increase in frequency (e.g., a child reinforced for building a house out of LEGO™ subsequently may arrange the pieces in many different ways). **Behavior maintenance** refers to how long a new behavior persists after the original contingencies are removed (e.g., an anorexic man who is taught to eat properly shows long-lasting effects of treatment if he maintains adequate weight for many years).

Dr. Don Bear at the University of Kansas has emphasized the importance of training behavioral generality and provides the following illustration:

> Suppose that a client characterized by hypertension has been taught systematic progressive relaxation techniques on the logic that the practice of relaxation lowers blood pressure a clinically significant amount, at least during the time of relaxation, and that the technique is such that relaxation can be practiced during all sorts of everyday situations in which the client encounters the kinds of stress that would raise blood pres-

sure if self-relaxation did not pre-empt that outcome. Suppose that the relaxation technique has been taught in the clinician's office, but is to be used by the client not there, but in the home, work, and recreation settings in which stress occurs. Thus, generalization of the technique across settings, as well as its maintenance after clinical treatment stops, is required. (Baer, 1982, p. 207)

To program generality of behavior change, Baer (1982) suggests a variety of procedures that affect stimulus and response generalization and behavior maintenance. Stimulus generalization of relaxation (or any other behavior) is promoted when the last few training sessions are given in situations that are as similar as possible to everyday settings. Second, when relaxation training is done in a variety of different contexts, such as different rooms with different therapists and different times of day, stimulus generalization increases. Finally, a therapist who trains relaxation in the presence of stimuli that elicit hypertension in everyday life is programming for stimulus generalization.

Response generalization is increased when the client is taught a variety of ways to obtain the same effect. For example, to relax and reduce blood pressure, the client may be taught meditation, progressive relaxation, and controlled breathing. In addition, a person may be taught to produce new forms of response, as when the therapist says, "Try to find new ways of relaxing and reducing blood pressure" and reinforces novel responses (e.g., Parsonson & Baer, 1978).

Behavior change may be programmed to last for many years if operant responses contact sources of reinforcement outside of the therapeutic setting. Applied behavior analysts who teach their clients skills that are reinforced by members of the social community are programming for behavior maintenance. This sort of programming has been called **behavior trapping** because, once learned, the new behavior is "trapped" by natural contingencies of reinforcement (e.g., Baer & Wolf, 1970; Stokes, Fowler, & Baer, 1978). The aversive consequences of hypertension are reduced when a person learns techniques of relaxation that decrease blood pressure and these practices are trapped by automatic negative reinforcement.

In fact, relaxation training has been used to reduce hypertension over a long time with generalized effects. Usually, hypertension is treated with drugs, but there are many difficulties, including side-effects of the drugs and failure by patients to follow the proposed treatment. Beiman, Graham, and Ciminero (1978) taught two hypertensive men to relax deeply. The men were taught to practice relaxation at home and when they were tense, anxious, angry, or felt under pressure. Blood pressure was monitored in a variety of everyday settings and during therapy sessions. Following behavior modification, both men had blood pressure readings within the normal range. These effects were maintained at a 6-month follow-up.

Focus on the Social Environment

From a behavioral point of view, the physical environment and social system requires change, not the person (Holland, 1978). Dr. James Holland at the University of Pittsburgh has been concerned with this issue:

Our contingencies are largely programmed in our social institutions and it is these systems of contingencies that determine our behavior. If the people of a society are unhappy, if they are poor, if they are deprived, then it is the contingencies embodied in institutions in the economic system, and in the government which must change. It takes changed contingencies to change behavior. (Holland, 1978, p. 170)

Behavior-change programs usually are more circumscribed in their focus than Holland recommends (but see Chapter 14 for a discussion of cultural design). Applied behavior analysts have seldom been in a position to change institutional contingencies. They have targeted more local contingencies involving family and community. In the case of Tammi, the social contingencies for talking about suicide were located in the family. When her parents stopped attending to such talk, she stopped saying that she wanted to kill herself. The focus of the intervention was on the family system rather than Tammi's neurosis.

Most behavior-change programs attempt to identify and alter significant variables that maintain target responses. As we have said, these variables are usually in the person's social environment. For this reason, treatment programs are often conducted in schools, hospitals, homes, prisons, and the community at large (see Tharp & Wetzel, 1969). Parents, teachers, friends, spouses, and others typically control significant sources of reinforcement that maintain another person's behavior. These individuals are often instructed in how to change contingencies of reinforcement to alter a client's behavior.

RESEARCH IN APPLIED BEHAVIOR ANALYSIS

In Chapter 2, we discussed A-B and A-B-A-B reversal designs for operant research. For single-subject research, basic or applied, the **A-B-A-B reversal design** has the highest level of internal validity—ruling out most extraneous factors. Recall that a baseline period (A_1) is followed by the introduction of the reinforcement procedure (B_1) and the target behavior changes. The inference is that the behavior change is caused by the presence of the reinforcement contingency. This assumption is tested by withdrawing the contingency of reinforcement (A_2) and observing whether the target behavior returns to baseline levels. If this occurs, a stronger test is made by again introducing the reinforcement procedure (B_2) and showing that the target behavior reliably changes in the expected direction.

While a reversal design is always preferred, there are practical and ethical difficulties that restrict its use in applied settings. In natural settings, behavior is often resistant to a reversal procedure. For example, a child's shyness may be altered by using contingencies of reinforcement to increase socially acceptable playing. If the reinforcement procedure is now withdrawn, the child will probably continue playing with other children. This may occur because the shy child's behavior is maintained by social reinforcement from playmates. In other words, the child's behavior is trapped by other sources of reinforcement. While this is a good result for the child, it is a bad outcome in terms of inference and research design. This is because the applied analyst cannot be sure that the original improvement in behavior was caused by his or her intervention.

Another difficulty with the reversal design in applied settings is that it requires the withdrawal of a reinforcement procedure that may improve behavior. For example, a psychiatric patient may be restrained with leather cuffs for biting his arms. A DRO procedure is implemented and arm biting is substantially reduced, to a point at which the cuffs are no longer necessary. Although we cannot be sure that the DRO contingency caused the reduction in self-injury, it would be cruel to remove the contingency only to show that it was effective. Thus, the A-B-A-B reversal design is sometimes inappropriate for ethical reasons.

Multiple Baseline Designs

To solve the problems raised by the A-B-A-B reversal design, applied behavior analysts have developed other single-subject designs. **Multiple baseline designs** demonstrate experimental control and help eliminate alternative explanations for behavior change. There are three major types of multiple baseline designs as first described by Hall et al. (1970). These designs are (a) multiple baseline across stimulus conditions, (b) multiple baseline across subjects, and (c) multiple baseline across behaviors.

Multiple Baseline across Stimulus Conditions. In this design, a reinforcement procedure is applied in one situation but is withheld in other settings. When behavior changes in the situation where it is reinforced, the contingency is applied to the same response in another setting. Hall and his associates (1970) used this design in a modification of children's tardiness in getting to class after recess or lunch.

Figure 13.2 shows the multiple baseline across stimulus conditions used by Hall and his colleagues (1970). The researchers used a "patriots chart" to modify lateness after lunch and after morning and afternoon recess. Children in the fifth grade who were on time for class had their names posted on the chart. As you can see, punctuality improved when the chart was posted. Notice that the chart was first posted after lunch time, but it was not introduced following morning or afternoon recess. The number of students who were late for class after lunch declined from about eight to less than two. This was not the case for the recess periods; the number of students who were tardy after recess remained at four or five. Next, the researchers continued to post the patriots chart after lunch, but they added the chart following the morning recess. When this occurred, all students were on time for class following both lunch and morning recess. Finally, when the chart was also posted following the afternoon recess, all students were on time for all three class periods. The multiple baseline across stimulus conditions demonstrates an effect of the intervention by staggering the introduction of the independent variable over time and settings.

Multiple Baseline across Subjects. A similar logic is used when an intervention is progressively introduced to different subjects who exhibit similar target behavior. In experiment 2, Hall and his colleagues (1970) attempted to improve three

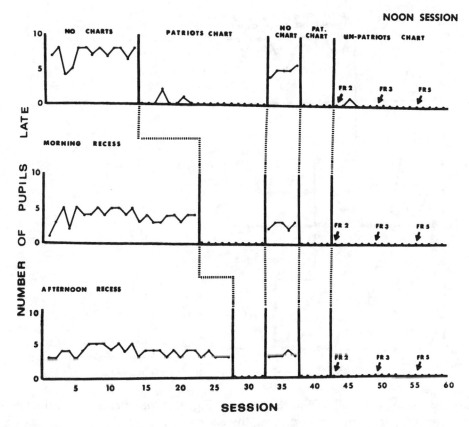

FIG. 13.2 The multiple baseline design across stimulus conditions used by Hall, Cristler, Cranston, and Tucker (1970, and reprinted with permission of the *Journal of Applied Behavior Analysis*).

students' scores on French quizzes. Modification involved a requirement to stay after school for tutoring if the student scored below a C on a quiz. The contingency was first introduced to Dave, then to Roy, and finally to Debbie. Figure 13.3 shows that Dave's quiz performance dramatically improved when the contingency was applied. The other students also showed improvement after the contingency went into effect. All of the students received grades of C or better when contingency management was used to improve their performance in the French class.

Multiple Baseline across Behaviors. A multiple baseline design across behaviors is used when a reinforcement procedure is applied progressively to several operants. In this case, the subject, setting, and consequences remain the same, but different responses are sequentially modified. Hall and his associates (1970) provided an example of this design when they modified the after-school reading, working on a Campfire honors project, and practicing the clarinet of a 10-year-old girl. The girl had to spend at least 30 minutes on an activity or else she had to go to bed early. She had to go to bed 1 minute earlier for every minute less than 30

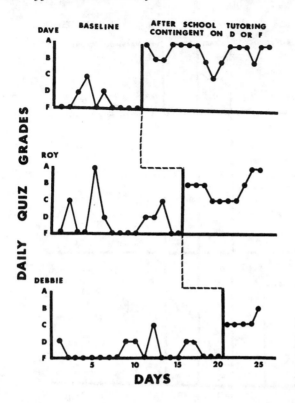

FIG. 13.3 The multiple baseline design across subjects used by Hall, Cristler, Cranston, and Tucker (1970, and reprinted with permission of the *Journal of Applied Behavior Analysis*).

she spent on an activity. As you can see from Fig. 13.4, practicing the clarinet was modified first, and time spent playing the clarinet increased from about 15 to 30 minutes. Next, both practicing the instrument and working on the Campfire project were targeted and both performances were at about 30 minutes. Finally, reading for book reports was modified and all three target responses occurred for 30 minutes. The avoidance contingency seems effective because each behavior changes when the contingency is introduced, but not before.

Multiple baseline and A-B-A-B reversal designs are the most frequently used research methods in applied behavior analysis. There are, however, many variations of these basic designs that may be used to increase internal validity or to deal with specific problems in the applied setting (e.g., Ulman & Sulzer-Azaroff, 1975). Often the basic designs are combined in various ways to be certain that the effects are due to the independent variable. In fact, Hall and his associates (1970) used a reversal phase in their experiment on tardiness and the patriots chart, but for reasons of clarity this was not shown in Figure 13.2. There are many other designs that are useful in a given situation. A **changing criterion design** involves progressive increases (or decreases) in the performance criterion for reinforcement. For example, a hyperactive child is reinforced for spending progressively more time on academic work. At first the child may be required to spend 3 minutes working quietly, then 5 minutes, then 10, and so on. The child's behavior is measured at each level of the criteria. A research example of this design is given in the section on self-control (see also Belles & Bradlyn, 1987).

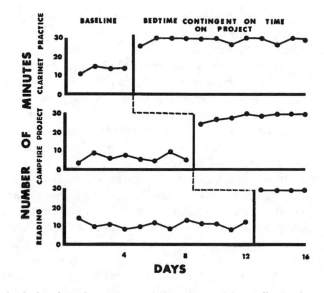

FIG. 13.4 The multiple baseline design across behaviors used by Hall, Cristler, Cranston, and Tucker (1970, and reprinted with permission of the *Journal of Applied Behavior Analysis*).

Issues of Measurement in Applied Behavior Analysis

It is relatively easy to define objectively an operant in the laboratory. Responses are defined by switch closures, and there is no dispute about their occurrence. When responses occur, they are recorded by computers and other electronic equipment. In the applied setting, definition and measurement of the behavior is much more difficult, especially when parents, teachers, and psychologists are used to identify problem behavior. In this regard, Kazdin (1989) has made the point that:

> identification of the target behavior may appear to be a relatively simple task. In a given setting (e.g., the home, school, or work place), there is general agreement as to the "problems" of the clients whose behaviors need to be changed and as to the general goals of the program. Global or general statements of behavioral problems are usually inadequate for actually beginning a behavior modification program. For example, it is insufficient to select as the goal alteration of aggressiveness, learning deficits, speech, social skills, depression, psychotic symptoms, self-esteem, and similar concepts. Traits, summary labels, and personality characteristics are too general to be of much use. Moreover, definitions of the behaviors that make up such general labels may be idiosyncratic among different behavior change agents (parents, teachers, or hospital staff). The target behaviors have to be defined explicitly so that they can actually be observed, measured, and agreed upon by individuals administering the program. (p. 54)

Kazdin goes on to discuss three criteria of an adequate response definition (see also Hawkins & Dobes, 1975). The first criterion is **objectivity.** This means that the response definition should refer to observable features of behavior in clearly specified situations. **Clarity** of definition is another requirement. This means that the description of the response can be read and then clearly restated by a trained research assistant or observer. Finally, the definition should be **complete** in the sense that all instances of the behavior are distinguished from all nonoccurrences. Thus, a troublesome student may be objectively defined as one who talks without permission when the teacher is talking and who is out of seat without permission during a lesson. The definition is clear in that it is easily understood and may serve as a basis for actual observation. Completeness is also shown since only these two responses are instances of the troublesome behavior class, and any other responses are not.

This definition of response assumes that there is a problem with the student's performance, not the teacher's judgment. The applied behavior analyst must be sensitive to the possibility that the teacher is too critical of the student. It is possible that many students talk without permission and leave their seats during lessons. The teacher, however, only gets upset when Anna is running about or talking during instruction. In this case, response definition may be accurate and modification successful, but the intervention is unfair. Applied behavior analysts must constantly be aware of whether they are part of the solution or part of the problem (Holland, 1978). If the problem lies with the teacher, it is his or her behavior that requires change.

Recording Behavior.   Once a suitable response has been defined, the next step is to record the behavior when it occurs. The simplest tactic is to record every instance of the response. Practically, this strategy may be very time-consuming and beyond the resources of most applied behavior analysts. One alternative is to count each instance of behavior only during a certain period of the day (e.g., lunch, recess, first class in the morning, and so on). This method of observation is called **event recording** for specified periods.

Another strategy is to select a block of time and divide the block into short, equal intervals. This is called **interval recording.** For example, a 30-minute segment of mathematics class may be divided into 10-second bits. Regardless of the number of responses, if the behavior occurs in a given 10-second segment, then the observer records it as a single event. One way this could be done is to have an observer wear a headset connected to a cassette tape recorder that plays a tape that beeps every 10 seconds. When the target behavior occurs, the observer records it on a piece of paper divided into segments that represent the 10-second intervals (see Figure 13.5). After each beep, the observer moves to the next interval.

FIG. 13.5 Interval recording method used in behavioral observation and measurement (from Martin & Pear, 1988, and republished with permission of Prentice Hall).

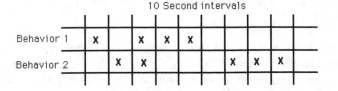

Time sampling is another method of recording used in applied behavior analysis. This technique samples behavior over a long time scale, with observations made at specified times throughout the day. For example, a patient on a psychiatric ward may be observed every 30 minutes, as a nurse does the rounds, and instances of psychotic talk are recorded. Again, the issue is whether the target behavior is occurring at the time of the observation, not how many responses are made.

When behavior is continuous, **duration recording** is a preferred method of observation. Continuous behavior involves responses like watching television, riding a bicycle, sitting in a chair, and so on. When behavior is continuous, an observer may use a stopwatch to record the duration of occurrence. When the person is sitting in a chair the watch is timing, and when the person does something else the watch is stopped.

Reliability of Observations.   No matter what method of recording behavior is used, **reliability of observation** is a critical issue. Briefly, reliability of observation involves the amount of agreement among observers who independently record the same response. For example, two observers may sit at the back of a classroom and use 10-second intervals to record the occurrence of Jessica's out-of-seat behavior. After 30 minutes of observation, 180 intervals of 10 seconds have been recorded by each researcher. One way to assess reliability is to count the number of times both observers agree that the behavior did or did not occur within an interval. This calculation can be expressed as a percentage agreement that varies from zero to 100%. Generally, applied behavior analysts strive for reliability of greater than 80% agreement.

FOCUS ON ISSUES
The Relationship Between Applied and Basic Research

Applied behavior analysis began with the extension of operant and respondent principles to the analysis and modification of human behavior. Such an extension was predicted by Skinner (1953) and led to the application of basic principles to a variety of human problems including improvement of teaching and learning (Keller, 1968), autistic behavior of children (Lovaas & Simmons, 1969; Risley, 1968), social interaction of children (Hart, Reynolds, Baer, Brawley & Harris, 1968), and classroom management (Barrish, Saunders, & Wolf, 1969). Other research concerned the basic analysis of human behavior in naturalistic settings (Baer et al., 1967; Gerwitz, 1969). Historically, the link between applied behavior analysis and basic behavioral research has been a successful strategy.

The early work in behavior analysis (applied and basic) was based on Skinner's (1953) pragmatic or practical philosophy. That is, a behavioral relationship was important if the relation was powerful in its effects and could be used to change the behavior of an individual. At this time, there was little distinction between applied and basic research. For instance, the *Journal of the Experimental Analysis of Behavior* was founded in 1958, and both applied and basic articles were represented in this journal. Flanagan, Goldiamond, and Azrin (1958) reported on "Operant Stuttering: The Control of Stuttering through Response Contingent Consequences," and Azrin (1958) published "Some Effects of Noise on Human Behavior." These articles are representative of a broad range of articles concerned with socially significant human behavior. They demonstrate that some behavior analysts were choosing to study behavioral relationships that had direct importance for human affairs. In the same journal, other researchers were investigating contingencies of reinforcement, using operant chambers, with a variety of organisms.

Because basic researchers were interested in application and applied researchers were interested in basic behavioral relationships, both fields shared a similar set of principles and philosophical assumptions. This **analytical pragmatism** resulted from a common education dealing with the philosophy of behavior and principles of conditioning (Epling & Pierce, 1986). Behavior analysts were well trained in basic science and in a philosophy that combined practical application with analysis. Little difference existed between applied and basic researchers, and indeed it was common at the time to refer to oneself as an operant conditioner.

The Separation of Applied and Basic Research

Over the years, there has been a separation of basic research and applied behavior analysis. Dr. Sam Deitz at Georgia State University was the first to describe the split between behavioral science and technology. In a 1978 article published in the *American Psychologist*, he stated:

> there does seem to be a strong trend toward change in the major emphasis of applied behavior analysis. That change is from discovering and investigating independent variables to applying previously discovered principles in order to improve [behavior]. The change is only now being proposed, but it seems to be already evidenced by the types of articles appearing in current issues of behavioral journals. The field seems to be shifting from *applied* behavior analysis to *applying* behavior analysis. (Deitz, 1978, p. 807)

Other researchers noted similar trends toward a "cure-help" approach to applied behavior analysis. These scientists concluded that the separation of basic and applied research would have a negative impact on an effective technology of behavior change. (Birnbrauer, 1979; Branch & Malagodi, 1980; Hayes et al., 1980; Michael, 1980; Pierce & Epling, 1980).

Dr. Don Baer at the University of Kansas agrees that applied behavior analysts are becoming more interested in treatment than in analysis, but views this shift as good news for a technological field. He compares the treatment orientation of applied behavioral researchers to the nonanalytical approach of most medical doctors. Baer (1981) recounted a story to support his contention that analysis is not a necessary component of behavioral technology. He was driving across the country to take a new job when his daughter became ill. At the first opportunity, he pulled into a small-town hospital and was surprised by the approach taken by the doctor.

There a doctor examined our daughter very briefly, remarked that her temperature was more than 103 degrees, noted some behaviors and some absences of other behaviors, asked questions about family allergy patterns, and then gave her an injection of something-mycin. The doctor advised that we continue on our way. When I expressed some amazement at that recommendation, he said that by the time that anything significant might happen, we would be in the next hospital-town; he would call the doctor there to alert him to our possible coming, but he thought that our daughter would probably be well by then anyway. I asked him what it was, then, that my daughter had; he said, in effect, that there was no way to be sure yet, if ever—and he implied that it was hardly worth knowing: either the something-mycin would have fixed it by then, or the next doctor would do something more effective, and perhaps more diagnostic. ... We drove on, amazed and apprehensive, but he was exactly correct: our daughter was cool and happy eight hours later and we drove without pause through the next hospital-town.

Obviously, I do not know the doctor at all, and so cannot specify his areas of ignorance. Still, it was obvious to me that he was being nonanalytic, standard, routinized, packaged, empirical—and effective. Behind his ability to do that stand generations of analytic, questioning, innovative, detail-devoted scientists, striving to relate the human condition—and especially its illnesses—to basic principles of nature, biology, and biochemistry. If it were not for them, he would not have been there with his very effective packages, his routine algorithm for when to apply them, and his simple empirical willingness to try another of them without amazement if the first choice did not work. But his back-up researchers probably were not, as individuals, particularly well equipped to dispense medicinal packages to a sick baby. And it probably had been a long time (if ever) since he had been equipped to analyze the mysteries of bacterial or viral infections in terms of human biochemistry. Still, when our baby was ill, it was he whom we needed. (Baer, 1981, p. 87)

In terms of applied behavior analysis, Baer is suggesting that those who apply behavioral technology are very much like physicians. Applied behavior analysts use standardized treatment packages that are effective in a given situation. For these practitioners (and their clients), the effectiveness of a behavior-change procedure is more important than an analysis of why the treatment works.

Although Baer's point is well taken, it seems to us that there is a place for analysis (i.e., searching for principles and laws of behavior) in applied behavior analysis. It is unreasonable to expect hospital personnel, social workers, probation officers, teachers, parents, and other users of behavior principles to focus on the discovery of basic processes. It is not unreasonable to expect specialists in behavior analysis, regardless of focus, to have an acquaintance with analysis and basic research.

In our view, applied behavior analysis is more than the application of behavioral technology—it is part of the science of human behavior (Skinner, 1953). Part of the goal of this science is to analyze social systems and design cultural change (see Chapter 14). Based on this perspective, experimental analyses of communication, status and power, interpersonal relationships, and other social processes are as important as the treatment of individual problems (Epling & Pierce, 1986).

APPLICATIONS OF BEHAVIOR PRINCIPLES

As noted throughout this book, behavior principles have been applied to many practical problems. In this section, we highlight a few well-known applications of operant and respondent conditioning and discuss the basic principles underlying the effectiveness of these techniques.

Premack Principle

The principle of reinforcement is usually described as contingency between an operant and an environmental consequence, $R \rightarrow S^r$. This description of reinforcement suggests that responses and consequences are two distinct classes of events. The first (R) is viewed as some action emitted by the organism, and the second (S^r) is seen as a stimulus. A rat presses a bar and receives food as a reinforcing stimulus.

Premack (1959, 1962) described a contingency in which one behavior was strengthened by the opportunity to engage in another performance. In this case, reinforcement is another action of the organism. Instead of saying that a rat presses the bar for food, we can say that bar pressing produces eating. The **Premack principle** states that a higher frequency behavior will reinforce a lower frequency behavior. This principle has wide applicability and was first demonstrated with laboratory animals.

In his 1962 experiment, Premack deprived rats of water for 23 hours and then measured their behavior in a setting in which they could run on an activity wheel or drink water. Of course, the animals spent more time drinking than running. Next, Premack arranged a contingency between running and drinking. The rats received a few seconds' access to a drinking tube when they ran on the wheel. Running on the wheel increased when it produced the opportunity to drink water—showing that drinking reinforced running. In other words, the rats ran on the wheel to get a drink of water.

At this point in the experiment, Premack (1962) gave the rats free access to water. When the rats were allowed to choose between drinking and running, they did little drinking and a lot more running. Premack reasoned that running would now reinforce drinking because running occurred at a higher frequency than drinking. The running wheel was locked and the brake was removed if the rats licked the water tube for a few seconds. Based on this contingency, Premack showed that drinking water increased when it produced running. That is, the animals drank water to get a chance to run on the wheel.

Generally, this experiment shows that drinking reinforces running when rats are motivated to drink. On the other hand, running reinforces drinking when running is the preferred activity. Thus, when behavior is measured in a situation that allows a choice among different activities, those responses that occur at higher frequency may be used to reinforce those that occur at a lower frequency. To identify effective reinforcers in an applied setting, the behavior analyst may simply look for what people do a lot of, and this can be made contingent on lower frequency behavior. If you watch television about 3 hours a night but only study for 1 hour, you can increase studying by setting a contingency between home-work and watching favorite programs. For example, you could require 1 hour of study for each hour of television viewing.

An early example of the Premack principle in an applied setting was reported by Homme et al. (1963). These investigators modified the behavior of nursery school children who engaged in a variety of disorganized activities. The children were running, screaming, pushing chairs around, and generally having a wonderful time. This behavior was viewed as annoying because the children ignored the teacher's instructions. The researchers reasoned that the teacher could get the children to follow more instructions if the higher frequency behaviors of running and screaming were made contingent on following instructions. For example, when the children were sitting quietly and attending, the teacher was told to ring a bell and tell them to run and scream. After the teacher rang the bell, the children usually began to scream and run around the classroom. At this time, the teacher rang the bell again and gave another instruction to do another activity. Eventually, the children earned tokens for engaging in low-probability behavior. These tokens could be used to buy opportunities to engage in higher probability operants like kicking a waste basket, throwing a plastic cup, and pushing an adult around in a caster-equipped chair. The modification was highly successful, and the children quickly learned to follow the teacher's instructions.

Self-Control

An important part of socialization involves learning to give up immediate gains for greater long-term benefits. It also involves accepting immediate aversive consequences for later positive outcomes. When people manage their behavior in such a way that they choose the more beneficial long-range consequences, they are said to show **self-control.** From a behavioral perspective, self-control occurs when a person emits a response that affects the probability of subsequent behavior.

A person who sets the alarm clock before going to bed is showing self-control if this response ensures that he or she gets up for classes in the morning. Setting the alarm may be called a controlling response because it alters conditions that affect subsequent behavior—getting up for school rather than sleeping. Getting up for school is the controlled response in the sense that its probability of occurrence is altered by the effects of the controlling response. In a behavioral view of self-control, both the controlling and controlled responses are determined by the species history and contingencies of reinforcement. That is, there is no self or internal agent that controls what you do; behavior that is said to show self-control is similar to other complex operants and is regulated by the same principles.

Skinner (1953) has discussed a variety of self-control techniques that people commonly use, involving controlling and controlled responses. **Physical restraint** is a simple but prevalent method of self-management in which a person physically prevents a subsequent response. For instance, a person may put a hand over his or her mouth to prevent laughter. In this case, the controlling response, clasping the mouth, prevents the controlled response of laughing in an awkward situation. Another technique is called **changing the stimulus conditions.** This occurs when a person manages the stimuli that control subsequent behavior. A student who must have a particular text for class could put the book by the front door. **Deprivation and satiation** can be used for self-control, as when an individual eats an apple before dinner to lower food consumption during the subsequent meal.

Manipulation of emotional conditions is also a self-control technique. Students may psyche themselves up to have the courage to protest a low grade. Here self-control involves rehearsing the unjust reasons for the low mark, thereby increasing the chances of protesting it. **Aversive stimulation** may be used in self-control. Students who say to themselves, "I may fail the course if I don't get the paper completed" increase the probability of writing it. People occasionally **use drugs** as a technique of self-management, as when a person has a few drinks to alleviate the stress of an upcoming talk or presentation (we do not recommend this because it negatively reinforces drinking alcohol).

Self-reinforcement and punishment are also used to manage behavior. As we wrote this book, we finished each day's effort by running a word count on the computer. Running the word count was self-reinforcement for writing (or punishment for not writing much). After making a fool of oneself at a party, a person may chastise or punish himself or herself in an attempt to reduce future acts of idiocy. Finally, just **doing something else** may be used to alter subsequent behavior. If you do not want to talk about what happened on your last date, you can change the topic of conversation to plumbing, politics, dry cleaning, the economy in Algeria, or some other interesting topic.

Modern behavioral researchers use behavior analysis of choice and preference (Chapter 10) to investigate the underlying processes that result in self-control (Ainslie, 1974; Logue, 1988b; Rachlin & Green, 1972). In the laboratory, self-control occurs when an organism chooses a larger, more delayed reinforcer rather than an immediate, smaller reward. The choice of the smaller, immediate reinforcer is called **impulsiveness**. For example, choosing an immediate payment of $50 now rather than $200 after 3 months is impulsive behavior.

The probability of an impulsive response varies with the relative amount of reinforcement and with the relative delay to reinforcement. A person is more likely to choose the delayed reinforcer if the amount is increased from $200 to $1,000 while the small, immediate payment is held constant at $50. Similarly, the larger payment of $200 is more likely to be selected if its delay is reduced from 3 months to 6 weeks (see Logue, Pena-Correal, Rodriguez, & Kabela, 1986, for research with humans).

One way to solve the problem of choosing the smaller, immediate reinforcer over the larger, delayed reinforcer is to make a commitment. A **commitment** is a controlling response made before the actual choice. The commitment ensures that the larger, delayed payoff is always chosen. People will make a commitment only if they benefit more from this behavior than from alternative action.

For example, when payday arrives at the end of the month, the value of spending $100 is greater than the value of saving it (i.e., having $1,200 at the end of a year). An important finding is that the worth of an immediate, smaller reinforcer ($100) is **discounted** more rapidly with time than the worth of a larger, delayed reinforcer ($1,200) (e.g., Ainslie, 1974; Rachlin & Green, 1972). This means that there is a time, prior to payday, when saving $1,200 over a year is more valuable than spending $100. This change in the value of a reinforcer with time is called **preference reversal**. Because of preference reversal, a customer will sign a contract (commitment) with the bank to debit his or her checking account $100 at the end of each month. The money is used to pay off a government savings bond that will yield $1,200 plus interest at maturity. The contract with the bank ensures that the customer always chooses to save rather than spend when his or her paycheck arrives.

A Case Study of Self-Control. In applied behavior analysis, self-control techniques may be taught to clients, who are then better able to manage their own behavior. As we have mentioned, one common technique for self-control is called self-reinforcement. An interesting study was conducted by Belles and Bradlyn (1987), who modified the behavior of a heavy smoker by arranging self-reinforcement and self-punishment over the telephone. The client was a 65-year-old man who lived 200 miles away from the clinic. The researchers arranged a treatment program with the client and his wife. For each day that he smoked less than a specified number of cigarettes, he added $3 to a savings fund that was used to buy items that he wanted. When he exceeded the agreed-on number of cigarettes, he had to send a $25 check to the therapist, who donated the money to a charity that was unacceptable to him. His wife verified the number of cigarettes he smoked each day by unobtrusively monitoring his behavior.

A **changing criterion design** was used to evaluate the effectiveness of the self-control procedure. In this design, the criterion for the number of cigarettes smoked each day was progressively lowered over 95 days. The effects of self-reinforcement are shown if the subject meets or falls below the criterion set by the researchers. Figure 13.6 shows the effects of the treatment. The target level for each period is shown by a horizontal line, and the client generally matched his behavior to this criterion. Notice that although the criterion generally decreased, the researchers occasionally set a value higher than a previous phase and the client's behavior changed in accord with the contingencies. After 81 days on the program, the client's cigarette consumption had declined from about 85 to 5 cigarettes each day. At this point, he was satisfied with his progress and said that he wanted to remain at this level. Follow-up reports on his smoking over 18 months showed that he continued to have only five cigarettes a day.

Behavior Analysis And Education

Behavior principles have been applied in a wide variety of educational settings (Sulzer-Azaroff, 1986). University students have shown better academic performance after being taught with Fred Keller's personalized system of instruction, or PSI (Keller, 1968; Kulik, Kulik & Cohen, 1980). In addition, learning has been accelerated for elementary school children (and others), by precision teaching (Lindsley, 1972). Athletic performance has been improved by applying behavior principles to physical education (Martin & Hrycaiko, 1983). Autistic children

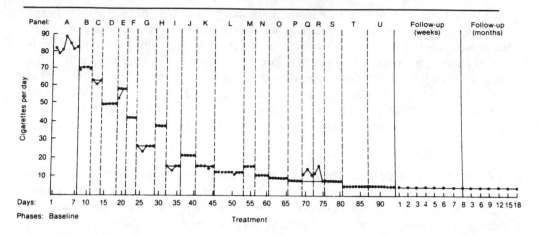

FIG. 13.6 A changing criterion design used in the modification of excessive smoking by Belles and Bradlyn (1987, and reprinted with permission of the *Journal of Behavior Therapy and Experimental Psychiatry*).

have benefited from the teaching of social and living skills (Lovaas, 1987). These are but a few of the many applications of behavior principles to education. In this section we focus on two examples, but there are many more educational applications than reported here.

A Personalized System of Instruction.

The traditional lecture method used to instruct college and university students has been largely unchanged for thousands of years. A teacher stands in front of a number of students and talks about his or her area of expertise. There are variations on this theme; students are encouraged to participate in discussion, to discover new facts for themselves, to reach conclusions by being led through a series of questions, and to be active rather than passive learners. During lectures, various forms of logic are used to arrive at conclusions, classroom demonstrations are arranged, and so on. Basically, however, the lecture method of teaching is the same as it has always been.

Dr. Fred Keller recognized that the lecture method of college teaching was inefficient and in many cases a failure. He reasoned that anyone who had acquired the skills needed to attend college was capable of successfully mastering most or all college courses. Some students might take longer than others to reach expertise in a course, but the overwhelming majority of students would be able to do so. If behavior principles were to be taken seriously, there were no bad students, only bad teachers.

In a seminal article, titled "Good-bye, teacher . . ." Fred Keller outlined a college teaching method based on principles of operant conditioning (Keller, 1968). Keller called his teaching method a personalized system of instruction, or PSI. Basically, PSI courses are organized such that students move through the course at their own pace. Some students may finish the course in a few weeks, others require a semester or longer.

Course material is broken down into many small units of reading and (if required) laboratory assignments. Students earn points (conditioned reinforcement) for completing unit tests and lab assignments. Mastery of the lab assignments and unit tests is required. If test scores are not close to perfect, the test (usually in a different form) is taken again. The assignments and tests build on one another so they must be completed in order.

Undergraduate proctors are recruited to assist with running the course. These individuals tutor students and mark unit tests and laboratory assignments. Proctors are, "chosen for [their] mastery of the course content and orientation, for [their] maturity of judgment, for [their] understanding of the special problems that confront ... beginner[s], and for [their] willingness to assist [with the course]" (Keller, 1968; p. 81). Lectures and class demonstrations are an optional privilege; students may or may not attend them. Lectures are scheduled once the majority of students in the class have passed a sufficient number of unit tests to indicate that they are ready to appreciate the lectures; no exams are based on these lectures. The course instructor designs the course, makes up the tests, delivers the optional lectures, adjudicates disputes, and oversees the course.

Comparison studies have evaluated student performance on PSI courses against performance for those students given computer-based instruction, audio-tutorial, traditional lecture-based teaching, visual-based instruction, and other programmed instruction methods. College students instructed by PSI outperformed students taught by these other methods when given a common final exam (see Lloyd & Lloyd, 1992 for a review). Despite this positive outcome, logistical problems in organizing PSI courses, teaching to mastery level (most students get an A for the course), and allowing students more time than the allotted semester to complete the course, have worked against the wide adoption of PSI in universities and colleges.

Teaching Autistic Children. Autistic children show an early lack of social interaction with parents, other family members, and peers. For example these children often resist being held and may have a tantrum if picked up or hugged. When autistic children get older they may be mistaken as deaf because they don't talk or even establish eye contact when talked to. These children often show repeated stereotyped patterns of behavior such as rocking back and forth, spinning a top, wiggling their fingers in front of their eyes and so on. More than 85% of autistic children fail to speak at an age when other children are highly verbal. The long-term outcome for this disorder is grim; the overwhelming majority of such children require extended care and supervision.

Ivar Lovaas, at the time of this writing a professor of psychology at the University of California at Los Angeles, has been working on the treatment of autism since the 1960s. Lovaas and his collaborators (Lovaas, 1966; 1977; 1987; McEachin, Smith, & Lovaas; 1993) have reported on the successful behavioral treatment of autistic children. Lovaas (1977) describes intensive behavioral interventions that increase social behavior, teach the child to speak, and eliminate self-stimulation. Most treated autistic children showed significant improvement in their daily functioning. Incredibly, when the treatment was applied to autistic children that were less than 30-months old, 50% of these children were later indistinguishable from normal school children. No other treatment of autistic children has produced such dramatic improvement (Lovaas, 1993; Schopler & Mesibov, 1994).

Because the treatment that Lovaas reported was highly effective, Joe Morrow and Brenda Terzich started a business devoted to behavioral intervention for autistic children (Morrow & Terzich, 1997, personal communication). The intervention they implemented was (and is) based on the treatment package described by Lovaas. Morrow and Terzich started their company, *Applied Behavior Consultants* or *ABC*, in 1987 in Sacramento, California. They concentrated on providing intensive in-home treatment for these children. Because they delivered an effective and well-designed treatment, the demand for their services quickly overwhelmed them. At this point they began hiring and training behavioral technicians.

As their business grew, they developed an in-home treatment technique that they continue to use today. Behavior technicians with some undergraduate training in behavior analysis are hired as behavior consultants. These people are then further trained by ABC staff to work with autistic children. When consultants are judged skilled enough to deliver behavioral services, they visit the homes of the client children. At this point, a behavioral assessment is conducted and an individualized treatment package is designed.

FIG. 13.7 Joe Morrow and Brenda Terzich.

Parents are taught the necessary behavioral skills for training their child. The treatment package includes specific intervention strategies for accomplishing behavioral outcomes. For example, the children are reinforced for making eye contact when the teacher talks to them. Appropriate life skills such as eating meals with utensils, dressing oneself, and personal hygiene (i.e., brushing teeth, combing hair, etc.) are reinforced with tokens and social approval. Verbal skills including manding and tacting are also targets for behavior change. ABC staff members monitor progress and, if necessary, advise program changes.

In 1994, Morrow and Terzich started a communication-based private school for autistic children that provides intensive behavioral intervention for more than 50 students at a time. The emphasis at the school is on verbal and academic behavior as well as social skills. An interesting innovation that they use in the school involves a picture-based communication program (Bondy & Frost, 1994) for children who have particular problems with spoken language. The children are reinforced for selecting picture icons that are exchanged for items that correspond with the icon.

Because of the success and subsequent demand for in-home behavioral treatment, ABC currently has more than 125 employees. Since the time they started (in 1987), more than 1000 autistic children have been treated by ABC. Each of these children have received a minimum of 40 hours a week of one-on-one behavior therapy. ABC has been able to reach such a large number of autistic children because of their emphasis on training parents to work with these youngsters (rather than directly providing therapy themselves). Although time-consuming, early-intensive behavior therapy has rescued many children from an otherwise isolated and impoverished life. Happily, this intervention is also much more cost-effective than providing a lifetime of supervision. The state of California has recognized both of these facts and provides most, or all, of the money for the program.

THE CAUSES AND PREVENTION OF BEHAVIOR PROBLEMS

In recent years, behavior analysts have focused attention on the factors that produce behavior problems. Animal models of disordered behavior have been developed that provide insight into the causes of problem behavior (see Epling & Pierce, 1992; Keehn, 1986). Other researchers have been concerned with promoting behavior related to physical health. The area of **behavioral medicine** includes behavior-change programs that target health-related activities such as following special diets, self-examination for early symptoms of disease, exercising, taking medicine, and so on (see Doleys, Meredith, & Ciminero, 1982; Friman, Finney, Glasscock, Weigel, & Christophersen, 1986). The idea is that many problems of behavior and health may be prevented before treatment is necessary.

Activity-Based Anorexia

Substantial evidence indicates that excessive physical activity is central to an understanding of human self-starvation, or anorexia (Pierce & Epling, 1991). Separate research areas indicate that, contrary to common sense, increasing amounts of physical exercise may reduce a person's appetite. Also, lowered food intake can induce physical activity. Thus, declining food intake produces activity and activity suppresses food intake. These two effects combine to produce an **activity-based anorexia** that occurs in animals and accounts for a significant number of cases of anorexia nervosa (Epling & Pierce, 1992).

Anorexia Nervosa.   A young woman goes on a severe diet and continues to the point of starvation. How can this person be anything but mentally disturbed? In fact, anorexia nervosa is currently classified as a neurotic disorder by psychiatrists and psychologists (see *Diagnostic and Statistical Manual*, 4th edition, *DSM IV*). Mental illness is suggested by the many symptoms that accompany willful starvation. These symptoms include fear of being fat, obsessive food rituals, distorted body image, and disturbed self-perception.

Notably, modern psychiatry has reinforced the view that cognitive and mental events cause abnormal human behavior. This is convincing to people, because unusual thoughts often accompany bizarre behavior. Although these thoughts may occur and are associated with disturbed eating, this evidence is not sufficient to claim that they are causes. One reason for this association may be that anorexics learn to label their emotional states and behavior in accord with the expectations of therapists, family, and friends.

The numerous and varied symptoms of anorexia also arise from starvation itself (Epling & Pierce, 1992; Keys, Brozek, Henschel, Mickelsen, & Taylor, 1950). Keys and his associates (1950) observed many of the symptoms of anorexia nervosa in psychologically healthy men who participated in a study of forced starvation. Symptoms similar to those found in anorexia nervosa developed as the men lost weight. On psychological tests the men became neurotic (a few scored in the psychotic range), they were obsessed with food, some became bulimic (excessive overeating), and so on. Importantly, these symptoms followed rather than preceded starvation—suggesting that they were not the causes of anorexia.

The study by Keys and his colleagues (1950) strongly suggests that starvation causes the symptoms of anorexia nervosa. If this is the case, then what determines starvation? Substantial evidence suggests that food restriction and excessive physical activity underlie most human anorexia.

Physical Activity and Anorexia.   Clinical reports of anorexia nervosa have viewed excessive physical activity as an interesting but unimportant symptom of the syndrome. For example, Feighner, Robins, Guze, Woodruff, Winokur, and Munoz (1972) have described diagnostic criteria that include periods of overactivity as one of six possible secondary symptoms. In the traditional view, activity is secondary because it is simply a way that the anorectic burns off calories. That is, physical activity reflects the patient's desire to lose weight.

Although this interpretation is widely accepted, there is evidence that it is wrong. Excessive physical activity appears central to many cases of human self-starvation (Epling & Pierce, 1992). The evidence for the importance of activity comes from a variety of sources. Controlled experiments with animals have shown that physical activity can make an animal give up eating when food is rel-

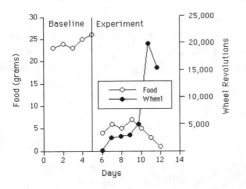

FIG. 13.8 Excessive running and reduction of food intake by an adolescent rat reported by Epling, Pierce, and Stefan (1983, and reprinted with permission of the *International Journal of Eating Disorders*).

atively abundant (Epling & Pierce, 1984, 1988). Research with humans has also suggested a link between activity and starvation. Beumont and his colleagues asked 25 anorexics to identify their symptoms and the order of occurrence (Beumont, Booth, Abraham, Griffiths, & Turner, 1983). Of the 28 reported symptoms, only manipulating food servings and increased sport activity were present in all patients. Generally, the ordering of the symptoms indicated that changes in dieting and food intake were followed by increased physical activity. Many other studies have documented excessive physical activity in anorexic patients (see Epling, Pierce, & Stefan, 1983, for a review).

Anorexia in Animals.

The process of activity anorexia begins when rats are fed a single daily meal and are allowed to run on an activity wheel. It is important to note that the size of the meal is more than adequate for survival. Also, animals are not forced to exercise on the wheel. They can choose to remain in an attached cage or just lie in the wheel. In fact, the animals start running, and this activity increases daily because of the food restriction.

As shown in Figure 13.8, wheel running rapidly increases to excessive levels. An adolescent rat may run up to 20 km a day at the peak. Ordinarily, these animals would run less than 1 km a day. This excessive activity is surprising because the animal is expending many more calories than it is consuming. For this reason, the activity is life-threatening.

A more startling effect is that food intake drastically declines as running becomes excessive. As you can see at the end of 1 week (Figure 13.8), the animal is eating very little. The rat is giving up eating in spite of increasing energy expenditure through wheel running. If this process is allowed to continue, the animal dies of starvation. The drop in running on the last day occurs because the rat is too weak to continue.

Motivational Basis of Eating and Running.

In Chapter 6, we discussed the interrelations of eating and running (Pierce et al., 1986). Recall that the research evidence indicates that rats will work more for an opportunity to run on a wheel as food deprivation increases. The animals bar pressed many more times for 60 seconds of wheel running as their body weights declined. Additionally, rats pressed a lever for food less when they had run on a wheel the night before a food session. This effect occurred even though the animals had several hours of rest before being placed in the operant chamber. The overall findings suggest that the reinforcing effectiveness of physical activity increased as a function of food deprivation. Also, the reinforcement value of eating food decreased when preceded by a bout of physical activity. These two reinforcement relations provide a behavioral account of the activity-anorexia cycle (see Chapter 6 for the biological basis of these reinforcement relationships).

Humans and Anorexia.   The seemingly willful starvation of animals appears similar to cases of human anorexia. For humans, social reinforcement can increase the tendency to diet or exercise. An individual may learn these responses to escape or avoid criticism for being overweight or to gain approval for being slim and fit. The type and intensity of dieting and exercise is initially regulated by the responses of others. However, once social reinforcement has encouraged food restriction, especially in the context of increasing exercise, the activity-anorexia cycle may be initiated. When the process starts, the person is trapped by the activity/food reduction cycle.

Humans self-impose diets for a variety of reasons. All diets do not generate excessive activity. The type, severity, and pattern of diet are important factors contributing to physical activity. For example, many anorexics change their meal pattern from several meals to one per day. This change in the number of meals may be important in generating activity anorexia. Other patterns of food intake may not lead to excessive activity, but evidence is lacking on this point at the moment.

Activity anorexia develops from an interplay of culture, behavior, and biology. Cultural practices and contingencies of reinforcement predispose some individuals to contact the activity-anorexia cycle. This cycle is the result of species evolution and is mediated by physiological mechanisms regulating eating and physical activity. Once initiated, the cycle of increasing activity and decreasing food intake is resistant to change.

Assessment, Treatment, and Prevention.   The activity-anorexia model has important practical implications. In our book *Solving the Anorexia Puzzle: A Scientific Approach* (Epling & Pierce, 1992), we outlined the criteria for assessment, treatment, and prevention of activity anorexia. In terms of assessment, the primary criteria involve a history of low and declining food intake, a history of excessive physical activity, and psychological symptoms that follow rather than precede weight loss. Treatment is based on traditional behavior-modification procedures but is directed at the responses that comprise the activity-anorexia cycle. For example, contingencies are arranged to stop excessive dieting and exercise. In addition, patients are taught how to eat and to discriminate between moderate and excessive levels of exercise.

Prevention of activity anorexia involves changing the sociocultural conditions that promote excessive dieting and exercising. Medical doctors are in the best position to call attention to the role of diet and exercise in the onset and maintenance of eating disorders. Self-help groups concerned with eating disorders may have members who recognize the biobehavioral processes involved in self-starvation. These groups can play an important role in preventing onset and relapse of activity anorexia. A second major function of self-help groups is education and social change. The groups may send speakers to schools, public meetings, and professional conferences. These groups may also lobby physicians, government agencies, private organizations, and public companies. Because of this active and organized involvement, self-help groups may be the most important source of prevention for activity anorexia.

ON THE APPLIED SIDE

MammaCare: Detection and Prevention of Breast Cancer

In 1980, breast cancer killed 36,000 women in the United States and was the leading cause of cancer deaths in women 25 to 74 years old. It is estimated that about 10% of women in the United States will eventually develop breast cancer—in 1980 there were over 100,000 new cases. In addition to loss of life, victims of breast cancer often undergo disfiguring surgery that may physically and psychologically disable them.

Early detection of a malignant tumor in the breast is a major weapon in the fight against breast cancer. At present, doctors do not know how to prevent breast cancer, but early detection significantly improves a woman's chances of survival. Importantly, the victims of the disease are almost always the first ones to detect the tumor. In most cases, however, women only detect the tumor after the cancer has reached an advanced stage. Regular and proficient self-examination by young women could substantially improve the detection of small tumors. Early detection would dramatically increase survival and lower the likelihood of disfiguring surgery.

Dr. Henry S. Pennypacker and his associates at the University of Florida have developed a behavioral program called **MammaCare** to teach women effective self-examination of their breasts (Hall, Adams, Stein, Stephenson, Goldstein & Pennypacker, 1980; Pennypacker, Bloom, Criswell, Neelakantan, Goldstein, & Stein, 1982). He began to work on this program because:

> like many before me, I took a degree in classical experimental psychology and began an academic career. I rapidly became uncomfortable with the hypocrisy inherent in my position: I was an "expert" in learning using none of my expertise in my work. My interest turned to education at all levels, partly because of the critical role it plays in the survival and evolution of the culture and partly because it looked like an easy place to make a contribution. How wrong I was! ... [W]ith hindsight ... I have a better understanding of the problems we face and general strategies needed to solve them. MammaCare is a step in that direction. (personal communication, February 22, 1989)

FIG. 13.9 Henry S. Pennypacker.

The MammaCare program is based on the assumption that women often are unable to detect small tumors simply because they have not been trained to do so. The pressure receptors of the fingertips allow for subtle discrimination of surface contour (e.g., from smooth to bumpy), as is clearly demonstrated by blind people who read Braille. It follows that women may be trained to detect small lesions in the breast related to cancerous tumors. An effective program must teach women to tell the difference between small tumors and the normal lumpiness of the breast itself.

Components of MammaCare.   An initial step involves discrimination training. The patient is trained to use her fingertips to discriminate small lesions from ordinary nodules in the breast. This training is accomplished with the used of silicone breast models that have been developed to match the physical properties of real breast tissue (Bloom, Criswell, Pennypacker, Catania, & Adams, 1982; Hall et al, 1980). A woman palpates the breast model in order to detect lumps of different hardness, located at various depths, and varying in lateral mobility. Detection of lumps functions as reinforcement that maintains searching for and reporting on abnormal breast tissue.

Once the patient is able to detect small lumps (e.g., diameter of 0.4 mm) with her fingertips, she is taught additional palpitation and search skills (Saunders, Pilgram, & Pennypacker, 1986). A technique of palpitation is trained which emphasizes breast examination using the pads of the fingers and multiple pressures. A vertical strips pattern of search is used because of greater success at detection when compared with concentric circles or radial spokes patterns (Saunders et al., 1986). The target of these procedures is to ensure that a woman's fingers contact a maximum volume of breast tissue during self-examination. In this phase, the woman learns palpitation and search on her own breast while being carefully evaluated by a trained professional.

As with all behavioral programs, simple but precise and objective measurement procedures are used to indicate a patient's proficiency at detection and thoroughness of self-examination. A patient must be at least 95% proficient before leaving the training center. This level of proficiency helps ensure that self-examination techniques become an integrated skill that may be practiced monthly as recommended.

A final component of the program ensures maintenance of self-examination by reinforced practice. After MammaCare training, each woman is given a take-home kit that contains a breast model that is matched to the firmness and nodularity of her own breast tissue. This breast model is used to update the patient's tactile skill just before she carries out the monthly self-examination. The practice model contains five small tumor simulations that the patient can find only if she performs the examination correctly. Based on this reinforced practice, a woman who finds nothing unusual during a breast examination can be almost certain that there was nothing there to detect.

Effectiveness of the Program.   Women who have learned the MammaCare method of breast self-examination are able to detect lesions as small as 0.4 mm in diameter. This compares favorably to the average tumor that women discover by accident, measuring 3.6 cm in diameter. It also compares well with conventional self-examination, in which women detect tumors in the 2.0-cm range. Evidence also shows that training in self-examination improves detection in actual breast tissue (Pennypacker et al., 1982, pp. 109–110). The greater effectiveness of a behavioral system of breast self-examination lies in the fact that the program directly teaches women what to feel for and how to search their breasts thoroughly.

Extending the Use of the Program.   The MammaCare program is now available to a greater number of women at a lower cost. Further research has resulted in a learning system that may be done at home, at the woman's convenience (MammaCare Learning System). The system includes a silicone breast model with simulated tumors, a step-by-step videocassette to train mastery-level proficiency in self-examination, and a practice kit that includes a second model, a written review manual, a reminder calendar, and a record booklet (for information write to The Mammacatch Corporation, 930 NW 8th Ave., Gainesville, FL 32601). A woman uses the learning system to master the self-examination skills and then is asked to perform a portion of the breast exam in the presence of a trained professional who can correct any problems.

Finally, the MammaCare system is now available to physicians or other health professionals through a special 2-hour clinical training course, with optional 3- and 5-day training seminars. Professional training is focused on those who must evaluate the breast self-examination skills of many women—including patients in a large medical practice or employees in a large organization. Also, women who complete the 5-day program may arrange to offer the 3-day course to professionals in their own neighborhood. In this way, an effective behavioral technology for breast self-examination is transmitted to a wider circle of health-care professionals, who in turn pass these skills on to more and more women.

KEY WORDS

A-B-A-B reversal design
Activity-based anorexia
Analytical pragmatism
Applied behavior
  analysis
Autism
Behavior maintenance
Behavior trapping
Behavioral contract
Behavioral medicine

Changing criterion
  design
Commitment (as
  controlling response)
Continuous recording
Controlled response
Controlling response
Differential
  reinforcement of
  other behavior (DRO)
Duration recording

Fear hierarchy
Interval recording
Multiple baseline designs
Personalized system of
  instruction
Premack principle
Response generalization
Self-control
Stimulus generalization
Time sampling

CHAPTER 14

Three Levels of Selection: Biology, Behavior, and Culture

1. What is the general form of causation for biology, behavior, and culture? Define three levels of selection.
2. Diagram and describe the contingencies at the three levels. How does selection by consequences operate at each level?
3. Discuss biological evolution as a fact and note the dispute over details.
4. Describe the process of natural selection as formulated by Darwin. What is evolution?
5. How does natural selection involve contingencies of survival? What happens when the contingencies of survival change?
6. Define phenotype and genotype. Discuss the interaction of genes and environment.
7. Identify two major sources of genetic variation and how each operates. In terms of embryonic development, what is the result of differences in genetic material?
8. Discuss differences in behavior as heritable characteristics using Barash's (1982) example of woodchucks, yellow-bellied marmots, and Olympic marmots. Explain the importance of natural selection for such behavioral differences.
9. Know what is meant by behavioral rigidity and give an example using the fixed-action pattern.
10. Describe the research of Scheller and Axel (1984) on the genetic control of egg laying in *Aplysia*.
11. Outline the components of the egg-laying sequence. Why is this experiment important for the study of relatively complex animal behavior?
12. Analyze the dance of the honeybee as genetic regulation of complex behavior. Point to the stimulus control exerted by the position of the sun. What is the survival value of the dance? How could the dance have evolved?

13. Under what conditions is behavioral rigidity likely to be selected? When does behavioral flexibility have survival value?

14. State the advantage of behavioral flexibility according to Skinner (1984).

15. Use an experiment by Hirsch and McCauley (1977) to show that conditioning is a heritable behavioral process. Talk about the variability in conditioning, and selection for (or against) behavioral flexibility.

16. Describe the biological advantage of reinforcement as a behavioral process. State Glenn's (1991) analysis of this problem.

17. Talk about operant selection and extinction using the example of a child's behavior and the sound of a rubber duck.

18. Discuss behavioral variation during extinction and its importance for human invention (e.g., electric light).

19. How does susceptibility to reinforcement supplement the survival value of eating and copulating? What happened when organisms evolved susceptibility to food and sexual reinforcement?

20. Show that susceptibility to reinforcement may be species specific. How can susceptibility to reinforcement occasionally lead to behavior that is not biologically adaptive?

21. In terms of determinants of social signals, what is the difference between the honeybee dance and human gestures (e.g., gesture for "come here")?

22. What role could stimulus equivalence play in communication by gestures?

23. Discuss the evolution of speech sounds, pointing to Skinner's (1986) analysis. What were three important steps in the evolution of speech sounds?

24. How did the evolution of speech sounds contribute to verbal behavior? Is manding for the benefit of the speaker or listener? What about tacting? Why?

25. Discuss verbal behavior and the coordination of action. Why does the listener provide reinforcement for the speaker's behavior? How could ways of speaking be selected by social reinforcement?

26. What is a cultural practice? Use the Roman phalanx to show the function of a cultural practice. Discuss how operants and practices are selected by consequences.

27. Know what is meant by metacontingency, and give an example based on education, science, and a technologically advanced culture. Why isn't the "best" educational practice always adopted?

28. Outline the origin of a food taboo for a troop of baboons in a zoo enclosure. How was the taboo transmitted? What maintained the cultural practice? Discuss Harris's (Harris, 1974) functional analysis of the origin and transmission of human cultural taboos.

29. Discuss cultural evolution in terms of adoption of innovations and metacontingencies. Cite examples of innovation by the infant Imo in a troop of Japanese macaque monkeys. How can cultural practices (e.g., transcription of books) remain unchanged over many generations?

30. How can selection by reinforcement and metacontingencies be used in cultural design?

31. Analyze the growth of human populations as a social problem. What kind of contingencies do Wiest and Squire (1974) suggest for modifying birth control practices?

32. What is the role of behavior analysis in the future?

Natural selection is one of the great scientific discoveries of humankind. Although most people know something about Darwin's theory of evolution, they seldom consider its implications for the behavior of organisms, especially humans. Contemporary behaviorists have, however, emphasized an evolutionary analysis, suggesting that principles of variation and selection are fundamental to any account of behavior.

Behavioral researchers have suggested that **selection by consequences** is the operating principle for biology, behavior, and culture. It is a general form of causation that goes beyond the push-pull mechanistic model of physics. With regard to biology, mutation and sexual reproduction ensure a range of variation in genes that code for the features of organisms. Some physical attributes are helpful in the sense of meeting the requirements of the environment. Organisms with these adaptive features survive and reproduce, passing their genetic material to the next generation. Organisms without these characteristics do not survive as well, and their genes are less represented in the subsequent population. Natural selection is therefore a form of selection by reproductive consequences that occurs at the biological level.

Selection by consequences has been extended to the level of behavior. Operant conditioning may be viewed as an expressed characteristic of many organisms, including humans. A major aspect of such conditioning is selection by the consequences of behavior. Organisms with an extensive range of operant behavior adjust to new environmental situations on the basis of reinforcement. Richard Dawkins (1986, p. 487), an eminent zoologist, noted that "the whole point of [behavioral-level] selection by consequences is that it can solve problems that [[genetic-level] selection has not solved." Organisms that increased or decreased behavior on the basis of reinforcing consequences were more likely to survive and reproduce. Thus, operant conditioning became a major mode of adaptation.

As noted throughout this book, operants are the physical units selected at the behavioral level. The process of selection and change of operants is analogous to evolution and natural selection at the genetic level. Emitted behavior varies in form and frequency. Those responses that meet the environmental requirements (both physical and social contingencies) are reinforced, increasing in frequency during the lifetime of an individual. Other responses that fail to satisfy the contingencies reduce in frequency or become extinct. Reinforcement is therefore an ontogenetic process that extends selection by consequences to the level of behavior.

A third level of evolution and selection occurs at the cultural level. The physical unit of selection at this level is the cultural practice. A **cultural practice** involves the interlocking operant behavior of many people. As with operants, cultural practices vary in form and frequency. Different ways of doing things are more or less successful in terms of efficiency, productivity, and survival of group members. For example, in terms of making automobiles, Henry Ford's assembly-line method produced more cars at less cost than other manufacturing systems. It also resulted in higher wages and more economic growth. These outcomes increased adoption of the assembly-line practice throughout the automotive industry. Generally, cultural practices are selected by such aggregate outcomes, increasing or decreasing the rate of adoption of the practice.

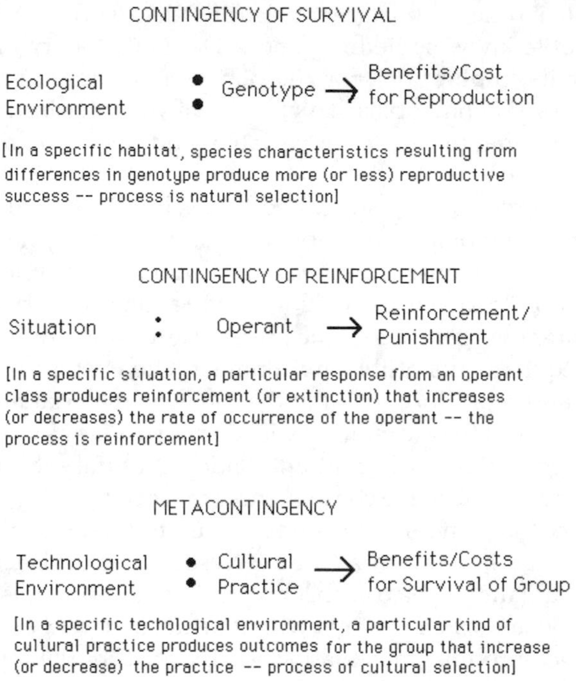

CONTINGENCY OF SURVIVAL

Ecological   •   Genotype →   Benefits/Cost
Environment   •   for Reproduction

[In a specific habitat, species characteristics resulting from
differences in genotype produce more (or less) reproductive
success -- process is natural selection]

CONTINGENCY OF REINFORCEMENT

Situation   :   Operant   →   Reinforcement/
                                   Punishment

[In a specific stiuation, a particular response from an operant
class produces reinforcement (or extinction) that increases
(or decreases) the rate of occurrence of the operant -- the
process is reinforcement]

METACONTINGENCY

Technological   •   Cultural   →   Benefits/Costs
Environment   •   Practice   for Survival of Group

[In a specific techological environment, a particular kind of
cultural practice produces outcomes for the group that increase
(or decrease) the practice -- process of cultural selection]

FIG. 14.1 Selection by consequences operates at three levels: biology, behavior, and culture.

In this chapter, selection by consequences is examined at the genetic, behavioral, and cultural levels (see Figure 14.1). In showing the parallels among these different levels, behavioral researchers seek to integrate the study of behavior with biology on the one hand and the social sciences on the other. The attempt is not to reduce behavior to biology, or culture to behavior. Rather, it is to show the common underpinnings of all life science in terms of the extension and elaboration of basic principles.

LEVEL 1: EVOLUTION AND NATURAL SELECTION

The theory of evolution is not merely speculation. Scientific research has shown that the major principles are well established. Based on this realization, the theory of evolution is a factual account of the origins of species. Even though most scientists accept the process of evolution, there are still disputes over details. For example, some evolutionary biologists claim that very rapid evolution can occur (e.g., Alvarez, 1982; Alvarez, Alvarez, Asaro, & Michael, 1980; Alvarez, Asaro & Michel, 1980; Alvarez, Asaro, Michel, & Alvarez, 1982) while others favor a more gradual elaboration of species characteristics (see Gould, 1989, for punctuated versus gradual evolution). Another issue involves the unit of selection. Some researchers emphasize the gene rather than the individual as the unit of selection.

From this perspective, the organism is simply the gene's way of "getting into the next generation" (Dawkins, 1976). All of these viewpoints are consistent with the major principle of natural selection. Thus, disagreements about how evolution operates do not challenge the fact of evolution (Barash, 1982).

Natural Selection

The evolutionary history of a species, or **phylogeny,** is the outcome of natural selection. Darwin (1859) showed how organisms change in accord with this principle. Based on a thorough analysis of life forms, Darwin concluded that reproductive success was the underlying basis of evolution. That is, individuals with more children pass on a greater number of their characteristics to the next generation.

Darwin noticed structural differences among members of sexually reproducing species. Except for identical (monozygotic) twins, individuals in the population vary in their physical features. Thus, birds like the thrush show variation in color of plumage, length of wings, and thickness of beak. Based on differences in their features, some individuals in a population are more successful than others at surviving and producing offspring. Differences in reproductive success occur when certain members of a species possess attributes that make them more likely to survive and reproduce in a given environment. Generally, individuals with features that meet the requirements of a habitat produce more offspring than others. As the number of descendants increases, the genetic traits of these individuals are more represented in the population. This process of differential reproduction is called *natural selection,* and the change in the genetic make-up of the species is evolution.

Contingencies of Survival

From a behavioral viewpoint, natural selection involves **contingencies of survival** (Skinner, 1986). The habitat or environment inadvertently sets requirements for survival of individuals. Members of a species who exhibit features appropri-

FIG. 14.2 Charles Darwin in his later years. Darwin discovered the principle of natural selection. (From Julia Cameron/ Corbis-Bettmann).

ate to the contingencies survive and reproduce. Those with less appropriate characteristics have fewer offspring and their genetic line may become extinct. Natural selection therefore occurs as particular organisms satisfy (or fail to satisfy) the contingencies of survival.

An important implication of a contingency analysis of evolution is that the requirements for survival may change gradually or suddenly. For example, during the time of the dinosaurs, the collision of a large asteroid with the earth may have drastically changed the climate, fauna, and temperature of the planet. Given these changes in environmental contingencies, dinosaurs could not survive. The smaller mammals, however, that possessed features more appropriate to the new habitat lived and reproduced. Changes in the contingencies may, therefore, occasionally favor characteristics that have advantages in a changed environment. This may occur even though these characteristics were a disadvantage in the past (see Gould, 1989, for a contingency view of evolution).

Phenotype, Genotype, and Environment

Evolutionary biologists distinguish between phenotype and genotype. An organism's **phenotype** refers to all the characteristics observed during the lifetime of an individual. For example, an individual's size, color, and shape are anatomical aspects of phenotype. Behavioral features include taste preferences, aggressiveness, shyness, and so on. Different phenotypic attributes of individuals may or may not reflect underlying genetic variation.

The **genotype** refers to the actual genetic make-up of the organism. Some observable characteristics are largely determined by genotype, while other features are strongly influenced by experience. But, as shown in Figure 14.3, most result from an interaction of genes and environment. Thus, the height of a person is attributable to both genes and nutrition. Evolution only occurs when the phenotypic differences among individuals are based on differences in genotype. If differences in height or other features did not result from genetic differences, selection for tallness (or shortness) could not occur. This is because there would be no genes for height to pass on to the next generation. People who engage in bodybuilding by lifting weights and taking steroids may substantially increase their muscle size (phenotype), but this characteristic will not be passed on to their children. Natural selection can only work when there are genes that underlie physical features.

FIG. 14.3 Phenotype is a product of geneotype and environment.

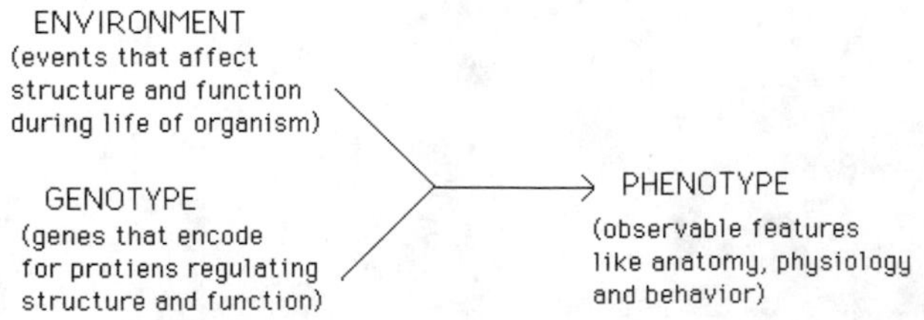

ENVIRONMENT
(events that affect
structure and function
during life of organism)

GENOTYPE
(genes that encode
for protiens regulating
structure and function)

PHENOTYPE
(observable features
like anatomy, physiology
and behavior)

Sources of Genetic Variation

There are two major sources of genetic variation: sexual recombination of existing genes and mutation. Genetic differences among individuals arise from sexual reproduction. This is because the blending of male and female genes produces an enormous number of combinations. Although sexual recombination produces variation, the number of genetic combinations is constrained by the existing pool of genes. In other words, there is a finite number of genes in a population, and this determines the amount of variation caused by sexual reproduction.

Mutation occurs when the genetic material (e.g., genes or chromosomes) of an individual changes. These changes are accidents that affect the genetic code carried by ovum or sperm. For example, naturally occurring background radiation may alter a gene site or a chromosome may break during the formation of sex cells or gametes. Such mutations are passed on to offspring, who display new characteristics. In most instances, mutations produce physical features that work against an organism's survival and reproductive success. However, on rare occasions mutations produce traits that improve reproductive success. The importance of mutation is that it is the source of new genetic variation. All novel genetic differences are ultimately based on mutation.

Natural selection depends on genetic variation attributed to sexual recombination and mutation. Genes code for proteins, which in turn regulate embryonic development and structural form. This means that differences in genes result in phenotypic differences in the structure (e.g., size and form of the brain) and physiology (e.g., release of hormones) of organisms.

Based on such differences in phenotype, some organisms are better adapted to meet the contingencies for survival arranged by the habitat. That is, some individuals exhibit features that satisfy the contingencies while others do not. Selection occurs when specific genes underlying these phenotypic features contribute to survival. Individuals with such characteristics have more offspring, ensuring that their genes occur at a higher frequency in the next generation.

EVOLUTION AND BEHAVIOR

Darwin (1871) recognized that the behavior of organisms was a heritable characteristic. The evolution of behavioral characteristics is shown in sociobiological studies of animal behavior. Woodchucks, yellow-bellied marmots, and Olympic marmots are three species of marmots that show differences in social behavior (Barash, 1973a, 1973b). There is evidence that the behavioral diversity of these marmots depends on natural selection (see Figure 14.4).

Variation in Social Behavior by Habitat

Woodchucks live at low elevations, primarily in food-abundant fields throughout the eastern United States. They are aggressive and solitary animals who associate only briefly at mating. The young are raised by the female woodchuck, who

FIG. 14.4 Olympic marmots studied by Barash (1973a, 1973b; reprinted from Barash, 1982, with permission of Elsevier, Amsterdam).

chases them out of the burrow as soon as they are weaned. Young woodchucks are completely on their own by the first year of life, and they are sexually mature by the second year. In contrast, Olympic marmots live at high elevations in Olympic National Park and inhabit the alpine meadows where there is a brief growing season. These animals are nonaggressive and highly tolerant of one another. Olympic marmots raise their pups in colonies, and the young disperse from the colony around the third year—becoming sexually active in the fourth year of life. Finally, yellow-bellied marmots live at medium elevations where there is an intermediate growing season. They are moderately aggressive and disperse their young in the second year.

Barash (1982) has pointed to the importance of natural selection in the behavioral differences of these marmots. He explains the process as follows:

> The most important environmental factor appears not to be elevation itself but, rather, the amount of food available to individuals of each species during a year. There is good evidence that aggression from adult marmots is instrumental in causing the young to disperse, to leave their colony of birth. It would clearly be adaptive for the adults to refrain from any aggressiveness that would precipitate the suicidal dispersal of their own undersized young. The progressively increasing need for delayed dispersal among marmot inhabitants of environments with progressively less available food may at least in part explain the striking correlation of marmot social systems with their environments. (Barash, 1982, p. 41)

The aggressive behavior of woodchucks functions to disperse the young at an early age. This is possible in a food-abundant environment where immature woodchucks may easily survive on their own. When food was scarce, cooperative behavior was selected and Olympic marmots became nonaggressive in accord with the longer caretaking requirements set by their habitat. Both aggressive and cooperative behavior may be adaptive depending on the contingencies of survival set by the environment.

Genetic Regulation of Behavior

Behavioral Rigidity. As we have noted, the behavior of organisms is always a phenotypic expression of genes and environment. Some behavioral characteristics are closely regulated by genes, and in such instances the environment plays a subsidiary role. For example, in some species, defense of territory occurs as a ritualized sequence of behavior called a **fixed-action pattern** (e.g., Tinbergen, 1951). The sequence or chain is set off by a specific stimulus, and the component responses are repeated almost identically with each presentation of the stimulus (see Chapter 3). The behavior pattern is based on a "genetic blueprint," and the environment simply initiates the sequence.

For example, the male stickleback fish will aggressively defend its territory from male intruders during mating season. The fish shows a fixed sequence of threatening actions that are elicited by the red underbelly of an intruding male. Tinbergen (1951) showed that this fixed-action pattern occurred even to cigar-shaped pieces of wood that had a red patch painted on the bottom of the stick. In addition, he showed that a male intruder with its red patch hidden did not evoke the threatening sequence. Generally, the male stickleback is genetically programmed to carry out the attack sequence given a specific stimulus at a particular moment in time.

FOCUS ON RESEARCH
Genetic Control of a Fixed-Action Pattern

Recently, Richard Scheller, a geneticist at Stanford University, and Richard Axel, a professor of pathology and biochemistry at Columbia University College of Physicians and Surgeons, reported on the genetic control of a complex behavioral sequence. Scheller and Axel (1984) used the techniques of recombinant DNA to isolate a subset of gene locations that control the egg-laying sequence of the marine snail (*Aplysia*).

Techniques of recombinant DNA are beyond the scope of this book, but the important thing is that these procedures can be used to identify gene sites that encode for specific neuropeptides. In the Scheller and Axel (1984) experiment, the researchers isolated a set of gene sites that coordinated the release of several peptides. These chemicals caused neurological changes that invariably produced the egg-laying sequence.

Using techniques of genetic manipulation, Scheller and Axel were able to "turn on" the gene sites that controlled a complex and integrated sequence of behavior. In this sequence, the snail first contracts the muscles of the reproductive duct and expels a string of

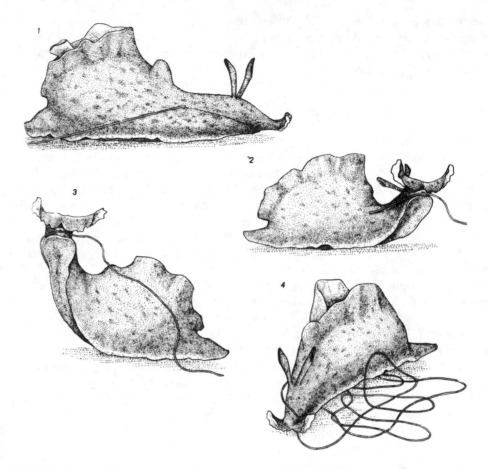

FIG. 14.5 The egg-laying sequence of the marine snail (*Aplysia*). The sequence involves (1) expelling a string of egg cases, (2) grasping the egg string by the mouth, (3) waving the head to draw the string out of the duct, and (4) affixing a triangle of string to a solid substance. This behavior was elicited by genetic procedures that activated the gene coding for egg-laying hormone (ELH) and other peptides associated with egg-laying behavior (from Scheller & Axel, 1984, and reprinted with the permission of *Scientific American*).

egg cases. Next, the animal grasps the egg string in its mouth and waves its head, behavior that typically functions to remove eggs from the duct. It then attaches the tangle of string to a solid surface. This behavioral sequence is shown in Figure 14.5. The fixed-action pattern was activated in an unmated snail by direct manipulation of the egg-laying hormone (ELH) gene.

The DNA sequences that control egg laying may play an important role in other aspects of this animal's behavior. For example, the genetic material that encodes for head-waving behavior may be duplicated and appear in other genes that regulate feeding. In this regard, Scheller and Axel (1984) suggested:

the same peptide may be incorporated in several different precursors encoded by different genes. Consider head waving in Aplysia. A characteristic waving of the snail's head takes place during feeding as well as during egg-laying. The same peptide or peptides could elicit the same behavioral component (head waving) in two very different contexts. To this end the head-waving peptide (or peptides) may be encoded in some other gene—one implicated in feeding behavior—as well as the ELH gene. In this way complex behaviors could be assembled by the combination of simple units of behavior, each unit mediated by one peptide or a small number of peptides. (p. 62)

When environments were stable and predictable, the replication of the same DNA sequence in a new genetic context may be one way that organisms evolved complex behavior. This solution involves using the same genetic code in different combinations. Although a high level of behavioral complexity may be achieved in this manner, the resulting behavior is tightly controlled by the underlying genetic context.

Some forms of animal communication are strongly determined by genotype. For example, the dance of the honeybee is a highly ritualized sequence of behavior that guides the travel of other bees (see Figure 14.6). After abundant foraging, a bee returns to the hive and begins to dance while other bees observe the performance. Subsequently, the bees who observe the dance fly directly to the foraging area in a so-called beeline.

The position of the sun with respect to food plays an important role in determining the initial dance. A bee may dance for several hours, and during this time the dance changes. These behavioral changes occur as the position of the sun with respect to food is altered by the rotation of the earth. That is, the bee's dancing corrects for the fact that the sun rises and falls over the course of a day.

The survival value of the dance relates to increased food supply for the hive. One problem is accounting for the occurrence of the dance before other bees responded to it—that is, before the dance had survival value. Presumably, the distance and direction that bees traveled had some effect on their behavior. Signs of fatigue and phototropic movements may have varied with distance and the position of the sun when they returned.

Bees that evolved sensitivity to what others did could respond to these aspects of behavior—relying on genes that coded for specific neurochemicals. Over time, natural selection favored variations in phototropic (and other) movements that made honeybee dancing more effective. Foraging bees would dance in conspicuous ways that allowed other bees to travel more accurately to the food source (for a similar analysis, see Skinner, 1986, p. 116).

Fixed-action patterns and the communication of bees are examples of behavior that is predominantly regulated by genes. In both instances, complex sequences of behavior are activated by specific stimuli and carried out in a highly ritualized manner. As shown in Figure 14.7, this form of behavior regulation was selected when the habitat of an animal was relatively stable and predictable.

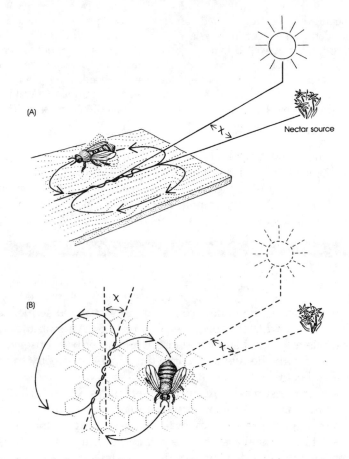

FIG. 14.6 The dance of a honeybee illustrates a phylogenetic form of communication in animals.

Behavioral Flexibility.   When organisms were faced with unpredictable and changing environments, natural selection favored those individuals whose behavior was flexible—adjusting on the basis of past experience. In this case, genes played a subsidiary role, coding for general processes of learning. These processes allowed an organism to adjust to changing environmental requirements throughout its life span. Flexibility of behavior in turn contributed to the reproductive success of the organism.

Skinner (1984) noted the survival advantage of behavioral flexibility:

> Reproduction under a much wider range of conditions became possible with the evolution of two processes through which individual organisms acquired behavior appropriate to novel environments. Through respondent (Pavlovian) conditioning, responses paired in advance by natural selection could come under the control of new stimuli. Through operant conditioning, new responses could be strengthened (reinforced) by events which immediately followed them. (p. 477)

In other words, respondent and operant conditioning are processes that are themselves genetically determined.

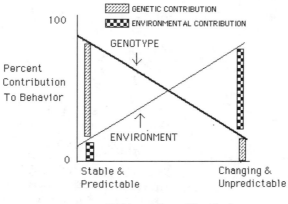

FIG. 14.7 When contingencies of survival are relatively stable and predictable, genetic regulation of behavior is predominant (e.g., fixed-action patterns) and the environment plays a subsidiary role. As contingencies of survival become more uncertain, the role played by the environment and conditioning increases, while direct genetic regulation of behavior declines.

There is evidence for the selection of conditioning. Hirsch and McCauley (1977) showed that the blowfly, *Phormia regina*, could be classically conditioned and that the process of conditioning was heritable. Blowflies can be trained to extend their proboscis (or snout) whenever water is applied to their feet, if they are given sugar that is paired with foot wetting. Even though this conditioned reflex is learned, the process of establishing the reflex can be modified dramatically by artificial selection.

Flies varied in the number of elicited responses to the conditioned stimulus on trials 8 through 15 and were assigned a conditioning score between zero and eight. Subjects with higher conditioning scores were selected and mated with each other, as were subjects with lower scores. A control group of flies was mated independent of their conditioning scores.

As shown in Figure 14.8, over seven generations, flies selected for conditioning showed increasingly more conditioned responses on test trials than their ancestors. When conditioning was selected against, each generation of flies showed less conditioned responses than the previous population. Flies mated regardless of conditioning scores (control) did not show a change over generations. At the end of seven generations, there was no overlap in the distribution of conditioning scores for the three groups—indicating that selection resulted in three separate populations of flies.

Hirsch and McCauley's (1977) experiment demonstrates that conditioning of a specific reflex has a range of variability. Based on this variation, selection can enhance the process of conditioning or eliminate it for distinct behavioral units. From a behavioral view, contingencies of survival continually mold the degree of behavioral flexibility of organisms—extending (or removing) the process of conditioning to a wide range of responses.

In the case of human evolution, natural selection produced a high degree of behavioral flexibility. This behavioral flexibility was not achieved by selection for a broader repertoire of conditioned reflexes. It involved the evolution of selection by

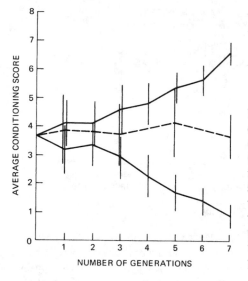

FIG. 14.8 Artificial selection for respondent conditioning in the blowfly, *Phormia regina*, reported by Hirsch and McCauley (1977). Flies mated for high-conditioning scores showed more conditioned responses over generations than flies that were randomly paired. Other flies that were mated on the basis of low-conditioning scores did progressively worse than their ancestors (data reprinted with permission of *Animal Behaviour*).

consequences as a behavioral process. That is, natural selection extended and elaborated the process of operant conditioning to most aspects of human behavior.

LEVEL 2: SELECTION BY REINFORCEMENT

The evolution of operant behavior allowed variation and selection to work throughout the lifetime of an organism. Many organisms evolved genetic programs that coded for operant processes. For some species, natural selection ensured that operant processes were extended to more and more aspects of behavior. Individuals who inherited an extensive capacity for operant conditioning could adjust to complex and changing situations on the basis of behavioral consequences. Selection by reinforcement therefore became a major mode of adaptation.

Selection for Operant Processes

Glenn (1991) noted the biological advantage of operant processes and selection by behavioral consequences:

> The instability of local environments and what might be considered a limit on behavioral complexity in genetic programs appears to have given rise to a less cumbersome and more rapid sort of variation and selection. Instead of building thousands of complex behavioral relations into DNA, evolution built a few programs for behavioral processes that allowed changing environments to build behavior repertoires "as needed" during the lifetime of individuals. A relatively small change in a bit of DNA could result in profound changes in the possibility for ontogenic adaptability if that change involved a gene for a behavioral process. All that was required as a first step was genetically uncommitted activity and susceptibility of that activity to selection by behavioral consequences. (p. 43)

The evolution of operant conditioning, a range of uncommitted behavior, and susceptibility to certain kinds of reinforcement resulted in a second level of selection. Behavioral selection supplemented and extended selection at the biological level (i.e., natural selection).

Operant Selection and Extinction

The unit of selection at the behavioral level is the operant. An operant is a unit of behavior comprised of responses that make contact with the environment (i.e., an operant class). Response forms vary from moment to moment, and some variations change the environment in ways that increase those forms. A child who manipulates a rubber duck in the bathtub may inadvertently squeeze it in ways that produce a squeaking sound. If the sound functions as reinforcement, the operant of squeezing the duck to make a sound increases over time.

If few (or no) response variations are reinforced, the operant decreases because of extinction. That is, all members of an operant class cease to exist when they no longer result in reinforcement. The sound device in the toy duckling may break, and squeezing it in different ways no longer has the characteristic effect. Over time, the child will squeeze the rubber duck less and less as the operant undergoes extinction.

Extinction not only eliminates operants but also generates behavioral variation. Greater variation in the behavior increases an individual's chances of contacting the prevailing contingencies. In the bathtub, the child may push the broken rubber duck under the water, emitting a response that has never occurred before. The effect of this behavior may be to generate bubbles on the surface that, in turn, reinforce the child's behavior.

A more profound example of extinction and behavioral variation concerns people trying new ways of doing things when old ways no longer work (or do not work well). Thomas Edison's invention of the electric light bulb involved behavioral variation and selection. To generate electric light, Edison collected and tested a variety of materials to produce an effective lamp filament (Etzkowitz, 1992, p. 1005). He was known as the trial-and-error inventor, but a better description of his performance is "trial and success." Invention occurs when novel forms of response (trying different filaments) are generated by extinction and the appropriate response (using a tungsten filament) has been selected by the prevailing contingencies of reinforcement (effective and efficient light).

Susceptibility to Reinforcement

Contingencies of reinforcement resemble contingencies of survival (Skinner, 1986). Many animals eat and copulate simply because these responses have contributed to survival. Male black widow spiders copulate and are then eaten by their mates. For these animals, copulating only has survival value for the species—passing on the genetic code even though the individual dies following the act. Other organisms evolved sensory systems that allowed food and sexual contact to reinforce behavior. That is, an animal whose actions resulted in sexual contact was more likely to act that way again. At this point, organisms had two redundant reasons for eating and copulating—survival of the species and reinforcement.

When food and sexual contact became reinforcing, new forms of behavior, indirectly related to eating and copulating, could be established. Animals could acquire new ways of finding, gathering, and processing foods based on reinforcement. Similarly, sexual reinforcement could establish and maintain a diversity of actions. These include looking at erotic objects, seeking out sexual partners, attracting a desirable mate, and performing a variety of sexual responses (e.g., genital contact with parts of body, position of intercourse, etc.).

Susceptibility to reinforcement may sometimes depend on the species and the particular behavior. Chaffinches *(Fringilla coelebs)* will peck a disk for food, but will not peck for contingent presentation of bird song. The same bird, however, will step on a perch for species-specific song, suggesting the biological preparedness of the response-reinforcer relationship (Hinde & Stevenson-Hinde, 1973; see also Chapter 5). Primates may also be susceptible to species-specific reinforcement. The work of Harlow and Zimmerman (1959) on mother-infant attachment suggests that "contact comfort" may function as reinforcement for infants staying close to and preferring their mothers. Infants who only received food reinforcement from their mothers did not show strong attachment behavior. These findings again suggest that the response-reinforcer relationship is biologically prepared.

Organisms who are susceptible to reinforcement may acquire behavior that is not adaptive (Pierce & Epling, 1988). One paradoxical byproduct of selection for operant conditioning is that people behave in ways that have distinct biological costs. Humans choose foods that are not healthful and engage in sexual behavior that is not related to procreation. In addition, conditioned reinforcement ensures that people come to value objects and events that are unrelated to survival. Conditioned reinforcement may shape behavior that decreases reproductive success. People learn to use birth control, love adopted children, risk their lives to help others, risk their lives to kill others, and some even kill themselves.[1] The point is that susceptibility to reinforcement has been adaptive, but this sensitivity may occasionally generate behavior with no adaptive value.

Evolution, Reinforcement, and Verbal Behavior

Social Signals.   As noted earlier, a honeybee signals the location of food by dancing in ways that affect the travel of other bees. This form of communication involves a high degree of genetic regulation. Genes also may code for general behavioral processes known as respondent and operant conditioning. Once these processes evolved, signaling could be acquired on the basis of an organism's interaction with the environment.

Skinner (1986) explained the acquisition of human gestures in terms of selection by consequence and susceptibility to aversive stimulation. He analyzed the contingencies as follows:

---

[1] We are not making a value judgment about these activities; the point is that these behaviors do not contribute to the biological definition of reproductive success.

One person can stop another by placing a hand on his chest, and if the person who is stopped finds the contact aversive, he will stop on later occasions before contact is made. The movement of the arm and hand changes from a practical response to a gesture. Once that happened, the topography can change until it would have little or no physical effect.

The gesture that means "Come here" is another example. It presumably originated as practical pulling but became effective as a gesture when people who were pulled moved quickly to avoid physical contact. The topography of the gesture still varies with distance, possibly because of visibility, but also as if some practical work remained to be done: When the parties are far apart, the whole arm is moved; when they are fairly near, only the forearm; and when they are close, only a hand or a finger. (pp. 116–117)

For Skinner, gesturing is behavior that results from social contingencies of reinforcement. A social contingency involves the behavior of two (or more) people who arrange stimuli and reinforcement for each other's actions.

The person who sees a surprising sight may pull a companion toward the view and be reinforced by the friend's reactions to the sight (see Figure 14.9). On later occasions, a pulling motion may occur before the companion is in reach. The friend may avoid being dragged to the sight by coming when the pulling motion is first made. The reinforcement contingencies composed of each person's behavior establish and maintain this social episode.

FIG. 14.9 How pulling a person to see a sight may have evolved into the gesture of pulling the arm toward the body.

Although social contingencies are clearly involved in human signs and gestures, other processes may play an important role. The research on stimulus equivalence discussed in Chapter 12 is relevant to signs and gestures (Sidman & Cresson, 1973). Humans easily distinguish equivalent stimulus classes, but other organisms do not. Gestures and signs may stand for or be equivalent to other stimulus classes. A smile, the spoken words "good job," and the gesture for "OK" (thumb and index finger make an *o*) become equivalent when they have a similar effect on behavior. Equivalence relations depend on discrimination of reflexivity (A = A and B = B), symmetry (if A = B then B = A), and transitivity (if A = B and A = C, then B = C). Complex transitivity relations seem to involve evolution of species-specific capacities for discrimination as well as general behavioral processes like operant conditioning.

Humans readily generate and respond to iconic or representational signs when there is a requirement to communicate but speaking is not possible (Kuschel, 1973; Meissner & Philpott, 1975). For example, Brown (1986) recounts a study that compared severely deaf children with a normal hearing group (Goldin-Meadow & Morford, 1985). The deaf children were raised by parents who refused to sign to them because they believed that signing would retard vocal speech. Each of the 10 deaf children independently acquired a similar repertoire of iconic signs. Presumably, particular ways of signing were more effective than others in altering the behavior of the parents. The hearing children also showed iconic signing that gradually diminished as vocal speech increased. This later finding suggests that speech has some advantages over gestures and iconic signs when speakers and listeners have normal hearing.

Speech Sounds.   Natural selection must have been important in the evolution of speech sounds. Compared with gestures and iconic signs, sounds can affect a listener's behavior when it is too dark to see, others are out of sight, or no one is looking at the speaker. Spoken sounds are also an advantage to speakers whose hands are full—warding off prey or holding weapons to attack an enemy. Additional benefits of speech sounds over gestures were noted by Skinner (1986):

> There are special advantages, however, in large operant repertoires, especially the enormous variety of available speech sounds. Gestures are not as conspicuously different as speech sounds and hence are fewer in number, and the sounds one produces are more like the sounds one hears than gestures are like the gestures one sees (because they are seen from a different point of view). One learns to gesture through movement duplication, but to speak through product duplication, which is more precise. (p. 117)

Most of the organs that allowed for speech sounds probably evolved for other reasons. The diaphragm was used in breathing, the tongue and jaws were involved in eating, and the lips could take in water by sucking and sipping. The vocal cords and pharynx did not play a direct role in survival, but may have evolved in social species who could benefit from the calls and cries of others (see Barash, 1982, on social alarms).

There were probably several other important steps in the evolution of human speech. One involved the extension of operant processes to a range of speech-relevant behavior. Each organ that contributed to speech was initially reflexive—the organism responding to specific stimulation. Survival must have been better served when reflexive behavior was supplemented by operant processes. An organism could breathe as a reflex elicited by high levels of circulating carbon dioxide, or it could hold its breath to avoid a predator. Based on natural selection, more and more speech-relevant behavior came under the control of its consequences. Compared with the great apes, humans made an evolutionary leap when the vocal apparatus was supplied with nerves (i.e., innervated) for operant regulation.

The step to operant regulation of the vocal musculature is not sufficient to account for speech. Evolution must have also resulted in the coordination of all the systems involved in the production of speech. The great apes have complete operant control of their hands but have not developed a sophisticated system of signs or gestures. Children show early iconic signing that shifts toward spoken words as more and more speech is acquired. Both iconic signing and spoken words require that the speaker and listener respond to abstract-stimulus relations along several dimensions. Thus, neural coordination of speech probably built on, and added to, specialized capacities for discrimination involving the visual, auditory, and motor systems. In less technical terms, humans evolved systems for symbolic behavior and these systems were eventually integrated with those of speech (Pierce & Epling, 1988).

Speech sounds are a large pool of uncommitted behavior. This behavior is spontaneously emitted at high frequency but plays no direct role in survival (Skinner, 1984). From a behavioral view, wide variation in spontaneous speech sounds allows for selection of vocal operants by reinforcement supplied by listeners. Thus, Osgood (1953) found that an infant's babbling included all the speech sounds that make up the different languages of the world. This suggests that a child's speech sounds could be shaped toward adult forms by reinforcement of successive approximations, and probably by modeling and generalized imitation. Evidence also indicates that a child's speech sounds become increasingly similar to the adults in the community. Speech sounds that occur frequently in the community increase over time, whereas infrequent sounds drop out of the repertoire (Irwin, 1948, 1952). The exact bases for these changes are not known, although the social reinforcement of speech sounds has some support (Moerk, 1990; Rheingold, Gewirtz, & Ross, 1959).

Verbal Behavior.   The evolution of operant processes, the coordination of speech systems, and a large variety of uncommitted speech sounds allowed for the regulation of vocal operants by others. A person in an English-speaking community learns to speak in accord with the verbal practices of the community. That is, the way a person speaks is attributable to the reinforcement practices of others. On a specific occasion, the community provides reinforcement for certain ways of speaking and withholds reinforcement or supplies aversive stimulation for other unacceptable responses. In this manner, the individual conforms to the customary practices of the community and, in so doing, contributes to the perpetuation of the culture.

In Chapter 12 on verbal behavior, we examined some of the verbal relations that are fundamental to speaking (as well as writing or signing). Verbal operants were distinguished in terms of mands and tacts. Recall that the mand is a verbal operant set up by the community for the benefit of the speaker. When a person is deprived of food, the response "Give me food" is reinforced only when a listener provides the meal. If it is raining, the response "Do you have an umbrella?" is reinforced when the other person gives you the umbrella and protects you from the rain. Because of these contingencies, mands are regulated by deprivation and aversive stimulation and the specific reinforcement supplied by a listener.

In contrast to mands, tact relations are set up for the benefit of listeners (the verbal community). The speaker who describes objects and relationships in the world supplies useful information to others. This information allows people in the community to learn from experiences of others, without testing the actual contingencies. A tact relation involves the control of a verbal operant by a specific discriminative stimulus. The child who correctly states the color of different objects (e.g., "That's a red ball") is tacting the stimulus property of color. In contrast to mands, tact relations are maintained by generalized reinforcement from others—such as approval, praise, or signs of correctness.

Verbal behavior allows people to coordinate their actions. When people observe rules, take advice, heed warnings, and follow instructions, their behavior is rule governed. Rule-governed behavior allows people to profit from what others say. If a fellow camper reports that a bear is near your tent, you can move the tent to a new camping site. A student looking for a good course may benefit from the advice of another student. In these examples, the listener or person who responds to the verbal report avoids an aversive event (the bear) or contacts positive reinforcement (a good course). Children are taught to follow advice and instructions. Parents and others provide simple verbal stimuli that set the occasion for reinforcement of the child's compliance. In this way, the child is taught to listen to what others say.

As we have noted, listeners benefit from the verbal reports of others. For this reason, listeners are inclined to reinforce the person who provides useful instructions. In a verbal community, people are taught to express their appreciation for the advice received from others. For example, in an English-speaking community, people say thank you and other variations of this response when given directions, advice, and instructions. These verbal responses by the listener reinforce the behavior of the speaker.

Verbal behavior evolved (level 2) in the sense that particular ways of speaking were more or less effective in regulating the behavior of the listener. Response variation ensured that many ways of speaking were tried and successful combinations of sounds were adopted by more and more people. At this point, many people were able to talk to one another on the basis of common standards for speech. These common linguistic practices by a verbal community were the underlying basis for a third level of selection: the selection and evolution of cultural practices.

LEVEL 3: THE SELECTION AND EVOLUTION OF A CULTURE

The evolution of operant processes and verbal behavior allowed for the emergence of human culture. Recently, Sigrid Glenn (1988, 1989; see also Lloyd, 1985) has proposed a behavior analysis of culture that builds on the works of Skinner (1953) and anthropologist Marvin Harris (1979). Although social scientists often talk about culture as the ideas and values of a group, a behavioral viewpoint suggests that a culture involves the usual ways of acting and speaking in a community. These customary forms of behavior (customs, mores, etc.) are the cultural practices of the group.

Cultural Practice

From a behavioral perspective, cultural practices involve the operant behavior of many people who compose the members of a culture. Each person's behavior provides stimulation and reinforcement for the actions of others. A **cultural practice** is therefore defined in terms of interlocking social contingencies—where the behavior of each person supports the behavior of other members of the community. The pattern of behavior that arises from the interlocking contingencies is the type of practice (e.g., what people do in that culture).

This view of culture suggests that what people do in a particular community is determined by the function of a practice. The ancient Romans adopted military tactics that were highly effective in most battles. For example, Roman soldiers would form a close body of men, called a phalanx, and interlock their shields as a common barrier against the enemy. Although there are many ways to conduct a battle, this military maneuver became popular because of its effectiveness. In other words, what people in a particular culture do is a function of the previous benefits and costs of that practice. With changes in technology (the products of a culture), the phalanx and the interlocking of shields became obsolete—the costs in terms of casualties and lost battles increased relative to the benefits.

Cultural practices are functionally similar to operants. Both operants and cultural practices are selected by consequences. Thus, a cultural practice increases when people have benefited from it. The practice of making water jars involves alternative sets of interlocking operants that result in a common outcome. One person gathers clay; another person makes the pot; and a consumer trades something for the jar. The common outcome of such a practice is greater efficiency in transporting and storing water. There are many ways of storing and transporting water, including shells, hollow leaves, woven baskets, clay pots, and indoor plumbing. The cultural form that predominates (e.g., plumbing) reflects the basic processes of selection by consequences. In terms of selection, operants are selected by contingencies of reinforcement and cultural practices are selected by metacontingencies.

Metacontingencies

Dr. Sigrid Glenn at the University of North Texas made an important contribution to the behavior analysis of culture when she first described the metacontingencies of cultural practices. **Metacontingencies** refer to contingent relations between cul-

FIG. 14.10 Sigrid Glenn.

tural practices and the effects of those practices for the group (Glenn, 1988). For example, competence in science is important for people who live in a technologically advanced culture. Scientific research produces a range of benefits for the general society. These include better medicine, more productive crop yields, new and better building materials, more efficient and longer-lasting appliances, and superior regulation of human behavior. Thus, a positive metacontingency exists between educational practices that increase scientific competence and long-term benefits to the group. This analysis suggests that teaching methods that promote science were selected, while alternative methods of education declined in popularity.

Metacontingency implies that there will be an increase in those forms of education that result in more and better trained students of science, but this may not occur. In complex cultures like the United States, competing (or concurrent) metacontingencies may mean that the "best" educational practice is not selected. A less than optimal form of scientific education may prevail for some time because teaching science is only part of the function of education. For example, the manifest function of education is to teach reading, writing, and arithmetic. The hidden or latent function of schooling includes keeping people out of the work force and categorizing them into high-, medium-, and low-status groups based on educational attainment. Thus, the form of education that predominates is one that has produced the most overall benefit to the community, group, or society. If the relative outcomes of an educational practice resulting in low scientific competence exceed those of a system that yields high scientific achievement, then the less adequate educational practice will predominate in the culture.

Origin, Transmission, and Evolution of a Cultural Practice

At the time of the writing of this book, we were unable to find a reference for a classic animal study concerned with establishing and transmitting a cultural taboo (see Pierce, 1991). We are not sure if this experiment was ever carried out;

however, it should be if it was not. Dr. Donald Heth, of the Department of Psychology at the University of Alberta, provided us with some details.

Origin and Transmission. Apparently, a troop of baboons (or chimpanzees) were kept in a zoo enclosure and were provided with a choice between a preferred food (bananas) and less appetizing laboratory chow. As expected, the baboons consistently chose to eat bananas.

Following a baseline period, the researchers established a negative reinforcement contingency for eating the less preferred food. Whenever any animal approached the bananas, the entire colony was drenched with water from a fire hose that was used to clean the enclosure. After exposure to this contingency, the troop attacked any member that approached the bananas. Eventually, all members of the troop were exclusively eating the less preferred laboratory chow and avoiding cold showers. The researchers then removed the reinforcement contingency—approaching and eating the bananas no longer resulted in being soaked with water. As you might expect, the group did not test the operating contingencies and continued to attack any member that went toward the preferred food. At this point, the contingencies had established a cultural taboo that was highly resistant to change.

Over time, new infants were born and raised in the colony. These infants had never been present when the original troop was soaked for eating the preferred food. The infants, however, learned to eat the laboratory chow rather than the bananas. As previously stated, the baboons would attack any member that went near the preferred food—and this social contingency applied to new members of the troop. In addition, modeling and imitation were apparently used for social training of the taboo, since all members of the troop ate the chow and rejected the bananas. Thus, social reinforcement and observational learning contributed to the maintenance of the food taboo, even though the original reinforcement contingencies had long since been removed.

Harris (1974) has provided a functional analysis of the origin and transmission of many human cultural practices. To illustrate, in India the cow is deified and beef is not eaten by many Hindus. This was not always the case—when the last ice age ended the peoples of Northern India raised and ate cattle, sheep, goats and many agricultural products. Cattle, however, have some advantages other than just providing meat; they may be easily herded and trained to pull plows or carts.

Population density increased greatly in the Ganges River valley and by 300 B.C. the people of the valley had destroyed the trees surrounding the river. As a result, the risk of drought increased and farms decreased in size. Small farms have little space for animals, but draft animals were essential for working the land and transporting agricultural products. Cows provided traction, milk, and meat, but the farmer who ate his cow lost milk production and a working animal.

Thus, the people of India faced a social trap involving the immediate benefit of eating beef and the long-term loss of the cows' other advantages. A cost/benefit analysis suggests it was better to keep a cow than eat it. To avoid this social trap, the cow was deified and eating beef became a cultural taboo. The Hindu community has maintained this practice into modern times. Other cultures have food taboos that may be analyzed in terms of the function of cultural practices. Until very recently, Catholics did not eat meat on Friday, many Islamic and Jewish people will not eat pork, and the Chinese people despise cow's milk (Harris, 1974).

Cultural Evolution.

Cultural evolution presumably begins at the level of the individual. Variation in individual behavior is reinforced by its technological effects. An inventor may discover a new way of making a wheel; a farmer finds a food crop that produces higher yields; and a teacher may find a novel way to teach reading. A culture is said to evolve when these innovations are adopted by the community.

Adoption of innovations depends on the metacontingencies facing the group. For example, a new food crop with higher yield is selected when the metacontingencies favor increased grain production. This could occur when a community is impoverished or when higher yielding crops support the feeding of domestic animals used for work or consumption. Higher yield crops may not be selected when food is overly abundant, when increased grain supply leads to problems of storage, or when a new crop attracts pests that spread disease.

The evolution of a cultural practice has been reported for a troop of Japanese macaque monkeys (Kawamura, 1959). A troop of macaques on Koshima Island are well known for their cultural innovations. In one example, an infant female called Imo began to wash sweet potatoes to remove the grit. This behavior was later observed in Imo's playmates and her mother, who taught it to another offspring. Imo was also among the first to take up swimming and to throw wheat kernels on the water. Throwing wheat on the water removed the sand that the kernels were mixed with, because the sand sank and the kernels floated. Both of these practices were eventually adopted by the entire troop (see Jolly, 1985, for more on animal culture).

A common observation is that cultural practices may remain unchanged over many generations. Persistence of a practice is illustrated by the baboons who continued to eat the less preferred food and in humans by the Jewish people's taboo for eating pork. Our analysis suggests that food taboos originated because of the aversive metacontingencies facing the group. As with behavioral (level 2) avoidance contingencies, the practices continued even though the metacontingency had changed. Thus, a practice may persist for many years because the members of the group who engage in it (i.e., avoidance of pork) fail to contact a change in the metacontingency. At the individual level, a person conforms to the taboo because the social contingencies arranged by the group (religious proclamations and sanctions) avert contact with a change in the physical environment.

Another reason that cultural practices persist over time is that the metacontingencies are stable and such practices, at least minimally, meet the contingencies. For centuries, the only way that books were manufactured was to have scribes make written copies. As a cultural practice, copying books allowed for more standardized transmission of knowledge than word of mouth. Better methods of food preparation, house construction, agriculture, waste disposal, and so on could be described in a common manner and passed from one generation to another. That is, transcription of books had survival value for human groups, ensuring the continuation of this practice. (Recall that in biology survival refers to the number of genes—or characteristics of organisms—that appear in the next generation. Culturally, survival refers to the transmission of a practice from one generation to the next.)

Transcription of books satisfied the metacontingencies of many cultures, but it was not the only way to produce books. The advent of the printing press allowed for an alternative form of transcription that was less costly and more productive. Thus, transcription by hand was replaced by the printing press even though both forms of the practice satisfied the existing metacontingencies. Innovation is therefore important in terms of whether a culture remains static or dynamic. In this view, innovation produces variation in cultural practices much as genetic mutation produces changes in species characteristics. In both cases, the new forms (species traits and cultural practices) do not depend on a change in the contingencies.

Generally, the analysis of cultural variation and metacontingencies provides a selectionist account of the evolution of group practices. Principles of behavioral and cultural selection may be used to design interventions that change cultural practices. The application of behavior modification to cultural practices is what Skinner has called "the design of a culture" (Skinner, 1948, 1953).

ON THE APPLIED SIDE

Design of Culture

Many governments throughout the world are faced with mounting population and declining food and resources (and many other problems). Economists, demographers, and other social scientists are frequently hired by government agencies to develop programs to help with these difficulties. Consultants often formulate plans of action based on assumptions of rational human choice or popular psychology. Because their analyses are based on assumptions that do not take contingencies into account, the programs are often ineffective (Hernandez, 1981). Behavior analysts are skilled at specifying the behavior classes that underlie the contingencies that support social behavior. Behaviorists can, for this reason, play a major role in the regulation of human social problems by providing analyses and research on controlling variables and designing new systems of reinforcement (see Lamal, 1997).

Consider the control of human populations (see Figure 14.11). Many scientists (and others) have suggested that people will eventually decimate the resources of the planet. They ask, "How can we stop this explosion of humanity?" A behavioral approach to human fertility has already been developed. As early as 1974, Wiest and Squire reported a reinforcement analysis of the adoption of birth control methods. They analyzed how different birth control methods were related to the time of use before sexual intercourse, the frequency of use, and the

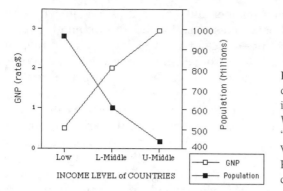

FIG. 14.11 Increasing population and declining resources as a function of the income level of countries (data are from *World Development Report 1989*, Table 1, "Basic Indicators," published by the World Bank through Oxford University Press). The low-income data are based on countries other than China and India.

sex of the user. The researchers noted that "contraceptive performances that are [dependent on sexual intercourse] . . . are difficult to measure directly simply because heterosexual behavior always occurs in private" (Wiest & Squire, 1974, pp. 251–252). One solution suggested by Wiest and Squire is to target behavior that is reliably correlated with contraceptive behavior. For example, research may show that talking about the negative consequences of unwanted pregnancies and the long-term advantages of a small family is positively correlated with contraceptive use. Reinforcement contingencies applied to talking about contraception could indirectly increase the use of contraceptive devices (e.g., Lovaas, 1961).

Wiest and Squire's analysis separates those who are "strongly motivated to avoid pregnancy" from people who want to have several children. The researchers suggest that little reinforcement is required to contact family planning agencies if pregnancy is not wanted. In these cases, how to use contraceptives may be the problem and teaching techniques of instruction and modeling could be employed.

On the other hand, it may be more difficult to alter the behavior of those who want children. One solution is that the "government might pay each female a monthly sum, beginning [at the time when she is able to conceive] until a birth occurs. The amount would increase as pregnancy risk became greater in early womanhood, and drop as the woman aged. This would regularly reward the successfully nonpregnant, and focus attention on the cost to a woman of bearing a child" (Wiest & Squire, 1974, p. 252). Although the authors do not mention it, a similar contingency could be applied to males who do not father children (e.g., payment to men for having a vasectomy). Importantly, this kind of intervention does not force reduced family size; it simply pays (reinforces) anyone who chooses to limit the number of children they have.

We are not advancing the argument that having many (or no) children is better or worse. We are suggesting that social problems such as overpopulation may be informed by a behavioral analysis of contingencies of reinforcement and metacontingencies.

There is a clear role for behavioral analysis in the study of society and culture. Behavior analysts are capable of designing socially important programs and policies (Glenwick & Jason, 1980; Lamal, 1991). Currently, behavioral researchers are tackling social problems at both the theoretical and applied levels. Experiments on social processes such as cooperation, competition, and exchange are being conducted (Molm, 1990; Schmitt, 1976, 1981, 1984), but more is required. Empirical research is needed on the transmission of cultural practices and the metacontingencies that regulate such practices (Pierce, 1991).

Dr. John Nevin at the University of New Hampshire is concerned with cultural practices that are designed to prevent armed conflict but, in fact, increase the probability of making war. In a recent article, Nevin (1988) suggested that the behavior of preventing war by threats of greater retaliation is counterproductive. This is because the actions of deterrence "form an operant class maintained by powerful contingencies of reinforcement. Therefore, any events that raise the probability of the military components of deterrence, such as a show of force in a time of crisis, also raise the probability of war, the very outcome that deterrence is intended to prevent" (p. 46). This analysis of deterrence leading to war received some support from the armed conflict that occurred after Iraq invaded Kuwait and was told by the United Nations to leave or "face the consequences."

The work of Nevin and other behaviorists suggests that our government and culture may profit from an analysis of contingencies operating on a large scale. Currently, the formation of policy and evaluation of government programs is conducted by politicians, bureaucrats, economists, and others. These public servants are not usually familiar with contingency management, and their planning could be improved by increased knowledge of behavior principles. Behavior analysts who help design social programs will thereby contribute to the science of human behavior and to the long-term survival of humankind.

KEY WORDS

Behavioral flexibility	Fixed-action pattern	Phenotype
Contingencies of survival	Genotype	Phylogeny
Cultural evolution	Metacontingencies	Selection by
Cultural practice		consequences

Glossary

A-B-A-B reversal design. The most basic single-subject research design. Also called a reversal design, it is ideally suited to show that an organism's behavior is regulated by specific features of the environment. The A-phase, or baseline, is used to measure behavior before the researcher introduces an environmental change. During baseline, the experimenter takes repeated measures of the behavior under study, and this establishes a criterion against which any changes (attributed to the independent variable) may be assessed. Following the baseline phase, an environmental condition is changed (B-phase) and behavior is measured repeatedly. If the independent variable, or environmental condition, has an effect, then the behavioral measure (dependent variable) will change—increase or decrease. Next, the baseline phase is reintroduced (A) and behavior is again measured. Since the treatment is removed, behavior should return to baseline levels. Finally, the independent variable is introduced again and behavior is reassessed (B). According to the logic of the design, behavior should return to a level observed in the initial B-phase of the experiment. This second application of the independent variable helps ensure that the behavioral effect is caused by the manipulated condition.

Absolute stimulus control. When operant responses are regulated by the physical properties of one stimulus (e.g., a red light), this is called absolute stimulus control. See also *relative stimulus control*.

Activity anorexia. Physical activity decreases food intake and declining food intake increases activity. This feedback loop is called activity anorexia, and a similar cycle occurs in many anorexic patients.

Ad libitum weight. The body weight of an organism that has free access to food 24 hours a day.

Adjunctive behavior. Also called interim behavior. On interval schedules of reinforcement, or time-based delivery of food, organisms may emit excessive behavior within the interreinforcement interval. For example, rats may drink up to three times their usual daily water intake (polydipsia) over a 1-hour session. This behavior immediately follows reinforcement and is a side-effect of periodic food delivery.

Analytical pragmatism. Behavior analysis is based on Skinner's pragmatic or practical philosophy. A behavioral relationship is important if the relation is powerful in its effects and can be used to change the behavior of an individual. Some behavior analysts choose to study behavioral relationships that have direct importance for human affairs. Other researchers investigate contingencies of reinforcement, using operant chambers, with a variety of organisms. Because basic researchers hold a pragmatic view and applied researchers are interested in analysis, both fields share a similar set of principles and philosophical assumptions called analytical pragmatism.

Applied behavior analysis. The use of behavior principles to solve practical problems.

Associative strength. During respondent conditioning, the term associative strength is used to describe the relation between the conditioned stimulus (CS) and the magnitude of the conditioned response (CR). In general, associative strength increases over conditioning trials and reaches some maximum level

Autistic children. Children who show an early lack of social interaction with parents, other family members, and peers. For example these children often resist being held and may have a tantrum if picked up or hugged. When autistic children get older they may be mistaken as deaf because they don't talk or establish eye contact when talked to. These children often show repeated stereotyped patterns of behavior such as rocking back and forth, spinning a top, wiggling their fingers in front of their eyes and so on.

Autoshaping. A respondent conditioning procedure that generates skeletal responses. For example, a key light is turned on a few seconds before grain is presented to a pigeon. After several pairings of key light and grain, the bird begins to peck the key. This effect was first reported as autoshaping, an automatic way to teach pigeons to key peck.

Avoidance. See *negative reinforcement.*

Backward chaining. A method used to train a chained performance. The basic idea is to first train behavior that is closest to primary reinforcement; once responding is established, links in the chain that are farther and farther from primary reinforcement are added. Each link in the chain is reinforced by the S^D (which is also a conditioned reinforcer) that signals the next component in the sequence.

Backward conditioning. In the respondent procedure backward conditioning, the US comes on before the CS. The general consensus has been that backward conditioning is unreliable, and many researchers question whether it occurs at all.

Baseline. The base rate of behavior against which an experimental manipulation is measured.

Behavior. Everything that an organism does, including covert actions like thinking.

Behavior analysis. Behavior analysis is a comprehensive experimental approach to the study of the behavior of organisms. Primary objectives are the discovery of principles and laws that govern behavior, the extension of these principles over species, and the development of an applied technology.

Behavior analysts. Researchers and practitioners of behavior analysis.

Behavior system. A species-specific set of responses related to a specific US. That is, for each species there is a behavior system related to procurement of food, another related to obtaining water, still another for securing warmth, and so on

Behavior trapping. The teaching of new behavior that, once established, is "trapped" by natural contingencies of reinforcement.

Behavioral contract. A behavioral plan of action that is negotiated between a client, child, spouse, etc. and concerned others. This plan usually includes a statement of target responses, consequences that follow different actions, and long-term goals. The contract objectively specifies what is expected of the person and the consequences that follow behavior.

Behavioral contrast. Contrast refers to a negative association between the response rates on the two components of a multiple schedule—as one goes up the other goes down. There are two forms of contrast, positive and negative. Positive contrast occurs when rate of response in an unchanged component of a multiple schedule increases with a decline in behavior in the other schedule. Negative contrast is defined when rate of response declines on the unaltered schedule and an increase in behavior occurs in the other component of the multiple.

Behavioral dynamics. An area of research that attempts to analyze schedule effects in terms of a few basic processes. Behavioral dynamics requires a high level of mathematical sophistication. Both linear and nonlinear calculus are used to model the behavioral impact of schedules of reinforcement. If performance on schedules can be reduced to a small number of fundamental principles, then reasonable interpretations may be made about any particular arrangement of the environment. Also, it should be possible to predict more precisely behavior based on knowledge of the operating contingencies and the axioms that govern reinforcement schedules.

Behavioral medicine. Behavior change programs that target health-related activities such as following special diets, self-examination for early symptoms of disease, exercising, taking medicine, and so on. In many instances, the idea is that problems of behavior that affect health may be prevented before treatment is necessary.

Behaviorism. The scientific philosophy of behavior analysis.

Bias. For the generalized matching equation, bias is indicated by variation in the value of k from 1. Generally, bias is produced by some unknown asymmetry between the alternatives on a concurrent schedule that affects preference over and above the relative rates of reinforcement.

Biological context. The evolutionary history and biological status of an organism are part of the context for specific environment-behavior interactions.

Blocking. In respondent conditioning, a CS that has been associated with a US blocks a subsequent CS-US association. A CS is paired with a US until the conditioned response reaches maximum strength. Following this conditioning, a second stimulus is presented at the same time as the original CS, and both are paired with the unconditioned stimulus. On test trials, the original CS evokes the CR but the second stimulus does not.

Break and run. A pattern of response, seen on a cumulative record, that occasionally develops on fixed-interval schedules. There is a long postreinforcement pause followed by a brief burst of responses that result in reinforcement.

Chain schedule of reinforcement. Two or more simple schedules (CRF, FI, VI, FR, or VR), each of which is presented sequentially and signaled by an S^D. Only the final or terminal link of the chain results in primary reinforcement. See also *homogeneous* and *heterogeneous chain schedules*.

Change in associative strength. A factor that affects the increment in associative strength on any one trial is the change in associative strength which is the difference between the present strength of the CS and its maximum possible value.

Changeover delay (COD). A control procedure that is used to stop rapid switching between alternatives on concurrent schedules of reinforcement. The COD contingency stipulates that responses do not have an effect immediately following a change from one schedule to another. After switching to a new alternative, a brief time is required before a response is reinforced. For example, if an organism has just changed to an alternative schedule that is ready to deliver reinforcement, there is a brief delay before a response is effective. As soon as the delay has elapsed, a response is reinforced. The COD contingency operates in both directions whenever a change is made from one alternative to another.

Changeover response. On a concurrent schedule, the response that an organism emits when it switches from one alternative to another. See also *Findley procedure*.

Changing criterion design. A research design primarily used in applied behavior analysis. The rate of target behavior is progressively changed to some new criterion (up or down). For example, the criterion for the number of cigarettes a person smokes each day could be progressively lowered over several months. The effects of the independent variable are shown if the subject meets or falls below the criterion for any set of days (e.g., the criterion is 20 cigarettes for week 3, but changes to 10 by week 6).

Choice. From a behavioral view, choice is the distribution of operant behavior among alternative sources of reinforcement.

Compound stimuli. In respondent conditioning, two (or more) conditioned stimuli (e.g., tone and light) called a compound are presented together and acquire the capacity to evoke a single conditioned response (e.g. salivation).

Concurrent-chains schedule. Two or more chain schedules that are simultaneously available. See also *chain schedule* and *concurrent schedules of reinforcement*.

Concurrent schedules of reinforcement. Two or more schedules of reinforcement (e.g., FR, VR, FI, VI) are simultaneously available. Each alternative is associated with a separate schedule of reinforcement and the organism is free to distribute behavior to the schedules.

Conditional discrimination. A discrimination that depends on the stimulus context. Consider a matching-to-sample experiment where a bird has been trained to match to triangles and squares based on the sample stimulus. To turn this experiment into a conditional-discrimination task, a red or green light illuminates the sample stimulus. The bird is required to match to the sample when the background light is green and to choose the noncorresponding stimulus when the light is red. Conditional matching to sample involves simultaneous discrimination of three elements in a display. The animal must respond to geometric form depending on the background color of the sample. It also must respond to the correspondence or noncorrespondence of the comparison stimuli. See also *matching to sample*.

Conditioned aversive stimulus. An aversive event that has acquired its effectiveness because of an organism's life or ontogenetic history.

Conditioned inhibition. In respondent conditioning, when a CS$^+$ is presented repeatedly without the US (extinction), the conditioned stimulus is said to acquire increasing amounts of inhibition, in the sense that its presentation suppresses the response.

Conditioned reflex. See *conditioned response* and *conditioned stimulus*.

Conditioned reinforcement. The presentation of a conditioned reinforcer and the subsequent strengthening of the operant that produced it.

Conditioned reinforcer. A reinforcing event that has acquired its effectiveness because of an organism's life or ontogenetic history.

Conditioned response (CR). An arbitrary stimulus, such as a tone, is associated with an unconditioned stimulus that elicits reflexive behavior (e.g., food elicits salivation). After several pairings, the stimulus is presented alone. If the stimulus now elicits a response (tone now evokes salivation), the response to the tone is called a conditioned response (CR).

Conditioned stimulus (CS). An arbitrary stimulus, such as a tone, is associated with an unconditioned stimulus that elicits reflexive behavior (e.g., food elicits salivation). After several pairings, the stimulus is presented alone. If the stimulus now elicits a response (tone evokes salivation), it is called a conditioned stimulus (CS).

Conditioned suppression. In conditioned suppression, a previously neutral stimulus (e.g., tone, light, etc.) is paired with an aversive US such as an electric shock. After several pairings, the originally neutral stimulus becomes a conditioned aversive stimulus (CS^{ave}). Once the CS^{ave} has been conditioned, its onset suppresses ongoing operant behavior. A rat may be trained to press a lever for food. After a stable rate of response is established, the CS^{ave} is introduced. When this occurs, the animal's lever pressing is suppressed.

Context of behavior. The ontogenetic and phylogenetic history of an organism plus the contextual stimuli that are present when conditioning occurs.

Contextual stimuli. In terms of operant and respondent conditioning, contextual stimuli are uncontrolled sights, sounds, smells, and so on that are the background for conditioning. These stimuli are conditioned at the same time that behavior is strengthened.

Contiguity. In respondent conditioning, contiguity refers to the temporal pairing of CS and US.

Contingencies of survival. The contingencies that regulate natural selection. The habitat or environment sets requirements for the survival of individuals. Members of a species who exhibit features appropriate to the contingencies survive and reproduce, and those with less appropriate characteristics have fewer offspring. Natural selection therefore occurs as particular organisms satisfy (or fail to satisfy) the contingencies of survival.

Contingency. In respondent conditioning, contingency refers to a correlation between CS and US. Rescorla (1972) has suggested that a positive correlation between CS and US, rather than the mere pairing of these stimuli, is necessary for conditioning. For operant conditioning, see *contingency of reinforcement*.

Contingency of reinforcement. A contingency of reinforcement defines the relationship between the occasion, the operant class, and the consequences that follow this behavior (e.g., SD: R → S^{r+}).

Contingency-shaped behavior. Operant behavior that is directly under the control of contingencies of reinforcement, as opposed to rule-governed behavior.

Continuous recording for specified periods. A tactic used in applied behavior analysis for assessing the rate of target behavior. Each instance of behavior is counted during certain periods of the day (e.g., lunch, recess, first class in the morning, and so on).

Continuous reinforcement (CRF). When each programmed response produces reinforcement (e.g., every lever press), the schedule is called CRF or continuous reinforcement.

Controlling stimulus (S). A stimulus or event that changes the probability of operant behavior. An S^D increases the probability of response, and an S$^{\Delta}$ makes responding less likely. An S^{ave} may increase or decrease the likelihood of operant behavior, depending on the operating contingency.

Correlation. As used in respondent conditioning, the percentage of conditioning trials in which the CS is followed by the US, and the percentage of trials in which the CS is not followed by the unconditioned stimulus. See also, contingency.

Cultural evolution. Cultural evolution begins at the level of the individual, when the behavior of a person is reinforced by technological effects. An inventor may discover a new way of making a wheel; a farmer finds a food crop that produces higher yields; and a teacher may find a novel way to teach reading. A culture is said to evolve when these innovations are adopted by the community.

Cultural practice. A cultural practice is defined in terms of interlocking social contingencies—where the behavior of each person supports the behavior of other members of the community. The pattern of behavior that arises from the interlocking contingencies is the type of practice (i.e., what people do in that culture).

Cumulative record. A real-time graphical representation of the rate of operant behavior. Each response produces a constant upward increment on the *y*-axis, and time is indexed on the *x*-axis. The faster the rate of response, the steeper the slope or rise of the cumulative record. See also *cumulative recorder*.

Cumulative recorder. A commonly used laboratory instrument that records the frequency of operant behavior in real time. For example, paper is drawn across a roller at a constant speed, and each time a lever press occurs a pen steps up one increment. When reinforcement occurs, this same pen makes a downward deflection. Once the pen reaches the top of the paper, it resets to the bottom and starts to step up again. See also *cumulative record*.

Delay-reduction hypothesis. Stimuli that signal a decrease in time to positive reinforcement, or an increase in time to an aversive event, are more effective conditioned reinforcers. Generally, the value of a conditioned reinforcer is attributed to its delay reduction—how close it is to reinforcement or how far it is from punishment.

Delayed conditioning. A respondent conditioning procedure in which the CS is presented a few seconds before the US occurs.

Delayed matching to sample. On a matching-to-sample task, the comparison stimuli are presented some time after the sample stimuli are turned off. See also *matching to sample*.

Dependent variable. What is measured in an experiment, commonly called an effect. In behavior analysis, the dependent variable is the behavior of organisms.

Deprivation operation. The procedure of restricting access to a reinforcing event. The effectiveness of a reinforcer is increased by withholding it.

Differential reinforcement. Reinforcement in the presence of one stimulus but not others.

Differential reinforcement of other behavior (DRO). Reinforcement for any behavior other than a target operant.

Differential response. When an organism makes a response in one situation but not in another, we say that the animal discriminates between the situations and makes a differential response.

Direct replication. The exact replication of an experiment.

Discriminated avoidance. Avoidance behavior that is emitted as a function of a warning stimulus. For example, a dog stops barking when its owner shouts, "Shut up!"

Discriminated extinction. Low-rate operant behavior that occurs as a function of an S^{Δ}. For example, the probability of putting coins in a vending machine with an "out of order" sign on it is very low.

Discrimination. When an organism makes a differential response to two or more stimuli, we can say the animal discriminates between them. This process is called discrimination.

Discrimination index (I_D). This index compares the rate of response in the S^D component to the sum of the rates in both S^D and S^{Δ} phases.

$$I_D = (S^D \text{ rate})/(S^D \text{ rate} + S^{\Delta} \text{ rate})$$

The measure varies between 0.00 and 1.00. Using the I_D measure, when the rates of response are the same in the S^D and S^{Δ} components, the value of I_D is 0.50, indicating no discrimination. When all responses occur during the S^D phase, the S^{Δ} rate is zero and I_D equals 1. Thus, a discrimination index of 1 indicates a perfect discrimination and maximum stimulus control of behavior. Intermediate values of the index signify more or less control by the discriminative stimulus.

Discriminative stimulus (S^D). The events that precede operants and set the occasion for behavior.

Discriminative-stimulus account of conditioned reinforcement. The hypothesis necessary for a stimulus to be an S^D in order for it to be a conditioned reinforcer. The hypothesis has been largely discounted, and the weight of the evidence supports Edmond Fantino's (1969b) delay-reduction hypothesis. See *delay-reduction hypothesis*.

Displacement behavior. Displacement behavior is observed in the natural environment and is characterized as irrelevant, incongruous, or out of context. The activity of the animal does not make sense given the situation, and the displaced responses do not appear to follow from immediately preceding behavior. Like adjunctive behavior (see definition in this glossary), displacement activities arise when consummatory activities like eating are interrupted or prevented.

Duration recording. When behavior is continuous, duration recording is a method of observation. An observer may use a stopwatch, or other timing device, to record the duration of behavior. When a person is sitting in a chair, the watch is timing; and when the person leaves the chair, the watch is stopped.

Echoic. When there is point-to-point correspondence between the stimulus and response, verbal behavior may be classified as echoic. A further requirement is that the verbal stimulus and the echoic response must be in the same mode (auditory, visual, etc.) and have exact physical resemblance (e.g., same sound pattern). An echoic is a class of verbal operants regulated by a verbal stimulus in which there is correspondence and topographic similarity between the stimulus and response. Saying "this is a dog" to the spoken stimulus "this is a dog" is an example of an echoic response in human speech.

Elicited. Respondent (CR) or reflexive (UR) behavior is said to be elicited in the sense that it is forced by the presentation of a stimulus (CS or US).

Emitted. Operant behavior is said to be emitted in the sense that it occurs at some probability in the presence of a discriminative stimulus, but the S^D does not force its occurrence.

Environment. All of the events and stimuli that affect the behavior of an organism. The environment includes events "inside the skin" like thinking, hormonal changes, and pain stimulation.

Errorless discrimination. In errorless discrimination, the trainer does not allow the organism to make mistakes by responding to the extinction stimulus. Initially S^D and S^Δ are very different, but differences between the stimuli are gradually reduced as training progresses. The procedure eliminates the aversive effects of extinction that are generated by other discrimination-training methods. For example, pigeons flap their wings in an aggressive manner and will work for an opportunity to attack another bird during the presentation of the S^Δ on a multiple schedule. This behavior does not occur when errorless discrimination is used in training.

Escape. See *negative reinforcement*.

Establishing operation. Formally, an establishing operation is defined as any change in the environment which alters the effectiveness of some object or event as reinforcement and simultaneously alters the momentary frequency of the behavior that has been followed by that reinforcement. Thus, an establishing operation has two major effects: (a) It increases the momentary effectiveness of reinforcement supporting operant behavior, and (b) it increases the momentary probability of responses that in the past produced such reinforcement. For example, the most common establishing operation is deprivation for primary reinforcement. This procedure has two effects. First, food becomes an effective reinforcer for any operant that produces it. Second, behavior that has previously resulted in getting food becomes more likely.

Experimental analysis of behavior. The method of investigation most commonly used in behavior analysis. The method involves breaking down complex environment-behavior relations into component principles of behavior. The analysis is verified by arranging experimental procedures that reveal the underlying basic principles and controlling variables. This involves intensive experimentation with a single organism over an extended period, rather than statistical assessment of groups exposed to experimental treatments.

External validity. External validity refers to the extent that an experimental finding generalizes to other behaviors, settings, and populations. That is, does the cause-and-effect relationship found in an experiment occur at different times and places, when the original conditions are in effect?

Extinction. The procedure of extinction involves the breaking of the contingency between an operant and its consequence. For example, a bar press that was followed by food reinforcement no longer produces food. As a behavioral process, extinction refers to a decline in the frequency of the operant when an extinction procedure is in effect. In both instances, the term *extinction* is used correctly.

Extinction burst. A rapid burst of responses that occurs when extinction is first implemented.

Extinction stimulus (S^Δ). An S^Δ, pronounced S-delta, is a stimulus that sets the occasion for a decrease in operant responses. For example, an "out of order" sign on a vending machine decreases the probability of putting money in the machine.

Extraneous sources of reinforcement (R_e). All nonprogrammed sources of reinforcement in a situation that affect behavior on a specified alternative. See also *quantitative law of effect*.

Facultative behavior. Collateral behavior generated by properties of a schedule of reinforcement. See also *adjunctive behavior*.

Fear hierarchy. The graduated set of stimulus items that are constructed by client and therapist to treat phobic responses in systematic desensitization. The items are ordered from least to most anxiety producing.

Findley procedure. A method used to present concurrent schedules in the operant laboratory. Separate schedules are programmed on a single key, and the organism may switch schedules (and associated S^Ds) by making a response on a CO or changeover key.

First-order conditioning. In first-order respondent conditioning, an apparently neutral stimulus is paired with an unconditioned stimulus. When this occurs, the control of the response to the US is transferred to the neutral stimulus, which is now called a conditioned stimulus (CS).

Fixed-action pattern. A sequence or chain of behavior set off by a specific stimulus. The component responses are repeated almost identically with each presentation of the stimulus. Fixed-action patterns are based on a "genetic blueprint," and the environment simply initiates the sequence. For example, the male stickleback fish will aggressively defend its territory from male intruders during mating season. The fish shows a fixed sequence of threatening actions that are elicited by the red underbelly of an intruding male.

Fixed interval (FI). A schedule of reinforcement in which an operant is reinforced after a fixed amount of time has passed. For example, on a fixed-interval 90-second schedule (FI 90 second), one bar press after 90 seconds results in reinforcement. Following reinforcement, another 90-second period goes into effect; and after this time has passed, another response will produce reinforcement.

Fixed ratio (FR). A response-based schedule of reinforcement that delivers reinforcement after a fixed number of responses are made. On a fixed ratio 10 (FR 10), the organism must make 10 responses for reinforcement.

Free operant method. In the free operant method, an organism may repeatedly respond over an extensive period of time. The organism is "free" to emit many responses or none at all. More accurately, responses can be made without interference from the experimenter.

Functional analysis of behavior. An analysis of behavior in terms of its products or consequences. Functionally, there are two basic types of behavior, operant and respondent. The term *respondent* defines behavior that increases or decreases because of the presentation of a stimulus (or event) that precedes the response. Such behavior is said to be elicited, in the sense that it reliably occurs when the stimulus is presented. There is a large class of behavior that does not depend on an eliciting stimulus. This behavior is called emitted and spontaneously occurs at some frequency. When emitted behavior is strengthened or weakened by the events that follow the response, it is called operant behavior. Thus, operants are emitted responses that increase or decrease depending on the consequences they produce.

Generality. An experimental result has generality when it is observed in different environments, organisms, and so on. For example, the principle of reinforcement generalizes over species, settings, responses, and reinforcers. In a pigeon, the peck-for-food relationship depends on deprivation for food in the immediate past. For humans, who have an extensive capacity for operant conditioning, going to a soda machine to get a cold drink is an effective contingency on a hot afternoon. In both examples, reinforcement is the operating principle.

Generalization gradient (operant). Generalization occurs when an organism responds to values of the S^D (or fewer responses to the S^Δ) that were *not* trained during acquisition. A generalization gradient is the function (graph) that relates stimulus values to a measure of response strength.

Generalization gradient (respondent). Generalization occurs when an organism shows a conditioned response to values of the CS that were *not* trained during acquisition. A generalization gradient is the function (graph) that relates stimulus values to a measure of response strength.

Generalized conditioned reinforcer. A conditioned reinforcer that is backed up by many other sources of reinforcement. Money is a good example of a generalized conditioned reinforcer. Cash may be exchanged for a large variety of goods and services.

Generalized matching law. Proportion equations like $B_a/(B_a + B_b) = R_a/(R_a + R_b)$ describe concurrent performance when alternatives differ only in rate of reinforcement. However, in complex environments, other factors also contribute to choice and preference. These factors arise from the biology and environmental history of the organism. For example, sources of error may include different amounts of effort for the responses, qualitative differences in reinforcement such as food versus water, a history of punishment, a tendency to respond to the right alternative rather than the left, and sensory capacities.

To include these and other conditions within the matching law, it is useful to express the law in terms of ratios rather than proportions (i.e., $B_a/B_b = R_a/R_b$). When relative rate of response matches relative rate of reinforcement, the ratio equation is simply a restatement of the proportional form of the matching law. A generalized form of the ratio equation may, however, be used to handle the situation in which unknown factors influence the distribution of behavior. These factors produce systematic departures from ideal matching but may be represented as two constants (parameters) in the generalized matching equation.

$$B_a/B_b = k(R_a/R_b)^a$$

In this form, the matching equation is known as the generalized matching law. In the equation, the coefficient k and the exponent a are values that represent two sources of error for a given experiment. When these parameters are equal to 1, the equation is the simple ratio form of the matching law. See also *matching law*.

Generalized social reinforcement. A generalized conditioned reinforcer that is also a social reinforcer. Praise is a social reinforcer backed up by many sources of reinforcement. See also *generalized conditioned reinforcer*.

Genotype. Genotype refers to the genetic make-up of the organism. Some observable characteristics are largely determined by genotype, other features are strongly influenced by experience, but most result from an interaction of genes and environment. Thus, the height of a person is attributable to both genes and nutrition.

Habituation. Habituation occurs when an unconditioned stimulus repeatedly elicits an unconditioned response. The frequent presentation of the US produces a gradual decline in the magnitude of the unconditioned response. When the UR is repeatedly evoked it may eventually fail to occur at all.

Heterogeneous chains schedule. A heterogeneous chain requires different responses for each link of the schedule. Dog trainers make use of heterogeneous chains when they teach complex behavioral sequences to their animals. In going for a walk, a seeing-eye dog stops at intersections, moves forward when the traffic is clear, pauses at a curb, avoids potholes, and finds the way home. Each of these different responses is occasioned by specific stimuli and results in conditioned reinforcement. See also *chain schedule*.

History. One kind of threat to internal validity. History refers to conditions changed at the same time as the manipulation of the independent variable. See also *internal validity*.

History of reinforcement. The reinforcement contingencies that an organism has been exposed to during its lifetime, including the resulting changes in behavior due to such exposure.

Homogeneous chains schedule. Operant chains are classified as homogeneous when the topography or form of response is similar in each link of the schedule. For example, a bird pecks the same key in each component of the chain. Each link in the schedule produces a discriminative stimulus for the next link, and the S^D is also a conditioned reinforcer for the behavior that produces it. See also *chain schedule*.

Hypothetical constructs. Nonobservable postulated events that are said to explain behavior. For example, Freud's mental device "ego" is a hypothetical construct. From a behavioral perspective, the difficulty is that the mental construct is not directly observable. That is, there is no objective way of getting information about such events except by observing the behavior of people.

Identity matching. In identity matching, the researcher presents a sample stimulus (e.g., red) and two options (e.g., red and green). The organism is reinforced for choosing the red option that corresponds to the sample (i.e., matching to sample). See also *matching to sample*.

Independent variable. What is manipulated or changed in an experiment, commonly called a cause. In behavior analysis, a change in the contingencies of reinforcement or the arrangement of events that precede and follow the behavior of an organism.

Information account of conditioned reinforcement. A hypothesis suggesting that a stimulus will become a conditioned reinforcer if it provides information about the occurrence of primary reinforcement. This notion has been largely discounted and replaced by Edmond Fantino's (1969b) delay-reduction hypothesis. See also *delay-reduction hypothesis*.

Instinctive drift. Species-characteristic behavior patterns that become more and more invasive during operant training.

Instrument decay. One threat to internal validity. In behavioral research, instrument decay refers to observers becoming better or worse at measuring the dependent variable. Such an effect can occur in reversal designs where repeated observations are made. See also *internal validity*.

Interim behavior. See *adjunctive behavior*.

Intermittent reinforcement effect. Intermittent reinforcement schedules generate greater resistance to extinction than continuous reinforcement (CRF).

Intermittent schedule of reinforcement. A schedule in which some rather than all operants are reinforced. In other words, an intermittent schedule is any schedule of reinforcement other than continuous (CRF).

Internal validity. When many extraneous variables are ruled out by an experimental design, the research has high internal validity. That is, changes in the dependent variable may be reasonably attributed to changes in the independent variable (cause → effect). Internal validity is the minimum requirement for all experiments.

Interreinforcement interval (IRI). The time between any two reinforcers.

Interresponse time (IRT). The time between any two responses.

Interval recording. A strategy used in applied behavior analysis to assess the rate of target behavior. A block of time is selected and divided into short-equal intervals, and if the target behavior occurs it is recorded once in an appropriate time bin. For example, a 30-minute segment of mathematics class may be divided into 10-second bins. Regardless of the number of responses, if the behavior occurs in a given 10-second segment, then the observer records it as a single event.

Interval schedules. Schedules of reinforcement that are based on the passage of time and one response after that time.

Intraverbal. An intraverbal is a class of verbal operants regulated by verbal discriminative stimuli. In everyday language, thematically related words (or sentences) are examples of intraverbals. For example, the verbal response "fish" to the spoken words "rod and reel" is an intraverbal; saying "water" to the written word *lake* is also intraverbal behavior. Thus, intraverbal stimuli arise from verbal behavior; a previous verbal response by a speaker is a stimulus for a subsequent verbal operant.

Latency. The time from the onset of one event to the onset of another. For example, the time it takes a rat to reach a goal box after it has been released in a maze.

Law of effect. A paraphrase of this law may be stated as the principle of reinforcement: Operants that produce positive reinforcers increase in frequency.

Law of intensity magnitude. As the intensity of a US increases, so does the magnitude or size of the unconditioned response.

Law of the latency. As the intensity of the US increases, the latency (time to onset) of the UR decreases.

Law of the threshold. At very weak intensities a stimulus will not elicit a response, but as the intensity of the eliciting stimulus increases there is a point at which the response is evoked. That is, *there is a point below which no response is elicited and above which a response always occurs.*

Learned helplessness. In the phenomenon called learned helplessness, an animal is first exposed to inescapable and severe aversive stimulation. Eventually the animal gives up and stops attempting to avoid or escape the situation. Next, an escape response, which under ordinary circumstances would be acquired easily, is made available but the animal does not make the response. The organism seems to give up and become helpless when presented with aversive stimulation.

Learning. Refers to the acquisition, maintenance, and change of an organism's behavior as a result of lifetime events.

Magazine training. Establishing an association (in time) between stimuli that precede reinforcement and the reinforcing event. For example, a rat is placed in an operant chamber and a microcomputer periodically turns on the feeder. When the feeder is turned on, it makes a click and a food pellet falls into a cup. Because the click and the appearance of food are associated in time you would, after training, observe a typical rat staying close to the food magazine and quickly moving toward it when the feeder is operated.

MammaCare. A behavioral program used to teach women effective self-examination of their breasts.

Mand. The word *mand* comes from the common English word *command*, but commands are only part of this operant class. The mand is a class of operants whose form is regulated by specific establishing operations (e.g., deprivation, aversive stimulation, etc.). When you say "give me the book," "don't do that," "stop," and so on, your words are regulated by motivational conditions (e.g., deprivation for the book, or by another person doing something unpleasant). In behavior analysis, these verbal responses are called mands.

Matching law. When two or more concurrent-interval schedules are available, relative rate of response matches (or equals) relative rate of reinforcement.

Matching to sample. A procedure used to investigate recognition of stimuli. For example, in a simple recognition procedure, a pigeon may be presented with three keys. A triangle is projected onto the center key. The triangle is the sample stimulus. To ensure that the bird attends to the sample, it is required to peck the sample key. When this happens, two sidekeys are illuminated with a triangle on one and a square on the other, called the comparison stimuli. If the bird pecks the comparison stimulus that corresponds to the sample, this behavior is reinforced and leads to the presentation of a new sample. Pecks to the noncorresponding stimulus result in extinction and the next trial.

Maturation. One source of invalidity in experiments is called maturation, which refers to biological or psychological processes that change over time. If these maturational changes occur at the same time as the manipulation of the independent variable, they (rather than the experimental treatment) could be responsible for the findings. See also *internal validity*.

Maximization. In this economic view of behavior, humans and other animals are like organic computers that compare their behavioral distributions with overall outcomes and eventually stabilize on a response distribution that maximizes overall rate of reinforcement.

Mechner notation. A notation system that describes the independent variables that produce operant behavior. For example, Mechner notation represents the way that schedules of reinforcement are arranged.

Melioration. An explanation of how organisms come to produce matching on concurrent schedules of reinforcement. In contrast to overall maximizing of reinforcement, Herrnstein (1982) proposed a process of **melioration** (doing the best at the moment). Organisms, he argued, are sensitive to fluctuations in the momentary rates of reinforcement rather than to long-term changes in overall rates of reinforcement.

Metacontingencies. Contingent relations between cultural practices and the effects of those practices for the group. For example, competence in science is important for people who live in a technologically advanced culture. Scientific research produces a range of benefits for the general society. These include better medicine, more productive crop yields, new and better building materials, more efficient and longer lasting appliances, and superior regulation of human behavior. Thus, a positive metacontingency exists between educational practices that increase scientific competence and long-term benefits to the group.

Mixed schedule of reinforcement. A mixed schedule is two or more basic schedules (CRF, FR, FI, VI, VR) presented sequentially in which each link ends with primary reinforcement (or in some cases extinction) and the component schedules are not signaled by discriminative stimuli. In other words, a mixed schedule is the same as an unsignaled multiple schedule.

Molar. Molar accounts of behavior are concerned with large-scale factors that regulate responding over a long period of time. For example, the average time between reinforcers for an entire session.

Molecular. Molecular accounts of behavior focus on small moment-to-moment relationships between behavior and its consequences. For example, the time between any two responses (IRT).

Multiple baseline across behaviors. A multiple baseline research design across behaviors is used when a reinforcement procedure is applied progressively to several operants. In this case, the subject, setting, and consequences remain the same, but different responses are modified sequentially.

Multiple baseline across stimulus conditions. In this research design, a reinforcement procedure is applied in one situation but is withheld in other settings. When behavior changes in the situation where it is reinforced, the contingency is applied to the same response in another setting.

Multiple baseline across subjects. A research design in which an intervention is introduced progressively for different subjects who exhibit similar target behavior. The same behavior (e.g., stealing) is first modified for subject 1, and baselines are collected for subjects 2 and 3. Next, the behavior of subject 2 is changed while the rate of target behavior for subjects 1 and 3 continues to be assessed. Finally, the treatment procedure is applied to subject 3.

Multiple baseline design. A class of research designs used primarily in applied behavior analysis. See *multiple baseline across behaviors, multiple baseline across stimulus conditions,* and *multiple baseline across subjects.*

Multiple schedule. A multiple schedule is two or more basic schedules (CRF, FR, FI, VI, VR) presented sequentially in which each link ends with primary reinforcement (or in some cases extinction) and *the component schedules are signaled by discriminative stimuli.* In other words, a multiple schedule is the same as a chain schedule, but each link produces primary reinforcement.

Negative automaintenance. Birds are autoshaped to peck a key, but in negative automaintenance food is not presented if the bird pecks the key. This is also called omission training because food reinforcement is omitted if key pecking occurs.

Negative contrast. See *behavioral contrast.*

Negative punishment. The removal of a positive reinforcer contingent on behavior is called negative punishment, and this procedure decreases operant behavior.

Negative reinforcement. When an operant response results in the removal or avoidance of an aversive event, the contingency is called negative reinforcement. If the response is made in the presence of the aversive stimulus, it is an escape response. When the operant prevents the aversive stimulus, it is an avoidance response. In both cases, the removal or prevention of an aversive event strengthens operant behavior.

Negative reinforcer. An event or stimulus that increases the frequency of operants when it is removed contingent on behavior. See also n*egative reinforcement.*

New-response method for conditioned reinforcement. First, a nonreinforcing stimulus is associated with a reinforcing event, and following this the stimulus is shown to increase the frequency of some operant behavior.

Nondiscriminated avoidance. Refers to the procedure used to train behavior or to avoidance responding (in which no warning stimulus is presented). Both uses are correct. See also *negative reinforcement.*

Omission training. See *negative automaintenance.*

Ontogenetic behavior. Each organism has a unique life history that contributes to its behavior. Ontogenetic behavior is caused by events that occur over the lifetime of an individual. Ontogenetic history builds on species history to determine when, where, and what kind of behavior will occur at a given moment. See also *phylogenetic behavior.*

Operant. An operant is behavior that operates on the environment to produce a change or consequence. Operants are selected in the sense that they increase or decrease as a function of the consequences they produce.

Operant aggression. Aggressive operant behavior that is reinforced by the removal of an aversive event. See also *negative reinforcement.*

Operant chamber. A laboratory device used to investigate operant conditioning. An operant chamber for a rat is a small, enclosed box that typically contains a lever with a light above it and a food magazine or cup connected to an external feeder. The feeder delivers a small food pellet when electronically activated.

Operant class. A class of related operant responses that may vary in topography but produce a common environmental consequence.

Operant conditioning. An increase or decrease in operant behavior as a function of the consequences that follow responses.

Operant level. The rate of an operant before any known conditioning. For example, the rate of key pecking before a peck-food contingency has been established.

Overmatching. In the generalized matching equation, a value of *a* greater than 1 indicates that changes in the response ratio (B_a/B_b) are larger than changes in the ratio of reinforcement (R_a/R_b). This outcome occurs because relative behavior increases faster than predicted from relative rate of reinforcement. See also *generalized matching law.*

Overshadowing. This effect occurs when a compound stimulus is used as the CS in a respondent conditioning experiment. For example, a light + tone (CS) may be presented at the same time and be associated with an unconditioned stimulus such as food. The most salient property of the compound stimulus comes to regulate exclusively the conditioned response. Thus, if a tone is more salient than a light, only the tone will evoke salivation.

Pain-elicited aggression. Respondent aggression or attack elicited by an aversive event. The same as respondent aggression.

Partial reinforcement effect. See *intermittent reinforcement effect.*

Peak shift. A shift in the peak of a generalization gradient away from an extinction (S^Δ) stimulus.

Personalized system of instruction (PSI). A college teaching method based on principles of operant conditioning and designed by Fred Keller (Keller, 1968). Keller called his teaching method a personalized system of instruction or PSI. Basically, PSI courses are organized such that students move through the course at their own pace and they are reinforced for completing small course units.

Phenotype. An organism's phenotype refers to anatomical and behavioral characteristics observed during the lifetime of the individual. For example, an individual's size, color, and shape are anatomical aspects of phenotype. Behavioral features include taste preferences, aggressiveness, and shyness. Different phenotypic attributes of individuals may or may not reflect underlying genetic variation.

Phylogenetic behavior. Environment-behavior relations that are based on the evolutionary history of a species are called phylogenetic. The reflex is one instance of phylogenetic behavior. Species history provides the organism with a basic repertoire of responses that interact with environmental conditions. See also *ontogenetic behavior.*

Phylogeny. The species history of an organism.

Polydipsia. Polydipsia or excessive drinking is adjunctive behavior induced by the time-based delivery of food. For example, a rat that is working for food on an intermittent schedule may drink as much as half its body weight during a single session. This drinking occurs even though the animal is not water deprived. See also *adjunctive behavior.*

Positive contrast. See *behavioral contrast.*

Positive punishment. The presentation of an aversive event contingent on behavior is called positive punishment, and it has the effect of decreasing operant behavior.

Positive reinforcement. The presentation of a reinforcing stimulus contingent on behavior is called positive reinforcement, and it has the effect of increasing operant behavior.

Positive reinforcer. A positive reinforcer is any stimulus or event that increases the probability of an operant that produces it.

Postreinforcement pause (PRP). The pause in responding that occurs after reinforcement on some intermittent schedules (e.g., FR, FI).

Power law for matching. See *generalized matching law.*

Preference. When several schedules of reinforcement are available concurrently, one alternative may be chosen more frequently than others. When this occurs, it is called preference for an alternative source of reinforcement.

Premack principle. A higher frequency operant will reinforce a lower frequency behavior.

Preparedness. Some relations between stimuli, and between stimuli and responses, are more likely because of phylogenetic history. This phenomenon has been called preparedness. For example, a bird that relies on sight for food selection would be expected to associate the appearance of a food item and illness, but rats that select food on the basis of taste quickly make a flavor-illness association.

Primary aversive stimuli. An aversive stimulus that has acquired its properties as a function of species history.

Primary reinforcer. A reinforcing stimulus that has acquired its properties as a function of species history.

Private behavior. Behavior that is only accessible to the person who emits it (e.g., thinking).

Punishing stimulus. A stimulus that decreases the frequency of an operant that produces it.

Punishment. A decrease in operant behavior when it is followed by an aversive stimulus or when reinforcement is withdrawn contingent on responding.

Quantitative law of effect. The matching law suggests that operant behavior is determined by rate of reinforcement for one alternative relative to all other known sources of reinforcement. Even in situations where a contingency exists between a single response and reinforcement, organisms may have several reinforced alternatives that are unknown to the researcher. Also, many of the activities that produce reinforcement are beyond experimental control. Thus, in a single-operant setting, multiple sources of reinforcement are operating. In this view, all operant behavior must be understood as behavior emitted in the context of other alternative sources of reinforcement.

Based on these ideas, an equation for the single operant is called the quantitative law of effect. The equation relates absolute response and reinforcement rates, using alternative sources of reinforcement as the context. The equation may be derived from a restatement of the proportional matching law and is written as $B_a/(B_a + B_e) = R_a/(R_a + R_e)$. In this equation, B_e refers to all behavior directed to extraneous sources of reinforcement, and R_e represents these sources.

Rate of response. The number of responses that occur in a given interval. For example, a bird may peck a key two times per second.

Ratio schedules. Response-based schedules of reinforcement.

Ratio strain. A disruption of responding that occurs when a ratio schedule is increased rapidly.

Reactive measurement. A threat to internal validity in an experiment. When a dependent variable changes just because it is measured, the effect is called reactive measurement. For example, a person may lose weight because he or she is weighed daily by a researcher who is conducting an experiment on different types of diets. See also *internal validity.*

Reflex. When an unconditioned stimulus elicits an unconditioned response (US→UR), the relationship is called a reflex.

Reflexivity. A one-to-one relationship (A = A) between stimuli. For example, a pigeon is presented with the color red on a sample key and the bird responds to a comparison key with the identical color (red). A child who is given a picture of a cat and then finds a similar picture in a set of photographs is showing reflexivity.

Reinforcement. An increase in the rate of operant behavior as a function its consequences. Also, the procedure of presenting a reinforcing consequence when a response occurs.

Reaction chains. Reaction chains are phylogeneticly prepared patterned sequences of behavior. An environmental stimulus sets off behavior that produces stimuli that set off the next set of responses in the sequence; these behaviors produce the next set of stimuli and so on. Presenting stimuli that prompt responses ordinarily occurring in the middle part of the sequence will start the chain at that point rather than at the beginning. Reaction chains are much like consecutive sets of reflexes where the stimuli that evoke the next response in the sequence is produced by the previous reflex.

Relative rate of reinforcement. When two or more sources of reinforcement are available (as on a concurrent schedule), relative rate of reinforcement refers to reinforcement delivered on one alternative divided by the sum of all alternatives.

Relative rate of response. When two or more sources of reinforcement are available (as on a concurrent schedule), relative rate of response refers to rate of response on one alternative divided by the sum of the rates on all alternatives.

Relative stimulus control. Relative stimulus control means that an organism responds to differences among the values of two or more stimuli. For example, a pigeon may be trained to peck in the presence of the larger of two triangles rather than to the absolute size of a triangle. See also *absolute stimulus control.*

Reliability of observation. In applied behavior analysis, reliability of observation involves the amount of agreement among observers who independently record the same behavior. One way to assess reliability is to count the number of times two observers agree that a target behavior did (or did not) occur. This can be expressed as a percentage agreement that varies from 0 to 100%. Generally, applied behavior analysts strive for reliability of greater than 80% agreement.

Repertoire. All the behavior an organism is capable of emitting on the basis of species and environmental history.

Rescorla-Wagner model. The basic idea of the Rescorla-Wagner model of respondent conditioning is that a conditioned stimulus acquires a limited amount of associative strength on any one trial. The term *associative strength* describes the relation between the CS and the magnitude of the conditioned response. In general, associative strength increases over conditioning trials and reaches some maximum level. A given CS can acquire only so much control over a conditioned response. This is the maximum associative strength for the CS. Thus, a tone (CS) that is paired with 1 gram of food will have maximum associative strength when the amount of conditioned salivation (CR) is about the same as the unconditioned salivation (UR) elicited by the gram of food (US). This magnitude sets the upper limit for the conditioned response. The CS cannot elicit a greater response than the one produced by the unconditioned stimulus.

Resistance to extinction. The perseverance of operant behavior when it is placed on extinction. Resistance to extinction is substantially increased when an intermittent schedule of reinforcement has been used to maintain behavior.

Respondent. A respondent is behavior that is elicited as a function of the previous pairing of a neutral stimulus with an unconditioned or biologically relevant stimulus. The new stimulus or CS evokes the CR, which is called a respondent. See also *conditioned response (CR)* and *respondent conditioning.*

Respondent aggression. Aggression elicited by the presentation of an aversive event. The same as pain-elicited aggression.

Respondent conditioning. Respondent conditioning occurs when an organism responds to a new event based on a history of association with a biologically important stimulus. The Russian physiologist Ivan Pavlov discovered this form of conditioning at the turn of the century. He showed that dogs salivated when food was placed in their mouths. This relation between the food stimulus and salivation is called a reflex and occurs because of the animal's biological history. When Pavlov rang a bell just before feeding the dog, it began to salivate at the sound of the bell. In this way, new features (sound of bell) controlled the dog's respondent behavior (salivation). Thus, presenting stimuli together in time (typically CS then US) is the procedure for respondent conditioning. If a CS comes to regulate the occurrence of a conditioned response (CR), respondent conditioning has occurred.

Respondent discrimination. Respondent discrimination occurs when an organism shows a conditioned response to one stimulus but not to other similar events. A discrimination procedure involves positive and negative conditioning trials. For example, a positive trial occurs when a CS$^+$ such as a 60-dB tone is associated with an unconditioned stimulus like food. On negative trials, a 40-dB tone is presented (CS$^-$) but never paired with food. Once a differential response occurs (salivation to 60 dB but not to 40), we may say that the organism discriminates between the tones.

Respondent extinction. The procedure of respondent extinction involves the presentation of the CS without the US after conditioning has occurred. As a behavioral process, extinction refers to a decline in the strength of the conditioned response when an extinction procedure is in effect. In both instances, the term *extinction* is used correctly.

Respondent generalization. Respondent generalization occurs when an organism shows a conditioned response to values of the CS that have not been trained. For example, if a tone of 375 Hz is paired with food, a dog will salivate at maximum level when this tone is presented. However, the animal may salivate to other values of the tone. As the tone differs more and more from 375 Hz, the CR decreases in magnitude.

Respondent level. The magnitude of the CR before any conditioning has taken place.

Response class. Operant responses that may vary in topography but produce the same or similar consequences. For example, saying "Please open the door" and physically opening the door are members of the same response class if both result in an open door.

Response-shock interval. On an avoidance schedule, the time from a response that postpones shock to the onset of the aversive stimulus (if another response is not emitted).

Run of responses. A fast burst of responding. For example, after the postreinforcement pause on a fixed-ratio schedule, an organism will rapidly emit the responses required by the ratio.

S-delta (S$^\Delta$). When an operant does not produce reinforcement, the stimulus that precedes the response is called an S-delta (S$^\Delta$). In the presence of an S-delta, the probability of emitting an operant declines.

S-S account of conditioned reinforcement. The hypothesis that it is necessary for a stimulus to be paired with a primary reinforcer in order for it to become a conditioned reinforcer. The hypothesis has been largely discounted, and the weight of the evidence supports Edmond Fantino's (1969b) delay-reduction hypothesis. See *delay-reduction hypothesis.*

Satiation. Repeated presentations of a reinforcer weaken its effectiveness, and for this reason rate of response declines. Satiation refers to this effect, and the repeated presentation of a reinforcer is called a satiation operation.

Scalloping. The characteristic pattern of response, seen on a cumulative record, that is produced by a fixed-interval schedule. There is a pause after reinforcement, then a few probe responses, and finally an increasingly accelerated rate of response until reinforcement.

Schedule of reinforcement. In relation to responses, a schedule of reinforcement is the arrangement of the environment in terms of discriminative stimuli and behavioral consequences.

Schedule-induced behavior. See *adjunctive behavior.*

Science of behavior. See *behavior analysis.*

Second-order conditioning. Second-order conditioning pairs two CSs ($CS_1 + CS_2$), rather than pairing a CS and US (CS + US). Pavlov (1927/1960) conducted experiments that demonstrated second-order conditioning. The tick of a metronome was paired with food. The sound of the metronome came to evoke salivation. Once the ticking sound reliably elicited salivation, Pavlov paired it with the sight of a black square ($CS_1 + CS_2$). Following several pairings of the metronome beat with the black square, the sight of the black square evoked salivation.

Selection by consequences. The causative principle for biology, behavior, and culture is selection by consequences. With regard to biology, mutation and sexual reproduction ensure a range of variation in genes that code for the features of organisms. Some physical attributes meet the requirements of the environment. Organisms with these adaptive features survive and reproduce, passing their genetic material to the next generation. Organisms without these characteristics do not survive as well and their genes are less represented in the subsequent population. Natural selection is therefore a form of selection by reproductive consequences that occurs at the biological level.

Selection by consequences has been extended to the level of behavior. Operant behavior is an expressed characteristic of many organisms, including humans. Organisms with an extensive range of operant behavior adjust to new environmental situations on the basis of the consequences that follow behavior. This kind of selection occurs over the life of the individual. Operants are the physical units selected at the behavioral level. The process of the selection and change of operants is analogous to evolution and natural selection at the genetic level. Reinforcement is therefore an ontogenetic process that extends selection by consequences to the level of behavior.

A third level of evolution and selection occurs at the cultural level. The physical unit of selection at this level is the cultural practice. A cultural practice involves the interlocking operant behavior of many people. As with operants, cultural practices vary in form and frequency. Different ways of doing things are more or less successful in terms of efficiency, productivity, and survival of group members. Generally, cultural practices are selected by aggregate outcomes, increasing or decreasing the rate of adoption of the practice.

Self-control. From a behavioral perspective, self-control occurs when a person emits a response that affects the probability of subsequent behavior in the following way: giving up immediate gains for greater long-term benefits or accepting immediate negative consequences for later positive outcomes. When people manage their behavior in such a way that they choose the more beneficial long-range consequences, they are said to show self-control.

Sensory preconditioning. Two stimuli, such as light and tone, are repeatedly presented together without the occurrence of a known US (preconditioning). Later, one of these stimuli is paired with an unconditioned stimulus and the other stimulus is tested for conditioning. Even though the second stimulus has never been directly associated with the US, it comes to evoke a conditioned response.

Shaping. The method of successive approximation or shaping may be used to establish a response. This method involves the reinforcement of closer and closer approximations to the final performance. For example, a rat may be reinforced for standing in the vicinity of a lever. Once the animal is reliably facing the lever, a movement of the head toward the bar is reinforced. Next, closer and closer approximations to pressing the lever are reinforced. Each step of the procedure involves reinforcement of closer approximations and nonreinforcement of more distant responses. Many novel forms of behavior may be shaped by the method of successive approximation.

Shock-shock interval. The scheduled time between shocks on an avoidance schedule.

Sign tracking. Sign tracking refers to approaching a sign (or stimulus) that signals a biologically relevant event. For example, dogs are required to sit on a mat and a stimulus that signals food is presented to the animal. When the food signal is presented, the dogs approach the stimulus and make food-soliciting responses to it.

Simultaneous conditioning. A respondent conditioning procedure in which the CS and US are presented at the same moment. Compared with delayed conditioning, simultaneous conditioning produces a weaker conditioned response.

Simultaneous discrimination. In simultaneous discrimination, the S^D and S^Δ are presented at the same time and the organism is reinforced for responding to the relative properties of one or the other. For example, a pigeon may be presented with two keys, both illuminated with white lights, but one light is brighter than the other. The bird is reinforced for pecking the dimmer of the two keys. Pecks to the other key are placed on extinction. After training, the pigeon will peck the darker of any two keys. See also *relative stimulus control*.

Single-subject research. Experimental research that is concerned with discovering principles and conditions that govern the behavior of single organisms. Each individual's behavior is studied to assess the impact of a given environmental variable.

Social disruption. A negative side-effect of punishment in which the person who delivers punishment and the context become conditioned aversive stimuli. Individuals will attempt to escape from or avoid the punishing person or setting.

Spontaneous recovery (operant). After a period of extinction, rate of response may be close to operant level. After some time, the organism is again placed in the setting and extinction is continued. Responding recovers, but over repeated sessions of extinction the amount of recovery decreases.

Spontaneous recovery (respondent). An increase in the magnitude of the CR after respondent extinction has occurred and after some time has passed.

Steady-state performance. Behavior that is stable in the sense that it does not change over time. For example, after transition from CRF to VI 30 seconds, a rat may press a lever at approximately the same rate day after day.

Stimulus class. Stimuli that vary across physical dimensions but have a common effect on behavior.

Stimulus control. A change in operant behavior that occurs when either an S^D or S^Δ is presented. When an S^D is presented, the probability of response increases; and when an S^Δ is given, operant behavior has a low probability of occurrence.

Stimulus equivalence. The presentation of one class of stimuli that occasions responses made to other stimulus classes.

Stimulus generalization. Stimulus generalization occurs when an operant that has been reinforced in the presence of a specific discriminative stimulus also is emitted in the presence of other stimuli. The process is called stimulus generalization because the operant is emitted to new stimuli that presumably share common properties with the discriminative stimulus.

Stimulus substitution. When a CS (e.g., light) is paired with a US (e.g., food) the conditioned stimulus is said to substitute for the unconditioned stimulus. That is, food evokes salivation and by conditioning the light elicits similar behavior.

Structural approach to classifying behavior. In the structural approach, behavior is analyzed in terms of its form or topography. For example, many developmental psychologists are interested in the intellectual growth of children. These researchers often investigate what a person does at a given stage of development. The structure of behavior is emphasized because it is said to reveal the underlying stage of intellectual development. See also *functional analysis of behavior*.

Successive approximation. See *shaping*.

Successive discrimination. A procedure used to train differential responding. The researcher arranges the presentation of S^D and S^Δ so that one follows the other. For example, a multiple schedule is programmed such that a red light signals VI food reinforcement, and this is followed by a green light that indicates that extinction is in effect.

Superstitious behavior. Behavior that is accidentally reinforced. For example, a parent may inadvertently strengthen aggressive behavior when a child is given his or her allowance just after fighting with a playmate. Switching from one alternative to another may be accidentally reinforced on a concurrent schedule if the alternative schedule has a reinforcement setup. In this case, the organism is accidentally reinforced for a change from one schedule to another.

Symbolic matching. In a matching-to-sample task, symbolic matching involves the presentation of one class of stimuli as the sample (e.g., geometrical forms) and another set of stimuli (e.g., different colors) as the options. Reinforcement depends on an arbitrary relation (e.g., triangle = red).

Symmetry. When stimulus class A is shown to be interchangeable with stimulus class B (if A = B then B = A), we may say that the organism shows symmetry between the stimulus classes.

Systematic desensitization. A behavioral technique used to treat phobias based on principles of classical conditioning. The first step in the procedure is to teach the client to relax; then a fear hierarchy is constructed. Next, the therapist reads the least-anxiety-provoking description on the hierarchy and asks the client to imagine himself or herself in that circumstance. If the person feels anxious, the same item is repeated; and following three or more successful repetitions, the next item on the hierarchy is presented.

Systematic replication. A way to increase the generality of an experimental finding by conducting other experiments in which the procedures are different (from the original research) but they are logically related. See also *direct replication*.

Tact. A class of verbal operants whose form is regulated by specific nonverbal discriminative stimuli. For example, a child may see a cat and say, "Look mom, a kitty." The word *tact* comes from the more familiar term *contact*. Tacts are verbal responses that make contact with the environment.

Tandem schedule. A tandem schedule is two or more basic schedules (CRF, FR, FI, VI, VR) presented sequentially in which only the final link ends with primary reinforcement (or in some cases extinction) and *the component schedules are not signaled by discriminative stimuli*. In other words, a mixed schedule is the same as an unsignaled chain schedule.

Teleological explanation. When behavior is accounted for in terms of future events, such an account is referred to as a teleological explanation.

Temporal pairing. In respondent conditioning, the pairing of the CS and US in time, See also *contiguity*.

Terminal behavior. On a schedule of reinforcement, as the time for reinforcement gets close, animals engage in activities related to the presentation of the reinforcer. For example, a rat will orient toward the food cup.

Textual. A class of verbal operants regulated by verbal stimuli where there is correspondence between the stimulus and response, but not topographical similarity. The most common example of textual behavior is reading out loud. The child looks at the text "See Dick, see Jane" and emits the spoken words "See Dick, see Jane."

Time sampling. A method of recording used mostly in applied behavior analysis. Behavior is sampled over a long time scale. The idea is to make observations at specified times throughout the day. For example, a patient on a psychiatric ward may be observed every 30 minutes, as a nurse does the rounds, and instances of psychotic talk are recorded.

Token economy. A reinforcement system based on token reinforcement; the contingencies specify when, and under what conditions, particular forms of behavior are reinforced. The system is an economy in the sense that tokens may be exchanged for goods and services, much like money is in our economy. This exchange of tokens for a variety of back-up reinforcers ensures that the tokens are conditioned reinforcers. Token economies have been used to improve the behavior of psychiatric patients, juvenile delinquents, pupils in remedial classrooms, medical patients, alcoholics, drug addicts, prisoners, nursing home residents, and retarded persons.

Topography. The physical form or characteristics of the response. For example, the way that a rat presses a lever.

Trace conditioning. A respondent conditioning procedure in which the CS is presented for a brief period, and after some time the US occurs. Generally, as the time between the CS and US increases, the conditioned response becomes weaker. When compared to delayed conditioning, trace conditioning is not as effective.

Transition-state performance. Behavior that is changing from one state to another as a function of a change in contingencies of reinforcement. For example, when CRF contingencies are changed to FR 10, responding is at first erratic but eventually stabilizes. See also *steady-state performance*.

Transitivity. When stimulus A = stimulus B and B = stimulus C, if an organism responds to stimulus A as equal to stimulus C, it is said to show transitivity. For example, if the written numbers one, two, three are equivalent to the arithmetic numbers 1, 2, and 3, the words and these arithmetic numbers are equivalent to sets {X}, {X,X}, and {X,X,X}, it logically follows that one, two, and three are equivalent to sets {X}, {X,X}, and {X,X,X} and the relationship is transitive.

Trans-situational. Once a stimulus is identified as reinforcing or punishing in one situation it may also be a reinforcer or punisher in other situations. Many, but not all, reinforcers and punishers have trans-situational properties.

Trial-and-error learning. A term coined by Thorndike (1898, 1911) that he used to describe results from his puzzle box and maze learning experiments. Animals were said to make fewer and fewer errors over repeated trials, learning by trial and error.

Two-key procedure. On a concurrent schedule of reinforcement, the alternative schedules are presented on separate response keys.

Unconditioned response (UR). All organisms are born with a set of reflexes (US → UR). These relationships are invariant and biologically based. The behavior elicited by the US is called the unconditioned response (UR).

Unconditioned stimulus (US). All organisms are born with a set of reflexes (US → UR). These relationships are invariant and biologically based. The eliciting event is called the unconditioned stimulus (US).

Undermatching. In the generalized matching equation, the exponent *a* takes on a value less than 1. This result is described as undermatching and occurs when changes in the response ratio are less than changes in the reinforcement ratio. See also *generalized matching law.*

Variable interval (VI). A schedule of reinforcement in which one response is reinforced after a variable amount of time has passed. For example, on a VI 30-second schedule, the time to each reinforcement changes but the average time is 30 seconds.

Variable ratio (VR). A response-based schedule of reinforcement in which the number of responses required for reinforcement changes after each reinforcer is presented. The average number of responses is used to index the schedule. For example, a rat may press a lever for reinforcement 50 times, then 150, 70, 30, and 200. Adding these response requirements for a total of 500, then dividing by the number of separate response runs (5), yields the schedule value, VR 100.

Verbal behavior. Verbal behavior refers to the vocal, written, and gestural performances of a speaker, writer, or communicator. This behavior operates on the listener, reader, or observer, who arranges for reinforcement of the verbal performance. Verbal behavior often has indirect affects on the environment. This contrasts with nonverbal behavior, which usually results in direct and automatic consequences. When you walk toward an object, you come closer to it. Verbal behavior, on the other hand, works through its affects on other people. To change the position of a lamp, the speaker states "Lift the lamp at the back of the room" to a listener, who is inclined to respond. Although verbal behavior is usually equated with speaking, vocal responses are only one of its forms. For example, a person may emit gestures and body movements that indirectly operate on the environment through their effects on others. A frown sets the occasion for others to remove some aversive event, while a smile may signal the observer to behave in ways that produce positive reinforcement.

Verbal community. The contingencies that regulate verbal behavior arise from the practices of people in the verbal community. The verbal community refers to the customary ways that people reinforce the behavior of a speaker.

References

ABRAMSON, L. Y., SELIGMAN, M. E. P., & TEASDALE, J. D. (1978). Learned helplessness in humans: Critique and reformulation. *Journal of Abnormal Psychology, 87,* 49–74.

AINSLIE, G. W. (1974). Impulse control in pigeons. *Journal of the Experimental Analysis of Behavior, 21,* 485–489.

ALLEN, C. M. (1981). On the exponent in the "generalized" matching equation. *Journal of the Experimental Analysis of Behavior, 35,* 125–127.

ALVAREZ, L. W. (1982). Experimental evidence that an asteroid impact led to the extinction of many species 65 million years ago. *Proceedings of the National Academy of Sciences, 80,* 627–642.

ALVAREZ, L. W., ALVAREZ, W., ASARO, F., & MICHEL, H. V. (1980). Extraterrestrial cause for the Cretaceous-tertiary extinction. *Science, 208,* 1095–1108.

ALVAREZ, L. W., ASARO, F., & MICHEL, H. V. (1980). Extraterrestrial cause for the Cretaceous-tertiary extinction—Experimental results and theoretical interpretation. *Science, 206,* 1095–1108.

ALVAREZ, W., ASARO, F., MICHEL, H. V., ALVAREZ, L. W. (1982). Iridium anomaly approximately synchronous with terminal eocene extinction. *Science, 216,* 886–888.

AMABILE, T. N. (1990). With you, without you: The social psychology of creativity, and beyond. In M. A. Runco & R. S. Albert (Eds.). *Theories of Creativity.* Newbury Park, CA.: Sage Publications.

ANGER, D. (1956). The dependence of Interresponse times upon the relative reinforcement of different interresponse times. *Journal of Experimental Psychology, 52,* 145–161.

ANREP, G. V. (1920). Pitch discrimination in a dog. *Journal of Physiology, 53,* 367–385.

ANTONITIS, J. J. (1951). Response variability in the white rat during conditioning, extinction, and reconditioning. *Journal of Experimental Psychology, 42 ,* 273–281.

APPEL, J. B. (1961). Punishment in the squirrel monkey *saimiri sciurea. Science, 133,* 36.

APPEL, J. B., & PETERSON, N. J. (1965). Punishment: Effects of shock intensity on response suppression. *Psychological Reports, 16,* 721–730.

ARBUCKLE, J. L., & LATTAL, K. A. (1988). Changes in functional response units with briefly delayed reinforcement. *Journal of the Experimental Analysis of Behavior, 49,* 249–263.

ARMSTRONG, E. A. (1950). The nature and function of displacement activities. *Symposia of the Society for Experimental Biology, 4,* 361–384.

AUTOR, S. M. (1960). *The strength of conditioned reinforcers as a function of frequency and probability of reinforcement.* Unpublished doctoral dissertation, Harvard University, Cambridge, MA.

AYLLON, T. (1963). Intensive treatment of psychotic behavior by stimulus satiation and food reinforcement. *Behavior Research and Therapy, 1,* 53–61.

AYLLON, T., & AZRIN, N. H. (1968). *The token economy: A motivational system for therapy and rehabilitation.* New York: Appleton-Century-Crofts.

AYRES, J. J. B., BENEDICT, J. O., & WITCHER, E. S. (1975). Systematic manipulation of individual events in a truly random control in rats. *Journal of Comparative and Physiological Psychology, 88,* 97–103.

AZRIN, N. H. (1956). Effects of two intermittent schedules of immediate and nonimmediate punishment. *Journal of Psychology, 42,* 3–21.

AZRIN, N. H. (1958). Some effects of noise on human behavior. *Journal of the Experimental Analysis of Behavior, 1,* 183–200.

AZRIN, N. H. (1959). Punishment and recovery during fixed ratio performance. *Journal of the Experimental Analysis of Behavior, 2,* 303–305.

AZRIN, N. H. (1960). Effects of punishment intensity during variable-interval reinforcement. *Journal of the Experimental Analysis of Behavior, 3,* 123-142.

AZRIN, N. H., HAKE, D. F., & HUTCHINSON, R. R. (1965). Elicitation of aggression by a physical blow. *Journal of the Experimental Analysis of Behavior, 8,* 55–57.

AZRIN, N. H., & HOLZ, W. C. (1961). Punishment during fixed interval reinforcement. *Journal of the Experimental Analysis of Behavior, 4,* 343–347.

AZRIN, N. H., & HOLZ, W. C. (1966). Punishment. In W. K. Honig (Ed.), *Operant behavior: Areas of research and application* (pp. 380–447). New York: Appleton-Century-Crofts.

AZRIN, N. H., HOLZ, W. C., & HAKE, D. (1963). Fixed-ratio punishment. *Journal of the Experimental Analysis of Behavior, 6,* 141–148.

AZRIN, N. H., HUTCHINSON, R. R., & HAKE, D. F. (1963). Pain-induced fighting in the squirrel monkey. *Journal of the Experimental Analysis of Behavior, 6,* 620.

AZRIN, N. H., HUTCHINSON, R. R., & HAKE, D. F. (1966). Extinction-induced aggression. *Journal of the Experimental Analysis of Behavior, 9,* 191–204.

AZRIN, N. H., HUTCHINSON, R. R., & SALLERY, R. D. (1964). Pain aggression toward inanimate objects. *Journal of the Experimental Analysis of Behavior, 7,* 223–228.

BACHRACH, A. J. (1962). *Psychological research: An introduction.* New York: Random House.

BADIA, P., HARSH, J., COKER, C. C., & ABBOTT, B. (1976). Choice and the dependability of stimuli that predict shock and safety. *Journal of the Experimental Analysis of Behavior, 26,* 95–111.

BAER, D. M. (1981). A flight of behavior analysis. *The Behavior Analyst, 4,* 85–91.

BAER, D. M. (1982). The role of current pragmatics in the future analysis of generalization technology. In R. B. Stuart (Ed.), *Adherence, compliance and generalization in behavioral medicine* (pp. 192–212). New York: Brunner/Mazel.

BAER, D. M., & GUESS, D. (1971). Receptive training of adjectival inflections in mental retardates. *Journal of Applied Behavior Analysis, 4,* 129–139.

BAER, D. M., & WOLF, M. M. (1970). The entry into natural communities of reinforcement. In R. Ulrich, T. Stachnik, & J. Mabry (Eds.), *Control of human behavior* (Vol. 2, pp. 319–324). Glenview, IL: Scott, Foresman.

BAER, D. M., WOLF, M. M., & RISLEY, T. R. (1968). Some current dimensions of applied behavior analysis. *Journal of Applied Behavior Analysis, 1,* 91–97.

BAKER, A. G. (1976). Learned irrelevance and learned helplessness: Rats learn that stimuli, reinforcers, and responses are uncorrelated. *Journal of Experimental Psychology: Animal Behavior Processes, 2,* 130–141.

BANDURA, A. (1973). *Aggression: A social learning analysis.* Englewood Cliffs, NJ: Prentice-Hall.

BANDURA, A. (1983). Psychological mechanisms of aggression. In R. G. Geen & E. I. Donnerstein (Eds.), *Aggression: Theoretical and empirical reviews* (Vol. 1, pp. 1–40). New York: Academic Press.

BANDURA, A., BLANCHARD, E., & RITTER, B. (1969). The relative efficacy of desensitization and modeling approaches for induced, behavioral, affective and attitudinal change. *Journal of Personality and Social Psychology, 13,* 173–199.

BARASH, D. P. (1973a). Social variety in the yellow-bellied marmot (*Marmota Flaviventris*). *Animal Behaviour, 21,* 579–584.

BARASH, D. P. (1973b). The sociobiology of the Olympic marmot. *Animal Behavior Monographs, 6,* 171–249.

BARASH, D. P. (1982). *Sociobiology and behavior.* Amsterdam: Elsevier.

BARKER, L. M., BEST, M. R., & DOMJAN, M. (Eds.). (1977). *Learning mechanisms in food selection.* Waco, TX: Baylor University Press.

BARON, A., & GALIZIO, M. (1983). Instructional control of human operant behavior. *The Psychological Record, 33,* 495–520.

BARON, R. A., & RICHARDSON, D. R. (1993). *Human aggression.* New York: Plenum Press.

BARON, R. A., RUSSELL, G. W., & ARMS, R. L. (1985). Negative ions and behavior: Impact on mood, memory, and aggression among Type A and Type B persons. *Journal of Personality and Social Psychology, 48,* 746–754.

BARRISH, H. H., SAUNDERS, M., & WOLF, M. M. (1969). Good behavior game: Effects of individual contingencies for group consequences on disruptive behavior in a classroom. *Journal of Applied Behavior Analysis, 2,* 119–124.

BAUM, M. (1965). An automated apparatus for the avoidance training of rats. *Psychological Reports, 16,* 1205–1211.

BAUM, M. (1969). Paradoxical effect of alcohol on the resistance to extinction of an avoidance response in rats. *Journal of Comparative and Physiological Psychology, 69,* 238–240.

BAUM, W. M. (1974a). Choice in free-ranging wild pigeons. *Science, 185,* 78–79.

BAUM, W. M. (1974b). On two types of deviation from the matching law: Bias and undermatching. *Journal of the Experimental Analysis of Behavior, 22,* 231–242.

BAUM, W. M. (1979). Matching, undermatching, and overmatching in studies of choice. *Journal of the Experimental Analysis of Behavior, 32,* 269–281.

BAUM, W. M. (1983). Studying foraging in the psychological laboratory. In R. L. Mellgren (Ed.), *Animal cognition and behavior* (pp. 253–278). New York: North-Holland.

BAUM, W. M. (1992). In search of the feedback function for variable-interval schedules. *Journal of the Experimental Analysis of Behavior, 57,* 365–375.

BAUM, W. M., & RACHLIN, H. C. (1969). Choice as time allocation. *Journal of the Experimental Analysis of Behavior, 12,* 861–874.

BEIMAN, I., GRAHAM, L. E., & CIMINERO, A. R. (1978). Self-control progressive relaxation training as an alternative nonpharmacological treatment for essential hypertension: Therapeutic effects in the natural environment. *Behavior Research and Therapy, 16,* 371–375.

BELKE, T. W., PIERCE, W. D., & POWELL, R. A. (1989). Determinants of choice for pigeons and humans on concurrent-chains schedules of reinforcement. *Journal of the Experimental Analysis of Behavior, 52,* 97–109.

BELLES, D., & BRADLYN, A. S. (1987). The use of the changing criterion design in achieving controlled smoking in a heavy smoker: A controlled case study. *Journal of Behavior Therapy and Experimental Psychiatry, 18,* 77–82.

BEM, D. J. (1965). An experimental analysis of self-persuasion. *Journal of Experimental Social Psychology, 1,* 199–218.

BENEDICT, J. O., & AYRES, J. J. B. (1972). Factors affecting conditioning in the truly random control procedure in the rat. *Journal of Comparative and Physiological Psychology, 78,* 323–330.

BENINGER, R. J., & KENDALL, S. B. (1975). Behavioral contrast in rats with different reinforcers and different response topographies. *Journal of the Experimental Analysis of Behavior, 24,* 267–280.

BERKOWITZ, L., & DONNERSTEIN, E. (1982). External validity is more than skin deep: Some answers to criticism of laboratory experiments. *American Psychologist, 37,* 245–257.

BERNARD, C. (1927). *An introduction to the study of experimental medicine.* New York: Macmillan. (Original work published 1865)

BEUMONT, A. L., BOOTH, S. F., ABRAHAM, D. A., GRIFFITHS, D. A., & TURNER, T. R. (1983). Temporal sequence of symptoms in patients with anorexia nervosa: A preliminary report. In P. L. Darby, P. E. Garfinkel, D. M. Garner, & D. V. Coscina (Eds.), *Anorexia nervosa: Recent developments in research* (pp. 129–136). New York: Alan R. Liss.

BIJOU, S., & BAER, D. M. (1978). *Behavior analysis of child development.* Englewood Cliffs, NJ: Prentice-Hall.

BIRNBRAUER, J. S. (1979). Applied behavior analysis, service and the acquisition of knowledge. *The Behavior Analyst, 2,* 15–21.

BLANCHARD, R. J. (1975). The effect of S⁻ on observing behavior. *Learning and Motivation, 6,* 1–10.

BLOOM, H. S., CRISWELL, E. L., PENNEYPACKER, H. S., CATANIA, A. C., & ADAMS, C. K. (1982). Major stimulus dimensions determining detection of simulated breast lesions. *Perception and Psychophysics, 32,* 251–260.

BLOUGH, D. S. (1959). Delayed matching in the pigeon. *Journal of the Experimental Analysis of Behavior, 2,* 151–160.

BLOUGH, D. S. (1982). Pigeon perception of letters of the alphabet. *Science, 218,* 397–398.

BOLLES, R. C. (1970). Species-specific defense reactions and avoidance learning. *Psychological Review, 77,* 32–48.

BOLLES, R. C. (1979). *Learning theory.* New York: Holt, Rinehart & Winston.

BONDY, A., & FROST, L. (1994). The picture exchange communication system. *Focus on Autistic Behavior, 9,* 1–19.

BORDEN, R. J., BOWEN, R., & TAYLOR, S. P. (1971). Shock setting behavior as a function of physical attack and extrinsic reward. *Perceptual and Motor Skills, 33,* 563–568.

BOREN, J. J. (1961). Resistance to extinction as a function of the fixed ratio. *Journal of Experimental Psychology, 4,* 304–308.

BOWER, G. H., & HILGARD, E. R. (1981). *Theories of learning.* Englewood Cliffs, NJ: Prentice-Hall.

BRADSHAW, C. M., RUDDLE, H. V., & SZABADI, E. (1981). Studies of concurrent performance in humans. In C. M. Bradshaw, E. Szabadi, & C. F. Lowe (Eds.), *Quantification of steady-state operant behavior* (pp. 79–90). Amsterdam: Elsevier/North-Holland.

BRADSHAW, C. M., & SZABADI, E. (1988). Quantitative analysis of human operant behavior. In G. Davey & C. Cullen (Eds.), *Human operant conditioning and behavior modification* (pp. 225–259). New York: John Wiley.

BRANCH, M. N., & MALAGODI, E. F. (1980). Where have all the behaviorists gone? *The Behavior Analyst, 3,* 31–38.

BRELAND, K., & BRELAND, M. (1961). The misbehavior of organisms. *American Psychologist, 16,* 681–684.

BREYER, N. L., & ALLEN, G. L. (1975). Effects of implementing a token economy on teacher attending behavior. *Journal of Applied Behavior Analysis, 8,* 373–380.

BRISTOL, M. M. (1976). Control of physical aggression through school- and home-based reinforcement. In J. D. Krumboltz & C. W. Thorensen (Eds.), *Counseling methods* (pp. 180–198). New York: Holt, Rinehart & Winston.

BROGDEN, W. J. (1939). Sensory pre-conditioning. *Journal of Experimental Psychology, 25,* 323–332.

BROWN, P. L., & JENKINS, H. M. (1968). Auto-shaping of the pigeon's key-peck. *Journal of the Experimental Analysis of Behavior, 11,* 1–8.

BROWN, R. (1958). *Words and things.* Glencoe, IL: Free Press.

BROWN, R. (1973). *A first language: The early stages.* Cambridge, MA: Harvard University Press.

BROWN, R. (1986). *Social psychology: The second edition.* New York: Free Press.

BROWN, R., & BELLUGI, U. (1964). Three processes in the child's acquisition of syntax. *Harvard Educational Review, 34,* 133–151.

BROWN, R., & FRASER, C. (1963). The acquisition of syntax. In C. N. Cofer & B. S. Musgrave (Eds.), *Verbal behavior and learning: Problems and processes* (pp. 158–209). New York: McGraw-Hill.

BROWNSTEIN, A. J., & PLISKOFF, S. S. (1968). Some effects of relative reinforcement rate and changeover delay in response-independent concurrent schedules of reinforcement. *Journal of the Experimental Analysis of Behavior, 11,* 683–688.

BUDNEY, A. J., HIGGINS, S. T., DELANEY, D. D., KENT, L., & BICKEL, W. K. (1991). Contingent reinforcement of abstinence with individuals abusing cocaine and marijuana. *Journal of Applied Behavior Analysis, 24,* 657–665.

BURGIO, L. D., & TICE, L. (1985). The reduction of seizure-like behaviors through contingency management. *Journal of Behavior Therapy and Experimental Psychiatry, 16,* 71–75.

BUSHELL, D., JR., & BURGESS, R. L. (1969). Characteristics of the experimental analysis. In R. L. Burgess & D. Bushell, Jr. (Eds.), *Behavioral sociology: The experimental analysis of social processes* (pp. 145–174). New York: Columbia University Press.

BYRNE, D. (1971). *The attraction paradigm.* New York: Academic Press.

CAMERON, J., & EISENBERGER, R. (1997). A meta-analysis of rewards and intrinsic interest. Paper presented at the *Society for Research in Child Development (SRCD),* Washington, DC.

CAMERON, J., & PIERCE, W. D. (1994). Reinforcement, reward and intrinsic motivation: A meta-analysis. *Review of Educational Research, 64,* 363–423.

CAMPBELL, D. T., & STANLEY, J. C. (1966). *Experimental and quasi-experimental designs for research.* Chicago, IL: Rand McNally.

CARR, E. G., & McDOWELL, J. J. (1980). Social control of self-injurious behavior of organic etiology. *Behavior Therapy, 11,* 402–409.

CARROLL, R. J., & HESSE, B. E. (1987). The effects of alternating mand and tact training on the acquisition of tacts. *The Analysis of Verbal Behavior, 5,* 55–65.

CATANIA, A. C. (1966). Concurrent operants. In W. K. Honig (Ed.), *Operant behavior: Areas of research and application* (pp. 213–270). Englewood Cliffs, NJ: Prentice-Hall.

CATANIA, A. C. (1973). The concept of the operant in the analysis of behavior. *Behaviorism, 1,* 103–116.

CATANIA, A. C. (1980). Autoclitic processes and the structure of behavior. *Behaviorism, 8,* 175–186.

CATANIA, A. C. (1984). *Learning.* Englewood Cliffs, NJ: Prentice-Hall.

CATANIA, A. C., & REYNOLDS, G. S. A. (1968). A quantitative analysis of the responding maintained by interval schedules of reinforcement. *Journal of the Experimental Analysis of Behavior, 11,* 327–383.

CHENEY, C. D., BONEM, E., & BONEM, M. (1985). Changeover cost and switching between concurrent adjusting schedules. *Behavioural Processes, 10,* 145–155.

CHENEY, C., & EPLING, W. F. (1968). *Running wheel activity and self-starvation in the white rat.* Unpublished manuscript, Department of Psychology, Eastern Washington State University.

CHILLAG, D., & MENDELSON, J. (1971). Schedule-induced airlicking as a function of body-weight in rats. *Physiology and Behavior, 6,* 603–605.

CHOMSKY, N. (1957). *Syntactic structures.* The Hague: Mouton.

CHOMSKY, N. (1959). Review of B. F. Skinner's verbal behavior. *Language, 35,* 26–58.

COHEN, P. S. (1968). Punishment: The interactive effects of delay and intensity of shock. *Journal of the Experimental Analysis of Behavior, 11,* 789–799.

CONDRY, J. (1977). Enemies of self-exploration: Self-initiated versus other-initiated learning. *Journal of Personality and Social Psychology, 35,* 459–477.

CONGER, R., & KILLEEN, P. (1974). Use of concurrent operants in small group research. *Pacific Sociological Review, 17,* 399–416.

COWLES, J. T. (1937). Food-tokens as incentive for learning by chimpanzees. *Comparative Psychology Monographs, 14,* 1–96.

CROSSMAN, E. K., TRAPP, N. L., BONEM, E. J., & BONEM, M. K. (1985). Temporal patterns of responding in small fixed-ratio schedules. *Journal of the Experimental Analysis of Behavior, 43,* 115–130.

CUMMING, W. W. (1966). A bird's eye glimpse of men and machines. In R. Ulrich, T. Stachnik, & J. Mabry (Eds.), Control of human behavior (pp. 246–256). Glenview, Ill: Scott Foresman & Co.

DAPCICH-MIURA, E., & HOVELL, M. F. (1979). Contingency management of adherence to a complex medical regimen in elderly heart patients. *Behavior Therapy, 10,* 193–201.

DARLEY, J. M., GLUCKSBERG, S., & KINCHLA, R. A. (1991). *Psychology.* Englewood Cliffs, NJ: Prentice Hall.

DARWIN, C. (1859). *On the origin of species by means of natural selection.* London: John Murray.

DARWIN, C. (1871). *The descent of man, and selection in relation to sex.* New York: Appleton-Century-Crofts.

DAVISON, M. C. (1969). Preference for mixed-interval versus fixed-interval schedules. *Journal of the Experimental Analysis of Behavior, 12,* 247–252.

DAVISON, M. C. (1972). Preference for mixed-interval versus fixed-interval schedules: Number of component intervals. *Journal of the Experimental Analysis of Behavior, 17,* 169–176.

DAVISON, M. C. (1981). Choice between concurrent variable-interval and fixed-ratio schedules: A failure of the generalized matching law. In C. M. Bradshaw, E. Szabadi, & C. F. Lowe (Eds.), *Quantification of steady-state operant behaviour* (pp. 91–100). Amsterdam: Elsevier/North-Holland.

DAVISON, M. C., & FERGUSON, A. (1978). The effect of different component response requirements in multiple and concurrent schedules. *Journal of the Experimental Analysis of Behavior, 29,* 283–295.

DAVISON, M. C., & McCARTHY, D. (1988). *The matching law: A research review.* Hillsdale, NJ: Lawrence Erlbaum Associates.

DAWKINS, R. (1976). *The selfish gene.* London: Oxford University Press.

DAWKINS, R. (1986). *The blind watchmaker.* New York: W. W. Norton.

DECI, E. L., & RYAN, R. M. (1985). *Intrinsic motivation and self-determination in human behavior.* New York: Plenum Press.

DeFRAN, R. H. (1972). *Reinforcing effects of stimuli paired with schedules of aversive control.* Unpublished doctoral dissertation, Bowling Green State University, Bowling Green, OH.

DEITZ, S. M. (1978). Current status of applied behavior analysis: Science versus technology. *American Psychologist, 33,* 805–814.

DE RISI, W. J., & BUTZ, G. (1975). *Writing behavioral contracts: A case simulation practice manual.* Champaign, IL: Research Press.

DE VILLIERS, P. (1977). Choice in concurrent schedules and a quantitative formulation of the law of effect. In W. K. Honig & J. E. R. Staddon (Eds.), *Handbook of operant behavior* (pp. 233–287). Englewood Cliffs, NJ: Prentice-Hall.

DEWS, P. B. (1963). Behavioral effects of drugs. In S. M. Farber & R. H. L. Wilson (Eds.), *Conflict and creativity* (pp. 138–153). New York: McGraw-Hill.

DEWS, P. B. (1969). Studies on responding under fixed-interval schedules of reinforcement: The effects on the pattern of responding of changes in requirements at reinforcement. *Journal of the Experimental Analysis of Behavior, 12,* 191–199.

DiCARA, L. V. (1970). Learning in the autonomic nervous system. *Scientific American, 222,* 30–39.

DINSMOOR, J. A. (1951). The effect of periodic reinforcement of bar-pressing in the presence of a discriminative stimulus. *Journal of Comparative and Physiological Psychology, 44,* 354–361.

DINSMOOR, J. A. (1952). A discrimination based on punishment. *Quarterly Journal of Experimental Psychology, 4,* 27–45.

DINSMOOR, J. A. (1977). Escape, avoidance, punishment: Where do we stand? *Journal of the Experimental Analysis of Behavior, 28,* 83–95.

DINSMOOR, J. A., BROWN, M. P., & LAWRENCE, C. E. (1972). A test of the negative discriminative stimulus as a reinforcer of observing. *Journal of the Experimental Analysis of Behavior, 18,* 79–85.

DINSMOOR, J. A., FLINT, G. A., SMITH, R. F., & VIEMEISTER, N. F. (1969). Differential reinforcing effects of stimuli associated with the presence or absence of a schedule of punishment. In D. P. Hendry (Ed.), *Conditioned reinforcement* (pp. 357–384). Homewood, IL: Dorsey Press.

DOLEYS, D. M., MEREDITH, R. L., & CIMINERO, A. R. (Eds.) (1982). *Behavioral medicine: Assessment and treatment strategies.* New York: Plenum Press.

DOLLARD, J., & MILLER, N. E. (1950). *Personality and psychotherapy.* New York: McGraw-Hill.

DONEGAN, N. H., & WAGNER, A. R. (1987). Conditioned diminution and facilitation of the UR: A sometimes opponent-process interpretation. In I. Gomezano, W. F. Prokasy, & R. F. Thompson (Eds.), *Classical Conditioning.* Hillsdale, N. J.: Erlbaum.

DOVE, L. D. (1976). Relation between level of food deprivation and rate of schedule-induced attack. *Journal of the Experimental Analysis of Behavior, 25,* 63–68.

DURLACH, P. J. (1982). Pavlovian learning and performance when CS and US are uncorrelated. In M. L. Commons, R. J. Herrnstein, & A. R. Wagner (Eds.), *Quantitative analysis of behavior: Acquisition* (Vol. 3, pp. 173–193). Cambridge, MA: Ballinger.

DURLACH, P. J. (1983). The effects of signalling intertrial USs in autoshaping. *Journal of Experimental Psychology: Animal Behavior Processes, 9,* 374–389.

EBBINGHAUS, H. (1964). *Memory* (H. A. Ruger & C. E. Bussenius, Trans.). New York: Dover. (Original work published 1885).

ECKERMAN, D. A., & LANSON, R. N. (1969). Variability of response location for pigeons responding under continuous reinforcement, intermittent reinforcement, and extinction. *Journal of the Experimental Analysis of Behavior, 12,* 73–80.

EGGER, M. D., & MILLER, N. E. (1962). Secondary reinforcement in rats as a function of information value and reliability of the stimulus. *Journal of Experimental Psychology, 64,* 97–104.

EGGER, M. D., & MILLER, N. E. (1963). When is reward reinforcing?: An experimental study of the information hypothesis. *Journal of Comparative and Physiological Psychology, 56,* 132–137.

EIBL-EIBESFELDT, I. (1975) *Ethology: The biology of behavior.* New York: Holt, Rinehart and Winston.

EISENBERGER, R. (1992). Learned industriousness. *Psychological Review, 99,* 248–267.

EISENBERGER, R., & ARMELI, S. (1997). Can salient reward increase creative performance without reducing intrinsic creative interest? *Journal of Personality and Social Psychology, 72,* 652–663.

EISENBERGER, R., & CAMERON, J. (1996). The detrimental effects of reward: Myth or reality? *American Psychologist, 51,* 1153–1166.

EISENBERGER, R., ARMELI, S., & PRETZ, J. (1998). Can the promise of reward increase creativity? *Journal of Personality and Social Psychology,* in press.

EKMAN, P., FRIESEN, W. V., & ELLSWORTH, P. (1972). *Emotion in the human face: Guidelines for research and an integration of findings.* New York: Pergamon Press.

ELLISON, G. D. (1964). Differential salivary conditioning to traces. *Journal of Comparative and Physiological Psychology, 57,* 373–380.

EPLING, W. F. & CAMERON, J. (1994) Gibbons on conditioned seeing. From Gibbons, E. (1970), *Stalking the Wild Asparagus: Field Guide Edition.* (pp. 28–32) Quotation Contributed to *The Journal of the Experimental Analysis of Behavior, 61,* 280.

EPLING, W. F., & PIERCE, W. D. (1983). Applied behavior analysis: New directions from the laboratory. *The Behavior Analyst, 6,* 27–37.

EPLING, W. F., & PIERCE, W. D. (1984). Activity-based anorexia in rats as a function of opportunity to run on an activity wheel. *Nutrition and Behavior, 2,* 37–49.

EPLING, W. F., & PIERCE, W. D. (1986). The basic importance of applied behavior analysis. *The Behavior Analyst, 9,* 89–99.

EPLING, W. F., & PIERCE, W. D. (1988). Activity-based anorexia: A biobehavioral perspective. *International Journal of Eating Disorders, 7,* 475–485.

EPLING, W. F., & PIERCE, W. D. (1990). Laboratory to application: An experimental analysis of severe problem behaviors. In A. C. Repp & N. N. Singh (Eds.), *Perspectives on the use of nonaversive and aversive interventions for persons with developmental disabilities* (pp. 451–464). Sycamore, IL: Sycamore Publishing Co.

EPLING, W. F., & PIERCE, W. D. (1992). *Solving the anorexia puzzle: A scientific approach.* Toronto: Hogrefe & Huber.

EPLING, W. F., PIERCE, W. D., & STEFAN, L. (1983). A theory of activity-based anorexia. *International Journal of Eating Disorders, 3,* 27–46.

EPSTEIN, R., LANZA, R. P., & SKINNER, B. F. (1980). Symbolic communication between two pigeons *(Columbia livia domestica). Science, 207,* 543–545.

EPSTEIN, R., & SKINNER, B. F. (1981). The spontaneous use of memoranda by pigeons. *Behavior Analysis Letters, 1,* 241–246.

ERNST, A. J., ENGBERG, L., & THOMAS, D. R. (1971). On the form of stimulus generalization curves for visual intensity. *Journal of the Experimental Analysis of Behavior, 16,* 177–80.

ERON, L. D., HUESMANN, L. R., DUBOW, E., ROMANOFF, R., & YARMEL, P. W. (1987). Aggression and its correlates over 22 years. In N. H. Crowell, R. J. Blanchard, I. Evans, & C. R. O'Donnel (Eds.), *Childhood aggression and violence: Sources of influence, prevention and control* (pp. 250–260). New York: Academic Press.

ESTES, W. K. (1944). An experimental study of punishment. *Psychological Monographs, 57* (Serial No. 3).

ESTES, W. K. (1969). New perspectives on some old issues in association theory. In N. J. Macintosh & W. K. Honig (Eds.), *Fundamental issues in associative learning* (pp. 162–189). Halifax, Nova Scotia: Dalhousie University Press.

ESTES, W. K., & SKINNER, B. F. (1941). Some quantitative properties of anxiety. *Journal of Experimental Psychology, 29,* 390–400.

ETTINGER, R. H., & McSWEENEY, F. K. (1981). Behavioral contrast and responding during multiple food-food, food-water, and water-water schedules. *Animal Learning & Behavior, 9,* 216–222.

ETZKOWITZ, H. (1992). Inventions. In E. F. Borgatta & M. L. Borgatta (Eds.), *Encyclopedia of sociology* (Vol. 2, pp. 1004–1005). New York: Macmillan.

FALK, J. L. (1961). Production of polydipsia in normal rats by an intermittent food schedule. *Science, 133,* 195–196.

FALK, J. L. (1964). Studies on schedule-induced polydipsia. In M. J. Wayner (Ed.), *Thirst: First international symposium on thirst in the regulation of body water* (pp. 95–116). New York: Pergamon Press.

FALK, J. L. (1969). Schedule-induced polydipsia as a function of fixed interval length. *Journal of the Experimental Analysis of Behavior, 9,* 37–39.

FALK, J. L. (1971). The nature and determinants of adjunctive behavior. *Physiology and Behavior, 6,* 577–588.

FALK, J. L. (1977). The origin and functions of adjunctive behavior. *Animal Learning & Behavior, 5,* 325–335.

FANTINO, E. (1965). Some data on the discriminative stimulus hypothesis of secondary reinforcement. *Psychological Record, 15,* 409–414.

FANTINO, E. (1967). Preference for mixed- *versus* fixed-ratio schedules. *Journal of the Experimental Analysis of Behavior, 10,* 35–43.

FANTINO, E. (1969a). Choice and rate of reinforcement. *Journal of the Experimental Analysis of Behavior, 12,* 723–730.

FANTINO, E. (1969b). Conditioned reinforcement, choice, and the psychological distance to reward. In D. P. Hendry (Ed.), *Conditioned reinforcement* (pp. 163–191). Homewood, IL: Dorsey Press.

FANTINO, E. (1977). Conditioned reinforcement: Choice and information. In W. K. Honig & J. E. R. Staddon (Eds.), *Handbook of operant behavior* (pp. 313–339). Englewood Cliffs, NJ: Prentice-Hall.

FANTINO, E., & LOGAN, C. A. (1979). *The experimental analysis of behavior: A biological perspective.* San Francisco, CA: W. H. Freeman.

FEIGHNER, J. P., ROBINS, E., GUZE, S. B., WOODRUFF, R. A., WINOKUR, G., & MUNOZ, R. (1972). Diagnostic criteria for use in psychiatric research. *Archives of General Psychiatry, 26,* 57–63.

FELDMAN, M. A. (1990). Balancing freedom from harm and right to treatment for persons with developmental disabilities. In A. C. Repp & N. N. Singh (Eds.), *Perspectives on the use of nonaversive and aversive interventions for persons with developmental disabilities* (pp. 261–271). Sycamore, IL: Sycamore Publishing Co.

FERSTER, C. B., CULBERTSON, S., & BOREN, M. C. P. (1975). *Behavior principles.* Englewood Cliffs, NJ: Prentice-Hall.

FERSTER, C. B., & SKINNER, B. F. (1957). *Schedules of reinforcement.* New York: Appleton-Century-Crofts.

FIELD, T, M., WOODSON, R., GREENBERG, R., & COHEN, D. (1982). Discrimination and imitation of facial expressions by neonates. *Science, 218,* 179–181.

FINDLEY, J. D. (1958). Preference and switching under concurrent scheduling. *Journal of the Experimental Analysis of Behavior, 1,* 123–144.

FIXSEN, D. L., PHILLIPS, E. L., PHILLIPS, E. A., & WOLF, M. M. (1976). The teaching family-model of group home treatment. In W. E. Craighead, A. E. Kazdin, & M. J. Mahoney (Eds.), *Behavior modification: Principles, issues, and applications* (pp. 310–320). Boston, MA: Houghton Mifflin.

FLANAGAN, B., GOLDIAMOND, I., & AZRIN, N. (1958). Operant stuttering: The control of stuttering behavior through response contingent consequences. *Journal of the Experimental Analysis of Behavior, 1,* 173–177.

FLORY, R. K. (1969). Attack behavior as a function of minimum inter-food interval. *Journal of the Experimental Analysis of Behavior, 12,* 825–828.

FRIMAN, P. C., FINNEY, J. W., GLASSCOCK, S. T., WEIGEL, J. W., & CHRISTOPHERSEN, E. R. (1986). Testicular self-examination: Validation of a training strategy for early cancer detection. *Journal of Applied Behavior Analysis, 19,* 87–92.

GALBICKA, G. (1992). The dynamics of behavior. *Journal of the Experimental Analysis of Behavior, 57,* 243–248.

GALTON, F. (1879). Psychometric experiments. *Brain, 2,* 149–162.

GAMZU, E. R., & SCHWARTZ, B. (1973). The maintenance of key pecking by stimulus-contingent and response-independent food presentations. *Journal of the Experimental Analysis of Behavior, 19,* 65–72.

GARCIA, J., & KOELLING, R. A. (1966). Relation of cue to consequence in avoidance learning. *Psychonomic Science, 4,* 123–124.

GARDNER, E. T., & LEWIS, P. (1976). Negative reinforcement with shock-frequency increase. *Journal of the Experimental Analysis of Behavior, 25,* 3–14.

GEEN, R. G. (1968). Effects of frustration, attack, and prior training in aggressiveness upon aggressive behavior. *Journal of Personality and Social Psychology, 9,* 316–321.

GELDER, M. G., & MARKS, I. M. (1966). Severe agoraphobia: A controlled prospective trial of behavior therapy. *British Journal of Psychiatry, 112,* 309–319.

GELDER, M. G., MARKS, I. M., WOLFF, H. E., & CLARKE, M. (1967). Desensitization and psychotherapy in the treatment of phobic states: A controlled inquiry. *British Journal of Psychiatry, 113,* 53–73.

GERWITZ, J. L. (1969). Mechanisms of social learning: Some roles of stimulation and behavior in early human development. In D. A. Goslin (Ed.), *Handbook of socialization theory and research* (pp. 57–212). Chicago, IL: Rand McNally.

GIBBON, J., & CHURCH, R. M. (1992). Comparison of variance and covariance patterns in parallel and serial theories of timing. *Journal of the Experimental Analysis of Behavior, 57,* 393–406.

GLAZER, H. I., & WEISS, J. M. (1976a). Long-term interference effect: An alternative to "learned helplessness." *Journal of Experimental Psychology: Animal Behavior Processes, 2,* 202–213.

GLAZER, H. I., & WEISS, J. M. (1976b). Long-term and transitory interference effects. *Journal of Experimental Psychology: Animal Behavior Processes, 2,* 191–201.

GLENN, S. S. (1988). Contingencies and metacontingencies: Toward a synthesis of behavior analysis and cultural materialism. *The Behavior Analyst, 11,* 161–179.

GLENN, S. S. (1989). Verbal behavior and cultural practices. *Behavior Analysis and Social Action, 7,* 10–14.

GLENN, S. S. (1991). Contingencies and metacontingencies: Relations among behavioral, cultural, and biological evolution. In P. A. Lamal (Ed.), *Behavioral analysis of societies and cultural practices* (pp. 39–73). New York: Hemisphere.

GLENWICK, D., & JASON, L. (1980). *Behavioral community psychology: Progress and prospects.* New York: Praeger.

GODDARD, M. J., & JENKINS, H. M. (1987). Effect of signaling extra unconditioned stimuli on autoshaping. *Animal Learning & Behavior, 15,* 40–46.

GOETZ, E. M., & BAER, D. M. (1973). Social control of form diversity and the emergence of new forms in children's blockbuilding. *Journal of Applied Behavior Analysis, 6,* 209–217.

GOLDIN-MEADOW, S., & MORFORD, M. (1985). Gesture in early child language: Studies of deaf and hearing children. *Merrill-Palmer Quarterly, 31,* 145–176.

GOLLUB, L. R. (1958). *The chaining of fixed-interval schedules.* Unpublished doctoral dissertation, Harvard University, Cambridge, MA.

GOLLUB, L. R. (1977). Conditioned reinforcement: Schedule effects. In W. K. Honig & J. E. R. Staddon (Eds.), *Handbook of operant behavior* (pp. 288–312). Englewood Cliffs, NJ: Prentice-Hall.

GONZALEZ, R. C., GENTRY, G. V., & BITTERMAN, M. E. (1954). Relational discrimination of intermediate size in the chimpanzee. *Journal of Comparative and Physiological Psychology, 47,* 385–388.

GOTT, C. T., & WEISS, B. (1972). The development of fixed-ratio performance under the influence of ribonucleic acid. *Journal of the Experimental Analysis of Behavior, 18,* 481–497.

GOULD, S. J. (1989) *Wonderful life.* New York: W. W. Norton.

GRANT, D. S. (1975). Proactive interference in pigeon short-term memory. *Journal of Experimental Psychology: Animal Behavior Processes, 1,* 207–220.

GRANT, D. S. (1981). Short-term memory in the pigeon. In N. E. Spear & R. R. Miller (Eds.), *Information processing in animals: Memory mechanisms* (pp. 227–256). Hillsdale, NJ: Lawrence Erlbaum Associates.

GREENE, W. A., & SUTOR, L. T. (1971). Stimulus control of skin resistance responses on an escape-avoidance schedule. *Journal of the Experimental Analysis of Behavior, 16,* 269–274.

GUESS, D. (1969). A functional analysis of receptive language and productive speech: Acquisition of the plural morpheme. *Journal of Applied Behavior Analysis, 2,* 55–64.

GUESS, D., & BAER, D. M. (1973). An analysis of individual differences in generalization between receptive and productive language in retarded children. *Journal of Applied Behavior Analysis, 6,* 311–329.

GUESS, D., HELMSTETTER, E., TURNBULL, H. R., & KNOWLTON, S. (1986). *Use of aversive procedures with persons who are disabled: An historical review and critical analysis* (Monograph No. 2). Seattle, WA: The Association for Persons with Severe Handicaps.

GUESS, D., SAILOR, W., RUTHERFORD, G., & BAER, D. M. (1968). An experimental analysis of linguistic development: The productive use of the plural morpheme. *Journal of Applied Behavior Analysis, 1,* 297–306.

GULLY, K. J., & DENGERINK, H. A. (1983). The dyadic interaction of persons with violent and nonviolent histories. *Aggressive Behavior, 7,* 13–20.

GUSTAFSON, R. (1989). Frustration and successful vs. unsuccessful aggression: A test of Berkowitz' completion hypothesis. *Aggressive Behavior, 15,* 5–12.

GUTTMAN, A. (1977). Positive contrast, negative induction, and inhibitory stimulus control in the rat. *Journal of the Experimental Analysis of Behavior, 27,* 219–233.

GUTTMAN, N., & KALISH, H. I. (1956). Discriminability and stimulus generalization. *Journal of Experimental Psychology, 51,* 79–88.

HAKE, D. F., DONALDSON, T., & HYTEN, C. (1983). Analysis of discriminative control by social behavioral stimuli. *Journal of the Experimental Analysis of Behavior, 39,* 7–23.

HAKENBERG, T. D., & HINELINE, P. H. (1987). Remote effects of aversive contingencies: Disruption of appetitive behavior by adjacent avoidance sessions. *Journal of the Experimental Analysis of Behavior, 48,* 161–173.

HALL, D. C., ADAMS, C. K., STEIN, G. H., STEPHENSON, H. S., GOLDSTEIN, M. K., & PENNYPACKER, H. S. (1980). Improved detection of human breast lesions following experimental training. *Cancer, 46,* 408–414.

HALL, G., & SUNDBERG, M. L. (1987). Teaching mands by manipulating conditioned establishing operations. *The Analysis of Verbal Behavior, 5,* 41–53.

HALL, R. V., CRISTLER, C., CRANSTON, S. S., & TUCKER, B. (1970). Teachers and parents as researchers using multiple baseline designs. *Journal of Applied Behavior Analysis, 3,* 247–255.

HALL, R. V., & HALL, M. C. (1982). *How to negotiate a behavioral contract.* Lawrence, KS: H. & H. Enterprises.

HANSON, H. M. (1959). Effects of discrimination training on stimulus generalization. *Journal of Experimental Psychology, 58,* 321–334.

HARLOW, H. F., & ZIMMERMAN, R. R. (1959). Affectional responses in the infant monkey. *Science, 130,* 421–432.

HARPER, D. N., & MCLEAN, A. P. (1992). Resistance to change and the law of effect. *Journal of the Experimental Analysis of Behavior, 57,* 317–337.

HARRIS, M. (1974). *Cows, pigs, wars, and witches.* New York: Vintage Books.

HARRIS, M. (1979). *Cultural materialism.* New York: Random House.

HART, B. M., REYNOLDS, N. J., BAER, D. M., BRAWLEY, E. R., & HARRIS, F. R. (1968). Effect of contingent and non-contingent social reinforcement on the cooperative play of a preschool child. *Journal of Applied Behavior Analysis, 1,* 73–76.

HAWKINS, R. P., & DOBES, R. W. (1975). Behavioral definitions in applied behavior analysis: Explicit or implicit. In B. C. Etzel, J. M. LeBlanc, & D. M. Baer (Eds.), *New developments in behavioral research: Theory, methods, and applications: In honor of Sidney W. Bijou* (pp. 167–188). Hillsdale, NJ: Lawrence Erlbaum Associates.

HAYES, S. C. (1987). A contextual approach to therapeutic change. In N. Jacobson (Ed.), *Psychotherapists in clinical practice: Cognitive and behavioral perspectives* (pp. 329–383). New York: Guilford Press.

HAYES, S. C. (1989a). Nonhumans have not yet shown stimulus equivalence. *Journal of the Experimental Analysis of Behavior, 51,* 385–392.

HAYES, S. C., RINCOVER, A., & SOLNICK, J. V. (1980). The technical drift of applied behavior analysis. *Journal of Applied Behavior Analysis, 13,* 275–285.

HEARST, E. (1961). Resistance-to-extinction functions in the single organism. *Journal of the Experimental Analysis of Behavior, 4,* 133–144.

HEARST, E., & JENKINS, H. M. (1974). *Sign tracking: The stimulus-reinforcer relation and directed action.* Austin, TX: Monograph of the Psychonomic Society.

HEINEMANN, E. G., & CHASE, S. (1970). On the form of stimulus generalization curves for auditory intensity. *Journal of Experimental Psychology, 84,* 483–486.

HEMMES, N. S. (1973). Behavioral contrast in pigeons depends upon the operant. *Journal of Comparative and Physiological Psychology, 85,* 171–178.

HENDRY, D. P. (1969). *Conditioned reinforcement.* Homewood, IL: Dorsey Press.

HERMAN, R. L., & AZRIN, N. H. (1964). Punishment by noise in an alternative response situation. *Journal of the Experimental Analysis of Behavior, 7,* 185–188.

HERNANDEZ, D. (1981). The impact of family planning programs on fertility in developing countries: A critical evaluation. *Social Science Research, 10,* 32–66.

HERRNSTEIN, R. J. (1961a). Stereotypy and intermittent reinforcement. *Science, 133,* 2067–2069.

HERRNSTEIN, R. J. (1961b). Relative and absolute strength of responses as a function of frequency of reinforcement. *Journal of the Experimental Analysis of Behavior, 4,* 267–272.

HERRNSTEIN, R. J. (1964a). Aperiodicity as a factor in choice. *Journal of the Experimental Analysis of Behavior, 7,* 179–182.

HERRNSTEIN, R. J. (1964b). Secondary reinforcement and the rate of primary reinforcement. *Journal of the Experimental Analysis of Behavior, 7,* 27–36.

HERRNSTEIN, R. J. (1970). On the law of effect. *Journal of the Experimental Analysis of Behavior, 13,* 243–266.

HERRNSTEIN, R. J. (1974). Formal properties of the matching law. *Journal of the Experimental Analysis of Behavior, 21,* 159–164.

HERRNSTEIN, R. J. (1979). Acquisition, generalization, and reversal of a natural concept. *Journal of Experimental Psychology: Animal Behavior Processes, 5,* 116–129.

HERRNSTEIN, R. J. (1982). Melioration as behavioral dynamicism. In M. L. Commons, R. J. Herrnstein, & H. Rachlin (Eds.), *Quantitative analyses of behavior: Vol 2. Matching and maximizing accounts of behavior* (pp. 433–458). Cambridge, MA: Ballinger.

HERRNSTEIN, R. J. (1990). Rational choice theory: Necessary but not sufficient. *American Psychologist, 45,* 336–346.

HERRNSTEIN, R. J., & DE VILLIERS, P. A. (1980). Fish as a natural category for people and pigeons. In G. H. Bower (Ed.), *The psychology of learning and motivation* (Vol. 14, pp. 60–95). New York: Academic Press.

HERRNSTEIN, R. J., & HINELINE, P. N. (1966). Negative reinforcement as shock frequency reduction. *Journal of the Experimental Analysis of Behavior, 9,* 421–430.

HERRNSTEIN, R. J., & LOVELAND, D. H. (1964). Complex visual concept in the pigeon. *Science, 146,* 549–551.

HERRNSTEIN, R. J., & LOVELAND, D. H. (1975). Maximizing and matching on concurrent ratio schedules. *Journal of the Experimental Analysis of Behavior, 24,* 107–116.

HERRNSTEIN, R. J., LOVELAND, D. H., & CABLE, C. (1976). Natural concepts in pigeons. *Journal of Experimental Psychology: Animal Behavior Processes, 2,* 285–302.

HIGGINS, S. T., BICKEL, W. K., & HUGHES, J. R. (1994). Influence of an alternative reinforcer on human cocaine self-administration. *Life Sciences, 55,* 179–187.

HILGARD, E. R., & MARQUIS, D. G. (1961). *Conditioning and learning.* New York: Appleton. (Original work published 1940).

HINDE, R. A., & STEVENSON-HINDE, J. (1973). *Constraints on learning: Limitations and predispositions.* New York: Academic Press.

HINELINE, P. N. (1970). Negative reinforcement without shock reduction. *Journal of the Experimental Analysis of Behavior, 14,* 259–268.

HINELINE, P. N. (1977). Negative reinforcement and avoidance. In W. K. Honig & J. E. R. Staddon (Eds.), *Handbook of operant behavior* (pp. 364–414). Englewood, Cliffs, NJ: Prentice-Hall.

HINELINE, P. N. (1984). Aversive control: A separate domain? *Journal of the Experimental Analysis of Behavior, 42,* 495–509.

HINELINE, P. N. (1989). Personal communication in letter of information and biography.

HINSON, R. E., POULOS, C. X., & CAPPELL, H. (1982). Effects of pentobarbital and cocaine in rats expecting pentobarbital. *Pharmacology Biochemistry & Behavior, 16,* 661–666.

HIROTO, D. S., & SELIGMAN, M. E. P. (1975). Generality of learned helplessness in man. *Journal of Personality and Social Psychology, 31,* 311–327.

HIRSCH, J., & McCAULEY, L. (1977). Successful replication of, and selective breeding for, classical conditioning in the blowfly *(Phorma regina). Animal Behaviour, 25,* 784–785.

HOCKETT, C. F. (1958). *A course in modern linguistics.* New York: Macmillan.

HOCKETT, C. F. (1968). *The state of the art.* The Hague: Mouton.

HOLLAND, J. G. (1978). Behaviorism: Part of the problem or part of the solution? *Journal of Applied Behavior Analysis, 11,* 163–174.

HOMME, L. E., deBACA, P. C., DEVINE, J. V., STEINHORST, R., & RICKERT, E. J. (1963). Use of the Premack principle in controlling the behavior of nursery school children. *Journal of the Experimental Analysis of Behavior, 6,* 544.

HOUSTON, A. (1986). The matching law applies to wagtails' foraging in the wild. *Journal of the Experimental Analysis of Behavior, 45,* 15–18.

HOYERT, M. S. (1992). Order and chaos in fixed-interval schedules of reinforcement. *Journal of the Experimental Analysis of Behavior, 57,* 339–363.

HUFFMAN, K., VERNOY, M., WILLIAMS, B., & VERNOY, J. (1991). *Psychology in action.* New York: John Wiley.

HUNG, D. (1980). Training and generalization of "yes" and "no" as mands in two autistic children. *Journal of Autism and Developmental Disorders, 10,* 130–152.

HUNT, H. F., & BRADY, J. V. (1955). Some effects of punishment and intercurrent anxiety on a simple operant. *Journal of Comparative and Physiological Psychology, 48,* 305–310.

HURSH, S. R. (1980). Economic concepts for the analysis of behavior. *Journal of the Experimental Analysis of Behavior, 34,* 219–238.

HURSH, S. R., NAVARICK, D. J., & FANTINO, E. (1974). "Automaintenance": The role of reinforcement. *Journal of the Experimental Analysis of Behavior, 21,* 112–124.

HUTCHINSON, R. R. (1977). By-products of aversive control. In W. K. Honig & J. E. R. Staddon (Eds.), *Handbook of operant behavior* (pp. 415–431). Englewood Cliffs, NJ: Prentice-Hall.

HUTCHINSON, R. R., AZRIN, N. H., & HUNT, G. M. (1968). Attack produced by intermittent reinforcement of a concurrent operant response. *Journal of the Experimental Analysis of Behavior, 11,* 489–495.

IRWIN, O. C. (1948). Infant speech: Development of vowel sounds. *Journal of Speech and Hearing, 13,* 31–34.

IRWIN, O. C. (1952). Speech development in the young child: 2. Some factors related to the speech development of the infant and the young child. *Journal of Speech and Hearing, 17,* 209–279.

JACKSON, R. L., ALEXANDER, J. H., & MAIER, S. F. (1980). Learned helplessness, inactivity, and associative deficits: Effects of inescapable shock on response choice escape learning. *Journal of Experimental Psychology: Animal Behavior Processes, 6,* 1–20.

JACOBSON, E. (1938). *Progressive relaxation.* Chicago, IL: University of Chicago Press.

JENKINS, H. M., & BOAKES, R. A. (1973). Observing stimulus sources that signal food or no food. *Journal of the Experimental Analysis of Behavior, 20,* 197–207.

JENKINS, H. M., BARRERA, F. J., IRELAND, C., & WOODSIDE, B. (1978). Signal-centered action patterns of dogs in appetitive classical conditioning. *Learning and Motivation, 9,* 272–296.

JOHNSTON, J. M., & PENNYPACKER, H. S. (1993). *Strategies and tactics of human behavioral research.* Hillsdale, NJ: Lawrence Erlbaum Associates.

JOLLY, A. (1985). *The evolution of primate behavior.* New York: Macmillan.

JONAS, G. (1973). *Visceral learning: Toward a science of self-control.* New York: Viking Press.

KAMIN, L. J. (1969). Predictability, surprise, attention, and conditioning. In B. A. Campbell & R. M. Church (Eds.), *Punishment and aversive behavior* (pp. 279–296). New York: Appleton-Century-Crofts.

KATZ, N. H. (1976). A test of the reinforcing properties of stimuli correlated with nonreinforcement. *Journal of the Experimental Analysis of Behavior, 26,* 45–56.

KAWAMURA, S. (1959). The process of sub-culture propagation among Japanese macaques. *Primates, 2,* 43–60.

KAZDIN, A. E. (1977). *The token economy: A review and evaluation.* New York: Plenum Press.

KAZDIN, A. E. (1982). *Single-case research designs: Methods for clinical and applied settings.* New York: Oxford University Press.

KAZDIN, A. E. (1983). Failure of persons to respond to the token economy. In E. B. Foa & P. M. G. Emmelkamp (Eds.), *Failures in behavior therapy* (pp. 335–354). New York: John Wiley.

KAZDIN, A. E. (1989). *Behavior modification in applied settings.* Belmont, CA: Brooks/Cole.

KAZDIN, A. E., & KLOCK, J. (1973). The effect of nonverbal teacher approval on student attentive behavior. *Journal of Applied Behavior Analysis, 6,* 643–654.

KEEHN, J. D. (1986). *Animal models for psychiatry.* London: Routledge & Kegan Paul.

KEEHN, J. D., & JOZSVAI, E. (1989). Induced and noninduced patterns of drinking by food-deprived rats. *Bulletin of the Psychonomic Society, 27,* 157–159.

KEITH-LUCAS, T., & GUTTMAN, N. (1975). Robust single-trial delayed backward conditioning. *Journal of Comparative and Physiological Psychology, 88,* 468–476.

KELLEHER, R. T., FRY, W., & COOK, L. (1959). Interresponse time distribution as a function of differential reinforcement of temporally spaced responses. *Journal of the Experimental Analysis of Behavior, 2,* 91–106.

KELLEHER, R. T., & GOLLUB, L. R. (1962). A review of positive conditioned reinforcement. *Journal of the Experimental Analysis of Behavior, 5,* 543–597.

KELLER, F. S. (1968). "Good-bye, teacher . . ." *Journal of Applied Behavior Analysis, 1,* 79–89.

KELLER, F. S., & SCHOENFELD, N. W. (1950). *Principles of psychology*. New York: Appleton-Century-Crofts.

KELLER, R. J., AYRES, J. J. B., & MAHONEY, W. J. (1977). Brief versus extended exposure to truly random control procedures. *Journal of Experimental Psychology: Animal Behavior Processes, 3,* 53–65.

KEYS, A., BROZEK, J., HENSCHEL, A., MICKELSEN, O., & TAYLOR, H. L. (1950). *The biology of human starvation*. Minneapolis: University of Minnesota Press.

KILLEEN, P. R. (1974). Psychophysical distance functions for hooded rats. *The Psychological Record, 24,* 229–235.

KILLEEN, P. R. (1975). On the temporal control of behavior. *Psychological Review, 82,* 89–115.

KILLEEN, P. R. (1985). Incentive theory IV: Magnitude of reward. *Journal of the Experimental Analysis of Behavior, 43,* 407–417.

KILLEEN, P. R. (1992). Mechanics of the animate. *Journal of the Experimental Analysis of Behavior, 57,* 429–463.

KIMMEL, E., & KIMMEL, H. D. (1963). Replication of operant conditioning of the GSR. *Journal of Experimental Psychology, 65,* 212–213.

KIMMEL, H. D. (1974). Instrumental conditioning of autonomically mediated responses in human beings. *American Psychologist, 29,* 325–335.

KINTSCH, W. (1965). Frequency distribution of interresponse times during VI and VR reinforcement. *Journal of the Experimental Analysis of Behavior, 8,* 347–352.

KIRBY, F. D., & SHIELDS, F. (1972). Modification of arithmetic response rate and attending behavior in a seventh-grade student. *Journal of Applied Behavior Analysis, 5,* 79–84.

KOHLER, W. (1927). *The mentality of apes* (2nd rev. ed., E. Winter, Trans.). London: Routledge & Kegan Paul.

KOHN, A. (1993). *Punished by rewards*. Boston: Houghton Mifflin.

KREBS, J. R., & DAVIES, N. B. (Eds.) (1978). *Behavioural ecology: An evolutionary approach*. Oxford: Blackwell Scientific Publications, Ltd.

KREMER, E. F. (1971). Truly random and traditional control procedures in CER conditioning in the rat. *Journal of Comparative and Physiological Psychology, 76,* 441–448.

KREMER, E. F., & KAMIN, L. J. (1971). The truly random control procedure: Associative or nonassociative effects in rats. *Journal of Comparative and Physiological Psychology, 74,* 203–210.

KULIK, C. C., KULIK, J. A., & COHEN, P. A. (1980). Instructional technology and college teaching. *Teaching of Psychology, 7,* 199-205.

KUSCHEL, R. (1973). The silent inventor: The creation of a sign language by the only deaf mute on a Polynesian island. *Sign Language Studies, 3,* 1–28.

LAMAL, P. A. (Ed.) (1991). *Behavioral analysis of societies and cultural practices*. New York: Hemisphere.

LAMAL, P. A. (Ed.) (1997). *Cultural contingencies: Behavior analytic perspectives on cultural practices*. Westport: Praeger.

LAMARRE, J., & HOLLAND, J. G. (1985). The functional independence of mands and tacts. *Journal of the Experimental Analysis of Behavior, 43,* 5–19.

LANE, H. (1961). Operant control of vocalizing in the chicken. *Journal of the Experimental Analysis of Behavior, 4,* 171–177.

LATTAL, K. A. (1984). Signal functions in delayed reinforcement. *Journal of the Experimental Analysis of Behavior, 42,* 239–253.

LATTAL, K. A., & ZIEGLER, D. R. (1982). Briefly delayed reinforcement: An interresponse time analysis. *Journal of the Experimental Analysis of Behavior, 37,* 407–416.

LAVIGNA, G. W., & DONNELLAN, A. W. (1986). *Alternatives to punishment: Solving behavior problems with non-aversive strategies*. New York: Irvington.

LAZAR, R. (1977). Extending sequence-class membership with matching to sample. *Journal of the Experimental Analysis of Behavior, 27,* 381–392.

LEA, S. E. G., TARPY, R. M., & WEBLEY, P. (1987). *The individual in the economy: A textbook of economic psychology*. Cambridge: Cambridge University Press.

LEAF, R. C. (1965). Acquisition of Sidman avoidance responding as a function of S-S interval. *Journal of Comparative and Physiological Psychology, 59,* 298–300.

LEE. V. L. (1981a). Prepositional phrases spoken and heard. *Journal of the Experimental Analysis of Behavior, 35,* 227–242.

LEE, V. L. (1981b). Terminological and conceptual revision in the experimental analysis of language development: Why. *Behaviorism, 9.* 25–53.

LEPPER, M. R., GREENE, D., & NISBETT, R. E. (1973). Undermining children's intrinsic interest with extrinsic reward: A test of the 'overjustification' hypothesis. *Journal of Personality and Social Psychology, 28,* 129–137.

LEWIS, P., GARDNER, E. T., & HUTTON, L. (1976). Integrated delays to shock as negative reinforcement. *Journal of the Experimental Analysis of Behavior, 26,* 379–386.

LINDSLEY, O. R. (1972). From Skinner to precision teaching: The child knows best. In J. B. Jordan & L. S. Robbins (Eds.), *Let's try something else kind of thing: Behavioral principles of the exceptional child* (pp. 1–11). Arlington, VA: The council for exceptional children.

LINSCHEID, T. R., & MEINHOLD, P. (1990). The controversy over aversives: Basic operant research and the side effects of punishment. In A. C. Repp & N. N. Singh (Eds.), *Perspectives on the use of nonaversive and aversive interventions for persons with developmental disabilities* (pp. 434–450). Sycamore, IL: Sycamore Publishing Co.

LLOYD, K. E. (1985). Behavioral anthropology: A review of Marvin Harris' *Cultural Materialism*. *Journal of the Experimental Analysis of Behavior, 43,* 279–287.

LLOYD, K.E., & LLOYD, M. E. (1992). Behavior analysis and technology in higher education. In R. P. West & L. A. Hamerlynck (Eds.) *Designs for excellence in education: The legacy of B.F. Skinner.* (pp. 147–160) Longmont, CO: Sopris West, Inc.

LOGUE, A. W. (1979). Taste aversion and the generality of the laws of learning. *Psychological Bulletin, 86,* 276–296.

LOGUE, A. W. (1985). Conditioned food aversion learning in humans. In N. S. Braveman & P. Bronstein (Eds.), *Experimental assessments and clinical applications of conditioned food aversions* (pp. 316–329). New York: New York Academy of Sciences.

LOGUE, A. W. (1988a). A comparison of taste aversion learning in humans and other vertebrates: Evolutionary pressures in common. In R. C. Bolles & M. D. Beecher (Eds.), *Evolution and learning* (pp. 97–116). Hillsdale, NJ: Lawrence Erlbaum Associates.

LOGUE, A. W. (1988b). Research on self-control: An integrating framework. *Behavioral and Brain Sciences, 11,* 665–709.

LOGUE, A. W., PENA-CORREAL, T. E., RODRIGUEZ, M. L., & KABELA, E. (1986). Self-control in adult humans: Variation in positive reinforcer amount and delay. *Journal of the Experimental Analysis of Behavior, 46,* 159–173.

LOVAAS, O. I. (1966). A program for the establishment of speech in psychotic children. In J. K. Wing (Ed.), *Early childhood autism* (pp. 115–144). Elmsford, NY: Pergamon.

LOVAAS, O. I. (1977). *The autistic child: Language development through behavior modification.* New York: Irvington

LOVAAS, O. I. (1987). Behavioral treatment and normal educational and intellectual functioning in young autistic children. *Journal of Consulting and Clinical Psychology. 55,* 3–9.

LOVAAS, O. I. (1993). The development of a treatment-research project for developmentally disabled and autistic children. *Journal of Applied Behavior Analysis, 26,* 617–630.

LOVAAS, O. I.,. & SIMMONS, J. Q. (1969). Manipulation of self-destruction in three retarded children. *Journal of Applied Behavior Analysis, 2,* 143–157.

LOWE, F. C. (1989). Personal communication in a letter of information and biography.

LOWE, F. C. (1979). Determinants of human operant behavior. In M. D. Zeiler & P. Harzem (Eds.), *Reinforcement and the organization of behaviour* (pp. 159–192). New York: John Wiley.

LOWE, F. C., BEASTY, A., & BENTALL, R. P. (1983). The role of verbal behavior in human learning: Infant performance on fixed-interval schedules. *Journal of the Experimental Analysis of Behavior, 39,* 157–164.

LOWITZ, G. H., & SUIB, M. R. (1978). Generalized control of persistent thumbsucking by differential reinforcement of other behaviors. *Journal of Behavior Therapy and Experimental Psychiatry, 9,* 343–346.

LUBINSKI, D., & MACCORQUODALE, K. (1984). "Symbolic communication" between two pigeons *(Columba livia)* without unconditioned reinforcement. *Journal of Comparative Psychology, 98,* 372–380.

LUBINSKI, D., & THOMPSON, T. (1987). An animal model of the interpersonal communication of introceptive (private) states. *Journal of the Experimental Analysis of Behavior, 48,* 1–15.

LUBOW, R. E. (1974). High-order concept formation in the pigeon. *Journal of the Experimental Analysis of Behavior, 21,* 475–483.

LUCAS, G. A., DEICH, J. D., & WASSERMAN, E. A. (1981). Trace autoshaping: Acquisition, maintenance, and path dependence at long trace intervals. *Journal of the Experimental Analysis of Behavior, 36,* 61–74.

MACCORQUODALE, K. (1970). On Chomsky's review of Skinner's Verbal Behavior. *Journal of the Experimental Analysis of Behavior, 13,* 83–99.

MACHADO, A. (1989). Operant conditioning of behavioral variability using a percentile reinforcement schedule. *Journal of the Experimental Analysis of Behavior, 52,* 155–166.

MACHADO, A. (1992). Behavioral variability and frequency dependent selection. *Journal of the Experimental Analysis of Behavior, 58,* 241–263.

MACHADO, A. (1997). Increasing the variability of response sequences in pigeons by adjusting the frequency of switching between two keys. *Journal of the Experimental Analysis of Behavior, 68,* 1–25

MACPHAIL, E. M. (1968). Avoidance responding in pigeons. *Journal of the Experimental Analysis of Behavior, 11,* 629–632.

MAIER, S. F. (1970). Failure to escape traumatic electric shock: Incompatible skeletal-motor responses or learned helplessness. *Learning and Motivation, 1,* 157–169.

MAIER, S. F., ALBIN, R. W., & TESTA, T. J. (1973). Failure to learn to escape in rats previously exposed to inescapable shock depends on nature of the escape response. *Journal of Comparative and Physiological Psychology, 85,* 581–592.

MAIER, S. F., & SELIGMAN, M. E. P. (1976). Learned helplessness: Theory and evidence. *Journal of Experimental Psychology: General, 105,* 3–46.

MAIER, S. F., SELIGMAN, M. E. P., & SOLOMON, R. L. (1969). Pavlovian fear conditioning and learned helplessness. In B. A. Campbell & R. M. Church (Eds.), *Punishment and aversive behavior* (pp. 299–342). New York: Appleton-Century-Crofts.

MAKI, W. S., & HEGVIK, D. K. (1980). Directed forgetting in pigeons. *Animal Learning & Behavior, 8,* 567–574.

MALOTT, R. W. (1988). Rule-governed behavior and behavioral anthropology. *The Behavior Analysts, 11,* 181–203.

MARKS, I. M. (1987). *Fears, phobias, and rituals.* New York: Oxford University Press.

MARR, J. M. (1992). Behavior dynamics: One perspective. *Journal of the Experimental Analysis of Behavior, 57,* 249–266.

MARSH, G., & JOHNSON, R. (1968). Discrimination reversal learning without "errors." *Psychonomic Science, 10,* 261–262.

MARTIN, D. G. (1991). *Psychology: Principles and applications.* Scarborough, Ontario: Prentice Hall.

MARTIN, G., & PEAR, J. (1996). *Behavior modification: What is it and how to do it.* Englewood Cliffs, NJ: Prentice Hall.

MARTIN, G.L., & HRYCAIKO, D. (1983). Behavior modification and coaching: Principles, procedures and research. Springfield, IL: Charles C. Thomas

MASSERMAN, J. H. (1946). *Principles of dynamic psychiatry.* Philadelphia, PA: Saunders.

MATSON, J. L., & TARAS, M. E. (1989). A 20 year review of punishment and alternative methods to treat problem behaviors in developmentally disabled persons. *Research in Developmental Disabilities, 10,* 85–104.

MATTHEWS, L. R., & TEMPLE, W. (1979). Concurrent schedule assessment of food preference in cows. *Journal of the Experimental Analysis of Behavior, 32,* 245–254.

MAZUR, J. E. (1983). Steady-state performance on fixed-, mixed-, and random-ratio schedules. *Journal of the Experimental Analysis of Behavior, 39,* 293–307.

MAZUR, J. E. (1990). *Learning and behavior.* Englewood Cliffs, NJ: Prentice Hall.

MCDONALD, J. S. (1988). Concurrent variable-ratio schedules: Implications for the generalized matching law. *Journal of the Experimental Analysis of Behavior, 50,* 55–64

MCDOWELL, J. J. (1981). On the validity and utility of Herrnstein's hyperbola in applied behavior analysis. In C. M. Bradshaw, E. Szabadi, & C. F. Lowe (Eds.), *Quantification of steady-state operant behaviour* (pp. 311–324). Amsterdam: Elsevier/North-Holland.

MCDOWELL, J. J. (1982). The importance of Herrnstein's mathematical statement of the law of effect for behavior therapy. *American Psychologist, 37,* 771–779.

MCDOWELL, J. J. (1986). On the falsifiability of matching theory. *Journal of the Experimental Analysis of Behavior, 45,* 63–74.

MCDOWELL, J. J. (1988). Matching theory in natural human environments. *The Behavior Analyst, 11,* 95–109.

MCDOWELL, J. J., BASS, R., & KESSEL, R. (1992). Applying linear systems analysis to dynamic behavior. *Journal of the Experimental Analysis of Behavior, 57,* 377–391.

MCEACHIN, J. J., SMITH, T., & LOVAAS, I. O. (1993). Long-term outcome for children with autism who received early intensive behavioral treatment. *American Journal on mental retardation, 97,* 359-372.

MCINTIRE, K. D., CLEARY, J., & THOMPSON, T. (1987). Conditional relations by monkeys: Reflexivity, symmetry, and transitivity. *Journal of the Experimental Analysis of Behavior, 47,* 279–285.

MCSWEENEY, F. K., ETTINGER, R. A., & NORMAN, W. D. (1981). Three versions of the additive theories of behavioral contrast. *Journal of the Experimental Analysis of Behavior, 36,* 285–297.

MCSWEENEY, F. K., MELVILLE, C. L., & HIGA, J. (1988). Positive behavioral contrast across food and alcohol reinforcers. *Journal of the Experimental Analysis of Behavior, 50,* 469–481.

MECHNER, F. (1959). A notation system for the description of behavioral procedures. *Journal of the Experimental Analysis of Behavior, 2,* 133–150.

MEEHL, P. E. (1950). On the circularity of the law of effect. *Psychological Bulletin, 47,* 52–75.

MEISSNER, M., & PHILPOTT, S. B. (1975). The sign language of sawmill workers in British Columbia. *Sign Language Studies, 9,* 291–308.

MELLITZ, M., HINELINE, P. N., WHITEHOUSE, W. G., & LAURENCE, M. T. (1983). Duration reduction of avoidance sessions as negative reinforcement. *Journal of the Experimental Analysis of Behavior, 40,* 57–67.

MENDELSON, J., & CHILLAG, D. (1970). Schedule-induced air licking in rats. *Physiology and Behavior, 5,* 535–537.

MEYER, D. R., CHO, C., & WESEMANN, A. F. (1960). On problems of conditioning discriminated lever-press avoidance responses. *Psychological Review, 67,* 224–228.

MEYER, L. H., & EVANS, I. M. (1989). *Non-aversive intervention for behavior problems: A manual for home and community.* Baltimore, MD: Paul H. Brookes.

MICHAEL, J. L. (1975). Positive and negative reinforcement, a distinction that is no longer necessary: Or a better way to talk about bad things. *Behaviorism, 3,* 33–44.

MICHAEL, J. L. (1980). Flight from behavior analysis. *The Behavior Analyst, 3,* 1–24.

MICHAEL, J. L. (1982a). Distinguishing between discriminative and motivational functions of stimuli. *Journal of the Experimental Analysis of Behavior, 37,* 149–155.

MICHAEL, J. L. (1982b). Skinner's elementary verbal relations: Some new categories. *The Analysis of Verbal Behavior, 1,* 1–3.

MICHAEL, J. L. (1984). Behavior analysis: A radical perspective. In B. L. Hammonds & C. J. Scheirer (Eds.), *Master lecture series: Psychology of learning* (Vol. 4, pp. 99-121). Washington, DC: American Psychological Association.

MICHAEL, J. L. (1988). Establishing operations and the mand. *The Analysis of Verbal Behavior, 6,* 3–9.

MICHAEL, J. L., WHITLEY, P., & HESSE, B. E. (1983). The pigeon parlance project. *The Analysis of Verbal Behavior, 1,* 6–9.

MILLENSON, J. R. (1967). *Principles of behavioral analysis.* New York: Macmillan.

MILLER, N. E. (1951). Learnable drives and rewards. In S. S. Stevens (Ed.), *Handbook of experimental psychology* (pp. 435–472). New York: John Wiley.

MILLER, N. E. (1960). Learning resistance to pain and fear effects overlearning, exposure, and rewarded exposure in context. *Journal of Experimental Psychology, 60,* 137–145.

MILLER, N. E. (1969). Learning of visceral and glandular responses. *Science, 163,* 434–445.

MILLER, N. E., & BANUAZIZI, A. (1968). Instrumental learning by curarized rats of a specific visceral response, intestinal or cardiac. *Journal of Comparative and Physiological Psychology, 65,* 1–7.

MILLER, N. E., & CARMONA, A. (1967). Modification of a visceral response, salivation in thirsty dogs, by instrumental training with water reward. *Journal of Comparative and Physiological Psychology, 63,* 1–6.

MILLER, N. E., & DiCARA, L. (1967). Instrumental learning of heart rate changes in curarized rats: Shaping and specificity to discriminative stimulus. *Journal of Comparative and Physiological Psychology, 63,* 12–19.

MILLER, N. E., & DWORKIN, B. R. (1974). Visceral learning: Recent difficulties with curarized rats and significant problems for human research. In P. A. Obrist, A. H. Black, J. Brener, & L. V. Dicara (Eds.), *Cardiovascular psychophysiology: Current issues in response mechanisms, biofeedback and methodology.* (pp. 295–331). Chicago, IL: Aldine.

MITCHELL, D., KIRSCHBAUM, E. H., & PERRY, R. L. (1975). Effects of neophobia and habituation on the poison-induced avoidance of extroceptive stimuli in the rat. *Journal of Experimental Psychology: Animal Behavior Processes, 104,* 47–55.

MOERK, E. L. (1972). Principles of dyadic interaction in language learning. *Merrill-Palmer Quarterly, 18,* 229–257.

MOERK, E. L. (1976a). Motivational variables in language acquisition. *Child Study Journal, 6,* 55–84.

MOERK, E. L. (1976b). Processes of language teaching and training in the development of mother-child dyads. *Child Development, 47,* 1064–1078.

MOERK, E. L. (1977a). *Pragmatic and sematic aspects of early language development.* Baltimore, MD: University Park Press.

MOERK, E. L. (1977b). Processes and products of imitation: Additional evidence that imitation is progressive. *Journal of Psycholinguistic Research, 6,* 187–202.

MOERK, E. L. (1980). Relationships between parental input frequencies and children's language acquisition: A reanalysis of Brown's data. *Journal of Child Language, 7,* 105–118.

MOERK, E. L. (1983a). A behavioral analysis of controversial topics in first language acquisition: Reinforcements, corrections, modeling, input frequencies, and the three-term contingency pattern. *Journal of Psycholinguistic Research, 12,* 129–155.

MOERK, E. L. (1983b). *The mother of Eve—as a first language teacher.* Norwood, NJ: Ablex.

MOERK, E. L. (1985a). Analytic, synthetic, abstracting, and world-class-defining aspects of verbal mother-child interactions. *Journal of Psycholinguistic Research, 14,* 263–287.

MOERK, E. L. (1985b). A differential interactive analysis of language teaching and learning. *Discourse Processes, 8,* 113–142.

MOERK, E. L. (1986). Environmental factors in early language acquisition. In G. J. Whitehurst (Ed.), *Annals of child development* (Vol. 3, pp. 191–235). Greenwich, CT: JAI Press.

MOERK, E. L. (1989). The LAD was a lady and the tasks were ill-defined. *Developmental Review, 9,* 21–57.

MOERK, E. L. (1990). Three-term contingency patterns in mother-child verbal interactions during first-language acquisition. *Journal of the Experimental Analysis of Behavior, 54,* 293–305.

MOLM, L. D. (1990). Structure, action, and outcomes: The dynamics of power in social exchange. *American Sociological Review, 55,* 427–447.

MORRIS, E. K. (1988). Contexualism: The world view of behavior analysis. *Journal of Experimental Child Psychology, 46,* 289–323.

MORRIS, E. K. (1992). The aim, progress, and evolution of behavior analysis. *The Behavior Analyst, 15,* 3–29.

MORROW, J., & TERZICH, B. (1997). Personal communication of research interest and biography.

MORSE, W. H. (1966). Intermittent reinforcement. In W. K. Honig (Ed.), *Operant behavior: Areas of research and application* (pp. 52–108). New York: Appleton-Century-Crofts.

MYERS, D. L., & MYERS, L. E. (1977). Undermatching: A reappraisal of performance on concurrent variable-interval schedules of reinforcement. *Journal of the Experimental Analysis of Behavior, 25,* 203–214.

MYERS, J. L. (1958). Secondary reinforcements: A review of recent experimentation. *Psychological Bulletin, 55,* 284–301.

MYERS, R. D., & MESKER, D. C. (1960). Operant conditioning in a horse under several schedules of reinforcement. *Journal of the Experimental Analysis of Behavior, 3,* 161–164.

MYERSON, J., & HALE, S. (1984). Practical implications of the matching law. *Journal of Applied Behavior Analysis, 17,* 367–380.

NEURINGER, A. J. (1986). Can people behave "randomly?": The role of feedback. *Journal of Experimental Psychology: General, 115,* 62–75.

NEVIN, J. A. (1988). The momentum of warmaking. *Behavior Analysis and Social Action, 2,* 46–50.

NEVIN, J. A. (1992). An integrative model for the study of behavioral momentum. *Journal of the Experimental Analysis of Behavior, 57,* 301–316.

NORMAN, W. D., & McSWEENEY, F. K. (1978). Matching, contrast, and equalizing in the concurrent lever-press responding of rats. *Journal of the Experimental Analysis of Behavior, 29,* 453–462.

NOTTERMAN, J. M. (1959). Force emission during bar pressing. *Journal of Experimental Psychology, 58,* 341–347.

OAH, S., & DICKINSON, A. M. (1989). A review of empirical studies of verbal behavior. *The Analysis of Verbal Behavior, 7,* 53–68.

O'BRIEN, F., & AZRIN, N. H. (1972). Developing proper mealtime behaviors of the institutionalized retarded. *Journal of Applied Behavior Analysis, 5,* 389–399.

O'BRIEN, R. M., & SIMEK, T. C. (1983). A comparison of behavioral and traditional methods for teaching golf. In G. L. Martin & D. Harycaiko (Eds.), *Behavior modification and coaching: Principles, procedures and research* (pp. 175–183). Springfield, IL: Charles C. Thomas.

O'KELLY, L. E., & STECKLE, L. C. (1939). A note on long enduring emotional responses in rats. *Journal of Psychology, 8,* 125–131.

O'LEARY, M. R., & DENGERINK, H. A. (1973). Aggression as a function of the intensity and pattern of attack. *Journal of Experimental Research in Personality, 7,* 61–70.

ORLANDO, R., & BIJOU, S. W. (1960). Single and multiple schedules of reinforcement in developmentally retarded children. *Journal of the Experimental Analysis of Behavior, 3,* 339–348.

OSGOOD, C. E. (1953). *Method and theory in experimental psychology.* New York: Oxford University Press.

OVERMIER, J. B., & SELIGMAN, M. E. P. (1967). Effects of inescapable shock upon subsequent escape and avoidance responding. *Journal of Comparative and Physiological Psychology, 63,* 28–33.

PAGE, S., & NEURINGER, A. J. (1985). Variability is an operant. *Journal of Experimental Psychology: Animal Behavior Processes, 11,* 429–452.

PAIVIO, A., & BEGG, I. (1981). *Psychology of language.* Englewood Cliffs, NJ: Prentice-Hall.

PALYA, W. L. (1992). Dynamics in the fine structure of schedule-controlled behavior. *Journal of the Experimental Analysis of Behavior, 57,* 267–287.

PAPINI, M. R., & BITTERMAN, M. E. (1990). The role of contingency in classical conditioning. *Psychological Review, 97,* 396–403.

PARROTT, L. J. (1987). Rule-governed behavior: An implicit analysis of reference. In S. Modgil & C. Modgil (Eds.), *B. F. Skinner: Consensus and controversy* (pp. 265–276). New York: Falmer Press.

PARSONSON, B. S., & BAER, D. M. (1978). Training generalized improvisation of tools by preschool children. *Journal of Applied Behavior Analysis, 11,* 363–380.

PATTERSON, G. R. (1976). The aggressive child: Victim and architect of a coercive system. In E. J. Mash, L. A. Hamerlynck, & L. H. Hendy (Eds.), *Behavior modification and families* (pp. 269–316). New York: Brunner/Mazel.

PATTERSON, G. R. (1982). *Coercive family processes.* Eugene, OR: Castalia.

PAUL, G. L. (1966). *Insight versus desensitization in psychotherapy.* Stanford, CA: Stanford University Press.

PAUL, G. L. (1968). Two-year follow-up of systematic desensitization in therapy groups. *Journal of Abnormal Psychology, 73,* 119–130.

PAUL, G. L. (1969a). Outcome of systematic desensitization I: Background, procedures, and uncontrolled reports of individual treatment. In C. M. Franks (Ed.), *Behavior therapy: Appraisal and status* (pp. 63–104). New York: McGraw-Hill.

PAUL, G. L. (1969b). Outcome of systematic desensitization II: Controlled investigations of individual treatment, technique variations, and current status. In C. M. Franks (Ed.), *Behavior therapy: Appraisal and status* (pp. 105–159). New York: McGraw-Hill.

PAVLOV, I. P. (1960). *Conditioned reflexes. An investigation of the physiological activity of the cerebral cortex* (G. V. Anrep, Trans.). New York: Dover. (Original work published 1927)

PEAR, J. J. (1985). Spatiotemporal patterns of behavior produced by variable-interval schedules of reinforcement. *Journal of the Experimental Analysis of Behavior, 44,* 217–231

PEAR, J. J., & WILKIE, D. M. (1971). Contrast and induction in rats on multiple schedules. *Journal of the Experimental Analysis of Behavior, 15,* 289–296.

PENNYPACKER, H. S. (1989). Personal communication of research and biography.

PENNYPACKER, H. S., BLOOM, H. S., CRISWELL, E. L., NEELAKANTAN, P., GOLDSTEIN, M. K., & STEIN, G. H. (1982). Toward an effective technology of instruction in breast self-examination. *International Journal of Mental Health, 11,* 98–116.

PEPPERBERG, I. M. (1981). Functional vocalizations by an African gray parrot (*Psittacus erithacus*). *Zeitschrift fur Tierpsychologie, 58,* 193–198.

PERIN, C. T. (1942). Behavior potentiality as a joint function of the amount of training and the degree of hunger at the time of extinction. *Journal of Experimental Psychology, 30,* 93–113.

PERONE, M., GALIZIO, M., & BARON, A. (1988). The relevance of animal-based principles in the laboratory study of human operant conditioning. In G. Davy & C. Cullen (Eds.), *Human operant conditioning and behavior modification* (pp. 59–85). New York: John Wiley.

PETERSON, C., & SELIGMAN, M. E. P. (1984). Causal explanations as a risk factor for depression: Theory and evidence. *Psychological Review, 91,* 347–374.

PETERSON, G. B., ACKIL, J. E., FROMMER, G. P., & HEARST, E. S. (1972). Conditioned approach and contact behavior toward signals for food or brain-stimulation reinforcement. *Science, 177,* 1009–1011.

PFAUTZ, P. L., DONEGAN, N. H., & WAGNER, A. R. (1978). Sensory preconditioning versus protection from habituation. *Journal of Experimental Psychology: Animal Behavior Processes, 4,* 286–292.

PIERCE, W. D. (1991). Culture and society: The role of behavioral analysis. In P. A. Lamal (Ed.), *Behavioral analysis of societies and cultural practices* (pp. 13–37). New York: Hemisphere.

PIERCE, W. D., & EPLING, W. F. (1980). What happened to analysis in applied behavior analysis? *The Behavior Analyst, 3,* 1–9.

PIERCE, W. D., & EPLING, W. F. (1983). Choice, matching, and human behavior: A review of the literature. *The Behavior Analyst, 6,* 57–76.

PIERCE, W. D., & EPLING, W. F. (1988). *Biobehaviorism: Genes, learning and behavior* (Working paper No. 88-5). Edmonton: Center for Systems Research, University of Alberta.

PIERCE, W. D., & EPLING, W. F. (1991). Activity anorexia: An animal model and theory of human self-starvation. In A. Boulton, G. Baker, & M. Martin-Iverson (Eds.), *Neuromethods: Animal models in psychiatry 1* (Vol. 18, pp. 267–311). Clifton, NJ: Humana Press.

PIERCE, W. D., EPLING, W. F., & BOER, D. P. (1986). Deprivation and satiation: The interrelations between food and wheel running. *Journal of the Experimental Analysis of Behavior, 46,* 199–210.

PIERREL, R., SHERMAN, G. J., BLUE, S., & HEGGE, F. W. (1970). Auditory discrimination: A three-variable analysis of intensity effects. *Journal of the Experimental Analysis of Behavior, 13,* 17–35.

PLATT, J. R. (1979). Interresponse-time shaping by variable-interval-like interresponse-time reinforcement contingencies. *Journal of the Experimental Analysis of Behavior, 31,* 3–14.

PLISKOFF, S. S., & BROWN, T. G. (1976). Matching with a trio of concurrent variable-interval schedules of reinforcement. *Journal of the Experimental Analysis of Behavior, 25,* 69–74.

POLING, A. (1978). Performance of rats under concurrent variable-interval schedules of negative reinforcement. *Journal of the Experimental Analysis of Behavior, 30,* 31–36.

POLING, A., NICKEL, M., & ALLING, K. (1990). Free birds aren't fat: Weight gain in captured wild pigeons maintained under laboratory conditions. *Journal of the Experimental Analysis of Behavior, 53,* 423-424.

POULOS, C. X., WILKINSON, D. A., & CAPPELL, H. (1981). Homeostatic regulation and Pavlovian conditioning intolerance to amphetamine-induced anorexia. *Journal of Comparative and Physiological Psychology, 95,* 735–746.

POWELL, R. W. (1968). The effect of small sequential changes in fixed-ratio size upon the post-reinforcement pause. *Journal of the Experimental Analysis of Behavior, 11,* 589–593.

PRELEC, D. (1984). The assumptions underlying the generalized matching law. *Journal of the Experimental Analysis of Behavior, 41,* 101–107.

PREMACK, D. (1959). Toward empirical behavioral laws: 1. Positive reinforcement. *Psychological Review, 66,* 219–233.

PREMACK, D. (1962). Reversability of the reinforcement relation. *Science, 136,* 235–237.

PREWITT, E. P. (1967). Number of preconditioning trials in sensory preconditioning using CER training. *Journal of Comparative and Physiological Psychology, 64,* 360–362.

RACHLIN, H. (1969). Autoshaping of key pecking in pigeons with negative reinforcement. *Journal of the Experimental Analysis of Behavior, 12,* 521–531.

RACHLIN, H. (1976). *Behavior and learning.* San Francisco: W. H. Freeman.

RACHLIN, H. (1992). Diminishing marginal value as delay discounting. *Journal of the Experimental Analysis of Behavior, 57,* 407–415.

RACHLIN, H., & GREEN, L. (1972). Commitment, choice and self-control. *Journal of the Experimental Analysis of Behavior, 17,* 15–22.

RAZRAN, G. (1949). Stimulus generalization of conditioned responses. *Psychological Bulletin, 46,* 337–365.

RESCORLA, R. A. (1966). Predictability and number of pairings in Pavlovian fear conditioning. *Psychonomic Science, 4,* 383–384.

RESCORLA, R. A. (1968). Probability of shock in the presence and absence of CS in fear conditioning. *Journal of Comparative and Physiological Psychology, 66,* 1–5.

RESCORLA, R. A. (1969). Conditioned inhibition of fear. In N. J. Mackintosh & W. K. Honig (Eds.), *Fundamental issues in associative learning* (pp. 65–89). Halifax, Nova Scotia: Dalhousie University Press.

RESCORLA, R. A. (1972). Informational variables in Pavlovian conditioning. In G. H. Bower & J. T. Spence (Eds.), *Psychology of learning and motivation* (pp. 1–46). New York: Academic Press.

RESCORLA, R. A. (1980). *Pavlovian second-order conditioning: Studies in associative learning.* Hillsdale, NJ: Lawrence Erlbaum Associates.

RESCORLA, R. A. (1989). Redundant treatments of neutral and excitatory stimuli in autoshaping. *Journal of Experimental Psychology: Animal Behavior Processes, 15,* 212–223.

RESCORLA, R. A., & WAGNER, A. R. (1972). A theory of Pavlovian conditioning: Variations in the effectiveness of reinforcement and nonreinforcement. In A. H. Black & W. F. Prokasy (Eds.), *Classical conditioning ll: Current research and theory* (pp. 64–69). New York: Appleton-Century-Crofts.

REVUSKY, S. H., & BEDARF, E. W. (1967). Association of illness with prior ingestion of novel foods. *Science, 155,* 219–220.

REVUSKY, S. H., & GARCIA, J. (1970). Learned associations over long delays. In G. H. Bower (Ed.), *The psychology of learning and motivation: Advances in research and theory* (Vol. 4, pp. 1–84). New York: Academic Press.

REYNOLDS, G. S. (1961a). An analysis of interactions in a multiple schedule. *Journal of the Experimental Analysis of Behavior, 4,* 107–117.

REYNOLDS, G. S. (1961b). Behavioral contrast. *Journal of the Experimental Analysis of Behavior, 4,* 57–71.

REYNOLDS, G. S. (1963). Some limitations on behavioral contrast and induction during successive discrimination. *Journal of the Experimental Analysis of Behavior, 6,* 131–139.

REYNOLDS, G. S. (1966a). *A primer of operant conditioning.* Glenview, IL: Scott, Foresman.

REYNOLDS, G. S. (1966b). Discrimination and emission of temporal intervals by pigeons. *Journal of the Experimental Analysis of Behavior, 9,* 65–68.

RHEINGOLD, H. L., GEWIRTZ, J. L., & ROSS, H. W. (1959). Social conditioning of vocalizations in the infant. *Journal of Comparative and Physiological Psychology, 52*, 68–73.

RILLING, M. (1977). Stimulus control and inhibitory processes. In W. K. Honig & J. E. R. Staddon (Eds.), *Handbook of operant behavior* (pp. 432–480). Englewood Cliffs, NJ: Prentice-Hall.

RISLEY, T. R. (1968). The effects and side-effects of punishing the autistic behaviors of a deviant child. *Journal of Applied Behavior Analysis, 1*, 21–34.

RIZLEY, R. C., & RESCORLA, R. A. (1972). Associations in second-order conditioning and sensory preconditioning. *Journal of Comparative and Physiological Psychology, 81*, 1–11.

ROGERS-WARREN, A., & WARREN, S. (1980). Mands for verbalization: Facilitating the display of newly trained language in children. *Behavior Modification, 4*, 361–382.

ROLL, J. M., HIGGINS, S. T., & BADGER, G. J. (1996). An experimental comparison of three different schedules of reinforcement of drug abstinence using cigarette smoking as an exemplar. *Journal of Applied Behavior Analysis, 29*, 495-505.

ROSCOE, B., MARTIN, G. L., & PEAR, J. J. (1980). Systematic self-desensitization of fear of flying: A case study. In G. L. Martin & G. L. Osborne (Eds.) *Helping in the Community: Behavioral Applications* (pp. 345–352). New York: Plenum.

ROUTTENBERG, A., & KUZNESOF, A. W. (1967). Self-starvation of rats living in activity wheels on a restricted feeding schedule. *Journal of Comparative and Physiological Psychology, 64*, 414–421.

ROZIN, P., & KALAT, J. (1971). Adaptive specializations in learning and memory. *Psychological Review, 78*, 459–486.

RUGGLES, T. R., & LEBLANC, J. M. (1982). Behavior analysis procedures in classroom teaching. In A. S. Bellack, M. Hersen, & A. E. Kazdin (Eds.), *International handbook of behavior modification and therapy* (pp. 959–996). New York: Plenum Press.

SANDERS, G. A. (1974). Introduction. In D. Cohen (Ed.), *Explaining linguistic phenomena* (pp. 1–20). Washington, DC: Hemisphere.

SAUNDERS, K. J. (1989). Naming in conditional discrimination and stimulus equivalence. *Journal of the Experimental Analysis of Behavior, 51*, 379–384.

SAUNDERS, K. J., PILGRAM, C. A., & PENNYPACKER, H. S. (1986). Increased proficiency of search in breast self-examination. *Cancer, 58*, 2531–2537.

SAVAGE-RUMBAUGH, S. E. (1984). Verbal behavior at a procedural level in the chimpanzee. *Journal of the Experimental Analysis of Behavior, 41*, 223–250.

SCHAEFER, H. H., & MARTIN, P. L. (1966). Behavior therapy for "apathy" of hospitalized patients. *Psychological Reports, 19*, 1147–1158.

SCHELLER, R. H., & AXEL, R. (1984). How genes control innate behavior. *Scientific American, 250*, 54–62.

SCHMITT, D. R. (1976). Some conditions affecting the choice to cooperate or compete. *Journal of the Experimental Analysis of Behavior, 25*, 165–178.

SCHMITT, D. R. (1981). Performance under cooperation and competition. *American Behavioral Scientist, 24*, 649–679.

SCHMITT, D. R. (1984). Interpersonal relations: Cooperation and competition. *Journal of the Experimental Analysis of Behavior, 42*, 377–384.

SCHNEIDERMAN, N. (1966). Interstimulus interval function of the nicitating membrane response of the rabbit under delay versus trace conditioning. *Journal of Comparative and Physiological Psychology, 62*, 397–402.

SCHOENFELD, W. N., ANTONITIS, J. J., & BERSH, P. J. (1950). A preliminary study of training conditions necessary for conditioned reinforcement. *Journal of Experimental Psychology, 40*, 40–45.

SCHOPLER, E., & MESIBOV, G.B. (1994). *Behavioral issues in autism.* New York: Plenum.

SCHRIER, A. M., & BRADY, P. M. (1987). Categorization of natural stimuli by monkeys (*Macaca mulatta*): Effects of stimulus set size and modification of exemplars. *Journal of Experimental Psychology: Animal Behavior Processes, 13*, 136–143.

SCHWARTZ, B. (1980). Development of complex stereotyped behavior in pigeons. *Journal of the Experimental Analysis of Behavior, 33*, 153–166.

SCHWARTZ, B. (1981). In pursuit of B. F. Skinner. *Swarthmore College Bulletin*, March, 12–16.

SCHWARTZ, B. (1982a). Failure to produce response variability with reinforcement. *Journal of the Experimental Analysis of Behavior, 37*, 171–181.

SCHWARTZ, B. (1982b). Reinforcement-induced stereotypy: How not to teach people to discover rules. *Journal of Experimental Psychology: General, 111*, 23–59.

SCHWARTZ, B. (1989). *Psychology of learning and behavior.* New York: W. W. Norton.

SCHWARTZ, B. (1990). The creation and destruction of value, *American Psychologist, 45*, 7–15.

SCHWARTZ, B., & GAMZU, E. (1977). Pavlovian control of operant behavior: An analysis of autoshaping and its implication for operant conditioning. In W. K. Honig & J. E. R. Staddon (Eds.), *Handbook of operant behavior* (pp. 53–97). Englewood Cliffs, NJ: Prentice-Hall.

SCHWARTZ, B., & LACEY, H. (1982). *Behaviorism, science, and human nature* (pp. 160-191). New York: W. W. Norton & Co.

SCHWARTZ, B., & WILLIAMS, D. R. (1972a). The role of response reinforcer contingency in negative auto-maintenance. *Journal of the Experimental Analysis of Behavior, 18*, 351–357.

SCHWARTZ, B., & WILLIAMS, D. R. (1972b). Two different kinds of key peck in the pigeon: Some properties of responses maintained by negative and positive response-reinforcer contingencies. *Journal of the Experimental Analysis of Behavior, 18*, 201–216.

SCOTT, J. F. (1971). Internalization of norms: A sociological theory of moral commitment. Englewood Cliffs, NJ: Prentice-Hall.

SEGAL, E. F. (1962). Effects of dl-amphetamine under concurrent VI DRL reinforcement. *Journal of the Experimental Analysis of Behavior, 5*, 105–112.

SELIGMAN, M. E. P. (1968). Chronic fear produced by unpredictable electric shock. *Journal of Comparative and Physiological Psychology, 66*, 402–411.

SELIGMAN, M. E. P. (1975). *Helplessness: On depression, development, and death.* San Francisco, CA: Freeman.

SELIGMAN, M. E. P., & MAIER, F. F. (1967). Failure to escape traumatic shock. *Journal of Experimental Psychology, 74*, 19.

SERDIKOFF, S. L. (1997). Personal communication on memory and remembering (9/25/97).

SHEARN, D. W. (1962). Operant conditioning of heart rate. *Science, 137*, 530–531.

SHERMAN, J. A. (1965). Use of reinforcement and imitation to reinstate verbal behavior in mute psychotics. *Journal of Abnormal Psychology, 70*, 155164.

SHERRINGTON, C. (1906) *The integrative action of the nervous system.* (2nd edition, 1947). New Haven, Connecticut: Yale University Press

SHIMP, C. P. (1969). The concurrent reinforcement of two interresponse times: The relative frequency of an interresponse time equals its relative harmonic length. *Journal of the Experimental Analysis of Behavior, 12*, 403–411.

SHIMP, C. P. (1992). Computational behavior dynamics: An alternative description of Nevin (1969). *Journal of the Experimental Analysis of Behavior, 57*, 289–299.

SHULL, R. L. (1979). The postreinforcement pause: Some implications for the correlational law of effect. In M. D. Zeiler & P. Harzem (Eds.), *Reinforcement and the organization of behaviour* (pp. 193–221). New York: John Wiley.

SHULL, R. L., & PLISKOFF, S. S. (1967). Changeover delay and concurrent schedules: Some effects on relative performance measures. *Journal of the Experimental Analysis of Behavior, 10*, 517–527.

SIDMAN, M. (1953). Two temporal parameters in the maintenance of avoidance behavior of the white rat. *Journal of Comparative and Physiological Psychology, 46*, 253–261.

SIDMAN, M. (1960). *Tactics of scientific research.* New York: Basic Books.

SIDMAN, M. (1962). Reduction of shock frequency as reinforcement for avoidance behavior. *Journal of the Experimental Analysis of Behavior, 5*, 247–257.

SIDMAN, M. (1989). *Coercion and its fallout.* Boston, MA: Authors Cooperative.

SIDMAN, M. (1994). *Equivalence relations and behavior: A research story.* Boston, MA: Authors Cooperative, Inc., Publishers.

SIDMAN, M., & CRESSON, O., JR. (1973). Reading and crossmodal transfer of stimulus equivalences in severe retardation. *American Journal of Mental Deficiency, 77*, 515–523.

SIDMAN, M., CRESSON, O., JR., & WILSON-MORRIS, M. (1974). Acquisition of matching to sample via mediated transfer. *Journal of the Experimental Analysis of Behavior, 22*, 261–273.

SIEGEL, S. (1972). Conditioning of insulin-induced glycemia. *Journal of Comparative and Physiological Psychology, 78*, 233–241.

SIEGEL, S. (1975). Conditioning insulin effects. *Journal of Comparative and Physiological Psychology, 89*, 189–199.

SIEGEL, S., & DOMJAN, M. (1971). Backward conditioning as an inhibitory procedure. *Learning and Motivation, 2*, 1–11

SIEGEL, S., HINSON, R. E., KRANK, M. D., & MCCULLY, J. (1982). Heroin "overdose" death: The contribution of drug-associated environmental cues. *Science, 216*, 436–437.

SIMIC, J., & BUCHER, B. (1980). Development of spontaneous manding in nonverbal children. *Journal of Applied Behavior Analysis, 13*, 523–528.

SKINNER, B. F. (1938). *The behavior of organisms.* New York: Appleton-Century-Crofts.

SKINNER, B. F. (1948). *Walden two.* New York: Macmillan.

SKINNER, B. F. (1950). Are theories of learning necessary? *Psychological Review, 57*, 193–216.

SKINNER, B. F. (1953). *Science and human behavior*. New York: Free Press.

SKINNER, B. F. (1957). *Verbal behavior*. New York: Appleton-Century-Crofts.

SKINNER, B. F. (1960). Pigeons in a pelican. *American Psychologist, 15*, 28–37.

SKINNER, B. F. (1968). *The technology of teaching*. New York: Appleton-Century-Crofts.

SKINNER, B. F. (1969). *Contingencies of reinforcement: A theoretical analysis*. New York: Appleton-Century-Crofts.

SKINNER, B. F. (1971). *Beyond freedom and dignity*. New York: Alfred A. Knopf.

SKINNER, B. F. (1974). *About behaviorism*. New York: Alfred A. Knopf.

SKINNER, B. F. (1979). *The shaping of a behaviorist*. New York: Alfred A. Knopf.

SKINNER, B. F. (1984). The evolution of behavior. *Journal of the Experimental Analysis of Behavior, 41*, 217–222.

SKINNER, B. F. (1986). The evolution of verbal behavior. *Journal of the Experimental Analysis of Behavior, 45*, 115–122.

SKINNER, B. F. (1988). An operant analysis of problem solving. In A. C. Catania & S. Harnad (Eds.), *The selection of behavior—The operant behaviorism of B. F. Skinner: Comments and consequences* (pp. 218–277). New York: Cambridge University Press.

SKINNER, B. F. (1989). Personal communication by telephone on Project Pigeon.

SMITH, M. C., & GORMEZANO, I. (1965). *Conditioning of the nictitating membrane response of the rabbit as a function of backward, simultaneous, and forward CS-UCS intervals*. Paper presented at the meeting of the Psychonomic Society, Chicago, IL.

SOBSEY, D. (1990). Modifying the behavior of behavior modifiers: Arguments for countercontrol against aversive procedures. In A. C. Repp & N. N. Singh (Eds.), *Perspectives on the use of nonaversive and aversive interventions for persons with developmental disabilities* (pp. 421–433). Sycamore, IL: Sycamore Publishing Co.

SOLOMON, R. L. (1969). Punishment. In D. Rosenhan & P. London (Eds.), *Theory and research in abnormal psychology* (pp. 75–119). New York: Holt, Rinehart & Winston.

SOLOMON, R. L., & BRUSH, E. S. (1956). Experimentally derived conceptions of anxiety and aversion. In M. R. Jones (Ed.), *Nebraska symposium on motivation* (pp. 212–305). Lincoln: University of Nebraska Press.

SOLZHENITSYN, A. (1973). *The first circle*. London: Collins Fontana Books.

SOWERS-HOAG, K. M., THYER, B. A., & BAILEY, J. S. (1987). Promoting automobile safety belt use by young children. *Journal of Applied Behavior Analysis, 20*, 133–138.

SQUIRES, N., & FANTINO, E. (1971). A model for choice in simple concurrent and concurrent-chains schedules. *Journal of the Experimental Analysis of Behavior, 15*, 27–38.

STADDON, J. E. R. (1977). Schedule-induced behavior. In W. K. Honig & J. E. R. Staddon (Eds.), *Handbook of operant behavior* (pp. 125–152). Englewood Cliffs, NJ: Prentice-Hall.

STADDON, J. E. R., & SIMMELHAG, V. L. (1971). The "superstition" experiment: A re-examination of its implications for the principles of adaptive behavior. *Psychological Review, 78*, 3–43.

STEVENSON-HINDE, J. (1983). Constraints on reinforcement. In R. A. Hinde & J. Stevenson-Hinde (Eds.), *Constraints on learning: Limitations and predispositions* (pp. 285–296). New York: Academic Press.

STIERS, M., & SILBERBERG, A. (1974). Lever-contact responses in rats: Automaintenance with and without a negative response-reinforcer dependency. *Journal of the Experimental Analysis of Behavior, 22*, 497–506.

STOKES, T. F., & BAER, D. M. (1977). An implicit technology of generalization. *Journal of Applied Behavior Analysis, 10*, 349–367.

STOKES, T. F., FOWLER, S. A., & BAER, D. M. (1978). Training preschool children to recruit natural communities of reinforcement. *Journal of Applied Behavior Analysis, 11*, 285–303.

STONEBRAKER, T. B., & RILLING, M. (1981). Control of delayed matching-to-sample using directed forgetting techniques. *Animal Learning & Behavior, 9*, 196–201.

STONEBRAKER, T. B., RILLING, M., & KENDRICK, D. F. (1981). Time dependent effects of double cuing in directed forgetting. *Animal Learning & Behavior, 9*, 385–394.

STORMS, L. H., BOROCZI, G., & BROEN, W. E., JR. (1962). Punishment inhibits an instrumental response in hooded rats. *Science, 135*, 1133–1134.

STROOP, J. R. (1935). Studies of interference in serial verbal reactions. *Journal of Experimental Psychology, 18*, 643–662.

STUART, R. B. (1971). Behavioral contracting with the families of delinquents. *Journal of Behavior Therapy and Experimental Psychiatry, 2*, 1–11.

SULZER-AZAROFF, B. (1986). Behavior analysis and education: Crowning achievements and crying needs. *Division 25 Recorder, 21*, 55–65.

SULZER-AZAROFF, B., & DE SANTAMARIA, M. C. (1980). Industrial safety hazard reduction through performance feedback. *Journal of Applied Behavior Analysis, 13,* 287–295.

SUNAHARA, D., & PIERCE, W. D. (1982). The matching law and bias in a social exchange involving choice between alternatives. *Canadian Journal of Sociology, 7,* 145–165.

SUNAHARA, F. D. (1980). *Social exchange theory and the matching law.* Unpublished doctoral dissertation, University of Alberta, Edmonton.

SUNDBERG, M. L. (1985). Teaching verbal behavior to pigeons. *The Analysis of Verbal Behavior, 3,* 11–17.

TAIT, R. W., & SALADIN, M. E. (1986). Concurrent development of excitatory and inhibitory associations during backward conditioning. *Animal Learning & Behavior, 14,* 133–137.

TAYLOR, S. P., & PISANO, R. (1971). Physical aggression as a function of frustration and physical attack. *Journal of Social Psychology, 84,* 261–267.

TERRACE, H. S. (1963). Discrimination learning with and without "errors." *Journal of the Experimental Analysis of Behavior, 6,* 1–27.

TERRACE, H. S. (1972). By-products of discrimination learning. In G. H. Bower (Ed.), *The psychology of learning and motivation* (Vol. 5, pp. 195–265). New York: Academic Press.

THARP, R. G., & WETZEL, R. J. (1969). *Behavior modification in the natural environment.* New York: Academic Press.

THOMAS, D. R., & SETZER, J. (1972). Stimulus generalization gradients for auditory intensity in rats and guinea pigs. *Psychonomic Science, 28,* 22–24.

THOMPSON, R. F. & SPENCER, W. A. (1966). Habituation: A model phenomenon for the study of neuronel substrates of behavior. *Psychological Review, 73,* 16-43.

THORNDIKE, E. L. (1898). Animal intelligence. *Psychological Review Monograph Supplements* (Serial No. 8).

THORNDIKE, E. L. (1911). *Animal intelligence.* New York: Macmillan.

TIMBERLAKE (1983). Rats responses to a moving object related to food or water: A behavior-systems analysis. *Animal Learning and Behavior, 11,* 309–320.

TIMBERLAKE (1993). Behavior systems and reinforcement: An integrative approach. *Journal of the Experimental Analysis of Behavior, 60,* 105–128.

TIMBERLAKE, W., & GRANT, D. L. (1975). Autoshaping in rats to the presentation of another rat predicting food. *Science, 190,* 690–692.

TINBERGEN, N. (1951). *The study of instinct.* Oxford: Oxford University Press.

TODD, J. T. , & MORRIS, E. K. (1992). Case histories in the great power of steady misrepresentation. *American Psychologist, 47,* 1441–1453.

TODD, J. T., & MORRIS, E. K. (1986). The early research of John B. Watson: Before the behavioral revolution. *The Behavior Analyst, 9,* 71–88.

TOWE, A. L. (1954). A study of figural equivalence in the pigeon. *Journal of Comparative and Physiological Psychology, 47,* 283–287.

TURNEY, T. H. (1982). The association of visual concepts and imitative vocalization in the mynah (*Gracula religiosa*). *Bulletin of the Psychonomic Society, 19,* 59–62.

TWINKLE, TWINKLE. (1991, January 4). *The Economist,* p. 91.

ULMAN, J. D., & SULZER-AZAROFF, B. (1975). Multielement baseline design is educational research. In E. Ramp & G. Semb (Eds.), *Behavior analysis: Areas of research and application* (pp. 377–391). Englewood Cliffs, NJ: Prentice-Hall.

ULRICH, R. E., & AZRIN, N. H. (1962). Reflexive fighting in response to aversive stimulation. *Journal of the Experimental Analysis of Behavior, 5,* 511–520.

ULRICH, R. E., WOLFF, P. C., & AZRIN, N. H. (1964). Shock as an elictor of intra- and inter-species fighting behavior. *Animal Behaviour, 12,* 14–15.

UPPER, D., LOCHMAN, J. E., & AVENI, C. A. (1977). Using contingency contracting to modify the problematic behaviors of foster home residents. *Behavior Modification, 1,* 405–416.

VAN HOUTEN, R., AXELROD, S., BAILEY, J. S., FAVELL, J. E., FOXX, R. M., IWATA, B. A., & LOVAAS, I. O. (1988). The right to effective treatment. *Journal of Applied Behavior Analysis, 21,* 381–384.

VARGAS, J. S. (1990). B. F. Skinner fact and fiction. *The International Behaviorology Association Newsletter, 2,* 8–11.

VAUGHN, W., JR. (1988). Formation of equivalence sets in pigeons. *Journal of Experimental Psychology: Animal Behavior Processes, 14,* 36–42.

VERHAVE, T. (1966). The pigeon as a quality control inspector. *American Psychologist, 21,* 109–115.

VILLAREAL, J. (1967). Shedule-induced pica. *Physiology and Behavior, 6,* 577–588.

WAGNER, A. R., & LAREW, M. B. (1985). Opponent processes and Pavlovian inhibition. In R. R. Miller & N. E. Spear (Eds.), *Information processing in animals: Conditioned inhibition* (pp. 233–265). Hillsdale, NJ: Lawrence Erlbaum Associates.

WAGNER, A. R., & RESCORLA, R. A. (1972). Inhibition in Pavlovian conditioning: Applications of a theory. In R. A. Boakes & M. S. Halliday (Eds.), *Inhibition and learning* (pp. 301–359). London: Academic Press.

WALLER, M. B. (1961). Effects of chronically administered chlorpromazine on multiple-schedule performance. *Journal of the Experimental Analysis of Behavior, 4,* 351–359.

WANCHISEN, B. A., TATHAM, T. A., & MOONEY, S. E. (1989). Variable-ratio conditioning history produces high- and low-rate fixed-interval performance in rats. *Journal of the Experimental Analysis of Behavior, 52,* 167–179.

WASSERMAN, E. A. (1973). Pavlovian conditioning with heat reinforcement produces stimulus-directed pecking in chicks. *Science, 181,* 875–877.

WATSON, J. B. (1903). *Animal education: An experimental study on the psychical development of the white rat, correlated with the growth of its nervous system.* Chicago, IL: University of Chicago Press.

WATSON, J. B. (1913). Psychology as the behaviorist views it. *Psychological Review, 20,* 158–177.

WATSON, J. B. (1936). John Broadus Watson. In C. Murchison (Ed.), *A history of psychology in autobiography* (Vol. 3, pp. 271–281). Worcester, MA: Clark University Press.

WATSON, J. B., & RAYNER, R. (1920). Conditioned emotional reactions. *Journal of Experimental Child Psychology, 3,* 1–14.

WAWRZYNCYCK, S. (1937) Badania and parecia *Spirostomum ambiguum major. Acta Biologica Experimentalis* (Warsaw), *11,* 57–77.

WEARDEN, J. H. (1983). Undermatching and overmatching as deviations from the matching law. *Journal of the Experimental Analysis of Behavior, 40,* 333–340.

WEARDEN, J. H., & BURGESS, I. S. (1982). Matching since Baum (1979). *Journal of the Experimental Analysis of Behavior, 38,* 339–348.

WEBBE, F. M., DEWEESE, J., & MALAGODI, E. F. (1978). Induced attack during multiple fixed-ratio, variable-ratio schedules of reinforcement. *Journal of the Experimental Analysis of Behavior, 20,* 219–224.

WEEKES, C. (1976). *Simple effective treatment of agoraphobia.* New York: Hawthorne Books.

WEINER, H. (1969). Controlling human fixed-interval performance. *Journal of the Experimental Analysis of Behavior, 12,* 349–373.

WEISS, B., & GOTT, C. T. (1972). A microanalysis of drug effects on fixed-ratio performance in pigeons. *Journal of Pharmacology and Experimental Therapeutics, 180,* 189–202.

WEISSMAN, N. W., & CROSSMAN, E. K. (1966). A comparison of two types of extinction following fixed-ratio training. *Journal of the Experimental Analysis of Behavior, 9,* 41–46.

WESTBROOK, R. F. (1973). Failure to obtain positive contrast when pigeons press a bar. *Journal of the Experimental Analysis of Behavior, 20,* 499–510.

WHALEY, D. L., & MALOTT, R. W. (1971). *Elementary principles of behavior.* Englewood Cliffs, NJ: Prentice-Hall.

WHITE, A. J., & DAVISON, M. C. (1973). Performance in concurrent fixed-interval schedules. *Journal of the Experimental Analysis of Behavior, 19,* 147–153.

WHITE, C. T., & SCHLOSBERG, H. (1952). Degree of conditioning of the GSR as a function of the period of delay. *Journal of Experimental Psychology, 43,* 357–362.

WIEST, W. M., & SQUIRE, L. H. (1974). Incentives and reinforcement: A behavioral approach to fertility. *Journal of Social Issues, 30,* 235–263.

WIKE, E. L. (1966). *Secondary reinforcement: Selected experiments.* New York: Harper & Row.

WILCOXON, H. C., DRAGOIN, W. B., & KRAL, P. A. (1971). Illness-induced aversions in rat and quail: Relative salience of visual and gustatory cues. *Science, 171,* 826–828.

WILLIAMS, A. R. (1997). Under the volcano: Montserrat. *National Geographic, 192 no.1,* 59–75.

WILLIAMS, B. A. (1974). The role of local interactions in behavioral contrast. *Bulletin of the Psychonomic Society, 4,* 543–545.

WILLIAMS, B. A. (1976). Behavioral contrast as a function of the temporal location of reinforcement. *Journal of the Experimental Analysis of Behavior, 26,* 57–64.

WILLIAMS, B. A. (1979). Contrast, component duration, and the following schedule of reinforcement. *Journal of Experimental Psychology: Animal Behavior Processes, 5,* 379–396.

WILLIAMS, B. A. (1981). The following schedule of reinforcement as a fundamental determinant of steady state contrast in multiple schedules. *Journal of the Experimental Analysis of Behavior, 12,* 293–310.

WILLIAMS, B. A. (1990). Pavlovian contingencies and anticipatory contrast. *Animal Learning and Behavior, 18,* 44–50.

WILLIAMS, B. A. (1992). Competition between stimulus-reinforcer contingencies and anticipatory contrast. *Journal of the Experimental Analysis of Behavior, 58,* 287–302.

WILLIAMS, C. D. (1959). The elimination of tantrum behavior by extinction procedures. *Journal of Abnormal and Social Psychology, 59,* 269.

WILLIAMS, D. R., & WILLIAMS, H. (1969). Automaintenance in the pigeon: Sustained pecking despite contingent non-reinforcement. *Journal of the Experimental Analysis of Behavior, 12,* 511–520.

WILLIAMS, J. L. & LIERLE, D. M. (1986). Effects of stress controllability, immunization, and therapy on the subsequent defeat of colony intruders. *Animal Learning & Behavior, 14,* 305–314.

WILSON, L., & ROGERS, R. W. (1975). The fire this time: Effects of race of target, insult, and potential retaliation on black aggression. *Journal of Personality and Social Psychology, 32,* 857–864.

WITOSLAWSKI, J. J., ANDERSON, R. B., & HANSON, H. M. (1963). Behavioral studies with a black vulture, Coragyps atratus. *Journal of the Experimental Analysis of Behavior, 6,* 605–606.

WOLFE, B. M., & BARON, R. A. (1971). Laboratory aggression related to aggression in naturalistic social situations: Effects of an aggressive model on the behavior of college students and prisoner observers. *Psychonomic Science, 24,* 193–194.

WOLFE, J. B. (1936). Effectiveness of token rewards for chimpanzees. *Comparative Psychology Monographs, 12,* 1–72.

WOLPE, J. (1958). *Psychotherapy by reciprocal inhibition.* Stanford, CA: Stanford University Press.

WYCKOFF, L. B., JR. (1952). The role of observing responses in discrimination learning. Part 1. *Psychological Review, 59,* 431–442.

WYCKOFF, L. B., JR. (1969). The role of observing responses in discrimination learning. In D. P. Hendry (Ed.), *Conditioned reinforcement* (pp. 237–260). Homewood, IL: Dorsey Press.

YAMAMOTO, J., & MOCHIZUKI, A, (1988). Acquisition and functional analysis of manding with autistic students. *Journal of Applied Behavior Analysis, 21,* 57–64.

ZEILER, M. D. (1977). Schedules of reinforcement: The controlling variables. In W. K. Honig & J. E. R. Staddon (Eds.), *Handbook of operant behavior* (pp. 201–232). Englewood Cliffs, NJ: Prentice-Hall.

ZEILER, M. D. (1992). On immediate function. *Journal of the Experimental Analysis of Behavior, 57,* 417–427.

ZETTLE, R. D., & HAYES, S. C. (1982). Rule-governed behavior: A potential theoretical framework for cognitive-behavior therapy. In P. C. Kendall (Ed.), *Advances in cognitive behavioral research and therapy* (Vol. 1, pp. 73–118). New York: Academic Press.

ZILLMANN, D. (1988). Cognition-excitation interdependencies in aggressive behavior. *Aggressive Behavior, 14,* 51–64.

ZIMBARDO, P. G. (1988). *Psychology and life.* Glenview, IL: Scott, Foresman.

ZIMMERMAN, J., & FERSTER, C. B. (1963). Intermittent punishment of S^{Δ} responding in matching-to-sample. *Journal of the Experimental Analysis of Behavior, 6,* 349–356.

Index

SUBJECTS